Essential
Study
Skills

SEVENTH EDITION

Linda Wong

WADSWORTH
CENGAGE Learning™

Australia • Brazil • Japan • Korea • Mexico • Singapore • Spain • United Kingdom • United States

WADSWORTH
CENGAGE Learning™

Essential Study Skills, Seventh Edition
Linda Wong

Publisher/Executive Editor: Annie Todd

Acquisitions Editor: Shani Fisher

Developmental Editor: Beth Kaufman

Assistant Editor: Daisuke Yasutake

Editorial Assistant: Cat Salerno

Media Editor: Amy Gibbons

Marketing Manager: Kirsten Stoller

Marketing Communications Manager: Stacey Purviance

Content Project Manager: Cathy Brooks

Art Director: Pam Galbreath

Print Buyer: Julio Esperas

Rights Acquisitions Specialist, image: Jennifer Meyer Dare

Senior Rights Acquisitions Specialist, text: Katie Huha

Production Service and Compositor: Integra Software Services, Inc.

Text Designer: Cia Boynton/Boynton Hue Studio

Cover Designer: Riezebos Holzbaur / Brie Hattey

Cover Image: (from left to right): Young man doing homework on rug/
© Frank & Helena/ Cultura/ Getty Images RF; Girl with study group/© Masterfile RF; Students at desk/© Image Source/ Image Source/ Getty Images RF

For product information and technology assistance, contact us at
Cengage Learning Customer & Sales Support, 1-800-354-9706

For permission to use material from this text or product,
submit all requests online at **www.cengage.com/permissions**
Further permissions questions can be emailed to
permissionrequest@cengage.com

Library of Congress Control Number: 2010931614

ISBN-13: 978-0-495-91350-4

ISBN-10: 0-495-91350-2

Wadsworth
20 Channel Center Street
Boston, MA 02210
USA

Cengage Learning is a leading provider of customized learning solutions with office locations around the globe, including Singapore, the United Kingdom, Australia, Mexico, Brazil, and Japan. Locate your local office at **international.cengage.com/region**

Cengage Learning products are represented in Canada by Nelson Education, Ltd.

For your course and learning solutions, visit **www.cengage.com.**

Purchase any of our products at your local college store or at our preferred online store **www.cengagebrain.com.**

Printed in the United States of America
3 4 5 6 14 13 12

Brief Contents

Contents

Preface

Essential Study Skills, Seventh Edition, empowers students to excel by using a meta-cognitive, multisensory approach throughout the textbook to provide students with essential study skills to increase their academic performance. Changing behaviors occurs most successfully when students understand *how* they learn, *what* skills they need to learn to use to perform well in college, and *which* strategies work most effectively to master different kinds of college materials. *Essential Study Skills*, Seventh Edition is an easy-to-use and easy-to-read textbook designed to encourage students to take greater responsibility for their learning, increase their self-confidence and motivation, and implement plans of action to achieve their academic and personal goals. This student-friendly textbook builds a strong foundation of essential study skills strategies designed to boost memory, integrate skills and concepts, and excel in the classroom. Freshmen, nontraditional, and returning students will benefit from the following student-friendly features used throughout this textbook to guide them through the process of acquiring strong essential study skills to use in all of their courses.

- Clear chapter learning objectives, a chapter outline, and a chapter mapping to grasp "the big picture" and key concepts in the chapter

- A direct, easy-to-read, step-by-step approach for learning a wealth of essential study skills strategies based on a metacognitive approach

- A concise, to-the-point format that uses easy-to-grasp bulleted points and clear examples of new concepts

- Marginal notes to highlight key concepts and define terminology

- Visually-appealing charts that summarize essential study skills strategies

- Self-assessment tools, Concept Checks, inventories, and checklists to monitor understanding and reinforce learning

- Engaging textbook exercises and group activities that reinforce skills

- Self-correcting Check Point and Chapter Review Questions to master the textbook content

- A clearly identifiable icon signaling activities, exercises, and interactive quizzes that are available on the comprehensive CourseMate student Web site

- A multi-color, visually appealing format that increases interest and improves comprehension by highlighting levels of information and important features

- Concise Learning Objectives Review with bulleted points

    Essential Study Skills, Seventh Edition, is also an instructor-friendly textbook that recognizes instructors' needs to have clearly defined goals, teachable strategies, clear examples, ready-to-use classroom materials, and a wealth of resources available at their fingertips to use to enhance classroom instruction and student performance. As an instructor, you will find the following easy-to-use resources provide you with essential tools to use to create a dynamic, engaging, and highly effective study skills course.

- A flexible format that allows you to select the most effective order to use to teach the topics of the twelve chapters and Appendix A, the new pull-out Essential Test-Taking Skills guide.

- Highly structured chapters with clear headings, subheadings, and bulleted points to use to introduce topics or use in class lectures or discussions.

- Abundant ready-to-use activities and materials that you select from to use for whole class, small groups, or as homework assignments.

- A printed version (NEW) and an online version of the Instructor Resource Manual (IRM) with suggestions and options for organizing your course, step-by-step teaching tips and directions, complete answer keys, lists of all available resources for each chapter, and reduced images of all available transparency masters for the course.

- A comprehensive Instructor Web site that includes all transparency masters, Power Point Slides, ready-to-use tests, enrichment activities, discussion topics, grading rubrics, and other useful teaching materials and tools.

- A new Appendix D with excerpts from a variety of content areas to use to reinforce reading, notetaking, and test-taking skills.

- A PowerLecture CD-Rom that contains the ExamView test-generating software with a test bank that has a minimum of 95 questions per chapter, Power Point slides, and other valuable instructor teaching tools.

WHAT'S NEW in the SEVENTH EDITION of ESSENTIAL STUDY SKILLS

Innovative features in the Seventh Edition provide instructors and students with new content and more comprehensive coverage of high-demand topics. These features include high-interest interactive learning tools and materials that better prepare students for a broader range of academic challenges they will encounter in their classes.

Critical Thinking and Transference Skills

As you examine the Seventh Edition, you will discover a sharper focus and emphasis on **critical thinking skills** and **the transference of skills to other content areas.** The goal of *Essential Study Skills* is not only to teach students how to use powerful study strategies to increase their academic performance, but also to teach students how to think on higher levels and how to interpret, evaluate, and apply what they are learning to other content areas as well as to their personal lives. In the previous edition, critical thinking skills were embedded in a variety of exercises; however, in the Seventh Edition, thinking critically, analyzing, discovering relationships, evaluating, and applying new skills are stated more directly. Following are the new critical thinking activities that are available for you to use to encourage your students to think on higher levels, engage in more challenging discussions, explore new ways to think about topics, and to apply or transfer the textbook skills to other content areas.

- **Critical Thinking Activities:** Each chapter now features a Critical Thinking Activity to use for class or small group discussions. These activities are open-ended and engage students in the process of paying closer attention to the integration of concepts, relationships beyond those stated in the textbook, and analysis of information they are studying.

- **Bloom's Taxonomy:** Many instructors use Bloom's Taxonomy to create learning objectives and structure higher-order questions to use on tests and in class discussions. In the newly revised Bloom's Taxonomy, the labels of the six levels have been changed from nouns to action verbs to reflect better the cognitive activities or processes involved in each level of the classification system. The order of the last two levels has changed from *synthesis* and *evaluation* to *evaluating* and *creating*. In addition, the lowest level, *knowledge* or *remembering*, includes newly defined subdivisions of remembering: factual, conceptual, procedural, and metacognitive knowledge, all of which appear throughout the Seventh Edition of *Essential Study Skills*.

- **Scientific Method of Inquiry:** Chapter 12 introduces students to the specific problem-solving steps of the Scientific Method of Inquiry. This model exemplifies the application of critical thinking skills to solve problems not only in areas of science, but also in everyday life situations.

- **Transfer These Skills:** Specific textbook exercises in Chapters 6–12 provide students with the opportunity to transfer the chapter skills to other textbooks they are using for other courses. The effectiveness of essential study skills involves knowing how to use the skills in textbooks with different structures, features, varied levels of difficulty, and content.

- **Evaluating Online Materials:** With the increased use of new technology and accessing the Internet for information, students have a greater need to know how to evaluate the accuracy and reliability of online materials. Chapter 8 includes critical thinking skills for evaluating online materials.

- **Appendix D:** Appendix D provides you with ready-to-use excerpts from psychology, public speaking, health care, health science technology, physical science, business, and literature textbooks to use to develop critical thinking skills. In addition to using these excerpts for specific textbook exercises, you may also use them for additional class discussions, content for lectures, or to practice reading, notetaking, and test-taking skills.

- **Discussion Topics:** Five discussion questions for each chapter appear online on both CourseMate and the Instructor Web site. These discussion topics encourage students to use higher-level critical thinking skills to respond to the questions. Discussion topics may be used for in-class or online discussions, or for writing assignments.

- **Critical Thinking, Critical Reading, and Critical Listening:** Preparing students to succeed in the academic world as well as in the world of work requires strengthening cognitive and communication skill levels: critical thinking, critical reading, and critical listening. *Essential Study Skills,* Seventh Edition, provides students with foundation skills to become more powerful thinkers, more in-depth readers, and more effective critical listeners.

Appendix A: Essential Test-Taking Skills

Students encounter the need to acquire essential test-taking skills at different times during a term for their various classes. The exciting, new Essential Test-Taking Skills guide provides a flexible format for acquiring essential test-taking skills whenever the need arises. Students can use this pull-out guide for independent study at any time during the present or future terms to prepare for upcoming tests. Instructors also may select the most appropriate time to teach these essential test-taking skills. Instructors have the option of using Appendix A in conjunction with Chapter 6, Preparing for Upcoming Tests, or as a separate topic at any time during the term. The following features make the Essential Test-Taking Guide a valuable resource for both students and instructors.

- The direct, step-by-step approach for learning sixty-five essential test-taking strategies includes clear explanations and examples.

- Easy-to-use strategies cover true-false, multiple-choice, matching, fill-in-the-blanks, listing, definition, short-answer, math, and essay test questions.

- Students learn how to read, understand, and interpret objective, recall, math, and essay test questions.

- Students may prepare for specific kinds of tests by going directly to the sections in Appendix A that address their test-taking needs.

- Using the systematic approaches for answering questions increases students' accuracy rates and grades on tests.

- Online practice quizzes provide students with practice applying the skills.

- The pull-out format encourages students to create a test-taking resource to use in future classes.

- Instructor resources for Appendix A include twenty-four transparency masters, Power Point slides, and teaching tips.

Your Chapter Mapping

The new feature "Your Chapter Mapping" at the beginning of each chapter instructs students to expand the key components of the chapter mapping with details that they identify after reading the information under each heading in the chapter. Developing and studying individual chapter mappings promotes multisensory learning, increases comprehension, and provides students with a study tool to use to recite, rehearse, and review important levels of information. The College Success Course-Mate (discussed in more detail below) also includes these chapter visual mappings.

Chapter 12: Carrying Your Skills Forward

This new chapter provides students with information about reading in the content areas, using Bloom's Taxonomy and the Scientific Method of Inquiry, plus culminating activities to use at the end of the term. This final chapter focuses students' attention on acknowledging the skills they have learned and carrying the skills forward to the next term and future courses.

New Technology and Online Resources

The extensive online materials for students and instructors have been updated to reflect the changes in the chapter content for Chapters 1–12 and Appendix A in the Seventh Edition. The new design of both the student and Instructor Web sites is user-friendly and facilitates the process of locating and accessing the abundant online materials.

College Success CourseMate

Cengage Learning's College Success CourseMate brings course concepts to life for students with interactive learning, study, and exam preparation tools that support the printed textbook.

Engagement Tracker

With CourseMate, instructors can use the included Engagement Tracker—a first-of-its-kind tool—to assess student preparation and engagement in the course. The tracking tools allow instructors to see progress for the class as a whole or for individual students, identify students at risk early in the course, uncover which concepts are most difficult for the class, and monitor time on task.

Interactive Teaching and Learning Tools

CourseMate provides quizzes, flashcards, videos, and many other interactive teaching and learning tools. These assets enable students to review for tests, prepare for class, and address the needs of their varied learning styles. College Success CourseMate also includes Chapter Profiles, Chapter Visual Mappings, Case Studies, Reflective Writing Assignments, Chapter Exercises and Forms, Discussion Topics, and other valuable resources. Enhanced Quizzes require students to use information they have learned from different sections of the chapter to answer objective questions. The rejoinders for these quiz questions contain links to the section of the eBook chapter students should read to better understand the concept.

Interactive eBook

In addition to interactive teaching and learning tools, CourseMate includes an interactive eBook. Students can take notes, highlight, search and interact with embedded media specific to their book. They can choose to use it as a supplement to the printed text, or as a substitute. Chapter 8 guides students through the process of navigating through an eBook chapter, using eBook special features, reading online, and using notetaking options. Students also learn that one of the greatest advantages of working in the eBook is that they can click on the online icon in the eBook and be routed directly to the online exercise or quiz. With the online materials, students have the option of printing their work or emailing it to their instructor.

 Look for this icon in the text denoting resources available in CourseMate, and access them at login.cengage.com.

Instructor Web Site

- **Chapter Links:** On the Instructor Web site under "Chapter Links," instructors will find printable forms, Topics In-Depth materials, ready-to-use answer keys for lengthier textbook exercises, inventories, and chapter-specific teaching materials.

- **Transparency Masters:** Transparency masters for all chapters and for Appendix A now appear in one location on the Instructor Web site. Transparencies are updated, use a fresh new format, and correlate directly with the new sequence of information in each chapter. While reduced images of all the transparencies appear in the IRM, the full-sized transparency masters appear online and are ready to download and convert into transparencies for classroom use. Ten transparencies are available for each chapter; twenty-four transparencies are available to support the presentation of test-taking skills in Appendix A. The IRM recommends that instructors prepare a special notebook with all of the transparency masters so they are available at their fingertips and ready to use. Instructors also have the option of printing and sharing these transparency masters with students before, during, or after lectures.

- **Discussion Topics:** As previously mentioned, five discussion topics for each chapter appear on CourseMate and the Instructor Web site.

- **New Enrichment Activities:** Instructors who teach multiple sections of study skills courses in a given term or over the course of several years sometimes choose to increase their motivation by using new exercises and activities that do not appear in the textbook. The Enrichment Activities online for each chapter provide instructors with new lesson plans and/or worksheet exercises to use in class. Instructor's enthusiasm and excitement about class materials spreads to students, so occasionally using enrichment activities to break the routine benefits both instructors and students.

- **ExamView Test Bank:** This exciting new product is a test-generating test bank that makes creating your own chapter, midterm, or final exams easy and quick to do. On the Instructor Web site you will find at least ninety-five new test questions for each chapter to use to create your own tests. The test bank is also available on the PowerLecture CD-Rom. With this instructional tool, you can use existing questions, or modify the questions to reflect your preferences for test questions.

- **PowerLecture CD-Rom:** The PowerLecture CD-ROM contains the test bank in the ExamView® test-generating software, instructor PowerPoint® slides, transparency masters, and a PDF of the Instructor's Manual.

- **Chapter Transition Guide:** On the Instructor Web site, you will also find a comprehensive transition guide for each chapter for instructors who have used previous editions of this text. This guide highlights changes made in chapters and in supporting materials.

Features Retained from the Sixth Edition

Instructors who have used previous editions of *Essential Study Skills* will find many familiar features continue to be an essential part of this student-oriented textbook:

Terms to Know, which now appear in the end-of-the-chapter materials, identify the key terms to learn.

Chapter Objectives and Chapter Outlines appear at the beginning of each chapter. These features provide students with the "big picture" of a chapter before they begin more in-depth reading. A color-coding system links the chapter objectives to the main headings throughout the chapter. The chapter objectives and an expanded chapter outline are available on both CourseMate and the Instructor Web site.

Chapter Profiles provide students with a self-correcting series of ten questions to assess their current attitudes and behaviors. Before beginning to work with a new chapter, students complete the profiles and record their responses on the Master Profile Chart in Appendix B. To show progress and changes made throughout the course, students complete the profiles again at the end of the term. Students may also complete and receive their Profile scores online on CourseMate.

Essential Strategies Charts appear throughout each chapter to highlight essential strategies presented in the chapter. The Essential Strategies Charts provide students with an overview of essential skills and a quick reference tool for reinforcing skills.

    Case Studies appear in every chapter. Two textbook case studies and four Web-only case studies present students with real-life student situations to analyze. Students then suggest strategies from the chapter to use to solve the case-study problems or increase student performance. Students may respond on paper or online with the option to print or e-mail their responses directly to their instructors.

    Reflective Writing Assignments provide students with opportunities to personalize the chapter content, discuss their current skills and attitudes, and integrate the chapter's skills with other study skills and personal experiences. Students can respond to the two Reflective Writing Assignments on paper, in journals, or online with the option to print or e-mail their responses directly to their instructors.

    Group Processing: A Collaborative Learning Activity in each chapter provides a small-group activity that enhances student interest; creates a forum for student interaction through brainstorming, discussion, and cooperative work. Group Processing Activities promote critical-thinking skills.

    Student Exercises to practice and reinforce skills appear throughout each chapter. These exercises may be used as homework assignments, for class discussions, or for small-group activities in the classroom. Exercises include excerpts from multiple disciplines, including social science and science. Instead of using or assigning all of the exercises in each chapter, instructors may select the exercises that are best suited for their students. Students do not have access to answer keys for exercises.

    Concept Checks in the margins provide students with questions to assess their understanding of concepts discussed in the adjacent paragraphs. Instructors may use these Concept Checks for class discussions, writing assignments, or selectively for "pop quizzes" to check that students are completing reading assignments. A complete list of all the Concept Checks is available on both CourseMate and the Instructor Web site.

    Check Points provide students with several questions to check how well they comprehended the information presented in the textbook. Check Points appear at the end of each main heading. Students use the answer keys in Appendix B to check their answers.

- ***Interactive Practice Quizzes*** refer students to CourseMate for interactive, self-correcting quizzes that reinforce the strategies and the concepts in the chapter and provide students with valuable feedback for each question. The Interactive Practice Quizzes are non-graded enrichment quizzes that help students hone their test-taking skills.

- ***Interactive Chapter Quizzes*** refer students to CourseMate. Four Interactive Chapter Quizzes are available for each chapter. Chapter Quiz 1 consists of ten fill-in-the-blanks questions to review chapter terminology. Chapter Quiz 2 consists of ten true/false questions. Chapter Quiz 3 consists of ten multiple-choice questions. Chapter Quizzes 1, 2, and 3 are scored online. Chapter Quiz 4 provides students with response boxes to write answers to two short-answer questions. Students may print or e-mail their responses to their instructor.

- ***Learning Objectives Review*** at the end of each chapter uses bulleted points to summarize the most important points for each of the chapter's objectives.

- ***Chapter Review Questions*** at the end of each chapter provide students with a tool to assess their understanding and recall of essential concepts, skills, and strategies discussed in the chapter. Answer keys for the Chapter Review Questions appear in Appendix B.

Instructor Overview

Essential Study Skills, Seventh Edition, continues its commitment to provide you with abundant materials to use to develop and teach your study skills course. To gain the most benefits from all the available resources, before beginning your adventure teaching your course, familiarize yourself with the following materials and resources:

- The textbook chapters and topics
- The textbook features used in each chapter
- Appendix A: Essential Test-Taking Skills
- Appendix B: Master Profile Chart and Answer Keys
- Appendix C: Exercises, Inventories, and Checklists
- Appendix D: Excerpts from Different Content Areas
- The Instructor Resource Manual (IRM)
  Table of Contents
  Introduction
  Part I: Planning Your Course
  Part II: Chapter-by-Chapter Resources
- The Instructor Web site for this textbook
  Transition Guide
  Instructor Resource Manual Online
  Expanded Outline and Objectives
  Concept Checks
  Chapter Links
  Transparency Masters
  Power Point Slides
  Ready-to-Use Chapter Test
  Grading Rubrics
  Enrichment Activities
  Discussion Topics
  Learning Options: Projects/Activities
  ExamView Test Bank
- The College Success CourseMate with Interactive eBook
- The PowerLecture CD-Rom and the ExamView Test Bank

Accessing Instructional Resources

To access instructor materials to accompany *Essential Study Skills*, Seventh Edition, visit CengageBrain.com. If you do not already have a Single Sign On account to access password protected content, you will be prompted to sign up for an account. **On this site you will also be able to request a printed copy of the Instructor Resource Manual and a copy of the PowerLecture CD-Rom.** If you have questions about any of these resources, contact your sales representative or contact Higher Ed customer service at 1 800.423.0563.

Dedication

The Seventh Edition of *Essential Study Skills* is dedicated to my son, Kailee Wong, who continuously pursues new learning opportunities and who exemplifies the characteristics of a life-long learner. I also dedicate this new edition to the thousands of educators who demonstrate an endless commitment to providing high quality, valuable educational experiences for their students, and to all students who strive to excel and benefit from their educational opportunities.

Acknowledgments

My appreciation is extended to the following reviewers who dedicated their time and expertise to contribute ideas to enrich this textbook and further strengthen the effectiveness of this instructor-friendly and student-friendly textbook. Thank you all for your contributions.

Jennifer McGregor, Tarleton State University
Eva A. O'Brian, Midlands Technical College
Mary J. Poole, Madisonville Community College
Kathryn O. "Kitty" Spires, Midlands Technical College
Kim Winford, Blinn College – Brenham

I extend my sincere appreciation for the outstanding editorial and production staff that has worked diligently with me through all the phases of creating the Seventh Edition of *Essential Study Skills*. Most readers of this textbook are unaware of the high degree of coordination, team-work, time commitment, and resources required to produce a new edition of a textbook and all its companion resources. The process is extensive and requires the utmost attention to details. I acknowledge your level of dedication and your utmost commitment to the development of this Seventh Edition. I appreciate and value you for your contributions. Thank you!

To the Student

Essential Study Skills, Seventh Edition, is designed to provide you with an array of study skills strategies that will unlock your learning potential and empower you with the essential skills to monitor and modify your learning strategies and help you improve your academic performance. Reading the following section carefully provides you with valuable information that explains how to get the most out of *Essential Study Skills,* Seventh Edition.

Quick Start Checklist

Go to the College Success CourseMate for a Quick Start Checklist to use to prepare for an upcoming term. Look for the Quick Start Checklist link on the left side of the home page screen. Click on it to learn about the following topics:

- Creating class schedules
- Familiarizing yourself with your campus
- Organizing your notebooks
- Selecting a system to record homework assignments
- Getting off to a good start on the first day of class
- Planning sufficient study time for your classes
- Other suggestions and tips for getting off to a good start

Steps to Access the College Success

CourseMate 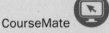 :

1. Log on to the College Success CourseMate via login.CengageBrain.com

2. You will be prompted to enter the Access Code that you received with your textbook. If you do not have an access code, you will be able to purchase one at CengageBrain.Com.

Starting the Term: Getting an Overview

As soon as you purchase this book, begin familiarizing yourself with the textbook. Read through this introductory section carefully, examine the Table of Contents, and familiarize yourself with the end matter that follows Chapter 12: Appendix A: Essential Test-Taking Skills; Appendix B: Master Profile Chart and Answer Keys; Appendix C: Exercises, Inventories, and Checklists; Appendix D: Excerpts; and the textbook index.

Essential Study Skills, Seventh Edition, has a College Success CourseMate to enhance your learning experience and strengthen your understanding of course materials. Each time you see this icon in your textbook, visit CourseMate for interactive practices and online materials. Your instructor may assign these exercises, or you may complete the exercises independently to strengthen your comprehension and learn content more thoroughly. Take time now to familiarize yourself with the wealth of online resources available to assist you throughout the term. As you click on the main menu for each chapter, you will see the following categories of your online materials:

- Interactive eBook
- Master Profile Chart
- Chapter Profile

- Chapter Visual Mapping
- Chapter Outline and Objectives
- Chapter Concept Checks
- Textbook Case Studies
- Web-Only Case Studies
- Reflective Writing Assignments
- Chapter Exercises and Forms
- Interactive Quizzes: Practice Quizzes, Chapter Quizzes, Enhanced Quiz
- Topics In-Depth
- Flashcard Drills
- Online Glossary
- Discussion Topics
- Appendix A: Essential Test-Taking Skills Guide

EBook

The College Success CourseMate for *Essential Study Skills*, Seventh Edition, has an interactive eBook for you to use with this textbook. If you have not yet experienced using an eBook, you are in for an exciting new learning experience! The eBook shows the exact pages that appear in this printed textbook. After accessing the eBook, you can turn the pages as you read, jump ahead or back to specific pages, sections, or headings in the chapter, highlight, and create notes. You can save time accessing specific online activities, exercises, or quizzes by simply clicking on the icon. You will be linked directly to the online activity, exercise, or quiz so you can begin working immediately. Most online quizzes are self-correcting, so you will get an immediate score. You will also have the option to print or email your results or responses to your instructor.

To learn more about your online eBook, look ahead to Chapter 8, pages 226–228 and take time to explore and navigate the eBook on the College Success CourseMate.

Starting Each Chapter

Surveying is an effective study strategy that provides you with an overview of a chapter before you begin the process of careful reading. Surveying familiarizes you with the topic, creates a mindset for studying, and prepares your memory to receive new information. Use the following steps for surveying a new chapter:

1. Read the *Chapter Objectives* that list learning goals or objectives for the chapter. The chapter objectives clearly indicate the skills you will learn and will be able to demonstrate when you finish studying the chapter. The color-coding used for the chapter objectives correlates with the color-coded headings throughout the chapter.

2. Read through the *Chapter Outline* for an overview of the organization and content of the chapter. You will find a copy of this chapter outline on CourseMate.

3. Complete the *Chapter Profile* before continuing to survey the chapter. This is not a graded assignment; answer the questions honestly. The profiles are

designed to examine your current attitude and habits in specific skill areas. These scores will be compared to end-of-the-term scores to show your progress and growth. You can complete the profile in the textbook, or you can complete it online on CourseMate.

4. Survey or skim through the chapter by reading the following items and features:

> All of the bold *headings* and *subheadings*
> The information that appears in the margins next to the paragraphs
> The figures and essential study skills charts
> The questions in the Check Points sections

5. Read through the *Terms to Know* that lists the course-specific terminology that you will learn to define; note the page number references for each term.

6. Read the *Learning Objectives Review* at the end of the chapter. Key points for each of the objectives provide you with additional insights about the content of the chapter.

7. Read through, but do not answer, the *Chapter Review Questions*. Plan to answer these questions after you have read the chapter carefully. For immediate feedback, you will be able to check your answers with the answer keys in Appendix B.

Using Chapter Features

In addition to the previously mentioned chapter features, you will encounter the following features designed to increase your comprehension and reinforce key concepts and skills in each chapter. Using these features consistently facilitates the process of mastering the concepts and skills in the chapter.

> *Your Chapter Mapping* shows you the basic skeleton or topic and the main headings used in the chapter. To create a visual study tool, expand the chapter mapping by connecting key words to show important details for each of the main headings. A copy of each chapter mapping also appears on CourseMate.
>
> *Definitions* in the margins provide a quick view of key terminology and definitions to learn. Review these definitions when you study for tests.
>
> *Concept Checks* in the margins provide you with study questions to assess your comprehension and promote critical thinking skills. For each Concept Check, answer the questions on paper, mentally, or out loud to yourself. At times, your instructor may ask you to use written responses. Return to these questions when you prepare for tests.
>
> *Check Points* in each chapter provide you with a short assessment tool to check your comprehension of information presented under each main heading in the chapter. Answer keys in Appendix B provide you with immediate feedback.
>
> *Exercises* appear throughout each chapter. Your instructor will assign some, but usually not all, of the exercises in the chapter. You will notice that the shorter exercises appear within the textbook chapter, and the longer exercises appear in Appendix C. For practice and enrichment, you may complete any of the

exercises that your instructor does not assign as homework or use as a class activity.

Transfer These Skills Exercises provide you with the opportunity to apply specific skills to other textbooks and courses. The skills you learn in this textbook work effectively for all of your courses.

Case Studies are exercises that describe student situations or problems. After reading a case study, identify the key issues or problems that are presented in the case study. Answer the question at the end of each case study by providing specific answers or suggestions that deal with the problem. Use specific strategies and terminology from the chapter in your answers. Case studies use open-ended questions, meaning there are many possible answers. They can be completed on paper or on CourseMate.

Practice Quizzes on CourseMate consist of self-correcting quizzes that provide you with additional practice and reinforcement of the skills in the chapter. You can complete these quizzes as many times as you wish. You will receive feedback and brief explanations with each answer.

Essential Strategy Charts appear in every chapter. These charts highlight key strategies to use to improve the way you study, process information, and master course content. Applying the essential strategies in these charts will increase your performance and academic success. Refer to these charts when you want to brush up on essential study skills or review for tests.

Terms to Know shows the course-specific vocabulary terms that you should know how to define. Practice defining these terms; look for the bold print words on the pages referenced. You can go to CourseMate for flashcard drills and an online glossary.

Chapter Review Questions provide you with practice test questions to assess your memory or recall of chapter concepts and key terms. Complete the Chapter Review Questions without referring to your textbook pages or your notes. Check your answers with the answer keys in Appendix B.

Chapter Quizzes and *Enhanced Quizzes* on CourseMate provide you with additional practice answering objective test questions and assessing your level of comprehension of chapter skills and concepts. Chapter Quizzes 1, 2, and 3 are interactive and self-correcting. Chapter Quiz 4 with two short-answer questions requires a written response that you can print or e-mail to your instructor. The Enhanced Quizzes link you to the heading in the e-textbook that covers the content of the quiz question.

Appendix A: Essential Test-Taking Skills

The exciting, new Essential Test-Taking Skills guide provides a flexible format for acquiring essential test-taking skills whenever the need arises. You can use this pull-out guide for independent study at any time during the present or future terms to prepare for upcoming tests. You may go directly to a specific section in Appendix A to prepare for a specific kind of test in one of your courses, such as a computerized multiple-choice test or an essay test. The Essential Test-Taking Skills Guide is a valuable resource for you to use in all of your courses. With the pull-out format, you can remove Appendix A to save as a resource to refresh your test-taking skills in future terms and courses. Using Appendix A addresses the following test-taking issues you may sometimes experience.

- *Do you sometimes struggle with taking tests because you have never really learned how to take tests?* Appendix A provides you with a direct, step-by-step approach for learning sixty-five essential test-taking strategies. Strategies include clear explanations and examples.

- *Do you sometimes have difficulty answering certain kinds of test questions?* Easy-to-use strategies provide you with the skills to answer true-false, multiple-choice, matching, fill-in-the-blanks, listing, definition, short-answer, math, and essay test questions.

- *Do you sometimes have difficulty understanding or interpreting questions?* Through easy-to read bulleted points, you will learn strategies for reading, understanding, and interpreting objective, recall, math, and essay test questions.

- *Do you sometimes get confused and waste valuable test-taking time trying to figure out how to move through a test?* In Appendix A, you will learn the value of using systematic approaches for answering questions. These approaches increase your accuracy rates and lead to higher grades on tests.

- *Do you want more practice applying test-taking strategies?* Twenty interactive quizzes for Appendix A are available on CourseMate. Navigate to Appendix A in the list of chapters, and then select the quizzes you wish to use to practice your test-taking skills.

Your instructor will provide you with additional information about using Appendix A. Your instructor may choose to discuss Appendix A in conjunction with Chapter 6: Preparing for Upcoming Tests, or your instructor may choose to discuss Appendix A at a different time during the term. Refer to your course syllabus or list of chapters and topics for the term.

A Note to You from the Author

Your goal is not to learn *about* study skills, but to learn to *use* powerful study skills to consistently achieve your goals and experience success. Learning is a lifelong process. Each time you are faced with a new learning situation—whether at school, at home, or at work—you can draw upon the skills you have learned in this textbook. By applying the skills of time management, goal setting, concentration, processing information, strengthening memory, reading comprehension, test-taking, and an array of additional strategies in this textbook, you will be prepared to experience the rewards of success … again and again and again. May my commitment to you, belief in you, and support of you in the learning process be reflected in the pages of this textbook.

—Linda Wong

1 Discovering and Using Your Learning Styles

© Image copyright Terry Chan, 2009. Used under license from Shutterstock.com

Understanding your individual style of learning can help you become a more effective learner. In this chapter, you will examine your preference for using your visual, auditory, or kinesthetic cognitive learning style (modality) for learning new information. By understanding your preferences, you can then select compatible multisensory learning strategies to boost your learning potential. You will gain additional insights about the way you learn by understanding the concepts of global and linear learners. Finally, you will learn about the eight intelligences that you already possess. Through this process of understanding more about yourself as a learner, you will quickly discover that you already have many skills and abilities that will contribute to your college success.

LEARNING OBJECTIVES

1. *Identify your preferred cognitive learning style and describe learning strategies you can use to utilize your preferred learning style and strengthen your other modalities.*

2. *Identify your linear- or global-learner tendency and discuss how it affects the way you process information.*

3. *Define the term* intelligences *and describe the common characteristics of each of Howard Gardner's eight intelligences.*

Access Chapter 1 Expanded Chapter Outline and Objectives in your College Success CourseMate, accessed through *CengageBrain.com.*

YOUR CHAPTER MAPPING

After reading information under each heading, return to the chapter visual mapping below. Add key words to show subheadings and important details related to each heading.

Access Chapter 1 Visual Mapping in your College Success CourseMate, accessed through *CengageBrain .com.*

Discovering and Using Your Learning Styles

ANSWER each profile question honestly. Your answers should reflect what you do, not what you wish to do. Check YES if you do the statement always or most of the time. Check NO if you do the statement seldom or never.

SCORE the profile. To get your score, give yourself one point for every answer that matches the answer key on page B2 in the back of your book. If you complete the profile online, the profile will be scored for you.

RECORD your score on the Master Profile Chart on page B1 in the column that shows the chapter number.

ONLINE: You can complete the profile and get your score online at this textbook's Web site.

Access Chapter 1 Profile in your College Success CourseMate, accessed through *CengageBrain.com*.

	YES	NO
1. I am aware of my learning style preference as a visual, auditory, or kinesthetic learner.	_____	_____
2. I can describe four or more effective learning strategies for each learning preference: visual, auditory, and kinesthetic.	_____	_____
3. When I study, I use a variety of learning strategies that capitalize on my learning style and preferences.	_____	_____
4. I usually study new information in a straightforward manner without spending time making creative study or review tools.	_____	_____
5. I know whether my thinking patterns reflect global (right-brain) or linear (left-brain) learning patterns.	_____	_____
6. When I initially begin processing new information, I am aware of my tendency to focus first on the "big picture" or focus first on the details.	_____	_____
7. I tend to use the same study methods for all of my classes even when my learning preferences differ from my instructor's style of presentation.	_____	_____
8. I recognize which of Howard Gardner's eight intelligences are strongest in me.	_____	_____
9. I have the potential to acquire new skills that will increase my abilities in the eight different intelligences.	_____	_____
10. I am confident that I can adjust my learning strategies to meet the demands of new learning situations or tasks.	_____	_____

QUESTIONS LINKED TO THE CHAPTER LEARNING OBJECTIVES:

Questions 1–4: objective 1   Questions 8, 9: objective 3

Questions 5–7: objective 2   Question 10: all objectives

Three Cognitive Learning Styles

 Identify your preferred cognitive learning style and describe learning strategies you can use to utilize your preferred learning style and strengthen your other modalities.

Learning is an individualized process; different educational and background experiences, personality traits, levels of motivation, and numerous other variables affect the way you learn. The term *cognitive* refers to thinking and reasoning processes, so **cognitive learning styles** refers to the general way people *prefer* to have information presented in order to problem solve, process, learn, and remember new information. **Figure 1.1** shows the three main cognitive learning styles. Understanding your cognitive learning style helps you select learning strategies that capitalize on your strengths and understand why learning in certain situations that are contrary to your learning style may be more difficult than anticipated.

Learning Style Preferences

Three commonly recognized cognitive learning styles, or **learning modalities,** are *visual, auditory,* and *kinesthetic.* Most people have a **learning style preference,** which is a tendency to use a *visual, auditory,* or *kinesthetic* modality when there is a choice of ways to learn and process new information. For example, a *visual learner* may prefer to read a manual or a textbook or learn from pictures, charts, or graphs. An *auditory learner* may prefer to be told how a new process or equipment works. A *kinesthetic learner* may prefer to be shown how a process or piece of equipment works and then be given an opportunity to try each step to learn the process.

Your learning style preference started in your childhood. As you matured, entered into the educational system, and were exposed to new learning situations, you learned to use, strengthen, and integrate all of your modalities. The childhood modality preference may still exist or you may have changed to a new modality preference as an adult, but as an adult with broadened skills, you are able, in most situations, to learn even when information is presented in a form that is not based on your preferred method of learning.

Understanding your learning style preference helps you select effective learning strategies that will boost your memory and your ability to recall information. As you take in and process information, your brain uses visual, auditory, and kinesthetic

Cognitive learning styles refers to the general way people *prefer* to have information presented in order to problem solve, process, learn, and remember new information.

Learning modalities refers to learning styles such as visual, auditory, or kinesthetic.

Learning style preference indicates a tendency to use a visual, auditory, or kinesthetic modality when there is a choice of ways to learn and process new information.

CONCEPT CHECK 1.1

In general terms, how do you go about learning something new? What study or learning techniques generally work best for you?

FIGURE 1.1 Cognitive Learning Styles

1. **Visual learners** learn and remember best by *seeing* and *visualizing* information.

2. **Auditory learners** learn and remember best by *hearing* and *discussing* information.

3. **Kinesthetic learners** learn and remember best by using large and small body *movements* and *hands-on experiences.*

(motor) codes to accept and move the information into different locations in your memory system. The following points are important to understand:

- When you use your strongest modality or your preferred learning style to take in and process information, learning can occur more efficiently and recalling information at a later time may occur more smoothly.

- Many learning strategies involve the use of more than one modality. In other words, more than one kind of coding into memory occurs. A *see-say-do* strategy utilizes all three modalities to process information into memory. We will learn more about this strategy later in this chapter.

- When you use more than one sensory channel to process information, you create a stronger impression of the information in your memory, so recalling information often occurs more rapidly.

EXERCISE 1.1

Learning Styles Inventory

PURPOSE: Identify your learning style preference and strength of your modalities. Understanding your learning style preference can guide your selection of study and learning strategies to use to be more effective and successful.

DIRECTIONS: Complete the following Learning Styles Inventory by reading each statement carefully. Check YES if the statement relates to you all or most of the time. Check NO if the statement seldom or never relates to you. There is no in-between option, so you must check YES or NO. Your first, quick response to a question is usually the best response to use.

	YES	NO
1. I like to listen and discuss information with another person.	_____	_____
2. I could likely learn or review information effectively by hearing my own voice on tape.	_____	_____
3. I prefer to learn something new by reading about it.	_____	_____
4. I often write down directions someone gives me so I do not forget them.	_____	_____
5. I enjoy physical sports and exercise.	_____	_____
6. I learn best when I can see new information in picture or diagram form.	_____	_____
7. I can easily visualize or picture things in my mind.	_____	_____
8. I learn best when someone talks or explains something to me.	_____	_____
9. I usually write things down so that I can look back at them later.	_____	_____
10. I pay attention to the rhythm and patterns of notes I hear in music.	_____	_____
11. I have a good memory for the words and melodies of old songs.	_____	_____
12. I like to participate in small-group discussions.	_____	_____
13. I often remember the sizes, shapes, and colors of objects when they are no longer in sight.	_____	_____

14. I often repeat out loud verbal directions that someone gives me. _____ _____

15. I enjoy working with my hands. _____ _____

16. I can remember the faces of actors, settings, and other visual details of movies I have seen. _____

17. I often use my hands and body movements when explaining something to someone else. _____ _____

18. I prefer standing up and working on a chalkboard or flip chart to sitting down and working on paper. _____ _____

19. I often seem to learn better if I can get up and move around while I study. _____ _____

20. I often refer to pictures or diagrams to assemble or install something new. _____ _____

21. I remember objects better when I have touched them or worked with them. _____ _____

22. I learn best by watching someone else first. _____ _____

23. I tend to doodle when I think about a problem or situation. _____ _____

24. I speak a foreign language. _____ _____

25. I am comfortable building or constructing things. _____ _____

26. I can follow the plot of a story when I listen to a book on tape. _____ _____

27. I often repair things at home. _____ _____

28. I can understand information when I hear it on tape. _____ _____

29. I am good at using machines or tools. _____ _____

30. I enjoy role-playing or participating in skits. _____ _____

31. I enjoy acting or doing pantomimes. _____ _____

32. I can easily see patterns in designs. _____ _____

33. I often know how to assemble, install, or fix something without referring to written directions. _____ _____

34. I like to recite or write poetry. _____ _____

35. I can usually understand people with foreign accents or dialects. _____ _____

36. I can hear many different pitches or melodies in music. _____ _____

37. I like to dance and create new movements or steps. _____ _____

38. I enjoy participating in activities that require physical coordination. _____ _____

39. I follow written directions better than oral ones. _____ _____

40. I can easily recognize differences between similar sounds. _____ _____

Exercise 1.1 (cont.)

41. I like to create or use jingles/rhymes to learn things.   _____   _____

42. I prefer classes with hands-on experiences.   _____   _____

43. I can quickly tell if two geometric shapes are identical.   _____   _____

44. I remember best things that I have seen in print, in diagrams, or in pictures.   _____   _____

45. I follow oral directions better than written ones.   _____   _____

46. I could learn the names of fifteen medical instruments more easily if I could touch and examine them.   _____   _____

47. I remember details better when I say and repeat them aloud.   _____   _____

48. I can look at a shape and copy it correctly on paper.   _____   _____

49. I can usually read a map without difficulty.   _____   _____

50. I can "hear" a person's exact words and tone of voice days after he or she has spoken to me.   _____   _____

51. I remember directions best when someone gives me landmarks, such as specific buildings and trees.   _____   _____

52. I have a good eye for colors and color combinations.   _____   _____

53. I like to paint, draw, sculpt, or be creative with my hands.   _____   _____

54. I can vividly picture the details of a meaningful past experience.   _____   _____

SCORING YOUR PROFILE

1. Ignore the NO answers. Work only with the questions that have a YES answer.

2. For every YES answer, look at the number of the question. Find the number in the following chart and circle that number.

3. When you finish, not all the numbers in the following boxes will be circled. Your answers will very likely not match anyone else's.

4. Count the number of circles for the Visual box and write the total on the line. Do the same for the Auditory box and Kinesthetic box.

Visual					Auditory					Kinesthetic				
3	4	6	7	9	1	2	8	10	11	5	15	17	18	19
13	16	20	22	32	12	14	24	26	28	21	23	25	27	29
39	43	44	48	49	34	35	36	40	41	30	31	33	37	38
51	52	54			45	47	50			42	46	53		
Total: _____					*Total:* _____					*Total:* _____				

ANALYZING YOUR SCORES

Highest Score   =   Preferred modality and way to process new information

Lowest Score   =   Weakest or least frequently used modality

Scores > 10   =   Frequently used modality

Scores < 10   =   Less frequently used modality

- If your two highest scores are the same, you use both modalities equally well.

- Your weakest modality and any modalities with scores lower than 10 may be the result of limited experiences that utilize this modality.

- Your weakest modality and any modalities with scores lower than 10 may be due to physical or neurological impairments, which may include learning disabilities.

    By learning to use new strategies, you can strengthen all three modalities.

Characteristics and Essential Strategies

As you read through the following common characteristics for each of the three types of learners or learning styles, relate this information to what you learned about yourself in the Learning Styles Inventory. Do you have the same or similar characteristics? Note that a person does not necessarily possess abilities or strengths in all of the characteristics but may instead demonstrate strengths in specific characteristics. Your strengths may reflect your educational or personal background. For example, an auditory learner may be strong in the area of language skills but may not have had the experience or the opportunity to develop skills with a foreign language or music. Finally, pay close attention to the variety of essential learning strategies that you can incorporate into your approach to learning. **Figure 1.2** summarizes essential strategies for each modality.

Visual Learners

Visual learners prefer to process and learn information in visual forms such as pictures, charts, or other printed information, such as lists or paragraphs. They learn and remember best by *seeing* and *visualizing* information. The following are additional characteristics of visual learners:

Visual learners prefer to process and learn information in visual forms such as pictures, charts, or printed information.

- Can easily recall information in the form of numbers, words, phrases, or sentences

- Can easily understand and recall information presented in pictures, charts, or diagrams

- Have strong visualization or visual memory skills and can look up (often up to the left) and "see" information

- Make "movies in their minds" of information they are reading

FIGURE 1.2	Essential Strategies for Visual, Auditory, and Kinesthetic Learners
VISUAL	Highlight textbooks and notes. Create movies in your mind. Create visual study tools. Visualize information. Add pictures. Be ready to write. Be observant.
AUDITORY	Participate in discussions. Ask questions. Verbalize. Recite frequently. Use tapes. Create rhymes, jingles, or songs. Use technology.
KINESTHETIC	Use hands-on learning. Create hands-on study tools. Get out of the chair. Use action-based activities. Use creative movement. Use a computer.

- Have strong visual–spatial skills that involve sizes, shapes, textures, angles, and dimensions
- Have a good eye for colors, design, visual balance, and visual appeal
- Pay close attention and learn to interpret body language (facial expressions, eyes, stance)
- Have a keen awareness of aesthetics, the beauty of the physical environment, and visual media

Visual learners often favor creating and using visual strategies when they study. Having something that they can *see*, examine for details, and even possibly memorize as a mental image is important and effective for visual learners. Following are essential strategies for visual learners. Use these strategies to strengthen and utilize your visual skills.

- **Highlight textbooks and notes.** Use colored highlighter pens to create a stronger visual impression of important facts, definitions, formulas, and steps. You can also write questions in the margins, highlight the answers, and then picture the answers as you review the questions.
- **Create movies in your mind.** Use your visual memory as a television screen with the information that you read or hear moving across the screen as a "movie with the cameras rolling." Practice reviewing the movie in your mind.
- **Create visual study tools.** Create visual mappings, hierarchies, and comparison charts to show levels of details. Color-code different levels of information.

CONCEPT CHECK 1.2

What factors contribute to the development of a learning style preference? Is your learning style preference always the same for all learning situations? Explain by giving examples.

- **Visualize information.** Visually memorize pictures, graphs, study tools, or small sections of printed information. Practice looking away, visualizing, and then checking the accuracy and details of your visual images.
- **Add pictures.** As you expand chapter visual mappings and hierarchies, or as you review your notes and study tools, add pictures to assist the recall of information.
- **Be ready to write.** Copy textbook information as information written in your own handwriting often is easier to visualize and recall than printed text. Create a habit of writing information and directions frequently as written information can be visually memorized and recalled.
- **Be observant.** Pay attention to details of objects and people. Observe nonverbal clues for body language that signal attitudes, feelings, or important points.

Auditory Learners

Auditory learners prefer to process and learn by hearing and discussing information. They prefer to have information presented to them verbally instead of, or in addition to, in writing. They learn by listening to others explain, debate, summarize, or discuss information about topics they are studying. Auditory learners, however, are not passive. Auditory learners like to *talk* and *listen* as they learn. They often get involved with discussions and learn by explaining information in their own words, expressing their understanding or opinions, and providing comments and feedback to other speakers. The following are additional characteristics of auditory learners:

- Can accurately remember details of information heard in conversations or lectures
- Have strong language skills, well-developed vocabularies, and an appreciation of words
- Have strong oral communication skills and are articulate
- Have "finely tuned ears" and may find learning a foreign language relatively easy
- Hear tones, rhythms, and notes of music, and often excel in areas of music
- Have keen auditory memories

Auditory learners often select learning strategies that code or process information through their auditory channel into memory. Following are essential strategies for auditory learners. Use these strategies to strengthen and utilize your auditory skills.

- **Participate in discussions.** Actively engage in group activities, discussions, study groups, and work with tutors. Express your ideas, paraphrase speakers, and summarize what you learn from lectures, conversations, and discussions.
- **Ask questions.** Show your interest and clarify information by asking questions. Practice recalling information and answers that you hear.
- **Verbalize.** Read out loud to activate your auditory channel. For difficult materials, read with exaggerated expression as the natural rhythm and patterns of language tend to group words into units of meaning when spoken.
- **Recite frequently.** Reciting involves stating information out loud, in your own words, in complete sentences, and without referring to printed information. Reciting provides you with feedback to gauge how well you remember and understand information.

> Auditory learners prefer to process and learn by hearing and discussing information.

- **Use tapes.** In difficult classes, request permission to tape lectures. Use the tapes to review and complete your notes after class. You can also read or recite main ideas, facts, details, or lists into a tape recorder to make your own study and review tapes. Your ability to recall information from tapes with your own voice may strengthen your auditory memory.

- **Create rhymes, jingles, or songs.** Short, catchy sayings or tunes that contain information you need to remember are effective study tools to recall information. Practice the rhymes, jingles, or songs multiple times as accuracy is important.

- **Use technology.** Check with your learning labs, library, and Internet resources for audio materials and products to reinforce learning.

Kinesthetic Learners

Kinesthetic learners prefer to process and learn information through large and small muscle movements and hands-on experiences. They learn best with "hands-on" learning that involves feeling, handling, using, manipulating, sorting, assembling, or experimenting with concrete objects or by using full body movement. Large and small muscles hold memory, so involving movement in the learning process creates muscle memory. The following are additional characteristics of kinesthetic learners:

> Kinesthetic learners prefer to process and learn information through large and small muscle movements and hands-on experiences.

- Learn best by working with physical objects and engaging in hands-on learning
- Learn well through movement, such as working at large charts, role-playing, dancing, or performing
- Work well with their hands in areas such as repair work, sculpting, or art
- Are well coordinated, with a strong sense of timing and body movements
- Often wiggle, tap their feet, or move their legs when they sit

Kinesthetic learners often prefer to use strategies that engage their small and large muscles in the learning process. Following are essential strategies for kinesthetic learners. Use these strategies to strengthen and utilize your kinesthetic skills.

- **Use hands-on learning.** Handle objects, tools, or machinery that you are studying. For processes, such as computer applications, repeat the hands-on learning applications several times to create muscle memory.

- **Create hands-on study tools.** Create flashcards that you can shuffle, spread out, sort, categorize, and review. Copy charts, diagrams, visual mappings, or hierarchies; cut them apart and practice reassembling the pieces.

- **Get out of the chair.** When you study, engage large muscle movements by using exaggerated hand expressions or body movements. Pace or walk with study materials in hand. Work at a chalkboard, white board, or flip chart to list, draw, practice, or rework problems. Use poster paper to create study tools, such as large visual mappings, charts, or timelines.

- **Use action-based activities.** Create ways to add action to the learning process; for example, if you are studying perimeters, tape off an area and walk the perimeter. Convert information you are studying into a game, such as Twenty-One Questions, Jeopardy, or Concentration. Review the information by playing the game with another student or group.

- **Use creative movement.** When feasible, incorporate drama, dance, pantomime, or role-playing into your study sessions.
- **Use a computer.** Type information and create notes, tables, and charts on the computer. Keyboard strokes help create muscle memory that you can use to simulate the actions and recall information.

GROUP PROCESSING

A COLLABORATIVE LEARNING ACTIVITY

Form groups of three or four students. Then complete the following directions.

Create a chart with three columns. Label the columns *Visual, Auditory,* and *Kinesthetic.* As a group, brainstorm different learning strategies or "things you can do when you study" that capitalize on each of the learning modalities. Use your own experiences and ideas for study strategies as well as ideas presented in this textbook. You may use the following examples to begin your chart.

Visual	Auditory	Kinesthetic
Use colored pens to highlight.	Talk out loud to study.	Make wall charts to review.

Multisensory Learning Strategies

Now that you are aware of your learning style and learning preference, you can begin the process of exploring new learning strategies, selecting some that utilize your strengths and some that help you "stretch" and strengthen your other modalities. As you experiment with the various essential learning strategies, strive to design *multisensory strategies*, strategies that combine two or more modalities. Explore combinations that help you *see* the information in new ways, *say* the information you are learning, and *do* some type of movement or hands-on activity. Incorporating *see-say-do* strategies benefits you in the following ways:

Multisensory strategies are learning strategies that combine two or more modalities.

- They boost your memory by coding information three different ways.
- They create stronger sensory paths into long-term memory.
- They provide you with multiple ways to access and recall information at later times.
- They add motivation and interest to the learning process and remind you that there is always more than one way to process information.

You can make a conscious effort to use multisensory strategies when you study by exploring ways to work with information using your visual, auditory, and kinesthetic modalities. The following examples show how easily you can encode information into memory using three sensory channels:

1. To learn a process to solve a difficult math problem:

    - **Say:** Verbalize the steps for a solution.
    - **Do:** Copy the steps into your notes.

CONCEPT CHECK 1.4

Why are multisensory strategies so effective? Give an example of using a see-say-do approach for a specific learning task.

- **See:** Color-code each step.
- **Say:** Recite the problem-solving steps for the problem.
- **Do:** Rework the problem multiple times. Check your accuracy.

2. To complete a complex computer project that must be done in the computer lab:

- **Say:** Discuss the lab project with another student.
- **Do:** Take notes on important points or steps.
- **Say:** Reread the notes out loud (verbalize) to check their clarity.
- **See:** Highlight key points or steps.
- **Do:** Perform the operation on the computer at least twice.

As you strive to design multisensory learning strategies, recognize that visual strategies often involve using pictures and colors and then taking time to rehearse or recall the visual images. Note that auditory strategies often involve **verbalizing**, which is the process of speaking or reading out loud to activate your auditory channel and build auditory memory. Verbalizing is less demanding on memory than reciting as you often look at printed information while talking. *Reciting* involves explaining information out loud, in complete sentences, and in your own words without looking at printed information. Kinesthetic strategies involve more active, hands-on approaches, which may include copying, assembling, constructing, or repeating a process multiple times.

Verbalizing involves speaking or reading out loud to activate your auditory channel and build auditory memory.

Reciting involves explaining information out loud, in complete sentences, and in your own words without looking at printed information.

Using Cognitive Modalities

EXERCISE 1.2

DIRECTIONS: Use Exercise 1.2 to identify one or more modalities used in various student activities (Part I) and then to solve a problem (Part II). Work by yourself, with a partner, or in a small group. Follow the directions for Part I and Part II.

PART 1: Read each statement below. Circle **V** (visual), **A** (auditory), or **K** (kinesthetic) to indicate the modality or modalities used by each student.

V A K **1.** To review sections of a chapter, Mark looks at the ceiling, mentally recalls pictures and graphs in the textbook, and then recites information about each one.

V A K **2.** Within the first week of every class, Sharon finds a "study buddy"— someone who wants to meet on a regular basis to discuss class work and topics.

V A K **3.** After each class, Cindy uses three different colors to highlight main ideas in her notes. She then makes flashcards for the terminology so she can recite the definitions and sort the cards into meaningful categories.

V A K **4.** Mark loves history and enjoys discovering relationships among different events. He tacks a long piece of paper across his bedroom wall so he can chart all kinds of events on a continuous time line.

V A K **5.** Liz types all her papers on a computer and then asks a tutor or a friend to read each paper out loud so she can listen to the way she expressed her ideas.

PART 2: Solve the following problem. Pay attention to the approach you use to find the answer.

A parent and a child are standing together on the sidewalk. They both start walking at the same time. Each person begins the first step with the right foot. The child must take three steps for every two steps the parent takes. How many steps must the child take until they both land again on the same foot?

1. How many steps did the child need to take?

2. Did they both land on the right foot or the left foot? _____

3. How did you solve this problem? _____

CHECK POINT 1.1

Answers appear on page B3

True or False?

_____ 1. The term *cognitive* refers to people's awareness of their surroundings.

_____ 2. To be considered a "visual learner," one must show strong signs of possessing all the characteristics of a visual learner.

_____ 3. To some degree, a person's learning style preference reflects his or her personal background and educational experiences.

_____ 4. Having a learning style preference means that a person is strong in only one of the three cognitive learning styles.

_____ 5. Multisensory learning strategies include some form of learning that involves two or all three learning modalities.

 Access Chapter 1 Practice Quiz 1: Cognitive Learning Styles under "Interactive Quizzes" in your college Success CourseMate, accessed through *CengageBrain.com*.

Linear and Global Learners

2 *Identify your linear- or global-learner tendency and discuss how it affects the way you process information.*

How humans process information and the factors that affect learning are areas of study that continue to expand. A multitude of theories, models, and inventories exist to assess and analyze thinking styles, emotional intelligence, and social intelligence as well as behavioral, personality, and psychological styles. These personal inventories are mere indicators of ways you tend to process, learn, or respond to your environment or to other people. The main goal behind these inventories is for you to understand yourself and the ways in which you process information, deal with people, and handle situations most effectively. Regardless of the model or inventory you use, keep in mind that no one learning style is better than another; each style is simply a distinctive way of learning, interacting, or responding.

Brain Dominance Theory

Research beginning in the late 1960s discovered that the human brain consists of two hemispheres or cortices that are connected by a complex network of nerve fibers called the *corpus callosum*. Though the two hemispheres are linked together neurologically, each hemisphere dominates specific kinds of mental activities and learning patterns. This research resulted in the Brain Dominance Theory. The ***Brain Dominance Theory*** is a cognitive model that identifies specific functions of the left hemisphere and the right hemisphere of the brain. **Figure 1.3** summarizes the functions of the right and the left hemispheres.

The Brain Dominance Theory suggests that people tend to have a preference for *initially* processing information through the left hemisphere (also referred to as the left brain) or the right hemisphere (the right brain). However, once they receive and start processing information from one side of the brain, the information then is shared with the other side of the brain, so both sides work together to process information—but in different ways. The result is the total processing of information using an array of functions. The following points are important for understanding total processing:

- Consider the mental activities involved in composing music. Is a composer more likely to be a linear or a global learner? Initially, you might respond that a composer is a global learner because composing involves rhythm, creativity, intuitive feelings, and imagination—functions of the right hemisphere of the brain. After the initial creative process begins, the composer activates linear functions in order to apply specific musical conventions such as writing the music in a logical, recognizable format. However, the composer could be a linear learner by first identifying a specific style or format for the composition and by analyzing the required elements—linear-type thinking. With a logical structure in mind, the composer could then activate the right hemisphere to bring creativity and

The Brain Dominance Theory is a cognitive model that identifies specific functions of the left hemisphere and the right hemisphere of the brain.

CONCEPT CHECK 1.5

As with multisensory learning, why is it important to use both linear-learner and global-learner strategies to process information?

FIGURE 1.3   Brain Dominance Theory

Brain Dominance Theory

Left Hemisphere	**Right Hemisphere**
Linear or Left-Brain Learners	*Global or Right-Brain Learners*
Logic	Generalized
Structured	Spatial
Sequences	Colors
Lists	Visualization
Specific details	Imagination/Creativity
Verbal language	Pictures, Graphs, Charts
Words and numbers	Intuition
Analytical	Interactive
Predictable	Rhythm

Source: Bernstein/Nash, *Essentials of Psychology*, Houghton Mifflin Company, © 2008, p. 70. Reprinted with permission.

imagination to the work. In other words, the process of composing, as well as all other kinds of learning, involves total processing with functions of both hemispheres; the variable is which hemisphere *begins* the process.

- To think of yourself as only a linear learner or as only a global learner limits your perception of yourself and your mental processing skills. Instead, think of yourself as a person who has a brain-hemisphere dominance for the initial intake of information, but who then combines learning activities that activate both brain hemispheres. Making a conscious effort to use a wide variety of study strategies, some linear and some global, will strengthen your ability to learn new information.

Left-Brain or Linear Learners

A *linear learner* is a person who initially processes information through the left hemisphere of the brain, which deals with logic, structured, and verbal information. The left hemisphere of the brain begins processing cognitive activities that involve logical sequencing, such as lists or steps, predictable patterns, verbal language (words), numbers, and analytical thinking. People who begin the initial learning or intake process by activating the left hemisphere first are referred to as left-brain or linear learners. Figure 1.3 summarizes the mental activities of left-brain and right-brain learners. The following are additional characteristics of linear learners:

- They prefer information that provides them with specific details, clearly defined steps, words, numbers, and logical arguments.
- Their initial focus is on the details followed by understanding the "big pictures" these details form.
- They tend to master information in the structured sequence in which it is presented.
- They tend to do well in straightforward, detail-oriented lectures and with textbooks that present information in a sequential, structured, and clear manner.
- They tend to prefer learning situations in which concepts, terminology, facts, details, applications, uses, and conclusions are clearly presented. In courses that require problem solving, such as science or mathematics, linear learners learn the fundamentals, such as problem-solving steps, and then proceed to apply the steps systematically to solve problems or answer questions.
- They tend to do well in science, mathematics, social sciences, and computer technology.

CONCEPT CHECK 1.6

What classroom approaches are best suited for linear learners?

Linear learners may experience some initial difficulty in courses that tend to be more right-brain oriented than left-brain or linear-learner oriented. For example, linear learners may initially flounder or feel frustrated in loosely structured learning environments, class discussions, group processes, or classes that require the learner to interpret passages, attach meanings to symbols, or find creative, self-discovery solutions for problems. Literature, poetry, creative writing, performing arts, career development, or personal development courses may be challenging and require the linear learner to make adjustments in his or her learning processes. Textbooks that do not use headings and subheadings in chapters, unstructured use of textbooks, multiple readings or sources of information, and lectures focusing more on anecdotal experiences than specific facts, data, or technical information may also cause initial frustration for the linear learner. **Figure 1.4** shows strategies a linear learner can use to impose more structure and organization to courses and course materials that tend to be more global-learner oriented.

FIGURE 1.4   Essential Strategies for Linear Learners in Global-Learning Situations

1. Ask for a summary of important points at the end of an open-ended or discussion-oriented class. List the significant points and the conclusions. After class, organize the information into a more meaningful format or structure.

2. During discussions, jot down the various points or opinions expressed. After class, organize the information into more meaningful lists or into charts.

3. When working with multiple sources of information, take notes from each source. Then use your organizational skills to integrate the information logically.

4. Add your own headings or subheadings to textbooks and lecture notes that lack the detailed organizational structure that works effectively for you.

Right-Brain or Global Learners

A global learner is a person who initially processes information through the right hemisphere of the brain, which deals with colors, visualization, creativity, and visual information.

A *global learner* is a person who initially processes information through the right hemisphere of the brain, which deals with colors, visualization, creativity, and visual information. The right hemisphere of the brain begins processing cognitive activities that involve spatial skills, pictures, colors, visual memories (visualizations), imagination, creativity, intuition, and rhythm. Because the right hemisphere deals with information in more generalized or big-picture patterns, people who begin the initial learning or intake process by activating the right hemisphere first are referred to as right-brain or global learners. (See Figure 1.3.) The following are additional characteristics of global learners:

- They first tend to see "the big picture," and then focus their learning on the details that develop the big picture concept.

- They enjoy learning details through discovery, experiment, exploration, discussion, brainstorming, or group processes. As a result, they tend to learn details in random order; they may not understand the details clearly until the *light bulb turns on,* and all the details come together and form the big picture.

- They prefer information in the form of pictures, charts, diagrams, and colorful visual stimuli.

- They enjoy using their creativity and intuition to process information, its meaning, and its applications. In problem-solving situations, they may take intuitive leaps to find solutions, sometimes creating their own problem-solving steps. They may be unable to explain to others how they arrive at their solutions.

- They do well in classes that involve learning communities, informally structured environments, discussions, group or cooperative learning activities, creative problem solving, and creative interpretation such as in literature, poetry, creative writing, performing arts, or personal development classes.

- To learn from textbooks, global learners often benefit from reading a chapter introduction, skimming through the entire chapter, and reading the summary. This helps them create a big picture before they begin learning specific details.

Global learners may experience some initial difficulty in courses that tend to be more left-brain oriented than right-brain or global-learner oriented. Teacher-directed or traditional lecture-based classrooms that focus on specific details, facts, steps, or processes without sufficient attention to the big picture may be challenging. Classroom

---

FIGURE 1.5   Essential Strategies for Global Learners in Linear-Learning Situations

1. When appropriate during a lecture, ask for specific examples or anecdotes to clarify factual information that is presented in a straightforward manner.

2. Ask instructors and other students questions about connections, relationships, trends, or themes when the details seem detached from the whole or the big picture.

3. Find a "study buddy," form a study group or an online chat group, or participate in tutoring or discussion

sessions so you can discuss course topics and interact with other students.

4. Add creativity to your lecture notes or course materials by adding colors, pictures, or diagrams to emphasize important points.

5. Rearrange information into charts or visual notes to show the big picture and the significant details.

6. Preview (survey) an entire chapter to get the big picture before reading the chapter for details.

---

environments with little opportunity to interact, use leadership skills, actively participate, or use hands-on learning may frustrate the global learner. In such classes, global learners may feel less engaged, and the learning process may feel impersonal or lacking creativity. **Figure 1.5** shows strategies a global learner can use to create a greater sense of involvement and interaction in a learning situation that tends to be more linear-learner oriented.

CONCEPT CHECK 1.7

How do preferred classroom approaches of global learners differ from preferred approaches of linear learners?

EXERCISE 1.3

Brain Dominance Inventory—Left/Right, Linear/Global Dominance

PURPOSE: The Brain Dominance Theory suggests that people tend to have a preference for initially processing information through the left hemisphere or the right hemisphere of the brain. Use this inventory as one way to identify yourself as a linear or a global learner.

DIRECTIONS: Answer all of these questions quickly; do not stop to analyze them. When you have no clear preference, choose the one that most closely represents your attitudes or behaviors.

_____ 1. When I buy a new product, I
   a. usually read the directions and carefully follow them.
   b. refer to the directions, but really try and figure out how the thing operates or is put together on my own.

_____ 2. Which of these words best describes the way I perceive myself in dealing with others?
   a. Structured/Rigid
   b. Flexible/Open-minded

_____ 3. Concerning hunches:
   a. I generally would not rely on hunches to help me make decisions.
   b. I have hunches and follow many of them.

Exercise 1.3 (cont.)

_____ **4.** I make decisions mainly based on
   a. what experts say will work.
   b. a willingness to try things that I think might work.

_____ **5.** In travelling or going to a destination, I prefer
   a. to read and follow a map.
   b. to get directions and map things out "my" way.

_____ **6.** In school, I preferred
   a. geometry.
   b. algebra.

_____ **7.** When I read a play or novel, I
   a. see the play or novel in my head as if it were a movie or TV drama.
   b. read the words to obtain information.

_____ **8.** When I want to remember directions, a name, or a news item, I
   a. visualize the information or write notes that help me create a picture or maybe even draw the directions.
   b. write structured and detailed notes.

_____ **9.** I prefer to be in the class of a teacher who
   a. has the class do activities and encourages class participation and discussions.
   b. primarily lectures.

_____ **10.** In writing, speaking, and problem solving, I am
   a. usually creative, preferring to try new things.
   b. seldom creative, preferring traditional solutions.

Source: Berko, et al., *Communicating,* "Learn by Doing" test, pp. 108–109, © 2007 by Pearson Education, Inc. Reproduced by Permission of Pearson Education, Inc.

SCORING

For items 1 through 5, give yourself one point for each **b** answer: _____

For items 6 through 10, give yourself one point for each **a** answer: _____

Total Score: _____

Circle your total points on the following scale.

Left   **1   2   3   4   5   6   7   8   9   10**   Right

INTERPRETATION

Scores of 1 or 2:	Left-brain tendency; highly linear
Scores of 3 and possibly 4:	Left-brain or linear tendency
Scores of 4 through 7:	Possibly no dominance; flexible in learning style
Scores of 8 and possibly 7:	Right-brain or global tendency
Scores of 9 and 10:	Right-brain tendency; highly global

Source: Berko, et al., *Communicating,* "Learn by Doing" test, pp. 108–109, © 2007 by Pearson Education, Inc. Reproduced by permission of Pearson Education, Inc.

Diverse Learners in the Classroom

As you sit in your classrooms, you can be assured that you are a member of a diverse group of learners. Students with visual-, auditory-, kinesthetic-, linear-, and global-learning style preferences sit side by side, taking in and processing information differently. You undoubtedly have experienced these differences in the classroom as some students seem to grasp information more readily while other students struggle with making sense of the new information.

Instructors' teaching styles often reflect their individual learning styles and preferences. Historically, the American approach to education favored the visual and linear learners. However, as instructors learned new teaching methods and perhaps even modified their learning style preferences, many instructional approaches became more compatible with a greater variety of learning styles. Inevitably, however, you will find yourself in a classroom with an instructor whose teaching style differs from your learning style preferences. To do well in such classes, vary your learning strategies to adjust to the instructor, the classroom approach, and the materials. Your goal as an adult learner is to increase your ability to perform well in a wide range of learning situations.

When you have the option, consider the following suggestions for identifying courses and instructors that are compatible with your learning style preferences:

1. Before enrolling in a course that offers several sections with different instructors, talk to other students, instructors, and counselors to learn more about the teaching and classroom styles of each instructor. *If you have a choice,* enroll in the section with the instructor who seems most compatible with your learning styles and preferences.

2. Find out what support services are available for the course. Are there study guides, study groups, supplemental computer instruction, or tutors available? If so, use them.

3. Find out what forms of assessment are used in the course. Are grades based solely on tests, or do grades include group or individual projects, assignments, or portfolios?

CHECK POINT 1.2

Answers appear on page B3

True or False?

_____ 1. The three cognitive learning styles are hands-on, visual, and kinesthetic.

_____ 2. Visual learners have strong memories for printed material and visualization; auditory learners have strong auditory memories for information they hear and discuss.

_____ 3. A study strategy that uses a multisensory approach incorporates more than one cognitive learning style or modality.

_____ 4. Linear learners often prefer using intuition, visually graphic materials, and interactive approaches to learn new information.

_____ 5. The Brain Dominance Theory states that people first take information into the left hemisphere of their brain and then integrate it with the right hemisphere.

 Access Chapter 1 Practice Quiz 2: Linear/Global Learners under "Interactive Quizzes" in your College Success CourseMate, accessed through *CengageBrain.com.*

some intelligences are more developed than others. The MI Theory also recognizes that people have the *potential* to activate and strengthen all eight intelligences. Following are several outcomes of the MI theory and research:

- Educators recognized the importance of incorporating more multi-intelligence based activities and approaches in classrooms for students of all ages.
- Effective training, experience, opportunities, and conducive environments have the potential to expand students' abilities and intelligences.
- Including skills of all eight intelligences in the classroom promotes individuals to reach greater levels of performance and fulfillment.
- A greater variety of talents and abilities are appreciated and acknowledged as being of special value and significance.

Intelligences Defined

In 1983, Gardner defined *an intelligence* as "the ability to solve problems or to create products that are valued within one or more cultural settings." In 1999, Gardner's definition of intelligences broadened. Gardner stated:

> I now conceptualize **an intelligence** as *biopsychological potential to process information that can be activated in a cultural setting to solve problems or create products that are of value in a culture.*

Gardner continued, "This modest change in wording is important because it suggests that intelligences are not things that can be seen or counted. Instead, they are potentials . . . that will or will not be activated, depending upon the values of a particular culture, the opportunities available in that culture, and the personal decisions made by individuals and/or their families, schoolteachers, and others." [From Howard Gardner, *Intelligence Reframed: Multiple Perspectives for The 21st Century,* 1999, pp. 33–34. Copyright © 1999 Howard Gardner. Reprinted by permission of Basic Books, a member of Perseus Books, L.L.C.]

CONCEPT CHECK 1.8

How does Gardner's theory of intelligences (MI) differ from the traditional theory of intelligence (IQ)? What abilities does MI add to the traditional IQ theory?

An intelligence is the potential to process information that can be activated in a cultural setting to solve problems or create products that are of value in a culture.

Access Chapter 1 Topics In-Depth: Scientific Criteria in your College Success CourseMate, accessed through *CengageBrain.com*.

EXERCISE 1.5

Definition of an Intelligence

Gardner's definition of an intelligence is perhaps easier to grasp by breaking the definition into the following five distinct parts. With a partner or in a small group, discuss each part, its significance in defining an intelligence, and your general reaction to the wording used as part of Gardner's definition of an intelligence.

1. biopsychological
2. potential
3. process information that can be activated in a cultural setting
4. information to solve problems or create products
5. solve problems or create products of value in a culture

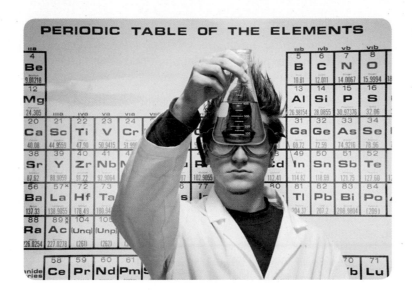

You possess interests, abilities, and learning styles unique to you. Learning to use your strengths and apply your abilities increases your academic performance. How do you use your talents, interests, and learning styles in your courses?

© Image Source/Getty Images.

Subintelligences

Gardner states that *subintelligences* are *core abilities* that are part of a larger individual intelligence. Each of the eight intelligences has subintelligences. For example, people can exhibit many different talents and abilities under the category of musical intelligence. Due to lack of opportunity, experiences, or training, a person with a high musical intelligence at a given time may not demonstrate a high level of all of the subintelligences of music. Singing, playing different instruments, composing, conducting, critiquing, and appreciating a variety of music require different skills, abilities, and processes. The level of accomplishment or mastery of subintelligences will vary among individuals, but the *potential exists* to activate, develop, and strengthen the various subintelligences of each intelligence. You will learn more about subintelligences (core abilities) in the following sections for each of the eight intelligences.

Subintelligences are core abilities that are part of a larger individual intelligence.

Linguistic Intelligence

Linguistic intelligence is the ability to use verbal and written language effectively. Common subintelligences (core abilities) of this intelligence include:

- A love of language—a curiosity, fascination, and sensitivity to words, their meanings, their ability to evoke feelings, and their usages (semantics)
- An interest in the structure of language (syntax) and the sounds used in a language (phonology)
- Sharp, detailed, vivid memories about written or spoken language
- The ability to excel in word games such as crossword puzzles or Scrabble
- The ability to create, recite, and remember puns, jingles, or poetry
- An ability to learn and speak foreign languages
- An ability to express ideas well in public (presentations, storytelling, or debates)
- An ability to express ideas well in writing (novels, articles, journals, prose, or poetry)

Linguistic intelligence is the ability to use verbal and written language effectively.

CONCEPT CHECK 1.9

Do individuals tend to demonstrate all of the subintelligences that belong to a specific intelligence? Do they have the potential to demonstrate all of the core abilities?

Following are common career options for people with strong linguistic intelligence:

author, journalist, editor, poet, newscaster, television announcer, motivational speaker, playwright, politician, consultant, lawyer

Logical-Mathematical Intelligence

Logical-mathematical intelligence is the ability to use logic, problem solving, analysis, and mathematical calculations effectively.

Logical-mathematical intelligence is the ability to use logic, problem solving, analysis, and mathematical calculations effectively. Other subintelligences (core abilities) include the ability to:

- Use sound reasoning, pattern identification, and sequential thinking
- Think both concretely and abstractly
- Understand and apply abstract numerical symbols and operations, and perform complex calculations
- Use systematic, logic-based, sequential problem-solving techniques and scientific methods to measure, hypothesize, test, research, and confirm results

Following are common career options for people with strong logical-mathematical intelligence:

mathematician, math or business teacher, scientist, computer programmer, accountant, tax expert, banker, researcher

Musical Intelligence

Musical intelligence is the ability to show an acute sensitivity and appreciation of musical patterns and elements, such as pitch, timbre, and harmony.

Musical intelligence is the ability to show an acute sensitivity and appreciation of musical patterns and elements, such as pitch, timbre, and harmony. People with these developed abilities may use vocal or instrumental music to express creativity, imagination, and the gamut of human emotions. Other subintelligences (core abilities) include:

- Skills in reading and writing (composing) music
- An understanding of music theory and symbols
- A passion for different types and structures of music
- Strong auditory memories for verbal and musical information
- Appreciation of various forms of musical expression: singing, chanting, humming, or drumming

Following are common career options for people with strong musical intelligence:

music teacher, composer, conductor, performer, sound engineer, filmmaker, television crew or director, marketing or advertising personnel

Bodily-Kinesthetic Intelligence

Bodily-kinesthetic intelligence is the ability to use precise body rhythms and movements, motor coordination skills, and other skills such as timing, balance, and flexibility.

Bodily-kinesthetic intelligence is the ability to use precise body rhythms and movements, motor coordination skills, and other skills such as timing, balance, and flexibility. People with high bodily-kinesthetic intelligence often prefer hands-on or activity-oriented tasks. Other subintelligences (core abilities) include:

- Dexterity and possibly strength and speed
- Well-developed gross (large) motor skills, an ability to judge how their bodies will respond to certain situations, and an ability to fine-tune and train their bodies to perform at higher levels
- Well-developed fine (small) motor skills, an ability to work well with their hands to create, modify, or fix objects, and an acute sensitivity "through their hands." For example, a mechanic unable to see inside an engine may be able to locate and fix a problem using only his or her hands.
- An enjoyment of physical exercise, sports, dancing, drama, role-playing, inventing, building, and repairing things

Following are common career options for people with strong bodily-kinesthetic intelligence:

dancer, athlete, actor, musician/instrumentalist (guitarist, drummer, pianist), dance teacher, choreographer, photographer, mime artist, painter, sculptor, surgeon, inventor, craftsperson

Spatial Intelligence

Spatial intelligence is the ability to use keen perceptions of patterns, shapes, textures, and visual skills. People with developed spatial intelligence often possess strong visual imagery or visualization skills, creativity, and active imaginations. Other subintelligences (core abilities) include:

- An ability to accurately perceive sizes, geometric forms, lines, curves, and angles in the physical world
- An ability to present their ideas graphically; for example, a gifted chess player can play a challenging game of chess blindfolded, or an architect can picture the floor plans of a building before drawing them
- Interest and abilities in the areas of fine arts, such as painting, sculpting, drawing, drafting, or photography

Following are common career options for people with strong spatial intelligence:

architect, designer, interior decorator, artist, painter, sculptor, fashion designer, landscaper, carpenter, contractor, graphic artist, advertiser, cartographer, inventor, pilot, surgeon

> Spatial intelligence is the ability to use keen perceptions of patterns, shapes, textures, and visual skills.

Interpersonal Intelligence

Interpersonal intelligence is the ability to use effective communication, social, leadership, and cooperative teamwork skills. Individuals with strong interpersonal intelligence participate actively in groups, create bonds with diverse groups of people, and feel a sense of global responsibility toward others. Other subintelligences (core abilities) include:

- The ability to interpret nonverbal clues that appear in the form of facial expressions, gestures, or general body language
- The ability to interpret the behavior, motivation, and intentions of others
- Enjoyment of socializing, helping others, sharing their skills, tutoring or teaching others
- The ability to contribute to the development of positive group dynamics

Following are common career options for people with strong interpersonal intelligence:

parent, tutor, teacher, therapist, counselor, healer, social activist, motivational speaker, workshop leader, religious leader, sociologist, actor, political organizer, salesperson

> Interpersonal intelligence is the ability to use effective communication, social, leadership, and cooperative teamwork skills.

Intrapersonal Intelligence

Intrapersonal intelligence is the ability to use skills related to personal growth, self-understanding, and self-motivation and to use intuition and spirituality. Individuals with strong intrapersonal intelligence use personal reflection and

> Intrapersonal intelligence is the ability to use skills related to personal growth, self-understanding, and self-motivation and to use intuition and spirituality.

self-motivation to achieve personal goals and potential. Other subintelligences (core abilities) include:

- Enjoyment of exploring their feelings, values, goals, strengths, weaknesses, and personal history
- The ability to interpret life experiences as lessons and guides to change aspects of their lives and to give their lives meaning
- An ability to project a sense of pride, self-esteem, confidence, self-responsibility, control, and empowerment
- An ability to be self-regulating, self-motivated, and goal-oriented
- An ability to adapt well to a wide variety of situations and circumstances

Following are common career options for people with strong intrapersonal intelligence:

psychiatrist, spiritual or personal counselor, self-help or motivational writer or speaker, philosopher, biographer

Naturalist Intelligence

> Naturalist intelligence is the ability to show a sensitivity to the physical world, which includes the balance of plants, animals, and the environment.

The *naturalist intelligence* is the ability to show a sensitivity to the physical world, which includes the balance of plants, animals, and the environment. People with strong naturalist intelligence are keen observers of nature's elements—such as daily, seasonal, and cyclical changes—and of the relationships in nature. Other subintelligences (core abilities) include:

- An ability to demonstrate detailed knowledge and expertise in recognizing and classifying plants and animals
- An ability to organize, classify, arrange, or group items and ideas into logical units or categories
- An ability to apply strong pattern-recognition talents to areas outside of the plant-animal world, such as with artists, poets, laboratory scientists, and social scientists

Following are common career options for people with strong naturalist intelligence:

meteorologist, geologist, botanist, herbologist, biologist, naturopath, holistic healer, medicine man, gardener, environmentalist

Recognizing Intelligences

EXERCISE 1.6

PURPOSE: Various activities activate specific intelligences by utilizing core abilities or subintelligences in the process. By analyzing specific tasks, you can more readily identify the intelligences that individuals activate and utilize.

DIRECTIONS

PART I: Work with a partner or in a small group. Discuss which of the eight intelligences is activated in each activity: linguistic, logical-mathematical, musical, bodily-kinesthetic, spatial, interpersonal, intrapersonal, or naturalist. You may identify more than one intelligence per activity.

1. Work as a group to create a student hand book for incoming freshmen.

   _____

2. Perform a scene from a book in a literature class.

   _____

3. Interview four people who work in the career field of interest to you, and then compile the results of the four interviews you conducted.

   _____

4. Select appropriate plants to use for experiments in an existing greenhouse on campus.

   _____

5. Collect and organize samples of music from five different cultural or ethnic groups.

   _____

6. Use a computer graphics program to create an eye-catching presentation about your heritage or cultural ties.

   _____

7. Construct a 3-D model that shows your idea for making better use of an existing space on campus.

   _____

8. Keep a daily journal or log to record your progress in reaching a specific goal.

   _____

9. Role-play a conflict resolution strategy.

   _____

10. Organize a small group of students to tutor elementary school students.

    _____

PART II: Review the core abilities or subintelligences of each of the eight intelligences. Discuss with your partner or the group which of the intelligences you believe are most developed in you. Explain your response.

Tests for Multiple Intelligences

Informal Multiple Intelligences inventories that use a linguistic or logical paper-pencil test to identify people's *preferences* or skills in using specific core abilities do exist, but there are no scientific tests at this time to assess intelligences defined as "the potential to process information that can be activated in a cultural setting to solve problems or create products that are of value in a culture." Valid, scientific assessment procedures would require that testers place individuals in settings where the individuals are required to activate specific intelligences. The following points from Howard Gardner about testing for intelligences and identifying additional intelligences provide further information about his MI Theory:

● "I would recommend that any intelligence be assessed by a number of complementary approaches that consider the several core components [subintelligences] of an intelligence. Thus, for example, spatial intelligence might be

CONCEPT CHECK 1.10

The I.Q. test results in an intelligence score. Why is it difficult to obtain test scores for each of Gardner's eight intelligences?

assessed by asking people to find their way around an unfamiliar terrain, to solve an abstract jigsaw puzzle, and to construct a three-dimensional model of their home." [Copyright © 2000 Howard Gardner. Reprinted by permission of Basic Books, a member of Perseus Books, L.L.C.]

- "Or if one wants to examine musical intelligence, one should expose people to a new melody in a reasonably familiar idiom and determine how readily they can learn to sing it, recognize it, transform it, and so on." [From Howard Gardner, *Intelligence Reframed.* Copyright © 1999 Howard Gardner, pages 80–81. Reprinted by permission of Basic Books, a member of Perseus Books, L.L.C.]

- In Gardner's book *Intelligence Reframed,* Gardner discusses spiritual and existential capabilities and whether or not they qualify as new intelligences. Gardner concludes that neither spiritual nor existential capabilities meet all eight scientific criteria used to categorize a set of abilities as an intelligence; therefore, neither can at this time be classified as a ninth intelligence. Gardner states, "Despite the attractiveness of a ninth intelligence, however, I am not adding existential intelligence to the list. I find the phenomenon perplexing enough and the distance from other intelligences vast enough to dictate prudence—at least for now. At most, I am willing . . . to joke about '8 1/2 intelligences.'" [p. 66].

CHAPTER 1
REFLECTIVE WRITING 2

On separate paper, in a journal, or online at this textbook's CourseMate Web site, respond to the following questions.

1. What academic major or career path interests you? How does your choice of careers reflect or not reflect your abilities or perceived intelligences as defined by Gardner?

2. What would be an ideal classroom environment and instructional approach for you that would

allow you to capitalize on your various learning styles and preferences? Use specific details to describe the classroom and the instructional approach.

Access Chapter 1 Reflective Writing 2 in your College Success CourseMate, accessed through *CengageBrain.com.*

Chapter 1 Critical Thinking

PURPOSE: Use your critical thinking skills to explore the relationships among the three different theories or perspectives on how people learn and process information: Cognitive Learning Styles, Brain Dominance, and Multiple Intelligences.

DIRECTIONS By yourself, with a partner, or in a small group, discuss answers to the following questions.

1. What relationships exist between cognitive learning styles and each of the eight intelligences?

2. Which intelligences do you think would be strongest for global learners? Explain your reasoning.

3. Which intelligences do you think would be strongest for linear learners? Explain your reasoning.

4. What relationships can you suggest exist between global and linear learners and the three cognitive learning styles?

CHECK POINT 1.3

Answers appear on page B3

True or False?

_____ 1. Howard Gardner has identified eight intelligences; each intelligence has core abilities called subintelligences.

_____ 2. To be considered intellectually strong in any one of the intelligences, a person must exhibit developed abilities in all of the core abilities for that intelligence.

_____ 3. Both IQ and MI tests are readily available to assess a person's intellectual abilities.

_____ 4. A person with a well-developed interpersonal intelligence may demonstrate leadership skills and work well with others.

_____ 5. In the MI Theory, an intelligence involves the potential to solve problems or create products that have value in a culture.

 Access Chapter 1 Practice Quiz 3: Multiple Intelligences under "Interactive Quizzes" in your College Success CourseMate, accessed through *CengageBrain.com*.

Learning Objectives Review

① *Identify your preferred cognitive learning style and describe learning strategies you can use to utilize your preferred learning style and strengthen your other modalities.*

- Visual, auditory, and kinesthetic are modalities related to three cognitive learning styles or learning preferences. Learning preferences reflect how individuals prefer to have information presented in order to problem solve, process, learn, and remember new information.

- Effective study strategies for each modality preference as well as *see-say-do* multisensory activities are available to use during the learning process.

② *Identify your linear- or global-learner tendency and discuss how it affects the way you process information.*

- The Brain Dominance Theory suggests that people prefer to *initially* process information through the left or the right hemisphere of the brain. After initial processing, information is shared with the other side of the brain for total processing.

Terms to Know

By yourself or with a partner, practice reciting or writing definitions for the following terms. You may also practice defining these terms by using the online flashcards or comparing your answers to the online glossary.

cognitive learning styles p. 5

learning modalities p. 5

learning style preference p. 5

visual learner p. 9

auditory learner p. 11

kinesthetic learner p. 12

multisensory strategies p. 13

verbalizes p. 14

recites p. 14

Terms to Know

Brain Dominance Theory p. 16

linear learner p. 17

global learner p. 18

Theory of Multiple Intelligences p. 23

an intelligence p. 24

subintelligences p. 25

linguistic intelligence p. 25

logical-mathematical intelligence p. 26

musical intelligence p. 26

bodily-kinesthetic intelligence p. 26

spatial intelligence p. 27

interpersonal intelligence p. 27

intrapersonal intelligence p. 27

naturalist intelligence p. 28

 Access Chapter 1 Flashcard Drills and Online Glossary in your College Success CourseMate, accessed through *CengageBrain .com.*

- Each hemisphere dominates specific kinds of cognitive activities and learning patterns. The left hemisphere focuses on structured, sequential, logically organized details. The right hemisphere focuses on generalized, big pictures and uses colors, creativity, visualization, and intuition in processing information.

- Linear learners are the left-brain learners. Global learners are the right-brain learners.

- By knowing how to use an array of learning strategies, students can adjust their approaches to instructors, classroom approaches, and course materials.

3 *Define the term intelligences and describe the common characteristics of each of Howard Gardner's eight intelligences.*

- Gardner identifies eight intelligences: linguistic, logical-mathematical, musical, bodily-kinesthetic, spatial, interpersonal, intrapersonal, and naturalist. General characteristics, skills, and career tendencies exist for each intelligence.

- Gardner uses a set of scientific criteria to qualify skills and abilities as an intelligence. More than a decade after identifying the original seven intelligences, Gardner added an eighth intelligence, the naturalist.

- Gardner defines intelligence as the "biopsychological potential to process information that can be activated in a cultural setting to solve problems or create products that are of value in a culture."

- Each of the eight intelligences has subintelligences (core abilities). A person may not exhibit developed abilities in all of the subintelligences.

Chapter 1 Review Questions

Answers appear on page B3

True or False?

_____ 1. Cognitive learning styles refer to the way people interact in group settings.

_____ 2. Learning styles indicate people's preferred ways of learning and processing new information.

_____ 3. Global learners tend to prefer creative, interactive, and intuitive approaches to learning new information.

_____ 4. Howard Gardner's Multiple Intelligences Theory claims that the eight intelligences reflect potential abilities that individuals can develop and strengthen.

_____ 5. The skills or abilities exhibited by a person with a well-developed logical-mathematical intelligence reflect characteristics of linear learners.

Multiple Choice

_____ 1. Which statement is *not* true about the Brain Dominance Theory?

    a. The human brain consists of two hemispheres that are linked together neurologically.

    b. Each hemisphere of the brain dominates specific kinds of mental activities.

    c. The majority of students are global learners.

    d. Both hemispheres share information to achieve total processing.

_____ 2. Linear learners

    a. are also referred to as left-brain learners.

    b. prefer information presented in logical, structured, and predictable ways.

    c. can learn to function effectively in "right-brain" oriented learning environments.

    d. exhibit all of the above.

_____ 3. Which of the following is *not* true about multisensory learning?

    a. It involves selecting strategies that utilize two or more modalities.

    b. It always requires verbalizing and reciting to process information.

    c. It provides multiple ways to access and recall information later.

    d. It focuses on strategies that use a combination of *see, say,* and *do* processes.

_____ 4. A person with a well-developed *naturalist intelligence* may exhibit

    a. strong pattern-recognition skills.

    b. the ability to organize and classify objects in the plant and animal world.

    c. a sensitivity to the cycles and balances in nature.

    d. all of the above.

Definitions

On separate paper, define each of the following terms.

1. Multisensory strategies
2. Reciting
3. Subintelligence
4. Intrapersonal intelligence

Short-Answer Question

Use complete sentences to answer the following question. Use information and terminology from this chapter. Write your answer on separate paper.

Question: The Theory of Multiple Intelligences contends that the traditional IQ tests are too limiting. What intelligences did Howard Gardner add to expand the concept of traditional intelligence and include a wider range of talents and abilities?

 Access Chapter 1 Chapter Quizzes 1–4 and Enhanced Quiz under "Interactive Quizzes" in your College Success CourseMate, accessed through *CengageBrain* .com.

Access all Chapter 1 Online Materials in your College Success CourseMate, accessed through *CengageBrain.com.*

2

Processing Information into Your Memory

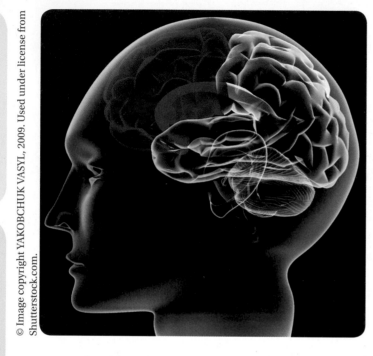

For centuries people have been fascinated by the workings of the human mind. Researchers and cognitive psychologists are now able to use sophisticated technology to study the human brain, its processing functions, and its complex structure. In this chapter, you will learn about a contemporary Information Processing Model that consists of three memory systems. Working memory, one of the three memory systems, is your conscious mind that is aware of all cognitive processes. You will learn processes and strategies to strengthen and use your working memory more effectively. By understanding *how* your mind processes information and *how* your memory works, you can use this information to increase your learning potential and to tailor or personalize your approach to learning different kinds of information.

LEARNING OBJECTIVES

1. *Explain how the three memory systems (sensory memory, working memory, and long-term memory) work to process information.*

2. *Explain four processes that work in your conscious mind: conducting memory searches, creating and using retrieval cues, tracking thought patterns, and rehearsing learned information.*

3. *Identify essential study skills strategies that strengthen working memory.*

1 **THE INFORMATION PROCESSING MODEL**

Input from the Physical World

Sensory Memory

Working Memory

Long-Term Memory

Output

2 **YOUR CONSCIOUS MIND AT WORK**

Conducting Memory Searches

Creating and Using Retrieval Cues

Tracking Your Thought Patterns

Rehearsing Learned Information

3 **ESSENTIAL STRATEGIES FOR WORKING MEMORY**

Limited Intake

Interest and Excitement

Learning Goals

Items in Lists

Spaced Practice

 Access Chapter 2 Expanded Outline and Objectives in your College Success CourseMate, accessed through *CengageBrain.com*.

YOUR CHAPTER MAPPING

After reading information under each heading, return to the chapter visual mapping below. Add key words to show subheadings and important details related to each heading.

 Access Chapter 2 Visual Mapping in your College Success CourseMate, accessed through *CengageBrain.com*.

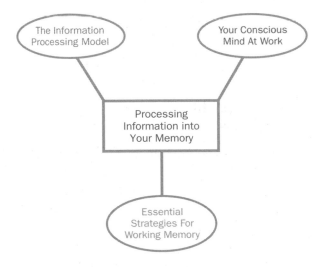

CHAPTER 2 PROFILE

INFORMATION PROCESSING

ANSWER, SCORE, AND RECORD your profile before you read this chapter. If you need to review the process, refer to the complete directions given in the profile for Chapter 1 on page 4.

ONLINE: You can complete the profile and get your score online at this textbook's CourseMate Web site.

 Access Chapter 2 Profile in your College Success CourseMate, accessed through *CengageBrain.com*.

	YES	NO
1. I have a general understanding of the kinds of mental activities and connections that take place when I learn new information.	___	___
2. I pay attention to the different kinds of information I receive on a regular basis from my senses: sight, sound, smell, taste, and touch.	___	___
3. I code all new information in a visual form so it is easy to remember or recall at a later time.	___	___
4. I monitor the speed that I take in information and the quantity of information that I try to learn at one time.	___	___
5. When I try to recall information from my memory, I use words, pictures, or other cues to find the information.	___	___
6. I am aware of my thought patterns and the way I connect ideas when I begin learning new information.	___	___
7. I take time to relate or associate new information to information that I already know.	___	___
8. When I need to learn items in a list, I give each item in the list an equal amount of my attention to learn.	___	___
9. When a subject is not very interesting to me, I find ways to create an interest and maintain a positive attitude.	___	___
10. I am confident in my ability to use effective strategies to boost my ability to process information without overloading working memory.	___	___

QUESTIONS LINKED TO THE CHAPTER LEARNING OBJECTIVES:

Questions 1–4: objective 1   Questions 8, 9: objective 3

Questions 5–7: objective 2   Question 10: all objectives

The Information Processing Model

 Explain how the three memory systems (sensory memory, working memory, and long-term memory) work to process information.

Understanding memory and information processing lays a strong foundation for many study skills strategies that you will learn in this textbook. Brain research, learning theories, and models of memory are complex and more detailed than we

will cover in this textbook, but understanding basic processes will equip you with essential information to help you increase your learning potential and tailor or personalize your approach to learning different kinds of information. (For information about four models of memory, read **Excerpt 1, Appendix D.** The Working Memory Information Processing Model in this chapter incorporates the key processes of four models of memory.)

Understanding how your mind processes and how your memory works is the first step to using the powerful process of metacognition. *Metacognition* is the process of understanding *how* you learn, *what* you need to learn, and finally, *which* strategies or techniques would be the most effective or the best matched to the learning task. Your ability to use metacognition effectively will increase as you acquire new study skills and strategies.

The *Information Processing Model* is a cognitive model that consists of three memory centers: *sensory memory, working memory,* and *long-term memory*. The Information Processing Model provides a foundation for understanding the kinds of mental activities and connections that are necessary for learning to take place. The model shown in **Figure 2.1** shows how sensory stimuli from the physical world move back and forth through the three memory systems when you process information.

Each part of the Information Processing Model plays an important role in the learning process. In this chapter, you will learn about each part of the Information Processing Model and become familiar with strategies that you can use to strengthen your memory and your ability to learn new information. In Chapter 3, "Using Twelve Principles of Memory," you will learn additional strategies that you can apply to any learning situation to increase your level of performance and improve your memory.

Input from the Physical World

The Information Processing Model begins with sensory input from the physical world. *Sensory input* refers to all the sensory stimuli from the physical world that we receive through our five senses—sight, sound, touch, taste, and smell. Sensory input comes in many forms: letters, numbers, words, visual images, sounds, smells, or tactile sensations, such as textures or the hardness or softness of objects. At this very second, you are receiving sensory input from your environment.

CONCEPT CHECK 2.1

Metacognition is the process of understanding what three things about the learning process?

Metacognition is the process of understanding *how* you learn, *what* you need to learn, and finally, *which* strategies or techniques would be the most effective or the best matched to the learning task.

The **Information Processing Model** is a cognitive model that consists of three memory centers: sensory memory, working memory, and long-term memory.

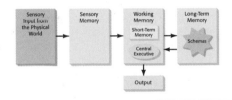

Sensory input refers to all the sensory stimuli from the physical world that we receive through our five senses—sight, sound, touch, taste, and smell.

FIGURE 2.1 The Information Processing Model

Sensory memory *is the first memory center; it holds stimuli for one or two seconds.* Working memory, *the second memory center, has two parts:* short-term memory *and the* central executive. Long-term memory, *the third memory center, contains schemas, or clusters of related information stored in long-term memory.*

Sensory Input from the Physical World → Sensory Memory → Working Memory (Short-Term Memory / Central Executive) → Long-Term Memory (Schemas) → Output

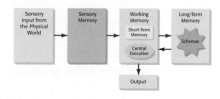

Sensory memory is a temporary storage center that receives and holds sensory input for one or two seconds before beginning to encode the information for further processing.

CONCEPT CHECK 2.2

How long does sensory memory hold sensory input? What is the value of the limited ability of sensory memory?

Encoding is the process of attaching codes to stimuli so your long-term memory can accept, understand, use, and store the sensory information.

CONCEPT CHECK 2.3

What are the four ways you encode information for further processing? What relationships do you see between these four kinds of encoding and the cognitive learning styles discussed in Chapter 1?

Sensory Memory

When you receive sensory input from the physical world, it enters into your sensory memory. *Sensory memory* is a temporary storage center that receives and holds sensory input for one or two seconds before beginning to *encode* the information for further processing. The following three points about sensory memory are important to understand:

- Sensory input is held briefly (one to two seconds) in sensory memory. One of two actions occurs: the stimuli are encoded or they are dumped.
- Information that you do not attend to, intentionally process, or that you simply ignore fades or becomes discarded quickly.
- This brief, temporary function of sensory memory works as a filter for the rest of your memory system. Without this filtering process, you would be bombarded with nonessential sensory stimuli. Your memory system would overload.

To see how quickly sensory memory receives and how briefly it holds on to sensory input, look briefly across the room you are in. Shut your eyes and move your head to the right. Open your eyes for a second and shut them again. Notice how the images you received remain for only a second or two and then fade. Imagine how overloaded your memory would become if your mind held onto the steady stream of sights, sounds, smells, tastes, and tactile sensations that you experience.

Encoding

As soon as you receive stimuli from your senses, your brain begins to prepare the information for your memory systems by encoding it. *Encoding* is the process of attaching codes to stimuli so your long-term memory can accept, understand, use, and store the sensory information. Encoding translates the stimuli into meaningful forms for long-term memory. The following are three important points about encoding information:

- The type of initial encoding depends on the type of sensory information that you receive. For example, visual stimuli are automatically encoded into horizontal and vertical lines, curves, moving lines, colors, or brightness.
- Even though some encoding occurs automatically, you can consciously or intentionally encode information specific ways so you can process it more effectively.
- Additional, more in-depth encoding occurs multiple times later in *working* memory.

Four Common Kinds of Encoding

Four common kinds of encoding are visual, linguistic, motor, and semantic. Each of these encoding systems prepare (code) stimuli for processing into your memory system. Understanding the different kinds of encoding can help you when you study. For example, if you see a diagram, a passage, or watch a demonstration, you can take the sensory stimuli from that learning experience and remind yourself that there are other ways to think about the information. As soon as your mind turns toward other ways to encode, for example, recalling the sounds you heard during the demonstration, or thinking of doing something similar to what was presented in a passage, you encode the stimuli in new ways. **Figure 2.2** summarizes the four common forms of encoding. The following provides you with additional details about each type of encoding.

FIGURE 2.2   Four Common Kinds of Encoding to Prepare Stimuli for Processing

1. **Visual Encoding**, also called *imaginal coding*, processes visual information.
2. **Linguistic Encoding**, also called *acoustical* or *auditory coding*, processes sounds and language information.
3. **Motor Encoding,** also called *physical* or *kinesthetic coding*, processes large and small muscle movement and physical movement.
4. **Semantic Encoding**, also called *conceptual* or *abstract coding*, processes general meanings of events or personal experiences (also called *episodic memories*).

Visual Encoding, also called *imaginal coding,* processes visual information, which includes the brightness, color, shapes, and locations of objects. It also processes pictures, diagrams, images of objects or people, and written symbols. You can use this form of encoding by doing the following:

- Make mental images or pictures in your mind of information.
- Notice colors, shapes, and spatial relationships of objects.
- Add movement to images to make "movies in your mind."
- Practice visualizing or recreating images.

> Visual encoding, also called *imaginal coding*, processes visual information.

Linguistic Encoding, also called *acoustical coding* or *auditory coding*, processes sounds and language information, such as letters, words, phrases, sentences, syntax, meanings, sounds, volume, pitch and rhythms. You can use this form of encoding by doing the following:

- Talk to yourself about the meaning of information.
- Read aloud and listen to your voice verbalize information.
- Use auditory memory to recall hearing the voice of an instructor or a speaker as he or she explained information.
- Use auditory memory to recall the sounds that occurred at a specific event.

> Linguistic encoding, also called *acoustical coding* or *auditory coding*, processes sounds and language information.

Motor Encoding, also called *physical coding* or *kinesthetic coding*, processes muscle- and physical-movement information. This encoding includes large muscle actions performed by full body movement and small muscle actions performed by hands or feet movement. You can use this form of encoding by doing the following:

- Make movements that illustrate the information.
- Use hand movements or gestures to explain information.
- Retrace shapes or objects.
- Manipulate parts of objects.

> Motor encoding, also called *physical coding* or *kinesthetic coding*, processes muscle- and physical-movement information.

Semantic Encoding, also called *conceptual coding* or *abstract coding*, processes the general meaning of an event or a personal experience. Semantic encoding includes processing categories, concepts, or abstract generalizations of something

> Semantic encoding also called *conceptual coding* or *abstract coding*, processes the general meaning of an event or a personal experience.

you have experienced. The memory is stored as one chunk or unit of memory called *episodic memory*, not as individual details. Semantic encoding may also include emotions and emotional responses to an event or experience. You can use this form of encoding by doing the following:

- Identify and think about concepts and generalizations as "big pictures" that embody images, senses, and emotions.
- Arrange information into categories of related concepts and recall yourself going through the process.
- Recall a chronological sequence of events or replay an experience in your mind. Include sensory and emotional response information.

You can use your understanding of the four kinds of encoding to code information in multiple ways. As you recall from Chapter 1, multisensory learning will be the result. For example, assume your geology instructor introduces the term *stalagmite* (a conical deposit of minerals that projects upward from the floor of a cavern or a cave). You hear the new information (linguistic coding). You instantly think about a time you saw or went inside a cave and saw a stalagmite (semantic coding). You draw a picture of a stalagmite (kinesthetic coding) and practice picturing it in your mind (visual coding). With you finger, you trace the shape in the air (kinesthetic coding). Within a matter of a few short seconds, you have moved the information into working memory and have strengthened the impression of the information by using multiple methods of encoding.

CONCEPT CHECK 2.4

What is working memory? What kinds of cognitive activities occur in working memory?

Encoding Information

EXERCISE 2.1

PURPOSE: You can translate sensory information that you receive into four different codes: visual, linguistic (auditory), motor (kinesthetic), and semantic (experiences of events). Your instructors use a variety of approaches to present information in ways that promote the use of different kinds of encoding.

DIRECTIONS: Work by yourself, with a partner, or in a small group to answer the following questions:

1. What was a main topic discussed in the previous class? _____

   _____

2. Complete the following chart to show the different kinds of codes you used for new information on the topic.

Visual Codes	
Linguistic Codes	
Motor Codes	
Semantic Codes	

Working Memory

Working memory (WM) refers to all cognitive processes or activities that occur in our conscious mind. In other words, *anything that you are aware of doing or thinking occurs in working memory.* Each time you pay attention to new information, rehearse, practice, recall, make connections, link information, retrieve concepts or details, get feedback, and achieve some form of output, you are in working memory. The following points help explain the variety of cognitive activities that occur in working memory:

- To understand new information, working memory searches for related information in long-term memory, activates it, and brings that information back into your working memory or your awareness.

- Working memory integrates the retrieved information with the new information to form a larger, stronger, or more comprehensive unit of meaning. Working memory then returns this expanded unit of meaning to long-term memory until it is needed and retrieved at a later time.

- As you work in new ways with new information, you encode the information on deeper levels using the same four kinds of coding as shown in Figure 2.2 (page 39). The effectiveness of your strategies to encode information on deeper levels directly affects your ability to retrieve or recall information at later times from long-term memory.

- As you work with information, your working memory rapidly moves encoded information both into and out of long-term memory. All in-depth learning and processing take place in working memory as you think about the material.

- When you work with *familiar* information (not new information), working memory holds a large "cloud of activated information." For example, if you are skilled at troubleshooting and correcting computer problems, as you work with computers, your working memory activates large amounts of information you already know about computers.

- Working memory manages all cognitive functions. Two parts of working memory are essential for working memory to function effectively:
  - A smaller, temporary storage center called *short-term memory*
  - The *central executive,* the administrator or the "C.E.O." (chief executive officer) of all working memory's operations

Short-Term Memory

Coded information from sensory memory that has been "tagged" for further processing moves into short-term memory. *Short-Term Memory (STM)* is a temporary storage center in working memory that receives and briefly holds sensory memory for further processing. If you do not give the information attention and encode it for processing, the information in short-term memory becomes discarded or dumped from memory. To keep *new* information active and to move it farther into memory for processing, you need to consciously work with the information. The following are important points about the limitations of short-term memory:

- **STM is limited in duration.** New information stays in short-term memory for up to thirty seconds. If there is no attempt to work further with the information, it fades and drops out of memory. For example, if you ask someone for a phone number or directions, unless you rehearse (practice) the information, encode it in a new way, or work with it, within thirty seconds you most likely will not recall accurately the phone number or the directions.

Working memory (WM) refers to all cognitive processes or activities that occur in our conscious mind.

Short-Term Memory (STM) is a temporary storage center in working memory that receives and briefly holds sensory memory for further processing.

CONCEPT CHECK 2.5

What are the limitations of short-term memory? What happens to information in this memory system?

- **STM is limited in capacity.** Short-term memory, on the average, holds fewer than nine items or "chunks" of new information at one time. The *Magic 7 ± 2 Theory* states that immediate memory span is 7 items, plus 2 (total 9 items) or minus 2 (total 5 items). Other studies show an average memory span of *new* information is three to five items or chunks of information. In either case, the number of items is limited. (See **Figure 2.3**.)

- **Short-term memory can become overloaded.** If too much new information enters short-term memory at one time, short-term memory becomes overloaded and some or all of the information is discarded. For example, if you are given twelve new items to learn at one time, short-term memory becomes overloaded and cannot begin to process all twelve items. However, if you break the list of items into three groups with four items each, your short-term memory can begin processing the first four items, then the second four items, and finally the last four items in your list.

- **Selective attention increases the size of your immediate memory span.** Selective attention involves consciously focusing your attention or paying attention to incoming information. It also involves a conscious effort to ignore insignificant or unrelated information. You will learn more about selective attention and its importance in the learning process in the section that follows.

The Central Executive

After learning about the functions and activities that occur in working memory, you may be wondering how our brains manage all these activities. Alan Baddeley, a British researcher and psychologist, introduced the concept that a specific part of the brain, referred to as the central executive, serves as the coordinator of brain activity. The *central executive* is the part of working memory that manages and coordinates the cognitive functions and the flow of information throughout the processing system. One analogy to use to grasp the functions of the central executive is to think of an executive of a large firm. He or she continually searches for relevant data needed to run the firm efficiently, activates information, sends out directives, initiates changes, and integrates all the operations of the firm. **Figure 2.4** shows the multiple functions of the central executive.

FIGURE 2.3   The Capacity of Short-Term Memory

LEARN BY DOING: Here is a test of your immediate memory span. Ask someone to read to you the numbers in the top row at the rate of about one per second; then try to repeat them back in the same order. Then try the next row, and the one after that, until you make a mistake. Your immediate memory span is the maximum number of items you can repeat back perfectly.

```
9 2 5
8 6 4 2
3 7 6 5 4
6 2 7 4 1 8
0 4 0 1 4 7 3
1 9 2 2 3 5 3 0
4 8 6 8 5 4 3 3 2
2 5 3 1 9 7 1 7 6 8
8 5 1 2 9 6 1 9 4 5 0
9 1 8 5 4 6 9 4 2 9 3 7
```

Source: From Bernstein/Nash, *Essentials of Psychology*, Houghton Mifflin Company, © 2008, page 215, Figure 6.3. Reprinted with permission.

FIGURE 2.4   The Multiple Functions of the Central Executive

The **central executive** in working memory:

1) Receives, organizes, and coordinates the flow of information throughout the memory system

2) Integrates data from the sensory centers and long-term memory

3) Initiates and controls deliberate actions and goal-directed behavior

4) Initiates and manages attention and planning

5) Activates decision-making functions of the conscious mind

EXERCISE 2.2

Labeling the Information Processing Model

PURPOSE: Familiarity with the skeleton or the structure of a model lays a foundation to which you can add or attach details. Focusing your attention on the structure of the Information Processing Model "refreshes your memory" and prepares you for adding more details to the model.

DIRECTIONS

1. Without referring to Figure 2.1, label the following chart to show *Sensory Input, Sensory Memory, Working Memory, Short-Term Memory, Central Executive, Long-Term Memory, Schemas,* and *Output.*

2. Add the arrows to the chart to show the direction of the flow of stimuli and information.

3. Check the accuracy of your work by comparing it to Figure 2.1.

Information Processing Model

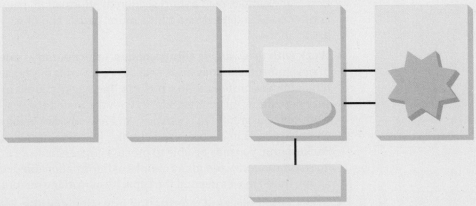

CONCEPT CHECK 2.7

What is selective attention? What kinds of activities can disrupt your selective attention?

Selective Attention

Selective attention is the process of focusing on or attending to specific sensory stimuli that are important to process further. Because sensory stimuli can fade or be dumped from your memory within one or two seconds, using *selective attention* helps you hold information in your sensory memory for a few seconds longer so you can begin processing it. Focusing your selective attention on what is important also involves ignoring stimuli that are not important to process further. For example, if you are in a room filled with talking people, you cannot take in and process all the conversations, all the visual stimuli, or all the other sensory stimuli in the room. Instead, you focus your selective attention on a specific conversation or on a smaller group of people, and you ignore the other stimuli.

Selective attention works when you study as well. As you read your textbook, the letters and words in a sentence enter your sensory memory. When you are using selective attention, you recognize that a sentence is important, select it for further cognitive processing and encoding, and immediately begin attaching meaning to the words. However, if you shift your focus from your book to a television screen, the sensory input of the printed sentence fades and the television image quickly replaces the textbook information. In other words, a second stimuli disrupted the encoding process you had started with the printed material. Consciously using selective attention will help you control and limit the sensory stimuli that you allow to enter into your memory systems.

Overload in Working Memory

Working memory can become overloaded when too many demands or cognitive activities are placed on it at one time. In such cases, WM operates less efficiently, resulting in incomplete or partial learning. To avoid overloading your working memory, do not attempt to take in too much new information too quickly. Cramming for tests or reading complex textbooks quickly, for example, are ineffective strategies that may overload working memory. Use the following tips to avoid placing excessive demands at one time on your central executive and working memory:

- **Monitor the speed you take in new information.** Work slowly enough to allow working memory sufficient time to retrieve meanings and related information from long-term memory and return them to working memory—a process that occurs each time you attempt to comprehend or attach meaning to new information. For example, read a short section of information, pause to think and make connections, and then read a little more, pause, and make new connections or associations.

- **Work with three to five chunks of new information at one time.** A "chunk" of new information may be as small as new words or phrases, or it may involve larger images or steps, as in a process. The size of chunks of information will vary depending on your familiarity with the material. For example, if you have a limited background in chemistry, you may need to break some sentences in a chemistry book into word-sized chunks; however, if you have a strong chemistry background, you may be able to process larger chunks of information. Trying to learn or memorize too many chunks of information too quickly or in too short of a time frame moves beyond the capacity of working memory,

- **Break larger pieces of information into smaller units.** Focus your attention on one unit at a time. For example, when reviewing your lecture notes, do not read an entire set of notes from start to finish without stopping. Instead, read a small section, pause to make associations, and check comprehension before moving to the next section of your notes.

- **Free up working memory by ignoring intrusive thoughts.** Intrusive thoughts, such as daydreaming, stress, general anxiety, or distractions (television, radio, stereo, or iPods) can occupy working memory space. By removing intrusive thoughts and distractions, you increase the amount of working memory available for thinking or for cognitive processes.

Long-Term Memory

Through a complex series of interactions, working memory sends information back and forth to the final memory center, long-term memory. *Long-term memory (LTM)* is a permanent storage center that holds chunks of information received from working memory. Unlike working memory that involves everything you are aware of thinking (your conscious mind), long-term memory simply exists as a storage center. You become aware of long-term memory only when your working memory activates parts of long-term memory to locate previously learned information or to imprint new information. The following are key points about long-term memory:

- Long-term memory has unlimited capacity; it never runs out of storage space.
- Long-term memory is your enormous mental filing cabinet, data center, or memory warehouse that permanently "files away" and stores coded information received from working memory.
- Information that you have rehearsed, coded clearly, linked to other related information, and have filed in a logical manner will be easier for you to locate in LTM than information that is disorganized, not linked to other ideas, or has not been processed effectively.
- Permanently stored information can be pulled back into working memory to be expanded, strengthened, or modified.
- Even though coded information is believed to be permanently imprinted in long-term memory, you may not always be able to access the information. Lack of use of the information may "bury" it deep into long-term memory or create "rusty doors" that make access to the information difficult or impossible.
- Stress, anxiety, sleep deprivation, states of emotional turmoil, or some medications may also temporarily block ready access to information stored in long-term memory.

Long-term memory (LTM) is a permanent storage center that holds chunks of information received from working memory.

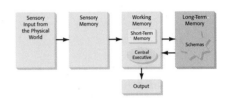

GROUP PROCESSING

A COLLABORATIVE LEARNING ACTIVITY

Form groups of three or four students. Then complete the following directions.

1. On large paper, create the chart shown on the right.

2. Brainstorm *specific topics* or kinds of information that members of your group have encountered in

any of their classes within the last two weeks that were *easy* for them to understand and learn. Record all the responses on the chart.

Easy to Learn	Why

Group Processing (cont.)

3. As a group, brainstorm all the reasons each topic may have been easy for the group member to learn. Record the reasons in the right column of the chart.

4. Create a second chart similar to the chart on the right. Repeat this process for *specific topics* or kinds of information that were difficult for group members to understand and learn. Brainstorm and record the reasons those topics may have been difficult to understand and learn.

5. Brainstorm specific topics or kinds of information that were difficult for group members to under-

stand and learn. Record all the responses on the chart.

Difficult to Learn	Why

6. Brainstorm and record reasons those topics may have been difficult to understand and learn.

7. Examine and summarize the results.

CONCEPT CHECK 2.9

How many schemas do you have in your long-term memory? Do you think they are housed in both hemispheres of your brain? Explain.

Schemas are sets of memories (clusters of related information) that store large concepts or frameworks in which other related ideas, facts, and details can be attached.

CONCEPT CHECK 2.10

What feelings did you experience the first time you sat behind the wheel to learn to drive a car? How do you feel now about driving a vehicle? What caused the change in your feelings?

Schemas in Long-Term Memory

As coded information enters long-term memory, it is categorized, *imprinted,* and stored with related clusters of information called schemas. **Schemas** are sets of memories (clusters of related information) that form large concepts or frameworks to which other related ideas, facts, and details can be attached. The following are important points about schemas:

- The number of schemas in a person's memory system is unlimited. For example, you already have schemas for concepts such as shelter, fast foods, pets, multiplication, cancer, global warming, taxes, loyalty, and football.

- The information in your schemas affects how you understand and process new information. For example, any new information you take in about football gets interpreted or understood based on what information about football you already have in your football schema. If you are an avid football fan, your football schema will include more information than the football schema of a person who seldom watches a game. Likewise, if you are or were a football player, your schema for football may vary considerably from that of an avid fan.

- When you do memory searches for information, your central executive scans long-term memory seeking to locate schemas with relevant information. For example, if you are trying to recall the Spanish word for "administration," through a series of associations and connections, you might scan the schemas related to Spanish, administration, and perhaps English-Spanish language patterns until you locate the answer, *administración.*

- If you encoded the information carefully, through memory searches, you will locate the sought-after information or answer to a question.

Forming and Expanding Schemas

Understanding the concept of schemas provides one explanation as to why learning new information sometimes is difficult and other times is relatively easy. For example, assume that you enroll in a French class, and this is your first experience studying a foreign language. At first, you may feel confused and struggle with the course until you begin to form a schema for French. As the course progresses, you will acquire skills that enable you to compare information, make connections, and establish a stronger schema. If your friend who already speaks Spanish enrolls in the same course, he or she already has foreign language schemas in long-term memory. Even though French is new to both of you, your friend most likely will feel fewer frustrations and will learn more quickly than you mainly because of the existence of schemas.

The following points are important to remember about the process of learning:

- When you start to learn something new or unfamiliar, the learning process at first may feel challenging, frustrating, or impossible because you lack schemas or a foundation for the new information.

- Once you begin learning basic concepts and related details for a new subject, you create a schema in long-term memory. Learning new information about the familiar topic becomes easier and more rewarding.

Throughout this textbook, you will be encouraged to think about schemas and background information that you already have in your LTM. You will also be encouraged to build strong schemas by connecting or associating new information to information you already know. As your knowledge expands, the learning experience becomes even more enjoyable, exciting, and rewarding.

EXERCISE 2.3

Textbook Case Studies

DIRECTIONS

1. Read each case study carefully. Respond to the question at the end of each case study by using strategies from Chapter 2 to answer each question. Answer in complete sentences.

2. Write your responses on paper or online at the CourseMate student Web site, Textbook Case Studies. You will be able to print your online response or e-mail it to your instructor.

CASE STUDY 1: By the end of the week, Curtis needs to read a thirty-page chapter and be prepared to discuss it in class. Curtis does not enjoy this textbook or course, so he tends to procrastinate. The night before class he spends one hour reading quickly through the chapter. He jots down a few words, phrases, and main ideas and shoves the list in his book so that he will be prepared for the class discussion the next day. Instead of a class discussion, however, the instructor gives a short quiz. Curtis unsuccessfully tries to recall information from his long-term memory, but he is only able to answer two of the ten questions. What strategies should Curtis have used to achieve better results?

CASE STUDY 2: Mary, normally a very confident student, needs to take a science class this term to fulfill a degree requirement. Before the class even begins, she worries about her ability to handle the course. She has never enjoyed science, and she knows that her background in science is weak. After the first week of class, Mary is frantic. She does not understand why she feels lost, confused, and defeated, and she does not know what to do to get on track. What strategies could you suggest Mary begin using to deal with her frustrations and get herself back on track?

 Access Chapter 2 Textbook Case Studies and Web-only Case Studies in your College Success CourseMate, accessed through *CengageBrain.com*.

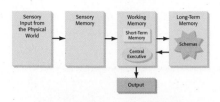

CONCEPT CHECK 2.11

What are the differences between recognition and recall forms of output?

Output

When you successfully move information through your information processing system, you will be able to show some form of *output* that demonstrates that memory and learning have taken place. *Output* may include *recognition tasks* that show that you recognize correct information or details when some kind of clue is provided. *Output* may also include *recall tasks* that demonstrate your ability to retrieve specific information or details imprinted in your LTM. In general, *recall tasks* are more difficult to perform than are *recognition tasks*. The following are examples of two forms of output:

Recognition Tasks

- Recognize the correct answer from a list of options, such as on a multiple-choice question or a quiz-show format
- Recognize parts of an object when the labels for the parts are provided
- Recognize familiar faces, pictures, sounds, or tunes

Recall Tasks

- Respond with a correct answer when no clues are provided
- Use specific steps from memory to solve a math problem, to perform a process or a procedure, or to create or construct a product
- Recall and explain information from memory with accurate details
- Use critical thinking skills to evaluate, draw a conclusion, or debate a point
- Write an effective essay or report without referring to printed sources of information

Chapter 2 Critical Thinking

ACTIVITY

DIRECTIONS

1. Read the following excerpt adapted from Bernstein and Nash's *Essentials of Psychology*, pages 70–71 (Houghton Mifflin, © 2008).

2. By yourself, with a partner, or in a small group, explore answers to the following questions.

   a. As you read the excerpt, did your working memory tap into an existing schema in long-term memory for hemispheres of the brain? If yes, how did previously learned information help you understand this excerpt? If no, explain what processes you did not use to associate new and old information.

   b. Compare and contrast the information you learned in Chapter 1 about the Brain Dominance Theory (page 16) and the information in this excerpt.

The Divided Brain: Lateralization

A striking suggestion emerged from observations of people with damage to the language centers of the brain. Researchers noticed that damage to specific areas of the left hemisphere interfered with the ability to use or understand language. Damage to those same areas in the right hemisphere usually did not cause such problems. Could it be that the right and left hemispheres of the brain serve different functions?

This idea was not entirely new. It had long been understood that most sensory and motor pathways cross over from one hemisphere to the other as they enter or leave the brain. As a result, the left hemisphere receives information from, and controls movement of, the right side of the body. The right hemisphere receives input from and controls the left side of the body. The image [at the right] shows the two hemispheres. The fact that the language centers . . . almost always occur on the left side of the brain suggests that each hemisphere might be specialized to perform some functions almost independently of the other hemisphere. Having these two somewhat specialized hemispheres allows the normal brain to perform some tasks more efficiently, particularly difficult ones. But the differences between the hemispheres should not be exaggerated. Remember, the corpus callosum usually integrates the functions of the "two brains." As a result the hemispheres

work closely together, each making up well for whatever lack of ability the other may have.

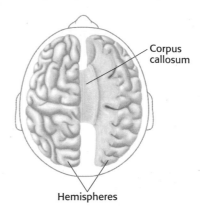

The Brain's Left and Right Hemispheres

The brain's two hemispheres are joined by the bundle of fibers knows as the corpus callosum. In this figure the hemispheres are separated so that the corpus callosum can be seen. The two cerebral hemispheres look nearly the same but perform somewhat different tasks. For one thing, the left hemisphere receives sensory input from, and controls movement on, the right side of the body. The right hemisphere senses and controls the left side of the body.

Bernstein/Nash, *Essentials of Psychology.* Houghton Mifflin Company, © 2008, pages 70–71. Reprinted with permission.

CHECK POINT 2.1

Answers appear on page B3

True or False?

____ 1. Recognition tasks involve more complex mental processes than recall tasks.

____ 2. Stimuli remain in sensory memory longer than they remain in short-term memory.

____ 3. All sensory memory is first encoded linguistically.

____ 4. Using selective attention is one way to hold information longer in your sensory memory and in your working memory.

____ 5. Working memory and long-term memory have unlimited capacities to store information.

 Access Chapter 2 Practice Quiz 1: Information Processing under "Interactive Quizzes" in your College Success CourseMate, accessed through *CengageBrain* .com.

CHAPTER 2
REFLECTIVE WRITING 1

On separate paper, in a journal, or online at this textbook's CourseMate Web site, respond to the following questions.

1. What current study practices can you change to avoid overloading your working memory?

2. What are the most interesting and valuable points you learned so far in Chapter 2 about the way your mind processes information?

Access Chapter 2 Reflective Writing 1 in your College Success CourseMate, accessed through *CengageBrain.com*.

Your Conscious Mind at Work

 Explain four processes that work in your conscious mind: conducting memory searches, creating and using retrieval cues, tracking thought patterns, and rehearsing learned information.

The majority of cognitive activities that are a part of learning occur in working memory. *What* you do in working memory and *how* you encode information in working memory have a major impact on how well you are able to locate information in long-term memory and show some form of *output*. Conducting memory searches, using retrieval cues, tracking your thought patterns, and rehearsing learned information are processes that you can use to increase the efficiency of accessing your long-term memory.

Conducting Memory Searches

As you have learned, working memory involves rapid and complex interactions with information you have stored in your long-term memory schemas. Working memory frequently uses memory searches to locate, activate, and bring learned information back into your conscious mind (working memory). A *memory search* involves linking together a series of facts, concepts, or previously learned associations in order to locate information stored in your long-term memory.

Sometimes a memory search is quick and the answer to a question immediately comes to mind; other times, your working memory requires more extensive searches to retrieve information. As an example, if someone asks you where you were born, for most people the answer is immediate. However, answering the question, "Where was your maternal grandmother born?" may require a more in-depth memory search to locate the answer. To identify the birth location of your maternal grandmother, you might need to "chat your way" to the answer by using associations:

> *"My mother was born in Detroit, Michigan, but her family had moved there right before she was born. I remember when we visited Michigan, we drove up to the northern peninsula and past the house in Copper Harbor where she grew up. I can still picture the little brown house at the end of the rocky road. I remember Grandma saying that she was born in that house."*

A **memory search** involves linking together a series of facts, concepts, or previously learned associations in order to locate information stored in your long-term memory.

If you are pressed for the exact address, perhaps no amount of memory searching will produce the answer, for it is likely that you never learned or imprinted the address into your memory. Sometimes after extensive memory searches, you will conclude that the information you are searching for was never clearly recorded in your long-term memory.

Creating and Using Retrieval Cues

Retrieval cues are words, phrases, pictures, graphics, or memory tricks (mnemonics) associated with units of information sent to long-term memory. Retrieval cues link one piece of information to another. Retrieval cues are an essential element of the learning process. Using a retrieval cue triggers memory of the information and its meaning. The following points about retrieval cues are important to understand:

- To attach or associate new information to your existing schemas, your working memory first uses retrieval cues to seek and locate information in long-term memory.
- Associations are powerful retrieval cues to link together chunks of information. Intentionally seek ways to relate the new information to information you already know. Actively use your background knowledge to create and activate associations.

Retrieval cues are words, phrases, pictures, graphics, or memory tricks (mnemonics) associated with units of information sent to long-term memory.

CONCEPT CHECK 2.12

Why are retrieval cues important in the process of conducting memory searches? How would a lack of clear retrieval cues affect your output?

EXERCISE 2.4

Memory Searches

PURPOSE: When you try to recall answers to questions, often you need to "chat to yourself" about the information and conduct memory searches for the answer. Sometimes you cannot find answers; perhaps the information was never learned, or if learned, it was not practiced on a regular enough basis to be accessible.

DIRECTIONS: In the following chart, read the questions and write the answer to as many of the questions as possible. Pay attention to your memory search process. Check one of the last three columns to show how you responded to the question.

Question	Answer	Immediately Knew the Answer	Needed to Do a Memory Search	I Do not Know
1. How many states are in the United States?				
2. Which state was the 49th state to join the Union?				
3. What is the capital city of New Mexico?				
4. What is the value of the Roman numeral XL?				
5. There are two cups in one pint. How many cups are in one gallon?				
6. Which fraction is smaller: 6/7 or 2/3?				
7. What is the name of your third grade teacher?				
8. What is photosynthesis?				

- Ask yourself questions such as: How is this similar to something I already know? Where have I seen or experienced something like this? How can I use this information?
- Take the time to create associations using words, pictures, symbols, or mnemonics (memory tools). In Chapter 3, you will learn about the powerful Memory Principle of Association. In Chapter 6 you will learn to create and use mnemonics.
- Use multisensory learning strategies to encode information in new ways and create multiple retrieval cues. By doing so, you will create retrieval cues that can help you access long-term memory through multiple memory paths.

Tracking Your Thought Patterns

Paying attention to the way you think and tracking your thought patterns increase your awareness of the complexity of thinking and learning. These processes also help you realize the importance of creating strong retrieval cues and making strong associations to link chunks of information. Jackson, a student like you, reads this test question: *What are three of Gardner's intelligences that rely heavily on physical movement and activity? Explain your answer.* The following reflects Jackson's thought patterns and processes:

Gardner... eight intelligences.... What are the eight intelligences? The first...language... oh yeah, we talked about the word lingua... Right, linguistic. The visual one is called... What the heck is that word? Architects have it. They work with space... oh right... spatial. Two people ones... I remember seeing the group of people I drew in my notes... interpersonal. The other is about me... intrapersonal. What was that chart I copied in my notes? Come on, think! I remember trees. The last one is about nature... the naturalist. Okay only three more to go. Oh yeah, the two M's... musical and mathematical... What's the last one? What did we talk about in the group when we listed people for each intelligence? Oh yeah, the other was Lance Armstrong and Michael Jordon... athletes. That's right, bodily-kinesthetic. Now I can use this to answer the question (His thoughts continued.)

Tracking your thought patterns as you conduct memory searches, use retrieval cues, and recall associations increases your awareness of the ways you organize and store information. When you attempt to recall learned information, do you give yourself sufficient time to activate these processes?

© Stockbyte/Getty Images.

Thought processes, schemas created, and memory searches vary from person to person. Heather approached the question from a different angle by recalling a memory tool (a mnemonic) that she created for the eight intelligences. She wrote the eight intelligences on a piece of paper and selected an initial letter for each intelligence: L, L, M, K, S, I, I, and N. She rearranged the letters to form two words: *SLIM LINK.* In order to use *SLIM LINK* to name the eight intelligences, she had to practice converting the letters to the original words to keep the information fresh and active. The following reflects Heather's thought patterns and processes:

Easy. I just need to write out the intelligences and then find the three that deal with physical movement and activity. SLIM LINK! S = spatial; L = linguistic; I = interpersonal; M = musical; L = logical-mathematical; I = intrapersonal; N = naturalist; and K = kinesthetic . . . I mean bodily-kinesthetic. Okay . . . let's see. Bodily-kinesthetic is one for sure. Interpersonal involves interacting with people, so that has movement and activity. Musical... that will be my third choice. Okay, now I just need to explain my reasoning . . . (Her thoughts continued.)

Tracking your thought patterns benefits you in many ways. First, it emphasizes the importance of having a variety of retrieval cues and associations to use. Second, it reveals weaknesses in your processing approaches when you did not consciously create strong retrieval cues. Finally, it activates your working memory and focuses your attention on specific details imprinted in your schemas.

Rehearsing Learned Information

Even when you have effectively learned and imprinted information in long-term memory, failure to rehearse the information may make recall of information difficult or impossible. Rehearsing frequently provides you with practice locating and retrieving chunks of information from your long-term memory schemas. Each time you rehearse or review, you keep the information active and accessible.

Speaking a foreign language is a good example of the necessity to practice frequently. Imagine that you learned to speak a foreign language as a child, but you have not practiced it for many years. You can still understand a few basic words in that language and you remember the general sentence structure used, but you have forgotten the vocabulary and can no longer speak the language fluently. The knowledge you have for speaking that language still exists in your schemas, but it is no longer accessible. However, by reviewing language lessons and materials and socializing with speakers of that language, you can reactivate the information stored in your schemas. You will be able to "relearn" the language in less time than you needed for the initial learning because of the schemas you previously formed.

Rehearsing learned information should be an ongoing process when you study. In Chapter 3, you will learn a variety of techniques for rehearsing and using ongoing review. For now, you can use the following three rehearsal strategies to strengthen the learning process:

- Include time on your study schedule to review information from your textbooks, lecture notes, and homework assignments.

- Create new study tools or new retrieval cues, or work with the information in new ways to avoid simply memorizing details. Your goal is to create a stronger impression of the information you are practicing.

- Use self-quizzing and other techniques that provide feedback. Self-quizzing involves a form of activity in which you test your accuracy and completeness of understanding.

CONCEPT CHECK 2.14

What are the benefits of frequently rehearsing information? What might happen to information in LTM that you do not practice frequently?

CHECK POINT 2.2

Answers appear on page B3

Multiple Choice

_____ 1. Encoding information using more than one sensory channel

  a. impacts your ability to show output.

  b. creates multiple retrieval cues.

  c. facilitates the process of conducting memory searches.

  d. does all of the above.

_____ 2. Which of the following is *not* true about memory searches?

  a. They produce immediate results.

  b. They involve using associations to connect related items.

  c. They scan schemas for relevant information.

  d. They activate previously learned information.

Check Point 2.2 (cont.)

_____ 3. You can make a strong impression of new information by

   a. thinking or pondering the new information.

   b. focusing your attention on details.

   c. rereading the information several times over several different days.

   d. doing all of the above.

_____ 4. Which of the following is *not* true about retrieval cues?

   a. They may involve words, pictures, or memory tools.

   b. They are created in sensory memory and reinforced in short-term memory.

   c. They link together chunks of information.

   d. They may include semantic encoding.

Access Chapter 2 Practice Quiz 2 Working Memory under "Interactive Quizzes" in your College Success CourseMate, accessed through *CengageBrain.com*.

EXERCISE 2.5

Working Memory Inventory

DIRECTIONS: Go to the Working Memory Inventory in Appendix C, page C1, to assess the effectiveness of the study skills strategies you currently use. You can retake this inventory at different times throughout the term.

Essential Strategies for Working Memory

3 *Identify essential study skills strategies that strengthen working memory.*

Understanding how you process information lays the foundation for learning how to use working memory effectively to become a more powerful learner. **Figure 2.5** summarizes twelve Essential Strategies for Strengthening Working Memory. You have learned about the first seven strategies in previous sections of this chapter. Following are details about the last five strategies listed in Figure 2.5.

Limited Intake

Limit the number of items and the speed at which you take in stimuli. Your working memory needs time to work, integrate, and process stimuli. Avoid overloading working memory or placing unreasonable demands on your processing system. Pay attention to and monitor your thinking processes. Reduce the number or sizes of chunks of information or slow down your "in-take speed" as soon as you realize you have overloaded your working memory.

FIGURE 2.5   Essential Strategies for Strengthening Working Memory

1. Use strategies for visual, linguistic, motor, and semantic encoding.
2. Break larger pieces of information into smaller units.
3. Free up working memory by ignoring intrusive thoughts.
4. Create and use associations to link together chunks of information.
5. Create retrieval cues to access information in LTM schemas.
6. Rehearse frequently.
7. Use self-quizzing and other techniques that provide feedback.
8. Limit the number of items and the speed at which you take in stimuli.
9. Create an interest and excitement in new information.
10. Set learning goals when you study.
11. Give additional rehearsal attention to items in the middle of lists.
12. Spread learning over several time periods.

Interest and Excitement

Create an interest and excitement in new information. You can create an interest in a subject by discussing it with other students, sharing the newly learned information with friends or family members, or finding meaningful ways to apply the new information in your life. Creating an interest adds an emotional charge to the learning process; working memory responds to emotional charges. Your interest level reflects your attitude toward a subject; your attitude affects the quality of a learning experience.

- If you have a *positive attitude* and are excited and motivated to learn about a subject, your mind is more alert and working memory becomes receptive to incoming stimuli.

- If you harbor *negative attitudes* toward the subject or the learning process, your short-term memory tends to "tag" the information as unimportant and ignores the incoming stimuli; it never moves into working memory for further processing.

Learning Goals

Set learning goals when you study. Goal-oriented behavior activates working memory. When you have an *intention* to learn, you create a purpose with desired outcomes. This builds motivation and momentum and engages your working memory in the learning process. You will learn more about setting learning goals and motivation in Chapters 4 and 5.

Items in Lists

Give additional rehearsal attention to items in the middle of lists. When you study and memorize items in a list, frequently you will remember items at the beginning of the list when your rehearsal or "memory work" began. This is called the *primacy*

CONCEPT CHECK 2.15

Explain how smaller units of information, associations, retrieval cues, and attitude affect the functioning of working memory.

CONCEPT CHECK 2.16

In your own words, what are the meanings of the primacy effect and the recency effect? How do they affect recall ability?

effect—the first items are easier to recall or remember. You will also have good recall of the last few items in a list. Remembering the last few items in a list is called the *recency effect,* which states that you will remember the items most recently practiced. The items in the middle of a list of items are the most difficult items to recall accurately. Therefore, when you study, give additional attention to rehearsing and recalling the most difficult items—the items in the middle of a list.

Spaced Practice

Spread learning over several time periods. Allowing time between study blocks and spreading contact with materials and tasks over several different time periods give working memory time to consolidate and integrate the new information into your long-term memory schemas. You will learn more about *spaced practice* in Chapters 3 and 4.

CHAPTER 2 REFLECTIVE WRITING 2

 On separate paper, in a journal, or online at this textbook's CourseMate Web site, respond to the following questions.

1. What did you learn about your study strategies when you took the Working Memory Inventory in Exercise 2.5? Be specific. If your instructor did not assign the inventory, go to Appendix C to complete it before answering this question.

2. What strategies have you learned in Chapter 2 that will help you process information more efficiently and use your working memory more effectively?

 Access Chapter 2 Reflective Writing 2 in your College Success CourseMate, accessed through *CengageBrain.com*.

CHECK POINT 2.3

Answers appear on page B3

True or False?

_____ 1. Trying to process large amounts of information quickly may overload your working memory.

_____ 2. Your interest level and attitude have little effect on the functions of working memory.

_____ 3. Working memory responds to emotional charges and goal-oriented behavior.

_____ 4. The items in the middle of a list are the easiest items to recall.

_____ 5. Intensive study blocks of three or more hours is an effective strategy to help working memory consolidate and integrate information without interruptions.

 Access Chapter 2 Practice Quiz 3 WM Strategies under "Interactive Quizzes" in your College Success CourseMate, accessed through *CengageBrain.com*.

Learning Objectives Review

1 *Explain how the three memory systems (sensory memory, working memory, and long-term memory) work to process information.*

- Metacognition is the process of understanding *how you* learn, *what* you need to learn, and *which* strategies or techniques would be the most effective or the best matched to the learning task. Understanding the Information Processing Model is the first step in learning to use the powerful process of metacognition.

- The Information Processing Model has three memory centers: sensory memory, working memory, and long-term memory. Each performs specific functions.

- Output, which may include *recognition tasks* and *recall tasks,* demonstrates that memory and learning have taken place.

- Encoding is the process of attaching codes to stimuli so long-term memory can process the stimuli. Visual, linguistic, motor, and semantic are the four kinds of codes that are used to encode information for long-term memory.

- Selective attention holds stimuli in sensory memory, and later in short-term memory and working memory, for further processing.

- Working memory refers to all cognitive processes that occur in your conscious mind. Short-term memory (STM), a temporary storage center in working memory, and the central executive are two parts of working memory.

- Using specific strategies helps you avoid overloading working memory.

- Long-term memory (LTM) with unlimited capacity is a permanent storage center that consists of schemas, which are sets or clusters of memory that store large concepts of related information.

2 *Explain four processes that work in your conscious mind: conducting memory searches, creating and using retrieval cues, tracking thought patterns, and rehearsing learned information.*

- Memory searches involve using associations to locate information in LTM.

- Retrieval cues help locate, activate, and retrieve information from LTM.

- Tracking your thought patterns increases your awareness of the way you think and evaluates your effectiveness in processing information.

- Rehearsing frequently provides you with practice locating and retrieving information from schemas in long-term memory. Study schedules should include review time and techniques that involve self-quizzing and feedback.

3 *Identify essential study skills strategies that strengthen working memory.*

- Twelve essential strategies can help you strengthen your working memory.

- Strategies include using four kinds of encoding, working with small units of information, ignoring intrusive thoughts, using associations and retrieval cues, rehearsing frequently, and self-quizzing.

Terms to Know

By yourself or with a partner, practice reciting or writing definitions for the following terms. You may also practice defining these terms by using the online flashcard programs or comparing your answers to the online glossary.

metacognition p. 37

Information Processing Model p. 37

sensory input p. 37

sensory memory p. 38

encoding p. 38

visual encoding, p. 39

linguistic encoding, p. 39

motor encoding, p. 39

semantic encoding, p. 39

working memory p. 41

short-term memory p. 41

Magic 7 ± 2 Theory p. 42

central executive p. 42

selective attention p. 44

long-term memory p. 45

schemas p. 46

memory search p. 50

retrieval cues p. 51

 Access Chapter 2 Flashcard Drills and Online Glossary in your College Success CourseMate, accessed through *CengageBrain.com.*

- Additional strategies include limiting the number of items and speed at which you take in stimuli, creating an interest, setting learning goals, focusing attention on items in the middle of lists, and spreading learning over several time periods.

Chapter 2 Review Questions

Answers Appear on Page B3

Matching

Match the terms below with the descriptions at the right. On the line, write the letter from the list at the right to show your answer.

_____ 1. Schemas

_____ 2. Long-term memory

_____ 3. Output

_____ 4. Selective attention

_____ 5. Sensory input

_____ 6. Semantic coding

_____ 7. Working memory

_____ 8. Sensory memory

_____ 9. Short-term memory

_____ 10. Central executive

a. Stimuli received by our five senses from the physical world

b. A memory with generalized meaning of a personal experience or event

c. A temporary storage center that holds stimuli for only a few seconds

d. Conscious memory that includes all mental activities that you are aware of performing

e. The part of working memory that coordinates brain activity

f. Includes recognition tasks and recall tasks

g. Clusters of related information in long-term memory

h. Permanent memory with unlimited capacity

i. The process of focusing on specific input or stimuli

j. A temporary storage center in working memory

True or False?

_____ 1. Short-term memory and working memory hold all sensory stimuli until all of the information is thoroughly learned.

_____ 2. Long-term memory can recognize and process linguistic, motor, visual, and semantic codes.

_____ 3. Most sensory input that you ignore in sensory memory fades or gets discarded from memory.

_____ 4. When you conduct a memory search for information, associations often work as retrieval cues to locate information.

_____ 5. Selective attention can delay or prevent stimuli from fading or being discarded.

_____ 6. People can control and direct what goes into long-term memory, but they cannot control or direct what goes into and out of the other memory systems.

_____ 7. The central executive of working memory coordinates many cognitive processes, responds to goal-oriented behavior, and makes decisions.

_____ 8. Creating an interest, setting learning goals, creating and using associations, and self-quizzing are strategies to use to strengthen working memory.

_____ 9. The Magic 7 ± 2 Theory refers to the range of items in immediate memory span.

_____ 10. Multisensory learning strategies involve using multiple forms of encoding.

Recall Question

In the space below, draw and label the parts of the
Information Processing Model.

Access Chapter 2
Chapter Quizzes 1–4
and Enhanced Quiz
under "Interactive
Quizzes" in your
College Success
CourseMate,
accessed through
CengageBrain.com.

Access all Chapter 2 Online Materials in your College Success CourseMate, accessed through *CengageBrain.com*.

3

Using Twelve Principles of Memory

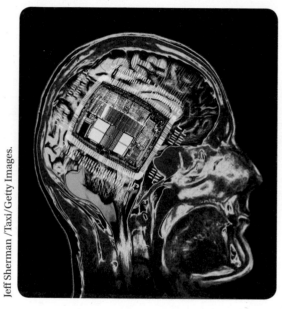

Jeff Sherman /Taxi/Getty Images.

The Twelve Principles of Memory discussed in this chapter lay a strong foundation for many study skills strategies you will learn in later chapters. The mnemonic (memory tool) SAVE CRIB FOTO provides you with a retrieval cue to trigger your memory and to recall quickly these twelve principles. These Principles of Memory represent cognitive processes that research shows build memory and improve cognitive performance. You can use these Principles of Memory to strengthen your memory and refine your study methods.

LEARNING OBJECTIVES

1 *Use the mnemonic* SAVE CRIB FOTO *to identify the Twelve Principles of Memory.*

2 *Explain how to use the Memory Principles of Selectivity, Association, Visualization, and Elaboration.*

3 *Explain how to use the Memory Principles of Concentration, Recitation, Intention, and Big and Little Pictures.*

4 *Explain how to use the Memory Principles of Feedback, Organization, Time on Task, and Ongoing Review.*

1 MEMORY MNEMONIC

2 THE FIRST FOUR PRINCIPLES OF MEMORY

Selectivity

Association

Visualization

Elaboration

3 THE MIDDLE FOUR PRINCIPLES OF MEMORY

Concentration

Recitation

Intention

Big and Little Pictures

4 THE LAST FOUR PRINCIPLES OF MEMORY

Feedback

Organization

Time on Task

Ongoing Review

 Access Chapter 3 Expanded Chapter Outline and Objectives in your College Success CourseMate, accessed through *CengageBrain.com*.

YOUR CHAPTER MAPPING

After reading information under each heading, return to the chapter visual mapping below. Add key words to show subheadings and important details related to each heading.

 Access Chapter 3 Visual Mapping in your College Success CourseMate, accessed through *CengageBrain .com*.

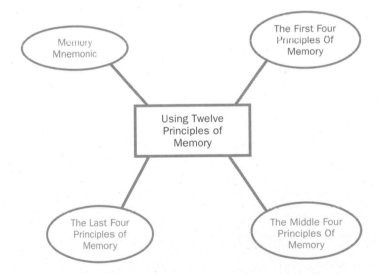

CHAPTER 3 PROFILE

Using Twelve Principles of Memory

ANSWER, SCORE, and **RECORD** your profile before you read this chapter. If you need to review the process, refer to the complete directions given in the profile for Chapter 1 on page 4.

ONLINE: You can complete the profile and get your score online at this textbook's CourseMate Web site.

Access Chapter 3 Profile in your College Success CourseMate, accessed through *CengageBrain.com*.

	YES	NO
1. I have a method for assessing the effectiveness of my study skills strategies and modifying or changing my approaches to learning.	_____	_____
2. I have problems identifying what textbook and lecture material is important to learn.	_____	_____
3. I take time to associate new information with familiar information and to visualize the associations.	_____	_____
4. I frequently use rote memory by memorizing specific details exactly as they are presented in a textbook.	_____	_____
5. I set goals and plan a course of action before I begin a learning task.	_____	_____
6. I recognize different levels of information in the materials I study.	_____	_____
7. I use self-quizzing and reciting to check my understanding and my memory.	_____	_____
8. I rearrange information into meaningful units or clusters so it is easier to learn and to remember.	_____	_____
9. I wait until close to test time before I practice the information that I previously read or studied.	_____	_____
10. I am confident in my ability to monitor, evaluate, and modify strategies I use to study.	_____	_____

QUESTIONS LINKED TO THE CHAPTER LEARNING OBJECTIVES:

Question 1: objective 1

Questions 2–4: objective 2

Questions 5–6: objective 3

Questions 7–9: objective 4

Question 10: all objectives

Memory Mnemonic

 Use the mnemonic SAVE CRIB FOTO *to identify the Twelve Principles of Memory.*

The Twelve Principles of Memory that you will learn in this chapter incorporate all of the working memory strategies you learned in Chapter 2. These Twelve Principles organize important memory principles and theories to assist you in

---

FIGURE 3.1   The Twelve Principles of Memory (SAVE CRIB FOTO)

1. **S**electivity: Select what is important to learn.

2. **A**ssociation: Associate or link together chunks of information.

3. **V**isualization: Picture in your mind the information you are learning.

4. **E**laboration: Work with information and encode information in new ways.

5. **C**oncentration: Stay focused and attend to specific stimuli.

6. **R**ecitation: Repeat information verbally in your own words.

7. **I**ntention: Create a learning goal with clearly defined desired outcomes.

8. **B**ig and Little Pictures: Recognize different levels of information.

9. **F**eedback: Check the accuracy of your learning and use forms of self-quizzing.

10. **O**rganization: Reorganize information in meaningful, logical ways.

11. **T**ime on Task: Dedicate and schedule ample time to learn.

12. **O**ngoing Review: Practice retrieving information from long-term memory.

CONCEPT CHECK 3.1

Using the mnemonic SAVE CRIB FOTO, what are the Twelve Principles of Memory? Which of these principles do you believe you already use effectively on a consistent basis? Which principles do you believe you will need to learn to use more effectively when you study?

---

becoming a more powerful learner. Understanding these Principles of Memory will help you in the following ways:

- Provide you with rationale for using the various steps in learning strategies
- Alert and activate your working memory (conscious mind) and hold stimuli in working memory longer to provide time for further processing
- Increase your awareness of the cognitive processes necessary for successfully learning new information and utilizing your working memory
- Empower you with guidelines to analyze, modify, and personalize your approach to learning course content

A *mnemonic* is a memory technique or a memory tool that serves as a bridge to help you recall information from long-term memory. You use memory tools on a regular basis every day to boost your memory and your ability to process information. In this chapter, the keyword mnemonic SAVE CRIB FOTO will help you recall quickly the Twelve Principles of Memory. In the mnemonic SAVE CRIB FOTO, each letter in these three words represents one of the Memory Principles. For mnemonics to work effectively, however, you must practice translating the mnemonic back into the original items it represents. **Figure 3.1** summarizes the twelve Principles of Memory. Carefully examine the cognitive process represented by each of the letters.

A **mnemonic** is a memory technique or a memory tool that serves as a bridge to help you recall information from long-term memory.

Memory Principles Inventory

EXERCISE 3.1

PURPOSE: The Memory Principles Inventory helps you identify which Principles of Memory you currently use effectively and which you need to strengthen. Understanding how you process information is the first step in the powerful process of using metacognition.

DIRECTIONS: Go to Appendix C, page C2, to complete the Memory Principles Inventory.

CHECK POINT 3.1

Answers appear on page B3

True or False?

_____ 1. Mnemonics are memory techniques that work as retrieval cues to trigger the recall of information in long-term memory.

_____ 2. SAVE CRIB FOTO uses the technique of chunking information into smaller, more manageable units.

_____ 3. Knowing a mnemonic for a list of items guarantees that you will be able to name all the items in a list without hesitancy or mistakes

CHAPTER 3 REFLECTIVE WRITING 1

On separate paper, in a journal, or online at this textbook's CourseMate Web site, respond to the following questions:

1. Based on the Exercise 3.1 Memory Principles Inventory results, which of the twelve Principles of Memory do you already use consistently and effectively? (See "Assessing Your Current Use of the Principles of Memory" that follows the inventory in Appendix C.) Do you agree with these results? Why or why not?

2. According to the inventory results, which Principles of Memory do you need to learn to use more consistently and effectively? Do you agree with these results? Why or why not?

Access Chapter 3 Reflective Writing 1 in your College Success CourseMate, accessed through *CengageBrain.com.*

Principles
SAVE
CRIB
FOTO

The First Four Principles of Memory

2 *Explain how to use the Memory Principles of Selectivity, Association, Visualization, and Elaboration.*

Selectivity, **A**ssociation, **V**isualization, and **E**laboration are the first four Principles of Memory. Focus your attention on the definitions, explanations, learning goals, and essential strategies for learning to use each of these principles. These principles, when used consistently throughout the learning process, result in a stronger, more efficient memory.

Selectivity

> *Selectivity* is the process of identifying and separating main ideas and important details from a larger body of information.

Selectivity is the process of identifying and separating main ideas and important details from a larger body of information. Trying to learn everything—every detail, every example, every word you read or hear—is not possible, certainly not reasonable, and would result in overloading your working memory. Using Selectivity helps you do the following:

- Identify and select what is important to attend to and learn
- Identify important concepts, main ideas, and significant supporting details

---

FIGURE 3.2   Essential Strategies for Using Selectivity

Learning Goal: To identify the information for further processing and to discard the information that is not relevant or important to process into memory.

- **Identify main ideas, concepts, or themes.** Use your course syllabus, the introduction in your textbook, and your lecture notes to help you identify the main ideas, concepts, or themes that receive frequent or repeated emphasis.

- **Identify important details by using chapter features.** Use lists of terminology, definitions, marginal notes, boxed features, steps or formulas to use to solve problems, chapter summaries, and chapter review questions to help you identify important details.

- **Use examples to grasp concepts, but do not focus on them as details to memorize.** Examples in textbooks and in lectures provide you with background information, capture your attention, and clarify concepts, but often they are not the details that you need to memorize or learn thoroughly.

- **Create study tools that show main ideas and important details.** In Chapters 7–11, you will learn about visual mappings, index cards, forms of notetaking, and other study tools that use Selectivity to identify main ideas and important details.

CONCEPT CHECK 3.2

What features in a textbook help you identify concepts or major categories of information? What textbook features help you identify and select important details to learn?

- Decide what to survey in a chapter, highlight in a textbook, write in your notes, and what to study for a test
- Identify what information you can ignore or not need to process further
- Avoid cluttering long-term memory schemas with insignificant, disorganized, and nonessential information
- Avoid overloading working memory

Each time you use Selectivity you will be honing your skills in identifying and pulling out important information and focusing your thoughts on main ideas and supporting details. **Figure 3.2** shows four Essential Strategies for Using Selectivity.

Association

Association is the process of forming visual or auditory cues to link together two or more items or chunks of information to process in memory. The associations that you form may consist of words, phrases, verbal expressions, pictures, familiar objects, numbers, tunes, personal experiences, familiar situations, or mnemonics. Using the Principle of Association helps you do the following:

- Hold new information longer in your working memory to provide time to begin encoding the information in new ways
- Connect and integrate new information with previously learned or familiar information
- Link together words, pictures, or sounds to form a stronger impression
- Create *retrieval cues* that are easy to remember and to use when you conduct *memory searches*
- Create *paired associations,* which are two items linked together in working memory, so that recall of one item triggers recall of the second item. Terms and definitions and pictures to words are examples of paired associations.

Principles
s**A**VE
CRIB
FOTO

Association is the process of forming visual or auditory cues to link together two or more items or chunks of information to process in memory.

Paired associations are two items that are linked together in working memory so that recall of one item triggers recall of the second item.

CONCEPT CHECK 3.3

How are paired associations used in a chain of associations? Give an example of a paired association you recall using recently.

FIGURE 3.3   Essential Strategies for Using Association

Learning Goal: To create a strong, vivid association between two or more items so one can serve as a memory cue to recall the other.

- **Create associations between new information and previously learned information.** Ask yourself: What do I already know about this? What schemas does this belong in? What is familiar and what is new?

- **Make associations vivid and detailed.** Identify the key parts of the information that you need to learn and then create clear associations with those details.

- **Visually link two items together into one image.** Instead of separating two items into two different images, form one picture that contains both images. To strengthen the image, add colors, sounds, and/or action.

- **Create and rehearse frequently paired associations and chains of associations.** Associations activate working memory and create ways to access long-term memory.

- **Associate the information you learned with the setting in which you learned it.** Ask yourself: Did I learn this from the textbook, from a lab project, in class, or from a homework assignment? Linking information to learning settings can be an effective association to use later as a retrieval cue.

- **Pay attention to your thought processes and associations.** Watch for ways associations are used in your textbook and as you process new information.

- Create and use a variety of mnemonics, which are paired associations, to assist recall of items represented by the mnemonic

- Create chains of associations to use in memory searches to recall information

Associations are an essential component of cognitive processing. Working memory creates associations on a regular basis; access into long-term memory often occurs through the use of associations. **Figure 3.3** shows six Essential Strategies for Using Association.

Visualization

Visualization is the process of making pictures or "movies" in your mind. Visualization is a powerful memory tool that involves visual encoding. For many students, and especially for visual learners, information presented in a visual or graphic form, such as a picture or a diagram, is often easier to process and recall than information presented in printed form such as paragraphs. The process of visualization involves "seeing" the pictures in your mind *without looking at the visual form itself.*

To visualize, close your eyes and strive to "see" the picture, the graphic, or the movie "on the inside of your eyelids." Another method for visualizing involves *looking up and to the left,* toward the ceiling, to retrieve the visual image. Looking up and to the left often signals that you are accessing visual information from the right hemisphere of your brain. Once you have pulled your visualization back into your working memory, check the accuracy of the image by referring back to the original visual form. Rehearse again with more accurate details if necessary. Using the Principle of Visualization helps you do the following:

- Activate your working memory to encode information visually
- Use and strengthen your visual memory skills

Visualization is the process of making pictures or "movies" in your mind.

Principles
sa**V**e
CRIB
FOTO

FIGURE 3.4   Essential Strategies for Using Visualization

Learning Goal: To create a strong visual image of important information that you can recall as needed from long-term memory.

- **Create a strong visual impression of the information.** As you encode and form a visual image, include details such as size, shape, color, brightness, and texture.
- **Attach additional meaning to the impression.** Think about its purpose, its uses, personal experiences related to the item, and similarities it has with other objects.
- **Practice or rehearse the information without looking at the physical form.** Visualizing occurs *in your mind*, so practice "seeing" objects or sequences of events in your imagination.
- **Check your accuracy.** Refer back to the physical object or printed passage. Compare the information in your visualization with the original information. Check for accuracy and the completeness of the details.
- **Rehearse frequently.** Keep the visualization active, accurate, and accessible by recalling the image frequently.

- Create memory cues to retrieve information from long-term memory
- Link drawings or pictures to mental images or impressions
- Create strong visual impressions by focusing attention on details of objects (such as medical instruments, a skeleton, rock samples, an electronic component, or a work of art)
- Clarify information and encode it visually by drawing a picture to represent the key elements. For example, after reading a textbook passage about the penetration of different kinds of radiation, a student drew the picture in the margin to clarify the concepts.
- Create *movies in your mind* as you read to increase comprehension and your ability to recall details from passages
- Visualize the characters, the setting, important details, and the unfolding action or sequence of events as soon as you begin reading
- Visualize the sequence of steps required to complete a specific process
- Strengthen visualizations by also verbalizing or reciting the details

CONCEPT CHECK 3.4

In what ways do you use visualization during a typical day? Give specific examples.

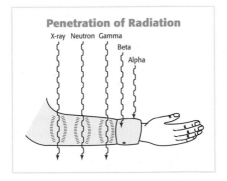

Penetration of Radiation

The Principle of Visualization has many uses. Throughout this textbook, you will encounter many study skills strategies that use the process. Note, however, that you can use this same principle for personal growth and performance by picturing yourself achieving specific goals, creating a mindset to concentrate on a task, studying productively for a test, or performing well in a specific area, such as competing in a sport or interviewing for a job. Read **Excerpt 2** in **Appendix D** for examples of ways you can apply this principle. **Figure 3.4** highlights five Essential Strategies for Using Visualization in academic or personal uses.

Elaboration

Elaboration, also called *elaborative rehearsal*, is the process of thinking about, pondering, or working with and encoding information in new ways.

Elaboration, also called *elaborative rehearsal,* is the process of thinking about, pondering, or working with and encoding information in new ways. Elaboration involves working with the information to achieve higher levels of comprehension and activate critical thinking skills. Using Elaboration helps you do the following:

- Personalize information during the encoding and rehearsal processes of learning
- Prepare information into meaningful, logically organized chunks of information that can be transferred to and accepted by long-term memory
- "Dig deeper" to clarify the meaning of new, unfamiliar information
- Generalize information and identify patterns or trends
- Identify relationships, such as cause-effect or comparisons and contrasts
- Integrate information from multiple sources or from previous learning
- Make stronger connections to other long-term memory schemas
- Understand how and why to use specific steps or processes
- Recognize applications of processes or other ways to use information

CONCEPT CHECK 3.5

How do elaborative rehearsal and rote memory differ?

Principles
SAV**E**
CRIB
FOTO

Rote memory is the process of using repetition to learn information *in the exact form* in which it was presented.

Elaboration forces you to move beyond rote memory. *Rote memory* is the process of using repetition to learn information *in the exact form* in which it was presented. Rote memory works for tasks such as memorizing a telephone number, the spelling of a word, or memorizing a direct quotation, but it is ineffective for learning factual information from textbooks because you give insufficient attention to comprehending the information or learning ways to manipulate or use the information. When you use rote memory for recalling textbook information, you may find yourself unable to respond to questions that present the information in a form other than the exact form you memorized.

As you will discover throughout this textbook, Elaboration or elaborative rehearsal occurs frequently as you work with and expand upon information you are studying. **Figure 3.5** provides you with six Essential Strategies for Using Elaboration.

FIGURE 3.5 Essential Strategies for Using Elaboration

Learning Goal: To work with, encode, and practice information in new ways to increase comprehension and application of information.

- **Encode and rehearse information in new ways.** Use the *see-say-do approach*; strive to elaborate using visual, auditory, and kinesthetic strategies.
- **Use your creativity to devise options for elaborating information:** copy it, condense it, group it into related categories, convert it to pictures, create visual mappings, or develop charts to show relationships, patterns or trends.
- **Notice similarities and differences between chunks of information.** Pay attention to and work with the details.
- **Weave big ideas or concepts together with their related details.** Creating visual mappings or timelines are two effective strategies for connecting different levels of information or weaving concepts together.
- **Use elaborative questioning by asking *why* and *how* questions.** *Why does this work this way? Why is this important? How can I use this? How can this apply to other situations?* To respond, you will need to use critical thinking and higher-level comprehension skills.
- **Use repetition but attach meaning and applications.** For steps and processes, such as in math problems, repetitive practice is essential. As you rework problems multiple times, notice the key elements of the problem, explain each step to yourself and why each step is important, mentally summarize the steps, and finally, think of other applications for the processes.

CHECK POINT 3.2

Answers appear on page B3

True or False?

_____ 1. Attempting to memorize large sections of information word by word shows effective use of the Memory Principles of Selectivity, Rote Memory, and Elaboration.

_____ 2. When you identify main ideas and important supporting details and then work to encode the information in new ways, you are using the Memory Principles of Selectivity and Elaboration.

_____ 3. Elaborative rehearsal may involve the use of creating multisensory study tools.

_____ 4. Asking *why* and *how* questions are important strategies for Elaboration.

_____ 5. The Memory Principle of Visualization involves creating strong visual impressions that work as retrieval cues for long-term memory.

Access Chapter 3 Online Practice Quiz 1 First Four Principles under "Interactive Quizzes" in your College Success CourseMate, accessed through *CengageBrain .com.*

GROUP PROCESSING

A COLLABORATIVE LEARNING ACTIVITY

1. Form groups of three or four students. Select one student to record your group's responses to the questions that follow the excerpt.

2. Read the excerpt "The Greenhouse Effect." Then study the picture a student drew to help clarify the information.

The Greenhouse Effect

A window pane transmits sunlight. It is nearly transparent, and much of the shortwave energy passes through. Only a little energy is absorbed to heat up the glass. However, the walls and furniture inside a room absorb a large part of the solar radiation coming through the window. The energy radiated from the furniture, unlike the original solar energy, is all long-wave radiation. Much of it is unable to pass out through the window pane. This is why the car seats get so hot on a hot, sunny day when all the windows are closed. Try putting a piece of glass in front of a hot object to see how the heat waves are cut off. A greenhouse traps energy in this way when the sun shines, and so does the atmosphere. From *Investigating the Earth,* American Geological Institute.

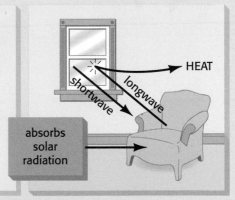

3. Discuss and record answers to the following questions. You may be asked to discuss your responses with the class.

a. Selectivity: What information in the excerpt is essential to understand, and what is nonessential? If you wish, you may highlight the essential details or cross out the nonessential details in the paragraph

b. Association: How did the student use the Principle of Association to comprehend the

information in the excerpt? What other associations can you create for the excerpt?

c. Visualization: Create a visual memory (visualization) of the drawing. Look away and practice recalling the image. What process did you use to visualize and recall the picture and its details?

d. Elaboration: What are three or more ways you could use the Principle of Elaboration to strengthen your understanding of the greenhouse effect?

The Middle Four Principles of Memory

> **3** *Explain how to use the Memory Principles of Concentration, Recitation, Intention, and Big and Little Pictures.*

The four middle Principles of Memory, *Concentration, Recitation, Intention,* and *Big and Little Pictures,* provide you with four more sets of strategies to use to strengthen your memory. Read this information carefully, for it lays the foundation for many study skills strategies discussed in later chapters.

Concentration

Concentration is the ability to block out distractions in order to stay focused on one specific item or task. Concentration is one of four *self-management skills* that you will learn about in Chapter 5. Using the Principle of Concentration can help you do the following:

- Monitor incoming stimuli and block out distractions that could interrupt your thought process or divide your attention
- Alert and activate working memory to focus on incoming stimuli
- Create a study environment conducive to learning
- Select appropriate strategies to increase and strengthen your ability to focus

You can strengthen your ability to concentrate by using active learning strategies when you study. *Active learning* is the process of using a variety of strategies that actively involve or engage you in the learning process. Active learning involves studying with a pen in your hand, taking notes, making diagrams, creating flashcards, writing questions and notes in the margins of your textbooks, and highlighting important information. Using active learning keeps you from shifting into *automatic pilot,* which is a state of mind in which you mechanically go through the motions without registering information into your memory. Active learning keeps your mind focused on one specific learning task.

Learning to use the Memory Principle of Concentration results in a disciplined and attentive mind that is receptive to the learning process. **Figure 3.6** shows five Essential Strategies for Using Concentration.

Principles

SAVE

CRIB

FOTO

Concentration is the ability to block out distractions in order to stay focused on one specific item or task.

Active learning is the process of using a variety of strategies that actively involve or engage you in the learning process.

CONCEPT CHECK 3.6

How does using active learning strategies affect concentration, working memory, and the use of automatic pilot?

FIGURE 3.6   Essential Strategies for Using Concentration

Learning Goal: To have a focused mind and undivided attention by blocking out disruptive thoughts and distractions.

- **Select a conducive learning environment that has limited distractions.**
- **Ask yourself a question about what you are studying.** As soon as you ask a question and begin to respond, you activate working memory. Your answer gives you a purpose and focuses your attention.
- **Limit your activities to one task.** Avoid disrupting your thought patterns by trying to multitask or by attending to other kinds of stimuli.
- **Use active learning strategies to stay engaged in the learning process.**
- **Use concentration strategies in Figure 5.2, page 123, to increase concentration when you study.**

Recitation

Recitation is the process of explaining information clearly, out loud in your own words, and in complete sentences without referring to printed materials. Reading information out loud encodes the information linguistically but reciting information out loud goes further: it requires you to pull the information out of your long-term memory and it becomes a form of self-quizzing with feedback.

Using flashcards is one excellent way to use the Principle of Recitation. Place the terms you need to learn on the fronts of the cards and the definitions on the backs of the cards. Look at the term on the front and explain the definition out loud without looking at the definition. After reciting, turn the card over to check your accuracy. You can use flashcards in the same way to write questions on the fronts of the cards and answers on the back. Using this method is much more effective than simply reading the information on each card.

Recitation is a powerful way to boost your memory. You will use recitation as you study notes, process textbook passages, use study tools such as flashcards or visual mappings, and as you prepare for tests. Using Recitation helps you do the following:

- Encode information linguistically and use your auditory channel to send information to your long-term memory
- Practice using your own words to explain ideas in a coherent manner
- Use effective strategies to practice or rehearse information to keep it active in memory
- Personalize the learning process and make explanations "your own"
- Use self-quizzing with feedback to check your level of accuracy and understanding

Throughout this textbook, you will learn that Recitation is an integral part of many study skills strategies. If initially you are uncomfortable talking out loud to yourself, remind yourself of the many benefits of reciting and the importance of being willing to try new approaches to learning. The more frequently you recite, the more comfortable you will become with this powerful Principle of Memory. **Figure 3.7** shows six Essential Strategies for Using Recitation.

Principles
SAVE
c**R**ib
FOTO

Recitation is the process of explaining information clearly, out loud in your own words, and in complete sentences without referring to printed materials.

CONCEPT CHECK 3.7

What do reading out loud and reciting have in common? Why is reciting a more effective process for testing comprehension?

FIGURE 3.7   Essential Strategies for Using Recitation

Learning Goal: To explain information clearly and in an organized, knowledgeable manner without looking at printed information.

- **Use a *Look-Away Technique* to recite information immediately.** After you read a passage, examine a graph, or read your notes, immediately look away and recite the information while it is fresh in your mind. Then, check your accuracy.

- **Use reciting to rehearse and retrieve information learned at an earlier time.** Reciting information hours, or even days, after the initial learning process keeps information active in your memory.

- **Explain information out loud to yourself or to someone else.** Explaining information in your own words improves comprehension and provides practice putting ideas together coherently.

- **Create paired associations between visual and verbal information.** Reciting information that first appeared in printed form creates an association and a retrieval cue for information encoded two different ways.

- **Use recitation to prepare for tests.** In testing situations, it is imperative that you can retrieve information quickly from long-term memory. Ongoing use of recitation helps you locate, practice explaining, and retrieve information quickly.

- **Use the feedback you get from reciting.** If you recite accurately, your confidence about learning the information increases. If you cannot express the information, or you recite inaccurate or incomplete information, return to the original material for further processing.

Principles
SAVE
CR▮B
FOTO

Intention is the process of creating a purpose or a goal to act or perform in a specific way.

Intention

Intention is the process of creating a purpose or a goal to act or perform in a specific way. Intention involves setting a *learning goal* that clearly states what you plan to accomplish and a *plan of action* that shows *how* you intend to achieve your goal. An underlying requirement for using the Principle of Intention is that you plan ample time to achieve your goal. Using the Principle of Intention helps you do the following:

- Focus on *what you need to learn*, a major component of metacognition
- Set learning goals so you know what you intend to accomplish. Do you want to:

  - familiarize yourself with new information?
  - use thorough reading to comprehend new information?
  - practice rehearsing new information?
  - practice retrieving or reviewing learned information?

- Help you select appropriate strategies to achieve your learning goal
- Identify and select appropriate strategies to study declarative (factual) information as well as procedural information (processes)

Setting specific learning goals provides you with options for your plan of action. For example, if your goal is to familiarize yourself with new information, options include surveying a chapter, reading introductory material, and reading the chapter summary in order to set up schemas for later details. If your goal is to comprehend new information, you select strategies to help you identify main ideas and details, create associations, use recitation and elaborative rehearsal strategies, and create study tools. If your learning goal is to review, you select strategies that challenge you to retrieve information from memory or rework problem sets with the goal to increase speed and accuracy.

The learning goals you set will vary depending on the kind of information you are learning or rehearsing. *Declarative knowledge* is information that includes facts, sets of details, definitions, concepts, events, or experiences. Learning a specific fact (one meter equals 100 centimeters), a set of details (three kinds of cognitive learning styles), a definition (Working memory refers to all cognitive processes that occur in our conscious mind), a concept (the Theory of Multiple Intelligences), or learning about an event (the oil spill in the Gulf of Mexico) or recalling an experience (a first job interview) all involve declarative knowledge in your working memory.

Declarative knowledge is information that includes facts, sets of details, definitions, concepts, events, or experiences.

Learning Goals, Plans of Action, and Strategies for Declarative Knowledge:

- Use activities that promote working with the information in new ways
- Elaborate, use elaborative rehearsal, and practice memory searches
- Create associations and retrieval cues

- Recite out loud without looking at printed materials
- Use a variety of activities to practice retrieval and use ongoing review

The second kind of information you may be working with is procedural knowledge. *Procedural knowledge* is information that involves steps or processes used to solve problems or create specific products with accuracy and speed. Every time you perform a series of steps (balance your checkbook), apply a sequence of rules (subtract a double-digit number from a triple-digit number), unconsciously perform a procedure (ride a bike or rollerblade), or repeat a habit without having to think consciously about the individual steps (conduct Internet searches), you are working with procedural knowledge in working memory.

> *Procedural knowledge* is information that involves steps or processes used to solve problems or create specific products with accuracy and speed.

Learning Goals, Plans of Action, and Strategies for Procedural Knowledge:

- Emphasize repetition of the original process *multiple times* over a period of several days and often over several months until it becomes automatic
- Perform the steps with the goal to increase speed and accuracy
- Explain each step in your words to verify your understanding
- Focus on understanding the steps and the processes to avoid rote memory

Figure 3.8 highlights three Essential Strategies for Using Intention. You will learn more about these strategies plus learn additional goal-oriented strategies in Chapter 4.

> **CONCEPT CHECK 3.8**
>
> *How does studying declarative (factual) information differ from studying procedural (processes) information?*

| **FIGURE 3.8** | Essential Strategies for Using Intention |

Learning Goal: To put yourself in a learning mode that identifies a purpose (a goal) and a plan of action for achieving your learning goal.

- **Identify a specific learning goal before you begin a learning activity.** Take the time to figure out and state clearly what you want to accomplish. Know your purpose.

- **Create a plan of action.** After identifying your goal, choose a set of activities that will produce the results that you desire. An organized plan of action motivates you to fulfill your intention to perform a specific task.

- **Determine if you are working with information that involves declarative knowledge or procedural knowledge.** Knowing the kind of information you are working with will help you select learning activities that involve working with the information in new ways, or working with the information through repetition.

Heinrich van den Berg/Gallo Images.

Declarative knowledge and procedural knowledge are integral parts of science and math courses. How does having declarative or factual knowledge help you understand and learn problem-solving processes? How does studying facts differ from studying steps and processes?

Principles
SAVE
CRI**B**
FOTO

Big and Little Pictures is a process of identifying different levels of information.

Big and Little Pictures

The Memory Principle of *Big and Little Pictures* is a process of identifying different levels of information. The "big pictures" are the schemas, themes, concepts, and main ideas. The "little pictures" are the supporting details, such as facts, definitions, examples, parts, or components of a larger concept. Both higher and lower levels of information are important in the learning process.

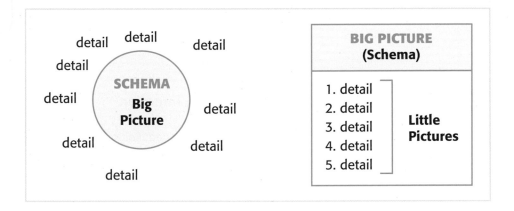

Many study strategies you use require an understanding of the Principle of Big and Little Pictures. In order to highlight textbooks, take notes, create visual mappings, make lists of information, or outline chapters, you need to understand the concept of different levels of information. Using the Principle of Big and Little Pictures helps you do the following:

CONCEPT CHECK 3.9

What problems might you encounter if you do not identify different levels of information in materials that you are studying?

- Identify levels of information: themes, concepts, main ideas, and supporting details (facts, definitions, functions, causes, effects, or steps in a process)
- Create or expand schemas in long-term memory
- Organize details under related headings or main ideas
- Organize information logically to improve memory searches and recall

> **FIGURE 3.9** Essential Strategies for Using Big and Little Pictures
>
> *Learning Goal:* To identify the different levels of information in the materials you are studying.
>
> - **Ask yourself questions that focus your attention on levels of the information.** Is this a recurring theme? Was this a chapter heading? Is this a main idea? Is this a schema? Is this a supporting detail?
> - **Organize details under appropriate schemas and connect them to the big picture.** Ask yourself, "Under what category does this detail belong? What are other related details? What big picture do these details support?"
>
> - **Create study tools that show levels of information.** Diagrams, lists, visual mappings, and outlines work effectively to show relationships.
> - **Use textbook marking and notetaking techniques to clearly show different levels of information.**
> - **Rehearse and recite by first identifying the big picture and then explaining the big picture by giving related details.**

The Memory Principle of Big and Little Pictures is sometimes referred to as seeing "the forest and the trees." If you focus only on the forest, you miss the meaning and beauty of individual trees. If you focus only on a few individual trees, you miss seeing how all the trees together make the forest. **Figure 3.9** shows five Essential Strategies for Using Big and Little Pictures.

Textbook Case Studies

EXERCISE 3.2

DIRECTIONS:

1. Read each case study carefully. Respond to the question at the end of each case study by using *specific* strategies discussed in this chapter. Answer in complete sentences.

2. Write your responses on paper or online at the CourseMate student Web site, Textbook Case Studies. You will be able to print your online response or e-mail it to your instructor.

CASE STUDY 1: Leia is having problems in many of her classes. She feels it is because no one ever taught her how to study or how to learn college level material. Leia is a global learner who quickly sees and grasps large concepts or big pictures. She is artistic and creative, but she does not see ways she can use those talents and interests when she studies. What strategies from the first eight Principles of Memory could Leia learn to use to be a more active, enthusiastic, and successful learner?

CASE STUDY 2: Eduardo spends far more time studying than do any of his other friends or classmates. His learning goal when he studies is to highlight almost every sentence in his textbook and then memorize the highlighted details. He rereads the highlighted information frequently. Eduardo does not understand why all his time and effort are not paying off. He does poorly on most tests. Which strategies for the first eight Principles of Memory would help Eduardo achieve better results on his tests?

 Access Chapter 3 Textbook Case Studies and Web-only Case Studies in your College Success CourseMate, accessed through *CengageBrain.com*.

CHECK POINT 3.3

Answers appear on page B3

Multiple Choice

_____ 1. Which of the following is *not* true about the Memory Principle of Recitation?

Recitation

a. involves adding linguistic or auditory codes to information.

b. when used correctly, provides you with immediate feedback.

c. is one way to use active learning when you study.

d. relies on rote memory to be effective.

_____ 2. Using the Memory Principle of Intention

a. provides a purpose for learning, which increases concentration.

b. involves goal-oriented behavior that activates working memory.

c. works with both declarative and procedural knowledge.

d. does all of the above.

_____ 3. The four Memory Principles represented by the mnemonic CRIB are

a. Clarification, Recitation, Intention, and Big and Little Pictures.

b. processes that involve thinking patterns and active learning behaviors.

c. memory processes that are unrelated to the first four Memory Principles of Selectivity, Association, Visualization, and Elaboration.

d. involved in all of the above.

 Access Chapter 3 Practice Quiz 2 CRIB Principles under "Interactive Quizzes" in your College Success CourseMate, accessed through *CengageBrain* .com.

The Last Four Principles of Memory

4 *Explain how to use the Memory Principles of Feedback, Organization, Time on Task, and Ongoing Review.*

As you have noticed by now, none of the Twelve Principles of Memory works solely by itself. For example, to use Selectivity you need to know how to use Big and Little Pictures; to use Visualization, you need to know how to form and use Associations. Before learning details about the last four Principles of Memory, complete Exercise 3.3.

Feedback

Feedback is the process of verifying how accurately and thoroughly you have or have not learned specific information. Feedback provides you with strategies to monitor your learning progress and the effectiveness of the learning strategies you chose to use. Using the Principle of Feedback helps you do the following:

- Monitor your progress during all stages of learning
- Use self-quizzing throughout the learning process. *Self-quizzing* is the process of testing yourself so you can receive feedback about the accuracy and completeness of your understanding.

Principles

SAVE

CRIB

FOTO

Feedback is the process of verifying how accurately and thoroughly you have or have not learned specific information.

Self-quizzing is the process of testing yourself so you can receive feedback about the accuracy and completeness of your understanding.

Working with the Twelve Principles of Memory

PURPOSE: Working with new information shortly after the initial learning process helps form a stronger impression, increases understanding, creates stronger associations, and personalizes the information.

DIRECTIONS:

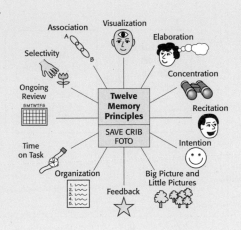

1. On your own paper, copy the visual mapping on the right, or go to the CourseMate Student Web site, Exercise 3.3, for a full-page worksheet for this visual mapping with graphics.

2. Add the following retrieval cue words to the visual mapping. Connect each cue word to the Principle of Memory it represents.

picking and choosing   *focusing*   *self-quizzing*

linking ideas   *explaining out loud*   *structuring logically*

seeing in your mind   *having a purpose or goal*   *using minutes/hours*

*working with and   *larger ideas and details*   *repeated practice*
expanding*

3. Review the first eight Principles of Memory. Attach additional cue words to each of the first eight principles. After reading about the final four principles, return to this visual mapping to attach additional cue words to each principle.

Access Chapter 3 Chapter Exercises in your College Success CourseMate, accessed through *CengageBrain .com*.

- Evaluate the effectiveness of your choice of study or learning strategies based on positive or negative feedback
- Adjust your strategies to achieve higher levels of performance and positive feedback
- Increase confidence, interest, concentration, and motivation

The **_Feedback Model_** is a model of a five-step process that provides you with feedback to assess your comprehension. Receiving feedback involves a sequence of steps: a learning goal—an action—feedback through self-quizzing—comparison to check accuracy—a positive or negative result that demonstrates if learning has taken or has not taken place. **Figure 3.10** shows the steps in the Feedback Model. Results from using this process can reveal both *positive* and *negative* feedback. **_Positive feedback_** is a response that shows you understand specific information. **_Negative feedback_** is a response that shows you have limited or inaccurate understanding of information. Both positive feedback and negative feedback are beneficial to you and your cognitive processes.

Positive Feedback

- Shows you that your memory of the information is accurate and thorough
- Reinforces and strengthens the mental impression of the information
- Creates new associations between questions and correct answers
- Motivates you and provides you with rewards for learning

Feedback Model is a model of a five-step process that provides you with feedback to assess your comprehension.

Positive feedback is a response that shows you understand specific information.

Negative feedback is a response that shows you have limited or inaccurate understanding of information.

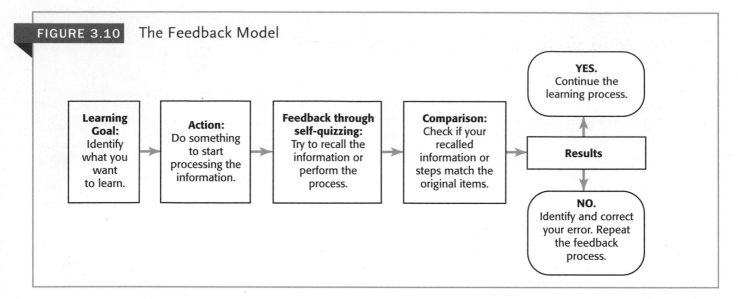

FIGURE 3.10   The Feedback Model

CONCEPT CHECK 3.10

How can you benefit from both positive feedback and negative feedback?

Negative Feedback

- Makes you aware of faulty or incomplete memory of information
- Provides you with the opportunity to modify your learning strategies or select completely different strategies to encode the new information in other ways
- Signals to you that you are not ready to move on to learning new information
- Motivates you to find new ways to clarify, understand, and process the information

The Principle of Feedback is valuable during all stages of learning: at the beginning stages of learning, during rehearsal stages, and during review stages of learning. **Figure 3.11** shows you six Essential Strategies for Using Feedback when you study.

FIGURE 3.11   Essential Strategies for Using Feedback

Learning Goal: To check your accuracy of remembering facts or processes and to adjust your study strategies if necessary.

- **Recite often.** Expressing information out loud, in complete sentences, and using your own words without looking at printed material is one of the most powerful forms of feedback.
- **Use Look-Away Techniques.** As you look away from printed material, *mentally rehearse and review, visualize an image of the material,* or *recite the information without looking.* Look-Away Techniques provide time for the information to gel or integrate with other information.
- **Create review study tools without referring to printed materials.** Write summaries, create lists, or write steps of a process from memory. Always check your accuracy by comparing your work to your textbook or your notes.
- **Rework math problems in the textbook and on homework assignments.** Procedural knowledge needs to be practiced multiple times. Feedback includes not only accurate answers, but also improved problem-solving speed.
- **Work with a partner to quiz each other.** Create sets of study questions, words to define, or problems to solve. Quiz a partner and have your partner quiz you.
- **Use self-quizzing strategies.** Use flashcards for definitions, study questions, or lists in a process for self-quizzing. Use the self-quizzing steps that are a part of notetaking and textbook reading strategies.

Organization

The Memory Principle of **Organization** is the process of creating a meaningful, logical structure or arrangement of *ideas* and information. It does *not* refer to organizing your workspace or your materials. One way to use this principle is to imitate the way authors and instructors organize information. Identifying their patterns of organization can help you follow their logic and understand the material more quickly.

Another way to use this principle is to organize information in new, meaningful ways—ways that make sense to you. Using the Principle of Organization helps you do the following:

- Examine information carefully to identify concepts, main ideas, and important details that you can reorganize, regroup, or rearrange in ways that are easier for you to memorize or learn
- Discover new ways to connect important details to "big ideas" or schemas
- Use your creativity to personalize the information
- Clarify or simplify information by creating meaningful study tools
- Reorganize information using strategies based on your learning style preferences
- Increase comprehension, concentration, interest, and motivation

In later chapters, you will learn an array of reading, notetaking, and study strategies that utilize the Principle of Organization. **Figure 3.12** shows four Essential Strategies for Using Organization.

Principles

SAVE

CRIB

F**O**TO

Organization is the process of creating a meaningful, logical structure or arrangement of *ideas* and information.

CONCEPT CHECK 3.11

What other Principles of Memory do you activate when you use the Principle of Organization?

FIGURE 3.12   Essential Strategies for Using Organization

Learning Goal: To organize information into meaningful chunks, to work with information in new ways to personalize and clarify it, and to create associations that connect levels of information.

- **Create original study tools to present information in new ways.** Develop index card questions, flashcards, visual mappings, hierarchies, formal outlines, Cornell notes or two-column notes, mnemonics, and drawings to reorganize information into original study tools.

- **Organize information into categories or lists.** To avoid working with isolated details, group related details together under one category, such as a topic, a main idea, or a theme.

- **Organize the information chronologically, or by time sequence.** Create time lines for a series of events (such as in history or social science courses), the development of a product (such as in business or marketing courses), or a process involving steps (such as in math, science, or writing courses).

- **Identify organizational patterns in the textbook.** Convert the information into diagrams or charts to show comparisons and contrasts, causes and effects, examples, definitions, processes, or whole-and-parts patterns.

Principles

SAVE

CRIB

FO**T**O

> Time on Task is the process of allocating sufficient time and spacing contact time effectively to learn, rehearse, and retrieve information in memory.

CONCEPT CHECK 3.12

What ineffective study habits can students eliminate by using the Principle of Time on Task for studying?

Time on Task

Time on Task is the process of allocating sufficient time and spacing contact time effectively to learn, rehearse, and retrieve information in memory. How you use time and how much time you spend on a learning task affect the quality of your learning experience. The ability to comprehend and remember what you have studied diminishes when you overload your memory system by trying to study too much information at one time (cramming) or by studying for a period of time (three or more continuous hours). Researchers also have found a high correlation between the amount of time spent studying and the grades earned in courses. Using the Principle of Time on Task helps you in the following ways:

- Dedicate sufficient time to studying, which includes rehearsing, creating associations, and using retrieval cues efficiently
- Eliminate ineffective study habits: cramming, spending insufficient quality time studying, or spending the minimal amount of time studying with hopes to simply "get by"
- Create and use effective time management schedules
- Use spaced practice with multiple contacts with information, spreading those contacts over several different time periods
- Increase your comprehension, retention, and recall of learned information
- Produce high quality work and earn higher grades

In Chapter 4, you will learn an array of time-management strategies that will help you monitor and use time effectively. **Figure 3.13** shows four Essential Strategies for Using Time on Task.

FIGURE 3.13   Essential Strategies for Using Time on Task

Learning Goal: To use time to your advantage by allocating sufficient time to the learning process and spacing practices effectively.

- **Do not rush the learning process.** The learning process and its many cognitive functions take time. When you read or study materials, take the time to pause, think about, work with, and process the information.

- **Plan sufficient study time for each course.** Use the 2:1 ratio (two hours of studying for every one hour in class) so you will have ample time to learn, practice, and review course information. (See Chapter 4.)

- **Use fifty-minute study blocks to study one subject.** Work with only one subject for fifty minutes to keep a strong mindset on the topic. Then, take a short break to give your working memory time to process or consolidate the information. After your break, return to the same subject, or move to a new subject.

- **Use time management strategies.** See Chapter 4 to learn about kinds of time management schedules, the 2:1 ratio, spaced practice, and additional time management strategies to develop Time on Task skills.

Ongoing Review

Ongoing Review is the process of practicing previously learned information. Even though information in long-term memory is considered to be permanent, without practicing retrieval or without using ongoing review, information can fade, become confused with other memories, or be difficult to locate and retrieve. Using the Principle of Ongoing Review helps you in the following ways:

- Reactivate the paths to information in long-term memory
- Practice using retrieval cues and associations created to assist you with memory searches and access to long-term memory schemas
- Use mental rehearsal to reinforce learning
- Keep learned information active and accessible

Ongoing Review is such a crucial step in the learning process that you will find it as the final step of most reading, notetaking, and study skills strategies. In addition to the strategies you will learn in later chapters, **Figure 3.14** shows four Essential Strategies for Using the Principle of Ongoing Review.

Principles
SAVE
CRIB
FOTO

Ongoing Review is the process of practicing previously learned information.

CONCEPT CHECK 3.13

How does using the Principle of Ongoing Review affect working memory and access to long-term memory schemas?

FIGURE 3.14   Essential Strategies for Using Ongoing Review

Learning Goal: To use time and effort on a regular basis to review previously learned information.

- **Include time each week to review previously learned information.** At the beginning of a study block, review information you studied the previous day. Also, allow some time each week to review notes, textbook information, homework assignments, or study tools created at earlier times.
- **Conduct memory searches frequently.** Practice locating and retrieving information quickly from your long-term memory. Track your thought processes, practice associations, recall where you learned specific information, and connect details to schemas when you review.
- **Use frequent repetition of steps and solutions for procedural knowledge.** Rework math or science problems to increase your accuracy and your problem-solving speed. Ongoing review leads to performing the steps more automatically.
- **Conduct a final review right before you know you will need to use the information.** Recently studied information is freshest in working memory (recency effect). Do a final review right before a test, a class discussion, a speech, or a performance task. This brings the information back into working memory.

CHAPTER 3
REFLECTIVE WRITING 2

On separate paper, in a journal, or online at this textbook's CourseMate Web site, respond to the following questions:

1. Which Principles of Memory would bring about the greatest changes in your study methods if you used them on a regular basis? Explain with details, including strategies you would add to your study methods.

2. What plan of action will you use to incorporate these Memory Principles into your study methods on a more regular basis?

Access Chapter 3 Reflective Writing 2 in your College Success CourseMate, accessed through *CengageBrain* *.com*.

CHECK POINT 3.4

Answers appear on page B3

Fill-in-the-Blank

Write one word (key term) per blank to complete each sentence.

1. _____, which can often be the result of recitation, is the process of verifying whether or not you understand and remember information.

2. When you rearrange, categorize, or present information in new ways, you are using the Memory Principle of _____.

3. The Principle of _____ on _____ promotes the use of time management skills.

4. Using the Memory Principle of Ongoing _____ promotes the practice of keeping information fresh in your mind and accessible from long-term memory.

Access Chapter 3 Practice Quiz 3 FOTO Principles under "Interactive Quizzes" in your College Success CourseMate, accessed through *CengageBrain* *.com*.

Chapter 3 Critical Thinking

PURPOSE: Strategies and skills you learned in previous chapters integrate well with information in this chapter. Use your critical thinking skills to identify relationships and associations between previously learned information and new information. Connecting and integrating information strengthen understanding and schemas in long-term memory.

DIRECTIONS: Work with a partner, in a small group, or by yourself to explore answers to the following questions. Be prepared to share your answers with the class.

1. Are the Twelve Principles of Memory more applicable to specific kinds of learning styles? Explain your answer with specific details.

2. We have three memory centers: sensory, working, and long-term. In which memory center are the Memory Principles most actively used? Explain your answer.

3. None of the twelve Principles of Memory works solely by itself. For example, to use Selectivity, you need to know how to use Big and Little Pictures. On paper, list all Twelve Principles of Memory. Across from each principle, list other principles that you activate when you use that specific principle effectively.

ACTIVITY

Learning Objectives Review

1 *Use the mnemonic* SAVE CRIB FOTO *to identify the Twelve Principles of Memory.*

- Mnemonics are memory tools that serve as bridges to help you recall information from long-term memory. SAVE CRIB FOTO is a keyword mnemonic for the Twelve Principles of Memory.

- To work effectively, you must practice translating each letter of the mnemonic into its original word.

2 *Explain how to use the Memory Principles of Selectivity, Association, Visualization, and Elaboration.*

- **S**electivity is the process of identifying and separating main ideas and important details from a larger body of information. Four essential strategies provide you with ways to use the Principle of Selectivity.

- **A**ssociation is the process of using visual or auditory cues to link together two or more items or chunks of information to process into memory. It involves memory searches, retrieval cues, paired associations, chains of associations, and using six essential strategies for the Principle of Association.

- **V**isualization is the process of making pictures or movies in your mind. Four methods for creating visualizations and five essential strategies can help you use the Principle of Visualization effectively.

- **E**laboration, also called *elaborative rehearsal,* is the process of working with and encoding information in new ways. Six essential strategies are available to help you use the Principle of Elaboration.

3 *Explain how to use the Memory Principles of Concentration, Recitation, Intention, and Big and Little Pictures.*

- **C**oncentration is the ability to block out distractions in order to stay focused on one specific item or task. Five essential strategies and using active learning can help you use the Principle of Concentration successfully.

- **R**ecitation is the process of explaining information clearly, out loud, in your own words, and in complete sentences without referring to printed materials. Six essential strategies, including Look-Away Techniques, show ways to use the Principle of Recitation.

- **I**ntention is the process of creating a purpose or a goal to act or perform in a specific way. Goals and plans of action will vary depending on the stage of learning and the kind of information: declarative knowledge or procedural knowledge. Three essential strategies show how to use the Principle of Intention.

Terms to Know

By yourself or with a partner, practice reciting or writing definitions for the following terms. You may also practice defining these terms by using the online flashcard programs or comparing your answers to the online glossary.

mnemonic p. 63

Selectivity p. 64

Association p. 65

paired associations p. 65

Visualization p. 66

Elaboration p. 68

rote memory p. 68

Concentration p. 70

active learning p. 70

Recitation p. 71

Intention p. 72

declarative knowledge p. 72

procedural knowledge p. 73

Big and Little Pictures p. 74

Feedback p. 76

self-quizzing p. 76

Feedback Model, p. 77

positive feedback, p. 77

negative feedback, p. 77

Organization p. 79

Time on Task p. 80

Ongoing Review p. 81

 Access Chapter 3 Flashcard Drills and Online Glossary in your College Success CourseMate, accessed through *CengageBrain.com.*

- **B**ig and Little Pictures is the process of identifying different levels of information: concepts, main ideas, and details. Five essential strategies can help you work with the Principle of Big and Little Pictures.

4 *Explain how to use the Memory Principles of Feedback, Organization, Time on Task, and Ongoing Review.*

- **F**eedback is the process of verifying how accurately and thoroughly you have, or have not, learned specific information. Key concepts include understanding the Feedback Model, the use of both positive and negative feedback, and six essential strategies for using the Principle of Feedback.

- **O**rganization is the process of creating a meaningful, logical structure or arrangement of ideas or information. Four essential strategies provide ways to use the Principle of Organization.

- Time on Task is the process of allocating sufficient time and spacing contact time effectively to learn, rehearse, and retrieve information. Four essential strategies show you how to begin using the Principle of Time on Task.

- **O**ngoing Review is the process of practicing previously learned information. Four essential strategies promote the use of the Principle of Ongoing Review on a regular basis.

Chapter 3 Review Questions

Answers appear on page B3

Matching

Match the terms below with the descriptions at the right. On the line, write the letter from the list at the right to show your answer.

_____ 1. Paired associations

_____ 2. Active learning

_____ 3. Self-quizzing

_____ 4. Declarative knowledge

_____ 5. Procedural knowledge

_____ 6. Goal—action—feedback—comparison—results

_____ 7. Look-Away-Techniques

_____ 8. Rote memory

_____ 9. SAVE CRIB FOTO

_____ 10. Elaborative rehearsal

a. Factual information, such as facts and definitions

b. The process of self-testing to check comprehension

c. Techniques to immediately check recall ability without looking at printed materials

d. A mnemonic for twelve cognitive processes that build and improve memory

e. Knowledge of steps to use for a procedure or process

f. Memorizing information in its exact form without emphasizing understanding

g. Two items linked together for processing

h. Using strategies to engage you in the learning process

i. Thinking about and practicing information in new ways

j. Steps in the Feedback Model

True or False?

_____ 1. The Memory Principle of Selectivity relies on the use of the Principles of Time on Task and Ongoing Review to work effectively.

_____ 2. You are using the Memory Principle of Visualization effectively when you glance at pictures, photographs, or charts.

_____ 3. The Memory Principles of Association, Intention, and Organization are usually used in elaborative rehearsal techniques.

_____ 4. Self-quizzing, reciting, and Look-Away Techniques are ways to get feedback about how well you are learning information.

_____ 5. More repetition and practice are often required for declarative knowledge than are required for procedural knowledge.

Short-Answer Question

On separate paper, answer the following question. Use complete sentences and use terminology from this chapter.

Question: What five Principles of Memory could you use to break the habit of using rote memory to learn and practice information? Explain your reasoning for choosing these five Principles of Memory.

 Access Chapter 3 Chapter Quizzes 1–4 and Enhanced Quiz under "Interactive Quizzes" in your College Success CourseMate, accessed through *CengageBrain .com*.

Access all Chapter 3 Online Materials in your College Success CourseMate, accessed through *CengageBrain.com*.

4

Becoming a Time Manager and a Goal Setter

© PNC/Digital Vision/Getty Images

Time management paired with goal setting is perhaps the most essential of all study skills, for it lays the foundation for you to have adequate time and structure to utilize all other study skills. Learning to use time management to balance your academic, work, and leisure time leads to greater productivity, more successes, and less stress. Learning to set goals provides you with well-defined plans of action to achieve specific results. Time management and goal-setting skills form a powerful partnership of lifelong skills that will benefit you in your academic, professional, and personal life.

LEARNING OBJECTIVES

1. Analyze your use of time and identify ways to create balance in your life.

2. Create and use effective term, weekly, and daily schedules to manage your time.

3. Explain how to use the four steps for writing goals and how to create a plan of action for immediate, short-term, intermediary, and long-term goals.

4. Demonstrate understanding and use of task schedules, goal organizers, the ABC Method, and self-management strategies for goal setting.

Access Chapter 4 Expanded Chapter Outline and Objectives in your College Success CourseMate, accessed through *CengageBrain.com*.

YOUR CHAPTER MAPPING

After reading information under each heading, return to the chapter visual mapping below. Add key words to show subheadings and important details related to each heading.

Access Chapter 4 Visual Mapping in your College Success CourseMate, accessed through *CengageBrain.com*.

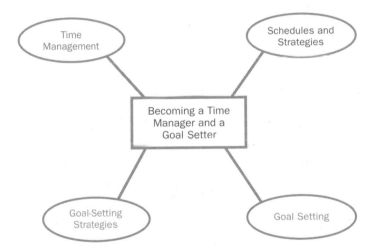

Becoming a Time Manager and a Goal Setter

ANSWER, SCORE, and **RECORD** your profile before you read this chapter. If you need to review the process, refer to the complete directions given in the profile for Chapter 1 on page 4.

ONLINE: You can complete the profile and get your score online at this textbook's CourseMate Web site.

 Access Chapter 4 Profile in your College Success CourseMate, accessed through *CengageBrain.com*.

	YES	NO
1. I use strategies to create a comfortable balance in my school, work, and leisure life.	____	____
2. I use a weekly schedule to organize my studying, work, and leisure time.	____	____
3. I try to make each scheduled day different so I do not get bored.	____	____
4. I often study for three hours or more in a row so I can stay current with my reading and homework assignments.	____	____
5. I usually study two hours during the week for every one hour in class.	____	____
6. I use a systematic four-step process for planning and setting goals.	____	____
7. I tend to have difficulty completing term-long projects on time.	____	____
8. I use task schedules to organize my short-term and study-block goals.	____	____
9. When faced with a list of short-term goals, I work to complete high-priority goals before working on goals with lower levels of importance.	____	____
10. I am confident that I have the skills necessary to manage my time effectively and to stay motivated to complete goals that I set.	____	____

QUESTIONS LINKED TO THE CHAPTER LEARNING OBJECTIVES:

Question 1: objective 1

Questions 2–5: objective 2

Question 6, 7: objective 3

Questions 8, 9: objective 4

Question 10: all objectives

Time Management

1 *Analyze your use of time and identify ways to create balance in your life.*

> Time management is a set of skills designed to help you monitor and use time effectively to increase performance and achieve goals.

Time management is a set of skills designed to help you monitor and use time effectively to increase performance and achieve goals. As a student, you will need to continually balance three main areas in your life: school, work, and leisure. How you spend your time in these three main areas will vary term by term and be influenced by your personal goals, needs, and interests. Imbalances in these three areas of life can lead to an array of negative consequences, including frequent frustration, low productivity, resentment, confusion, or a lack of motivation. The Pie of

Life and the Increase-Decrease Method in the next sections will help you do the following:

- Identify the areas of your life that are not receiving sufficient time to flourish
- Make adjustments and manage your time in new ways to achieve goals and create a more productive and rewarding balance in your life

The Pie of Life

The *Pie of Life* is a graphic representation that shows how much time you dedicate to each of the three main areas of your life: *school, work,* and *leisure.* **Figure 4.1** shows the activities, responsibilities, and commitments that are a part of each section of the Pie of Life.

A balanced Pie of Life is not necessarily divided into three equal parts. The amount of time dedicated to school, work, and leisure vary according to an individual's circumstances, goals, and values. Consider the different Pies of Life for the following students:

- A student who lives in a dorm and does not work while attending school
- A student who works a graveyard shift and attends college full-time
- A student who lives at home and has few responsibilities other than school
- A student who attends school full-time on an athletic scholarship
- A student who is a single parent and who is enrolled in college part-time
- A full-time student who has three children and family responsibilities

You can begin the process of analyzing your use of time by examining **Figure 4.2**. The first circle in Figure 4.2 shows a Pie of Life divided into three equal parts for *school, work,* and *leisure.* Think about your current use of time for these three main areas of the Pie of Life. Then, divide the second circle into a pie that shows the *estimated amount of time* you currently spend per week in each of the three areas. In the last circle, adjust the lines to show your *ideal* Pie of Life that reflects the balance that you wish to obtain.

> The **Pie of Life** is a graphic representation that shows how much time you dedicate to each of the three main areas of your life: *school*, *work*, and *leisure*.

Access Chapter 4 Topics In-Depth: Interactive Pie of Life in your College Success CourseMate, accessed through *CengageBrain.com.*

CONCEPT CHECK 4.1

What does it mean to have a "balanced Pie of Life?" What areas of life need to be examined to achieve a healthy balance?

FIGURE 4.1	Three Main Areas of the Pie of Life

School	Work	Leisure
Classes	*Work/Job*	*Family time*
Homework	*Parenting*	*Social time with friends*
Study/review time	*Household chores*	*Recreation*
Tutoring	*Errands, shopping*	*Exercise*
Study groups	*Volunteer work*	*Personal "alone" time*
Test preparation	*Committee work*	*Hobbies*
Lab projects		*Television, movies, music*
Meetings		*Computer time*
Conferences		*Church*
Team practices/games		

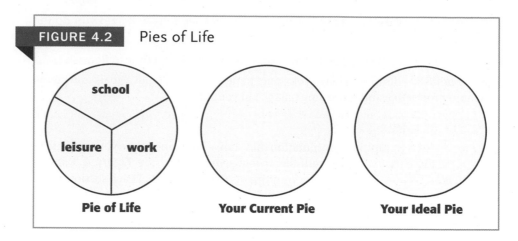

FIGURE 4.2   Pies of Life

Achieving your ideal Pie of Life requires a willingness to examine the ways you currently use time and to commit to exploring new strategies that will improve your time-management and goal-setting skills. Change is not always easy, but the benefits of having a more balanced life make the process rewarding and worthwhile.

EXERCISE 4.1

How You Use Time

PURPOSE: Creating a more effective balance of time in your life begins with an awareness of your daily patterns, habits, and priorities for using time. Keep a log of how you spend your time for three complete days. After analyzing the results of your three-day time log, you can begin applying time-management strategies to create a more effective balance in your life. (A form for a 7-day time log is available on this textbook's CourseMate student Web site.)

DIRECTIONS: Go to Exercise 4.1 in Appendix C, pages C5–C6. Complete the following steps:

1. **Step 1:** On the chart, record all your activities for three days. *Be specific.* For example, you might write: in class, met with tutor, lab work, team practice, job, laundry, television, gym, hobby, e-mail, talked on phone, commuted, napped, or ate dinner.

2. **Step 2:** After completing your three-day log, count the number of hours spent each day in the areas shown on the final chart. Some activities may fit into more than one category; however, count them only once in the most appropriate category.

3. **Step 3: Class Discussion:** How do the results of your three-day log match your ideal Pie of Life as shown in Figure 4.2 on page 90? Explain.

Access Chapter 4 Topics In-Depth: 7-Day Time Log in your College Success CourseMate, accessed through *CengageBrain.com.*

The Increase-Decrease Method

The *Increase-Decrease Method* involves increasing or decreasing time used in one area of life in order to make more time for another area of life. You only have so many hours in a week. If your Pie of Life is unbalanced, you have two choices:

The Increase-Decrease Method involves increasing or decreasing time used in one area of life in order to make more time for another area of life.

1. Learn more efficient ways to study, do household chores, or finish projects at home or at work. In other words, spend less time by becoming more focused, efficient, and productive.

2. Use the Increase-Decrease Method to change the boundaries in your Pie of Life. Begin by identifying the section of your Pie of Life that needs more time in order to create a better balance in your life. As you increase time in this section, you will need to decrease time allocated to one or both of the remaining sections of your pie. For example, if your goal is to increase the amount of time allocated to *school,* you will need to decrease the time you spend in the area of *work* and/or *leisure.*

Using the Increase-Decrease Method to bring you closer to achieving an ideal balance involves learning new skills. At times, ways to increase one area and decrease one or both of the other areas in order to achieve balance are obvious and possible to do. Other times, however, you will need to use your creative problem-solving and brainstorming skills to find increase-decrease solutions for your personal situations, obligations, and goals. Do not be too quick to say, "That won't work," or "That's not possible in my situation." Finding a better balance often involves a willingness to change old behaviors and routines and to give possibilities the opportunity to work for you.

CONCEPT CHECK 4.2

How does the use of the Increase-Decrease Method for one main area of your life affect the other two areas of your Pie of Life? Explain with specific examples.

EXERCISE 4.2

Using the Increase-Decrease Method to Find Time

INSTRUCTIONS

1. Work with a partner. The following three students want suggestions that will help them increase a specific area of their Pie of Life. Several suggestions appear for each student.

2. With your partner, brainstorm additional suggestions for each student. Include ways to reduce the other two areas of their Pie of Life. You may also refer to and include the suggestions available on the CourseMate student Web site for Exercise 4.2.

3. Identify the area in your Pie of Life that you would like to increase. With your partner, brainstorm solutions for your specific situation.

SUGGESTIONS FOR STUDENT 1: I want to increase my *leisure* time with family and friends.

1. Reduce time spent on leisure activities done alone, such as time on the computer.

2. Reduce time spent on chores by learning to do them more efficiently.

3.

4.

Exercise 4.2 (cont.)

SUGGESTIONS FOR STUDENT 2: I want to increase my *school* time so I can earn better grades.

1. Schedule "quality" social time; decrease "spur of the moment" socializing.

2. Make better use of time between classes to study or review.

3.

4.

SUGGESTIONS FOR STUDENT 3: I want to increase my *work* (employment) time so I will have fewer financial stresses.

1. Talk to employer about adding a few extra hours on the weekend.

2. Seek new strategies for budgeting and managing existing income.

3.

4.

SUGGESTIONS FOR ME: I want to increase _____

1.

2.

3.

4.

 Access Chapter 4 Exercises: Exercise 4.2 in your College Success CourseMate, accessed through CengageBrain .com.

CHECK POINT 4.1

Answers appear on page B3

True or False?

_____ 1. Balance in the areas of school, work, and leisure often results in less stress, greater productivity, and a more positive lifestyle.

_____ 2. For realistic balance in one's daily life, a person should allocate equal time to school, work, and leisure activities.

_____ 3. The majority of *school* time in the Pie of Life occurs within the classroom.

_____ 4. The main goal of the Increase-Decrease Method is to encourage students to increase their school and study time by decreasing their social and leisure time.

_____ 5. The concept of *work* includes more than an income-earning job.

 Access Chapter 4 Practice Quiz 1: Balance under Interactive Quizzes in your College Success CourseMate, accessed through CengageBrain.com.

Schedules and Strategies

2 *Create and use effective term, weekly, and daily schedules to manage your time.*

Well-designed schedules serve as road maps to guide you through the months of a term, through the week, and through each day. Rather than being at the mercy of time, schedules empower you and give you the ability to take control of time. With schedules, *you* create goals and plans for how you wish to spend your time. Your skills as a time manager become lifelong skills that benefit you well in school, at home, and in your chosen career.

Term Schedules

A *term schedule* is a month-by-month calendar that shows important events and deadlines for the entire term. You can use a regular calendar, a monthly planner, an electronic organizer, or a computer calendar program for each month in your current academic term. At the beginning of each term, create your term schedule by adding the items to your calendar that appear in **Figure 4.3**.

Access Chapter 4 Topics In-Depth: Quick Start Forms in your College Success CourseMate, accessed through *CengageBrain.com*.

CONCEPT CHECK 4.3

What potential problems can you avoid by using a term schedule? Why is it important for you to have a "big picture" of the term?

A **term schedule** is a month-by-month calendar that shows important events and deadlines for the entire term.

EXERCISE 4.3

Create a Term Schedule

PURPOSE: Create a term schedule that provides you with an overview of the term and serves as a guide when you create your weekly schedule.

DIRECTIONS: Gather together your campus calendar, the syllabus from each of your courses, and your personal calendar of events to create a term schedule.

1. Use a month-by-month planner or calendar. On your calendar, enter the items shown in Figure 4.3.

2. Place your month-by-month calendars in the front of your notebook, or if you are using an electronic calendar program, refer to the monthly calendar at the beginning of each week when you create your weekly schedule.

3. Update your term calendar throughout the term with deadlines for new assignments or significant events.

Access Chapter 4 Topics In-Depth: Quick Start Forms in your College Success CourseMate, accessed through CengageBrain.com.

FIGURE 4.3   Items to Include on Your Term Schedule

1. Important deadlines for special projects, reports, and writing or lab assignments that appear on your course syllabi

2. Scheduled tests, midterms, and final exams

3. Special events, meetings, workshops, or conferences

4. Holidays

5. Scheduled times for tutors, study groups, or other support services

6. Personal appointments on or off campus

A weekly schedule is a detailed plan that serves as a guide for creating a manageable, daily plan for each day of the week.

Weekly Schedules

A *weekly schedule* is a detailed plan that serves as a guide for creating a manageable, daily plan for each day of the week. While term schedules provide you with an overview of important events and deadlines on a month-to-month basis, weekly schedules focus your attention on details and requirements for the upcoming week. Using a weekly schedule helps you maintain a focus and helps you organize, monitor, and regulate your use of time.

Unlike a time log made *after* you complete activities or tasks, a weekly time-management schedule is made *before* you engage in the activities. The weekly schedule becomes your *plan,* your guide, and your structure for the week. **Figure 4.4** shows a well-planned weekly schedule. A well-planned weekly schedule includes the following characteristics:

- **A realistic, balanced Pie of Life for** *school, work,* **and** *leisure*
- **Adequate time for study blocks:** Study blocks are scheduled throughout the week so you study on a regular basis, not just when you have assignments due or a test the following day.
- **Effective use of all blocks of time:** You "tighten up" your schedule to avoid wasted blocks of time, such as an hour between classes or an hour or two after dinner.
- **Blocks of time for work and leisure time activities:** Your schedule shows your hours of employment. If your work hours change weekly, your weekly schedule reflects these changes. Your weekly schedule also shows time set aside for household chores, errands, exercise, recreation, social and family time, and daily routines, such as getting ready in the morning, commuting, or preparing and eating meals.
- **Strong, consistent patterns:** Patterns, such as specific times for studying specific classes, eating meals, doing chores, or engaging in recreation help you follow your schedule to the point that it becomes routine and habitual.
- **Time allocated to work on personal goals:** For example, if you want to jog three times a week or spend time in the park with your children twice a week, your schedule shows time set aside for those goals.
- **A routine time to sleep each night:** Going to bed about the same time each night helps stabilize your internal clock and your sleep-awake patterns. Short nights occasionally followed by long nights of sleep disrupt your normal rhythm and a more natural flow of energy.

CONCEPT CHECK 4.4

If you were to analyze another student's weekly schedule, what criteria would you use to evaluate its effectiveness?

 Access Chapter 4 Topics In-Depth: Quick Start Forms in your College Success CourseMate, accessed through *CengageBrain .com*.

Five Steps to Create a Weekly Time-Management Schedule

Using a systematic approach to create your weekly time-management schedule helps you plan sufficient time for important areas of your daily life. **Figure 4.5** provides you with a five-step approach for developing your weekly time-management schedule. The following points will help you develop and use your weekly schedule effectively:

- Each Sunday spend a few minutes planning your schedule for the upcoming week.
- Keep your weekly schedule in the front of your notebook or in your electronic organizer. Refer to your weekly schedule whenever you wish to make new plans or set up appointments.
- Use your schedule for the entire term. On occasion, you may need to make minor changes in your schedule to accommodate special events or work schedules.
- Apply the strategies discussed in the following five steps for creating a weekly time-management schedule.

FIGURE 4.4   Example of Weekly Time-Management Schedule

WEEKLY TIME-MANAGEMENT SCHEDULE

For the week of _____

Time	Monday	Tuesday	Wednesday	Thursday	Friday	Saturday	Sunday
12–6 AM	SLEEP ──→						
6–7:00	SLEEP ──→						
7–8:00	Get up, get ready, eat breakfast ───────────────→					SLEEP	SLEEP
8–9:00	Commute to school ──────────────────────→					Get up	Get up
9–10:00	PE Class	Study Math	PE Class	Study Math	PE Class	Breakfast	Breakfast
10–11:00	Math Class	Math Class	Math Class	Math Class	Study Math	Career Class	Get ready
11–12 NOON	Study Math	LUNCH	Study Math	LUNCH	with TUTOR	Study Career	CHURCH
12–1:00	LUNCH	Computer Class	LUNCH	Computer Class	LUNCH	ERRANDS	CHURCH
1–2:00	Reading Class	Computer Class	Reading Class	Computer Class	Reading Class	LUNCH	LUNCH
2–3:00	Study Reading	Lab-Study Computer	Study Reading	Lab-Study Computer	Study Reading	CHORES	LEISURE
3–4:00	Study Reading	Lab-Study Computer	FLEX	Lab-Study Computer	FLEX	CHORES	LEISURE
4–5:00	Commute home ───────────────────────→					CHORES	LEISURE
5–6:00	DINNER ──────────────────────────────→						LEISURE
6–7:00	LEISURE	LEISURE	LEISURE	LEISURE	WORK	WORK	DINNER
7–8:00	Study Reading	WORKOUT	Study Math	WORKOUT	WORK	WORK	Study Math
8–9:00	Study Reading		Study Computer		WORK	WORK	Study Computer
9–10:00	LEISURE		LEISURE		WORK	WORK	FLEX
10–11:00	LEISURE	↓	LEISURE	↓	WORK	WORK	PLAN WEEK
11–12 AM	SLEEP ──────────────────────────→				WORK	WORK	SLEEP

> **FIGURE 4.5**   Five Steps for Creating a Weekly Time-Management Schedule
>
> **1.** Write in all your fixed activities.
> **2.** Write in your fixed study blocks for each class.
> **3.** Add two or three flexible study blocks.
> **4.** Add time for personal goals and personal responsibilities.
> **5.** Schedule leisure, family, and social time.

Step 1: Write your fixed activities. Fixed activities are those activities that do not vary much from week to week. On your weekly schedule, write the following fixed activities in the appropriate time blocks:

1. Class times
2. Work schedule (employment)
3. Daily routines: getting ready in the morning; commuting
4. Meals: breakfast, lunch, and dinner
5. Special appointments
6. Sleep

Step 2: Write your fixed study blocks. **Fixed study blocks** are well-planned blocks of time set aside to study specific subjects during the course of the week. With effective fixed study blocks, you place a high priority on having sufficient time to complete your reading and homework assignments, create study tools, use elaborative rehearsal, and practice retrieving information through ongoing review.

Step 3: Add several flexible study blocks. **Flex study blocks** are flexible blocks of time on a weekly schedule that you use only when you need them. Flex blocks are safety nets for extra study time. Identify two or three hours each week that you can hold in reserve in case you need additional time to study for a specific class, prepare for a test, or complete a special project. On your weekly schedule, write *FLEX* for these time blocks. Unlike fixed study blocks, which you should use each time they appear on your schedule, if you do not need to use the flex blocks, *convert them to free time.*

Step 4: Add time for personal goals and responsibilities. Schedule time blocks to work specifically on important goals or personal responsibilities. If you do not set aside time specifically for these important goals, tasks, or responsibilities, you may find yourself postponing or procrastinating about them or ignoring them completely.

Step 5: Schedule leisure, family, and social time. Label the remaining time on your schedule as *family, social,* or *leisure.* For the upcoming week, you can specify specific plans for time blocks, such as "swimming," "movie," or "entertaining," or you can leave the time blocks open and flexible to do whatever you decide to do on that day. Having family, social, and leisure time is important for mental and physical health and strong relationships. If you do not have adequate time on your schedule for these activities, explore ways to use the Increase-Decrease Method to find more social and leisure time.

Fixed study blocks are well-planned blocks of time set aside to study specific subjects during the course of the week.

Flex study blocks are flexible blocks of time on a weekly schedule that you use only when you need them.

CONCEPT CHECK 4.5

What are the five steps to create a weekly schedule? Why are the first three steps focused on school?

Five Basic Time-Management Strategies

Your fixed study blocks on your weekly schedule help you organize your time and your academic commitments. Effectively using the five Basic Time-Management Strategies in **Figure 4.6** as you plan your fixed study blocks increases the effectiveness of your weekly schedule.

Use the 2:1 ratio to schedule fixed study blocks. The *2:1 ratio* is a time-management technique that involves studying two hours for every one hour in class. Studying in college means more than just doing homework. The 2:1 ratio provides you, in most cases, with sufficient time not only to take notes, memorize, and elaborate on course work, but to rehearse or review to keep information in long-term memory "fresh" and accessible. The 2:1 ratio applies to the majority of college courses that require reading and homework assignments. For example, if your writing class meets for three hours each week, schedule six hours of studying *for the writing class* each week.

> 2:1 ratio is a time-management technique that involves studying two hours for every one hour in class.

Use the 3:1 ratio for independent study or online courses. The *3:1 ratio* is a time-management technique that involves studying nine hours a week for three-credit independent study or online courses. Even though independent study and online courses offer students flexibility, they often require a higher level of self-discipline, dedication, and time commitment to complete successfully. For three-credit independent study or online courses that have few or no in-class hours, you need to schedule a minimum of *nine hours* per week for coursework. Use the course syllabus to create a term schedule and your personal week-by-week schedule of assignments to insure that you complete the course in a timely manner.

> 3:1 ratio is a time-management technique that involves studying nine hours a week for 3-credit independent study or online courses.

Use spaced practice. *Spaced practice,* also known as *distributed practice,* is a time-management strategy that involves making multiple contacts with new information and spreading this contact over several days or weeks. Spaced practice limits the length of a study block and spreads study blocks out over time. Using spaced practice increases comprehension, retention, motivation, concentration, and productivity. You will spend less time rereading and relearning information. Following are important points to understand about spaced practice:

> Spaced practice, also known as *distributed practice*, involves making multiple contacts with new information and spreading this contact over several days or weeks.

- You will understand and recall information better for a subject if you study it for one hour six times a week, or two hours three times a week, rather than study it for six hours on the same day.
- The breaks or rest intervals between every fifty-minute study block give your memory system time to sort, process, and connect information. The Topics

Access Chapter 4 Topics In-Depth: Spaced Practice in your College Success CourseMate, accessed through *CengageBrain.com*.

FIGURE 4.6   Five Basic Time-Management Strategies

- Use the 2:1 ratio for most classes.
- Use the 3:1 ratio for independent study and online courses.
- Use spaced practice.
- Avoid using marathon studying.
- Use trading time sparingly.

In-Depth: Spaced Practice on the CourseMate student Web site discusses the impact study breaks have on comprehension and retention.

- After studying two or three hours (with short breaks between each fifty-minute study block), change to a different kind of activity, such as a leisure or social activity. Your thinking processes do not shut down when you step away from the books for a few hours. When you return to studying, you will be more alert and receptive to new information.

Avoid marathon studying. *Marathon studying,* also known as *massed practice,* occurs when you study more than three hours in a row. Three or more continuous hours of studying without a break leads to problems with productivity, concentration, and retention. Avoiding marathon studying will also help you avoid overloading working memory.

Marathon studying *is* acceptable in some learning situations that involve a creative flow of ideas or energy. Learning tasks such as painting, sculpting, constructing a model, or writing a research paper may benefit from marathon studying because tapping into the same channel of creativity and thought patterns at a later time may be more difficult to achieve. In such situations, scheduling longer study blocks is acceptable.

Use trading time sparingly. *Trading time* is a time-management technique that allows you to trade or exchange time blocks for two activities within the same day. Use trading time when you need flexibility in your schedule to adjust to a special event. For example, if you want to participate in an unexpected social activity that will occur during your 7:00–9:00 PM study block, trade the study block with a 2:00–4:00 block of time you had set aside to spend with friends. Use trading time cautiously. If you trade time blocks too frequently, you will lose the sense of routine, and your self-discipline to follow your schedule may decline.

Marathon studying, also known as *massed practice,* occurs when you study more than three hours in a row.

CONCEPT CHECK 4.6

What are the major differences between spaced practice and massed practice? When is spaced practice preferred over massed practice?

Trading time is a time-management technique that allows you to trade or exchange time blocks for two activities within the same day.

GROUP PROCESSING

A COLLABORATIVE LEARNING ACTIVITY

Form groups of three or four students. You will need to have a chart to record information. Select one member of your group to be the group recorder. Complete the following directions.

1. Divide a large chart into two columns. In the left column write all the problems the members of your group have encountered with managing time. List as many different ideas or problems as possible.

2. After you have a list of common problems, brainstorm possible solutions. Write the possible solutions in the right column. You may provide more than one possible solution for each problem. Be prepared to share your list of problems and possible solutions with the class.

Access Chapter 4
Practice Quiz 2:
Using Schedules under
"Interactive Quizzes"
in your College
Success CourseMate,
accessed through
CengageBrain.com.

Essential Strategies for Scheduling Fixed Study Blocks

Learning to become a time manager involves a willingness to adjust behaviors, attitudes, and ways you use time. To succeed, anticipate change, be willing to relax or replace your old patterns, and be patient with yourself as you make the necessary adjustments. Creating an effective weekly schedule helps you get off to a good start and experience the benefits of using time management. **Figure 4.7** provides you with seven essential strategies to use as you schedule your fixed study blocks.

Label and use each study block for one specific subject. Labeling a block "study" does not provide you with a specific study plan and tends to promote an ineffective habit of studying whatever feels to be of the greatest urgency. Instead, use specific labels such as *Study English, Study Math,* or *Study Psychology.* Plan to use the entire study block for one subject. Jumping from one subject to another within an hour block disrupts the process of creating a "mindset" for the subject matter. Use the entire fifty-minute study block to review previous work, complete the current assignment, make notes or other study tools, and review. At the end of fifty minutes, give yourself a *ten-minute break* before moving into the next hour of studying.

Schedule at least one study block every day of the week. By spreading your study times throughout the entire week, you will be using spaced practice and will experience less stress and frustration. Studying long hours during the weekdays and then engaging mainly in leisure or social activities on the weekend is ineffective.

Schedule a math study block every day. Math involves working with steps and processes, the kind of knowledge that requires repetition, repetition, and more repetition. Studying math on a daily basis provides essential time for repetition and to practice increasing problem-solving speed and accuracy. When possible, schedule a math study block right after your math class; on the days of the week that you do not have a math class, schedule your math study block during your alert times of the day.

Study during your most alert times of the day. Study when you feel the most mentally sharp, alert, and focused, not when you know your body and eyes are physically fatigued. Mornings, midafternoons, and early evenings are often the most productive times to study. Studying late at night or right after a meal is often less productive. Use "low energy or low attention times" for tasks that do not require high cognitive functioning.

CONCEPT CHECK 4.7

What strategies or guidelines can you use to schedule study blocks for your most difficult class, a math class, a Spanish class, and a history lecture class?

FIGURE 4.7   Essential Strategies for Scheduling Fixed Study Blocks

- Label and use each study block for one specific subject.
- Schedule at least one study block every day of the week.
- Schedule a math study block every day.
- Study during your most alert times of the day.
- Schedule your hardest or least-liked subject early in the day.
- Schedule a study block right *before* a class that involves discussions or student participation.
- Schedule a study block right *after* a lecture or a math class.

Schedule your hardest or least-liked subjects early in the day. By placing the hardest or least-liked subjects first on your study priorities, you are able to use a more alert mind and focused attention to tackle the assignments and process new information.

Schedule a study block right before a class that involves discussion or student participation. This puts you in the mindset for the course, refreshes your memory of key concepts, and provides you with time to rehearse as needed.

Schedule a study block right after a lecture or a math class. Taking notes is your main task during a lecture class. By scheduling a study time right *after* the class, you can review your notes, compare them with other students' notes, fill in missing details, and reorganize your notes in more meaningful ways while the information is still fresh in your mind. Scheduling a study time right *after* a math class reinforces the processes and provides immediate practice working problem sets or applications while the class explanations are fresh in your memory.

Using effective time-management strategies provides you with the tools to become a successful time manager. As you learn to use your weekly schedule, you may at times recognize that you are wandering from your time-management plan. Do not be hard on yourself or discard the schedule. Instead, recognize that change requires adjustments. Return to your schedule and get yourself back on track.

Exercise 4.4 guides you through the process of creating your weekly time-management schedule. Examine the effectiveness of your schedule during the first three weeks of using it. If you do not follow your plans for some of the scheduled blocks of time, analyze the situations to identify what happened. Adjust your schedule the following week if necessary. As you learn these skills, remember that the time-management skills you learn now are highly prized skills recognized and admired in both the work force and the academic world.

Creating Your Weekly Schedule

DIRECTIONS: Go to Exercise 4.4 in Appendix C, pages C7–C8 for a weekly time-management form and a Time-Management Self-Assessment Checklist. Photocopy the weekly schedule form to use for this exercise or download the form from online Chapter 4 in the Topics In-Depth: Quick Start Forms. Complete the following directions.

Step 1: Use the steps diagrammed on the following page to create a weekly time-management schedule. Use a pencil at first so you can rearrange time blocks and make adjustments as needed to create a manageable and realistic schedule.

Step 2: Mentally walk through each day on your schedule to determine that it is realistic. Make adjustments if necessary.

Step 3: Complete the Time-Management Self-Assessment Checklist on page C8 in Appendix C. Use that information to make any necessary adjustments on your schedule.

Step 4: Color-code your schedule so it is easier to see at a glance. Use one color for your classes; another for study times; and a third for leisure, family, and social time. Use a fourth color for work or leave the spaces without color coding.

Step 5: Make a copy of your schedule to keep in the front of your notebook if your instructor asks you to turn in your original schedule and the Self-Assessment Checklist.

EXERCISE 4.4

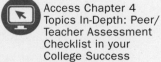

Step 6: Begin following your schedule as soon as possible. Several times during the day, indicate on your schedule how often you followed it as planned. Create a code system such as using stars for blocks that worked as planned and checks for blocks that you did not follow according to the plan.

Access Chapter 4 Topics In-Depth: Peer/ Teacher Assessment Checklist in your College Success CourseMate, accessed through *CengageBrain.com*.

Step 7: Use your schedule for a full seven days. After you have used your schedule for a full week, your instructor may ask you to turn in your first schedule and the Time-Management Self-Assessment Checklist.

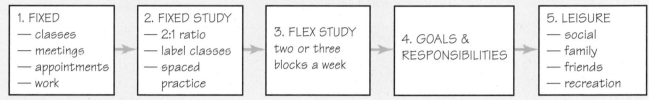

1. FIXED	2. FIXED STUDY	3. FLEX STUDY	4. GOALS &	5. LEISURE
— classes	— 2:1 ratio	two or three	RESPONSIBILITIES	— social
— meetings	— label classes	blocks a week		— family
— appointments	— spaced			— friends
— work	practice			— recreation

Daily Schedules

A *daily schedule* is a specific list of tasks that you plan to achieve over the course of a day. It is your "To-Do List" that helps you move through the day efficiently. Use an index card, a daily planner, or an electronic organizer for your daily schedule. Each night before you go to bed, take a few minutes to prepare your daily schedule for the next day's activities. Keep the schedule in a convenient place for quick reference. In **Figure 4.8**, after examining the example of the daily schedule on the left, make a daily schedule for yourself in the box on the right.

> A **daily schedule** is a specific list of tasks that you plan to achieve over the course of a day.

CHECK POINT 4.2

Answers appear on page B3

Matching

Match the terms on the left with the shortened definitions or descriptions on the right. Write the letter of the definition next to the word in the left column.

_____ 1. flex blocks   a. often require more than the hours associated with the 2:1 ratio

_____ 2. 2:1 ratio   b. occurs with marathon studying

_____ 3. spaced practice   c. best to schedule study block right before class

_____ 4. massed practice   d. distributed practice

_____ 5. trading time   e. study blocks set to study specific courses

_____ 6. online courses   f. set of monthly calendars with deadlines and events

_____ 7. lecture classes   g. two or three blocks of time set aside as "safety nets"

_____ 8. speech classes   h. best to schedule study block after class

_____ 9. fixed study blocks   i. a formula for allocating sufficient time to study in most courses

_____ 10. term schedule   j. an exchange of two blocks of time within the same day

Access Chapter 4 Practice Quiz 3: TM Strategies under "Interactive Quizzes" in your College Success CourseMate, accessed through *CengageBrain.com*.

FIGURE 4.8   Example of a Daily Schedule

TO DO WEDNESDAY:

8–9:00 AM   Study Psy.
             Read & notes for
             pages 95–116

CLASSES   Regular schedule

1–3:00 PM   Study Algebra
             —Redo Ex. 6 #2–5
             —Do Ex. 7 odd numbers
             —Make study flash cards

3–5:00 PM   —Start laundry
             —Grocery shop
             —Read mail
             —Finish laundry

MY DAILY SCHEDULE FOR TOMORROW:

CHAPTER 4 REFLECTIVE WRITING 1

On separate paper, in a journal, or on this textbook's CourseMate Web site, respond to the following questions.

1. What are the major adjustments you have had to make in your attitude, behavior, or use of time as you learn to become a more effective time manager? How has your Pie of Life changed since you began using time management? Be specific.

2. What are the most difficult times of the day for you to "stay on schedule"? What areas of time management are most difficult for you to implement? Discuss the time-management strategies you can use to overcome these difficulties.

Access Chapter 4 Reflective Writing 1 in your College Success CourseMate, accessed through *CengageBrain* .com.

Goal Setting

 Explain how to use the four steps for writing goals and how to create a plan of action for immediate, short-term, intermediary, and long-term goals.

Goals are well-defined plans aimed at achieving specific results.

Goals are well-defined plans aimed at achieving specific results. Goal setting and time management go hand in hand. Effective time management requires effective goal setting. You can use your blocks of time more effectively when you have a clear goal of what you want to accomplish during specific times. Your goals become your road maps to guide you to your desired outcomes.

Different Kinds of Goals

Goals can be defined and organized in a variety of ways, such as educational goals, financial goals, or organizational goals. The length of time required to achieve the desired outcome is another way to categorize goals. The following are four kinds of goals defined by time:

- An *immediate goal* is a well-defined plan to achieve specific results within a few hours to a few days. For example, completing a list of errands, organizing your desk to create an ideal study area, washing and detailing your car, or cleaning out a closet are immediate goals that you can achieve within a few days.

- A *short-term goal* is a well-defined plan to achieve specific results within as little as a week or as long as three months. To create a plan for a short-term goal, you may want to break the goal into smaller steps or a series of immediate goals. For example, to organize your records and receipts and complete your tax return may take several weeks or as long as three-months. Likewise, to gather information, do research, write a draft, and complete the final version of a research report for a class is a term-long project, but it is considered a short-term goal because you can complete it within a few months.

- An *intermediary goal* is a well-defined plan to achieve specific results within a time period of one or two years. Completion of an intermediary goal often is the result of completing a series of short-term goals that serve as benchmarks, motivators, and links to the completion of the longer goal.

- A *long-term goal* is a well-defined plan to achieve specific results after several years. Completion of a long-term goal often is the result of completing a series of intermediary goals. **Figure 4.9** demonstrates the relationship of immediate, short-term, and intermediary goals to the long-term educational goal of acquiring a four-year degree.

An immediate goal is a well-defined plan to achieve specific results within a few hours to a few days.

A short-term goal is a well-defined plan to achieve specific results within as little as a week or as long as three months.

An intermediary goal is a well-defined plan to achieve specific results within a time period of one or two years.

A long-term goal is a well-defined plan to achieve specific results after several years.

 Access Chapter 4 Practice Quiz 4: Kinds of Goals under "Interactive Quizzes" in your College Success CourseMate, accessed through *CengageBrain .com*.

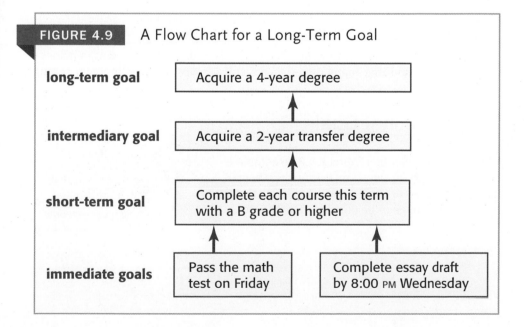

FIGURE 4.9   A Flow Chart for a Long-Term Goal

long-term goal	Acquire a 4-year degree
intermediary goal	Acquire a 2-year transfer degree
short-term goal	Complete each course this term with a B grade or higher
immediate goals	Pass the math test on Friday / Complete essay draft by 8:00 PM Wednesday

Your Long-Term Educational Goal Flow Chart

DIRECTIONS

1. Use **Figure 4.9** as a model for this exercise, or use the form online in the CourseMate student Web site, Exercise 4.5. On your paper, make boxes in your flow chart for "long-term educational goal," "intermediary goals," "short-term goals," and "immediate goals." Allow ample space for specific details about your goals.

2. Write your specific long-term educational goal in the box on the top of your flow chart.

3. Locate a printed page of a catalog or brochure that shows the classes and requirements you need to complete your program or degree. List those in the box for "intermediary goals."

4. Complete your flow chart by adding items in the boxes for "short-term goals" for this term, and "immediate goals" for the next few days.

 Access Chapter 4 Exercises: Exercise 4.5 in your College Success CourseMate, accessed through *CengageBrain.com*.

A Four-Step Approach for Achieving Goals

Many people have good intentions and a strong desire or motivation to succeed by achieving their goals; however, many of these same people fall short of making their goals a reality. Frequently, the inability to achieve goals begins with the lack of a sound process or strategy to write and plan effective goals. In other cases, people shy away from goal setting because of attitudes such as the following:

- I have a fear of failure, or I have a fear of success.
- It's better not to try than to try and not succeed.
- I'll just get discouraged, frustrated, or embarrassed, so why bother?
- I've never been a goal setter and I'm doing okay.
- I have never learned how to set goals and don't know where to start.

Fortunately, by learning to write effective goals and to use strategies to achieve goals, you will find that many of your fears and reasons for avoiding goal setting

Initial Thoughts about Personal Goals

DIRECTIONS: Go to the CourseMate student Web site, Exercise 4.6, to complete the Initial Thoughts about Personal Goals chart for this term, the next two years, and the next five years. This exercise is designed to encourage you to begin thinking about where you are and where you want to go or be during different time periods of your life.

 Access Chapter 4 Exercises: Exercise 4.6 in your College Success CourseMate, accessed through *CengageBrain .com*.

vanish. One easy way to begin the process of becoming a goal setter is to identify a *specific, realistic immediate goal* that you can achieve within a few hours. Select strategies to complete the goal. One success at completing a goal leads the way to more successes and combats reasons for shying away from goal setting.

The ***Four-Step Approach for Achieving Goals*** is a process to set and achieve goals by using these steps: Specific, Target, Steps, and Rewards. **Figure 4.10** shows these four steps.

Step 1: Set Specific Goals

Take the time to do a personal inventory to identify what it is that you wish to achieve. When your goal is clear, specific, and realistic, you have a vivid picture or vision of the desired outcome. To simply say, "I will do better" or "I want something new" results in vague and immeasurable goals. To say, "I will be a millionaire tomorrow" is not realistic for most people. Before you commit to a goal, evaluate whether the goal is clear, specific, and realistic for you.

Step 2: Set a Specific Target Date and Time

Procrastinators (people who put off doing something) seldom achieve goals. You can reduce or eliminate procrastination by setting a *specific target date* (deadline) and even *a specific time* to finish the steps involved in reaching your goal. The target date and time work as a form of motivation to keep you moving forward and on time.

Step 3: Identify Steps

On paper, list the individual steps you will need to work through to achieve your goal. For goals with multiple steps, list specific target dates and times for completing each step. Schedule time on your weekly schedule to complete each step. When you use this method of breaking one large goal into several smaller ones, you gain momentum each time you achieve a smaller goal by its targeted time.

Step 4: Plan a Reward

You can acknowledge and celebrate the completion of a goal with a reward. You can use that reward as an incentive—a motivator—to achieve your goal. You can use two kinds of rewards in your goal-setting plan: extrinsic rewards and intrinsic rewards.

Extrinsic rewards are material things or activities that are awarded when a goal is achieved. Buying a CD, going to a movie, going out to dinner, or planning a short trip are examples of extrinsic rewards. An extrinsic reward is a strong motivator only if you use it *after* you achieve the goal. You must also withhold the reward if you do not achieve the goal.

Intrinsic rewards are emotions or feelings that a person experiences when a goal is achieved. An increased self-esteem, pride, relief, joy, more confidence, or immense satisfaction are examples of intrinsic rewards. For any rewards to work as motivators, select rewards that truly represent what you *want* and can look forward to receiving.

The Four Step Approach for Achieving Goals is a process to set and achieve goals by using these steps: Specific, Target, Steps, and Rewards.

Long-term goals are the result of the accomplishment of multiple intermediary, short-term, and immediate goals. Do you have clear vision for your long-term educational goal? What intermediary goals must you complete to reach your long-term goal?
© Image copyright buket bariskan, 2009. Used under license from Shutterstock.com.

Extrinsic rewards are material things or activities that are awarded when a goal is achieved.
Intrinsic rewards are emotions or feelings that a person experiences when a goal is achieved.

FIGURE 4.10   Four Steps for Achieving Goals (STSR)

1. **Specific:** Set specific, clear, and realistic goals.
2. **Target:** Set a specific target date and time to complete each goal.
3. **Steps:** Identify the individual steps involved in reaching the goal.
4. **Reward:** Plan a reward for yourself when you reach the goal.

A Plan of Action

The four steps for writing and achieving goals become your *plan of action*. Creating a plan of action for any goal increases the likelihood that you will complete the goal. Each of the four steps for writing and achieving goals activates your working memory and helps you build momentum to succeed:

Step 1 helps you clarify what you wish or intend to achieve.

Step 2 increases your awareness of time and activates your time-management skills.

Step 3 motivates you to identify and organize the tasks involved.

Step 4 builds motivation for you to follow through with your plan of action.

You can use these four powerful steps for a plan of action to tackle high-priority tasks that need to be done immediately at work, to organize and complete household chores, to achieve personal goals, or to organize a study block or a project for school.

For example, assume that you have set an immediate goal to organize your study area at home. Your plan of action may include the following details for each step of the goal-setting process.

Step 1—Set a specific goal: Organize my desk to create an ideal study area.

Step 2—Set a target date and time: Have it done by this Sunday at 4:00.

Step 3—Identify the individual steps I need to work through:

1. Sort/organize paperwork stacked on my desk (bills, mail, class notes, and homework).

2. For each class, put current assignments and notes into my notebooks in chronological order.

3. Put all older notes and assignments into file folders. Label according to class and file each folder in a file box or cabinet.

4. Organize my work surface: textbooks, dictionary, supplies, and other materials.

5. Get rid of any remaining clutter. Empty wastepaper basket.

Step 4—Identify a reward: Extrinsic: Go out for pizza and a movie with friends.

CONCEPT CHECK 4.9

Why is each step of the four-step goal-setting process important? What would happen if you omitted any one of the steps?

Achieving an Immediate Goal

EXERCISE 4.7

PURPOSE: Select an immediate goal that you can complete within the next day or two. Use the four goal-setting steps to tackle a small task that you would like to accomplish but keep putting off doing.

DIRECTIONS

1. Use all four steps for planning your goal. On a separate piece of paper or online under Exercise 4.7, answer the following questions.

   Step 1: What is your *specific* goal?

   Step 2: What are the *target date* and *time* to complete this goal?

   Step 3: What are the individual *steps* you must complete to achieve the goal? List each step.

   Step 4: What is your planned reward?

2. Implement your plan of action. Begin working to complete each step as soon as possible.

3. After your target date and time pass, respond to the following question: Did you achieve your goal by the target date and time? If yes, explain what contributed to your success. If no, describe the obstacles that interfered with the process.

Access Chapter 4 Exercises: Exercise 4.7 in your College Success CourseMate, accessed through *CengageBrain.com*.

Goals for Term-Long Projects

Preparing for a major test, such as a midterm or a final exam, is one kind of term-long project that you will face as a student. In Chapter 6, pages 159–162, you will learn about the five-day study plan, which is a goal-oriented approach for organizing and managing your time and your review materials for major tests.

Another kind of term-long project occurs when early in the term instructors assign a project, such as a research report, that is not due until the middle or the end of the term. Following are situations students often face with term-long projects:

- **False sense of time:** Rather than start immediately, they believe the project will not take long. They begin to work on the project too close to its due date, often neglecting their other study times and classes in order to meet the deadline.

- **Procrastination:** Not sure how to manage the project, students postpone starting. Instead of identifying the steps that need to be done and beginning the project as soon as it is assigned, they wait too long to begin and run out of time. This creates unnecessary stress and lowers the quality of the work.

When faced with term-long projects, use the strategies in **Figure 4.11** to guide you through the steps to complete your project on time. Taking time to create a plan

> **CONCEPT CHECK 4.10**
>
> *What potential problems can you avoid by using all five steps to set goals and create a plan of action for a term-long project?*

FIGURE 4.11   Setting Goals for a Term-Long Project

1. **Step 1: Break the assignment into specific tasks.** Analyze the project carefully until you can identify the individual tasks involved for the entire project. List these tasks or steps on paper.

2. **Step 2: Estimate the time needed for each task.** Estimate the number of hours you think you will need to complete each task. Base this estimate on your past experiences with similar projects. Write the estimates next to each task.

3. **Step 3: Double the estimated time needed for each task.** To avoid running short on time or to counteract underestimating the time you will need, double your estimate. Doubling your estimated time also gives you a safety net to deal with any unforeseen problems. Planning too much time for a project always is better than running out of time to finish a project or having too little time to produce quality work that you are proud to turn in.

4. **Step 4: Record target dates on your term calendar for each task.** Plan target dates and times to complete each step. Identify time each week on your weekly schedule to work on specific steps for the term-long project. If you finish a task ahead of schedule, adjust your calendars and begin working on the next task.

5. **Step 5: Begin immediately.** Do not waste time or add unnecessary stress by procrastinating. Give yourself all the time possible to produce a quality project that reflects your abilities.

FIGURE 4.12   Example Format for Planning a Term-Long Project

STEP 1: List the tasks	STEP 2: Estimated time	STEP 3: Doubled time
1.	3 hrs.	6 hrs.
2.	3 hrs.	6 hrs.
3.	2 hrs.	4 hrs.
4.	4 hrs.	8 hrs.
5.	5 hrs.	10 hrs.
	Time Needed:	34 hrs.

STEP 4: Schedule time on your term schedule and your weekly time-management schedule to complete each task.

Weeks 1 and 2: Do Task 1 (6 hours).
Weeks 3 and 4: Do Task 2 (6 hours).
Week 5: Do Task 3 (4 hours)
Weeks 6 and 7: Do Task 4 (8 hours).
Weeks 8 and 9: Do Task 5 (10 hours).
Step 5: Begin immediately.

of action and scheduling time on your term and weekly time management schedules for each step of the plan will result in completion of your project on time. This process also provides you with sufficient time to produce quality work that reflects your abilities. **Figure 4.12** shows the format to use to create your plan of action for a term-long project.

CHECK POINT 4.3

Answers appear on page B3

True or False?

_____ 1. Setting a specific target date to complete a goal can help reduce or eliminate procrastination.

_____ 2. Extrinsic rewards include positive feelings, a sense of pride, and relief.

_____ 3. Not all immediate and short-term goals are subgoals of long-term goals.

_____ 4. Lack of goal-setting strategies, lack of a clear direction, and lack of procrastination are the three main reasons people do not complete goals.

_____ 5. When planning a term-long project, you should double the estimated time you anticipate needing for only the most difficult tasks on your plan of action.

 Access Chapter 4 Practice Quiz 5: Setting Goals under "Interactive Quizzes" in your College Success CourseMate, accessed through *CengageBrain* .com.

ACTIVITY

Chapter 4 Critical Thinking

PURPOSE: The term *study skills* refers to a variety of skills and strategies integrated or linked together. As you begin to use one type of study skill or strategy, you activate others. Use your critical thinking skills to explore the relationships between the following paired items.

DIRECTIONS: By yourself, with a partner, or in a small group, explain the relationship between each of the following paired items. You may be asked to discuss the relationships in class.

1. goal setting and weekly schedules
2. goal setting and intrapersonal intelligence
3. 2:1 ratio and elaborative rehearsal
4. goal setting and Principle of Time on Task
5. goal setting and the Principle of Intention
6. spaced practice and working memory

Goal-Setting Strategies

④ *Demonstrate understanding and use of task schedules, goal organizers, the ABC Method, and self-management strategies for goal setting*

Using the four steps for setting and achieving goals is the starting point for becoming an effective goal setter. These four steps work effectively to create task schedules, which are a reduced version of a daily schedule. **Figure 4.13** shows five Essential Strategies for Goal Setting. Explanations of each strategy follow.

Task Schedules

A *task schedule* is a step-by-step plan for completing a specific task in a specific block of time. **Figure 4.14** shows how to incorporate the four goal-setting steps into task schedules. Taking a few minutes at the beginning of a block of time to create a task schedule structures the block of time for you. Task schedules also help you do the following:

A **task schedule** is a step-by-step plan for completing a specific task in a specific block of time.

- Increase your efficiency
- Waste less time trying to decide what to do or where to begin

---

FIGURE 4.13   Essential Strategies for Goal Setting

- Use the four steps for setting and achieving goals.
- Use task schedules to plan specific tasks for specific blocks of time.
- Use goal organizers to think about and carefully plan a course of action.
- Use the ABC Method to prioritize your goals.
- Use self-management strategies to monitor and manage your goals.

> **FIGURE 4.14** Example of a Task Schedule for a Study Block
>
> **Step 1—Specific goal:** Review math class and do math homework pp. 26–33.
>
> **Step 2—Target date and time:** Wednesday, 10:00–11:00 AM
>
> **Step 3—Individual steps:**
>
> **1.** Review class notes and rework class problem sets.
>
> **2.** Read pages 26–32. Highlight key points. Study examples.
>
> **3.** Do even-numbered problems on p. 33.
>
> **4.** Check answers with answer key. Study/rework any incorrect problems.
>
> **Step 4—Reward:** Extrinsic: Watch my favorite show on television.

CONCEPT CHECK 4.11

How could you use a task schedule today? How can a task schedule help you use time more effectively?

- Motivate you to identify what you need to do and to create a plan of action
- Set immediate goals for study blocks, household chores, or job-related tasks
- Perform in a time-efficient and an organized, logical manner

EXERCISE 4.8

Textbook Case Studies

DIRECTIONS

1. Read each case study carefully. Respond to the question at the end of each case study by using *specific* strategies discussed in this chapter. Answer in complete sentences.

2. Write your responses on paper or online at the CourseMate student Web site, Textbook Case Studies. You will be able to print your online response or e-mail it to your instructor.

CASE STUDY 1: Julian always seems to be caught off-guard. He is surprised when he arrives in class and hears that a specific assignment is due that day. He seldom has his assignments done on time. Sometimes he does not remember them, and other times he runs out of time. He prefers to do all his studying on the weekends, so when an assignment is due in the middle of or at the end of the week, he never has it completed. What suggestions would you give to Julian so he might modify his approach to his assignments?

CASE STUDY 2: Ronnie is an "overachiever" and a "supermom" who can't say no to friends or family members. Ronnie is an avid, organized goal setter. Every Sunday she writes a new list of goals for the week. Throughout each day, she adds more goals to her lists and then works on whichever goals seem most pressing until something or someone sidetracks her. By the end of a typical day, she has accomplished few goals, and she finds herself shuffling the unfinished goals into the list of goals for the next day. By Saturday, she feels defeated; she has multiple lists of goals that she failed to achieve during the week. How can Ronnie become a more successful goal setter?

 Access Chapter 4 Textbook Case Studies and Web-only Case Studies in your College Success CourseMate, accessed through *CengageBrain.com*.

Goal Organizers

A *goal organizer* is a chart that consists of six questions to help you plan a course of action to achieve a specific goal. **Figure 4.15** shows the questions used in a goal organizer. You can go to the CourseMate student Web site for a goal-organizer form to use. As you use a goal organizer, you will find that it helps you do the following:

- Identify a specific goal and its importance to you
- Increase awareness and prepare you to deal with possible obstacles you may encounter as you work on your goal
- Utilize the support of other people and resources

The ABC Method

The *ABC Method* is a goal-setting strategy to prioritize your goals according to rank of importance. If you try to achieve too many goals at one time, you may find that you complete few or none of your goals. Instead of developing positive feelings about goal setting, you end up feeling overwhelmed, frustrated, or defeated. The solution is to take a few minutes to organize your goals from most important or urgent to least important or urgent. The result will be a logically sequenced list of goals that serve as a road map for greater productivity and goal-setting success. **Figure 4.16** shows the steps of using the ABC Method.

Self-Management

Self-management involves monitoring and managing your progress for achieving your goals. As you recall, adjusting your strategies is one of the essential components of using metacognition. Goal setting is an art that requires practice and refinement. Strive to strengthen your goal-setting skills by using the following strategies to increase your success with each goal that you set.

- **Break larger goals into smaller goals:** Break a large task or goal into smaller steps or a series of steps called subgoals. By using this "chunking down technique," your larger goal becomes more manageable and realistic. Completing each of the subgoals or smaller steps brings you closer to achieving the larger goal.
- **Evaluate the importance of a goal:** Goals, especially long-term goals, can become outdated due to changes in values or life circumstances. If a goal is no

Access Chapter 4 Topics In-Depth: Quick Start Forms in your College Success CourseMate, accessed through *CengageBrain* .com.

A **goal organizer** is a chart that consists of six questions to help you plan a course of action to achieve a specific goal.
The **ABC Method** is a goal-setting strategy to prioritize your goals according to rank of importance.

CONCEPT CHECK 4.12

What is the definition of the Memory Principle of Intention? How is this principle used when you create a goal organizer or use the ABC Method?

| FIGURE 4.15 | The Goal Organizer |

1. What is your goal?
2. What benefits will you gain by achieving this goal?
3. What consequences will you experience by *not* achieving this goal?
4. What obstacles might you encounter while working on this goal?
5. How can you deal with the obstacles effectively if they occur?
6. What people or resources could help you with achieving this goal?

> **FIGURE 4.16**   ABC Method to Prioritize Goals
>
> 1. List all the goals your want to achieve within a specific time period.
>
> 2. Use the letter "A" to label your highest priority goals—the most important goals or the goals that you must complete in order to start other related goals.
>
> 3. Use the letter "B" to label the goals of medium importance and less urgency to complete.
>
> 4. Use the letter "C" to label the goals of lowest importance and urgency— the goals you wish to complete after you achieve your "A" and "B" goals.
>
> 5. Prioritize the goals within your "A" list. Identify the order in which you will work on each "A" list goal. Continue prioritizing your "B" and "C" list goals.
>
> 6. Use goal-setting strategies to begin working on your sequenced list of goals. As you complete one goal, start on the next.

CONCEPT CHECK 4.13

If goal setting is an art, then what strategies or tools does a goal setter need to refine to master the art? What are primary characteristics of an effective goal setter?

longer of value to you, replace it with a new, more significant goal. Do not, however, abandon a goal because it is more difficult to achieve or requires more from you than you had originally anticipated.

- **Analyze your goal-setting strategies:** At times when you do not achieve a goal by a specific target date, or you do not get the desired outcome, turn such situations into learning experiences. Ask yourself the following kinds of questions to gain personal insights about yourself and your goal-setting processes. Use your responses to adjust your approach the next time you create a similar goal.

  Was the goal that I set unrealistically high or too low?
  Did I feel a lack of purpose or unchallenged?
  Was the goal high on my priority list of importance?
  Did I think through the steps carefully when I planned the goal?
  Did I allot sufficient time on my weekly schedule to work on the goal?
  Was I motivated? Did I really apply effort and follow my plan of action?
  What would I do differently if I were to set this goal again?

- **Monitor your progress:** Create an easy-to-use method, such as checkmarks or stars, to track your progress, show that you are meeting target dates, and completing the steps of a goal. Tracking your progress on a calendar, a checklist, or in a personal journal can help you monitor your progress and motivate you to stay on course to achieve your goals.

- **Keep your goals in the forefront:** If on occasion you find yourself struggling with your goal-setting plans, your motivation dwindles, your momentum temporarily stalls, or you find yourself ignoring your goals, write your goals on index cards. Place these cards around your house and in your notebook as a constant reminder to spend time each day working toward the outcome. Use the Chapter 5 strategies of visualizing, positive self-talk, affirmations, and other strategies for building and maintaining motivation.

CHAPTER 4
REFLECTIVE WRITING 2

On separate paper, in a journal, or online at this textbook's CourseMate Web site, respond to the following questions.

1. Which time-management and goal-setting strategies in this chapter are potentially the most valuable or beneficial for you? Explain with specific details.

2. What is your plan of action to implement these strategies in your daily and weekly routines?

 Access Chapter 4 Reflective Writing 2 in your College Success CourseMate, accessed through *CengageBrain*.com.

CHECK POINT 4.4

Answers appear on page B3

True or False?

_____ 1. Immediate and short-term goals are the only goals that are well-defined plans of action designed to achieve specific results.

_____ 2. If a goal seems too overwhelming, you should discard it and write only immediate goals that you can achieve in one day.

_____ 3. A person who sets too many goals and tries to achieve them all simultaneously would benefit from using the ABC Method.

_____ 4. A goal organizer helps a person identify the importance of a goal, plan ways to deal with

obstacles, and use resources to help achieve success.

_____ 5. Effective goal managers monitor their progress and adjust their goal-setting strategies to increase success and productivity.

 Access Chapter 4 Practice Quiz 6: Goal-Setting Strategies under "Interactive Quizzes" in your College Success CourseMate, accessed through *CengageBrain.com*.

Learning Objectives Review

1 *Analyze your use of time and identify ways to create balance in your life.*
- Analyzing the way you spend time in the three main areas of your Pie of Life helps you find a healthy, fulfilling balance in your school, work, and leisure life.
- The Increase-Decrease Method helps you adjust the boundaries of your Pie of Life in order to achieve greater balance.

2 *Create and use effective term, weekly, and daily schedules to manage your time.*
- Term schedules provide you with an overview or a big picture of all the deadlines and special events for the term; weekly schedules provide you with a

Terms to Know

By yourself or with a partner, practice reciting or writing definitions for the following terms. You may also practice defining these terms by using the online flashcard programs or comparing your answers to the online glossary.

time management p. 88
Pie of Life p. 89
Increase-Decrease Method p. 91
term schedule p. 93

Access Chapter 4 Flashcard Drills and Online Glossary in your College Success CourseMate, accessed through *CengageBrain* *.com*.

seven-day plan to balance your activities; and daily schedules provide you with organized lists of goals and tasks to complete on specific days.

- Use a five-step plan for organizing an effective weekly schedule: show fixed activities, fixed study blocks, flex blocks, time for personal goals, and family, social, and leisure time.

- Basic time-management strategies include understanding the 2:1 ratio, the 3:1 ratio, spaced practice, marathon studying, and trading time.

- Seven essential strategies for scheduling effective study blocks guide you through the process of creating an effective weekly schedule. The Time-Management Self-Assessment Checklist helps you evaluate your schedule.

3 *Explain how to use the four steps for writing goals and how to create a plan of action for immediate, short-term, intermediary, and long-term goals.*

- Goals are well-defined plans aimed at achieving a specific result. Immediate, short-term, intermediary, and long-term are four kinds of goals based on the length of time required to complete and achieve the goal.

- Using a four-step approach for achieving goals (STSR) enhances your performance and success in achieving your desired outcomes. S = specific, clear, realistic goals; T = target date; S = steps involved; and R = intrinsic or extrinsic reward.

- Goal setting for term-long projects includes listing tasks, estimating time, doubling estimated time for each task, scheduling tasks, and beginning immediately.

4 *Demonstrate understanding and use of task schedules, goal organizers, the ABC Method, and self-management strategies for goal setting.*

- Task schedules help you create a plan of action for a specific block of time. Goal organizers encourage you to think carefully about a goal and your plan of action.

- The ABC Method is a strategy that helps you prioritize your goals and focus your attention first on the high-priority goals.

- Five strategies help you monitor and manage your progress with setting and achieving goals.

Chapter 4 Review Questions

Answers appear on page B3

True or False?

_____ 1. Time management is a plan for organizing your time, and goal setting is a plan for using your time constructively to achieve desired outcomes.

_____ 2. A weekly schedule reflects some of the tasks and target dates shown on a term schedule.

_____ 3. An effective weekly schedule helps you avoid wasted time, tighten up your available time, and plan for important tasks or activities.

_____ 4. Extrinsic and intrinsic rewards should be awarded only after a person completes a specific goal.

Multiple Choice

_____ 1. A well-planned term schedule

  a. shows only midterm and final exams.

  b. reflects academic and personal time lines and commitments.

  c. states your weekly goals and shows your daily homework assignments.

  d. accomplishes all of the above.

_____ 2. When you use a fifty-minute study block effectively, you

  a. spend time reviewing each of your courses.

  b. create a mindset that focuses on only one subject.

  c. cover as many textbook pages as possible by reading fast.

  d. begin by identifying which class has an assignment due the next day.

_____ 3. An effective weekly time-management schedule includes

  a. eight hours of studying on weekends.

  b. adequate time to use the 2:1 ratio, elaborative rehearsal, and spaced practice.

  c. three or more flex blocks and three times set aside for trading time.

  d. all study blocks completed by 9:00 PM.

_____ 4. A goal organizer

  a. is a four-step approach for writing short-term goals.

  b. shows that you have thought about benefits, consequences, and strategies to face obstacles related to a specific goal.

  c. is used every time you plan a task in a daily organizer.

  d. does all of the above.

_____ 5. If you feel overwhelmed because you have too many goals, you can

  a. use the ABC Method to prioritize your goals.

  b. evaluate the importance of each goal and then discard the most difficult ones.

  c. write all your goals on index cards and post them around your house.

  d. visualize yourself completing all the goals ahead of schedule.

_____ 6. Setting goals for a term-long project

  a. begins by listing all the tasks required to finish the project.

  b. includes doubling the amount of time you estimate you need for each task.

  c. involves writing target dates on your term calendar and your weekly schedule.

  d. involves all of the above.

_____ 7. Which of the following is *not* a recommended goal-setting strategy to keep yourself motivated?

  a. Visualize yourself achieving your goal.

  b. Use a checklist or a journal to track your progress.

  c. Select meaningful intrinsic or extrinsic rewards that motivate you.

  d. Write your goals in a safe place so other people cannot see them and possibly discourage you from achieving your goals.

_____ 8. The primary purpose of the Increase-Decrease Method is to

  a. help you find ways to increase your social time each week.

  b. find a more satisfying and productive balance in your Pie of Life.

  c. move you toward having a Pie of Life that shows an equal amount of time each week for school, work, and leisure.

  d. decrease the amount of time you need to study each day.

Short-Answer Questions

On separate paper, answer the following questions. Use complete sentences and terminology from this chapter in your answers.

1. Define *spaced practice* and explain how using spaced practice assists information processing in working memory.

2. In your opinion, what are the five most important strategies to use to become an effective goal setter? Briefly explain why each is important.

 Access Chapter 4 Chapter Quizzes 1–4 and Enhanced Quiz under "Interactive Quizzes" in your College Success CourseMate, accessed through *CengageBrain .com*.

Access all Chapter 4 Online Materials in your College Success CourseMate, accessed through *CengageBrain.com*.

CHAPTER OUTLINE

Access Chapter 5 Expanded Chapter Outline and Objectives in your College Success CourseMate, accessed through CengageBrain.com.

YOUR CH

*After re
visual
import*

5

Developin Self-Mana

© Image copyright Andresr, 2009. Used under license from Shutterstock.com.

reduce, and eliminate *stress* and *procras* put you in greater control of your life.

LEARNING OBJECTIV

① *Define concentration and id distractions and maintain a*

② *Define motivation and discu strategies to strengthen mo*

③ *Define stress and identify st stress management.*

④ *Define procrastination and i effective procrastination ma*

Self-Management Skills

ANSWER, SCORE, and **RECORD** your profile before you read this chapter. If you need to review the process, refer to the complete directions given in the profile for Chapter 1 on page 4.

ONLINE: You can complete the profile and get your score online at this textbook's CourseMate Web site.

 Access Chapter 5 Profile in your College Success CourseMate, accessed through *CengageBrain.com*.

		YES	NO
1.	I have little control over the people or things that break my concentration when I am studying.		
2.	I often study with the radio, stereo, or television turned on.		
3.	I use effective strategies to block out internal and external distractors when I study.		
4.	I use effective strategies, such as visualizations, positive self-talk, and affirmations to boost my motivation and keep my momentum going.		
5.	I am motivated when I study and believe in my ability to do well.		
6.	I use a variety of relaxation techniques to manage my stress.		
7.	My level of stress often reduces my performance or ability to concentrate.		
8.	I recognize when and why I procrastinate, and then I take action to combat the sources of my procrastination.		
9.	I tend to procrastinate when faced with unpleasant or uninteresting tasks.		
10.	I am confident that I have adequate self-management skills to monitor and manage my concentration, motivation, stress, and procrastination.		

QUESTIONS LINKED TO THE CHAPTER LEARNING OBJECTIVES

Questions 1–3: objective 1   Questions 8, 9: objective 4

Questions 4, 5: objective 2   Question 10: all objectives

Questions 6, 7: objective 3

Self-management is the ability to use strategies to deal constructively and effectively with variables that affect the quality of your personal life.

Concentration is the ability to block out *external* and *internal distractors* in order to stay focused on one specific item or task.

Concentration

① *Define concentration and identify strategies to block out distractions and maintain a focused, disciplined mind.*

Self-management refers to the ability to use strategies to deal constructively and effectively with variables that affect the quality of your personal life. A successful self-manager uses his or her skills to monitor, orchestrate, and adjust or redirect thinking or behavior patterns in order to increase personal satisfaction and performance of regular daily functions. **Figure 5.1** show the six common sets of self-management skills.

Concentration is the ability to block out *external* and *internal distractors* in order to stay focused on one specific item or task. Concentration is a flighty process;

FIGURE 5.1   The Six Common Sets of Self-Management Skills

- Time Management
- Goal Setting
- Concentration
- Motivation
- Stress Management
- Procrastination Management

CONCEPT CHECK 5.1

What are common internal and external distractors you encounter when you study? What effects do they have on your thought processes?

you can concentrate one minute and then easily become distracted and lose that concentration the very next. The following are important points about concentration:

- Concentration requires a concerted effort on your part to train or discipline your mind.
- Concentration involves monitoring not only your thoughts and emotions, but also your environment.
- External and internal distractors consume space in working memory, disturb your brainwave patterns, and affect the flow of stimuli throughout your memory system. You can use effective strategies to train your mind and your attention to not respond to external and internal distractors.
- *External distractors* are disruptions caused by things in your physical environment. Noises, people, television, enticing or harsh weather, clutter, and lighting are examples of external distractors.
- *Internal distractors* are disruptions that occur inside you physically or emotionally. Worries, stress, anxiety, depression, sickness, hunger, pain, daydreams, and anticipation of upcoming events are examples of internal distractors.

> **External distractors** are disruptions caused by things in your physical environment.
> **Internal distractors** are disruptions that occur inside you physically or emotionally.

An Ideal Study Area

An ideal study area is a specific area designated as your place to concentrate and focus on studying. You organize this area so it is conducive to learning, has few or no distractions, and helps you focus your attention on your learning tasks. Creating an ideal study area will help you do the following:

- Increase your ability to concentrate
- Promote the use of selective attention on specific tasks and goals
- Increase motivation and academic performance
- Reduce the tendency to procrastinate
- Reduce or eliminate the effects of internal and external distractors

Creating an ideal study area may require some thoughtful planning and rearranging of furniture or materials, but the time spent will bring positive results. During this process, pay careful attention to three elements in your physical environment: the noise level, the lighting, and the workspace.

The Noise Level

People have different tolerance levels to noise. Some students are able to concentrate only in a completely silent environment; other students can tolerate minor noises without becoming distracted. A final group of students try to convince themselves that they can concentrate and study in noisy environments because they like to study in specific areas, such as a cafeteria, or they like to study with the television or music turned on. However, research shows that noisy environments interrupt the steady flow of thought processes and brainwave patterns, thus causing concentration to turn on and off and on and off in split-second intervals. Following are additional important points about the noise level in your study area:

- Music with lyrics and frequent variations in rhythm interrupt thought processes. If you wish to have music in the background, soft, classical, or instrumental music (especially baroque music) does not cause the on-and-off pattern and actually may enhance learning by helping the mind be more receptive to new information.

- Auditory and visual stimuli from television take up space in working memory, thus reducing the amount of working memory available to process information efficiently. The best advice is to turn the television off when you are studying.

- Various noise levels in your study environment do impact the quality of learning, so consciously increase your awareness of the noise level around you. Be willing to change your study location or adjust your existing learning space until you find the best suited level of noise (or silence) for you.

The Lighting

Proper lighting is important in any study area. If you have too little light, your eyes can easily become strained and tired. Some lighting can create shadows or glare on your books. To avoid many of the problems created by poor lighting, have *two* sources of light in your study area. This may include an overhead light and a desk lamp or two lamps in different locations. Two sources of lighting may seem like a minor detail, but sometimes ignoring small details leads to vision and concentration problems.

The Workspace

Trying to study in an area that lacks sufficient space to spread out your textbooks, open your notebooks, take notes as you read, or use other study materials and supplies creates distractions. You can do the following to create a workspace conducive to concentration:

- Remove clutter, which creates distractions.
- Limit the amount of visual stimuli, such as photographs or memorabilia.
- Create a work surface that has ample room for your notebooks, textbooks, and supplies.
- Select a comfortable chair that is an appropriate height for the table and for your legs.
- Avoid trying to study on the floor, in a recliner, on a couch, or on a bed.

CONCEPT CHECK 5.2

What constitutes an ideal study area? How do these characteristics affect working memory processes?

My Ideal Study Area

EXERCISE 5.1

PURPOSE: Your physical environment impacts your ability to use selective attention and to concentrate. To increase concentration, examine your physical space and modify it so it is more conducive to studying.

DIRECTIONS:

1. In the following chart, the items on the left are physical elements that can hinder or strengthen concentration. In the middle column, describe each physical element as it currently exists in your typical study area at home and at school.

2. In the right column, describe the changes you could make to your study area at home and your study area at school to create more ideal study areas.

Home	Current Study Area	Ideal Study Area
Noise		
Movement Nearby		
Lighting		
Chair		
Work Surface		
Supplies		
School	Current Study Area	Ideal Study Area
Noise		
Movement Nearby		
Lighting		
Chair		
Work Surface		
Supplies		

Essential Concentration Strategies for Studying

You have already learned an array of strategies from Chapters 2 and 3 to increase concentration and promote effective use of your working memory for cognitive processes. **Figure 5.2** summarizes seven Essential Concentration Strategies for Studying. Explanations of each strategy follow.

FIGURE 5.2 Essential Concentration Strategies for Studying

- Set learning goals with plans of action.
- Be an active learner.
- Chunk information.
- Create a study ritual.
- Begin with a warm-up activity.
- Use mental rehearsal.
- Use the Take-Charge Technique.

Set Learning Goals

Knowing *what* you plan to do and *how* you plan to achieve your goals gives you a purpose, a motivation to stay focused, and a "mission" to achieve. At the beginning of a study block, identify your specific intentions for your time. Setting learning goals activates your working memory and initiates the process of creating a plan of action to achieve the goals.

Be an Active Learner

Active learning discourages you from reading or working in a detached, mechanical way. Active learning engages you in the learning process, increases concentration, and helps you avoid internal distractors, such as sleepiness, boredom, or disinterest. Be an active learner by studying with a pen in hand, taking notes, highlighting textbooks, writing questions, and creating study tools, such as diagrams, flashcards, and visual notes.

Chunk Information

Chunking is the process of breaking larger assignments or sections of information into smaller, more manageable units that working memory can handle.

Chunking is the process of breaking larger assignments or sections of information into smaller, more manageable units that working memory can manage. Trying to take in too much information too rapidly overloads working memory and results in loss of concentration and ineffective learning.

Create a Study Ritual

A study ritual is a series of steps or a consistent routine that allows you to get started quickly on a task.

A *study ritual* is a series of steps or a consistent routine that helps you to get started quickly on a task. Instead of wasting time trying to decide what to do or where to begin, a study ritual moves you directly into the mindset of studying. For example, your study ritual might be to use a quick relaxation or visualization technique, create a task schedule, and do a *warm-up activity*.

Begin with a Warm-Up Activity

Warm-ups are activities at the beginning of a study block that shift thoughts and create a mindset for studying and concentrating.

Warm-ups are activities at the beginning of a study block that shift thoughts and create a mindset for studying and concentrating. Warm-ups activate working memory and long-term memory. They also set up frameworks, schemas, or big pictures for new information. *Previewing* (skimming through a new chapter or assignment to get an overview) and *reviewing* previous work are effective warm-up activities.

Use Mental Rehearsal

Mental rehearsal is the process of creating a picture or a movie in your mind that shows you performing effectively.

Mental rehearsal is the process of creating a picture or a movie in your mind that shows you performing effectively. The image that you hold of yourself as a learner often affects the behaviors you exhibit. Use mental rehearsal to replace any negative images of yourself as a learner with positive images of yourself as a learner who stays focused and achieves learning goals. For example, picture yourself beginning an assignment, working with ease, writing answers on a test with confidence, or studying without distractions.

Use the Take-Charge Technique

The Take-Charge Technique involves taking responsibility for your environment by seeking an alternative place to study or by modifying the existing environment so it has few or no distractions.

The *Take-Charge Technique* involves taking responsibility for your environment by seeking an alternative place to study or by modifying the existing environment so it has few or no distractions. You do not want to waste your valuable time trying to study in an environment filled with distractions. When you *take charge* of your environment, you exhibit a willingness to let go of old habits and try new strategies to increase your ability to concentrate and your overall performance. Following are several examples of ways students used the Take-Charge Technique.

- Robert, a student with a short attention span and limited tolerance for noise, was trying to study in the library, but there were too many whispering conversations and movement around him. He *took charge* by moving to an empty conference room without the noise of people or foot traffic.
- Joel, a student who grew up in a large, busy, noisy household, tried to study in the cafeteria. After realizing how little he accomplished there, Joel *took charge.* He moved to a quieter place in the back of the library. At home, he turned on a small fan to provide some nondistracting background noise as total silence was a distractor for him.
- Heather studied in the student lounge, but the fluorescent lighting bothered her eyes and her vision. She *took charge* by moving to a room with windows, which provided some natural lighting. At home, she also had problems with her eyes when she studied, so in addition to the ceiling light, she added a desk lamp in order to have two sources of lighting.
- Marshall liked studying at his kitchen table, but often he was not productive. He realized how often he was getting up to eat or drink. To increase his efficient use of time, Marshall *took charge.* He replaced the kitchen items on the table with a box of his study materials so the table felt more like a desk. He moved the chair so he faced away from the refrigerator and the pantry.

CONCEPT CHECK 5.3

Explain the benefits of using each of the concentration strategies for studying that appear in Figure 5.2.

Techniques to Manage Distractors

When you find yourself distracted and having trouble concentrating, the first step is to analyze the situation to determine the source of your distraction. Is it caused by an *internal distractor* or an *external distractor?* The second step is to select an appropriate technique to use to address the concentration problem. **Figure 5.3** summarizes seven quick, easy-to-use techniques to reduce or eliminate distractors. Familiarize yourself with each technique and practice using it several times to increase your ability to stay focused and manage distractors.

- The ***Say No Technique*** involves resisting the urge to participate in an external or internal distraction. Assertively just *say no* when friends or family members ask you to drop your study schedule and participate in an activity with them. Train yourself to *say no* and to stay focused when you want to get a snack, turn on the television, day dream, make phone calls, or text friends.

The **Say No Technique** involves resisting the urge to participate in an external or internal distraction.

FIGURE 5.3 Techniques to Manage Distractors

- Say No
- No Need
- Red Bow
- Check Mark
- Mental Storage Box
- Tunnel Vision
- Emotional E Words

CONCEPT CHECK 5.4

Which of the techniques do you predict will work effectively to deal with your internal and external distractors? Explain how each will affect your concentration.

The No Need Technique is the process of training yourself not to look up and not to break your concentration to attend to minor, familiar distractions.

The Red Bow Technique involves using a symbol to signal to others that you do not want to be interrupted or disturbed.

The Check Mark Technique involves keeping a score card to record and reduce the number of distractions that you allow into your working memory.

The Mental Storage Box Technique involves placing any internal distractors into an imaginary box, putting a lid on the box, and shoving that box aside to be dealt with at a later time.

The Tunnel Vision Technique involves picturing yourself in a tunnel and training your mind to stay centered and on course.

The Emotional E Words Technique involves refocusing your mind by using words that begin with e to create a positive attitude.

- The *No Need Technique* is the process of training yourself not to look up and not to break your concentration to attend to minor, familiar distractions. Wherever you are studying, you know minor distractions and predictable noises will occur. Force yourself to keep your eyes and your attention on your own work. Tell yourself, "There is *no need* to look."

- The *Red Bow Technique* involves using a symbol, such as a red bow, to signal to others that you do not want to be interrupted or disturbed. Place this bow or symbol on your door or in your work area to signal to others that you do not want to be disturbed.

- The *Check Mark Technique* involves keeping a score card to record and reduce the number of distractions that you allow into your working memory. Each time you lose your concentration during a study block, make a check mark on a score card you keep on your desk. At the end of your study block, count the number of checks. Set a goal each time you study to reduce the number of check marks.

- The *Mental Storage Box Technique* involves placing any internal distractors into an imaginary box, putting a lid on the box, and shoving that box aside to be dealt with at a later time. Before you begin studying, identify any concerns, worries, or emotions that might interrupt your concentration. Place them inside your *mental storage box*. Tell yourself that you will deal with the contents of the box at a more appropriate time, and then do so.

- The *Tunnel Vision Technique* involves picturing yourself in a tunnel and training your mind to stay centered and on course. In this one-way, single-lane tunnel, if your mind wanders, steer it back into the center of the tunnel to avoid banging into the walls. Stay on course and focused on reaching the end of the tunnel.

- The *Emotional E Words Technique* involves refocusing your mind by using words that begin with *e* to create a positive attitude and self-image. For example, you might repeat to yourself words such as *effortless, enthusiastic, excited, energetic, eager, effective, efficient, essential, excelling, excellent, expert, exhilarating,* or *educated.* Mentally rehearse seeing yourself exhibiting these qualities.

CHECK POINT 5.1

Answers Appear on Page B3.

True or False?

_____ 1. Using concentration strategies effectively increases working memory space for cognitive functions.

_____ 2. You can focus your mind more quickly on studying when you set learning goals, create a study ritual, and do a warm-up activity.

_____ 3. A person's physical environment has less of an impact on concentration than his or her emotional state of mind.

_____ 4. The Take-Charge, Emotional *E* Words, and the Red Bow techniques are designed to deal only with external distractors.

 Access Chapter 5 Practice Quiz 1: Concentration under "Interactive Quizzes" in your College Success CourseMate, accessed through *CengageBrain.com*.

CHAPTER 5
REFLECTIVE WRITING 1

On separate paper, in a journal, or online at this textbook's CourseMate Web site, respond to the following questions:

1. *What* distractors do you encounter most frequently when you study? Be specific.

2. *When* and *where* do you have the most problems concentrating when you study? What techniques

can you learn to use more consistently to combat these problems?

Access Chapter 5 Reflective Writing 1 in your College Success CourseMate, accessed through *CengageBrain.com*.

Motivation

 Define motivation and discuss factors that affect motivation and strategies to strengthen motivation.

Motivation is the feeling, emotion, or desire that moves a person to take action. This internal driving force has the power to help you achieve goals, change behaviors, and "push on," not give up, and persevere. The strength of your motivation to achieve a specific goal or task often determines the intensity and determination for achieving the goal. High motivation equates to success; low motivation equates to lower achievement, lower performance, and incompletion of goals. Using the self-management set of skills and strategies for increasing motivation helps you acquire a stronger interest, curiosity, and excitement for learning and reaching new goals.

Motivation is the feeling, emotion, or desire that moves a person to take action.

Intrinsic and Extrinsic Motivation

Two forms of motivation drive people to achieve their goals: intrinsic and extrinsic motivation. *Intrinsic motivation* is the driving force to take action that comes from within you. Intrinsic motivation is the most powerful and effective form of motivation because you "own" it, and you give it personal meaning, importance, and conviction. The following are common sources of intrinsic motivation:

- A desire to fulfill a basic need, such as food, shelter, or financial comfort
- An internal desire to engage in behaviors or actions that bring intrinsic rewards, such as feelings of pride, joy, increased self-esteem or personal satisfaction
- A desire to affirm your self-image, live by your values, and prove your abilities to yourself

The second type of motivation is extrinsic motivation. *Extrinsic motivation* is the driving force to take action that comes from sources outside of yourself. Actions based on extrinsic motivation are often more difficult to achieve than actions based on intrinsic motivation. Having someone tell you that you *must* do something or you *must* behave in a certain way is a weak motivator and often ineffective. For extrinsic motivation to work, strive to find a purpose or a value in complying with the external expectations. In other words, strive to convert your extrinsic motivation to intrinsic

Intrinsic motivation is the driving force to take action that comes from within you.

CONCEPT CHECK 5.5

How do intrinsic and extrinsic motivation differ? Why is intrinsic motivation so powerful?

Extrinsic motivation is the driving force to take action that comes from sources outside of yourself.

motivation so your main purpose is to achieve for yourself—not for the main purpose of pleasing others. The following are common sources of extrinsic motivation:

- Imposed expectations tied to retaining a job or fulfilling requirements such as those for an academic or athletic scholarship
- A desire to obtain an *extrinsic reward,* such as a prestigious award, a coveted prize, or a monetary reward for work or performance
- A desire to receive positive responses, praise, acceptance, or recognition from parents, family members, peers, co-workers, or a specific social group

Motivation, Self-Esteem, and Self-Efficacy

Developing and strengthening your motivation generates new desire and drive to tackle new challenges. Success breeds more success and strengthens the intensity and power of motivation. In turn, this chain of positive results affects your self-esteem and your self-efficacy (your belief in your abilities). Higher self-esteem and self-efficacy equate to higher levels of motivation and achievement; low self-esteem and low self-efficacy equate to lower motivation and achievement. The following sections show the important relationship between motivation and self-esteem and between self-esteem and self-efficacy.

Motivation and Self-Esteem

> **Self-esteem** is the perception you have of yourself as a human being.

Why are some people more motivated, more productive, and more successful than others? Part of the answer may be tied to their self-esteem. *Self-esteem* is the perception you have of yourself as a human being. This self-perception is the result of the way you interpret or remember past experiences, choices, behaviors, decisions, and consequences. This self-perception also reflects your memory of past reactions of acceptance or rejection from family members, friends, teachers, or coworkers. An individual's self-esteem, sense of worthiness, and degree of personal pride may be high or low depending on these self-perceptions or memories of the past.

Individuals with high self-esteem tend to be highly motivated and experience a cycle of positive results. They exhibit self-confident behaviors and tend to show less hesitancy or resistance to trying something new or adjusting to change. Their positive attitudes guide them through many difficult situations with a sense of optimism and plans of action to move forward.

Individuals with low self-esteem exhibit opposite characteristics. They are less driven to achieve goals and perceive more situations as failures. Obstacles are more difficult to overcome and often are accompanied by feelings that they lack control of events that occur in their lives. A sense of negativity surfaces in multiple aspects of their lives. **Figure 5.4** shows self-esteem cycles for individuals with low and individuals with high self-esteem.

Motivation and Self-Efficacy

> **CONCEPT CHECK 5.6**
>
> *How does the self-esteem cycle of a person with high self-esteem differ from the self-esteem cycle of a person with low self-esteem? How does the level of self-esteem affect motivation?*

> **Self-efficacy** is the belief in your abilities to accomplish a specific task at a specific level of performance.

Self-efficacy is the belief in your abilities to accomplish a specific task at a specific level of performance. Achievements, pleasant learning experiences, positive attitudes, and supportive environments cultivate high self-efficacy for specific tasks or types of activities. A person with high self-efficacy in one area will exhibit a sense of self-confidence and motivation to succeed at new tasks related to that area. However, the same person may have a low sense of self-efficacy for an unfamiliar area or for a task that is outside of his or her realm of experiences or comfort zone. The self-confidence, motivation, and belief in one's own abilities may be questioned or challenged.

FIGURE 5.5   The Expectancy Theory of Motivation

Expectancy Theory, developed by Victor Vroom, is a very complex model of motivation based on a deceptively simple assumption. According to expectancy theory, motivation depends on how much we want something and on how likely we think we are to get it. Consider, for example, the case of three sales representatives who are candidates for promotion to one sales manager's job. Bill has had a very good sales year and always gets good performance evaluations. However, he isn't sure he wants the job because it involves a great deal of travel, long working hours, and much stress and pressure. Paul wants the job badly but doesn't think he has much chance of getting it. He has had a terrible sales year and gets only mediocre performance evaluations from his present boss. Susan wants the job as much as Paul, and she thinks she has a pretty good shot at it. Her sales have improved significantly this past year, and her evaluations are the best in the company.

Expectancy theory would predict that Bill and Paul are not very motivated to seek the promotion. Bill doesn't really want it, and Paul doesn't think he has much of a chance of getting it. Susan, however, is very motivated to seek the promotion because she wants it *and* thinks she can get it.

Source: Pride/Hughes/Kapoor, *Business, 7e*, Houghton Mifflin Company, © 2007, page 312. Reprinted with permission.

---

activities such as giving speeches.) Use the following steps to imprint positive images of yourself into your memory:

1. Close your eyes. Create a picture or an image of yourself, and "watch yourself" performing effectively in a specific situation. For example, see yourself working through the steps to perform a math equation, or studying in an ideal study area without encountering distractions, or standing comfortably and confidently in front of your class to give a speech.

FIGURE 5.6   Essential Strategies to Increase Motivation

- Plan to Succeed by Setting Goals
- Visualize Success
- Use Positive Self-Talk
- Use Affirmations
- Let Go of the Past; Focus on the Present
- Use Self-Management Skills to Monitor Your Progress

2. Visualize or "see" yourself receiving the rewards for your behavior or performance. Feel the sense of pride, accomplishment, or success.

3. Practice "rerunning" the visualization several times and recalling it from memory to use as a motivator.

Use Positive Self-Talk

Self-talk is that ever-busy inner voice that monitors, critiques, and ultimately affects your behavior, choice of actions, self-esteem, as well as your level of confidence and motivation. Your self-talk may be positive or negative. The following points about self-talk are important to understand:

- *Positive self-talk* is the internal conversation that focuses on positive qualities, words of encouragement, and statements that reflect a high self-esteem.

- *Negative self-talk* is the critical inner voice that focuses on negativity, low self-image, and statements of doubt. Negative self-talk may tell you that you *can't do something, don't have the ability, are not worthy of the reward,* or *will not succeed.* Intrinsic motivation quickly dwindles when negative self-talk takes over.

- Instantly when you hear negative self-talk, choose to manage your thoughts by turning those statements around and counteracting with positive self-talk. Use positive-self talk statements, such as "I have the ability to do this," or "I am willing to work hard for this because this is something I am worthy of receiving." Knowing the importance of and using intrinsic motivation, quickly turn negative self-talk into constructive, powerful, positive self-talk.

Use Affirmations

Affirmations are positive statements used as motivators. Affirmations help change your basic belief systems, your self-image, and the direction you are moving to make changes in your life. Use the following suggestions for writing and using affirmations:

- **Use positive words and tones.** Avoid using words such as *no, never, won't.* Say, for instance, "I complete my written work on time," rather than "I will never turn in a paper late again."

- **Write affirmations in the present tense.** Using present tense in your affirmations creates a belief system that a specific behavior already exists. To support the belief, actions or behaviors change to match the beliefs. Say, for example, "I eat healthy food," rather than "I will stop eating junk food soon," or "I complete assignments on time," rather than "I will get better at completing my assignments on time."

- **State your affirmation with certainty and conviction.** Avoid using words such as *want to, try,* or *hope to.* Say, for instance, "I exercise for thirty minutes every day," rather than "I want to exercise more each day," or "I manage my time well," rather than "I hope I can use my time-management schedule."

- **Keep the affirmation short and simple; repeat it often.** Brief, simple affirmations are easier to remember and repeat. Reinforce the affirmation by repeating frequently. You can place your affirmation on cards around your house or inside your notebook.

Let Go of the Past; Focus on the Present

In many ways, we are the reflection of our past. Past experiences are strong influencing factors of who we are today, and understanding those influencing factors is important for self-understanding and growth. The expression, "Let it go," is often easier said than done, but it merits our attention. Choose to shift your attention to

---

Positive self-talk is an internal conversation that focuses on positive qualities, words of encouragement and statements that reflect a high self-esteem.

Negative self-talk is the critical inner voice that focuses on negativity, low self-esteem, and statements of doubt.

Affirmations are positive statements used as motivators.

CONCEPT CHECK 5.9

Which Principles of Memory are active when you use these strategies: set goals, visualize success, positive self-talk, and affirmations?

the present and accentuate the positive elements that you are creating in your life at this very moment.

Use Self-Management Skills to Monitor Your Progress

Using self-management skills puts you in charge of your actions and promotes making adjustments that are in your best interest. To increase your motivation, ask yourself the following kinds of questions:

Are my incentives important to me and realistic for me to obtain?
Am I using intrinsic or extrinsic motivation?
What strategies can I use to strengthen my intrinsic motivation?

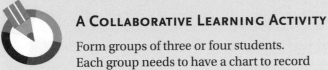

GROUP PROCESSING

A COLLABORATIVE LEARNING ACTIVITY

Form groups of three or four students. Each group needs to have a chart to record information. Select one group member to be the group recorder. Complete the following directions.

1. Divide a large chart into two columns and two rows. In the top left box, write as many different internal and external distractors that you might encounter when you study.

2. In the bottom left box, write situations in which students lack motivation.

3. In the top right box, across from the internal and external distractors, brainstorm and then list techniques or strategies that you can use to combat each distractor.

4. In the bottom right box, brainstorm and list techniques or strategies you can use to increase motivation for each situation.

5. Be prepared to share your chart with techniques with the class.

Internal/External Distractors	Techniques/Strategies
Lack Motivation	Techniques/Strategies

CHECK POINT 5.2

Answers Appear on B3

True or False?

_____ 1. Extrinsic motivation based on physical or monetary awards tends to be the most powerful form of motivation.

_____ 2. Self-esteem and self-efficacy are based on other people's perceptions of you.

_____ 3. Self-esteem affects motivation, and motivation affects self-esteem.

_____ 4. As extrinsic motivators gain momentum, they may become intrinsic motivators.

_____ 5. Creating positive self-images and using positive words can alter your self-esteem.

 Access Chapter 5 Practice Quiz 2: Motivation under "Interactive Quizzes" in your College Success CourseMate, accessed through *CengageBrain.com*.

Stress Management

> ③ *Define stress and identify strategies and techniques for effective stress management.*

Stress is a reaction or response to events or situations that threaten or disrupt our normal patterns or routines. Stress is the wear and tear on our bodies due to physical, emotional, cognitive, and behavioral responses. The following are important points about stress:

> **Stress** is a reaction or response to events or situations that threaten or disrupt our normal patterns or routines.

- Some stress is normal as we move through life making decisions and changing directions in our personal, work, and academic lives.

- In some situations, stress is beneficial. Stress can compel us to take action and to move in new directions. The increased adrenaline from stress can help us perform at higher levels.

- As stress increases, our ability to deal with and control the stress decreases.

- Early warning signs that stress is becoming more intense and moving into the danger level include headaches, backaches, insomnia, fatigue, anxiety attacks, mood swings, depression, forgetfulness, carelessness, and irritability.

- Excessive stress hinders performance and affects our cognitive abilities. Excessive stress affects working memory and long-term memory and reduces our ability to concentrate, solve problems, and make wise decisions.

- Excessive stress from unresolved issues has physical consequences: increased pulse rate, faster breathing, higher blood pressure, a weakening of the immune system a decrease in the production of endorphins (a neurochemical that makes us feel happy), ulcers, heart attacks, strokes, and clinical depression.

- Excessive stress may become anxiety. Test anxiety is one kind of excessive stress that hinders performance and results in physical, emotional, cognitive, and behavioral consequences.

- Learning to manage stress is a lifelong skill that affects the quality of life and longevity.

Stressors

> **Stressors** are situations or actions that cause stress.

Stressors are situations or actions that cause stress. How you *perceive* and *handle* external situations or stressors—rather than the situations themselves—is the cause of stress. Taking some form of action to reduce or eliminate stressors empowers you to have greater control over your stress and to alter your perception of external situations. For example, if an upcoming test is a stressor, you can create a plan of action and use specific techniques to take control of the situation. Other stressors, such as the terminal illness of a loved one, are out of your immediate control; the only control you have is how you handle your reaction to the stressor.

Stressors may be positive or negative. Divorce, personal injury, loss of a job, or family problems are negative stressors. Events such as marriage or a vacation may be positive stressors. The number of stressors you face, both positive and negative, at one time affect your overall stress level. In 1967, Dr. Thomas H. Holmes and Dr. Richard H. Rahe developed a "stress test," the Social Readjustment Rating Scale (SRRS), to help individuals identify their stress levels. The stressors and the stress scores on SRRS remain applicable today. (See Exercise 5.2.)

CONCEPT CHECK 5.10

How does your perception of a stressor affect your level of stress? Explain with specific examples.

EXERCISE 5.2

Stress Test

DIRECTIONS: Go to Exercise 5.2 in Appendix C, page C9, to complete the Social Readjustment Rating Scale. You will be asked to circle all the events (stressors) you have experienced in the last twelve months. Each event has a point value. After totaling all the point values for events, you will be able to find your stress level score.

Healthy Lifestyle

A basic look at your lifestyle patterns begins by looking specifically at your lifestyle choices in the areas of nutrition, exercise, and sleep. Your lifestyle choices influence your level of stress and the ways you respond to a variety of stressors. When you feel stress, especially when stress is becoming excessive, take time to examine your habits, behaviors, and lifestyle choices. Create goals and motivation to convert unhealthy lifestyle behaviors to the positive, healthier options that can help you reduce and cope with stress. Unchecked, negative lifestyle behaviors affect your quality of life and your longevity. **Figure 5.7** shows the lifestyle behaviors that affect the leading causes of death in the United States.

Nutrition

You are what you eat. Unfortunately, people experiencing stress frequently turn to fast foods and snacks that are high in sugar and fat. Foods high in sugar often produce an energy surge as they increase blood sugar in the body. However, the increased blood sugar quickly drops, thus leaving the individual feeling less energetic than before eating the high-sugar foods or snacks. Foods high in sugar may

---

FIGURE 5.7 Lifestyle Behaviors That Affect the Leading Causes of Death in the United States

This table shows five of the leading causes of death in the United States today, along with behavioral factors that contribute to their development

Cause of Death	Alcohol	Smoking	Diet	Exercise	Stress
Cancer	×	×	×		?
Heart disease	×	×	×	×	×
Stroke	×	×	×	?	?
Lung disease		×			
Accidents and injury	×	×			×

Source: Bernstein/Nash, *Essentials of Psychology,* Houghton Mifflin Company, © 2008, p. 391. Reprinted with permission.

lead to diabetes, obesity, heart disease, and other health issues. (Read **Excerpt 3 Maintaining a Normal Weight,** in Appendix D.) Foods high in fat contribute to health problems, such as heart problems, high cholesterol, and increased blood pressure. Using the following nutritional guidelines can help you begin making healthier lifestyle choices:

- **Complex Carbohydrates:** Instead of eating foods loaded with sugar, choose foods that break sugars down more slowly and release energy over a more sustained period of time. Complex carbohydrates, such as those found in grains, cereals, rice, pasta, bread, and potatoes, protect blood levels from the roller coaster effect of highs and lows.

- **Fruit and Vegetables:** Consume three to four helpings of fruits and vegetables each day. In addition to providing you with essential vitamins and minerals, these foods increase your brain's production of serotonin, a brain chemical that stabilizes mood swings and promotes a sense of happiness. Multivitamins can supplement your dietary needs for vitamins and minerals, but they are not a substitute for good eating.

- **Items to Avoid:** Limit your use of nicotine, caffeine, and alcohol; avoid nonprescription drugs. People often use more of these products when under stress, but they are not effective ways to cope with stress, and their health consequences may lead to more serious problems.

- **Preparation and Planning:** Take time to plan healthy meals and shop for groceries with nutritional value. Set aside fifteen to thirty minutes three times a day to sit down, enjoy a relaxing meal, and give your system time to digest food, instead of "eating on the run."

- **Snacks:** To avoid unhealthy snacks, take a few minutes each day to pack a bag of healthy snacks to eat between meals. Sliced fruit, nuts, or health bars bring greater benefits than potato chips, candy bars, or fast food.

Exercise

Physical activity reduces the physiological effects of stress. Plan twenty to thirty minutes a minimum of three times a week to exercise (walk, run, swim, bike, lift weights, do aerobics, or play basketball, baseball, soccer, or golf). Consider signing up for a physical education course, a yoga class, an intramural sport, or a community exercise program. Explore the option of tuning in to a televised or an interactive exercise program. In addition to reducing your stress level and giving yourself a mental break from thinking about the stressor, the benefits of regular exercise are many:

- **Mental Break:** Exercising not only reduces your stress level, but it provides you with a mental break by shifting your attention away from the stressor.

- **Oxygen to the Brain:** Exercise gets oxygen moving more smoothly to your brain. Your concentration level increases, and information enters and moves through your memory system more efficiently.

- **Healthy Heart:** Exercise improves your cardiovascular system thus reducing your risk of more serious health conditions that may result from prolonged stress.

- **Stronger Body:** Exercise strengthens your body, making it more resistant to the physical and emotional effects of stress. A healthy body becomes better equipped to handle stress, resist illnesses, and feel less fatigue.

CONCEPT CHECK 5.11

How do your nutrition and level of exercise affect stress? How do they affect your brain and cognitive processes?

Sleep

Stress can disrupt your regular sleep patterns and sleep deprivation can cause stress, creating a vicious cycle of fatigue of the body and diminished cognitive functioning. Under stress, some people sleep too little while others sleep too much. People who sleep too little may experience symptoms of *insomnia*, the inability to fall asleep. (Insomnia is a common sleep disorder in which the inability to fall asleep or stay asleep persists for more than one month.) People who sleep too much may be using excessive sleep to avoid feeling overwhelmed or helpless and to escape from the world and avoid dealing with their sources of stress. The following guidelines can help you obtain a healthy lifestyle that includes adequate sleep:

- **Eight Hours of Sound Sleep:** On your weekly time management schedule, plan to get eight hours of sound sleep per night.
- **Sleep Pattern:** Strive to achieve a regular, predictable pattern of sleep throughout the week. Sleeping eight hours during the week and then five hours per night on the weekends, or sleeping six hours during the week and ten hours during the weekend creates the need for your body to keep adjusting to an irregular schedule. You will find your days to be more productive, your body more resilient, and your mind sharper on a more consistent basis when you have an established pattern of sleep.
- **Relaxation Strategies:** When faced with a night of tossing and turning, the inability to fall asleep has the tendency to create more stress and anxiety as you are fully aware of your need for sleep but are not able to fall asleep. During such times, instead of focusing on your sources of stress, engage yourself in relaxation techniques that help reduce tension, stress, or anxiety. Relax in a prone position, listen to soft music, visualizing pleasantries, or practice progressive relaxation techniques. A relaxed body and state of mind are the next best thing to restful sleep.
- **Professional Advice:** If your inability to fall asleep and get a good night's sleep, or your inability to limit your nightly sleep to eight hours persists for more than one month, underlying medical conditions, medications, or more deep-seeded issues may be affecting your sleep patterns. Consult a counselor or a physician to discuss your sleep disorder.

Essential Strategies for Managing Stress

Managing stress involves an active participation on your part to change habits, behaviors, and emotional attitudes. After analyzing your stress levels and stressors, create a plan of action to implement effective stress-management strategies that include coping and relaxation techniques to reduce your reaction to stressors and to decrease stress. **Figure 5.8** shows Essential Strategies for Managing Stress.

FIGURE 5.8   Essential Strategies for Managing Stress
- Choose a healthy lifestyle in the areas of nutrition, exercise, and sleep.
- Use cognitive, emotional, behavioral, and physical coping strategies.
- Use relaxation strategies.
- Strengthen intrapersonal skills.

Coping Strategies

Coping strategies are cognitive and behavioral strategies used to manage and overcome stressors and difficult situations. **Figure 5.9** shows examples of coping methods for four main types of coping methods: cognitive, emotional, behavioral, and physical.

Coping strategies are cognitive and behavioral strategies used to manage and overcome stressors and difficult situations.

Cognitive coping strategies involve changing the way you think and perceive stressors.

- *Cognitive coping strategies* involve changing the way you think and perceive stressors. Instead of perceiving a situation as hopeless, frightening, or insurmountable, use motivational strategies, such as positive self-talk, affirmations, and visualizing success to alter your perception of the situation. Look at the situation as a learning experience and an opportunity to use your problem-solving skills to create a plan of action to overcome the situation.

Emotional coping strategies involve identifying and expressing your emotions to others.

- *Emotional coping strategies* involve identifying and expressing your emotions to others. Having a strong, positive social support network of friends, family, and coworkers provides you with an outlet to share your emotions, analyze the reality of situations, brainstorm solutions, and receive support and encouragement. Many research studies show that social interaction can reduce stress, improve overall health and the immune system, stimulate cognitive processes, and stave off depression. Keeping emotions to yourself or bottling-up your stress and frustrations may result in catastrophic thinking, a state of mind in which your perception of the problem becomes distorted and the severity of the problem becomes greatly exaggerated. Left unchecked, your stress level increases and your ability to manage the stress decreases.

Behavioral coping strategies involve changing patterns or behaviors to overcome stress.

- *Behavioral coping strategies* involve changing patterns or behaviors to overcome stress. For example, if you toss and turn at night, feel immobilized during the day, and feel more stress than usual about an upcoming test, you can reduce your stress by implementing time management, goal-setting, and test-preparation strategies. Your plan of action becomes your plan to select behaviors that combat the source of the stress. Perhaps instead of an upcoming test, your stressor is a specific task that you procrastinate about doing, such as finalizing financial aid papers, applying for a scholarship, or filing your taxes. Changing your behavior by using strategies to increase motivation, set goals, and stop procrastination will eliminate the stressor.

Physical coping strategies involve the use of physical activity to reduce or eliminate your responses to specific stressors.

- *Physical coping strategies* involve the use of physical activity to reduce or eliminate your response to specific stressors. Engaging in activities that create positive emotions reduces the intensity of your emotional reaction to stress and

CONCEPT CHECK 5.12

Briefly describe strategies to use for each of the four kinds of coping strategies.

| FIGURE 5.9 | Methods for Coping with Stress |

Type of Coping Method	Examples
Cognitive	Thinking of stressors as challenges rather than as threats; avoiding perfectionism
Emotional	Seeking social support; getting advice
Behavioral	Implementing a time-management plan; when possible, making life changes to eliminate stress
Physical	Progressive relaxation training; exercise; meditation

Source: Bernstein/ Nash, *Essentials of Psychology,* 4e, Houghton Mifflin Company, © 2008, p. 414. Reprinted with permission.

the tendency to dwell on negative situations. Redirect your emotions by spending time on a favorite hobby or activity that involves physical movement. Exercise and using relaxation techniques reduce the physiological effects of stress. The following section provides you with easy-to-use relaxation techniques to cope with stress.

Relaxation Techniques

Relaxation techniques can help you reduce your stress levels, improve your emotional health, and create a state of mind and body that perhaps can best be described as "Ahhhhhhh." In this state, the body is not tense and the mind is not wandering; you are open and ready to receive new information or expand on previously learned information. Relaxation techniques help you manage emotional situations, such as anxiety, nervousness, tension, stress, apprehension, hyperactivity, restlessness, and feelings of defeat, frustration, or being overwhelmed. The following are six relaxation techniques that are easy to learn and require only a few minutes of your time.

- The *perfect place technique* involves taking a mental vacation and visualizing a perfect, stress-free place to relax. Use the following steps for this technique:

  1. Close your eyes, breathe in slowly, and visualize a perfect place where you feel relaxed, confident, safe, comfortable, and content.

  2. Continue breathing in and out slowly as you create this mental picture of a perfect place. Make your image more vivid by adding sounds, smells, sights, tastes, and tactile sensations.

  3. Use the power of association to recall the mental picture and the soothing sensations of this perfect place whenever you need to separate yourself in a healthy way from stress and stressful situations.

- The *soothing mask technique* involves using your imagination to create and pull a mask over your face to block out reactions to stress. Use the following steps for this technique:

  1. Close your eyes and place your hands on the top of your head.

  2. Slowly move your hands down your forehead, down your face, and to your neck. As you do this, picture your hands gently pulling a *soothing mask* over your face, removing worries, fears, or stresses from your mind.

  3. Keep your eyes closed for another minute. Feel the soothing mask resting on your face, blocking out stressful thoughts or feelings. As you practice this technique, you will be able to visualize the soothing mask without using your hands.

- The *relaxation blanket technique* involves visualizing yourself pulling a soft, warm blanket up to your neck to release tension. Use the following steps for this technique:

  1. As you sit comfortably in your chair, close your eyes, and focus your attention on your feet.

  2. Imagine yourself pulling a soft, warm blanket up over your feet, up over your legs, lap, and chest until the blanket is snuggled around your shoulders and against your neck. Focus on the way your body feels warm and relaxed.

  3. Keep your eyes closed for another minute as you enjoy the warmth and comfort of the blanket.

CONCEPT CHECK 5.13

What effects can relaxation techniques have on the body and on the mind? Which relaxation techniques are most beneficial for you?

The perfect place technique involves taking a mental vacation and visualizing a perfect, stress-free place to relax.

The soothing mask technique involves using your imagination to create and pull a mask over your face to block out reactions to stress.

The relaxation blanket technique involves visualizing yourself pulling a soft, warm blanket up to your neck to release tension.

The breathing by threes technique involves inhaling and exhaling slowly as a way to reduce stress.

- The *breathing by threes technique* involves inhaling and exhaling slowly as a way to reduce stress. Use the following steps for this technique:

  1. Count to three as you inhale slowly through your nose, Count to three as you hold your breath. Finally, count to three as you exhale slowly.

  2. Repeat this several times. You will feel your body begin to slow down and relax.

The deep breathing technique involves taking deep breaths and exhaling slowly as a way to reduce stress.

- The *deep breathing technique* involves taking deep breaths and exhaling slowly as a way to reduce stress. Use the following steps for this technique:

  1. Take a deep breath to fill your lungs. You may think your lungs are full, but there is room for one more breath of air. Inhale once again.

  2. Now slowly exhale and feel your body relax.

  3. Repeat this deep breathing several times. If you feel lightheaded or dizzy after trying this exercise, discontinue and use an alternative relaxation technique.

The deep muscle relaxation technique involves tensing and releasing different groups of muscles as a way to reduce stress.

- The *deep muscle relaxation technique* involves tensing and releasing different groups of muscles as a way to reduce stress. Use the following steps for this technique:

  1. Identify the areas of your body where you feel tension.

  2. Make a clenched fist tight enough so that you can feel your fingers pulsating. Breathe several times, feel the tension in your fingers and your hands, and then breathe slowly as you uncurl your fists until they are totally relaxed. Pay close attention to the different sensations as you go from tense to relaxed.

  3. Continue this with other muscle groups that tend to hold tension: shoulders, arms, lower back, legs, chest, fingers, or face. As you work to release tension from your different muscle groups, your total body moves into a state of greater relaxation.

Intrapersonal Skills

As you recall from Chapter 1, intrapersonal intelligence involves developing skills related to personal growth, self-understanding, self-motivation, intuition, and spirituality. Intrapersonal skills shift your focus from the outside world to your internal world—your thoughts, feelings, reactions, inspirations, and personal goals. Following are four ways to use your intrapersonal skills to reduce or eliminate stress and strengthen your self-management skills.

1. **Take time to center yourself.** Engage in a mind-calming activity such as meditation, yoga, prayer, or biofeedback to center yourself and return to a state of calmness and serenity. Sitting in a sauna, soaking in a hot tub or warm bath, or sitting near a fountain of water can also be a mind-calming experience. Centering activities provide a way to block out and temporarily shield yourself from the rest of the world.

2. **Keep a journal.** In a journal, describe your feelings or concerns privately and tap into some of your innermost thoughts in a nonthreatening way. Putting your emotions on paper often reduces the intensity of the emotions, disperses some of the negative energy, and helps you discover solutions or new directions to take with the situation.

3. **Strive to strengthen self-esteem.** As you recall from Figure 5.4, positive self-talk, high achievement, positive perception of self and others, rewarding

CONCEPT CHECK 5.14

What is the focus of intrapersonal skills? What is the relationship of intrapersonal skills to increasing motivation and reducing stress?

relationships, and improved self-confidence are characteristics of high self-esteem, which often reflect fewer stressors than the characteristics associated with low self-esteem. Using strategies to boost your confidence, your self-perception, and your self-esteem provides you with additional coping strategies to reduce the effects of stressors.

4. **Use your executive function.** Chaos, disorganization, and clutter create stress. Not being able to organize materials or assignments, locate important papers or information, or structure tasks in logical ways create stressors and immobilize your ability to perform effectively. To help working memory organize and process tasks efficiently, create personal goals to become a high-performing, outstanding executive of your activities, cognitive processes, and your surroundings. In some cases, you may need to slow down your pace and focus your attention on a given task so you can devise or structure a plan that is based on a logical, meaningful, and efficient approach. Gaining a greater sense of personal organization results in less stress and more rewarding accomplishments.

Strategy and Technique Review

EXERCISE 5.3

You have learned an array of strategies and techniques to increase concentration and motivation and reduce stress. To keep these strategies and techniques fresh in your memory, follow the directions below.

DIRECTIONS

1. With a partner or in a small group, take turns giving a three-part definition for each of the terms listed in this exercise.
   - Name the term and a larger category to which it belongs (concentration, motivation, or stress management)
   - Define the term.
   - Add one additional detail about using the strategy or technique.

2. For additional practice, go to this textbook's CourseMate Web site to practice reciting and writing definitions for terminology.

affirmations, *p. 132*	chunking *p. 124*	emotional coping
behavioral coping	cognitive coping	strategies *p. 138*
strategies *p.138*	strategies *p. 138*	emotional *e* words *p. 126*
breathing by threes *p. 140*	deep breathing *p. 140*	mental rehearsal *p. 124*
check mark *p. 126*	deep muscle	mental storage box *p. 126*
negative self-talk *p. 132*	relaxation *p. 140*	study ritual *p. 124*
no need *p. 126*	positive self-talk *p. 132*	take-charge *p. 124*
perfect place *p. 139*	red bow *p. 126*	tunnel vision *p. 126*
physical coping	relaxation blanket *p. 139*	visualize success *p. 130*
strategies *p. 138*	say no *p. 125*	warm-ups *p. 124*
	soothing mask *p. 139*	

- **Do I tend to procrastinate about beginning a specific task?** If you drag your feet and make excuses to avoid beginning a task, the source of your procrastination may be due to lack of motivation, lack of confidence in your ability to do the work, confusion about what steps are involved, or uncertainty about how to begin to tackle the task. Breaking the task down, setting goals, identifying incentives and placing the task higher on your priority list can help you break through your procrastination pattern.

- **Do I start tasks but then procrastinate during the middle of the process?** When procrastination sets in during the middle of a process, you may have lost interest, motivation, or a sense of purpose in persevering to completion. Other times you may find procrastination in the middle of a process occurs due to time-related issues: you underestimated the length of time needed, you have other demands on your time that seem more urgent, or you fail to use your time management skills and schedules. As soon as your momentum starts shifting, create a plan of action that utilizes strategies to boost your time management, goal-setting, and motivation skills.

- **Do I procrastinate close to the end of the completion of a task?** Procrastinating close to the completion of a task or project is a way to quit to avoid the final results. The underlying cause may be related to fear: fear of being evaluated or judged on your work, fear of failure, or fear of success. People who fear success become concerned that excellence on performance will put pressure on them to repeat that level of excellence on future tasks as well. Use strategies such as visualizing success, positive self-talk, incentives, and a goal organizer to motivate yourself to finish the task.

- **Do I tend to start multiple tasks, jumping from one to another, and making less important tasks seem more important or urgent?** This behavior is a common sign of the onset of procrastination. Procrastinators can get so caught up in this whirlwind behavior that they do not realize all the busy work is a mask for avoiding specific tasks. When you find yourself scurrying around, sometimes aimlessly keeping busy, take time to identify the task you are avoiding. Use the ABC Method for goal-setting by listing and then prioritizing the tasks you need to accomplish. Focus your attention on the tasks with highest importance and refrain from dedicating time to the less urgent or lower-priority tasks.

Why You Procrastinate

CONCEPT CHECK 5.16

Why is it important to analyze behavior patterns to identify when and why you procrastinate? Give examples of when and why procrastination may occur.

Reasons for procrastinating vary for different tasks, situations, and individuals. In some cases, procrastinating will not have any serious consequences. For example, procrastinating about moving a stack of magazines to the garage or putting your compact disks back in their cases has no dire consequences. In other cases, procrastinating leads to increased stress and additional problems. Procrastinating about paying your bills, studying for a test, or filling your tires with air will have more serious consequences, some of which could alter your goals or course for the future.

We all procrastinate at one time or another. When you are aware of *when* you procrastinate, "dig deep" to uncover your reason for putting off something important that needs to be done. What behavior or underlying belief triggers your procrastination? As you learned in the previous section, the sources or reasons for procrastinating may be tied to lack of interest, lack of confidence, confusion or lack of know-how, time management issues, fear of failure, or fear of success. As you conduct an honest search for the reasons you procrastinate, you may discover additional behaviors or beliefs that trigger this self-defeating pattern of behavior. The following graphic shows common reasons for procrastinating. Understanding both *when* and *why* you procrastinate is the beginning step to overcome the learned behavior of postponing or avoiding productive activity. To learn more about procrastination and its causes, read **Excerpt 4** in Appendix D.

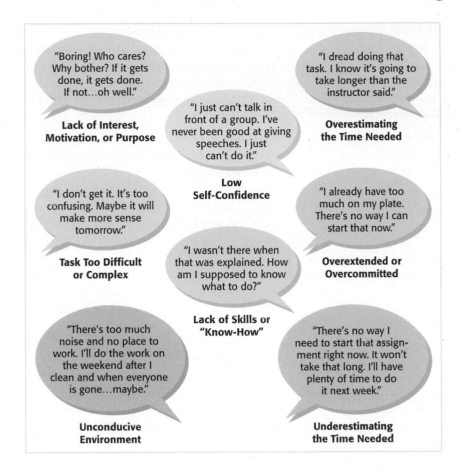

Procrastination Management Strategies

EXERCISE 5.5

PURPOSE: By applying self-management skills and strategies, you can combat the multiple reasons for procrastinating.

DIRECTIONS: Work as a group, with a partner, or by yourself to complete the following directions.

1. On separate paper, create the following chart. In the first column, list ten reasons people procrastinate. You may use any ten reasons discussed in this chapter and in Excerpt 4 in Appendix D.

2. In the second column, list strategies a person could use to combat each reason for procrastinating. You may use strategies from previous chapters, this chapter, Excerpt 4 in Appendix D, and from your personal experiences.

Reason	Strategies
Lack of motivation	• *Use goal organizer to identify importance* • *Break task into steps; use rewards for completing each step*

Essential Strategies to Combat Procrastination

Learning to reduce or eliminate procrastination can empower you, enhance your self-esteem, strengthen your self-discipline, and put you in greater control of your life. In addition to the time management, goal setting, motivation, and other self-management strategies that you have already learned, the following are ten additional strategies to combat procrastination.

- **Strategy 1: Use your intrapersonal intelligence.** Explore *when* and *why* you procrastinate about a specific task. Use those insights to identify appropriate strategies to deal directly with the underlying issues.

- **Strategy 2: Identify a purpose and meaning.** Avoid labeling a task as "meaningless, stupid, or boring" or expressing a negative attitude toward a task, as these attitudes and behaviors lower motivation and negatively impact your self-image. Find a purpose or a valid reason for the task. Use a goal organizer; identify the benefits.

- **Strategy 3: Create an interest.** Engage a family member, a tutor, or a study group to work with you on the task. Seek alternative sources of information, such as a video, Internet searches, magazines, or books related to the topic. Once you become familiar with the topic, interest often increases.

- **Strategy 4: Take charge of the situation.** Identify and list the steps you need to do to break the cycle of procrastination about a specific task. Gather up all the supplies or materials you need to get started. Create a goal or a plan of action. Select an appropriate work environment. *Take charge* and take responsibility of the situation.

- **Strategy 5: Prioritize and stick to the order.** When you feel overwhelmed or overextended, make a list of tasks that must be done. Use the ABC Method to prioritize them by their importance or prioritize them by completion date requirements. Tackle the high-priority tasks first. Schedule time on your weekly schedule to work on these tasks.

- **Strategy 6: Relax your personal standards.** If you tend to be a perfectionist, lower your unrealistically high standards or expectations. You can continue to produce quality work without always having to "be the best." Avoid spending excessive time redoing parts of a task or the final outcome, such as a paper, when your work already shows quality.

- **Strategy 7: Be flexible and willing to change.** Be willing to give up the attitude that "I have always done things this way" or the false belief that "I work best under pressure or stress." Be willing to try new strategies and to create new behavior patterns that have the potential to produce higher quality work and less stress.

- **Strategy 8: Face your fear of failure.** Focus on your positive traits, your accomplishments, and the skills you have acquired. Use positive self-talk, affirmations, and emotional *e* words to negate self-doubts, self-criticism, and fear of failure. Build your self-confidence by mentally rehearsing the steps of the task several times before you begin.

- **Strategy 9: Visualize success.** Create a mental picture of yourself working through a task, feeling positive about your work, and completing the task on time.

- **Strategy 10: Make a contract with yourself.** Make a contract with yourself to stop using excuses for not getting things done. Begin by creating a plan of action (a goal). Push yourself to "just do it." End your contract with an incentive, such as an extrinsic reward.

CONCEPT CHECK 5.17

When *and* why *did you recently procrastinate? Be specific. Which of the strategies in this chapter could you have used to stop your procrastination?*

**CHAPTER 5
REFLECTIVE WRITING 2**

On separate paper, in a journal, or online at this textbook's CourseMate Web site, respond to the following questions:

1. Which strategies or techniques in Chapter 5 will you use to become a more effective self-manager? Be specific.

2. How will implementing these strategies or techniques benefit you?

Access Chapter 5 Reflective Writing 2 in your College Success CourseMate, accessed through *CengageBrain.com*.

ACTIVITY

Chapter 5 Critical Thinking

PURPOSE: The concept of self-management involves an integration of many different study skills and learning theories. Learning to use strategies from one category, such as motivation, can strengthen your self-management skills in other areas, such as goal setting, concentration, stress management, and procrastination management. Each time you see relationships between concepts and sets of skills, identify how they are interrelated, and recognize the chain reaction that occurs between various behaviors, you are using your critical thinking skills to understand information on a deeper level.

DIRECTIONS: By yourself, with a partner, or in a small group, explore answers to the following questions.

1. How does managing procrastination affect self-esteem?

2. How does a person's level of motivation affect concentration and stress?

3. How can stress management affect concentration, motivation, and procrastination?

4. How does a person's self-esteem cycle affect his or her self-talk and self-efficacy?

5. How do self-management skills affect the operations of working memory?

CHECK POINT 5.4

Answers appear on page B3

True or False?

_____ 1. Procrastination is a learned behavior that can be reduced or eliminated.

_____ 2. Low self-efficacy can be one reason for procrastinating.

_____ 3. If a person starts a task and later procrastinates, he or she may fear failure or find the task to be too complex or difficult.

_____ 4. Procrastination often involves selecting high-priority tasks over low-priority tasks.

_____ 5. For a chronic procrastinator, procrastination always begins right before he or she is close to completing the task.

Access Chapter 5 Practice Quiz 4: Procrastination under "Interactive Quizzes" in your College Success CourseMate, accessed through *CengageBrain.com*.

Terms to Know

By yourself or with a partner, practice reciting or writing definitions for the following terms. In addition, practice and review definitions for specific strategies and techniques listed in Exercise 5.3 on page 141. You may also practice defining these terms by using the online flashcard programs or comparing your answers to the online glossary.

self-management p. 120

concentration p. 120

external distractors p. 121

internal distractors p. 121

motivation p. 127

intrinsic motivation p. 127

extrinsic motivation p. 127

self-esteem p. 128

self-efficacy p. 128

Incentive Theory of Motivation p. 129

Expectancy Theory of Motivation p. 130

stress p. 134

stressors p. 134

coping strategies, p. 138

procrastination p. 143

 Access Chapter 5 Flashcard Drills and Online Glossary in your College Success CourseMate, accessed through *CengageBrain.com*.

Learning Objectives Review

1 *Define concentration and identify strategies to block out distractions and maintain a focused, disciplined mind.*

- Self-management is the ability to use strategies to deal constructively and effectively with variables that affect the quality of your personal life. Concentration is a self-management set of skills.

- Concentration is the ability to block out external and internal distractors in order to stay focused on one specific item or task.

- An ideal study area involves careful attention to elements in your physical environment: noise, lighting, and workspace.

- You can use specific strategies to increase your concentration when you study, manage distractors, and free up your working memory for cognitive processes.

2 *Define motivation and discuss factors that affect motivation and strategies to strengthen motivation.*

- Motivation is the feeling, emotion, or desire that moves a person to take action.

- Intrinsic and extrinsic motivation are two forms of motivation that drive people to achieve goals. In general, intrinsic motivation is more powerful than extrinsic motivation.

- A person's self-esteem and self-efficacy are factors that affect motivation. You can use specific strategies to boost self-esteem and develop a stronger sense of self-efficacy.

- The Incentive Theory of Motivation and the Expectancy Theory of Motivation are two theories of motivation that help explain what motivates people to take action and change behaviors.

- Strategies to increase motivation, such as visualizing success, using positive self-talk, and using affirmations also increase self-esteem and create a stronger sense of self-efficacy.

3 *Define stress and identify strategies and techniques for effective stress management.*

- Stress is a reaction or a response to events or situations that threaten or disrupt our normal patterns or routines. Stress is normal and can be beneficial. Excessive stress has physical consequences and can hinder performance and cognitive functioning.

- Stressors, which can be positive or negative, are situations or actions that cause stress.

- Stress-management techniques include choosing a healthy lifestyle (nutrition, exercise, and sleep); using cognitive, emotional, behavioral, and physical coping strategies; using relaxation techniques; and implementing strategies that focus on intrapersonal skills.

4 *Define procrastination and identify strategies and techniques for effective procrastination management.*

- Procrastination is a learned behavior that involves putting off, postponing, or avoiding something until a later time. Identifying *when* and *why* you procrastinate is the beginning step to combating procrastination.
- Ten strategies can be used to overcome procrastination and take action to complete tasks.

Chapter 5 Review Questions

Answers appear on page B3

Fill-in-the-Blanks

Write one word (key term) per blank to complete each sentence.

1. _____ distractors are disruptions caused by things in your physical environment.

2. _____ are situations or actions that cause stress.

3. The _____ Theory of Motivation states that people are motivated by the rewards that they may receive for their actions or performance.

4. _____ motivation is the most effective kind of motivation because you strive to accomplish something to please yourself.

5. Self-_____ is the belief in your ability to achieve a specific task at a specific level of performance.

6. Cognitive, emotional, behavioral, and physical are four kinds of _____ strategies designed to decrease or overcome stress.

7. A healthy lifestyle involves making wise choices in the areas of nutrition, sleep, and _____.

8. _____ is the process of putting off something for a later time or choosing low-priority tasks over high-priority tasks.

Multiple Choice

_____ 1. Concentration is
   a. the ability to block out distractions and focus on only one item or task.
   b. one of the Twelve Principles of Memory.
   c. a mental discipline that involves training your mind to maintain a focus.
   d. all of the above.

_____ 2. Which techniques would work well for a student who wants to stop wasting the first half hour of a study block trying to "get started" on studying?
   a. Warm-up activities and using the Take-Charge Technique.
   b. Chunking technique and mental rehearsal.
   c. Setting learning goals and creating a task schedule.
   d. All of the above.

_____ 3. Procrastination
   a. may stem from lack of interest, fear of failure, or faulty beliefs.
   b. occurs when low-priority tasks take the place of high-priority tasks.
   c. is a learned behavior that can be altered by using effective strategies.
   d. involves all of the above.

_____ 4. Which of the following strategies are *not* designed to convert a person's negative attitude to a positive attitude?

   a. Tunnel vision, intrinsic rewards, and deep breathing.

   b. Mental rehearsal and positive self-talk.

   c. Affirmations and emotional *e* words.

   d. Seeing success and strategies to increase self-esteem.

_____ 5. Which of the following statements is *not* true about stress?

   a. Stress is normal and can help people move in new directions.

   b. Prolonged stress may affect physical, emotional, behavioral, and cognitive functions.

   c. Excessive stress requires prescription medications in order to avoid physical damage to the body.

   d. You can reduce stress by using cognitive, emotional, behavioral, or physical coping strategies.

_____ 6. Which of the following helps decrease or eliminate the habit of procrastination?

   a. Taking time to understand *when* and *why* procrastination occurs

   b. Using a weekly schedule, a task schedule, and goal organizers

   c. Creating a stronger interest in the task and finding a purpose for completing the task

   d. All of the above

Access all Chapter 5 Online Materials in your College Success CourseMate, accessed through *CengageBrain.com*.

Short-Answer Questions

On separate paper, answer the following questions. Use complete sentences and details and terminology from this chapter.

1. Discuss specific strategies you can use to improve your self-management skills in any one of the following areas: concentration, motivation, stress management, or procrastination management.

2. Define and briefly explain how to use *any three* of the following techniques.

   Chunking

   Mental Storage Box

   Positive Self-Talk

   Affirmations

   Take-Charge

   Warm-Ups

Access Chapter 5 Chapter Quizzes 1–4 and Enhanced Quiz under "Interactive Quizzes" in your College Success CourseMate, accessed through *CengageBrain .com*.

6 Preparing for Upcoming Tests

© Image Source/Getty Images

Tests in college are a standard method to assess your understanding of course material. As you approach the middle of a term and midterm exams, understanding kinds of test questions and learning strategies to prepare effectively for tests, take tests, manage test anxiety, and use mnemonics to boost your memory provide you with the essential skills to perform well on tests. The removable Essential Test-Taking Skills Guide in Appendix A provides you with specific strategies and skills for objective, recall, math, and essay tests.

LEARNING OBJECTIVES

1. *Identify and explain effective strategies for preparing for tests.*

2. *Identify and explain effective strategies for performing well on tests.*

3. *Identify and explain effective strategies for managing test anxiety.*

4. *Identify and explain ways to use mnemonics to prepare for tests.*

CHAPTER OUTLINE

Access Chapter 6 Expanded Chapter Outline and Objectives in your College Success CourseMate, accessed through *CengageBrain.com*.

YOUR CHAPTER MAPPING

After reading information under each heading, return to the chapter visual mapping below. Add key words to show subheadings and important details related to each heading.

Access Chapter 6 Visual Mapping in your College Success CourseMate, accessed through *CengageBrain.com*.

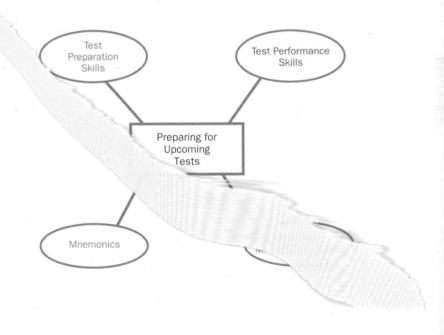

Preparing for Upcoming Tests

ANSWER, SCORE, and **RECORD** your profile before you read this chapter. If you need to review the process, refer to the complete directions given in the profile for Chapter 1 on page 4.

ONLINE: You can complete the profile and get your score online at this textbook's CourseMate Web site.

Access Chapter 6 Profile in your College Success CourseMate, accessed through *CengageBrain.com.*

	YES	NO
1. I use the twelve Principles of Memory when I study and prepare for tests.		
2. I understand the different skills required to answer objective, recall, and essay questions.		
3. I make a five-day study plan and summary notes to prepare for major tests.		
4. I use the survival technique of cramming for most tests.		
5. On tests, I answer one question, or guess at an answer if necessary, and then move to the next question.		
6. I use associations, memory searches, and visualizations to try to recall information to answer test questions.		
7. When I take tests, I tend to forget information that I studied, or I "go blank."		
8. I am often nervous, feel sick, or have physical problems (headache, stomachache, clammy hands) right before a test or during a test.		
9. I create mnemonics for information that is difficult to remember.		
10. I am confident in my test-preparation and test-taking skills and abilities.		

QUESTIONS LINKED TO THE CHAPTER LEARNING OBJECTIVES:

Questions 1–3: objective 1   Question 9: objective 4

Questions 4–6: objective 2   Question 10: all objectives

Questions 7, 8: objective 3

Test Preparation Skills

1 *Identify and explain effective strategies for preparing for tests.*

In college, tests indicate how well you have prepared, the effectiveness of your study methods, and your test-taking skills. By using the strategies in this chapter, you will learn how to enter testing situations with more confidence and preparedness, which will lead to better results and rewards for your work and effort.

Applying Memory Principles and Strategies

You have already learned about the Twelve Principles of Memory and an array of strategies to develop and strengthen self-management skills. As you progress through this chapter, you will notice that many of these same principles and strategies apply equally as well to test-preparation and test-taking situations. Managing your time, setting specific kinds of goals, concentrating while reviewing, staying motivated, managing your stress, and refraining from procrastinating continue to be important as you prepare for upcoming tests. Exercise 6.1 provides you with an opportunity to examine how well you have integrated the Twelve Principles of Memory and related strategies into your customized approach to learning.

CONCEPT CHECK 6.1

What Principles of Memory do you activate when you prepare for tests?

EXERCISE 6.1

Assessing Your Strategies Inventory

Go to Exercise 6.1, Appendix C, page C10, for the Assessing Your Strategies Inventory. Use this inventory to assess your application of the Twelve Principles of Memory to the study methods you currently use. Use the results from the inventory to modify your approach to learning and include to a greater degree strategies based on the Twelve Principles of Memory. Return to this inventory several times throughout the term to assess your application of the principles to a specific course or to your overall study methods.

Understanding Kinds of Test Questions

Understanding types of test questions is the first step in the process of strengthening your test-preparation and test-taking skills. **Figure 6.1** provides you with information about the different test-question formats you will encounter on your tests. To learn more about each kind of test question, refer to the **Essential Test-Taking Skills Guide** in **Appendix A.** For now, the following common test-question formats will help you begin to anticipate what to expect on upcoming tests.

FIGURE 6.1   Test Question Formats

Kind of Question	Level of Difficulty	Includes	Requires
Recognition: Objective Questions	Easiest	True-False Multiple-Choice Matching	Read and recognize whether information is correct; apply a skill and then recognize the correct answer.
Recall Questions	More demanding	Fill-in-the-Blanks Listings Definitions Short Answers Problem-Solving	Retrieve the information from your memory and then respond.
Essay Questions	Most difficult	Essays	Retrieve the information from memory, organize it, and use effective writing skills to respond.

True-False Questions

True-false questions are objective questions that require you to recognize if a statement is true or false. Mark a question *true* only when the complete statement is true and accurate. If any part of the statement is false or inaccurate, you must mark the statement as *false.* Following is an example of a true-false question:

_____ 1. An intermediary goal is a short goal that you set to complete in between two immediate goals. (Answer: False)

Multiple-Choice Questions

Multiple-choice questions are objective questions that require you to select the best answer from a group of options to complete an opening statement. At times, more than one option may complete the statement accurately, but only one option is the best, most inclusive, or most complete answer. Multiple-choice questions may show three, four, or five options. Sometimes the last option includes "all of the above," which means every option is accurate. Following is an example of a multiple-choice question:

_____ 1. Kinds of encoding to prepare stimuli for long-term memory include:

    a. linguistic and visual coding

    b. motor coding

    c. semantic coding

    d. all of the above   (Answer: d)

Matching Questions

Matching questions are objective questions that require you to match items in the left column with items in the right column. Matching questions often test your ability to match terminology with definitions; people, places, or dates with descriptions, characteristics, or events; or match causes and effects. Following is a partial example of the matching question format:

_____ 1. reciting   a. learning styles

_____ 2. linear learner   b. processes information first through the left brain hemisphere

_____ 3. learning modalities   c. explaining out loud, in your own words without referring to printed information

(Answers: 1. c, 2. b, 3. a)

Fill-in-the-Blanks Questions

Fill-in-the-blanks questions are recall questions that require you to write a term or a word on each blank line to complete the statement. Words that complete these statements are often vocabulary or terminology words. Correct answers often require that you spell the words in the blanks correctly. Following is an example of a fill-in-the-blanks question:

1. _____ is the process of postponing a task for a later time. (Answer: Procrastination)

Listing Questions

Listing questions are recall questions that require you to generate a list of items from memory to answer a question. *Closed questions* require specific items in the answer. *Open-ended questions* have a variety of possible answers. Listing questions often begin with one of these direction words: *list, name,* or *what are.* Unless the directions ask you to add details about each item, your answer simply lists the items. Following is an example of a listing question that is a closed question that requires a specific answer.

   1. List the three memory systems in the Information Processing Model.

      (Answer:) 1. sensory memory

              2. working memory

              3. long-term memory

Definition Questions

Definition questions are recall questions that require you to define and expand upon a vocabulary term. Simply writing a word-for-word textbook definition is not sufficient. Instead, you can use a three-part definition: 1. Identify the category to which the term belongs. 2. Define the term. 3. Give one more detail about the term. You learned to use this definition approach in Chapter 5, Exercise 5.3. Following is an example of a definition question.

> 1. What is the definition of the Take-Charge Technique?
> (Answer: The Take-Charge Technique is a concentration technique. It involves taking responsibility for your environment by seeking alternative places to study or by modifying your existing place of study so you have few or no distractions. When you use this technique, you find solutions rather than blame others for your inability to concentrate.)

Definition questions are recall questions that require you to define and expand upon a vocabulary term.

CONCEPT CHECK 6.3

What are the five kinds of recall question formats? Why are they often considered more demanding than recognition questions?

Short-Answer Questions

Short-answer questions are recall questions that require you to pull information from memory to write a short answer to a question. Often times you can answer the question in five to seven sentences. Direction words for short-answer questions include *discuss, tell, identify, describe, explain why, explain how,* and *when.* Short-answer questions may be closed or open-ended questions. Following is an example of a short-answer question.

> 1. Explain how the last step in the four-step approach for achieving goals affects a
>   person's motivation.
> (Answer:) The last step in the four-step approach for achieving goals is to identify a reward to receive when you finish the goal. The reward is the incentive and the motivation to complete the steps on time. Both intrinsic and extrinsic rewards can be used for motivation. Without having a reward in mind, motivation may dwindle and interest in completing the task may fade.

Short-answer questions are recall questions that require you to pull information from memory to write a short answer to a question.

Problem-Solving Questions

Problem-solving questions are recall questions that require you to apply a series of steps to solve a problem. Problem-solving questions may involve story problems or solving a mathematical equation. Usually your answer must show all the steps used to solve the problem. Following is an example of a problem-solving question:

> 1. Use the power rule to solve the following equation: $(2^3)^4 = ?$
> (Answer:) $(2^3)^4 = 2^{3 \times 4} = 2^{12} = 4{,}096$

Problem-solving questions are recall questions that require you to apply a series of steps to solve a problem.

Essay Questions

Essay questions require you to retrieve information from memory and organize it into several paragraphs with main ideas that are related to a thesis statement. Essay questions involve higher level thinking, organizational, and writing skills. You will learn

Essay questions require you to retrieve information from memory and organize it into several paragraphs with main ideas that are related to a thesis statement.

more about essays in the **Essential Test-Taking Skills Guide** in **Appendix A.** Following is an example of an essay question that requires multiple paragraphs in your response.

1. Compare and contrast the functions and capabilities of sensory memory, working memory, and long-term memory.

ACTIVITY

Chapter 6 Critical Thinking

PURPOSE: Critical thinking involves the use of a variety of cognitive processes. *Application* of information is one critical thinking process that involves applying and integrating information to new situations. Writing and answering practice test questions is one effective way to apply what you have learned to the creation of study tools.

DIRECTIONS: By yourself, with a partner, or in a small group, write one *objective* and one *recall* question for each of the following topics discussed in previous chapters. Your instructor may ask you to give your questions to your partner, to another group, or to the class to answer.

1. Linear and Global Learners
2. Multiple Intelligences
3. Feedback Model
4. One of the Twelve Principles of Memory

5. Kinds of Time-Management Schedules
6. Motivation
7. Procrastination
8. Test Anxiety

Organizing Your Materials

Preparing for a test requires additional time and organization, both of which can be demanding in a schedule that already is filled with other demands from your courses and in your personal life. The following suggestions can help you organize your materials in a time-efficient and effective manner.

Pay Attention to Test Details

Find out as much as you can about the test from your instructor and from other students. Listen carefully to your instructor's description of the test and the topics or chapters that the test will cover. Take notes on materials or topics your instructor emphasizes that you should review or need to know. If your instructor indicates the kinds of test questions that will appear on the test, jot these down as you may use different strategies to prepare for different kinds of test questions. Talk to other students who have already completed the course and tutors who are familiar with the course. Ask them for study suggestions and about the kinds of test questions to expect. Remember, however, that instructors do change test questions and formats, so do not feel overly confident about an upcoming test based on information you obtained from previous students or from tutors. If previous tests are available to examine, take the time to look at and practice with the tests.

Gather Your Course Materials

Review your course syllabus and class assignment sheets so you know specifically which chapters and topics will be included on the test. Gather together and organize your notes and assignments, chapter by chapter. Identify topics that received special attention in class or through assignments as these may receive greater attention on the test. Pulling together and organizing your materials before you begin the serious review process promotes effective and efficient use of time.

Predict Test Questions

Predicting test questions is an excellent method for preparing for tests and reducing test anxiety. Predicting test questions becomes easier after you have taken one or two tests from a specific instructor and have a sense of the types of tests he or she uses. Even though effective test preparation should include studying all the important material thoroughly so you are well prepared for any type of test question, you may prefer to modify your test-preparation strategies to reflect specific testing formats when the instructor announces the formats in advance. **Figure 6.2** shows the kind of information to study and the type of practice to use when you predict specific kinds of question formats will appear on a test.

Create Summary Notes

Summary notes are specific notes that include concepts, definitions, details, steps, or other information that you need to review further before the day of the test. If you have used effective learning strategies and ongoing review, as you review your textbook and lecture notes, you will recognize concepts, facts, and terms that you already know well. These do not need to appear on your summary notes. Your summary notes are special sets of notes for information that you know you need to give more attention to and study further. **Figure 6.3** shows a variety of formats that are commonly used for summary notes. You will learn more about these formats in Chapters 10 and 11.

Organizing Your Time: A Five-Day Study Plan

A *five-day study plan* is a plan of action that helps you organize your materials and time to review for a major test, such as a midterm or a final exam. This plan promotes spaced

> **CONCEPT CHECK 6.4**
>
> *How do the summary notes you create during the five-day study plan differ from your regular textbook and lecture notes?*

> **Summary notes** are specific notes that include information that you need to review further before the day of the test.

> A **five-day study plan** is a plan of action that helps you organize your materials and time to review for a major test, such as a midterm or a final exam.

FIGURE 6.2	Predicting and Studying for Different Kinds of Tests

If You Predict ...	Study This Kind of Information:	Practice May Include:
Objective Questions	• Definitions of key terms • Categories or lists of information • Details: names, dates, theories, rules, events	• Writing and later answering true-false, multiple-choice, and matching questions • Working with a study partner to exchange practice questions
Recall Questions	• Information presented in lists • Definitions of terminology • Cornell recall columns (Chapter 9) • Questions formulated before, during, and after reading • Chapter summaries • Details on visual notes (Chapter 11) • Problem-solving examples and prototypes	• Reciting and using Look-Away Techniques • Writing summaries and answers to questions to practice expressing ideas • Writing and answering fill-in-the-blanks, listings, and definitions questions • Reworking math problems • Writing the problem-solving steps • Working with a study partner to exchange practice questions
Essay Questions	• Themes • Relationships • Major concepts	• Outlining chapters to see headings and relationships • Reviewing notes for recurring themes • Using strategies in the Essential Test-Taking Skills Guide in Appendix A

FIGURE 6.3   Formats Commonly Used for Summary Notes

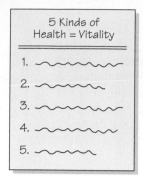

Lists/categories of information to remember

Comparison charts to compare or contrast different subjects studied

Notes based on topics that include textbook and lecture information

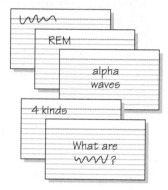

Flashcards of categories, terminology, and study questions

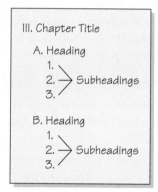

Chapter outlines made by using headings and subheadings

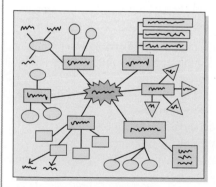

Visual mappings for individual chapters or topics that appear in several different chapters

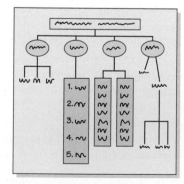

Large hierarchies made on poster paper to include several topics or chapters

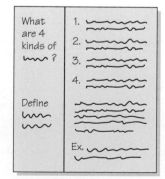

Cornell notes with study questions on the left for self-quizzing (see Chapter 9)

practice and ongoing review; it reduces tendencies to procrastinate, cram, or have test anxiety. The five-day study plan is based on the same four-step approach for setting goals that you learned in Chapter 5. Use the following steps to create a five-day study plan.

Step 1: Be Specific and Realistic

Begin by making a list of all the topics and materials that you need to review for the upcoming test. Following is an example for a sociology course.

Terminology	Lecture Notes	Textbook Notes
Study Guides	Chapter Reviews	Homework Assignments
Guest Speaker Notes	Notes from Video	Two Discussion Papers

Step 2: Set Target Days and Times

Organize specific blocks of time on days 1, 2, 3, and 4 for review sessions. On day 5, dedicate all of your study time to reviewing your *summary notes.* Mark the study/ review days and times on your calendar or your weekly schedule. Coordinate these times with other students if you are going to review with a study partner or study group.

Day 1	Day 2	Day 3	Day 4	Day 5
Monday Review Times:	Wednesday Review Times:	Friday Review Times:	Saturday Review Times:	Sunday Final Review Times:
8–9:00 AM	8–9:00 AM	8–9:00 AM	10:00 AM–12:00 PM	2–4:00 PM
3–5:00 PM	3–5:00 PM	3–5:00 PM	4–6:00 PM	7–9:00 PM

Step 3: Identify the Steps and a Plan of Action

Identify which chapters and which materials you will review on day 1, day 2, day 3, and finally on day 4. To avoid wasting review time, create a pattern or plan for reviewing each time you sit down. For example, your plan may be to use this sequence of review activities: review study guide, review chapter summary, review textbook notes, review terminology, review homework, review class handouts, and review lecture notes. Throughout this review process, plan to make *summary notes for the information you feel you need to review further* on day 5 and right before the test. Following is an example of a plan of action.

Example of a Plan of Action

Monday	Wednesday	Friday	Saturday	Sunday
8–9:00 AM (Ch. 1) class study guide homework Q handouts	8–9:00 AM (Ch. 2) study guide homework Q video notes	8–9:00 AM (Ch. 3) class study guide handouts homework Q	10–12:00 PM (Ch. 4) study guide (no handouts) homework Q 2 short papers	2–4:00 PM Review summary notes; self-quiz on Ch. 1 & 2
3–5:00 PM (Ch. 1) lecture notes textbook notes Notes-Guest speaker	3–5:00 PM (Ch. 2) lecture notes textbook notes	3–5:00 PM (Ch. 3) lecture notes textbook notes	4–6:00 PM (Ch. 4) lecture notes textbook notes	7–9:00 PM Review summary notes; self-quiz on Ch. 3 & 4

Step 4: Plan a Reward

Use an intrinsic reward at the end of each daily review time: the satisfaction that the studying is under control. Choose an intrinsic or an extrinsic reward for yourself *after* you complete your five-day study plan *and* after you complete the test.

For shorter tests, such as unit tests or tests for a module, you can use the same steps as those shown in the five-day study plan, but your plan will cover fewer days and less content. The important point is to identify what needs to be done and create a plan of action that organizes your time and your materials so you can review and prepare efficiently and thoroughly.

EXERCISE 6.2

Transfer These Skills

 PURPOSE: Creating summary notes and organizing a five-day study plan are two important processes you can use to organize your materials and your time for an upcoming test. Both take time but each has the potential to increase your test-taking performance.

DIRECTIONS: Unless your instructor provides you with alternative directions, choose to do one of the following assignments to demonstrate your ability to transfer skills from this chapter to other courses. On your paper, identify the course, the instructor, and the assignment option you selected.

1. For any one of your classes, create summary notes for an upcoming test. Use a variety of summary note formats. Remember, your summary notes reflect only the information that you know you need to study further to prepare for the test.

2. For any one of your classes, create a five-day study plan that shows the specific topics you need to review, the target dates and times for reviewing, the steps and your plan of action, and your reward. Use the format shown on page 161 for each step of the five-day study plan.

Reviewing for Upcoming Tests

Before beginning the review process, complete all reading or homework assignments so you do not need to mix review time with new learning time. If you have used ongoing review prior to the announcement of a test, you will find that preparing for a test will involve *reviewing* and not *studying to learn* information for a test. Preparing for tests becomes a matter of "brushing up" or "refreshing" your memory. If you did not dedicate adequate time for ongoing review each week, you now will need to dedicate more time to prepare for a test. Begin the review process by using the Essential Strategies for Reviewing for Tests shown in **Figure 6.4**. Details for each strategy follow.

Review Notes and Study Tools

After you have organized your notes and study tools by chapter, use *Look-Away Techniques* that involve reciting, visualizing, or writing the information from memory. The feedback you receive will indicate your ability to recall information accurately, or it will signal to you information that you need to place into summary notes to study and review further. (Review Figure 3.11, Essential Strategies for Using Feedback, p. 78.)

FIGURE 6.4   Essential Strategies for Reviewing for Tests

- Review notes and study tools.
- Practice associations, visualizations, and mnemonics.
- Review terminology.
- Rework math problems or series of steps.
- Review with others.
- Use the recency effect.

Practice Associations, Visualizations, and Mnemonics

Associations, visualizations, and mnemonics are three memory tools and strategies that provide you with effective retrieval cues to recall information from long-term memory. Practicing associations may involve reciting definitions for terminology, linking key words to a chart or a graphic in the textbook, or associating a list of people or events to their achievements or significance. Practicing visualizations may involve using Look Away Techniques to retrieve the visual image or impression of a visual mapping, or it may involve replaying a movie in your mind of a series of steps or actions. In a later section, you will learn about mnemonics and ways to practice or rehearse these memory tools. Actively practicing these processes strengthens your recall ability and integrates information from throughout the chapter or the term.

Review Terminology

Understanding the course terminology provides you with a strong foundation that will help you answer questions, think through information, and conduct memory searches to find correct answers. With a partner or by yourself, practice reciting or writing definitions for all the terminology in the chapters that will be included on the test. Practice using the three-part definition format that includes a category for the word, a formal definition, and one additional detail to expand the definition. Use any online flashcard drills or vocabulary exercises available for your textbook.

Rework Math Problems or Series of Steps

To process procedural knowledge requires repetition, repetition, and more repetition in order to increase speed and accuracy. Rework textbook, classroom, and homework problems. Review the prototypes or models of problems you memorized for different types of equations. Verbalize the steps you use to solve the problems. Check your accuracy by referring back to the solution to each problem.

Review with Others

Review sessions are an effective way to receive immediate feedback about the topics you understand clearly and those that you need to review further. Review sessions also provide you the opportunity to verbalize, explain information in your own words, and answer practice test questions. *Study groups* are also an effective way to prepare for tests. If a study group does not exist, you can create one with members of your class. To be effective and time-efficient, a study group needs to have structure;

CONCEPT CHECK 6.5

How do each of the review strategies test your ability to retrieve learned information from long-term memory?

therefore, establish clear guidelines or expectations so the study group is not seen as a casual, socializing event. As members of the group, you could agree to:

- Individually write practice test questions to present to the group
- Take turns leading a discussion for a specific topic that will be covered on the test
- Have each student summarize important information for specific chapters and provide group members with a set of summary notes for those chapters
- Bring study tools, such as flashcards, to use to quiz each other

Use the Recency Effect

> The recency effect states that the items you will remember more easily are items that you most recently practiced.

The *recency effect* states that the items you will remember more easily are items that you most recently practiced. When using a five-day study plan, you utilize this recency effect when the fifth day of this plan is the day before a test. You can also utilize this recency effect by reviewing summary notes one final time right before you go to bed the night before a test. For the greatest impact, avoid placing any other kinds of stimuli, such as television or a movie, between your review time and your sleep. As you sleep, your mind may continue thinking about and integrating the information you reviewed. You can also gain the benefits of the recency effect by reviewing summary notes one final time the day of the test or the hour before the test.

EXERCISE 6.3

Academic Preparation Inventory

PURPOSE: Your grades on tests often reflect the effectiveness of your study and review strategies. Identifying your strengths and weaknesses before a test and after you receive test results provides you with an opportunity to identify which strategies work and which you need to modify or replace.

DIRECTIONS: Go to Exercise 6.3 in Appendix C, page C11, to complete the inventory.

CHECK POINT 6.1

Answers appear on page B3

True or False?

_____ 1. Students who do not use ongoing review or a five-day study plan may need to resort to last minute cramming.

_____ 2. Participating in small study groups is always more effective and productive than using your time to review by yourself.

_____ 3. One effective strategy is to study thoroughly the day before a test and then enjoy a movie or some type of recreational activity at night before you go to sleep.

_____ 4. The feedback you receive from Look-Away Techniques can help you determine what information to put into summary notes.

 Access Chapter 6 Practice Quiz 1: Preparing for Tests under "Interactive Quizzes" in your College Success CourseMate, accessed through *CengageBrain .com*.

CHAPTER 6
REFLECTIVE WRITING 1

On separate paper, in a journal, or online at this textbook's CourseMate Web site, respond to the following questions:

1. For the majority of test-taking situations you encounter, do you enter the classroom feeling confident and well-prepared for the test? Explain your answer.

2. What specific test-preparation techniques do you use regularly? Are they effective for you or do you

need to learn to use better test-preparation strategies? Explain your answer by giving specific details.

3. Overall, are you satisfied or dissatisfied with grades you receive on tests? Explain your answer by giving specific details.

Access Chapter 6 Reflective Writing 1 in your College Success CourseMate, accessed through *CengageBrain.com*.

Test Performance Skills

2 *Identify and explain effective strategies for performing well on tests.*

Feeling slightly nervous or apprehensive when you first enter the classroom or when the instructor distributes the test is a normal reaction to testing situations. Strive to use strategies to calm your nerves, establish a positive state of mind, and mentally prepare to do well on the test. The following are strategies to establish a positive mindset for tests:

- Arrive to class early. Rushing in at the last minute or arriving late adds stress and does not allow you time to mentally prepare.

- Use positive self-talk, a quick relaxation or visualization technique, or a concentration technique to focus your mind.

- Focus only on yourself; ignore other students and their nervous reactions to the test.

- If you have a few minutes before the test is distributed, mentally rehearse information from your summary notes. Or, if allowed, review your summary notes one final time.

- Listen carefully to the directions. Your instructor may announce corrections on the test, suggestions for completing the test, the amount of time available for the test, and other important directions.

Essential Test-Taking Strategies

The **Essential Test-Taking Skills Guide** in **Appendix A** provides you with sixty-five easy-to-use strategies for all test question formats. The strategies are easy-to-read and understand so you can use a self-study approach at any time during the term. When you know an upcoming test will focus on a specific type of test question, you may refer to that specific section in Appendix A to prepare for the test. You can remove the Essential Test-Taking Skills Guide and place it in your notebook for quick reference for taking tests in any of your classes.

For now, you can begin strengthening your test-taking skills by using the Essential Strategies for Taking Tests in **Figure 6.5**. You can use these strategies from the beginning to the end of a test-taking situation. Details for each strategy appear in the following sections.

Immediate Response

Immediate Response, the first level of response to a test question, involves immediately knowing the answer. As soon as you read the question, you are able to provide an answer with confidence and certainty. The question automatically triggers an association with information in your long-term memory. This is the payoff or reward for effective studying.

Strategy: When there is no immediate response, move to the next level of response, the delayed response.

Delayed Response

Delayed Response, the second level of response to a test question, involves carefully rereading a question and conducting memory searches for the answer. After reading the question a second time, go into "retrieval mode" by using an association, visualization, mnemonic, or auditory cue to help locate and retrieve the answer from your long-term memory. Think of things you know that are related to the question as this process may trigger a chained association and the answer may "pop" into memory. If that process doesn't produce an answer, try using these steps:

1. Mentally ask yourself questions to see if your questions trigger an association. *When did we discuss this? What chapter is this from? What other things belong in a category with this term? Is it a vocabulary term?*

2. Try *visualizing* the information as it appeared in your notes, in your study tools, in the class lecture, or in the textbook.

3. Try tapping into your *auditory memory* by recalling your instructor's words or your own words when you recited the information or discussed it with other students or in class.

Strategy: If no answer surfaces, *place a small check mark next to the question* and leave the question unanswered at this time. Plan to return to this question later when you use assisted response.

Assisted Response

After you have answered with confidence and certainty as many questions on the test as possible, return to the unanswered questions that you marked with a check mark. Carefully reread each question to see if you can now answer it. Information from other questions may trigger an association to help you answer the question now. If you still cannot answer the question, use assisted response.

Assisted Response, the third level of response to a test question, involves using other questions in the test to assist you with answering a question. Begin by identifying a key word in the question. Then *skim through the test* looking for other questions that have that key word. Reread those questions to see if they trigger an appropriate answer for your unanswered question. Often the test itself can assist you with finding answers for questions.

Strategy: If none of these strategies result in an answer, move to the next level of response, educated selection.

Educated Selection

Educated Selection, also called *educated guessing,* is the fourth level of response to a test question that involves using a variety of strategies to increase your odds in selecting the correct answer. This strategy involves the use of logic and thinking skills, so in actuality, it is more than mere guessing. This educated selection (or educated

---

Immediate response, the first level of response to a test question, involves immediately knowing the answer.

Delayed response, the second level of response to a test question, involves carefully rereading a question and conducting memory searches for the answer.

CONCEPT CHECK 6.7

What four levels of answering questions do effective test-takers use? Briefly describe each.

Assisted response, the third level of response to a test question, involves using other questions in the test to assist you with answering a question.

Educated selection, also called *educated guessing,* is the fourth level of response to a test question that involves using a variety of strategies to increase your odds in selecting the correct answer.

guessing) response is a last-resort strategy that may increase your odds for selecting the correct answer, but it does not guarantee a correct answer. Use educated selection only when all else fails.

Strategy: See **Essential Test-Taking Skills Guide** in **Appendix A** for educated selection strategies for objective test questions.

Computerized Tests

Computerized tests usually consist of multiple-choice questions. These tests may be written by the instructor, but more often they consist of questions from a test bank generated by the textbook author or publisher. Some of the test banks randomly assign test questions of varying levels of difficulty; other test banks allow the instructor to tag which questions to use on a test.

Taking computerized tests has both advantages and disadvantages. One advantage is that you receive immediate feedback and a score for your test. When you answer correctly, the positive feedback increases your confidence level. Another advantage is that usually the time limit to complete a test is less rigid than when you take a test in class. Because you can control the pace for answering questions, you may feel less stress. One disadvantage is that any negative feedback that indicates an incorrect answer may cause stress and frustration. Also, most computerized tests do not allow you to go back to previous questions to change answers or use the test-taking strategy of assisted response. Finally, you usually do not get a printed copy of the test to review later when you study for your final exam.

If you have not already experienced computerized testing, chances are good that you will at some time during your college career. For practice taking computerized tests, go to the CourseMate Web site for this textbook. Complete the Practice Quizzes and Chapter Quizzes at the end of each chapter. **Figure 6.7** summarizes seven Essential Strategies for Taking Computerized Tests. Following are details about these strategies.

Know the Rules for Computerized Testing

Prior to taking a computerized test, gather as much information as possible about the rules for computerized testing. Ask questions such as the following: *Is there a tutorial or practice test? May I take the test more than once? Is there a time limit for completing the test? May I have blank scratch paper and pen to work out problems or to organize my thoughts? Will I be able to get a printed version of the test to use for studying after the test is scored?*

> **CONCEPT CHECK 6.8**
>
> *Do you prefer computerized tests over paper-pencil tests? Why or why not?*

| FIGURE 6.7 | Essential Strategies for Taking Computerized Tests |

- Know the rules for computerized testing.
- Allow yourself ample time to complete the test.
- Understand the computer and the testing software commands.
- Read and choose answers carefully.
- Learn from incorrect answers.
- Use relaxation techniques.
- Discuss your test-taking experience.

Allow Yourself Ample Time to Complete the Test

For many students, taking computerized tests requires more time than taking tests in the classroom. Therefore, you will want to avoid going into the computer lab when you are rushed or pressed for time. Select a time of day when you feel mentally sharp and best able to concentrate. When you enter the lab, choose a computer that is not in the line of a steady flow of traffic so you will experience fewer distractions. Finally, do not postpone taking the test or wait until close to the final deadline set to complete the test.

Understand the Computer and the Testing Software Commands

Ask for help if you are unfamiliar with the computer, need help logging on, or do not understand how to select or change answers. Ask for help if you do not know how to save your test results. Read all the directions carefully. Notice whether or not the software program allows you to return to previous questions or change previous answers.

Read and Choose Answers Carefully

Read the beginning of the multiple-choice question carefully. Try to complete the question in your own words. Then, examine the options given as possible answers before selecting your answer. The **Essential Test-Taking Skills Guide** in **Appendix A** explains how to combine the opening of a multiple-choice question with each option to form true-false statements to help you identify the correct answers. The strategies for multiple-choice questions used for paper-pencil tests are the same as those used for computerized tests.

Do not answer too quickly. Once you have decided on your answer, reread the opening part of the question with the option you believe completes the statement correctly. You can often avoid careless mistakes by double-checking an answer before selecting it as your final answer.

Learn from Incorrect Answers

Do *not* immediately move to the next question when you receive feedback that your answer is incorrect. Instead, use this feedback as a learning opportunity. Reread the question and if the correct answer is provided, study the correct answer. Similar information may appear in another question, so the feedback may help you answer later questions correctly. This strategy also keeps your mind focused on the materials and reduces the tendency to move too hastily to the next question.

Use Relaxation Techniques

Pause and use a short relaxation technique if you find yourself tensing up, feeling discouraged, or getting irritated. Working memory needs to remain free of mental clutter; stress or anxiety affect thinking processes. Breathing by threes, using positive self-talk, or stretching your arms, rolling your shoulders, or shaking out your hands help reduce stress.

Discuss Your Test-Taking Experience

Before you leave the test, jot down any questions that concerned or confused you. Discuss these questions with your instructor. Make a brief list of topics you need to review or study further. After taking several tests, if you remain uncomfortable with computerized tests, ask lab assistants or your instructor for additional test-taking strategies. Talk to other students to learn their strategies. Ask your instructor if there is an option to take a paper-pencil or written test.

Learning from Your Tests

Do you sometimes receive your graded tests, look at the grade, and then stick the test into your notebook or backpack? A more effective approach involves using the tests for valuable feedback and then analyzing the effectiveness of your learning strategies. With the information you learn from analyzing your test, create a plan of action to adjust your study and learning strategies to bring even greater results on your next test.

Examine the Questions You Answered Correctly

Understanding what processes you used to answer questions correctly helps you recognize what is working for you. Answer the following questions:

- What strategies did I use to learn this information?
- What was the original source of the information? Did I learn the information in class, through a homework assignment, from the textbook, or from a combination of sources?
- Was the information new to me or did I already know this information at the time it was presented?

Look for Patterns of Errors

Repeat the process you used to examine the questions you correctly answered. For example, perhaps the information that you missed the most frequently appeared mainly in the textbook or as information presented in class during lectures. This feedback makes you more aware of the need to focus greater attention on your textbook reading skills and strategies or on your notetaking skills for class lectures.

Correct Your Errors

You want to override or erase incorrect information and replace it with accurate information. Create and practice new associations so the next time you need to retrieve that information from your schemas, you will recall accurate information. Frequently during the course of a term, previously learned information appears again on future tests or as knowledge upon which new information is built. Therefore, taking time to learn the correct information strengthens the memory schema with accurate details.

> ### CONCEPT CHECK 6.9
>
> *How can you use graded tests to improve your understanding and future performance on tests? Be specific.*

CHECK POINT 6.2

Answers appear on page B3

True or False?

_____ 1. Students who use metacognition use test results to analyze and modify their choice of learning strategies to use for that specific course.

_____ 2. Once you mark an answer, you should never go back and change that answer.

_____ 3. The third level of response to answer test questions involves using other parts of the test to search for clues to answer a question.

_____ 4. When taking computerized tests, it is important to move through the test as quickly as possible to avoid forgetting information that appeared in earlier questions.

_____ 5. Educated selection is also referred to as educated guessing.

 Access Chapter 6 Practice Quiz 3: Performing on Tests under "Interactive Quizzes" in your College Success CourseMate, accessed through *CengageBrain.com*.

Practice Test-Taking Skills

Read the information in the **Essential Test-Taking Skills Guide** in **Appendix A.** Then go to Exercise 6.4 in Appendix page C12–C15 to practice test-taking skills for objective and recall questions. You may work by yourself, with a partner, or in a small group to complete this exercise. If your instructor does not assign Exercise 6.4, you can complete the exercise by yourself or later as a review tool to prepare for a midterm exam in this course.

Test Anxiety Management Skills

3 *Identify and explain effective strategies for managing test anxiety.*

> **Test anxiety** is excessive stress that hinders a person's ability to perform well *before* or *during* a test.

In Chapter 5, you learned that *stress* is defined as your reaction or response to events or situations that threaten to disrupt your normal pattern or routine. With normal stress, a person is aware of the stress, aware of the source of the stress, and still able to control his or her reaction or responses. Stress specifically related to an upcoming test can be beneficial and motivate people to perform on higher levels; however, excessive stress that becomes test anxiety creates negative responses and consequences.

Anxiety occurs when the level of stress is excessive to the point that it hinders performance. Using the stress-management techniques in Chapter 5 helps prevent stress from accelerating to the level of anxiety, but for individuals who do experience a bout with anxiety, knowing how to manage it can reduce its effects, duration, and intensity. When people experience a bout of anxiety, they no longer recognize the source of the excessive stress and have little or no control of the situation. They are reactionary rather than oriented to problem solving.

Test anxiety is a specific form of anxiety. **Test anxiety** is excessive stress that hinders a person's ability to perform well *before* or *during* a test. Test anxiety before and during a test can exhibit its presence in physical, emotional, cognitive, and behavioral forms. For example, a student might become ill, emotionally distraught, experience confused or disorganized thinking, or use avoidance strategies to procrastinate studying for a test. During a test, test anxiety affects cognitive processing and can immobilize thinking skills. A student may "go blank," make excessive careless mistakes, mark answers in the wrong place, or quit due to frustration. **Figure 6.8** shows common symptoms related to test anxiety.

©Images Source/Getty

Reviewing with other students and using available resources, such as online practice tests, can help you prepare for tests, strengthen your test-taking skills, and reduce or eliminate test anxiety. What other strategies can you use to control test anxiety and its effects on your performance?

FIGURE 6.8	Symptoms Related to Test Anxiety		
Physical Symptoms of Anxiety	Rapid heartbeat Upset stomach, nausea Abnormal nervousness Tight muscles, tension	Blurred vision Increased blood pressure Shakiness	Headaches Clammy palms More than normal sweating
Emotional Symptoms of Anxiety	Fear, anger, frustration Irritable, short-tempered Fatigue	Feelings of hopelessness or lack of control of a situation	"Fight or flight" feelings Anxious, nervous, panicky Depressed
Cognitive Symptoms of Anxiety	Mind filled with intrusive thoughts Poor concentration Inaccurate or limited recall Confusion, disorientation	Impulsive responses Negative self-talk Lack of clear thinking Misdirected attention "Going blank"	Fixating on one item too long Careless mistakes Overemphasis on negative thoughts
Behavioral Symptoms of Anxiety	Crying, sobbing Strained facial expressions	Slumped posture Procrastination	Shaky voice Aggressive behavior

EXERCISE 6.5

Test Anxiety Inventory

PURPOSE: Some students may experience test anxiety, which impacts their test performance; other students may experience test-related stress that actually motivates them to perform well. This inventory provides you with information about test anxiety indicators you may experience.

DIRECTIONS: Go to Exercise 6.5 in Appendix C, page C16, to complete this inventory.

Sources of Test Anxiety

Test anxiety is a *learned behavior*. As such, it can be unlearned. If you experience test anxiety, begin by analyzing the source of your anxiety. In other words, what triggers your test anxiety? Sometimes listening to the kinds of comments you make about tests will help you identify the source of your test anxiety. *Under-preparedness, past experiences, fear of failure,* and *poor test-taking skills* are four common sources of test anxiety.

Under-Preparedness

Students who do not apply study skills on a regular basis often need to resort to *cramming,* which is an attempt to learn large amounts of information in a short period of time. Cramming is a survival technique that often backfires. Frequently, students who cram become even more aware of how much *they do not know*

CONCEPT CHECK 6.10

What symptoms might you exhibit if you experience test anxiety? If you have test anxiety, does it appear before or during a test?

Feeling under-prepared can create test anxiety and lead to poor test performance. Following are student comments that indicate under-preparedness:

- I am nervous about this test because I did not have enough time to study or review.
- When I started reviewing, I realized how much I still needed to learn.
- Everyone else seems to know more than I do. I should have studied more.
- I can't keep up; there's too much information to learn in this class.

Past Experiences

As you recall, low self-esteem is often the result of past experiences that left a person with a negative self-image or perception of his or her limited ability to perform well. Having experienced frustration, disappointment, or a sense of failure in past testing situations can create a cycle of negative self-talk, self-doubt, low self-esteem, and low self-confidence. Often times, students who have experienced negative past experiences lay the blame for poor performance on other people instead of taking responsibility for their test results. Following are student comments that reflect test anxiety due to past experiences:

- I never get decent grades on tests.
- I did not do well on the last test, so this test probably won't be any different.
- Instructors write tricky tests that are not fair and are designed to flunk most students.
- Tests make me feel stupid and embarrassed.

Fear of Failure

Another source of procrastination is the fear of failure. This same fear of failure is a source of test anxiety for many students. They fear the negative consequences of poor grades, which in turn increases stress levels which may trigger test anxiety. Following are student comments that reflect test anxiety triggered by the fear of failure:

- I am so worried that my grades will disappoint my parents.
- I am so concerned that my grades will affect my scholarship.
- If I don't pass this test with a good grade, my GPA for the term is ruined.
- A bad grade on this test will prove that I am in way over my head and shouldn't even be taking this class.

Poor Test-Taking Skills

For many students, the source of test anxiety is linked directly to the lack of test preparation skills and the lack of test-taking skills. Taking tests requires understanding kinds of test questions as well as how to read and interpret questions accurately, conduct memory searches for answers, select answers carefully, and write appropriate answers.

Following are student comments that reflect that poor test-taking skills are the source of test-anxiety:

- I have never learned how to be a good test-taker.
- I get nervous taking tests because I do not really know how to answer different kinds of questions.
- I make a lot of mistakes because I have problems understanding the directions or the kind of answers that are expected.
- I never have enough time on tests to really show how much I know.

CONCEPT CHECK 6.11

What is test anxiety? When and why does it occur?

GROUP PROCESSING

A COLLABORATIVE LEARNING ACTIVITY

1. Form groups of three or four students. Your group will need to have a chart to record responses. Select one member of your group to be the group recorder.

2. Create the following chart. In the "Strategies" column, brainstorm and list strategies students could use to "unlearn" the behaviors and beliefs that cause test anxiety. Use your knowledge of strategies for Principles of Memory, self-management skills, as well as strategies from this chapter to recommend strategies to combat sources of test anxiety.

Source	Strategies
Under-preparedness	
Past Experiences	
Fear of Failure	
Poor Test-Taking Skills	

Access Chapter 6 Topics In-Depth: Strategies to Reduce Test Anxiety in your College Success CourseMate, accessed through *CengageBrain* .com.

Strategies to Use *Before* a Test

In the Group Processing Activity, you and members of your group listed an array of strategies from previous chapters to deal with test anxiety. Following are a few such strategies that may have appeared on your lists.

- Set learning goals.
- Use ongoing review.
- Recognize your strengths.
- Use Look-Away Techniques.
- Mentally rehearse.
- Use schedules.
- Use affirmations.
- Improve motivation.
- Make summary notes.
- Predict test questions.
- Use effective study strategies.
- Use positive self-talk.
- Recite and use feedback.
- Create plans of action.
- Review with a partner.

Two new strategies, locus of control and systematic desensitization, also work effectively to help students with test anxiety reduce their excessive stress before a test.

Locus of Control

Locus of control is the degree to which a person feels power to control circumstances in his or her life. Individuals with an *internal locus of control* feel that they

Locus of control is the degree to which a person feels power to control circumstances in his or her life.

FIGURE 6.9   Locus of Control

External Locus of Control	Internal Locus of Control
• I did not do well because my instructor does not like me.	• I need to adjust my attitude—quickly.
• This test is totally unfair.	• I take full responsibility; I was not prepared for this test.
• I could not study because of my children.	• I forgot to study the charts.
• All the questions were trick questions.	• I need to find more time to myself to study.
• I failed the test because it was poorly written.	• I am going to talk to the tutor about my test-taking strategies.
• My instructor did not even take the time to try to understand what I wrote.	• I am going to use more ongoing review every week.
• My instructor did not understand my situation.	• I am going to work to improve my writing skills.
• The textbook didn't explain this clearly.	• I can learn from this experience.

CONCEPT CHECK 6.12

How do the behavior and attitudes of a person with an external locus of control differ from a person with an internal locus of control? Be specific.

Systematic desensitization is an anxiety-reducing strategy that involves a series of activities designed to reduce strong negative emotional reactions to an upcoming situation.

CONCEPT CHECK 6.13

What fear have you ever had that escalated to the degree that the thing you feared became greatly over-exaggerated? How could you use systematic desensitization to deflate such a fear?

have the power to control most situations or circumstances in their lives. They exhibit self-confidence and a high sense of self-efficacy. When they do not do as well as expected, they accept responsibility for outcomes and use problem-solving techniques to create plans for improvement. Students with an internal locus of control experience test anxiety less frequently than students with an external locus of control.

Individuals with an *external locus of control* relinquish control and see other people or other situations as having the power and control over their circumstances. They blame others for their personal shortcomings instead of accepting personal responsibility. They tend to have low self-esteem, low confidence in their abilities, and high levels of frustration. Students with an external locus of control experience test anxiety more frequently and to greater degrees. To reduce test anxiety, the locus of control needs to shift from external to internal. **Figure 6.9** shows how attitudes and statements differ between people with an external and an internal locus of control.

Systematic Desensitization

Systematic desensitization is an anxiety-reducing strategy that involves a series of activities designed to reduce strong negative emotional reactions to an upcoming situation. You can use this strategy before the day of a test by replacing your fear-based thoughts with positive thoughts that emphasize the successes you have already experienced. Systematic desensitization stops the fear from accelerating and getting blown out of proportion. You can use systematic desensitization in the following ways:

1. **Reduce your emotional response to trigger words.** Make a list of specific situations or words that trigger your test anxiety. For example, "There will be a test next Monday" may trigger early test anxiety. After you have your list of *trigger situations or words,* visualize yourself reacting differently to those situations or words. See yourself responding in a more positive and constructive way. "Good. I have time to make a five-day plan, or I have stayed current with my work, so I can be ready for this test."

2. **Predict and write practice test questions.** Decide on an appropriate amount of time to answer the test questions. Create a test environment as close as

possible to the real thing. If the classroom in which you will take a test is empty, be in that room when you take your practice test.

Strategies to Use *During* a Test

You can reduce or eliminate most test anxiety that occurs during a test by using the essential strategies for taking tests shown in **Figure 6.5**, page 166. The following strategies address specific symptoms that you might experience during a bout with anxiety during a test.

- **You go "blank" and are unable to recall the needed information.**

  Strategies: 1. Use a quick relaxation technique to calm yourself down.

   2. Use positive self-talk. Become your own cheerleader.

   3. Reread the question in a whisper voice. Go into retrieval mode by conducting a new memory search. If necessary, place a check mark to return to the question later. Do not stay stuck on the question.

- **Your eyes start jumping from the printed line or skip over words when you read.**

  Strategies: 1. Use your arm, a blank index card, or a blank piece of paper to block off the rest of the test. Restricting your vision so you only see the question that you are contemplating helps your eyes stay focused on a line of information.

   2. Use your pencil to point to each word as you read silently. Doing this keeps your eyes from skipping words or jumping to other lines of print.

- **You notice yourself making excessive careless mistakes in selecting or marking the correct answer.**

  Strategies: 1. Slow down the reading and answering process.

   2. Activate your auditory channel by mouthing or quietly whispering the words as you read the directions, questions, and options for answers.

   3. Highlight key words in the questions. Check to ensure that your answer relates to the key words.

   4. Before moving to the next question, ask yourself: Does this answer make sense?

- **Your mind shifts away from the test and your concentration begins fading quickly.**

  Strategies: 1. Become more active and interactive with the test. Circle direction words and highlight key words in directions and questions.

   2. Use positive self-talk and force yourself to keep your eyes on the test. "I can do this. My eyes and my mind stay focused on the paper. I can figure this out."

By using the strategies in this chapter for preparing for and taking tests, you will see changes in your study habits and strategies and in your test results. These changes also affect your level of confidence, your self-esteem, your locus of control, and your ability to manage test anxiety.

CONCEPT CHECK 6.14

What may happen to your eyes, your concentration, and your cognitive skills when you are experiencing test anxiety? How can you combat these effects?

Textbook Case Studies

DIRECTIONS

1. Read each case study carefully. Respond to the question at the end of each case study by using *specific* strategies discussed in this chapter. Answer in complete sentences.

2. Write your responses on paper or online at the CourseMate student Web site, Textbook Case Studies. You will be able to print your online response or e-mail it to your instructor.

CASE STUDY 1: Adolpho has not been in school for fifteen years. He never learned how to study or take tests. He works hard, and he is able to respond in class and in study groups to questions that are related to the current assignment. However, when it is time to take tests that cover several chapters of information, he freezes and goes blank. What test-preparation and test-taking strategies would you recommend Adolpho start using?

CASE STUDY 2: Jenny does not study much for her communications class because she is taking the class for pass/no pass rather than a letter grade. As the end of the term approaches, she realizes that she may not have enough points to pass the class. She intends to deal with the situation the way she usually deals with tests—cramming in the day or two before the final exam. What test-preparation strategies would you suggest that Jenny use during the final two weeks of the term?

Access Chapter 6 Textbook Case Studies and Web-Only Case Studies in your College Success CourseMate, accessed through *CengageBrain.com*.

CHECK POINT 6.3

Answers appear on page B3.

True-False?

_____ 1. Students who have an internal locus of control frequently make excuses and see others as the source of their test anxiety.

_____ 2. Students with test anxiety may exhibit physical, emotional, cognitive, or behavioral symptoms of excessive stress.

_____ 3. Test anxiety is a learned behavior caused mainly by poor test-taking skills.

_____ 4. When test anxiety occurs during a test, your eyes may jump around on the page, your mind may go blank, or you may have confused thinking.

_____ 5. Systematic desensitization is a process used to reduce your emotional response to an upcoming situation.

Access Chapter 6 Practice Quiz 4: Test Anxiety under "Interactive Quizzes" in your College Success CourseMate, accessed through *CengageBrain.com*.

Mnemonics

4 *Identify and explain ways to use mnemonics to prepare for tests.*

Mnemonics are memory tools that serve as bridges to help you recall information from long-term memory. Mnemonics always involve creating some form of an association. You may want to use mnemonics, but sparingly, to create associations and retrieval cues for information that is otherwise difficult to recall. If you use mnemonics too extensively, they increase the amount of information you need to remember. If you do not memorize the mnemonic in its exact form, or if you do not practice translating the mnemonic back into its original meaning, it can hinder and confuse you rather than help you recall information accurately. In the CourseMate student Web site, Topics In-Depth: Kinds of Mnemonics, you can learn more about using different kinds of mnemonics. In this section, the focus will be on creating acronyms, acrostics, word associations, picture associations, and the Loci Method for information that you want to remember and be able to retrieve from memory when you are taking tests.

Mnemonics are memory tools that serve as bridges to help you recall information from long-term memory.

CONCEPT CHECK 6.15

What mnemonics have you created and used? Explain how they are helpful memory cues.

Acronyms

An *acronym* is a word or phrase made by using the first letter of key words in a list of items to remember. An acronym forms an association and works as a retrieval cue to recall the original items in the list. The mnemonic SAVE CRIB FOTO is an acronym for the Twelve Principles of Memory. A classic acronym is the word *HOMES* for the five Great Lakes in the northern United States: <u>H</u>uron, <u>O</u>ntario, <u>M</u>ichigan, <u>E</u>rie, and <u>S</u>uperior. For any acronym to work, you must practice translating the letters of the acronym back into the original words that the letters represent. For example, if you are asked to name the Great Lakes or name the Twelve Principles of Memory, giving the answer "HOMES" or "SAVE CRIB FOTO" would not suffice for an answer.

An *acronym* is a word or phrase made by using the first letter of key words in a list of items to remember.

Use the following steps to create an acronym:

1. **List items:** Write the list of items you need to remember.

2. **Write letters:** On paper, write the **first letter** of each item in the list. If an item in the list consists of more than one word, select only one key word to use for that item.

3. **Rearrange letters:** Unless the items in the list must be learned in the original order, rearrange the letters to form a word or a phrase. If you do not have at least one vowel (*a, e, i, o, u,* and sometimes *y*), you will not be able to create an acronym that is a real word in English. A real word is easier to recall than a nonsense word, so strive to rearrange the letters to create a real word or phrase.

4. **Practice:** Practice translating your acronym. For your acronym to be useful to you, memorize the acronym, repeat it several times, and practice translating it back to the original words in the list of items.

 Access Chapter 6 Topics In-Depth: Kinds of Mnemonics in your College Success CourseMate, accessed through *CengageBrain.com.*

Acrostics

If you are not able to create an acronym, you can always use the first letter of each key word to create an acrostic. An *acrostic* is a *sentence* made by using the first letter of key words in a list of items to remember. You can use the letters in their original order, or you can rearrange the letters to create the sentence. A classic example of an acrostic is the sentence, *<u>P</u>lease <u>e</u>xcuse <u>m</u>y <u>d</u>ear <u>A</u>unt <u>S</u>ally*. The first letters of each

An *acrostic* is a sentence made by using the first letter of key words in a list of items to remember.

How is an acrostic different than an acronym? Which is easier to use? Why do you think so?

word in this sentence represent the order of operations in math problems: parentheses, exponents, multiplication, division, addition, and subtraction. Note that you cannot add additional words to the sentence. Use acrostics sparingly as they tend to be more difficult to use effectively and result in one more piece of information you need to remember. As with acronyms, you must practice translating the acrostic into the original words for items in your list.

EXERCISE 6.7

Creating Acronyms and Acrostics

PURPOSE: Acronyms are a common type of mnemonic used to remember items in a list. When you cannot create an acronym, you can create an acrostic.

DIRECTIONS: Create an acronym or an acrostic as indicated for the following items.

1. A pediatrician's advice for food a child should eat when he or she has a stomach flu: bananas, applesauce, toast, rice. (Letters to use: b a t r) Acronym:_____

2. Ten body systems in humans: skeletal, digestive, muscular, endocrine, circulatory, nervous, reproductive, urinary, respiratory, and integumentary. (Letters to use: s d m e c n r u r i) Acronym:_____

3. The seven coordinating conjunctions used to form compound sentences: for, and, nor, yet, but, so, or. (Letters to use: f a n y b s o) Acronym:_____

4. Vertical structures of the atmosphere, beginning with the closest to the Earth: troposphere, stratosphere, mesosphere, and thermosphere. (Letters to use: t s m t) Acrostic:_____
_____

5. Skeletal (bone) structure of the arm: humerus, ulna, radius, carpals, phalanges. (Letters to use: h u r c p) Acrostic:_____
_____

Word Associations

If you have strong language or musical skills, you can use those skills to create word associations that use *rhymes, jingles, short songs,* and *raps* that work as memory tools to recall information. The following examples of word associations demonstrate the use of linguistic and musical skills to create mnemonics:

- Use *i* before *e* except after *c* or when sounded like *a* as in *neighbor* and *weigh*.
- In fourteen hundred and ninety-two, Columbus sailed the ocean blue.
- Spring forward; fall back (daylight-saving time).
- Who invented dynamite? *Alfred Nobel had quite a fright when he discovered dynamite.*
- Which way should you turn to open a jar or tighten a bolt? *Righty tighty, lefty loosy*

- What is the difference between *stalagmites* and *stalactites?* (Stalagmites are deposits of minerals that project upward from the floor of a cavern; stalactites project downward from the ceiling of a cavern.) You can use this jingle to differentiate between the two: *When the mites go up, the tights come down.*
- Use a familiar tune. Create lyrics with information you need to learn and sing them to a favorite tune or melody such as "Happy Birthday" or "Rudolph the Red-Nosed Reindeer."

Picture Associations

To use picture associations effectively, you need to actively look for and think about ways to create simple associations that will be easy to remember and use to recall information. Actively search for a familiar object or picture to use in your association. Visualize the shape and colors of the objects. Sometimes you can recall picture associations easier if you exaggerate some part of an object by making it larger than its real size or if you turn them into whimsical cartoon figures. Add sounds and smells to the association when appropriate. **Figure 6.10** shows a picture association for Gardner's eight intelligences.

If you are adding letters to your picture, use large, bold capital letters. The following are suggestions for using picture associations to remember different kinds of information:

1. **To remember a person's name:** Associate the name with an object or another person you know with that name.

2. **To remember a definition:** Associate the meaning with an object that has a similar characteristic.

3. **To remember a specific number:** Find and visualize a number pattern within the number.

4. **To remember a cause-effect relationship:** Picture the items as an action movie.

The Loci Method

The *Loci Method* is a mnemonic technique that involves associating items or topics with specific rooms in a familiar building. *Loci* (pronounced lo-si), which means *locations,* dates back to the early times of Greek orators, who could deliver lengthy

The Loci Method is a mnemonic technique that involves associating items or topics with specific rooms in a familiar building.

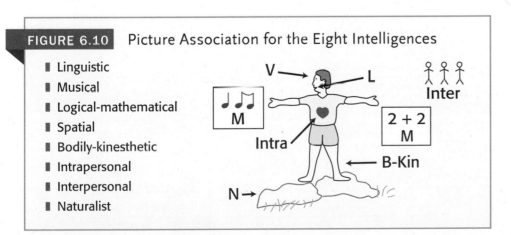

FIGURE 6.10 Picture Association for the Eight Intelligences

- Linguistic
- Musical
- Logical-mathematical
- Spatial
- Bodily-kinesthetic
- Intrapersonal
- Interpersonal
- Naturalist

CONCEPT CHECK 6.18

What Principles of Memory are activated when you use the Loci Method?

speeches without any written notes by making instead mental notes that associated parts or topics of their speeches with familiar rooms or locations in a building. As they mentally walked through each room, they visualized items in the rooms that they associated with the topic to be discussed and then used this structure to deliver organized, fluent speeches. You can also use the Loci Method to memorize points you want to make in a speech, in an essay, or in a discussion. Use the following steps for the Loci Method:

1. **Items:** Make a list of the items you need to remember.

2. **Floor plan:** Draw a floor plan of a familiar location.

3. **Pictures:** On paper or mentally, attach pictures. Attach a picture of the first item you need to remember inside the first location or room on your floor plan. Walk through the floor plan, attaching one item to each room. You can exaggerate the size or shape of the picture or hang it in an unusual position to make it stand out in your memory.

4. **Practice:** Visually practice (visualize) walking through all the rooms and reciting the important information associated with the items in the rooms.

In the following example, a student used the Loci Method for a speech about the end of the economic boom in the 1970s. He sketched the floor plan and numbered eight locations on the floor plan. He later realized he only needed to use five locations. At each of the first five locations, he mentally attached a picture that represented the topic he wanted to present in his speech. In the following list, the bold faced items show the topics he would discuss in chronological order. After memorizing the floor plan and the objects, he practiced *visualizing* and *reciting* his speech.

1. At the front door, picture a poster that says "**350 percent increase in oil prices**."

2. In the hallway, picture rows of oil barrels with large Xs on them for **Arab oil embargo**.

3. In the cafeteria, picture food prices: hamburgers $7.50, milk $3.00 for **high retail prices**.

4. In the lounge, picture posters on the walls of closed auto factories for **slump in auto industry**.

5. In the hall, picture people lined up for job interviews for **high unemployment**.

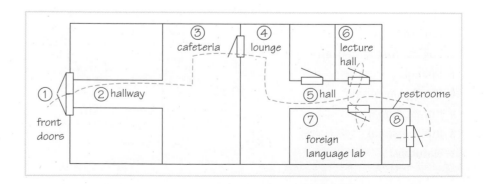

EXERCISE 6.8

Transfer These Skills

DIRECTIONS

1. Identify a series of steps, a sequence of events, or a list of points that you want to include in a speech, an essay, or a discussion for one of your current classes.

2. Draw a floor plan of a familiar building. Number the rooms to show the order that you will mentally walk. In each room, attach a picture that represents the item you need to remember.

3. Practice mentally walking through your building and reciting the information represented by the pictures in each room. Your instructor may ask you to recite your information in class.

CHECK POINT 6.4

Answers appear on page B3

True or False?

_____ 1. You will always be able to locate any information paired with a mnemonic and stored in long-term memory.

_____ 2. In acronyms, each letter at the beginning of each word in a sentence represents a specific item in a list of items you want to remember.

_____ 3. When you use mnemonics, you also use Memory Principles of Association, Visualization, Recitation, and Elaboration.

_____ 4. You can use picture or word associations, jingles, acronyms, or acrostics as retrieval cues to help with later recall of specific information.

Access Chapter 6 Practice Quiz 5: Using Mnemonics under "Interactive Quizzes" in your College Success CourseMate, accessed through *CengageBrain.com*.

CHAPTER 6
REFLECTIVE WRITING 2

On separate paper, in a journal, or online at this textbook's CourseMate Web site, respond to the following questions.

1. Which specific skills in this chapter will help you the most in terms of preparing for tests, performing well on tests, and managing test anxiety? Discuss at least four skills and include specific strategies you intend to use.

2. How does your attitude toward taking tests affect your ability to perform well? How does your current attitude toward taking tests differ from your attitude at the beginning of the term? Explain with details.

Access Chapter 6 Reflective Writing 2 in your College Success CourseMate, accessed through *CengageBrain.com*.

Terms to Know

By yourself or with a partner, practice reciting or writing definitions for the following terms. You may also practice defining these terms by using the online flashcard programs or comparing your answers to the online glossary.

true-false questions, p. 156

multiple-choice questions, p. 156

matching questions, p. 156

fill-in-the-blanks questions, p. 156

listing questions, p. 156

closed questions 156

open-ended questions 156

definition questions, p. 157

short-answer questions, p. 157

problem-solving questions, p. 157

essay questions, p. 157

summary notes p. 159

five-day study plan p. 159

recency effect, p. 164

four levels of response p. 167

immediate response, p. 168

delayed response, p. 168

assisted response, p. 168

educated selection, p. 168

test anxiety, p. 172

locus of control, p. 175

systematic desensitization. p. 176

mnemonic, p. 179

acronym p. 179

acrostic p. 179

the Loci Method p. 181

 Access Chapter 6 Flashcard Drills and Online Glossary in your College Success CourseMate, accessed through *CengageBrain.com.*

Learning Objectives Review

1 *Identify and explain effective strategies for preparing for tests.*

- Three kinds of questions you will encounter on college tests include: recognition (objective) questions, recall questions, and essay questions.
- Effective strategies to prepare for an upcoming test include organizing your materials and your time. Skills include creating summary notes, predicting test questions, creating a five-day study plan, and reviewing notes, terminology, and study tools.

2 *Identify and explain effective strategies for performing well on tests.*

- Seven essential strategies to use during the process of taking tests help you work through tests in an organized and confident way.
- By using the four levels of response for answering questions, you can respond to questions in four stages: immediate response, delayed response, assisted response, and educated selection (educated guessing).
- Computerized tests differ from paper-pencil tests. Seven essential strategies provide you with ways to boost your computerized test performance.
- You can learn from your tests by examining correct answers, looking for patterns of errors for incorrect answers, and correcting errors.

3 *Identify and explain effective strategies for managing test anxiety.*

- Test anxiety is excessive stress that affects performance. Symptoms of test anxiety may be physical, emotional, cognitive, or behavioral.
- Four common sources of test anxiety include: under-preparedness, past experiences, fear of failure, and poor test-taking skills.
- Locus of control and systematic desensitization are two new strategies you can use to reduce test anxiety before a test.
- Test anxiety is a learned behavior that can be "unlearned" by using effective test anxiety management strategies before and during a test.

4 *Identify and explain ways to use mnemonics to prepare for tests.*

- Mnemonics are memory tools that serve as bridges to help you recall information from long-term memory.
- Five kinds of mnemonics work effectively for academic materials: acronyms, acrostics, word associations, picture associations, and the Loci Method.
- For any mnemonic to work effectively, you need to learn the mnemonic in its exact form and practice translating the mnemonic into the words or items it represents.

Chapter 6 Review Questions

True or False?

_____ 1. Effective use of mnemonics involves creating acronyms and acrostics for every chapter in your textbook.

_____ 2. You can use the recency effect by doing a final review one or two hours before the time of a test.

_____ 3. A person with an external locus of control often shows a strong sense of self-confidence and a personal responsibility for outcomes.

_____ 4. Recall questions include listing, multiple-choice, definition, and short-answer questions.

_____ 5. Summary notes are a compilation of all of your textbook and lecture notes organized chapter by chapter.

Multiple Choice

_____ 1. Effective test-preparation skills

    a. reduce the necessity to cram for tests and use rote memory techniques.

    b. include time-management and goal-setting techniques.

    c. involve making summary notes and predicting, writing, and answering practice test questions.

    d. include all of the above.

_____ 2. In a five-day study plan, you

    a. begin by listing the topics and materials you need to review.

    b. use the same steps that you use to write effective goals.

    c. may set aside more than one study block for each day in the plan.

    d. do all of the above.

_____ 3. Which of the following statements is *not* true about test anxiety?

    a. A person's self-esteem and locus of control may contribute to test anxiety.

    b. Test anxiety is productive and beneficial for many students.

    c. A person's lack of test preparation and test-taking skills may trigger test anxiety.

    d. Test anxiety is a learned behavior that can be altered, eliminated, or "unlearned."

_____ 4. Cramming

    a. is a survival technique used for under-preparedness.

    b. uses most of the Memory Principles.

    c. processes large amounts of information efficiently.

    d. is highly effective when used the day before a test.

_____ 5. Which of the following is *not* an effective test-taking strategy?

    a. Leave some questions temporarily unanswered when taking a test.

    b. Read directions and questions carefully to avoid unnecessary mistakes.

    c. Do not feel that you must work through the test questions in the order that they appear on the test.

    d. Your original answer is usually the correct one, so avoid returning to questions to change the original answer.

Definitions

On separate paper, write a definition for the following terms. Each answer should include a three-part definition.

1. Internal locus of control

2. Acronym

3. Summary notes

4. Test anxiety

Short-Answer Questions

On separate paper, answer the following questions. Include details and chapter terminology in your answers.

1. Explain how associations are used in the first three levels of response for answering test questions.

2. Discuss four specific test-taking strategies that you can use to boost your test performance.

3. What are the advantages and disadvantages of using mnemonics such as acronyms and acrostics?

 Access Chapter 6 Chapter Quizzes 1–4 and Enhanced Quiz under "Interactive Quizzes" in your College Success CourseMate, accessed through *CengageBrain .com*.

Access all Chapter 6 Online Materials in your College Success CourseMate, accessed through *CengageBrain.com*.

Chapter Notes

7

Strengthening Your Reading Skills

© Stockbyte/Getty Images

Strengthening your reading skills requires a variety of reading strategies, flexibility, and reading goals as you work with different kinds of textbooks and different levels of reading. Surveying is a strategy that provides you with an overview and helps you establish schemas for new information. Working with paragraph elements, such as topics, main ideas, supporting details, definitions of terminology and meanings of unfamiliar words, strengthens your reading skills and comprehension. Applying the skills in this chapter will increase your textbook reading performance and comprehension.

LEARNING OBJECTIVES

1 *Explain different purposes for reading, how to create reading goals, and how to use essential reading strategies when you read college textbooks.*

2 *Explain how to survey different kinds of reading materials and why surveying is important.*

3 *Explain how to identify and use paragraph elements (topics, main ideas, and key details) to strengthen reading skills.*

4 *Explain the importance of learning definitions of terminology and discuss strategies to use to identify definitions in paragraphs.*

Access Chapter 7 Expanded Chapter Outline and Objectives in your College Success CourseMate, accessed through *CengageBrain.com*.

YOUR CHAPTER MAPPING

After reading information under each heading, return to the chapter visual mapping below. Add key words to show subheadings and important details related to each heading.

Access Chapter 7 Visual Mapping in your College Success CourseMate, accessed through *CengageBrain.com*.

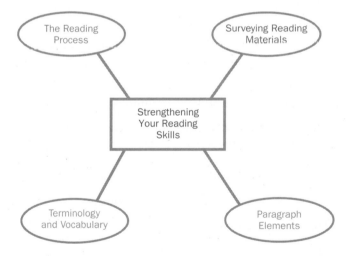

to strengthen your college textbook comprehension: overview reading and thorough reading.

Overview Reading

Overview reading is the process of skimming or surveying reading materials without interruption in order to form a big picture or create a schema for the topic before engaging in thorough reading. Overview reading creates a mindset for more in-depth learning that will follow. You can use overview reading to:

- Survey a new textbook, chapter, or a test.
- Get a sense of the flavor of a short story, essay, play, or short excerpt by reading without stopping or pausing to analyze. This type of overview reading often stirs your imagination, creates an emotional connection with the words, immerses you in the material, and keeps the unity of the plot and the characters' actions moving steadily forward.
- Get a sense of the material in a difficult or complex section or chapter of a textbook without focusing on immediately understanding the details. Reading *slowly* all the way through can provide you with basic background information, lay a foundation for more thorough reading, and alert you to sections that seem confusing or complicated.

Reading Flexibility for Thorough Reading

Thorough reading is the process of reading slowly and systematically in order to comprehend and process printed information. *Thorough reading* requires you to be flexible in your reading approach so you can adjust to various levels of difficulty in both content and readability. Some textbooks are easy to read and understand; others require a considerable amount of attention and effort. In any given textbook, you may be able to read some sections more quickly, and then you need to slow down the reading process for more difficult sections. Following are important points about using flexibility during thorough reading:

- Selecting an appropriate amount of material to read before pausing to think about or work with information prevents overloading your working memory.
- For textbooks with relatively easy levels of difficulty, stop at the end of each *page* to think about the information, create visual images of the material, and associate it to other information in long-term memory.
- For textbooks with average levels of difficulty, stop at the end of each *paragraph* to think about and process the information. Take time to identify main ideas, important details, and meanings of terminology. Use this read-pause approach after each paragraph for most textbooks.
- For textbooks with difficult reading levels and complex content, stop at the end of *each sentence* or *group* of sentences to check understanding and think about and process the information.
- *Chunking* information into meaningful sized units gives your working memory sufficient time to grasp, associate, and integrate information for understanding. It also helps you avoid going into *automatic pilot,* which results in little or no information registering in your memory.

Overview reading is the process of skimming or surveying reading materials without interruption in order to form a big picture or create a schema for the topic before engaging in thorough reading.

CONCEPT CHECK 7.1

What is the purpose of overview reading? When is overview reading appropriate for college textbooks? When is it not appropriate?

Thorough reading is the process of reading slowly and systematically in order to comprehend and process printed information.

 Access Chapter 7 Practice Quiz 1: Purposes for Reading under "Interactive Quizzes" in your College Success CourseMate, accessed through *CengageBrain* .com.

CHAPTER 7
REFLECTIVE WRITING 1

On separate paper, in a journal, or online at this textbook's CourseMate Web site, respond to the following questions.

1. What are your reading habits and interests? How often do you engage in recreational reading? What kinds of materials do you enjoy reading?

2. What type of reading is difficult or challenging for you? What specific difficulties do you encounter frequently?

Access Chapter 7 Reflective Writing 1 in your College Success CourseMate, accessed through *CengageBrain.com.*

Reading Goals and Plans of Action

Creating reading goals activates working memory. Your central executive responds to goal-oriented behavior and plans of action. Creating reading goals reflects your intention, your purpose, and your desired outcomes. To create a reading goal, ask yourself, "What is my purpose for reading this?" Then create a plan of action to achieve your goal. For example, if the purpose is to become familiar with a textbook and its features, your plan of action is to survey the textbook at the beginning of the term. If your goal is to familiarize yourself with a new chapter, your plan of action is to survey the chapter. Following are additional examples of the kinds of reading goals and plans of action you may implement as you read:

Goal:	Understand the main ideas and details.
Plan of Action:	Underline or highlight main ideas and key words in details in each paragraph. Take time to identify relationships and make associations. Take notes.
Goal:	Learn the course-specific terminology.
Plan of Action:	Identify terminology. Create flashcards for definitions.
Goal:	Do more in-depth learning of the chapter content.
Plan of Action:	Take notes to show relationships and link details together. Create study tools to use to practice rehearsing and retrieving information from long-term memory.

CONCEPT CHECK 7.2

How does thorough reading differ from overview reading? Which of these two kinds of reading do you use more frequently?

CONCEPT CHECK 7.3

... ... goals and you set during your last study block? Be specific. How does specifying a reading goal and a plan of action affect your reading performance?

Essential Reading Strategies

Reading for understanding is a complex process that involves many cognitive functions. As you read a chunk of information, your working memory retrieves related information to help you understand new information. Working memory then integrates the new information with retrieved information and returns the unit of information back into long-term memory and the appropriate schemas. This interaction and exchange of information between the memory systems happens quickly and continually throughout the reading process. **Figure 7.2** shows nine Essential Strategies for Reading Textbooks. You can use these strategies to assist working memory with the process of reading.

FIGURE 7.2   Essential Strategies for Reading Textbooks

- **Begin with an attitude to learn.** A positive, inquisitive, receptive attitude signals working memory that this information is important.

- **Create reading goals.** Know your intention before you begin any type of reading. Are you reading for pleasure or reading to acquire specific knowledge? Are you reading to get an overview or reading for more in-depth understanding?

- **Be patient and do not rush the reading process.** Reading is an intake and an encoding process that requires time for your mind to mull over, absorb, process, and integrate the new information.

- **Relate new information to existing schemas in your long-term memory.** Thinking about associations and linking different chunks of information lead to greater comprehension. Ask questions such as *What do I already know about this topic? How is it similar and how is it different from previous learning or past experiences? What are the important points and details?*

- **Recognize different levels of information as you read.** Strive to become an analytical reader who can recognize major themes, large concepts (schemas), main ideas, and important supporting details.

- **Learn terminology and definitions.** Knowing definitions of key terms lays the foundation for more complex learning and provides you with tools to communicate subject matter effectively to others.

- **Use spaced practice or spaced studying.** Spreading the reading process and activities over several different time periods actually cuts down total learning time. Avoid *marathon studying,* or in this case, *marathon reading,* which can overload your working memory.

- **Use elaborative rehearsal and active learning techniques as you read.** Actions that engage you in the reading and learning process help you maintain attention and concentration, encode information in new ways, and make stronger impressions of the information for memory.

- **Include some form of feedback as you study.** Use self-quizzing, reciting, and Look-Away Techniques to check the thoroughness and accuracy of your comprehension and memory.

CHECK POINT 7.1

Answers appear on page B4

Multiple Choice

_____ 1. Which of the following is *not* true about the reading process?

    a. Reading is a complex process of recalling and creating associations.

    b. You can use overview reading to become familiar with new material before reading and studying the details more thoroughly.

    c. Chunking information into appropriate sizes gives your working memory time to process and integrate information.

    d. When you have strong reading skills, your reading goal may be to use your *automatic pilot* to read many of your college textbooks.

_____ 2. Effective textbook reading strategies include

    a. selecting meaningful and manageable sizes of information to process at one time.

    b. identifying a purpose and a process to use for reading a textbook.

    c. using spaced practice and including rehearsal techniques to reinforce concepts.

    d. all of the above.

Access Chapter 7 Practice Quiz 2: The Reading Process under "Interactive Quizzes" in your College Success CourseMate, accessed through *CengageBrain.com.*

Surveying Reading Materials

 Explain how to survey different kinds of reading materials and why surveying is important.

Surveying is the process of previewing or skimming information to get an overview. As you learned in the section on overview reading, you can use surveying to get the big picture and set up schemas for all kinds of reading materials. You can also use surveying to preview tests. Surveying is an effective part of the reading process because surveying:

- Enhances your motivation and your interest in the material
- Breaks inertia or the tendency to procrastinate about starting the reading process
- Boosts confidence in your ability to master new material
- Provides you with a general idea about the length and difficulty level of the material
- Helps you set realistic goals and manage your reading and studying time effectively

Surveying a Textbook

Surveying a new textbook before you begin reading specific chapters acquaints you with the book's philosophy, organization, and special features; it also provides you with suggestions for using the book more effectively. Surveying a textbook is a process that usually requires less than thirty minutes of your time at the beginning of the term. **Figure 7.3** shows the parts of a textbook to examine when you survey.

The Table of Contents

The *table of contents* provides you with an overview of the topics in the textbook, the organization of the topics (chronological or thematic), chapter headings and subheadings, page numbers, and other textbook features. Carefully examine the table of contents as it is the "roadmap" for the textbook. You can use the table of contents to quickly locate a chapter, view the major headings and subheadings in the chapter, or check the length of chapters you are assigned to read.

The Introductory Materials

The *introductory materials* may include sections titled *Preface, Introduction, To the Teacher,* and *To the Student.* The **preface** (pronounced *prĕf is,* not *prē face')* or the *introduction* provides insight into the philosophy, objectives, and structure of the

> **CONCEPT CHECK 7.4**
>
> *Even though surveying requires little of your time, how does it benefit you?*

Surveying is the process of previewing or skimming information to get an overview.

The preface, or the introduction, in a textbook provides insight into the philosophy, objectives, and structure of the book.

FIGURE 7.3   Surveying a Text book

Front Matter: title page, copyright page, tables of contents, and introductory information

Back Matter: appendix, glossary, references/bibliography, and the index

book, and may include background information about the author. Read the student-oriented introductory materials carefully for valuable suggestions, study strategies, and explanations of textbook features that will help you learn the textbook content and use the book effectively.

The Appendix

The *appendix* is the part in the back of a book that contains supplementary materials that were not included within the chapters. The appendix might include answer keys; additional exercises; practice tests; supplementary readings; or important tables, graphs, charts, or maps. It may also include documents, such as the Bill of Rights or the Constitution, that are important but not included in the chapter due to their length, which would break the flow or disrupt the overall structure of the chapter. You will find that appendixes in textbooks have a wide variety of supplementary materials; some textbooks may have several appendixes.

The Glossary

The *glossary* is a minidictionary in the back of a book that contains definitions of course-specific terminology. The glossary appears after the appendix. Definitions in a glossary are limited to the word meanings used in the textbook; however, to learn more about a term, you can refer to a standard college dictionary. Bold, italic, or colored print within textbook chapters often indicates words that appear in the glossary. If your textbook does not have a glossary, you can create your own glossary for each chapter. Use the following strategies with textbooks that do have a glossary.

- Each time you see words in special print in a chapter, locate the terms in the glossary to see if the glossary provides more details or clarifies the definition.
- As you encounter terminology as you read your chapters, place a star next to or highlight those terms in the glossary. Use the glossary as a review tool to prepare for tests.
- Make separate definition cards or vocabulary sheets with the definitions of key terms to review to prepare for tests.

The Index

The *index* is an alphabetical listing of significant topics that appear in the book. The index is one of the most frequently used sections in the back of a textbook. You can use the index to quickly locate pages throughout the textbook that refer to a specific topic. In some textbooks you might find a *subject index,* an *author index,* or an *index of illustrations.* Frequently, topics are cross-referenced so they appear in more than one place in the index. The following strategies will help you use the index effectively:

- When you hear an unfamiliar term during a class discussion or lecture, write the word in your notes or in the margin of your textbook. After class, locate the term in the index of your book and read the pages indicated for explanations.
- When you are assigned a specific topic for a research paper, an essay, a writing assignment, a project, or a test, begin by locating the topic in the index. Then turn to the page numbers provided in the index to read or review the information.

The **appendix** is the part in the back of a book that contains supplementary materials that were not included in the chapters of the book.

CONCEPT CHECK 7.5

What kinds of information might you find in the back matter of a textbook? What are the benefits of surveying back matter in a textbook?

The **glossary** is a minidictionary in the back of a book that contains definitions of course-specific terminology.

The **index** is an alphabetical listing of significant topics that appear in the book.

EXERCISE 7.1

Surveying This Textbook

PURPOSE: Surveying a textbook, designed to familiarize you with the textbook structure and features, takes fifteen to thirty minutes. Surveying a chapter, designed to help you create a mindset for a new topic and get an overview or a big picture of upcoming information, usually takes less than twenty minutes.

DIRECTIONS:

Part I: Survey the front and the back section of this textbook. Then answer the following questions on separate paper or online at this textbook's CourseMate Web site.

1. What did you learn from reading the introductory information? How did it help familiarize you with this textbook?

2. What kind of information appears in the appendixes?

3. The glossary for this textbook is online. Explain how to access the online glossary.

4. Explain how you have already used the index this term.

Part II: After reading "Surveying a Chapter," survey a chapter in this textbook that you have not yet read. Then answer the following questions on separate paper or online at this textbook's CourseMate Web site.

1. Which features helped you begin to formulate a big picture of the chapter?

2. What benefits did you gain by examining visual materials?

3. What kinds of information in the margins helped you understand the new content?

4. What end-of-the-chapter features did you survey? What benefits did you gain by surveying these features?

 Access Chapter 7 Chapter Exercises: Exercise 7.1 in your College Success CourseMate, accessed through *CengageBrain.com*.

Surveying a Chapter

Surveying a chapter before beginning the process of careful, thorough reading is a *warm-up* activity you can use at the beginning of a study block to help you focus your mind, create interest, and form a big picture of the chapter.

The benefits of surveying a chapter are numerous, yet doing so generally requires fewer than twenty minutes. For longer chapters, you can modify the process by surveying as many pages of the chapter as you think you realistically

CONCEPT CHECK 7.6

What should you examine when you survey a chapter? How long should the process take you?

can cover in one or two study blocks; survey the remaining pages at the beginning of a later study block. Following are the parts of a chapter to include in surveying:

- **Introductory Materials:** Read the title of the chapter carefully; take a moment to think about the topic and relate the topic to information you already know. Read any lists, paragraphs, or visual materials that state the objectives for the chapter or introduce the chapter's content.

- **Headings and Subheadings:** Different font colors and different formats or designs in a chapter differentiate headings from subheadings. Move through the chapter by glancing over the headings and subheadings to see the skeletal structure of the chapter. Later, if you wish, you can use the headings and the subheadings to create a chapter outline.

- **Visual Materials:** Examine visual materials, such as charts, graphs, diagrams, pictures, and photographs. Read the information and the captions that appear with the visual materials.

- **Marginal Notes:** Marginal notes may be brief explanations, short definitions, lists of key points or objectives, or study questions that appear in the margins of the textbook pages. Marginal notes provide you with background details and emphasize important points to learn.

- **Terminology:** Skim over the terminology to get a general idea of terms you will need to learn. During surveying, do not spend time reading definitions for all the terminology.

- **End-of-the-Chapter Materials:** Read the chapter summary, list of key concepts, chapter review questions, or any other end-of-the-chapter materials. These materials highlight or summarize the important concepts and information you should learn in the chapter.

 Access Chapter 7 Practice Quiz 3: Surveying a Textbook under "Interactive Quizzes" in your College Success CourseMate, accessed through *CengageBrain.com*

Surveying an Article or an Essay

Using surveying to preview an article, an excerpt, an essay, or any other short reading requires a minimal amount of time but can provide you with valuable information. Use the following steps to survey short readings:

1. **Think about the title.** Without reading the article or essay, what does the title mean to you? What do you predict that article will be about? What understanding or opinions do you already have about the subject?

2. **Identify the author.** If you are familiar with the author, think about the information you already know about the author. If there is a footnote or a byline about the author's affiliations with specific groups or organizations, additional publications, or other personal information, read it carefully and think of ways it might relate to the subject matter and the author's point of view.

3. **Read and think about any introductory material.** Introductory material for short articles often provides necessary background information about the topic and/or the author.

CONCEPT CHECK 7.7

Even though articles and essays are shorter, why is surveying still beneficial?

4. **Read the first paragraph carefully.** The thesis statement, the main point or purpose of the entire article, often appears in this paragraph.

5. **Skim through the rest of the article.** Read the headings, subheadings, and side notes.

6. **Read the concluding paragraph.** The concluding paragraph often restates the thesis statement and summarizes the main ideas in the article.

EXERCISE 7.2

Transfer These Skills

Surveying before beginning the process of careful, thorough reading works effectively as a *warm-up activity* at the beginning of a study block. Select any textbook you are currently using. At the beginning of a study block, survey a new chapter. Then answer the following questions on your own paper or online at this textbook's CourseMate Web site.

1. Write the name of your textbook as well as the chapter number and title.

2. How did the introductory materials in the chapter help you focus your attention on the new chapter?

3. What was the value of reading all headings and sub-headings in the chapter?

4. What other special features in the chapter did you examine during surveying?

5. What end-of-the-chapter materials appeared in this chapter? How did they help you obtain a big picture of the chapter?

Access Chapter 7 Chapter Exercises: Exercise 7.2 in your College Success CourseMate, accessed through *CengageBrain.com*.

CHECK POINT 7.2

Answers appear on page B4

True or False?

_____ 1. Not taking the time to survey reading materials may reduce motivation, reduce your ability to relate information quickly to a schema, and increase procrastination.

_____ 2. Surveying is a process that is used only to become familiar with the front and back sections of a new textbook.

_____ 3. Surveying a chapter involves overview reading.

_____ 4. Surveying a chapter involves reading headings, subheadings, visual materials, all the marginal notes, all the definitions, and all the review questions.

Access Chapter 7 Practice Quiz 4: Surveying under "Interactive Quizzes" in your College Success CourseMate, accessed through *CengageBrain.com*.

GROUP PROCESSING

A COLLABORATIVE LEARNING ACTIVITY

Form groups of three or four students. Then complete the following directions.

1. Individually, think of the last complete chapter that you read in any one of your textbooks. On separate paper, make a chronological list of the steps or processes you used to complete the chapter.

2. Put all the lists together so that you and the members of your group can compare them. Do any of you use the same process? What do the lists have in common? Which approach seems most comprehensive? Be prepared to share your discussion with the rest of the class.

Paragraph Elements

> The **topic** of a paragraph is a word or a phrase that states the subject of a paragraph.

③ *Explain how to identify and use paragraph elements (topics, main ideas, and key details) to strengthen reading skills.*

For most textbooks, *thorough reading* involves reading one paragraph at a time; stopping to understand, analyze, and digest the important information in the paragraph; and then moving on to the next paragraph to repeat the process. You can understand the contents of a paragraph more easily when you can identify the three paragraph elements shown in **Figure 7.4** and understand their relationship to each other.

© Digital Vision/Getty Images

Understanding, integrating, and processing textbook information are processes that you cannot rush. Strategies that focus on analyzing key elements in paragraphs help you unlock the meaning of printed passages. What strategies do you use to increase your reading comprehension and manage your textbook assignments?

The Topic of a Paragraph

The *topic* of a paragraph is a word or a phrase that states the subject of a paragraph. Every paragraph has a topic that tells what the author is writing about in a paragraph. By identifying the topic, you activate working memory and pull an appropriate schema into your conscious mind.

As you read a paragraph, begin looking for details that tell more about, explain, or give examples of the topic.

FIGURE 7.4	Three Paragraph Elements

1. **The topic of the paragraph:** the subject
2. **The main idea of the paragraph:** the author's main point
3. **The important details of the paragraph:** details that support the main idea

These details cluster together to form meaning. You can use the following strategies to identify the topic sentence of a paragraph:

- Use overview reading to read the entire paragraph without stopping.
- Ask yourself: *In one word or one phrase, what is this paragraph about?*
- If you cannot state the topic, glance through the paragraph again and ask yourself: *Is one word repeated several times in the paragraph? Does that word work as the topic?*

The Main Idea

The *main idea* of a paragraph states the author's most important point about the topic of the paragraph. The *topic sentence,* also called the *main idea sentence,* is the sentence in a paragraph that includes the topic and states the author's main point or main idea for the paragraph. Sometimes after you read a paragraph, you can quickly identify the topic sentence; other times, you may need to reread the paragraph and actively search for the most important sentence that represents the main idea of the paragraph. The topic sentence is an essential key for understanding the information in a paragraph. Use the following tips to help you locate the topic sentence:

- **The topic sentence is like an umbrella**. It needs to be broad enough for all of the other sentences and supporting details in the paragraph to "fit under it." In a well-written paragraph, each sentence relates to or supports the topic sentence. Ask yourself the following questions to help you identify the topic sentence:
  - What is the topic (subject) of this paragraph?
  - Is there a big picture or an "umbrella sentence" that contains this topic word?
  - What is the main idea the author wants to make about the topic? Which sentence states the main idea?
  - Which sentence is large enough to encompass the content of the paragraph?
  - Do all the important details in the paragraph fit under this sentence?
- **Examine the first, the last, and then the sentences in the middle of the paragraph**.
  - *First Sentence*: Topic sentences appear most frequently as the first sentence of paragraphs. This is particularly true in textbooks.
  - *Last Sentence*: If the first sentence is not the "umbrella sentence," check the last sentence. Sometimes the last sentence summarizes the main point of the paragraph and thus states the main idea.
  - *Other Sentences*: If the first and the last sentences do not state the main idea, carefully examine each sentence in the body of the paragraph.

Highlight Topic Sentences

Highlighting or underlining the complete topic sentence in a paragraph is one way to make it stand out in your mind. Read the paragraph about knowledge workers (topic) in Example 1. Notice how highlighting the topic sentence creates a clearer impression of the topic and the author's most important point about the paragraph.

CONCEPT CHECK 7.8

What specific kinds of information (elements) should you look for in a paragraph? How are they related to each other?

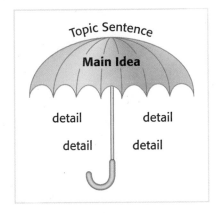

The main idea of a paragraph states the author's most important point about the topic of a paragraph.

The topic sentence, also called the *main idea sentence,* is the sentence in a paragraph that includes the topic and the author's main point for the paragraph.

Access Chapter 7 Practice Quiz 5: Find Main Ideas under "Interactive Quizzes" in your College Success CourseMate, accessed through *CengageBrain.com*.

CONCEPT CHECK 7.9

What techniques can you use to identify the topic sentence in a paragraph? How will identifying the topic sentence improve comprehension?

Example 1

Topic: Knowledge Workers

Knowledge workers, including, for example, computer scientists, engineers, and physical scientists, pose special challenges for managers. They tend to work in high-technology firms and are usually experts in some abstract knowledge base. They often like to work independently and tend to identify more strongly with their profession than with any organization—even to the extent of defining performance largely in terms recognized by other members of their profession.

From Griffin. *Principles of Management*. Houghton Mifflin Company, © 2008, page 213. Reprinted with permission.

In Example 2, the first sentence is an example of the biological approach that may be used by psychologists; however, the second sentence clearly states the main idea and is the sentence to highlight.

Example 2

Topic: Biological Processes

Investigating the possibility that aggressive behavior or schizophrenia, for example, might be traceable to a hormonal imbalance or a brain disorder reflects the biological approach to psychology. As its name implies, the biological approach assumes that behavior and mental processes are largely shaped by biological processes. Psychologists who take this approach study the psychological effects of hormones, genes, and the activity of the nervous system, especially the brain. Thus, if they are studying memory, they might try to identify the changes taking place in the brain as information is stored there. Or if they are studying thinking, they might look for patterns of brain activity associated with, say, making quick decisions or reading a foreign language . . .

From Bernstein et al. *Psychology*, 5e. Houghton Mifflin Company, © 2002, page 3. Reprinted with permission.

CONCEPT CHECK 7.10

What is an implied main idea? Why do textbooks infrequently use implied main ideas?

Write Implied Main Ideas in the Margin

On occasion, you will encounter a paragraph that has *no stated main idea,* which means you will not find a topic sentence in the paragraph. This occurs when the main idea is *implied.* If you are not able to locate a topic sentence after carefully examining the first sentence, the last sentence, and the sentences in the remainder of the paragraph, look carefully at the details in the paragraph. Draw your own conclusion about the main idea. Write the main idea in the margin. Example 3 shows a paragraph with an *implied* main idea.

Example 3

Topic: Written Records

Some of the world's earliest civilizations have left written records that we cannot yet decipher and might never be able to read. These include India's Harappan civilization, which was centered in the Indus valley from before 2500 to some time after 1700 BCE; and the Minoan civilization of the Aegean island of Crete, which flourished from roughly 2500 to about 1400 BCE; and the African civilization of Kush, located directly south of Egypt, which reached its age of greatness after 800 BCE; but with much earlier origins as a state. For many other early civilizations and cultures we have as yet uncovered no written records. This is the case of mysterious peoples who, between approximately 6000 BCE and the first century CE, painted and carved thousands of pieces of art on the rocks of Tassili n'Ajjer in what is today the central Saharan Desert. It is also true of the Olmec civilization of Mexico, which appeared around 1200 BCE.

Supporting
details

Formulated Main Idea:
We cannot use written records to learn about some early civilizations.

From Alfred J. Andrea and James Overfield, *The Human Record, 3rd ed.*, p. 34. Copyright © 1998 by Houghton Mifflin Company. Used with permission.

Important Details

Supporting details in a paragraph are facts, explanations, causes and effects, examples, and definitions that develop, support, or prove the main idea. In a well-developed paragraph, the details in each sentence must relate to the topic and the topic sentence, which states the main idea. Your goal as a reader is to use *Selectivity* to identify the important details that you need to learn and the details that provide understanding but are not essential to learn. Use the following tips to identify important supporting details:

Supporting details in a paragraph are facts, explanations, causes and effects, examples, and definitions that develop, support, or prove the main idea.

- Ask yourself: What details would I want to include in my explanation of the main idea to someone else? You can *highlight or underline the key words or phrases* in that paragraph that you would use in your explanation.

- Identify specific details that can serve as *retrieval cues* or associations to trigger recall of information later from your long-term memory. If the paragraph has multiple examples, select several, but not all, of the examples as memory cues.

- Be selective. Do not mark words such as *to, and, with, also,* and *in addition* because they are not key memory trigger words. Also, you do not need to mark a key word or the topic that appears multiple times.

- Carefully examine bulleted lists of information and notes that appear in the margins of your textbook. Key supporting details to learn often appear in these lists or notes.

CONCEPT CHECK 7.11

What kinds of information in a paragraph can function as supporting details? How can you create a stronger impression of these details?

The purpose of marking your textbooks, which includes highlighting or underlining, is to draw your attention to the most important information to study and to reduce the amount of information you need to review. Excessive marking defeats the purpose, so always be selective and limit the amount of highlighting or underlining you use in each paragraph. In Example 4, notice how a student highlighted the topic sentence completely and used Selectivity to identify and highlight only key words or phrases.

Example 4

Topic: Stalactites

Stalactites are stony travertine structures, resembling icicles, that hang from cave ceilings. They form as water, one drop at a time, enter the roof of a cave through a crack and deposits minute amounts of calcium carbonate. Initially, the center of each growing stalactite is a hollow tube, resembling a soda straw, through which the next drop enters the cave. Eventually precipitated travertine clogs the tube, causing the water to drip down the stalactite's outer surface, where it continues to deposit travertine and creates the irregular icicle shape of a typical stalactite.

From Chernicoff/Fox. *Essentials of Geology*. Houghton Mifflin Company, © 2006, page 203. Reprinted with permission.

EXERCISE 7.3

Identifying Topic Sentences and Supporting Details

DIRECTIONS: By yourself or with a partner, carefully read each of the paragraphs in Exercise 7.3 in Appendix C. Highlight or underline the sentence that you think is the topic sentence for each paragraph. Then, selectively highlight or underline key supporting details. You may be asked to compare your responses with other students' answers.

CHECK POINT 7.3   Answers appear on page B4

True or False?

_____ 1. A topic sentence is also known as a main idea sentence.

_____ 2. In textbooks, the topic sentence appears most frequently as the last sentence in a paragraph.

_____ 3. To identify a topic of a paragraph requires that you first identify the main idea.

_____ 4. When highlighting or underlining supporting details in a paragraph, Selectivity is required to help you avoid over-marking.

Access Chapter 7 Practice Quiz 6: Paragraph Elements under "Interactive Quizzes" in your College Success CourseMate, accessed through *CengageBrain.com*.

Textbook Case Studies

DIRECTIONS

1. Read each case study carefully. Respond to the question at the end of each case study by using *specific* strategies discussed in this chapter. Answer in complete sentences.

2. Write your responses on paper or online at the CourseMate student Web site, Textbook Case Studies. You will be able to print your online response or e-mail it to your instructor.

CASE STUDY 1: Justine reads all her textbooks the way that she reads paper-back books. She starts at the beginning of the chapter and does not stop until she reaches the end of the chapter. She often finds that she needs to reread chapters two or three times before she can retain the information. What methods can Justine use to comprehend a textbook chapter better and spend less time rereading?

CASE STUDY 2: The instructor spent half the class time talking about a concept that was unfamiliar to Simon. Simon had not had a chance to read the last three chapters, so he thought perhaps the concept appeared in those chapters. When he sat down to work with a study partner, Simon started flipping through the chapters page by page and eventually located the section of information. What strategies would help Simon be a more efficient reader and student?

Access Chapter 7 Textbook Case Studies and Web-Only Case Studies in your College Success CourseMate, accessed through *CengageBrain.com*.

Terminology and Vocabulary

4 *Explain the importance of learning definitions of terminology and discuss strategies to use to identify definitions in paragraphs.*

Course-specific vocabulary and definitions are other details you will encounter in many college textbooks. Understanding course-specific terminology and definitions is one powerful way to strengthen your reading skills and lay a foundation for understanding the remainder of the paragraph. **Figure 7.5** summarizes five Essential Strategies for Working with Terminology.

As you read with an alert mind, you will notice many ways terminology and definitions appear in paragraphs. Sometimes an entire paragraph defines one specific term. Other times, as in Example 5, the paragraph defines several key terms. As shown in Example 5, circling the key terms and highlighting key words in the definitions help focus your attention on the information you need to learn.

CONCEPT CHECK 7.12

What consequences might you experience if you do not spend ample time learning definitions of terminology? What strategies can you use to learn definitions for key terms?

FIGURE 7.5 Essential Strategies for Working with Terminology

- **Use bold or special print in textbooks to help identify terminology.** In most textbooks, the definition of the term is within the same sentence or in the following sentence.
- **Circle terminology words and highlight key words.** Circling the terminology words distinguishes them from other types of details in a paragraph, and selectively highlighting key words in the definition narrows your focus and reinforces the *paired associations.*
- **Use word clues and punctuation clues to identify the definitions.**
- **Use the textbook glossary to verify and learn more about the terminology words.**
- **Make definition cards or vocabulary sheets to recite, rehearse, and review definitions.**

Example 5

Topic: Changing Shape of the Earth's Continents

Have continents grown in more recent geologic time? Bordering North America on both the Atlantic and the Pacific coasts are rocks that are no more than 600 million years old. Recently gathered evidence indicates that many of these fault-bounded rock bodies, called **displaced terranes**, originated elsewhere but were transported by plate motion and attached, or *accreted*, to our continent by collisions. Some may have been island arcs that formed in an ocean basin and then were towed to a continental margin by subduction of the intervening ocean plate. Others are probably **microcontinents**, pieces of continental lithosphere broken from larger distant continents by rifting or transform faulting.

From Chernicoff, Fox. *Essentials of Geology,* p. 241. © 2003, Houghton Mifflin.

Word Clues to Identify Definitions

CONCEPT CHECK 7.13

What are common word clues? How do word clues help you identify definitions?

A word clue, such as *defined as, is/are,* or *known as,* link the vocabulary word to its definition that appears in another part of the same sentence.

A *word clue,* such as *defined as, is/are,* or *known as,* links the vocabulary word to its definition that appears in another part of the same sentence. In other words, a word clue links the two parts of a *paired association.* **Figure 7.6** shows word clues used frequently in sentences to define terminology.

When you search for the words in a sentence that define a word in bold or special print, *be selective;* do not automatically highlight all the surrounding words. Read and think carefully about which words are essential words for the definition. If your textbook has a glossary, refer to the glossary definition if you have difficulty separating the definition part of a sentence from other kinds of details.

In many textbooks, the terminology word appears first and is then followed by its definition. However, the definition may appear before the terminology word, or the terminology word may be inserted within parts of the definition. Reading and

---

FIGURE 7.6 Common Word Clues in Definition Sentences

also	defined as	referred to as	known as	is/are called
is/are	to describe	mean/means	which is	or

Word Clue: known as

For a time, researchers believed that anyone who displayed the pattern of aggressiveness, competitiveness, and nonstop work known as "Type A" behavior was at elevated risk for heart disease.

Word Clue: are called

Efforts to reduce, eliminate, or prevent behaviors that pose health risks and to encourage healthy behaviors are called health promotion.

From Bernstein/Nash. *Essentials of Psychology*, 2e. Houghton Mifflin Company, © 2002, page 368. Reprinted with permission.

thinking carefully are essential for using information within a sentence to define a word. Above, examine the two examples that use word clues to help locate definitions for terminology.

Punctuation Clues to Identify Definitions

Punctuation clues, such as commas, dashes, parentheses, and colons, signal the definition of terminology within the sentence. The punctuation clues separate the definition from the other words in the sentence. Use the punctuation clues to help identify the words that are important parts of the definition and words that you should highlight for emphasis. Be aware, however, that each of these punctuation marks may serve other functions in sentences, so their appearance does not automatically mean they are functioning as definition clues. **Figure 7.7** shows the four kinds of punctuation clues with example sentences.

Punctuation clues, such as commas, dashes, parentheses, and colons, signal the definitions of terminology within the sentence.

FIGURE 7.7   Four Kinds of Punctuation Clues for Definitions

Punctuation Clue		Example Sentence with Example Highlighting
Commas	, ,	Stress may also intensify **functional fixedness**, the tendency to use objects for only one purpose.
Dashes	— —	**Chronic stressors**—stressors that continue over a long period of time—include such circumstances as living near a noisy airport, being unable to earn a decent living, residing in a high-crime neighborhood, being the victim of discrimination, and even enduring years of academic pressure.
Parentheses	( )	Stressors trigger a process that begins when the brain's hypothalamus activates a part of the autonomic nervous system, which stimulates the **medulla** (inner part) of the adrenal glands.
Colon	:	A related phenomenon is **catastrophizing**: dwelling on and overemphasizing the possible negative consequences of an event.

Source: Bernstein/Nash. *Essentials of Psychology 2ED.* Houghton Mifflin Company, © 2002, page 368. Reprinted with permission.

Using Punctuation and Word Clues

DIRECTIONS: Work with a partner or by yourself to complete this exercise. In the following sentences, use punctuation and word clues to identify the definitions of the words in bold print. Underline or highlight the key words that define the terms. Be selective; include only words that are a part of the definition.

1. The unit of electric charge is called the **coulomb** (C), after Charles Coulomb (1736–1806), a French scientist who studied electrical effects. [p. 167]

2. Waves with relatively low frequencies, or long wavelengths, are known as **radio waves** and are produced primarily by causing electrons to **oscillate**, or vibrate, in an antenna. [p. 122]

3. The fourth and final factor in reaction rate is the possible presence of a **catalyst**, a substance that increases the rate of reaction but is not itself consumed in the reaction. [p. 326]

4. **Thermodynamics** means the dynamics of heat and deals with the production of heat, the flow of heat, and the conversion of heat to work. [p. 107]

5. The **neutron number** (N) is, of course, the number of neutrons in a nucleus. [p. 230]

6. The chemical reactivity of the elements depends on the order of the electrons in the energy levels in their atoms, which is called the **electron configuration**. [p. 272]

7. The outer shell of an atom is known as the **valence shell**, and the electrons in it are called the **valence electrons**. [p. 273]

From Shipman et al., *An Introduction to Physical Science, 10th ed.* Copyright © 2003. Reprinted by permission of Houghton Mifflin, Inc.

Definition Cards or Vocabulary Sheets

Understanding and being able to define course-specific terminology lays a strong foundation for understanding textbook information and being well-prepared for tests. More than 60 percent of most test questions are based directly on knowing and understanding the course terminology. To learn definitions and prepare for tests, preparing study tools to practice and review definitions is beneficial.

Create Definition Cards

One effective study tool involves using index cards to create a set of definition cards. On the front side of your index card, write the term. If you wish, include the chapter and the page number. On the back of your index card, write important information about the term. **Figure 7.8** shows an example of a definition card. To prepare for questions that test your understanding of terminology, write three kinds of information on the backs of your cards:

- The **category** to which the word belongs
- The **formal definition**
- One or more **additional details** to expand the definition

Use your definition cards for self-quizzing and immediate feedback. Look at the front and then recite the information on the back. Turn the card over to check your accuracy. You can sort the cards into two piles: ones you know and ones you need to review further. If you anticipate fill-in-the-blanks questions, reverse the order. Read the back and then *name and spell* the word on the front. Check your accuracy.

Create Vocabulary Sheets

Another way to study terminology and definitions is to create vocabulary sheets for each chapter. Vocabulary sheets are a form of *two-column notes*. In the left column, write the term. In the right column, write the three parts of a definition (the category, the definition, and one or more details). By creating vocabulary sheets, you create your own glossary of terms. **Figure 7.9** shows the beginning of a vocabulary sheet. To study from a vocabulary sheet, cover up the right column with a piece of paper. Say the word and recite the definition. Remove the paper. Check your accuracy. Reverse the order. Cover the left column, read the right column, and then *say and spell* the term.

FIGURE 7.8   Example of a Definition Card

Front

Acronym

Back

— A Mnemonic

— A word or phrase made by using the first letter of key words in a list of items to remember

— Forms an association and works as a retrieval cue

FIGURE 7.9   Example of a Vocabulary Sheet

Terminology	Chapter 6
Acrostic	— A mnemonic — A word or phrase made by using the first letter of key words in a list of items to remember — Forms an association and works as a retrieval cue.
Acronym	

CONCEPT CHECK 7.15

How does the information you write on vocabulary sheets differ from the information you write on definition note cards? How do you use the Memory Principles of Selectivity, Recitation, and Feedback when studying from these study tools?

EXERCISE 7.6

Transfer These Vocabulary Skills

DIRECTIONS: Select any chapter that you have already studied in one of your textbooks. Create a set of definition cards or vocabulary sheets for the course-specific terminology in the chapter. After creating your study tool, practice reciting the terminology and the definitions.

Meanings of Unfamiliar Words

Identifying and learning terminology and definitions definitely strengthen your reading skills and comprehension of paragraph-level information. However, paragraphs may contain other words, general words, that are unfamiliar to you. If you have limited understanding of a word in a paragraph, or if you just skip over an unfamiliar word, your understanding of the paragraph may be limited or inaccurate.

For example, do you know the meaning of the word *travertine* in Example 4? Do you know the meaning of *accrete, subduction, lithosphere,* and *rifting* in Example 5? If not, when you read these words in the previous examples, did you skip over them or did you use a dictionary to look up the meaning? Any time you encounter unfamiliar words, recognize that understanding the meanings of those words increases your understanding of the paragraph. **Figure 7.10** summarizes four Essential Strategies to Use with Unfamiliar Words. Use these strategies to increase your vocabulary and learn the meanings of unfamiliar words.

Use Word Structure Clues

Word structure clues involve using the meanings of prefixes, suffixes, base words, and roots to determine the general meaning of unfamiliar words. If using word structure clues results in a vague understanding of the word, refer to a dictionary or glossary for a more complete definition. **Figure 7.11** shows the four word parts used in word structure clues plus a word structure model.

> **Word structure clues** involve using the meanings of prefixes, suffixes, base words, and roots to determine the general meaning of unfamiliar words.

| **FIGURE 7.10** | Essential Strategies to Use with Unfamiliar Words |

- Use word clues and punctuation clues to identify definitions within the sentence.
- Use word structure clues to determine general meanings of words.
- Use context clues to determine general meanings of words.
- Use glossaries and dictionaries to look up meanings of unfamiliar words.

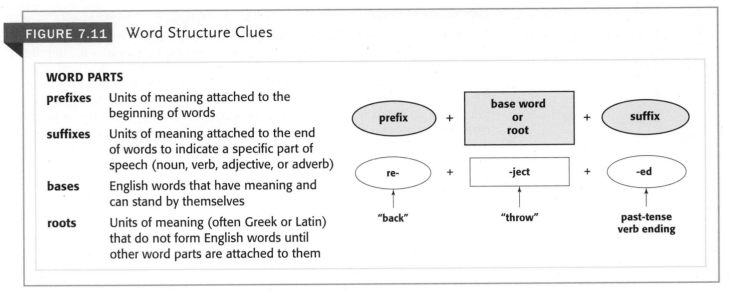

| FIGURE 7.11 | Word Structure Clues |

WORD PARTS

prefixes Units of meaning attached to the beginning of words

suffixes Units of meaning attached to the end of words to indicate a specific part of speech (noun, verb, adjective, or adverb)

bases English words that have meaning and can stand by themselves

roots Units of meaning (often Greek or Latin) that do not form English words until other word parts are attached to them

prefix + base word or root + suffix

re- + -ject + -ed
"back"   "throw"   past-tense verb ending

Using word structure clues to understand and recall terminology is an extremely valuable skill in science and health science courses, for much of the terminology used in those courses derives from Greek or Latin roots and word parts. (For a list of prefixes, suffixes, and roots and their meanings, go to the CourseMate student Web site, Topics In-Depth: Meaning of Word Parts.) Learning the meanings of structural word parts can save you time, increase your comprehension, and expand your vocabulary. Do you know the meanings of the following common roots?

anthro	derma	migra	phone	aqua	graph	ology
audio	helio	osteo	psych	biblio	hydro	ped
bio	macro	pathos	theo	cred	micro	phobia

CONCEPT CHECK 7.16

What do you tend to do when you encounter an unfamiliar word when you read? Do you do something to figure out the meaning, or do you skip over the word?

 Access Chapter 7 Topics In-Depth: Meaning of Word Parts in your College Success CourseMate, accessed through *CengageBrain.com*.

The Muscular System

Read **Excerpt 5** in **Appendix D**. Circle the key terms in bold print. Underline or highlight key words in the definition for each term. Then, unless your instructor gives different directions, create flashcards or a vocabulary sheet for these terms.

Context clues are words in a sentence or in surrounding sentences that provide hints about the general meanings of unfamiliar words.

Use Context Clues

Context clues are words in a sentence or in surrounding sentences that provide hints about the general meanings of unfamiliar words. By carefully reading the sentence with the unfamiliar word and then rereading the surrounding sentences, you can often pick up hints or context clues about the *general* meaning of the word. Sometimes you simply get a "sense" of the meaning of a word by understanding the examples linked to it, relating it to personal experience, or drawing a logical conclusion. Other times, specific kinds of words signal the meaning of the unfamiliar word. **Figure 7.12** shows five categories of words that often function as context clues to provide you with general meanings of unfamiliar words.

Once you have identified the meaning of an unfamiliar word, you can *substitute a familiar word for the unfamiliar word* to convert formal textbook language into

FIGURE 7.12   Kinds of Context Clues

Context Clue	Definition	Strategy	Example Sentence
Synonyms	words with exact or similar meanings	Try substituting a familiar word (a synonym) for the unfamiliar word.	*probity:* The judge has a keen sense of recognizing a person's honesty and integrity. For that reason, the *probity* of the witness was not questioned.
Antonyms	words with opposite meanings	An unfamiliar word is understood because you understand its opposite.	*impenitent:* Instead of showing shame, regret, or remorse, the con artist was *impenitent.*
Contrasts	words that show an opposite or a difference	Look for words such as *differ, different, unlike,* or *opposite of* to understand the differences.	*thallophyte:* Because the fungi is a *thallophyte,* it differs from the other plants in the garden that have embedded roots and the rich foliage of shiny leaves and hardy stems.
Comparisons or **Analogies**	words or images that indicate a likeness or a similarity	Look for the commonality between two or more items.	*cajole:* I sensed he was trying to *cajole* me. He reminded me of a salesman trying to sell me a bridge.
Examples	examples that show function, characteristics, or use of the term	Look for ways that the examples signal the meaning of the term.	*implosion:* *Implosions* are not rare in Las Vegas. The most recent one collapsed an old, outdated casino to make room for a new megaresort. Dust and debris filled the air, but the nearby buildings suffered no damage.

a less formal, more personal conversational tone. Above the words in a paragraph that were unfamiliar to you, write a more common or familiar word. Reread the paragraph, but this time, read using the common or familiar words. The following example shows how this technique of substituting words adds clarity and improves comprehension of a difficult paragraph.

CONCEPT CHECK 7.17

Without referring to a dictionary, what strategies can you use to understand the meaning of unfamiliar words in a paragraph that are not course-specific vocabulary terms?

Few if any philosophies are as enigmatic [puzzling] as Daoism—the teachings of the Way (Dao). The opening lines of this school's greatest masterpiece, *The Classic of the Way and Virtue [morality]* (*Dao De Jing*), which is ascribed to [associated with] the legendary [famous] Laozi, immediately confront [challenge] the reader with Daoism's essential paradox [contradiction]: "The Way that can be trodden [walked] is not the enduring [lasting] and the unchanging Way. The name that can be named is not the enduring and unchanging name." Here is a philosophy that purports [claims] to teach the Way (of truth) but simultaneously [at the same time] claims that the True Way transcends [exceeds] human understanding. Encapsulated [Contained] within a little book of some five thousand words is a philosophy that defies [resists] definition, spurns [rejects] reason, and rejects words as inadequate.

From Alfred J. Andrea and James Overfield, *The Human Record, 3rd ed.*, p. 93. Copyright © 1998 by Houghton Mifflin Co. Reprinted with permission.

CHAPTER 7
REFLECTIVE WRITING 2

On separate paper, in a journal, or online at this textbook's CourseMate Web site, respond to the following questions:

1. The reading process is complex and cannot be taught in one chapter of a textbook. However, by learning about and applying specific reading strategies, you can strengthen your reading skills. What strategies in this chapter will help you strengthen your reading skills?

2. On a scale of one to ten, with ten showing the most ability, how would you rate your ability to read and understand the textbooks you are currently using? What additional skills do you feel you need to acquire in order to rate yourself on an even higher level? Explain with details.

Access Chapter 7 Reflective Writing 2 in your College Success CourseMate, accessed through *CengageBrain.com*.

ACTIVITY

Chapter 7 Critical Thinking

PURPOSE: The term "critical thinking" involves an array of thinking skills. *Application* and *Synthesis* are two critical thinking skills. Learning to recognize and use higher level thinking skills increases your reading comprehension and your overall understanding of new material.

DIRECTIONS

1. Read **Excerpt 1** in **Appendix D**. Underline the main ideas in each paragraph, circle terminology, and highlight key words for the definitions.

2. Read the following description of two critical thinking skills: application and synthesis.

APPLICATION: Application involves applying information in meaningful ways.

SYNTHESIS: Synthesis involves integrating information and seeing connections or relationships.

3. Answer the following questions. Unless your instructor gives you other directions, write your answers on separate paper.

Question 1: Explain how you can use each model of memory to improve the way you process information in your courses.

Question 2: Explain how the Working Memory Model incorporates each of the models of memory discussed in Excerpt 1.

CHECK POINT 7.4

Answers appear on page B4

True or False?

_____ 1. Learning meanings of word parts can often help you learn terminology in health science and other science courses.

_____ 2. Study tools to rehearse and review terminology should show a category for the word, the definition, and at least one more detail that shows you understand the term.

_____ 3. You may be able to use word structure, punctuation, context, or word clues to determine the meaning of an unfamiliar word you encounter while reading.

_____ 4. Commas, quotation marks, semicolons, and dashes are the four common punctuation clues that help signal or identify definitions.

 Access Chapter 7 Practice Quiz 7: Terminology under "Interactive Quizzes" in your College Success CourseMate, accessed through *CengageBrain.com*.

Terms to Know

By yourself or with a partner, practice reciting or writing definitions for the following terms. You may also practice defining these terms by using the online

Learning Objectives Review

❶ *Explain different purposes for reading, how to create reading goals, and how to use essential reading strategies when you read college textbooks.*

• Reading is an active process of inputting information, encoding meaning, and creating associations—a process that cannot be rushed. By recognizing and using four purposes for reading (recreational, overview, thorough, and comparative), you can adjust your reading goals and strategies to match the task.

- Reading flexibility guidelines suggest the length of material you should read before pausing to think about and work with the information.
- Reading goals activate working memory. Before starting a reading task, create a reading goal and a plan of action to make the best use of your time and achieve desired results.
- Nine essential reading strategies can help you strengthen your reading skills.

2 *Explain how to survey different kinds of reading materials and why surveying is important.*

- Surveying is the process of previewing or skimming to get an overview. Surveying can be used to familiarize yourself with textbooks, chapters, articles, essays, or tests.
- Surveying a textbook involves examining four parts in front and four parts in back of a textbook.
- Surveying a chapter involves examining six parts of the chapter before reading: introductory materials, headings and subheadings, visual materials, marginal notes, terminology, and end-of-chapter materials.
- Surveying an article or an essay involves examining six parts of the printed materials.

3 *Explain how to identify and use paragraph elements (topics, main ideas, and key details) to strengthen reading skills.*

- Thorough reading for most textbooks involves reading one paragraph at a time and then pausing to analyze paragraph elements: topic, main ideas, and important details.
- The topic of a paragraph is the subject of the paragraph. The main idea states the author's most important point about the topic; it appears in the topic sentence. Strategies help you identify the topic and the topic sentence in a paragraph.
- Important supporting details in a paragraph include facts, explanations, causes and effects, examples, and definitions that develop, support, or prove the main idea.

4 *Explain the importance of learning definitions of terminology and discuss strategies to use to identify definitions in paragraphs.*

- Five essential strategies can help you work effectively with terminology.
- Creating index cards (flashcards) or vocabulary sheets are effective study tools to rehearse definitions of terminology.
- Use word clues, punctuation clues, word structure clues, and context clues to identify general meanings of unfamiliar words you encounter when you read.
- Substituting familiar words for unfamiliar words boosts your comprehension and recall ability.

Terms to Know

flashcard programs or comparing your answers to the online glossary.

purposes for reading p. 191

overview reading p. 192

thorough reading p. 192

surveying p. 195

preface, p. 195

appendix, p. 196

glossary, p. 196

index, p. 196

topic p. 200

main idea p. 201

topic sentence p. 201

supporting details p. 203

word clues p. 206

punctuation clues p. 207

word structure clues p. 210

context clues p. 212

 Access Chapter 7 Flashcard Drills and Online Glossary in your College Success CourseMate, accessed through CengageBrain.com.

Chapter 7 Review Questions

Answers appear on page B4

True or False?

_____ 1. Learning the meanings of common prefixes, suffixes, and roots can sometimes help you unlock the general meanings of unfamiliar words you encounter in textbooks.

_____ 2. When you study from vocabulary sheets or definition cards, you are working with paired associations and using recitation and feedback.

_____ 3. Understanding the main idea of a paragraph helps you identify important details and understand the overall meaning of the paragraph.

_____ 4. One suggestion for saving time when you read is to skip over unfamiliar words as long as you understand the general meaning of the main idea of the paragraph.

_____ 5. When you use punctuation clues to define words, the definitions always appear between the two punctuation marks.

_____ 6. To read all college textbooks, you should first read through the entire chapter and then reread the chapter, stopping at the end of each page to take notes.

_____ 7. Marathon reading may overload your working memory and hinder your ability to process information effectively.

_____ 8. Overview reading involves identifying key ideas, determining the organization used in each paragraph, and analyzing the different parts of the overall topic.

Locating Definitions

In the following sentences, underline or highlight only the words in the sentence that define the term in bold print.

1. The advantage of the **binary system**, which uses only the digits 0 and 1, is that each position in a numeral contains only one of two values. (p. 134)

2. A **point** may be regarded as a location in space with no breadth, width, or length. (p. 253)

3. The property shared by these three numeration systems is that they are **additive**; that is, the values of the written symbols are added to obtain the number represented. (p. 118)

4. We have already studied **perimeter** (the length of the boundary of a polygon) and the **area** (the space enclosed by the polygon). (p. 395)

5. Primes that differ by 2 are called **twin primes**, and the smallest twin primes are 3 and 5. (p. 160)

From Bello and Britton. *Topics in Contemporary Mathematics, 6th ed.* Copyright © 1997. Houghton Mifflin Company.

Short-Answer Questions

Write your answers on separate paper.

1. How does surveying assist working memory?

2. Why is it important to understand and be able to define course-specific terminology?

Access Chapter 7 Chapter Quizzes 1–4 and Enhanced Quiz under "Interactive Quizzes" in your College Success CourseMate, accessed through *CengageBrain.com*.

Access all Chapter 7 Online Materials in your College Success CourseMate, accessed through *CengageBrain.com*.

Chapter Notes

8

Learning from College Textbooks

©JGI/Daniel Grill/Jupiter Images

Many college students have reading habits and use techniques that they have established over many years of reading, yet those habits and techniques may be inadequate to handle the demands of college-level reading and comprehension. By using the comprehension skills and strategies in this chapter, you can replace old reading habits and techniques with more effective ones designed to strengthen your reading skills and improve comprehension of textbook materials.

LEARNING OBJECTIVES

1. *Define active reading and discuss active reading strategies, reading from online sources, and textbook reading systems to use with college textbooks.*

2. *Define and discuss the seven organizational patterns used to organize details in paragraphs.*

3. *Explain and use strategies to read and interpret six kinds of graphic materials.*

Access Chapter 8 Expanded Chapter Outline and Objectives in your College Success CourseMate, accessed through *CengageBrain.com*.

YOUR CHAPTER MAPPING

After reading information under each heading, return to the chapter visual mapping below. Add key words to show subheadings and important details related to each heading.

Access Chapter 8 Visual Mapping in your College Success CourseMate, accessed through *CengageBrain.com*.

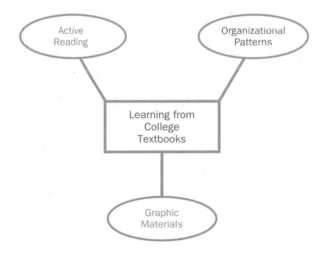

Learning from College Textbooks

ANSWER, SCORE, and **RECORD** your profile before you read this chapter. If you need to review the process, refer to the complete directions given in the profile for Chapter 1 on page 4.

ONLINE: You can complete the profile and get your score online at this textbook's CourseMate Web site.

		YES	NO
1.	I often go into "automatic pilot" when I read a textbook: I do not pay enough attention to the details and do not monitor my understanding.	_____	_____
2.	The system I use to read textbooks includes surveying and some form of writing questions about the chapter content.	_____	_____
3.	I use a variety of strategies when I read, and I adjust my strategies as needed to comprehend difficult-to-understand sections of information.	_____	_____
4.	I only verbalize, visualize, or ask myself questions about content when the information is difficult to understand.	_____	_____
5.	I know how to evaluate online materials for reliability and accuracy.	_____	_____
6.	I use clue words and the order of details in paragraphs to identify the organizational patterns used by the authors.	_____	_____
7.	I often have difficulty following the author's line of reasoning.	_____	_____
8.	I know how to interpret information on pie charts, flow charts, tables, bar graphs, and line graphs.	_____	_____
9.	I pose questions, compare data, and look for patterns and trends when I study visual materials.	_____	_____
10.	I am confident in my ability to read all kinds of textbooks and select the most effective reading strategies for each textbook.	_____	_____

QUESTIONS LINKED TO THE CHAPTER LEARNING OBJECTIVES

Questions 1–5: objective 1   Questions 8, 9: objective 3

Questions 6, 7: objective 2   Question 10: all objectives

Active Reading

 Define active reading, and discuss active reading strategies, reading from online sources, and textbook reading systems to use with college textbooks.

Comprehending what you read is a complex process that involves active learning and active reading. *Active reading* is the process of using effective strategies to engage working memory to achieve specific reading goals. Active reading places

Active reading is the process of using effective strategies to engage working memory to achieve specific reading goals.

heavy demands on your working memory, requires your undivided attention, and cannot be done quickly or effortlessly. Your working memory requires time to:

- Attach meaning to printed words
- Associate chunks of new information with previously learned information
- Analyze information by identifying its individual parts, characteristics, patterns, and relationships
- Integrate information into existing schemas to form generalizations
- Evaluate the logic and accuracy of information
- Apply the information to new situations or to solve problems

CONCEPT CHECK 8.1

What kinds of demands does reading place on working memory? What demands does it place on your central executive?

CHAPTER 8
REFLECTIVE WRITING 1

On separate paper, in a journal, or online at this textbook's CourseMate Web site, respond to the following questions:

1. Which of your textbooks is the most challenging for you this term? Explain the kinds of challenges it presents and why the textbook is difficult for you to use effectively.

2. Do you use the same or different reading processes for all of your textbooks? Explain your answer.

Access Chapter 8 Reflective Writing 1 in your College Success CourseMate, accessed through *CengageBrain.com.*

Active Reading Strategies

Active readers commit themselves to the reading process by creating a mindset that reflects their intention to engage actively in the reading process, comprehend content, process the information, and achieve reading goals. Use the following strategies to become a more active reader and active learner:

- **Create a plan of action.** Instead of haphazardly tackling a textbook chapter or procrastinating about reading assignments, select an appropriate, systematic reading system to use to move you into the reading process and achieve your specific reading goals. Your plan of action may also include a specific *warm-up activity* to use at the beginning of each study block.

- **Identify paragraph elements and definition clues for terminology.** Use the skills you learned in Chapter 7 for identifying main ideas and important supporting details in paragraphs. Use word, punctuation, definition, word structure and context clues to grasp meanings of terminology or unfamiliar words.

- **Interact with printed materials.** Use the active learning strategies discussed in Chapter 3: take notes, make diagrams, make study tools, write questions, and highlight. Read with a pen in your hand so you are ready to write as you read.

- **Verbalize and visualize information.** Reading out loud (verbalizing) activates your auditory channel. Hearing yourself read can clarify information because

CONCEPT CHECK 8.2

What is active reading? Explain at least six reading strategies active readers use when they read textbooks.

the natural tendency, without any conscious effort, is to read in clusters or meaningful groups of words or phrases. When you talk or reason out loud, your own words may help you identify what you understand and which sections of information you do not clearly understand.

Visualizing converts information from printed form (left brain) into pictures or visual images (right brain). Create strong visual impressions of the information or convert the information into a *movie in your mind.*

- **Select appropriate strategies for factual and procedural knowledge.** As you read, ask yourself: *Is this mainly factual (declarative) knowledge or is this procedural knowledge?* If you are working mainly with factual knowledge, focus your attention on identifying specific details of significance. If you are working mainly with procedural knowledge, focus your attention on the steps in the process. As you prepare to work with the information, select strategies best-suited to learn, rehearse, and review the information.

- **Identify organizational patterns, levels of information, and relationships.** Strive to "get into the author's head" by identifying patterns the author used in paragraphs to organize details. When you can identify the organizational pattern in a paragraph, the details used in the paragraph make more sense because you see their function.

  Authors develop concepts in headings or subheadings through a series of paragraphs. Examine the relationship of paragraphs to the headings or subheadings to understand the purpose or function of each paragraph. Likewise, the details in paragraphs develop the main ideas of the paragraphs, so examine the details to understand how they relate to the main ideas.

- **Ask questions to control your attention**. As you ask questions, your mind begins to search for answers. You might ask yourself: *What don't I get here? How do these details fit together? What is the author trying to say here?*

- **Use available graphic materials.** Examine graphic materials as they often clarify information in the paragraphs. Shift back and forth between the printed text and the visual graphic until you can integrate the two forms used to explain a concept.

- **Use all available resources.** Active readers are resourceful readers. They take advantage of textbook resources, Web site enrichment materials, supplementary videos, computer lab software, lab manuals, study guides, tutors, or study groups.

Active reading involves developing an awareness of the strategies you use and monitoring your comprehension. As you read different types of material, become keenly aware of sections of material you understand and sections of material that puzzle you or are difficult to understand. For difficult material, try using the following strategies to unlock the meaning of information and improve your comprehension.

- **Be persistent.** Stay with a paragraph or section of material until you comprehend it. Reread the difficult section of material slowly at least one more time. Use strategies to analyze the paragraph, identify paragraph structure or patterns, and find relationships among the details and the main idea. Understanding later concepts may rely on understanding information in the difficult paragraph, so do not move on or skip the paragraph just because it is difficult.

- **Adjust your reading rate.** Slow down the intake process, which means slow down your reading rate. For difficult materials, you may need to read individual

CONCEPT CHECK 8.3

What is the role of metacognition in the process of reading and understanding college textbooks?

sentences or phrases slowly to allow your working memory time to make associations and attach meanings to words.

- **Chunk up or chunk down.** Consciously control the size of information you are trying to understand. When you *chunk up,* you look beyond the paragraph to determine how the paragraph fits into the bigger picture. Place the paragraph or section in context with the surrounding material. Reread the previous paragraphs and read ahead to the following paragraph or paragraphs to find the natural flow or progression of information. When you *chunk down,* you break the information into smaller units, perhaps as small as individual sentences, or phrases, to identify the meanings of details.

- **Convert information into pictures.** Draw pictures of the information presented in paragraphs. As you reread a paragraph, begin drawing a picture of the significant details. The process often forces you to find the relationships and the important details.

Acknowledging the complexity of reading and understanding textbook material supports the fact that reading is an active, not a passive, process that requires effort, attention, commitment, and effective reading skills. **Figure 8.1** summarizes the thirteen active reading strategies for you to use to strengthen your reading skills.

Reading from Online Sources

In this age of technology, for many people the computer is an integral part of daily personal and professional life. We use the Internet for e-mail, banking, travel plans, shopping, information searches, online courses, and reading e-books. Needless to say, many additional uses of computers occur in the work environment as most businesses and professions now rely heavily on computers for the majority of their operations and transactions. The more we integrate technology into our lives, the greater is the need to learn new skills to use the online sources of information cautiously and effectively.

FIGURE 8.1   Essential Active Reading Strategies

- Create a plan of action.
- Identify paragraph elements and definition clues for terminology.
- Interact with printed materials.
- Verbalize and visualize information.
- Select appropriate strategies for factual and procedural knowledge.
- Identify organizational patterns, levels of information, and relationships.
- Ask questions to control your attention.
- Use graphic materials.
- Use all available resources.
- Be persistent.
- Adjust your reading rate.
- Chunk up or chunk down.
- Convert information into pictures.

---

224   **CHAPTER 8** Learning from College Textbooks

EXERCISE 8.1

Textbook Reading Inventory

Go to Appendix C, page C18, to complete the Textbook Reading Inventory, Exercise 8.1.

CONCEPT CHECK 8.4

Why is it important to use critical reading skills when you read online materials? How can you evaluate online materials?

Reading Information from Web Sites

Information on any given topic is at your fingertips within a few keystrokes. Access is easy and search results often produce abundant sites to access for information. However, not all information found on the Internet is accurate or reliable. Because anyone can post almost anything on the Internet without having the information evaluated, authenticated, or scrutinized for accuracy, you need to read online materials carefully. When you are using the Internet to search for information for academic purposes, such as writing a report or preparing for a speech, accept the information as accurate only after careful examination. Following are points to consider when you read and intend to use Web site information for academic purposes:

- Are there spelling or grammatical errors? Question the quality and credibility of information when you see spelling errors and grammatical errors as these "red flags" indicate the Web site is an informal personal posting.

- Can information presented as facts be proven or verified by data, research, or objective evidence? If not, the information may be subjective but camouflaged to look objective.

- Even though statements may sound objective or authoritative, are they really expressing an opinion in an attempt to convince the reader to accept a specific point of view? Words such as *should, would,* and *must* often signal a subjective point of view and an opinion.

- Is the information an online publication, such as a wiki encyclopedia entry or a personal blog? Even though the information may be accurate or informative, it has a greater potential to be incomplete, biased, inaccurate, and lack reference to the writer's credentials.

Using Internet sources for academic purposes is common when gathering information for research reports, essays, presentations, or speeches. Critical reading is essential to avoid accepting and using information that is not reliable, does not reflect quality, or is not useful. Cindy Griffin, author of *Invitation to Public Speaking*, offers the following suggestions for evaluating Internet information.

Is the information reliable? Check the domain in the URL. Is it .com (a commercial enterprise that might be trying to sell something), .org (a non-profit organization, more interested in services and issues than in commerce), .edu (an education institution), or .gov (a government agency)? What bias might those operating the site have about your topic? Do they make any disclaimers about the information they post on the site? What makes this information reliable or not?

Is the information authoritative? URLs that include a tilde (~) often indicate that a single individual is responsible for the information on a website. Can you find the person's credentials posted on the site? Can you contact the person and ask for credentials? Can you find the person's credentials in any printed sources, such as a *Who's Who* reference? Regardless of whether the material was authored by a single person, an organization, an institution, or a company, is the author an expert on the subject of the site?

How current is the information? Many web pages include a date that tells you when it was posted or last updated. If you don't see such a date, you may be able to find it in your browser's View or Documents menu. If you determine that the website is current, is the time frame relevant to your subject or arguments? You may find great information, but if it doesn't relate to the time frame of your speech, it's not relevant or ethical to use.

How complete is the information? Much of the text posted on the Internet consists of excerpts from printed materials, and what is left out may be of more use than what is included. For example, a site may contain one paragraph from a newspaper article, but that paragraph may not reflect the overall message of the article. If you want to use an excerpted portion of a printed work, you must locate the complete work to ensure that you are using that material accurately.

Is the information relevant? Many interesting facts and stories appear on the web, but be sure those you use as supporting material do more than just tell a great story. Your information must help you develop your thesis…Ask yourself whether the information fits your needs. Does it help develop your main ideas, or does it take you in a different direction?

Is the information consistent and unbiased? Is the information you find consistent with information you find on other sites, from printed sources, or from interviews? Can you find other sources to support the statements, claims, and facts provided by the website? If the information is inconsistent with other sources, it may reflect new findings about a topic, but it also may reflect an unfounded or unsubstantiated claim. Many sites only present one side of an issue. To guarantee a less biased presentation and more comprehensive picture of your topic, search at a number of different sites and be sure to cross-check what you find against information you obtain from more established sources such as books and other printed documents. Be wary of outrageous or controversial claims that can't be checked for accuracy or aren't grounded in reasonable arguments or sources.

From: Griffin. *Invitation to Public Speaking, 3e.* @2009 Wadsworth, Cengage Learning, p. 126.

Reading and accepting online materials as accurate and valid require you to use critical reading and critical thinking skills. (See Chapter 12) **Figure 8.2 Did This Section Click?** provides you with a useful checklist to evaluate online resources in terms of reliability, quality, and usefulness. The figure begins with an activity, which your instructor may assign or you may wish to do on your own. The term *blind peer review* refers to the process "whereby scholars in the field assess articles submitted for publication before the articles are published." (Watkins, Corry, p. 41–42).

FIGURE 8.2   Did This Section Click?

Evaluate an online news article from one of today's websites [for example, http://www.nytimes.com/college/students/, http://www.cnn.com, http://www.wsj.com]. using the following table. Place a check mark next to each criterion as you review the resource. You should also copy this table and use it to evaluate online resources that you plan to use in papers and other assignments in your college courses.

RELIABILITY	QUALITY	USEFULNESS
Contact information included	Avoids broad generalizations	Relates to your goals
Satisfactory author credentials	Up-to-date resources and references	Relates to your writing or research outline
Publication has a respectable reputation	Consistency of facts	Appropriate or similar audience
Sponsoring organization(s) of the author and/or publication are identified	Appropriate grammar and spelling	Appropriate level of detail for your goals
Blind peer-review process	From an online database	
Contacted author provided additional information	Bias or one-sided perspectives	
	Comprehensive review	
	Citations and references are accurate and complete	
	Resource is original source	
	Support or corroboration of facts	

Source: From Watkins, *E-Learning Companion,* 3E. © 2011 Wadsworth, a part of Cengage Learning, Inc. Reproduced by permission. www.cengage.com/permissions.

Reading from Online E-Books

E-books (electronic books) offer a new technology and way to read books online, or on electronic readers, such as the Kindle or Sony Reader systems. Textbooks, such as this book, that have an e-book option provide you with alternative access to textbook information. Reading e-books may require some adjustments from the way you typically read traditional books, but they also offer interactive features that are not available in traditional textbooks.

Learn to navigate the *Essential Study Skills* Interactive e-book   To access this textbook's interactive e-book, you must have a passkey that gives you permission to log onto this textbook's CourseMate Web site, accessible from www.CengageBrain.com. (If your textbook was not bundled with this resource, you can purchase a passkey online, too.) Once you have accessed the CourseMate for *Essential Study Skills,* click on "Interactive e-book." You will find useful navigational tools along the top of the e-book. Practice using the e-book by doing the following:

- Move the cursor to "Contents" in the upper left corner. When you click on "Contents," you will see a Table of Contents. Click on the chapter you want to read. A new column of information will appear that shows you the chapter headings. If you want to go to a specific chapter heading or part of the chapter, click on the words for the heading. If you want to begin reading from the first page of the chapter, click on "Chapter Objectives" at the top of the list of headings in the chapter. The first page of the selected chapter appears on the screen.

- Explore the interactive e-book functions by moving your cursor to the icons in the upper-right corner. Click on each of the following to see how it works:
- **Double Page:** Two pages appear side-by-side on the screen.
- **Single Page:** One textbook page appears on the screen.
- **Zoom In:** Zoom in on the page to enlarge the print size from 100% to 120%, 140%, 180%, or 200%.
- **Zoom Out:** Zoom out for a more "bird's eye" view: 80%, 60%, or 40%.
- **Highlighter:** Turn the highlighter on; highlight main ideas and important supporting details. Your highlights will be collected for a quick view of the items you've marked up by clicking on "My highlights."
- **Notes and Bookmarks:** Click the bookmark or note to save your place or type a note just like you would if you were marking a spot in your printed textbook. Your bookmarks notes will also appear in one place, under "My Notes" or "My Bookmarks."
- **Search**: If you are looking for a specific piece of information, use the Search feature to find content anywhere in the text.
- **Page Number:** Find the page number box. Click > to go to the next page, or click < to return to a previous page.
- **Print:** Click to print the page you are currently viewing.

As you read, notice any online icons that appear in the margins next to the following chapter features: outline, visual mapping, exercises, Check Points, Chapter Review Questions, Topics In-Depth, or Terms to Know. When you are ready to work on a Reflective Writing or Case Study exercise, a practice or a chapter quiz, or a flashcard drill, simply click on the icon. You will be linked immediately to the online interactive materials. This feature is one of the greatest advantages to reading the textbook online.

Use essential reading strategies for e-books Many of the essential strategies for reading textbooks you learned in Chapter 7 apply equally as well to reading e-books. (Review Figures 7.2, 7.7, and 7.10). When you read e-books, reading skills such as recognizing levels of information, learning terminology, using spaced practice, using various kinds of clues to unlock the meaning of unfamiliar words are essential reading skills to strive to use as you read the textbook online. The Essential Active Reading Strategies in Figure 8.1 also apply to reading your e-book online. To increase understanding, you still need to identify paragraph elements, interact with material, visualize and verbalize, ask questions, understand graphic materials, adjust reading rate, and chunk up or down to work with the appropriate size or unit of information at one time.

Surveying a new e-book chapter If your e-textbook begins a chapter with a chapter outline, you can create a big picture of the chapter by reading through the chapter outline and the main headings of the chapter. You can click to move from page to page through the e-book, stopping to examine charts, marginal notes, and key terms. You can finish surveying a new e-book chapter by reading the end-of-the-chapter material.

Taking notes when you read e-books As you will learn in Chapter 9, an effective study strategy involves reading thoroughly, highlighting important information, and then using the highlighting to help you identify and select the important information to put in your notes. For many e-textbooks, such as the multimedia e-book for this textbook, you have two interactive features that encourage you to take notes while you are reading

CONCEPT CHECK 8.5

How does reading from an e-book differ from reading a traditional textbook?

online: the *highlighter* so you can highlight directly on the e-book pages and the *pen* that opens a space for you to type brief notes or questions about the information you are reading. Use the following Essential Strategies for Taking E-Book Notes:

- **Use the Read-Record-Recite Cycle.** Read a paragraph or a short section of information, pause to record what is important, and recite what you recorded. (See page 230.)

- **Use the highlighter and notes features in your e-textbook.** Record important information by using the highlighter to highlight main ideas and important supporting details. Use the "notes" feature to write brief notes about the information you read. If your e-textbook does not have these interactive features, instead of highlighting, go directly to taking notes on separate notebook paper. Before moving to a new paragraph or section of information, recite the important points you put in your notes.

- **Make Computer Notes.** If the "notes" feature does not provide you with sufficient space to take notes or write definitions close to the bold-faced terms in the text, you have another option. First, highlight important information. If you are using a computer with Windows 7, open a separate window, open Word, and write notes in your Word file. Use your highlighting as a guide to help you select which information is important to write in your notes.

- **Cut and paste notes.** If your e-textbook allows you to cut and paste materials from the textbook, you have another notetaking option. Cut and paste your highlighting and your notes into a Word file. Take time then to reorganize your notes if necessary and expand your notes with additional information. Save your Word file.

- **Write notes on notebook paper.** Return to the e-book chapter. Use your highlighting and notes as guides to help you select which information is important to write in notes you create on separate paper. This is the same process used for traditional textbooks: transfer important highlighting and marginal notes into notes on separate paper.

Many of the rehearsal strategies that you would use for a traditional textbook do not take place in the textbook; they take place on separate paper or on index cards or flashcards. The same is true for rehearsal strategies for information you are learning from an e-textbook. Most elaborative rehearsal strategies for both the traditional textbook and the e-textbook are done outside of the book. Reading by itself is not sufficient to learn and apply textbook information, so do not throw away the pens and paper as you will still need them as you study.

The SQ4R Reading System

Using a systematic approach for reading textbook chapters may take more time than you are used to spending for reading a chapter, but you will process and comprehend the information more thoroughly, eliminate the need to reread chapters multiple times in order to learn the content, and in the long run, save valuable study time.

One of the first textbook reading systems, SQ3R, was developed by Francis E. Robinson in 1941. The letters represent a five-step process: survey, question, read, recite, and review. In other courses and textbooks, you may encounter different reading systems, but upon close examination, you will notice that other reading systems often use different labels for steps very similar to those in SQ3R. The reason is that the steps and activities used in the SQ3R are powerful and proven to increase comprehension and enhance learning.

SQ4R is a six-step system for reading and comprehending textbook chapters: **s**urvey, **q**uestion, **r**ead, **r**ecord, **r**ecite, and **r**eview. SQ4R adds a fourth "R" to remind students to record important information (take notes). As with any approach, skipping

Access Chapter 8 Practice Quiz 1: SQ4R under "Interactive Quizzes" in your College Success CourseMate, accessed through *CengageBrain.com*

SQ4R is a six-step system for reading and comprehending textbook chapters: survey, question, read, record, recite, and review.

any one step weakens the system. To gain the most benefit from this system, use all six steps shown in **Figure 8.3** each time you use the SQ4R system.

Step One: Survey the Chapter

Use the steps discussed in Chapter 7 for surveying a chapter (page 197). This first step of SQ4R should require less than twenty minutes of your time, but it will provide you with an overview of the chapter and will begin the process of activating or creating schemas upon which you can attach details.

Step Two: Write Questions

The *question step of SQ4R* involves turning the chapter title, each heading, and each subheading into a question. The ten or twenty minutes it takes to write questions is time well spent. You get one additional overview of the chapter, and you create a purpose for reading, focus your attention on upcoming information, and activate working memory. Use the following suggestions when you write your questions:

- **Strive to use a variety of questions**. Each question word elicits a different kind of response. For example, answers to questions that begin with the following words elicit the specific kinds of responses:

  What...response: specific facts   **Why....response:** reasons
  How...response: steps or processes   **When...response:** time periods
  Which....response: specific items   **Who....response:** specific people
  Where...response: specific locations

- **Modify or delete some words in headings and subheadings** if necessary. Write the questions directly in your textbook next to the title, headings, or subheadings, or write them on notebook paper or index cards, leaving space to write the answers later. Following are examples of questions for the beginning of this chapter. The italic print shows words added to the title, heading, and subheadings to create questions.

  > **Title:** *How can I* **Learn from College Textbooks**?
  > **Heading:** *What is* **Active Reading**?
  > **Subheading:** *Which* **Active Reading Strategies** *do I need to learn to use?*

If you are reading an e-textbook, you may not be able to write questions directly across from the title, headings, or subheadings, but you can use the "notes" feature to create a list of questions for the title, headings, and subheadings. You can then transfer these notes to a Word file or copy them on separate paper. If you are using the tradition textbook in addition to the e-textbook, you can write your questions in the traditional textbook.

CONCEPT CHECK 8.6

What are the six steps in the SQ4R reading system? How do they differ from any other reading system you have previously used?

The **question step of SQ4R** involves turning the chapter title, each heading, and each subheading into a question.

| FIGURE 8.3 | The Six Steps of SQ4R |

1. **Survey** the chapter to get an overview.
2. Write **Questions** for each heading and subheading.
3. **Read** the information, one paragraph at a time.
4. **Record** by selecting a form of notetaking to record information.
5. **Recite** the important information from the paragraph.
6. **Review** the information learned in the chapter.

Step Three: Read Carefully

Some students feel that they should be able to "read fast" to get through chapters. Others read chapters—only to find at the end of the chapters that they must reread the chapter because they do not remember much of what they read the first time. The *read step of SQ4R* involves reading *carefully* and *thoroughly*. Use the following three suggestions for the *read step* of SQ4R:

- **Decide if overview reading of chapter contents would be beneficial.** Because overview reading involves reading straight through without pausing, use it sparingly. Overview reading is beneficial for difficult or unfamiliar content to help you begin to form schemas or to give you a "flavor for" the materials before beginning the process of thorough reading. Do not take notes or highlight when your intention is to do overview reading only.

- **Begin thorough reading.** For most textbooks, you should read *one paragraph at a time* and then stop to dissect, analyze, and comprehend the content of the paragraph.

- **Use active reading strategies to unlock the meaning of difficult paragraphs.** Review Figure 8.1 for thirteen active reading strategies.

The read step of SQ4R involves reading *carefully* and *thoroughly*.

CONCEPT CHECK 8.7

How does thorough reading in Step 3 of SQ4R differ from overview reading and recreational reading?

Step Four: Record Information

The *record step of SQ4R* involves stopping at the end of a paragraph or section of information to take notes or record important information you will need to study further. Taking time to record information (take notes) benefits you in many ways:

1. Your notes become a reduced or a condensed form of the information you need to study and learn.

2. Taking notes keeps you actively involved in the learning process and reduces the tendency for you to read without processing information clearly.

3. Taking notes holds information in working memory and provides more time for you to encode it for your long-term memory.

4. Creating a set of notes requires identification of key concepts and attention to key details and relationships among the details—processes that lead to improved comprehension. In Chapters 9 and 10, you will learn a variety of notetaking options to use:

The *record step of SQ4R* involves stopping at the end of a paragraph or section of information to take notes or record important information.

Annotation	Cornell Notes	Two- or Three-Column Notes
Outline Notes	Visual Mappings	Hierarchies
Comparison Charts	Index Card Notes	

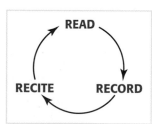

The *recite step of SQ4R* involves reciting the important points you read in the paragraph and recorded in your notes without looking at printed materials.

The Read-Record-Recite Cycle is a thorough reading strategy that involves reading a section of information, taking notes, and explaining the information out loud before moving to new information.

Step Five: Recite

The *recite step of SQ4R* involves reciting the important points you read in the paragraph and recorded in your notes without looking at printed materials. After reciting, look back at the textbook or your notes to check your accuracy.

Continue to move through the chapter by using the Read-Record-Recite Cycle. The *Read-Record-Recite Cycle* is a thorough reading strategy that involves reading a section of information, taking notes, and explaining the information out loud before moving to new information. You can use the Read-Record-Recite Cycle for traditional and e-textbooks. When you have completed this cycle for the entire chapter, move on to the final step of SQ4R.

Step Six: Review

The *review step of SQ4R* involves using immediate and ongoing review. Following are activities you can use to review the content in the chapter:

- Answer the chapter review questions that appear at the end of the chapter.
- Answer the questions you formulated during the *question step*.
- Study and recite from the notes that you took in the *record step*.
- Write a summary. In paragraph form, summarize the important concepts and details.
- Create additional study tools, such as flashcards, outlines, study tapes, or visual notes.
- Rework problems. Rework problems from class or from your textbook. Compare the steps you used and your answers with those in the textbook. For language courses, copy sentences or grammatical exercises from the textbook. Rework the assignment, diagram the sentences, or identify parts of speech within sentences. For math books, rework problem sets. Check your accuracy.

> The review step of SQ4R involves using immediate and ongoing review.

> **CONCEPT CHECK 8.8**
>
> *What would be the consequences of skipping the S step of SQ4R? What would be the consequences of skipping each of the remaining five steps of SQ4R?*

EXERCISE 8.2

Transfer These SQ4R Skills

PURPOSE: Learning to use a reading system, such as SQ4R, requires practice. With practice, the system becomes more comfortable and automatic.

DIRECTIONS: Use any textbook from one of your courses. Use all six steps of SQ4R for a new chapter. On separate paper, briefly summarize the activities you performed during each step.

EXERCISE 8.3

SQ4R and Principles of Memory

PURPOSE: Effective study skills strategies are powerful because they support learning theories and research. Understanding the reasons for using specific steps emphasizes the importance of using each step when you study.

DIRECTIONS: Work with a partner or in a small group. On separate paper, copy the SQ4R chart on the right. Label the six steps of SQ4R. Then, for each step of SQ4R, discuss which of the Twelve Principles of Memory (SAVE CRIB FOTO) are used in that step. Using any method you prefer, attach the appropriate Memory Principles to each section of the chart. Be prepared to share your results with the class.

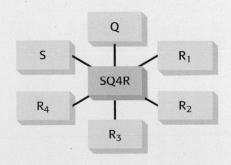

The Triple Q Reading System

The Triple Q System is an active reading system that focuses on formulating questions *before, during,* and *after* reading a chapter. After *surveying* the chapter, you can begin the process of formulating questions. **Figure 8.4** shows the three Q's in the Triple Q system.

> The Triple Q Reading System is an active reading system that focuses on formulating questions *before, during,* and *after* reading a chapter.

Q_1 Write Questions Before You Read

Use the same suggestions for writing Q_1 questions as shown previously for the *question step* of SQ4R. Formulate a variety of questions for the title, headings, and subheadings by using the words *what, why, how, when, which, who,* and *where.*

Q_2 Write Questions During the Reading Process

After you read and identify important concepts and details in a paragraph, think about the information and predict possible test questions that you might later encounter on the material. Then, do the following:

- In the margin, *write one or two study questions or test questions* that can be answered by the information in the paragraph. Use the *what, why, how, when, which, who,* and *where* question words as well as the following question words frequently used on tests:

List	Define	Describe	Identify	Discuss	Compare
Calculate	Show	Classify	Explain	Contrast	Solve

- Return to the paragraph. *Highlight key words* in the paragraph that provide details for answers to your questions. As shown in **Figure 8.5**, you can use different colors of highlighter pens to differentiate details if you wish.

If you are using an e-textbook, this Triple Q Reading System may not be an effective reading system to use because you may not be able to write questions in the margins next to key words. If your "notes" feature does not allow you to place notes in the margins next to important text, select a different reading approach or return to the traditional textbook to use this reading method.

CONCEPT CHECK 8.9

How do the questions you write in the Q_1 differ from the questions you write for the Q_2 and Q_3 steps?

FIGURE 8.4   The Triple Q Reading System

Step	When to Use	What to Do
Q_1	Before reading	Write questions for the title, headings, and subheadings in a chapter.
Q_2	During the reading process	After reading a paragraph, write one or two study questions in the margin next to the paragraph. Highlight key words in the paragraph that answer each question.
Q_3	After reading a chapter	Write chapter questions to use to review the chapter and prepare for tests. Practice answering all your questions.

FIGURE 8.5	Using Q_1 and Q_2 Steps in an Excerpt

When does achievement motivation develop? List factors that influence development of achievement motivation. How can parents support or undermine development of ach. motivation? Important point	***Development of Achievement Motivation*** Achievement motivation develops in early childhood under the influence of both genetic and environmental factors. As described in the personality chapter, children inherit general behavioral tendencies, such as impulsiveness and emotionality, and these tendencies may support or undermine the development of achievement motivation. The motivation to achieve is also shaped by what children learn from watching and listening to others, especially their parents. Evidence for the influence of parental teachings about achievement comes from a study in which young boys were given a task so difficult that they were sure to fail. Fathers whose sons scored low on achievement motivation tests often became annoyed as they watched their boys work on the task, discouraged them from continuing, and interfered or even completed the task themselves (Rosen & D'Andrade, 1959). A much different response pattern emerged among parents of children who scored high on tests of achievement motivation. Those parents tended to (1) encourage the child to try difficult tasks, especially new ones; (2) give praise and other rewards for success; (3) encourage the child to find ways to succeed rather than merely complaining about failure; and (4) prompt the child to go on to the next, more difficult challenge (McClelland, 1985). Other research with adults shows that even the slightest cues that bring a parent to mind can boost some people's efforts to achieve a goal (Shah, 2003).

Source: Bernstein/Nash. Essentials of Psychology, p. 317. Houghton Mifflin Company, © 2009. Reprinted with permission.

Q3 Write Questions After Reading a Chapter

Writing chapter questions after you finish reading a chapter while the information is fresh in your memory eliminates the need to spend time predicting and writing questions later when you prepare for tests. These questions also provide you with study tools to use to rehearse information, to self-quiz, and to use as a warm-up activity at the beginning of a study block.

Questions by themselves are not sufficient for building memory. *Answering* the questions, reciting, and reviewing the answers are the processes that build memory. Use the following three strategies for maximum benefits from your questions.

- **Recite answers**. Cover up the printed text. Recite by using your own words to answer the Q_1, Q_2, and Q_3 questions. Refer to your textbook to check the accuracy and completeness of the information you recite.

- **Create notes**. On separate paper or on index cards, copy the questions and provide the answers. These notes become valuable study tools to review and prepare for tests.

- **Review your questions and answers**. You can use your questions and answers as a warm-up activity at a beginning of a study block, for a quick review before a related lecture or discussion, as quizzing materials in a study group, or to prepare for an upcoming test.

A Customized Reading System

SQ4R and Triple Q are effective textbook reading systems, but they are not the only systems available for you to use. A *Customized Reading System* is a system you design for

A **Customized Reading System** is a system you design for a specific textbook based on the author's suggestions and the chapter features.

CONCEPT CHECK 8.10

When is a Customized Reading System appropriate to use? How does a reader know what steps to include in a Customized Reading System?

a specific textbook based on the author's suggestions and the chapter features. Your goal with this system is to establish a consistent routine to use to read and study each chapter.

Step 1: Use the Author's Suggestions

Carefully read the To the Student or the Preface information in the front of the textbook. List the author's suggestions for reading and using the textbook.

Step 2: Use the Chapter Features

Examine the chapter features in the first few chapters. In some textbooks, such as composition and math textbooks, the chapter format and the chapter features "dictate" a reading process for you to use—work through each section and each feature in the order presented. For example, the textbook structure may begin with definitions of terminology, then move to an example or a prototype with explanations, and then provide problem sets to solve by applying the steps shown in the prototype or example.

Step 3: Create Your Customized System

Using the information learned by surveying, create a list of steps that you will use consistently and habitually to read and comprehend the information in each chapter. (See **Figure 8.6.**) To work successfully, your customized approach to reading the textbook should:

- Utilize effective study skills strategies and the Twelve Principles of Memory
- Incorporate at least one form of notetaking to organize and record information
- Include reworking problem sets or portions of homework assignments
- End with review activities

FIGURE 8.6 A Customized Reading System for a Math Textbook

Step 1: Read the introduction, goals, and objectives.

Step 2: **Read the definitions.** Create a vocabulary sheet or definition flashcards each time you encounter new terminology, formulas, equations, and symbols.

Step 3: **Study examples until you understand the problem type and steps involved.** Choose one example to memorize as a *prototype*. Create meaningful notes.

Step 4: **Practice new skills.** Rework the example problems. Check your accuracy.

Step 5: **Do new problem sets.** These usually mirror the problem types shown by the examples. Pay attention to underlying patterns. Apply the steps; check work.

Step 6: **Do mixed problem sets.** Look for underlying patterns. Match problem types to prototypes you have memorized. Apply the steps; check answers.

Step 7: **Do the real-world story problems.** Look for familiar underlying patterns. Apply RSTUV steps (Appendix A, Strategy 51, page A34). Check work. Be sure to label units in the solution.

Step 8: **Review the chapter.** Read the chapter summary. Do review problems. Rework several examples and problems from the chapter. Recite and study the terminology, formulas, equations, and problem-solving steps.

CHECK POINT 8.1

Answers appear on page B4

True or False?

_____ 1. Surveying a chapter is a recommended reading strategy and is the first step in many reading systems.

_____ 2. You should use active reading strategies only for complex, difficult textbooks.

_____ 3. A student who uses metacognition adjusts strategies when initial strategies do not result in comprehending textbook information.

_____ 4. A Customized Reading System designed for one textbook can be used effectively for all other textbooks.

_____ 5. SQ4R works effectively for traditional textbooks but not for e-textbooks.

 Access Chapter 8 Practice Quiz 2: Active Reading under "Interactive Quizzes" in your College Success CourseMate, accessed through *CengageBrain.com*.

EXERCISE 8.4

Textbook Case Studies

DIRECTIONS

1. Read each case study carefully. Respond to the question at the end of each case study by using *specific* strategies discussed in this chapter. Answer in complete sentences.

2. Write your responses on paper or online at the CourseMate student Web site, Textbook Case Studies. You will be able to print your online response or e-mail it to your instructor.

CASE STUDY 1: Cecilia does not have problems reading the textbook words, but she often has problems figuring out what she can do to study and practice the information. She usually just rereads the chapter one or two times more. What strategies will help Cecilia become a more active reader?

CASE STUDY 2: Several of Jeremy's "get-by" reading strategies that he acquired in high school are proving to be ineffective for his college textbooks. His current strategies involve looking through a chapter, reading the notes in the margins, examining graphs and charts, and reading the summary. He then reads only the sections of information that appear to have new or unfamiliar information. Jeremy visited the tutoring center to learn more effective strategies for his geology textbook. If you were the tutor Jeremy visited, what strategies would you recommend he begin using for his geology textbook?

 Access Chapter 8 Textbook Case Studies and Web-Only Case Studies in your College Success CourseMate, accessed through *CengageBrain.com*.

Organizational Patterns

 Define and discuss the seven organizational patterns used to organize details in paragraphs.

Organizational patterns are paragraph patterns that writers use to present details in a logical, meaningful order. Understanding organizational patterns helps you unlock the meaning of what you read, identify relationships among the details within a paragraph, and follow the internal logic and natural progression of information. Paragraphs may exhibit characteristics of more than one organizational pattern, but one dominant pattern reflects the purpose of the paragraph. In the following sections you will learn more about each pattern, its clue words, and diagram formats you can use to convert information into visual forms. A sample paragraph clarifies the key elements for each organizational pattern. You will encounter the following seven organizational patterns in your college textbooks:

- chronological pattern
- process pattern
- comparison or contrast pattern
- definition pattern
- examples pattern
- cause/effect (causal) pattern
- whole-and-parts pattern

The Chronological Pattern

The **chronological pattern** presents details in a logical time sequence.

Chronological Pattern	Clue Words	Diagram for This Pattern
▌ Details are presented in a logical time sequence: *chronological order.* ▌ Details happen in a specific, fixed order to reach a conclusion or an ending. ▌ This pattern is often used to tell a story (a narrative) or explain a sequence of events.	when then before next after first second finally	1. → 2. → 3. → 4. → Conclusion or Ending

Excerpt Demonstrating the Chronological Pattern

While commercial farming was spreading, cattle ranching—one of the West's most romantic industries—was evolving. Early in the nineteenth century herds of cattle, introduced by the Spanish and expanded by Mexican ranchers, roamed southern Texas and bred with cattle brought by Anglo settlers. The resulting longhorn breed multiplied and became valuable by the 1860s, when population growth increased demand for beef and railroads facilitated the transportation of food. By 1870, drovers were herding thousands of Texas cattle northward by Kansas, Missouri, and

Wyoming. On these long drives, mounted cowboys (as many as 25 percent of whom were African-American) supervised the herds, which fed on open grassland along the way. At the northern terminus—usually Abilene, Dodge City, or Cheyenne—the cattle were sold to northern ranches or loaded onto trains bound for Chicago and St. Louis for slaughter and distribution.

From Mary Beth Norton, David M. Katzman, Paul D. Escott, and Howard Chudacoff, *A People and a Nation, 5th ed.,* p. 496. Copyright © 1998 Houghton Mifflin Company. Used with permission.

The Process Pattern

The *process pattern* presents a specific procedure or order of steps to use to do, create, repair, or solve problems.

CONCEPT CHECK 8.13

What is the purpose of a process pattern? Does it tend to emphasize declarative or procedural knowledge?

The process pattern presents a specific procedure or order of steps to use to do, create, repair, or solve problems.

Process Pattern	Clue Words	Diagram for This Pattern
▌ Details explain a procedure or how something works. ▌ Details may provide directions to complete a specific series of steps to do, create, repair, or solve something. ▌ Steps must be done in chronological order. ▌ Outcome is a finished product or a solution. ▌ Science, social science, and mathematics textbooks use this pattern frequently.	steps process procedure first second before after when as soon as next finally outcome result	1. → 2. → 3. → 4. → End Product or Solution

Excerpt Demonstrating the Process Pattern

Frost Wedging Water expands in volume by about 9% when it turns to ice. When water enters pores or cracks in a rock and the temperature subsequently falls below 0 degrees C (32 degrees F, the freezing point of water), the force of the expanding ice greatly exceeds that needed to fracture even solid granite. The cracks then become enlarged, often loosening or dislodging fragments of rock. This enlargement allows even more water to enter the crack, and the process is repeated. This frost wedging process is the fastest, most effective type of mechanical weathering. It is most active in environments where surface water is abundant and temperatures often fluctuate around the freezing point of water.

Source: Chernicoff/Fox, *Essentials of Geology,* p. 185. Houghton Mifflin, © 2003.

The Comparison/Contrast Pattern

The *comparison or contrast pattern* shows similarities and/or differences for two or more subjects.

CONCEPT CHECK 8.14

What clues signal that a paragraph is a comparison/contrast paragraph? Can a paragraph with a comparison/contrast pattern show more than two subjects?

The comparison or contrast pattern shows similarities and/or differences for two or more subjects.

Learning how to read and interpret graphic materials helps you understand data, identify relationships, and see trends. What kinds of graphic materials do you frequently encounter in your textbooks?

- *Photographs, illustrations,* and *diagrams,* which include cartoons, sketches, and drawings, provide background information and clarify concepts.
- *Pie charts* show and compare parts (sectors) to a whole.
- *Flow charts* show levels of organization or the directions in which information flows.
- *Tables* use columns and rows to organize information on various topics or to show data to use to solve problems.
- *Bar graphs* use vertical or horizontal bars to show frequency of occurrence of different subjects or data and to show trends.
- *Line graphs* plot information on a grid to form one continuous line to show trends and compare data.

A **caption** is a short explanation that accompanies a graphic.

A **legend** defines or gives values for the symbols used in the graphic.

Many graphic materials include captions and legends to help you interpret the information. A **caption** is a short explanation or description that accompanies a graphic. A **legend** defines or gives values for the symbols used in the graphic. Captions and legends provide you with essential information for understanding and interpreting the graphic materials, so read them carefully.

To gain the greatest benefits from graphic materials, use the eight Essential Strategies for Working with Graphic Materials in **Figure 8.7**.

FIGURE 8.7   Essential Strategies for Working with Graphic Materials

- **Carefully read the features in the graphic.** Read the titles, captions, legends, and labels that appear with graphic materials.
- **Examine the details carefully.** Look at sizes, colors, spatial positions, likenesses and differences, relationships, patterns, and trends.
- **Verbalize or "string ideas together."** Talk to yourself about the information. Use some of your own words to explain the information and the relationships you see.
- **Visualize the graphic.** Create a strong visual image or impression of the basic features of the graphic. Practice using this as a retrieval cue to recall and rehearse information.
- **Ask yourself questions about the content.** Create questions about specific parts of the graphic

materials, questions that compare two or more items, and questions that focus on the cause-effect relationships, trends, and patterns.

- **Copy important graphic materials into your notes.** Unless the graphic materials are too complex, include them in your notes. Color-code the parts of the graphics and add labels and captions. For more complex graphics, list important points you learned from the graphic and list textbook page references for later review.
- **Expand the graphic materials in your notes.** Add your own reminders, details, or explanations to the graphics you copied into your notes.
- **Write a short summary under the graphics in your textbook or in your notes.**

Apply These Skills

EXERCISE 8.6

DIRECTIONS: As you read through this section about Graphic Materials, start looking in your textbooks for examples of each type of visual graphic. Note the name of the textbook and the page number as this information will be helpful for the Group Processing-A Collaborative Learning Activity on page 250. Your instructor may ask you to photocopy one or more examples you find and to write questions next to each visual graphic that will help you understand the information presented in the diagrams, charts, tables, or graphs.

Photographs, Illustrations, and Diagrams

Survey any textbook and you will see an array of photographs, illustrations, and diagrams. Examine the illustration in **Figure 8.8**. You could apply the Essential Strategies for Working with Graphic Materials (Figure 8.7) by asking the following kinds of questions and performing the suggested activities to learn from this illustration:

1. What did you learn by reading the caption?

2. What are the important details in the diagram?

3. What does the diagram show? Verbalize or explain the flow of information in the diagram.

4. Visualize the basic structure of the graphic. After studying the diagram, use a Look-Away Technique. Practice using your visual memory to recall the diagram.

5. Next to or below the illustration, create two questions about the details.

6. Next to or below the illustration, write a short summary about the graphic.

| FIGURE 8.8 | The Hydrologic Cycle |

All of the water that falls from the atmosphere onto the Earth's surface eventually enters the vast oceanic reservoir through one or more of the pathways of the cycle.

Precipitation · Evaporation · Run-off · Ground water · Ocean

Ebbing/Wentworth. *Introductory Chemistry.* Houghton Mifflin Company, © 1998, p. 426. Reprinted with permission.

Pie Charts

Pie charts, also called circle graphs, show a whole unit (100 percent) divided into individually labeled parts or sectors. Pie charts are based on a whole-to-parts organizational pattern. **Figure 8.9** clearly shows the seven "selves" of a "whole person" as presented in a textbook for counselors; each sector of the pie is of equal proportion. If you were enrolled in the class using this textbook, after reading more detailed descriptions about each category of information, you could copy the chart into your notes and attach key words or phrases to each sector.

For some pie charts, you may need to estimate the percentage represented by each sector of the chart, or you may need to convert data into percentages. Frequently, however, pie charts provide exact percentages, making comparison of sectors easier and more accurate. (See **Figure 8.10**.) After examining the basic parts of a pie chart,

> **Pie charts,** also called circle graphs, show a whole unit (100 percent) divided into individually labeled parts or sectors.

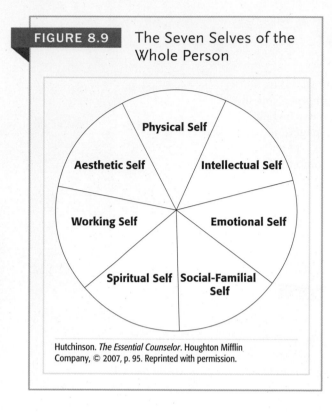

FIGURE 8.9   The Seven Selves of the Whole Person

Physical Self
Aesthetic Self
Intellectual Self
Working Self
Emotional Self
Spiritual Self
Social-Familial Self

Hutchinson. *The Essential Counselor*. Houghton Mifflin Company, © 2007, p. 95. Reprinted with permission.

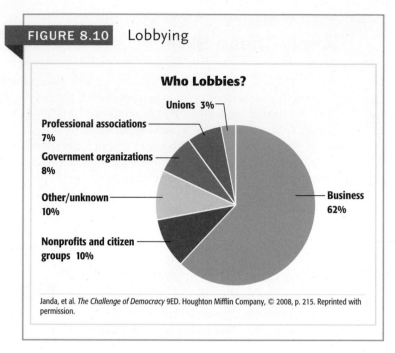

FIGURE 8.10   Lobbying

Who Lobbies?

Unions 3%
Professional associations 7%
Government organizations 8%
Other/unknown 10%
Nonprofits and citizen groups 10%
Business 62%

Janda, et al. *The Challenge of Democracy* 9ED. Houghton Mifflin Company, © 2008, p. 215. Reprinted with permission.

CONCEPT CHECK 8.20

Discuss the way pie charts and flow charts organize information. What reading strategies work well to understand both kinds of visual graphics?

Flow charts, also called organizational charts, show levels of organization or a directional flow of information from one level or topic to another.

compare and contrast sectors, make generalizations about the categories of information, and pose questions about the information.

Flow Charts

Flow charts, also called organizational charts, show levels of organization or a directional flow of information from one level or topic to another. To remember information in flow charts, use the Essential Strategies in Figure 8.7, page 242: *Read*; *Examine*; *Verbalize/String Ideas Together*; *Visualize*; *Question*; *Copy*; *Expand*; and *Summarize*. In Chapter 5, you learned about the Expectancy Theory. **Figure 8.11** condenses one full textbook page of information about the Expectancy Theory into an easy-to-comprehend flow chart. You could use the following kinds of activities to learn from this type of flow chart:

1. Read the title, the caption, and examine the details in the chart.

2. Verbalize or string ideas together to explain the chart.

3. Create a visual impression of the chart. Look away and practice visualizing the chart.

4. Formulate two questions about the details in the chart.

5. Copy the chart on your own paper. Expand your chart in some way.

6. Next to or below your chart, write a short summary about the important information to remember.

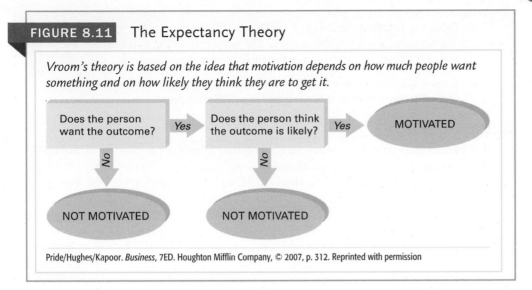

FIGURE 8.11 The Expectancy Theory

Vroom's theory is based on the idea that motivation depends on how much people want something and on how likely they think they are to get it.

Pride/Hughes/Kapoor. *Business*, 7ED. Houghton Mifflin Company, © 2007, p. 312. Reprinted with permission

Tables

Tables, also called comparison charts, grids, or matrixes, use columns and rows to organize information on various topics or to show data to use to solve problems. Tables require careful reading as they often contain a considerable amount of data in the boxes or the *cells* of the chart. In **Figure 8.12**, notice the four columns of information: Storage System, Function, Capacity, and Duration. Then notice the three rows of subjects: Sensory memory, Short-term and working memory, and Long-term memory. When tables appear without lines that divide columns and rows, you can add those lines to the table if doing so will help you see the information more clearly. Following are examples of activities to use to understand tables.

1. **Read the title and the caption.** Verbalize or string ideas together to explain the table.

2. **Visually memorize the skeleton of the chart.** The skeleton consists of the titles or labels for the columns and the rows. Look away and recite the skeleton.

> Tables, also called comparison charts, grids, or matrixes, use columns and rows to organize information on various topics or to show data to use to solve problems.

CONCEPT CHECK 8.21

Describe where you will find each of the following on a table: rows, columns, and cells. How can you read or string together the information in tables?

FIGURE 8.12 Storing New Memories Table

Storage System	Function	Capacity	Duration
Sensory memory	Briefly holds representations of stimuli from each sense for further processing	Large: absorbs all sensory input from a particular stimulus	Less than 1 second
Short-term and working memory	Holds information in awareness and manipulates it to accomplish mental work	Five to nine distinct items or chunks of information	About 18 seconds
Long-term memory	Stores new information indefinitely	Unlimited	Unlimited

From Bernstein/Nash. *Essentials of Psychology*. Houghton Mifflin Company, © 2008, p. 391. Reprinted with permission.

3. **Read the information in each cell for the first column.** For example, read: *The function of sensory memory is... The function of STM and WM is... The function of LTM is...* Repeat the process by reading across the rows.

4. **Create questions based on the table.** Ask questions that compare the different cells, the different columns, and the different rows.

Bar Graphs

> Bar graphs use vertical or horizontal bars to show frequency of occurrence for different subjects or data being graphed and to show trends.

Bar graphs use vertical or horizontal bars to show frequency of occurrence for different subjects or data being graphed and to show trends. To read bar graphs, begin by reading the title and the caption. Then read the label that appears on the *horizontal line* called the *x axis* and on the *vertical* line, called the *y axis.* Notice that one axis identifies the data that is being graphed while the other axis shows the frequency of an occurrence or event, which may be shown in percentages, quantities, or a unit of measurement. Finally, use the height (or the length) of the bars to obtain information about each bar; compare the information. As you encounter bar graphs in your textbooks, you will notice a variety of formats may be used to graph information.

Histograms

Sometimes a bar graph shows a *range of values* on the *x axis,* or the base of the chart. When this occurs, as in **Figure 8.13**, the bar graph is known as a *histogram.* Notice the kinds of questions you can ask to understand the information in a histogram.

Double Bar Graph

Other times, as shown in **Figure 8.14,** you will find *double bar graphs* that show two kinds of data. The *legend* for double bar graphs defines the colors of each of the bars. Notice the kinds of questions you can ask to understand the information in a double bar graph.

CONCEPT CHECK 8.22

How do histograms, double bar graphs, and horizontal bar graphs differ? What do they have in common?

FIGURE 8.13   Stress Duration and Illness

Two hundred seventy-six volunteers were interviewed about recent life stress, then infected with a cold virus. As shown [below], the longer a stressor had lasted, in months, the more likely a person was to catch the cold. Over time, stress breaks down the body's immune system.

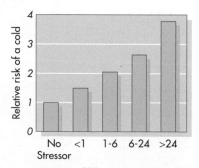

Questions:

1. How does the caption help you understand the bar graph?
2. Which axis shows the data being graphed? What do the number ranges represent?
3. Look at the vertical axis, the frequency data axis. What do the numbers represent?
4. What are *two* questions you could ask about this data?
5. What generalization could you make based on the data in the chart?

Brehm/Kassin/Fein. *Social Psychology*, 5ED. Houghton Mifflin Company, © 2002, p. 515. Reprinted with permission.

FIGURE 8.14 Sources of Capital for Entrepreneurs

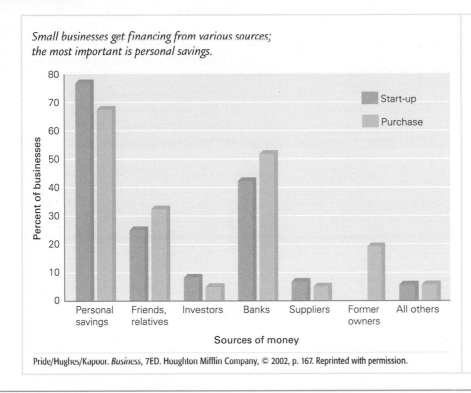

Small businesses get financing from various sources; the most important is personal savings.

[Bar graph with y-axis "Percent of businesses" ranging 0 to 80, x-axis "Sources of money" with categories: Personal savings, Friends/relatives, Investors, Banks, Suppliers, Former owners, All others. Legend: Start-up, Purchase]

Pride/Hughes/Kapoor. *Business*, 7ED. Houghton Mifflin Company, © 2002, p. 167. Reprinted with permission.

Questions:

1. What did you learn by reading the caption and the legend?
2. What information appears on the x axis? What appears on the y axis?
3. Estimate the percentages for each bar. Write the percentages on the top of the bars.
4. What *two comparison* questions could you pose for data in Figure 8.14?

Horizontal Bar Graphs

In horizontal bar graphs, the subjects being graphed appear on the *y axis*. The length of the bars shows the frequency rate. Because exact percentages or data appear at the end of the bars to avoid possible misinterpretations, the frequency axis is not labeled. Notice these features in **Figure 8.15** on page 248 and the kinds of questions you can ask to understand the information.

Line Graphs

Line graphs, also called linear graphs, plot points on a coordinate grid or graph to form one continuous line to show trends and compare data. When you encounter line graphs, carefully read the *horizontal axis* and the *vertical axis* and then look for trends as well as increases, decreases, and changes in the occurrence of a particular action or event.

Single Line Graphs

Figure 8.16 is an example of a single line graph. By examining the information, you can quickly notice a trend: a decline in the number of work force members belonging to unions. After identifying the trend, examine and compare the data for various years; look for patterns and ask yourself questions. Use the two coordinates to learn about any specific point on the graph. For example, in Figure 8.16, by drawing

CONCEPT CHECK 8.23

What kinds of information will you find on the horizontal axis and the vertical axis in line graphs? What type of information can you often learn from line graphs?

Line graphs, also called linear graphs, plot points on a coordinate grid or graph to form one continuous line to show trends and compare data.

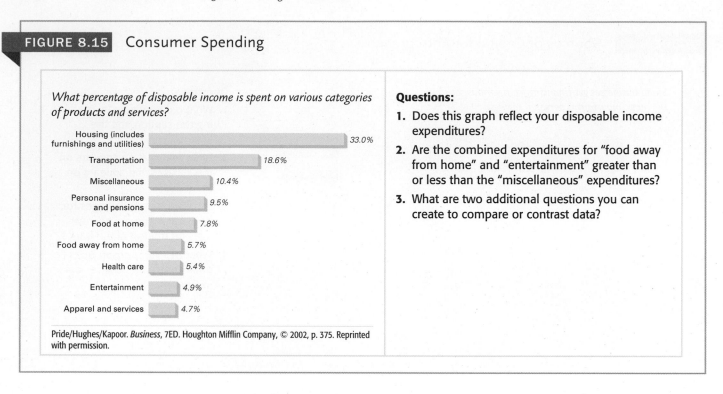

FIGURE 8.15 Consumer Spending

What percentage of disposable income is spent on various categories of products and services?

- Housing (includes furnishings and utilities) — 33.0%
- Transportation — 18.6%
- Miscellaneous — 10.4%
- Personal insurance and pensions — 9.5%
- Food at home — 7.8%
- Food away from home — 5.7%
- Health care — 5.4%
- Entertainment — 4.9%
- Apparel and services — 4.7%

Questions:

1. Does this graph reflect your disposable income expenditures?

2. Are the combined expenditures for "food away from home" and "entertainment" greater than or less than the "miscellaneous" expenditures?

3. What are two additional questions you can create to compare or contrast data?

Pride/Hughes/Kapoor. *Business*, 7ED. Houghton Mifflin Company, © 2002, p. 375. Reprinted with permission.

a vertical line from 1991 to the line in the graph, and then drawing a horizontal line from that point to the percentage axis, you learn that 16 percent of the work force belonged to a union in 1991. Ask yourself questions, such as *How does that percentage compare to the percentage in 2005? What are the percentage differences between 1985 and 1995? 1995 and 2005?*

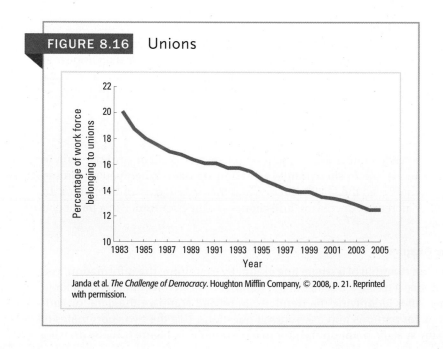

FIGURE 8.16 Unions

Janda et al. *The Challenge of Democracy*. Houghton Mifflin Company, © 2008, p. 21. Reprinted with permission.

Double Line Graphs

Double line graphs show two line graphs within one chart. Double line graphs are used to compare trends and patterns between the two subjects. In **Figure 8.17**, the individual lines are labeled. In other double bar graphs, legends may be used to define line colors or line patterns used in the graph. Notice the kinds of questions you can ask to understand information in double line graphs.

FIGURE 8.17   Retrieval Failures and Forgetting

Tulving and Psotka (1971) found that people's ability to recall a list of items was strongly affected by the number of other lists they learned before being tested on the first one. When retrieval cues were provided on a second test, however, retroactive interference from the intervening lists almost disappeared.

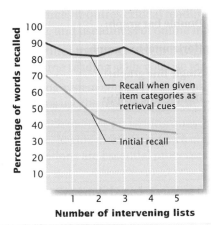

Bernstein/Nash. *Essentials of Psychology.* Houghton Mifflin Company, © 2008, p. 230. Reprinted with permission.

Questions:

1. How does the caption help you interpret the graph?

2. What happened when a person learned two additional lists and was tested on the first list without using any retrieval cues? What happened when retrieval cues were provided for a second test?

3. What is retroactive interference?

4. What can you conclude or summarize after studying this graph?

CHECK POINT 8.3

Answers appear on page B4

True or False?

_____ 1. In most cases, you can interpret and understand graphic materials by reading the caption and briefly glancing at the details.

_____ 2. "Stringing ideas together" is a strategy that involves using your own words to explain the information and the relationships between data in graphic materials.

_____ 3. Because graphic materials effectively condense printed information into visual forms, students should always copy the illustrations, graphs, or charts into their notes.

 Access Chapter 8 Practice Quiz 4: Graphic Materials under "Interactive Quizzes" in your College Success CourseMate, accessed through *CengageBrain.com.*

Developing Notetaking Skills

©Flying Colours Ltd/Digital Vision/Getty Images

Effective notetaking is an essential skill for college students. In this chapter, you will learn about five powerful notetaking systems that lead to greater academic success: annotation, the five-step Cornell Notetaking System, two-column notes, three-column notes, and outline notes. After learning to use all five notetaking systems, you will be equipped with the skills and ability to use the combinations of notetaking systems that are best matched to your individual textbooks and your preferences.

LEARNING OBJECTIVES

1. Discuss the rationale for taking notes and effective strategies to use with all notetaking systems.

2. Discuss and apply strategies for marking or annotating textbook passages.

3. Discuss and apply the five steps of the Cornell system for taking notes.

4. Discuss and apply effective strategies for creating two- and three-column notes.

5. Discuss and apply effective strategies for taking informal outline notes.

Access Chapter 9 Expanded Chapter Outline and Objectives in your College Success CourseMate, accessed through *CengageBrain.com*.

YOUR CHAPTER MAPPING

After reading information under each heading, return to the chapter visual mapping below. Add key words to show subheadings and important details related to such heading.

Access Chapter 9 Visual Mapping in your College Success CourseMate, accessed through *CengageBrain. com*.

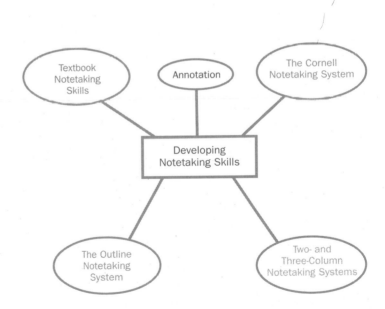

Developing Notetaking Skills

ANSWER, SCORE, and **RECORD** your profile before you read this chapter. If you need to review the process, refer to the complete directions given in the profile for Chapter 1 on page 4.

ONLINE: You can complete the profile and get your score online at this textbook's CourseMate Web site.

 Access Chapter 9 Profile in your College Success CourseMate accessed through *CengageBrain.com*.

	YES	NO
1. I am selective when I take notes; I write down only the important ideas and details.	_____	_____
2. I spend significantly more time rereading chapters than I spend studying from my notes.	_____	_____
3. I highlight main ideas and only short phrases in my textbook to avoid highlighting too much.	_____	_____
4. I write short notes or use abbreviations in the margins of my textbook.	_____	_____
5. I copy as much word-for-word information as I can so my notes are accurate and detailed.	_____	_____
6. I recite, reflect upon, and review my textbook notes.	_____	_____
7. I use the same notetaking system for all of my textbooks.	_____	_____
8. My notes summarize important charts, graphs, or pictures in the textbook.	_____	_____
9. I avoid using an outline notetaking system because it is too confusing.	_____	_____
10. I am confident about my ability to take effective notes and use a variety of notetaking systems for all my textbooks.	_____	_____

QUESTIONS LINKED TO THE CHAPTER LEARNING OBJECTIVES:

Questions 1, 2: objective 1   Questions 7, 8: objective 4

Questions 3, 4: objective 2   Question 9: objective 5

Questions 5, 6: objective 3   Question 10: all objectives

Textbook Notetaking Skills

 Discuss the rationale for taking notes and effective strategies to use with all notetaking systems.

Textbooks are a focal point for learning and mastering course content. Sometimes students are fooled by the fact that they seem to understand and temporarily remember what they read, so they feel there is no need to record notes. However, over time, information can fade or become confused with new information. Creating and using well-developed notes provide you with study tools to use to rehearse and review information so it remains active in your memory. In addition, research shows a high correlation between notetaking skills and test performance. The better students' notes are the better are their grades.

The Importance of Notetaking

In this chapter you will learn five notetaking systems that you can use to take notes from your textbooks. Your goal is to learn how to use all five systems so you can then select the most appropriate system to use for your various textbooks. In some cases, you may decide to use two notetaking systems for one textbook. For example, you might decide to annotate the textbook *during* the reading process and then convert the annotations to Cornell notes, two- or three-column notes, or outline notes *after* you finish reading the chapter. The combinations of notetaking systems you use will be your decision based on what works best for you and for your textbooks. In Chapter 11, you will learn four additional notetaking systems that you can use to take textbook notes.

The following important points about textbook notes provide you with additional rationale for taking the time to create and use textbook notes effectively:

- Notetaking involves condensing or reducing large amounts of information into more manageable units that are easier to study and review.

- Notetaking requires you to think carefully about information, break it down, analyze it, and select what is important to learn. If you have difficulty understanding what you are reading, you will have difficulty taking notes. Using the reading strategies in Chapters 7 and 8 will strengthen your reading skills and make it possible for you to develop meaningful notes.

- Notetaking encodes information kinesthetically and visually. When you practice reciting your notes, you encode the information linguistically. Thus, when you use all the recommended steps in the notetaking processes, notetaking becomes a multisensory activity that helps create a strong impression of information in your memory.

- Studying from well-developed notes is more time efficient than reading and rereading chapters of information. Effective textbook notes save you time in the long run.

- Learning to use specific notetaking systems is achieved more comfortably by first learning to use the systems to take textbook notes because you can control the pace, refer back to printed information, and learn the systems without the pressure of lecture situations.

Essential Strategies for Textbook Notetaking

In the following sections, you will learn about five notetaking systems: annotation, Cornell notes, two-column notes, three-column notes, and outline notes. Each notetaking system differs in its structure, but all work effectively when you use the eight Essential Strategies for Textbook Notetaking as shown in **Figure 9.1**.

CONCEPT CHECK **9.1**

What are the benefits of having well developed notes for your textbooks?

CONCEPT CHECK **9.2**

Does the notetaking process include all twelve Principles of Memory? Explain your answer.

FIGURE 9.1   Essential Strategies for Textbook Notetaking

- **Understand what you read before taking notes.** Read a paragraph or chunk of information, pause, think about the information, be sure that you understand it, and then take notes.

- **Be selective.** Your notes should be a *condensed* version of the textbook, not a word-for-word copy of the textbook pages. Capture only the important concepts, main ideas, and supporting details in your notes.

- **Paraphrase or reword.** Shorten textbook explanations or information by using your own words to state main ideas and important details as long as your wording presents the information accurately.

- **Include textbook reminders in your notes.** Instead of copying large charts or lengthy sections of important text, write a reminder in your notes to see page XX in the textbook.

- **Label your notes.** As you progress through the term, you will have many pages of notes. To avoid confusion, include textbook chapter numbers and number each page of your notes.

- **Use spaced practice.** Make several contacts with your notes over different periods of time. You can use them as a warm-up activity to put you in the mindset of the subject the next time you sit down to study, or you can schedule time each week to review your notes for the week.

- **Use feedback strategies.** Use Look-Away Techniques, such as reciting or visualizing, to check the completeness and accuracy of your learning.

- **Review your notes.** Use immediate review to create a strong impression in memory. Use ongoing review to keep information active and accessible in working memory.

CHECK POINT 9.1

Answers appear on page B4

True or False?

_____ 1. Taking textbook notes on textbooks that are easy to understand is not necessary.

_____ 2. Students' test performance and grades are linked to the quality and use of their notes.

_____ 3. Textbook notes should be condensed versions of textbook information.

_____ 4. Notetaking encodes information in new ways and creates stronger memory impressions of material.

 Access Chapter 9 Practice Quiz 1 Textbook Notes under "Interactive Quizzes" in your College Success CourseMate, accessed through *CengageBrain* .com.

CHAPTER 9
REFLECTIVE WRITING 1

On separate paper, in a journal, or online at this textbook's CourseMate Web site, respond to the following questions.

1. What kinds of notes do you currently take when you read your textbooks? Have your textbook notes proven to be effective? Why or why not?

2. What are the benefits you will gain by taking and studying from textbook notes?

Access Chapter 9 Reflective Writing 1 in your College Success CourseMate, accessed through CengageBrain.com.

Annotation

❷ *Discuss and apply strategies for marking or annotating textbook passages.*

Annotating is the process of highlighting, underlining, making marginal notes, or marking specific information in printed materials. By using this active learning process that involves interacting with printed text and holding information longer in your working memory, you reduce the risk of information fading or being displaced before you have time to process it.

> **Annotating** is the process of highlighting, underlining, making marginal notes, or marking specific information in printed materials.

Annotating Important Information

Figure 9.2 shows five annotation strategies for marking or annotating your textbooks. Whenever you see the term *marking,* it includes *highlighting* or *underlining,* whichever is your preference. Highlighting (using different colors of highlighter pens) is preferred by most students because it tends to make information stand out more than underlining. However, you may substitute underlining for highlighting if you prefer.

Chapter 7 introduced you to highlighting topic sentences and key words or phrases, and it introduced you to the notion of marking your textbook by circling terminology. In addition to the above annotation strategies, you will learn to number steps or lists of information in paragraphs and make marginal notes. **Figure 9.2** shows the five Essential Strategies for Annotating or Marking Textbooks.

CONCEPT CHECK 9.3

What should you highlight or mark? How can you avoid over-marking?

FIGURE 9.2   Essential Strategies for Annotating or Marking Textbooks

- Highlight the **complete topic sentence,** which states the main idea.
- Selectively highlight **key words or phrases** that support the topic sentence.
- **Circle terminology** and **highlight key words** in the definitions.
- **Enumerate steps** or lists of information.
- Make **marginal notes** to emphasize important ideas and integrate information.

Enumerate Steps or Lists of Information

Enumerating means "numbering." A paragraph with a topic sentence that uses words such as *kinds of, reasons, advantages, causes, effects, ways,* or *steps* often has a list of supporting details that you should be able to identify. For example, if a topic sentence states there are "five reasons" for something, you should be able find those five reasons in the paragraph. The following kinds of words signal the individual items to number in a paragraph:

Enumerating means "numbering."

- *Ordinals:* **Ordinals** are words that signal a numbered sequence of items. Ordinals, or "number words," such as *first, second,* or *third,* help you identify the individual items.

Ordinals are words that signal a numbered sequence of items.

- *Placeholders:* Placeholders are words that substitute for ordinals. Words such as *next, another,* and *finally* signal additional items that belong in the list of items you are enumerating.

Enumerating or numbering serves as a memory device, for it is easier to remember a fixed quantity of items than it is an unknown quantity of items. To enumerate, simply write the numerals (1, 2, 3) on top of the individual items in the paragraph that appear by an ordinal or a placeholder word. Often times, you will find that writing a brief list of the items in the margin as marginal notes is also helpful. Notice how enumeration is used in **Figure 9.3**.

CONCEPT CHECK 9.4

What is the value of enumerating items in your notes? Give examples of words that signal that a possible list of items will follow in the paragraph.

Write Marginal Notes

Marginal notes are brief notes written in the margins of textbook pages. Marginal notes give you a glimpse at the important points in a paragraph. To avoid cluttered or difficult-to-read marginal notes, be selective and brief. The following are kinds of information that work effectively as marginal notes:

Marginal notes are brief notes written in the margins of textbook pages.

numbered lists of key ideas	short definitions of terms
study questions	comments or reactions
diagrams or pictures	key words to define
definitions of unfamiliar terms	questions to ask in class
? for unclear information	

FIGURE 9.3   Marking a Paragraph, Enumerating and Making Marginal Notes

The earth system contains a number of interconnected subsystems, often described as "environmental spheres." The four major subsystems are the ① atmosphere or the ocean of air that overlies the entire earth's surface; the ② hydrosphere or the water of the surface and near-surface regions of the earth; the ③ lithosphere or the massive accumulation of rock and metal that forms the solid body of the planet itself; and the ④ biosphere or the layer of living organisms of which we are a part. All four respond in various ways to the flow of energy and materials through the earth system.

Earth System
1. atmosphere
2. hydrosphere
3. lithosphere
4. biosphere

From Holt/Atkinson. *Reading Enhancement and Development.* Houghton Mifflin Company, © 1995, p. 218–219. Reprinted with permission.

Using brackets and abbreviations in the margins helps you avoid cluttered margins:

- **Use Brackets for Large Sections of Information:** Rather than over-mark or clutter the margins with too many details, draw a bracket next to large sections of information or entire paragraphs that are densely written. You can add a note or abbreviation next to the bracket.

- **Use Abbreviations to Call Attention to Specific Kinds of Information:** You can use abbreviations next to brackets to draw your attention to sections you want to return to for further studying. The following are abbreviations you may want to use:

EX. = example or examples	**Q.** = question
DIFF. = differences	**CE.** = cause-effect
SUM. = summary	**RE.** = reasons why…?
F. = important fact	**REL.** = important relationship
IMP. = important to reread	**FORM.** = formula
DEF. = lengthy definition	**H.** = hypotheses

Essential Strategies to Study from Annotations

To be truly effective, you need to practice using your annotations by personalizing, reciting, and working with the information in new ways. Simply rereading your highlighted notes can give you a false sense that you "know" the information and have processed it into your long-term memory. **Figure 9.4** shows five Essential Strategies for Studying from Annotations. Use these strategies after you finish reading a paragraph, a group of paragraphs, or an end of a section in your textbook.

Reread Out Loud

When you reread only the marked information, it will sound broken or fragmented; however, you will hear yourself stating only main ideas and important supporting details. Read slowly so that your working memory has time to absorb the key points and to make associations.

Verbally String Ideas Together

Stringing ideas together is the process of adding your own words to convert annotated text into full sentences and explanations. So this time, instead of reading fragmented annotated text, you use the annotations as guides to help you string ideas together more coherently. Verbalizing in this manner personalizes information as you state it in less formal language. Use transition words, such as *therefore, however,*

CONCEPT CHECK 9.5

Why is rereading your highlighted and marked textbook not sufficient for boosting and challenging your memory? What steps should follow rereading your annotations?

Stringing ideas together is the process of adding your own words to convert annotated text into full sentences and explanations.

FIGURE 9.4	Essential Strategies for Studying from Annotations

- Reread out loud only the marked annotations.
- Verbally string the ideas together by adding your own words.
- Recite without looking.
- Write summaries or make a second set of notes.
- Use spaced practice, immediate review, and ongoing review.

The Cornell Notetaking System

 Discuss and apply the five steps of the Cornell system for taking notes.

The *Cornell Notetaking System* is a five-step notetaking process used to take notes from textbooks or from lectures. This powerful notetaking system was designed by Dr. Walter Pauk at Cornell University more than forty-five years ago when he recognized students' need to learn how to take more effective notes. Many college and university instructors consider this the most effective notetaking system for college students.

The *Five R's of Cornell* are record, reduce, recite, reflect, and review. The goal of the Cornell Notetaking System is to take notes that are so accurate and detailed that you *may not need to go back to the book to study*. To avoid weakening this powerful system, use all five *R*'s shown in **Figure 9.5** to record and study your notes.

Preparing to Take Notes

To prepare your notebook paper for Cornell notes, draw a two-and-one-half-inch margin down the left side of your notebook paper. Only do this on the front side of your notebook paper as you will not be taking notes on the backsides. (The backsides are reserved for information you may want to list or summarize in the reflect step of this notetaking system.) At the top of the first page, write the course name, chapter number, and date. For all the following pages, just write the chapter number and the page number of your notes. Instead of drawing the line to create the wider margin, you may want to ask your campus bookstore if it carries Cornell or "law notebook" paper with the wider left margin.

Step One: Recording

The *record step* in the Cornell system involves taking notes in the right column. Read each paragraph carefully, decide what information is important, and then record that information on your paper. Your notes should be a *reduced version* of the textbook. Be selective. **Figure 9.6** shows the standard format for recording notes. Carefully read the information in Figure 9.6 to learn techniques for recording information in your notes.

Tips for Recording Notes

The headings and subheadings in the textbook are the *skeleton,* or outline, of the chapter. They serve as guides for identifying main categories of information. Details for your notes come from information under each heading. An effective notetaker

---

The Cornell Notetaking System is a five-step notetaking process to use to take notes from textbooks or from lectures.

The Five *R's* of Cornell are record, reduce, recite, reflect, and review.

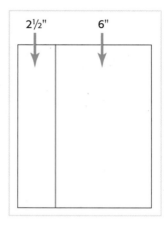

The record step in the Cornell system involves taking notes in the right column.

CONCEPT CHECK **9.6**

What are the Five R's of Cornell? Do these steps incorporate all Twelve Principles of Memory? Why or why not?

| **FIGURE 9.5** | The Five R's of Cornell |

1. **Record** your notes in the right column.
2. **Reduce** your notes into the recall column on the left.
3. **Recite** out loud from the recall column.
4. **Reflect** on the information that you are studying.
5. **Review** your notes immediately and regularly.

FIGURE 9.6   The Record Step of the Cornell System

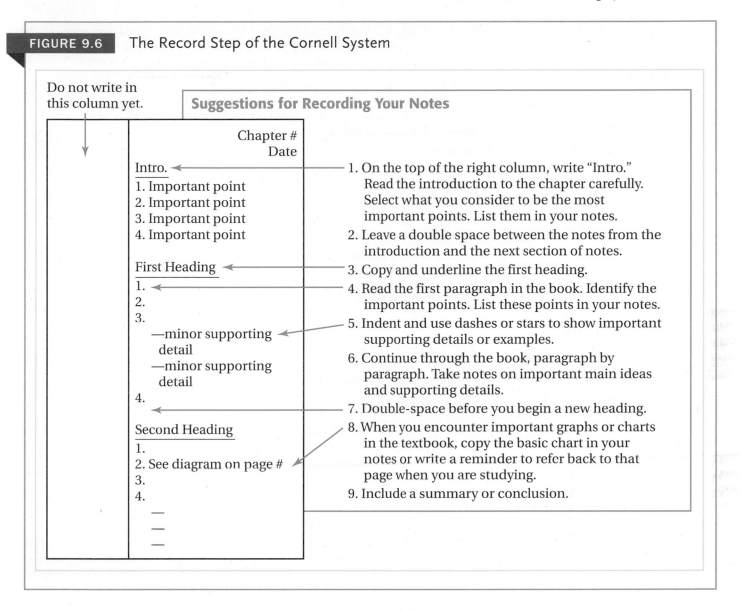

Do not write in this column yet.

Suggestions for Recording Your Notes

Chapter #
Date

Intro.
1. Important point
2. Important point
3. Important point
4. Important point

First Heading
1.
2.
3.
   —minor supporting detail
   —minor supporting detail
4.

Second Heading
1.
2. See diagram on page #
3.
4.
   —
   —
   —

1. On the top of the right column, write "Intro." Read the introduction to the chapter carefully. Select what you consider to be the most important points. List them in your notes.

2. Leave a double space between the notes from the introduction and the next section of notes.

3. Copy and underline the first heading.

4. Read the first paragraph in the book. Identify the important points. List these points in your notes.

5. Indent and use dashes or stars to show important supporting details or examples.

6. Continue through the book, paragraph by paragraph. Take notes on important main ideas and supporting details.

7. Double-space before you begin a new heading.

8. When you encounter important graphs or charts in the textbook, copy the basic chart in your notes or write a reminder to refer back to that page when you are studying.

9. Include a summary or conclusion.

organizes the details and gives them structure so they do not appear to be an endless stream of random details. Use the following tips to organize your notes:

- **Introduction:** If the chapter has an introductory paragraph that lists key ideas presented in the chapter, create a heading that says Introduction and list the key ideas.

- **Headings and Subheadings:** Copy the textbook headings and the subheadings into your notes. Underline them so they stand out as main categories or topics. Do not number or letter the headings.

- **New Headings:** If you wish to regroup or reorganize information into headings or subheadings that are more helpful for understanding topics, you can create your own headings or subheadings in your notes.

- **Marginal Notes:** Carefully read marginal notes (or sidebars) that may appear in your textbooks. If this information does not appear within the regular text, include important points from the marginal notes in your notes.
- **Double Spacing Between Headings:** To avoid crowded or cluttered notes that are difficult to study, leave a double space between each new heading or section of your notes. This visually groups or chunks the information into smaller units, which will help your memory.
- **Sufficient Information:** Your notes need to show the big picture and the small pictures (details), so be sure to record sufficient information to be meaningful later.
- **Meaningful Phrases or Short Sentences:** Shorten or paraphrase information. Avoid using only individual words or short phrases that may lose their meaning when you return to them later. If phrases by themselves are not meaningful units of thought, convert them into short sentences.
- **Annotations:** If you have already highlighted or annotated the information, move the same information into your notes.
- **Number Details:** Number the ideas as you include them in your notes. Numbering helps you create a stronger impression about the number of important points under each heading, and it breaks the information into smaller, more manageable units.
- **Minor Details:** You will frequently encounter minor details that belong under an idea that you already numbered. Indicate these details by *indenting* and then using *dashes* or *stars* before writing the details. Unless you are comfortable with the levels of information in formal outlining, avoid more complicated formal outlining that mixes numbering and lettering. Just use the dashes.
- **Graphs and Charts:** You can *copy* smaller graphic materials into your notes or *summarize* the conclusions you make after studying the visual materials. For larger visual materials, simply include a reminder in your notes to go to a specific textbook page to review the materials. In some way, your notes should reference graphic materials as they contain valuable information.

Write a Summary or a Conclusion

Summaries or conclusions pull the main ideas together to help you see the big picture. If the book has a summary, include the summary as the last heading in your notes. If there is no summary, write your own paragraphs to summarize the chapter.

Step Two: Reducing

After you have finished taking notes for the chapter, you are ready to close the book and reduce your notes one step further. The *reduce step* in the Cornell system involves condensing notes into the recall column. The *recall column* is the left column in the Cornell notes that shows headings, key words, and study questions. **Figure 9.7** shows the standard format to use to reduce notes in the recall column. Use the following tips to create an effective recall column that you can use during step three, reciting.

- **Copy Headings:** To structure and organize your recall column, copy the headings from the right column into the left column and underline them. The headings should appear directly across from the headings in your notes.
- **Reread Your Notes:** Reread a section of your notes. If your notes seem vague or incomplete, go back to the book, reread, and add more details to your notes.
- **Study Questions:** Under the headings in your recall column, write brief study questions about the information in the right column. Your study questions can be in an abbreviated form such as *Why? Name the 6... Related to* X *how?*

CONCEPT CHECK 9.7

What strategies can you use to organize your textbook notes so they clearly show headings and subheadings?

The reduce step in the Cornell system involves condensing notes into the recall column on the left.

The recall column is the left column in the Cornell notes that shows headings, key words, and study questions.

CONCEPT CHECK 9.8

What are the do's and the don't's for creating and using the recall column?

FIGURE 9.7   Reciting from the Recall Column

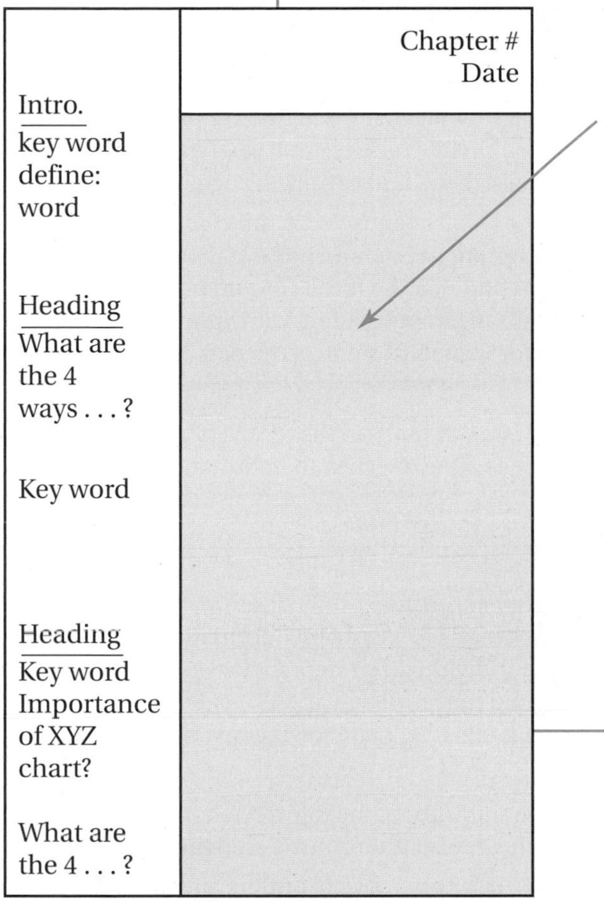

Suggestions for Reciting

Chapter #
Date

Intro.
key word
define:
word

Heading
What are
the 4
ways . . . ?

Key word

Heading
Key word
Importance
of XYZ
chart?

What are
the 4 . . . ?

1. Cover up the notes on the right.

2. Start at the top of the recall column. Read the heading and the first key word or question.

3. Explain the information. Talk out loud in complete sentences.

4. If you do not remember the information, uncover the right column. Reread the information. Cover it up and try reciting it again.

5. Move through your notes in this manner.

6. Adjust the recall column by adding new key words if needed.

- **Key Words to Define:** In your recall column, across from your notes that define a key term, write *def.* and the *key word* to cue you later to recite the definition for the word.

- **Do Not Write Too Much:** Do not clutter the recall column with too much information. Do not write answers to your study questions, definitions, or completed lists of information. You want to challenge yourself in the next step to see if you can recall the information from memory.

Step Three: Reciting

The *recite step* in the Cornell system involves using information in the recall column to explain information out loud in your own words without referring to detailed notes. To avoid the tendency to look at your notes as you recite, use a blank piece of paper to cover your notes on the right side of your paper.

> The recite step in the Cornell system involves using information in the recall column to explain information out loud in your own words without referring to detailed notes.

CONCEPT CHECK 9.9

Why does reciting occur in so many learning strategies? How is it used in the Cornell system?

Access Chapter 9 Topics In-Depth: Cornell with SQ4R in your College Success CourseMate, accessed through *CengageBrain.com*.

The **reflect step** in the Cornell system involves thinking seriously, comprehending, and using elaborative rehearsal strategies to work with information in new ways.

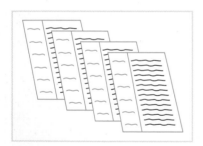

CONCEPT CHECK 9.10

How do the reflect and the review steps of the Cornell Notetaking System create stronger impressions of information in your memory? What benefits would you miss if you avoid using these steps?

The **review step** in the Cornell system involves using immediate and ongoing review.

Immediate review is the process of rehearsing information before you end a learning task.

Figure 9.7 shows the format of headings, study questions, and key words to use to trigger reciting.

Begin reciting by looking at and then telling about the information in the recall column. Use the following tips to recite from the recall column.

- **Explain in Complete Sentences:** Answer the questions, define terms, and tell what you remember about the key words. Talk out loud in complete, coherent sentences.
- **Use Feedback:** After reciting a section of information, pull down the paper that covered the right column. Check your accuracy and the completeness of your recited information. If you have difficulty reciting, or if you "go blank," pull down the paper, reread your notes, cover them, and try reciting again.
- **Adjust the Recall Column:** If the recall column lacks sufficient cues to direct your reciting or focus you on the important points, add more key words or study questions to the recall column. If you find that the recall column provides you with too much information that results in simply reading with little information left to recite from memory, cross out (or whiteout) some of the details before you recite again.

Track Your Progress: If you wish, star items in the recall column that you recited with accurate details. Check or place an arrow next to information that you need to practice further.

Step Four: Reflecting

The *reflect step* in the Cornell system involves thinking seriously, comprehending, and using elaborative rehearsal strategies to work with information in new ways. The reflect step is a creative and highly individualized step, so no two students will create identical study tools or use the same rehearsal activities. Decide *what works best for you* and the materials you are studying. Use the following tips for reflecting on your notes.

- **Think and Ponder:** Take time to think about the topic, relationships among details, and the importance of the information you are studying.
- **Line Up Your Recall Columns:** To see an informal outline and an overview of all the information in your set of notes, arrange the pages of your notes so you can see a lineup of all the recall columns.
- **Write a Summary:** Look only at the information in the recall columns. Write a summary using full sentences and paragraphs to summarize the main ideas and important details.
- **Write on the Back Sides of Your Notes:** Use the back sides of your notes to make lists of information, write study questions, add diagrams or charts, or jot down questions you want to ask in class.
- **Make Study Tools:** Reinforce your learning by creating study tools that you can use throughout the term: index card notes, visual mappings, charts, or mnemonics.

Step Five: Reviewing

The *review step* in the Cornell system involves using immediate and ongoing review. *Immediate review* is the process of rehearsing information before you end a learning task. Use immediate review with your notes after you finish the reflect step. This review helps create a stronger impression of the information before you set it aside and move on to something new.

Ongoing review is the process of practicing information days and even weeks after the initial learning occurred. Ongoing review keeps information active and accessible in your memory system. You can use Look-Away Techniques to rehearse the information by visualizing or reciting the information in the recall columns of your notes and study tools you created during the reflect step. Ongoing review saves you time in the long run; when you prepare for tests or exams, you will not need to cram or spend excessive time "relearning" information.

> **Ongoing review** is the process of practicing information days and even weeks after the initial learning occurred.

EXERCISE 9.2

Taking Notes on Forgetting Theories

DIRECTIONS

1. Go to **Excerpt 7** in **Appendix D.** In the excerpt "Forgetting Theories," annotate each paragraph in the excerpt. Demonstrate what you have learned about highlighting, circling terminology, and marking your textbook.

2. Use your annotations to help select the important information to transfer to a set of Cornell notes. Use the tips on pages 265 for recording notes in the right column. Finally, use the tips on page 267 to create a recall column.

3. To evaluate your notes, Go to **Appendix C,** page C21 for the Cornell Notetaking Self-Assessment Checklist. Use the checklist to evaluate your notes.

4. Your instructor may provide you with additional directions. You may be asked to turn in your notes with the checklist, or you may be asked to practice reciting your notes in class with another student or in a small group. You may also be asked to compare your notes to a set of sample notes that your instructor will show you for comparison and discussion.

 Access Chapter 9 Topics In-Depth: Forgetting Theories in your College Success CourseMate, accessed through *CengageBrain.com.*

EXERCISE 9.3

Transfer These Skills

 PURPOSE: Learning to use a new notetaking system effectively requires practice using the system for taking notes from a variety of textbooks.

DIRECTIONS: Follow your instructor's directions to do *one* of the following notetaking assignments.

1. Take notes on any two pages of information from a textbook you are using in another course this term. Your notes should begin with a textbook heading. Your instructor may ask to meet with you to compare your notes to the textbook pages or may ask you to include photocopies of the two textbook pages when you turn in your notes.

2. Take notes on a printed or an online excerpt or article assigned by your instructor.

3. Take notes on a specific excerpt in Appendix D that your instructor assigns for this notetaking exercise.

CHECK POINT 9.3

Answers appear on page B4

True or False?

_____ 1. The Five *R*'s of Cornell are *read, record, recite, reflect,* and *review.*

_____ 2. Headings are used to help organize information in both columns of Cornell notes.

_____ 3. An effective recall column includes questions without answers and terminology without the written definitions.

_____ 4. The Memory Principles of Selectivity, Elaboration, Recitation, Feedback, and Ongoing Review are used each time you create and study your Cornell notes.

 Access Chapter 9 Practice Quiz 3: Cornell Notes under "Interactive Quizzes" in your College Success CourseMate, accessed through *CengageBrain.com.*

GROUP PROCESSING

A COLLABORATIVE LEARNING ACTIVITY

Form groups of three students. Complete the following directions. Compile the responses on a large group chart.

1. Across the top of your chart, draw the five pictures shown below.

2. As a group, brainstorm and list all the important points you remember about each of the Five *R*'s of Cornell. Do not refer back to your textbook. You may be asked to share your chart with the class.

1. Record	2. Reduce	3. Recite	4. Reflect	5. Review

Two- and Three-Column Notetaking Systems

4 *Discuss and apply effective strategies for creating two- and three-column notes.*

Two-Column and Three-Column Notetaking Systems are alternatives to the Cornell Notetaking System. Unlike the Cornell system where you begin taking notes in the right column, in the two- and three-column notetaking systems, you begin taking notes in the left column. In two- and three-column notes, you begin by writing the topic/subject, category, key word, or study question in the *left* column. The remaining column(s) show important details. As with all notetaking systems, to work effectively you need to spend time rehearsing the information, using feedback activities, and incorporating immediate and ongoing review in your study blocks.

The Two-Column System

The *Two-Column Notetaking System* shows topics, vocabulary terms, and/or study questions in the left column and details or explanations in the right column. Two-column notes are a simplified version of Cornell notes. In this notetaking system, you can vary the width of each column to suit your needs and preferences. Creating two-column notes is a two-step process:

- **Step 1: Write in the Left Column:** Write a topic, vocabulary term, or a study question in the *left column.*

- **Step 2: Write in the Right Column:** Directly across from the item in the left column, write details or explanations. As with Cornell notes, be brief but not so brief that the information loses meaning over time. You can number details, use bullets for items in a list, or simply write the information in meaningful phrases or short sentences.

Two-column notes are easy to create and use when you take textbook or lecture notes. They are informal and reflect your preferences for the kinds of information you want to appear in each column. (See Examples 1, 2, and 3.) Use the following tips to create, rehearse, and review your two-column notes:

- **Be selective.** Do not clutter your notes with unnecessary information.

- **Use the read-record-recite cycle.** Read one paragraph, pause your reading, and then take notes on paper. Usually your first action will be to write a topic or a subject in the left column that reflects the main idea of the paragraph. Then, in the right column, add the important supporting details. Continue this process as you work through the chapter.

- **The items in the left column will vary.** Sometimes for a specific paragraph you will want to place more than one entry in the column on the left. For example, if the paragraph defines several key terms, you will have several key terms in the left column instead of only one word representing the topic of the paragraph.

- **Space your notes.** Leave a space between each new item or group of related items in your notes. You do not want the right-hand column to look like a non-stop, steady flow of information. By placing a space between new sections of information, you create groups of information that clearly show which details belong together.

- **Sketch diagrams or charts.** When you encounter diagrams or charts, you may sketch them in the left column and summarize them in the right column. Or, you may write a question about the chart in the left column and sketch the chart in the right column.

- **Practice your notes.** Cover the right column and recite. After you recite lists of information, definitions, or answers to study questions, remove the paper to check the accuracy and completeness of your answer. Reread, cover the notes, and recite again if necessary.

- **Highlight difficult sections of your notes.** Use colored pens to highlight sections in the right column that you want to identify quickly for additional practice or review.

- **Use immediate and ongoing review.**

The Two-Column Notetaking System shows topics, vocabulary terms, or study questions in the left column and details or explanations in the right column.

CONCEPT CHECK 9.11

How is the Two-Column Notetaking System different from the Cornell system? In what ways are they similar?

Notice in the following examples the kinds of information and topics you can use to develop two-column notes.

EXAMPLE 1: Forgetting Theories	
Five Theories	5 theories explain why info may be forgotten or inaccessible in memory
Def.—Decay Theory	1. A forgetting theory that occurs in STM; stimuli too weak or unattended to
What happens to stimuli in STM?	2. Stimuli decays or fades away
	3. Ignored stimuli decay from STM within 28 seconds

EXAMPLE 2: Multiplying Negative and Positive Numbers	
When both numbers are positive	Answer is positive. Example: $4 \times 9 = 36$
When both numbers are negative	Answer is positive. Example: $-5 \times -4 = 20$
When one number is positive and the other is negative	Answer is negative. Example: $(-3) \times 4 = -12$

EXAMPLE 3: Practice Visualization (Excerpt 2 in Appendix D)	
What is self-fulfilling prophecy?	1. Imagining worse-case scenarios and negative images in mind, increase anxiety and set up self-fulfilling prophecy.
	2. Self-fulfilling prophecy: images you hold set you up to perform in the negative way imagined
2 solutions?	Two solutions: Use visualization & affirmations

Two-Column Notes about the Forgetting Curve

EXERCISE 9.4

DIRECTIONS: Read the following excerpt one paragraph at a time, pause, and then create two-column notes. Use a combination of topics, key terms to define, and study questions in the left column. Note: If you wish, annotate the excerpt before taking notes.

HOW DO WE FORGET?

Hermann Ebbinghaus, a German psychologist, began the systematic study of memory and forgetting in the late 1800s, using only his own memory as his laboratory. He read aloud a list of nonsense syllables, such as POF, XEM, and QAL, at a constant pace, and then tried to recall the syllables.

Ebbinghaus devised the *method of savings* to measure how much he forgot over time. This method compares the number of repetitions (or trials) it takes to learn a list of items and the number of trials needed to relearn that same list later.

Any difference in the number of learning trials presents the *savings* from one learning to the next. If it took Ebbinghaus ten trials to learn a list and ten more trials to relearn it, there would be no savings. Forgetting would have been complete. If it took him ten trials to learn the list and only five trials to relearn it, there would be a savings of 50 percent.

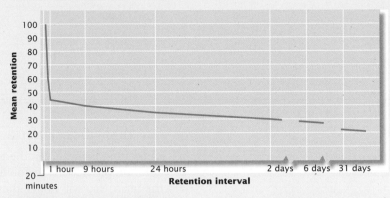

Ebbinghaus's Curve of Forgetting

Ebbinghaus found that most forgetting occurs during the first nine hours after learning, and especially during the first hour.

Ebbinghaus's research produced two lasting discoveries. One is the shape of the forgetting curve shown on the right. Even when psychologists have substituted words, sentences, and stories for nonsense syllables, the forgetting curve shows the same strong initial drop in memory, followed by a more moderate decrease over time... Of course, we remember sensible stories better than nonsense syllables, but the shape of the curve is the same no matter what type of material is involved... Even the forgetting of events from daily life tends to follow Ebbinghaus's forgetting curve (Thomson, 1982).

Ebbinghaus also discovered just how long-lasting "savings" in long-term memory can be. Psychologists now know from the method of savings that information about everything from algebra to bike riding is often retained for decades... So, although you may forget something you have learned if you do not use the information, it is very easy to relearn the material if the need arises, indicating that the forgetting was not complete.

Source: Bernstein, Nash. *Essentials of Psychology,* Houghton Mifflin Company, © 2008, pp. 227–228. Reprinted with permission.

The Three-Column System

The Three-Column Notetaking System shows topics, vocabulary terms, or study questions in the left column followed by two categories of details in the remaining two columns. As you will notice in the following examples, the two categories of information will vary depending on the textbook content. It will be up to you to decide how to label each column in your notes and how wide to make each column.

> The Three-Column Notetaking System shows topics, vocabulary terms, or study questions in the left column followed by two categories of details in the remaining two columns.

Use Three-Column Notes for Comparative Reading

In one set of notes, you can record information from two different sources for one specific topic. For example, if you are asked to read two separate articles about global warming, the global warming topics would appear in the left column. What each of the sources says about each topic would appear in the middle and the right columns.

Example: Comparative Reading		
Topic	Article 1	Article 2
Greenhouse Effect		
Climate Changes		
Burning Fossil Fuels		
Deforestation		

Use Three-Column Notes to Define Terms

In the first column, list the term or course-specific vocabulary word. In the center column, provide the textbook definition. In the third column, add details related to the term. You will notice that this format is very similar to the three-part definition you learned to write in Chapter 7.

Example: Definitions and Applications		
Topic/Concept	Definition or Explanation	Details
continental shelf	shallow, sloping area located around the margins of continents	Average depth 400 feet. On average stretch out from land 45 miles. About 90% of all fish and shellfish harvested from continental shelves.

Table "Continental Shelf" adapted from *Science of Earth Systems*, First Edition, by Stephen Butz, p. 419.

Use Three-Column Notes for Math Problems.

Begin by copying the original math problem into the first column. Then, skip the middle column. In the third column, write the steps to solve the problem. When you are ready to review, fold the third column back so you cannot see the problem-solving steps. Rework the problem in the middle column. Unfold the third column to check your accuracy.

Example: Math Problems		*Fold this column back until you rework the problem.*
Original Math Problem	Space to Rework the Problem.	Original Solution from Textbook or Class.
Leave the answer in exponential form: $4^5 \times 4^7$		$4^5 \times 4^7 = 4^{5+7} = 4^{12}$

CONCEPT CHECK 9.12

Why are three-column notes more useful at times than two-column notes? What categories of information can you use to label the second and third columns?

Use the Three-Column Notes for Math Terminology

As in all courses, math courses require you to learn math terminology. The terminology may be a specific vocabulary term, a symbol, or a formula. Learning the definitions along with explanations lays the foundation for you to apply this knowledge to solve equations. In the following example, notice how the first column shows the symbol or the term, the second column provides examples, and the third column explains the process.

Example: Math Terminology		
Key Words	Examples	Explanations/Rules
$-n$	$-n$	Opposite of any number.
	If $n = s$, Then $-n = -s$	
	$-(-10) = 10$ $-(-15)(-15) = -15$	Count the number of signs; even means +, odd means −
	Opposite of $-x$ is x	
Rational	Rational numbers are fractions (¼, ½, ¾)	A/B, $B/0$ is rational Division by 0 undefined.
Numerator Denominator	numerator/denominator N/D	Numerator on top Denominator on bottom (D = Down).

Adapted from Paul Nolting. *Math Study Skills Workbook.* Houghton Mifflin Company, © 2000, pp. 50–51. Reprinted with permission.

Use Three-Column Notes to Combine Textbook and Lecture Notes

Write the topic in the left column. Create textbook notes for the topic in the middle column. Because class lectures may present topics in an order different than your textbook notes, taking lecture notes directly in the right column is often not feasible. Instead, use another form of notetaking, such as Cornell notes, to take lecture notes. After the lecture, return to your three-column notes. Add additional key points from the lecture to complete your three-column notes. For example, you may want to include clarification or examples that were presented in the lecture but were not in the textbook.

Example: Combining Textbook and Lecture Notes		
Topic/Concept	Textbook	Instructor/Lecture
Product life cycle	1. Introduction 2. Growth 3. Maturity 4. Decline	Class example: 3M (Post-it Notes) Sony digital cameras

Flying Colours Ltd/Digital Vision/Getty

Creating notes from your math textbooks provides you with study tools to learn the skills. Which notetaking system works best for your math textbooks?

Study Your Three-Column Notes

Use recitation to study from your three-column notes. Cover the middle or the right-hand column, recite the information, and then check your accuracy. Continue to study from your three-column notes by covering the remaining columns, reciting, and then checking the accuracy of your explanations. For math notes that involve equations, rework the problems, and then compare your results with the original problem and solution.

CHECK POINT 9.4

Answers appear on page B4

True or False?

_____ 1. Three-column notes are always more difficult to create than two-column notes.

_____ 2. Unlike the Cornell system, you begin two-column notes by writing first in the left column.

_____ 3. The notetaker can use questions, terminology, diagrams, or key words for topics in the left column of two- or three-column notes.

_____ 4. You should always read the entire chapter before taking two-column notes.

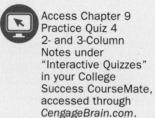

Access Chapter 9 Practice Quiz 4 2- and 3-Column Notes under "Interactive Quizzes" in your College Success CourseMate, accessed through *CengageBrain.com*.

Textbook Case Studies

EXERCISE 9.5

Access Chapter 9 Textbook Case Studies and Web-Only Case Studies in your College Success CourseMate, accessed through *CengageBrain.com*.

DIRECTIONS

1. Read each case study carefully. Respond to the question at the end of each case study by using *specific* strategies discussed in this chapter. Answer in complete sentences.

2. Write your responses on paper or online at the CourseMate student Web site, Textbook Case Studies. You will be able to print your online response or e-mail it to your instructor.

CASE STUDY 1: Labrishun learns by writing information and studying from handwritten information. After Labrishun had taken Cornell notes on two different chapters in her math textbook, she noticed that her notes were longer than the textbook chapters. She realized she had been copying everything from the textbook into her notes. What notetaking strategies or systems would you suggest Labrishun consider using?

CASE STUDY 2: With Cornell notes, Joey has learned to condense information effectively into the right column. However, in his recall column, Joey makes lists of important information, writes definitions for key terms, and writes study questions with their answers. He reads all the information out loud. What adjustments does Joey need to make in the way he uses his Cornell notes so he tests his memory more effectively?

The Outline Notetaking System

5 *Discuss and apply effective strategies for taking informal outline notes.*

Formal outlines are highly structured, logically organized, detailed notes that show levels of information and relationships among main ideas and details. Formal outlines use Roman numerals, capital letters, Arabic numerals, lowercase letters, and numerals inside parentheses to show the relationship of the larger concepts to the smaller details. You may already be familiar with formal outlines because many composition instructors require formal outlines with your essays or papers. **Figure 9.8** shows the different levels of information in a formal outline.

Following are the standard requirements or rules that you must follow when you develop a formal outline:

- **Alignment:** When you indent to show a lower level of information, place the new letter or the new number directly below the first letter of the first word that appears in the line above. For example, in Figure 9.8, notice how the "A" for the subtopic appears directly below the "M" for the main heading.

- **Two or More Subtopics:** Each level in the formal outline must have *at least two subtopics* under each category. If you do not have two items [A, B; 1, 2; a, b; or (1), (2)], try renaming the larger category so you do not end up with only one item under that category.

- **Roman Numerals:** Use Roman numerals for main topics. Roman numerals from one to fifteen are written as follows: I, II, III, IV, V, VI, VII, VIII, IX, X, XI, XII, XIII, XIV, and XV.

- **Arabic Numerals:** Use Arabic numerals (1, 2, 3, 4...) for supporting details.

- **Wording:** Most outlines consist of key words and short phrases; full sentences are seldom used.

Informal Outlines

Outlines provide a *skeleton* or an overview of the basic structure of printed materials, or in this case, of a complete chapter. Some textbooks provide basic chapter outlines in the chapter introductory materials. These chapter outlines often include only

---

| FIGURE 9.8 | Example of a Formal Outline |

Title:

I. Main headings or topics use Roman numerals.
   A. Subtopics use capital letters.
   B. Subtopic
      1. Supporting details use Arabic numerals.
      2. Supporting detail
         a. Minor details use lowercase letters.
         b. Minor detail
            (1) Subideas of minor details use Arabic numerals inside parentheses.
            (2) Subideas of minor details
   C. Subtopic

The **Outline Notetaking System** involves using an informal outline structure for notes.

CONCEPT CHECK 9.13

How can formal outlining be simplified so outline notes become easier to create?

the chapter's headings and subheadings. For this textbook, a basic chapter outline appears at the beginning of each chapter and an expanded outline appears online on the CourseMate Web site for this textbook

The ***Outline Notetaking System*** involves using an informal outline structure for notes. If you are not comfortable with the formal outline structure, get confused about which letter or number to use for a detail, or you feel it is too "cumbersome," you can modify the outlining rules and simplify the labeling. **Figure 9.9** shows the beginning of an informal outline for this chapter. When you create informal outline notes, use the following guidelines for your notes.

- Use Roman numerals for headings.
- Use capital letters for subheadings.
- Use Arabic numbers for details.
- Use dashes for all other levels of minor details.

Outlining Before the Reading of a Chapter

You can use informal outlining for textbook notes *before, during,* or *after* reading a chapter. If your textbook does not provide a chapter outline, create a basic outline that shows only *headings* and *subheadings* before you begin reading. This outline provides you with an overview of the chapter. Later you can use your basic outline for self-quizzing by reciting what you know about each heading and subheading and adding clue words.

Outlining During the Reading of a Chapter

Some students prefer to use an informal outline to take textbook notes *during* the reading process. Creating outline notes during the reading process results in more comprehensive notes than outlines created before reading as an overview activity. Use the following tips to create outline notes as you read a chapter:

- **Headings and Subheadings:** Use the headings and the subheadings in your text-book as the skeleton for your outline. Use Roman numerals (I, II, III, ...) to label main headings. Use capital letters in the outline to label subheadings.

FIGURE 9.9   The Beginning of an Informal Outline

Chapter 9

I. Textbook Notetaking Skills

   A. Introduction

      1. Textbooks focal point for learning

      2. Info can fade or become confused, so important to take notes.

      3. Research—High correlation between notetaking skills and test performance.

   B. The Importance of Notetaking

      1. Learn 5 notetaking systems

      2. May want to use 2 notetaking systems for one textbook

      3. Rationale for taking notes:

         -condense large amounts of info

         -Think, break it down, analyze, select info for notes

- **Details under Subheadings:** After labeling the subheading, read a paragraph under the subheading, pause, identify the important information, and then transfer that information into your notes. Number the individual items or details.

- **Minor Details:** Your informal outline is your personal set of notes, so use a clear, organized method for showing minor details. You may simply use dashes to show individual minor details instead of the more formal lettering or numbering system.

CONCEPT CHECK 9.14

How do outline notes show different levels of information? How does understanding levels of information assist your memory?

Outlining After the Reading of a Chapter

Some students find value in creating informal outlines *after* they read the chapter. These outline notes summarize information in a new way and reinforce relationships between headings and subheadings. They also become effective study or review tools. In the following section, you will learn how to study, recite, and review from informal outline notes.

Creating Outline Notes

EXERCISE 9.6

PURPOSE: Before you can know whether or not you like using a specific kind of notetaking system, you need to experience creating and studying from notes created with each system.

DIRECTIONS

1. Create a set of outline notes for this chapter. The beginning of the outline appears in Figure 9.9. As you develop your chapter outline, include at least three levels of information: the heading, the subheading, and important supporting details. Compare your outline to the Chapter 9 expanded outline on the student CourseMate Web site.

2. Work with a partner. Practice reciting and explaining information about each line of information in your outline.

Studying from Outline Notes

Outlines provide an excellent study tool to practice reciting and to give you immediate feedback about your level of understanding and recall of textbook information. Use the following tips to study from your outlines.

- **Read and explain line by line.** Begin with the first Roman numeral on your outline. Read the information on that line of the outline. Recite what you know about the topic. Speak in complete sentences. Move to the next line of information. Recite what you know; strive to integrate and link ideas together and explain relationships.

- **Check your accuracy and completeness of information.** As you recite, you will quickly become aware of your familiarity with the topic. Refer to your textbook to check your accuracy or to see what kinds of information you did not include in your reciting.

- **Add clue words to the right of the lines in your outline.** You can break away from the general structure of the outline at this point by jotting down key words or details that you did not initially include in your reciting. These clue words can guide you through the reciting process the next time you use your outline to review the contents of the chapter. Notice the clue words in the following example of an outline.

B. Stress Responses
    1. Physical Stress Responses: The GAS *general adaptation syndrome*   alarm / resistance / exhaustion
    2. Emotional Stress Responses   fear, anger / diminish, persist, severe
    3. Cognitive Stress Responses —— ruminative thinking; catastrophizing
    4. Behavioral Stress Responses

- **Use the outline to write a summary.** Many students learn and remember information more readily when they use their own words to explain and connect information in a logically sequenced manner and when they express themselves in writing. You can use the levels of information in your outline to organize and to write a summary. Include main ideas and briefly mention important supporting details.

CHECK POINT 9.5

Answers appear on page B4

True or False?

_____ 1. You can use formal or informal outlining to take textbook notes.

_____ 2. Informal outline notes do not use Roman or Arabic numerals.

_____ 3. Reciting is one effective way to study from outlines.

_____ 4. Outline notes should always be created after you read the entire chapter.

 Access Chapter 9 Practice Quiz 5 Outline Notes under "Interactive Quizzes" in your College Success CourseMate, accessed through *CengageBrain.com.*

CHAPTER 9 REFLECTIVE WRITING 2

On separate paper, in a journal, or online at this textbook's CourseMate Web site, respond to the following questions.

1. In what ways can taking textbook notes improve your performance in your classes?

2. Which notetaking system works best for each of your textbooks? Make a list of all the classes you are enrolled in this term. After carefully examining the textbooks for each class, state which notetaking system works best for each textbook and briefly explain why that system is the best choice to use.

Access Chapter 9 Reflective Writing 2 in your College Success CourseMate, accessed through *CengageBrain.com.*

Chapter 9 Critical Thinking

ACTIVITY

PURPOSE: Critical thinking involves analyzing and comparing information, which includes different points of view, and integrating information from different sources about the same subject. When reading information on one subject from two different sources (comparative reading), you can use three-column notes to show different definitions or opinions about the same subject.

DIRECTIONS

1. Read the following excerpt that explains Maslow's Hierarchy of Needs. The five levels of needs influence human behavior and motivation.

2. Create a set of three-column notes. In the left column of your notes, write the five levels of needs. In the second column, write details to explain each of the needs. For this exercise, focus on taking notes on only the five levels of needs and not on critics' or Alderfer's response to Maslow's Hierarchy of Needs.

3. In **Excerpt 8, Appendix D,** read "Maslow's Hierarchy of Needs." In the third column of your notes, add details about each need based on the information in Excerpt 8. You do not at this time need to take notes on Kohlberg's moral levels.

4. Your instructor may expand this exercise by asking critical thinking questions about Alderfer's point of view in the excerpt or Kohlberg's moral levels as they relate to Maslow's Hierarchy of needs (Excerpt 8).

Maslow's Hierarchy

Maslow (1970) suggested that human behavior is influenced by a hierarchy, or ranking, of five classes of needs or motives. He said that needs at the lowest level of the hierarchy must be at least partially satisfied before people can be motivated by ones at higher levels. From the bottom to the top of Maslow's hierarchy, these five motives are as follow:

1. *Physiological,* such as the need for food, water, oxygen, and sleep.

2. *Safety,* such as the need to be cared for as a child and to have a secure income as an adult.

3. *Belongingness and love,* such as the need to be part of groups and to participate in affectionate sexual and nonsexual relationships.

4. *Esteem,* such as the need to be respected as a useful, honorable individual.

5. *Self-actualization,* which means reaching one's full potential. People motivated by this need explore and enhance relationships with others; follow interests for intrinsic pleasure rather than for money, status, or esteem; and are concerned with issues affecting all people, not just themselves.

Maslow's Hierarchy of Motives

Abraham Maslow saw human motives as organized in a hierarchy in which motives at lower levels come before those at higher levels. According to this view, self-actualization is the essence of mental health; but Maslow recognized that only rare individuals, such as Mother Teresa or Martin Luther King, Jr., approach full self-actualization. Take a moment to consider which level of Maslow's hierarchy you are focused on at this point in your life. Which level do you ultimately hope to reach?

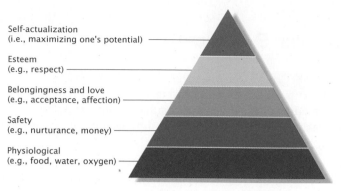

Self-actualization
(i.e., maximizing one's potential)

Esteem
(e.g., respect)

Belongingness and love
(e.g., acceptance, affection)

Safety
(e.g., nurturance, money)

Physiological
(e.g., food, water, oxygen)

Maslow's hierarchy has been very influential over the years, partly because the needs associated with basic survival and security do generally take precedence over those related to self-enhancement of personal growth... But critics see the hierarchy as too simplistic. It doesn't predict or explain, for example, the motivation of people who starve themselves to draw attention to political or moral causes. Further, people may not have to satisfy one kind of need before addressing others; we can seek to satisfy several needs at once. Finally, the ordering of needs within the survival/security and enhancement/growth categories differs from culture to culture, suggesting that there may not be a single, universal hierarchy of needs.

To address some of the problems in Maslow's theory, Clayton Alderfer (1969) proposed *existence, relatedness, growth (ERG) theory,* which places human needs into just three categories: *existence needs* (such as for food and water), *relatedness needs* (e.g., for social interactions and attachments), and *growth needs* (such as for developing one's capabilities). Unlike Maslow, Alderfer doesn't assume that these needs must be satisfied in a particular order. Instead, he sees needs in each category as rising and falling from time to time and from situation to situation. When a need in one area is fulfilled, or even if it is frustrated, a person will be motivated to pursue some other needs. For example, if a breakup frustrates relatedness needs, a person might focus on existence or growth needs by eating more or volunteering to work late.

Source: Bernstein/Nash. *Essentials of Psychology. Houghton Mifflin Company,* © 2008, pp. 320–321. Reprinted with permission.

Terms to Know

By yourself or with a partner, practice reciting or writing definitions for the following terms. You may also practice defining these terms by using the online flashcard program or comparing your answers to the online glossary.

annotating p. 259

enumerating p. 260

ordinals p. 260

Learning Objectives Review

1 *Discuss the rationale for taking notes and effective strategies to use with all notetaking systems.*

- Taking effective notes before, during, and after the reading process affects your ability to learn information, combats forgetting, and shows a high correlation to test performance.

- Eight essential notetaking strategies—including being selective, paraphrasing, and using spaced practice—work effectively for all notetaking systems.

2 *Discuss and apply strategies for marking or annotating textbook passages.*

- Annotating textbooks includes highlighting or underlining, marking, enumerating, and making marginal notes. Selectivity is essential when annotating.
- Marginal notes may include key terms, short questions, and abbreviations for kinds of information or sections of the text marked with a bracket.
- Studying from annotations involves rereading, stringing ideas together, reciting, and using additional activities to reinforce the learning.

3 *Discuss and apply the five steps of the Cornell system for taking notes.*

- The Cornell Notetaking System is a five-step process for taking comprehensive notes. The Five *R's* of Cornell are *record, reduce, recite, reflect,* and *review.*
- The **record step** occurs in the right column. The **reduce** and the **recite steps** occur in the left column, the recall column.
- The **reflect step** involves activities that personalize and reinforce the information.
- The **review step** involves immediate and ongoing review.

4 *Discuss and apply effective strategies for creating two- and three-column notes.*

- Two-column notes show topics, vocabulary terms, or study questions in the left column and details or explanations in the right column. Rehearse and review by reciting columns.
- Three-column notes can be used for comparative reading, terminology with two additional categories of information, and math notes. Rehearse and review by reciting.

5 *Discuss and apply effective strategies for taking informal outline notes.*

- Formal outlines follow specific rules for ordering and labeling levels of information. You can use formal outlines for notes, or you can modify the lower levels of information to create informal outline notes.
- You can use informal outline notes for a textbook before, during, or after the reading process.
- Studying from outline notes involves reading each line of the outline, reciting information, checking accuracy, and adding clue words to assist with reciting.

Terms to Know

marginal notes p. 260

stringing ideas together p. 261

Cornell Notetaking System p. 264

the Five *R*'s of Cornell p. 264

record step p. 264

reduce step p. 266

recall column p. 266

recite step p. 267

reflect step p. 268

review step p. 268

immediate review p. 268

ongoing review p. 269

Two-Column Notetaking
    System p. 271

Three-Column Notetaking
    System p. 273

Outline Notetaking System p. 278

 Access Chapter 9
Flashcard Drills and
Online Glossary
in your College
Success CourseMate,
accessed through
CengageBrain.com.

Chapter 9 Review Questions

Answers appear on page B4

True or False?

_____ 1. It is always best to read the whole chapter first and then go back to take notes.

_____ 2. All notetaking systems should result in a reduced version of textbook information.

_____ 3. If you are short on time, you will not weaken the system if you skip the fourth step of Cornell or skip rereading annotations and stringing ideas together.

_____ 4. It is not necessary to take notes on graphs, charts, or pictures because they are always easy to remember.

_____ 5. Annotating involves a variety of processes: marking main ideas, circling terminology, writing marginal notes, and possibly using abbreviations next to brackets.

_____ 6. Too much information in the Cornell recall column causes you to read and not do much reciting.

_____ 7. You can add more questions or key words to the Cornell recall column or outline notes if there are too few cues to help you recite.

_____ 8. The left column in two- and three-column notes usually shows terminology, study questions, or topics.

Application

Select *one* form of notetaking to take organized notes on the following excerpt.

Causes and Characteristics of Earthquakes

An **earthquake** is a trembling of the ground caused, most often, by the sudden release of energy in underground rocks. Most earthquakes occur where rocks are subjected to the stress associated with tectonic plate movement—that is, near plate boundaries. . . . The application of such stress may cause rocks to deform elastically and to accumulate *strain energy,* which builds until the rocks either shift suddenly along preexisting faults or rupture to create new faults. The result—earthquakes.

The precise subterranean spot at which rocks begin to rupture or shift marks the earthquake's **focus**... Approximately 90% of all earthquakes have a relatively shallow focus, located less than 100 kilometers (60 miles) below the surface; indeed, the focus of virtually all catastrophic quakes lies within 60 kilometers (40 miles) of the surface. Large earthquakes seldom occur at greater depth because heat has softened rocks there and robbed them of some of their ability to store strain energy. A few earthquakes, however, have occurred at depths as great as 700 kilometers (435 miles). Deeper than this level, higher temperatures and pressures cause stressed rocks to deform plastically, rather than rupture or shift.

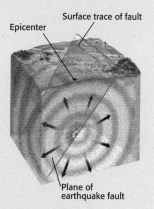

Epicenter   Surface trace of fault

Plane of earthquake fault

The point on the Earth's surface directly above any earthquake's focus is its **epicenter**. The greatest impact of a quake is generally felt at the epicenter, with the effect decreasing in proportion to the distance from the epicenter. After a major earthquake, the rocks in the vicinity of the quake's focus continue to reverberate as they adjust to their new positions, producing numerous, generally smaller earthquakes, or *aftershocks.* Aftershocks may continue for as long as one or two years after the main quake, shaking and further damaging already-weakened structures.

Source: Chernicoff/Fox. *Essentials of Geology.* Houghton Mifflin Company, © 2003, pp. 198–199. Reprinted with permission.

 Access Chapter 9 Chapter Quizzes 1-4 and Enhanced Quiz under "Interactive Quizzes" in your College Success CourseMate, accessed through *CengageBrain.com.*

Access all Chapter 9 Online Materials in your College Success CourseMate, accessed through *CengageBrain.com.*

Listening and Lecture Notes

ANSWER, SCORE, and **RECORD** your profile before you read this chapter. If you need to review the process, refer to the complete directions given in the profile for Chapter 1 on page 4.

ONLINE: You can complete the profile and get your score online at this textbook's CourseMate Web site.

Access Chapter 10 Profile in your College Success CourseMate, accessed through CengageBrain.com.

	YES	NO
1. I use different listening goals or purposes for different kinds of listening situations.		
2. I often feel unprepared for class and unfamiliar with the lecture topic when I enter the classroom.		
3. I am familiar with key words used in lectures that signal headings, main ideas, and important supporting details.		
4. I know how to use several different kinds of notetaking systems, so I select the one that is best suited for each class, the instructor, and the content.		
5. I avoid using outline notes—even when the instructor provides a basic outline before a lecture.		
6. I stop taking notes when the speaker sidetracks from the topic.		
7. I spend time going over my notes and filling in missing information as soon after the lecture as possible.		
8. I do not take notes when instructors provide me with copies of Power Point slides used in class lectures because all of the information appears on the slides.		
9. I frequently paraphrase, abbreviate, and use shortened sentences in my lecture notes.		
10. I am confident in my ability to use effective listening and lecture notetaking skills in my classes.		

QUESTIONS LINKED TO THE CHAPTER LEARNING OBJECTIVES:

Questions 1–3: objective 1   Questions 7–9: objective 3

Questions 4–6: obective 2   Question 10: all objectives

Listening Skills

❶ *Discuss factors that influence the quality of listening, the four kinds of listening, and essential listening strategies for lectures.*

Listening is a process that involves taking in auditory stimuli, holding the stimuli in working memory long enough to attach meaning to the words, and understanding the words you hear. Hearing, which involves receiving auditory stimuli and

Listening is a process that involves taking in auditory stimuli, holding the stimuli in working memory long enough to attach meaning to the words, and understanding what you hear.

sound waves, does not automatically assure that you are *listening*. Hearing is only the starting point of listening; listening is an *active process* that engages the listener in a variety of cognitive processes.

We use four kinds of verbal communication skills to communicate with others: listening, speaking, reading, and writing. Daly and Engleberg, in the textbook *Presentations in Everyday Life,* state that listening is our number-one communication activity. Although percentages vary from study to study, **Figure 10.1** shows how most of us divide up our daily communication time.

The Listening Process

Even though the largest percentage of our communication activities involve listening, listening skills are often the weakest of our communication skills.

One study of college students found that listening occupies more than half of their communicating time. In the corporate world, executives may devote more than 60 percent of their workday listening to others.

Yet, despite all of the time we spend listening, most of us aren't very good at it. For example, immediately after listening to a short talk, most of us cannot accurately report 50 percent of what was said. Without training, we listen at only 25 percent efficiency. And of that 25 percent, most of what we remember is distorted or inaccurate. *Source:* Daly/Engleberg, *Presentations in Every Day Life.* Houghton Mifflin Company, © 2001, p. 29, 30. Reprinted with permission.

So, why is listening such a difficult process? One answer is that our poor listening habits may be the result of the *lack* of training or instruction on how to be good listeners. Another answer lies in understanding how our memory systems function. Consider the cognitive processes that we must activate in order to receive and understand spoken information, and consider the challenges we face in listening situations:

- As soon as our sensory memory accepts auditory input, within a matter of seconds we need to identify information as important to avoid losing the stimuli completely.
- Because of the limited capacity and duration of short-term memory, once stimuli are in short-term memory, we need to attend to or concentrate on them to keep them active in working memory for further processing. Without attention, the stimuli will drop out of our memory system and not be processed.

CONCEPT CHECK 10.1

Why is listening a more active, complex process than hearing?

FIGURE 10.1   Percentage of Time Used in Four Communication Activities

Communication Activity	Percentages
Listening	40–70
Speaking	20–35
Reading	10–20
Writing	5–15

Engleberg/Daley, *Presentations in Every Day Life, 2e,* Allyn and Bacon, ©2007, p. 29, 30

- To understand what we hear, we need to continuously tap into long-term memory to associate the new information with information we already know or understand. In a rapid-fire manner, information moves back and forth between working memory and long-term memory, building in strength as we integrate old and new information.

- The process is complicated and requires undivided attention, yet fluctuating attention is a natural process. We listen, tune out briefly, refocus on listening, and continue with this fluctuation. At times, we may tune-out to avoid over-loading our working memory if too much new information is coming in at one time. Other times we may tune-out because there is too little new or challenging information presented, we are bored, or we fail to control internal or external distractions.

- Inability to concentrate during the entire listening process may be the result of discrepancies in speaking and thinking rates. (See Figure 10.9.)

- Our attention during the listening process at times may be weakened by the need to attend to visual stimuli as well. Our processing centers need to attend not only to auditory stimuli, but also to visual stimuli in the form of Power Point slides, overhead transparencies, or other visual materials used by the speaker.

Effective listening requires rapid-fire shifting of attention to multiple stimuli and tasks. To be an effective listener, one must commit to the process of developing effective listening skills and eliminating ineffective listening habits or patterns. Developing effective listening skills will benefit you not only in the academic setting, but also in your personal life. Strengthening effective listening skills is a topic of interest in more than college courses; businesses, organizations, and counseling settings all stress the importance of becoming an effective listener. **Figure 10.2** shows effective and less effective listening skills.

Influencing Factors

Good listening is similar to concentration: it is here one second and then it is gone. Effective listening involves a willingness to eliminate poor listening habits, which are learned behaviors and which are influenced by internal and external distractions. You may begin listening to a speaker with the complete intention of "staying tuned in," listening attentively, following the ideas, and making every effort to understand the information, but then your thoughts suddenly shift and you find yourself doodling, daydreaming, or attempting to multitask by engaging in tasks unrelated to listening to the speaker. Interferences, including both listener interference and speaker interference, can cause disruptions in the listening process.

Listener Interference

"*Interference* is anything that stops or hinders a listener from receiving a message." In *Invitation to Public Speaking*, author Cindy Griffin explains bad listening habits that stem from listener interference:

> You may be surprised to learn that most listening challenges stem from poor listening habits. Consider the following list of bad listening habits. Can you identify times you've done some of the following?
>
> - Think you're not interested in the subject before the speech really gets going.
> - Assume you know what the speaker is going to say before it's even said.

CONCEPT CHECK 10.2

How do the actions or behaviors of an effective listener differ from the actions or behaviors of a poor listener?

CONCEPT CHECK 10.3

What factors influence your listening effectiveness?

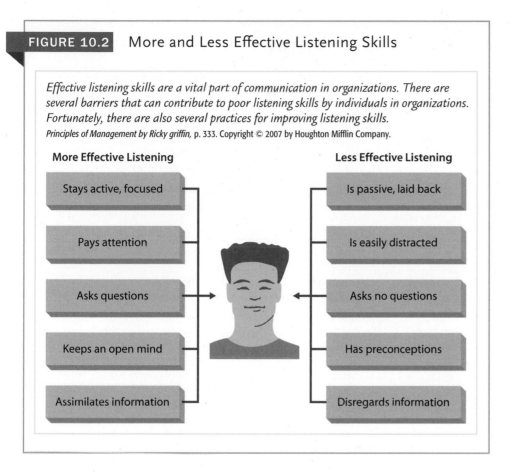

FIGURE 10.2   More and Less Effective Listening Skills

Effective listening skills are a vital part of communication in organizations. There are several barriers that can contribute to poor listening skills by individuals in organizations. Fortunately, there are also several practices for improving listening skills.

Principles of Management by Ricky griffin, p. 333. Copyright © 2007 by Houghton Mifflin Company.

More Effective Listening	Less Effective Listening
Stays active, focused	Is passive, laid back
Pays attention	Is easily distracted
Asks questions	Asks no questions
Keeps an open mind	Has preconceptions
Assimilates information	Disregards information

- Get so focused on the details that you miss the bigger point.
- Adopt a passive physical stance-turning away, crossing arms, making hostile eye contact.
- Pay attention to distractions or create them yourself.
- Be so preoccupied with the message that you miss the message.
- Tune out difficult information.
- Tune out information you don't agree with, or argue with the speaker's message in your own mind.
- Prepare your response while the speaker is speaking.
- Daydream or pretend you are listening when you really aren't.

At one time or another, most of us have fallen into many of these habits. We may think we've heard all there is to hear on a subject, so we begin daydreaming or simply pretend to listen. We become so enamored of or so frustrated with a speaker that we forget to listen to the content of a speech.

From: Griffin, *Invitation to Public Speaking, 3e,* © 2009 Wadsworth, a part of Cengage Learning, Inc. Reproduced by permission. www.cengage.com/permissions.

As a listener, you may bring additional factors into the listening process that interfere with your ability to listen effectively. **Figure 10.3** shows five personal factors that influence your listening skills and that you need to monitor, control, and adjust to become an effective listener.

FIGURE 10.3   Personal Factors That Influence Listening Skills

Your Attitude *Positive attitude enhances listening ability; negative attitude hinders it.*	Your interest level in the topic Your attitude toward the subject Your attitude toward the speaker
The Topic *Familiarity enhances listening; lack of background hinders it.*	Your familiarity with the words, terminology, or topic Your personal background and cultural experiences Difficulty level of the course or presentation Quantity of information presented
External Distractors *Ability to block out distractors enhances listening; attending to distractors hinders it.*	Noise and movement in the listening environment Room temperature or lighting Interruptions or disruptions by others in the room
Physical Factors *Comfort, proximity to speaker, and positive physical and emotional state enhance listening; opposites of these factors hinder it.*	Length of time required to remain seated Sitting posture during the lecture Seating location in relation to the speaker Personal physical and emotional state at the time
Learning Style Preferences *Similar listening styles of listener and speaker enhance understanding; different listening styles may challenge understanding. Linear learners often are linear listeners; global learners often are global listeners.*	Linear listeners tend to listen for logical, sequential details and may not use concerted effort to see the "big picture." Global listeners tend to listen for the "big picture" and may not use concerted effort to identify important supporting details.

Speaker Interference

Sometimes poor listening stems from characteristics or behaviors speakers bring to the listening situation. However, you cannot lay blame for poor listening on the speaker; it is your responsibility to adjust to the speaker and use effective strategies to reduce the interferences that occur due to the speaker. Following are examples of speaker interferences that you may be challenged to deal with in classroom lecture situations.

CONCEPT CHECK 10.4

Explain the negative impact that listener interferences and speaker interferences have on the listening process.

- **Complicated or technical information:** Lack of familiarity with a topic makes listening and understanding information difficult to do. The tendency is to "tune-out" rather than work to understand. To reduce the negative response to complicated or technical information, you can read ahead in your textbook to gain familiarity with the topic and begin to create memory schemas for the subject.

- **Tone of voice and speech patterns:** Some tones of voice, for example an unusually high pitched or low pitched voice, a soft, quiet tone, or a booming, assertive tone of voice, can bother or annoy you as a listener. The same is true for speech patterns, such as over-using unnecessary phrases such as "You know," speaking rapidly, or speaking slowly with long pauses can hinder your ability to listen effectively. Because a speaker's tone of voice or speech patterns likely are not going to change, you need to take responsibility to change your attitude and seek ways to adapt to the speaker's characteristics. Strive to focus your attention on the information and not on the voice or speech patterns. Over time, you will become more accustomed to the tone and speech patterns and will find that they have less impact on your ability to listen effectively.

- **Poorly organized presentation of information:** As an effective listener and a critical listener, there will be times that you recognize that the speaker is presenting information in an unorganized, difficult-to-follow, or loosely structured manner. The poor organization of information becomes a distractor. When the speaker sidetracks, the tendency often is for you to tune-out and lose focus. When you attempt to start listening again, you may find the information even more confusing. In this chapter, you will learn strategies to maintain a focus when faced with these lecture situations.

In the following sections, you will learn about four different kinds of listening and effective strategies to use to overcome interferences linked to poor listening habits. Becoming an effective listener requires work on your part; listening to learn does not *just happen* without effort.

EXERCISE 10.1

Classroom Listening Factors Inventory

DIRECTIONS: Go to Exercise 10.1 in Appendix C for a listening inventory to increase your awareness of behaviors and attitudes that influence your ability to listen during classroom lectures. Your responses will provide you with insights on ways to strengthen your classroom listening skills.

Kinds of Listening

Just as there is more than one way to read a book, write a paper, or speak to others, there is more than one way to listen. Different reading, writing, speaking, or listening activities involve different purposes or learning goals. For example, your purpose for:

- *reading* differs when you read a movie review, a magazine, a newspaper, a novel, a research report, and a textbook.
- *writing* may range from capturing feelings and memories in a diary, expressing yourself through poetry, communicating with a friend, writing a short story or an essay, summarizing an article, answering test questions, or preparing a report.
- *speaking* may be to gain someone's support, share personal experiences, vent emotions, teach or inform, clarify a situation, persuade, or promote.
- *listening* may be to understand new information, interpret and analyze a speaker's message, relate to another person's feelings, or enjoy and appreciate a message.

Understanding your listening goal each time you approach a listening situation can help you select appropriate strategies to strengthen your listening skills. **Figure 10.4** shows four kinds of listening and the listening goals for each.

CONCEPT CHECK 10.5

What are different kinds of listening goals that you might establish in your classes? Explain.

FIGURE 10.4   Kinds of Listening and Listening Goals

Kinds of Listening	The Listening Goal is to...
Active Listening	Understand and learn new information
Critical Listening	Understand, interpret, examine, and analyze a speaker's message
Empathic Listening	Understand and relate to another person's feelings and emotions
Appreciative Listening	Enjoy, appreciate, and acknowledge a speaker and his or her message

---

Active Listening

Active listening is the process of concentrating intently on a speaker's message with the goal of understanding the information as it is presented. Many of your college active listening experiences will occur in classroom settings: in lectures, in labs, in small groups, or in partner activities. The Essential Listening Strategies for Lectures in the following section apply directly to active listening situations.

Active listening is the process of concentrating intently on a speaker's message with the goal of understanding the information as it is presented.

Critical Listening

Critical listening is the process of concentrating intently on a speaker's message with the goals of understanding, interpreting, analyzing, and critiquing the content of the message. Critical listening is a higher, more complex form of listening that involves critical thinking skills. Following are important points about critical listening:

Critical listening is the process of concentrating intently on a speaker's message with the goals of understanding, interpreting, analyzing, and critiquing the content of the message.

- Critical listening is difficult, if not impossible, to do without pre-existing background knowledge and familiarity with the topic.
- In addition to hearing the speaker's message without distorting it, critical listening requires separating your emotions and opinions from those of the speaker.
- Only after you hear the speaker's full message will you be able to analyze, evaluate, or critique the validity or logic of the information.
- For more information about Critical Listening, read **Excerpt 9: How to Listen Critically** in **Appendix D.**
- Critical listening challenges working memory due to the number of cognitive processes involved. For this reason, notetaking strategies for critical listening situations may differ from notetaking strategies used in active listening situations. To reduce the possibility of overloading working memory, focusing attention on the content of the message becomes more important than taking detailed notes.
- Notes taken during critical listening situations, such as with debates, may summarize important points in an argument with less recording of each step or detail in the presentation.

Empathic Listening

Empathic listening is the process of concentrating intently on a speaker's words with sincere intent to understand that person's feelings, emotions, and thoughts

Empathic listening is the process of concentrating intently on a speaker's words with sincere intent to understand that person's feelings, emotions, and thoughts related to a specific topic or situation.

related to a specific topic or situation. Your listening goal is to *empathize* or relate to the other person. Following are important points about empathic listening:

- Empathic listeners pay attention to people's verbal and nonverbal clues in order to identify the emotion being exhibited (anger, frustration, disappointment, resentment, excitement, enthusiasm, self-pride, and so on) and relate to the speaker's situation, feelings, or point of view.

- In many empathic listening situations, the speaker wants someone to listen and understand; he or she does not necessarily want to be consoled or given advice.

- Empathic listening skills are valuable in college courses that use group activities that encourage or require students to interact on more personal levels. Listen to and observe what the person wants to communicate to you.

- Empathic listeners avoid being judgmental and avoid criticizing, making negative comments, or telling the other person that he or she is "wrong." Instead, they use positive words or gestures to communicate that they *understand* the feeling or the situation—even if they do not agree with the other person.

Appreciative Listening

Appreciative listening is the process of listening to a speaker for the purpose of enjoying, appreciating, and acknowledging the speaker and the message in positive ways. Being drawn into a story by a captivating storyteller, laughing at an instructor's humorous anecdotes or examples in a lecture, marveling at the ease with which a student gives a class presentation, listening to an actor practice a scene from an upcoming play, or listening to someone describe a vacation to an exotic location are examples of appreciative listening. The following points are important about appreciative listening:

Appreciative listening is the process of listening to a speaker for the purpose of enjoying, appreciating, and acknowledging the speaker and the message in positive ways.

- Appreciative listening is not a passive, laid-back process. To feel the richness of words, to be moved emotionally by a message, or to experience overwhelming gratitude for a speaker and his or her message all require that you, the listener, take an active role by paying close attention to details, connecting with the speaker, and allowing emotional responses to occur.

- You can demonstrate your appreciation through nods of agreement, eye contact, facial expressions, compliments or expressions of gratitude, and, when appropriate, applause.

Using Four Kinds of Listening

EXERCISE 10.2

PURPOSE: We engage in all four types of listening on a regular basis. By recognizing the type of listening involved in a situation, we can adjust our listening goals and strategies to the situation.

DIRECTIONS: Read the following descriptions of listening situations. Then write one of the following letters to indicate which kind of listening would be the most effective for each situation.

AC = Active   **C** = Critical
 E = Empathic   **AP** = Appreciative

_____ **1.** A debate about storing the nation's nuclear waste at Yucca Mountain in Nevada

_____ **2.** A lecture that reviews a psychology textbook chapter

Exercise 10.2 (cont.)

_____ **3.** Four students' project that involves a ten-minute skit

_____ **4.** A debate in a political science class between two guest speakers

_____ **5.** An instructor's explanation of the steps to use to complete a lab project

_____ **6.** A class discussion about the author's purpose and the thesis of a short story

_____ **7.** A student expressing frustration about a disagreement with a tutor

_____ **8.** An instructor reading three of his favorite poems written by American poets

_____ **9.** A candidate for a county commissioner position giving a campaign speech

_____ **10.** An instructor expressing his or her opinion about job reductions on campus

CONCEPT CHECK 10.7

What strategies can you use to become a more effective listener each time you enter into a lecture situation?

Essential Listening Strategies for Lectures

Replacing poor listening habits with effective listening habits will benefit you in the classroom, in your personal life, and in your place of employment. The essential strategies for effective listening in this section focus on becoming an effective listener in the classroom. However, you can apply or modify the same strategies to strengthen your listening skills in all areas of your life. The following essential strategies are effective strategies to begin the process of becoming an active and a critical listener:

- **Create a clear listening goal.** Enter the classroom with an *intention* to listen to learn. Exhibit a positive attitude toward the subject, the speaker, and the experience. Strive to follow the speaker's chain of thoughts, sequence of details, relationships, examples, and logic.

- **Use concentration strategies.** Free up working memory space by eliminating as many external and internal distractors as possible, including disruptive thoughts. Make a concerted effort to maintain undivided attention.

- **Familiarize yourself with the topic *before* class.** Become familiar with the terminology, main concepts, and key details by previewing the chapter that will be discussed in class; read the chapter if time permits. Instead of hearing information for the first time, you will have already activated or started new schemas in your long-term memory for the information.

- **Keep an open mind.** Avoid prejudging information or the speaker. Set personal opinions aside so you can hear the speaker's message as it is presented.

- **Activate your visual skills.** Try to visualize information as it is presented. Turn on the "movie in your mind" to create a visual association with the verbal information.

- **Express an interest in the topic.** When appropriate, ask questions about points of interest or points that are confusing or unclear. Ask clarifying questions and paraphrase what you hear to check the accuracy of your understanding.

In your classes, you will use your listening skills for partner or small group activities, during discussions, and during question-answer or review sessions. However, classroom lectures and presentations will place the greatest demands on your listening skills. Taking effective lecture notes requires you to use effective listening skills to help you identify and capture main ideas and details for your notes.

Quality notes show the structure, the levels of information, and sufficient details to support main ideas. If your notes are too brief and lack sufficient details, they will not be very helpful when you need to study the information or prepare for tests. By listening carefully for key words, you will be better equipped to identify main ideas and shifts made to supporting details. **Figure 10.5** shows six Essential Listening Strategies to Use for Lectures.

Listen for Key Words Signaling Headings

Many instructors introduce a new topic or category of information by using signal words. You can use these signal words to help you organize lecture information. The words in the following list often signal a new heading for your notes. When the words are repeated, they signal supporting details. For example, if the instructor says, "Let's look at the major *causes* of global warming," the word *causes* signals a new heading. As the lecture progresses, the instructor will use the word *causes* several more times to identify and explain each individual cause, which you can then number as details. Following are key words to listen for as they may help you identify major headings or topics.

advantages	effects	parts	steps
benefits	factors	principles	solutions
causes	findings	purposes	techniques
characteristics	functions	reasons	types of
conclusions	kinds of	rules	uses
disadvantages	methods	stages	ways

Listen for Main Ideas

Main ideas are the main points the instructor makes about a specific topic or heading. Often times your instructor will use transition words to connect or move

---

FIGURE 10.5 Essential Listening Strategies to Use for Lectures

1. Listen for key words signaling headings.
2. Listen for main ideas.
3. Listen for terminology and definitions.
4. Listen for supporting details.
5. Listen for verbal clues.
6. Listen for the conclusion.

Notetaking Systems for Lectures

CONCEPT CHECK 10.9

What strategy can you use when an instructor wanders off course during a lecture and discusses information that seems to be out of sequence or order?

❷ *Explain how to use Cornell, Two-Column, Three-Column, and Outline Notes for taking lecture notes; explain how to use the Book Notes System.*

Being familiar and comfortable with a variety of notetaking systems allows you to select the most appropriate and effective notetaking system to use for specific lecture styles and course content. **Figure 10.6** shows notetaking systems that are recommended for specific kinds of lectures; however, you can select from the other options if they seem better suited to your notetaking needs.

FIGURE 10.6 Lecture Notetaking Options

	Cornell Notes	Two-Column Notes	Three-Column Notes	Outline Notes
Lectures *Mostly declarative knowledge: facts, definitions, examples, explanations*	✔ Show headings. Number details. Create recall column.	✔ Write topics, terminology, and questions in the left column. Number details in the right column.		✔ Use I, II, III for topics. Use A,B,C for main ideas. Use 1, 2, 3 for details. Add a recall column if you wish.
Discussions		✔ Write questions or topics in the left column. Write comments and explanations in the right column.		
Math or Procedural Knowledge content *Steps, processes, equations*		✔ Write the topic, process, or equation in the left column. Write the steps and the solution in the right column.	✔ Write the process or equation in the left column; write the steps in the middle column; write explanations in the right column. *OR* ✔ Leave the middle column empty for reworking the problem later.	
Power Point Presentations		✔ Write slide number in the left column. Write and number details in the right column.	✔ Write the slide number in the left column. Sketch the slide in the middle column. Add notes or comments in the right column.	

Cornell, Two-Column, Three-Column, and Outline Notes

In Chapter 9, you learned how to take notes using the Cornell System, Two-Column Notes, Three-Column Notes, and Outline Notes. You can use all four of these notetaking systems for lecture notes. Select the notetaking system that you are most comfortable using and that best suits the type of lecture and material presented.

Dealing with Sidetracking

During the course of a lecture, you may find that the instructor *sidetracks* by discussing information that does not seem to fit within the order or the outline of the topics. When you recognize that the instructor has sidetracked, continue to take notes on the *sidetracked information* as it may be important. Write sidetracked information on the *back side* of the previous page of notes, or include sidetracked information in your regular notes but place these notes inside a box to separate them from your regular notes. (See **Figure 10.7.**) You can use this method of recording information that is presented out of order or sequence in the lecture for all four notetaking systems.

Completing Lecture Outline Notes

In some lectures, the instructor may provide you with a partial outline of the lecture at the beginning of the class. With the partial outline as the skeleton of the main topics in the lecture, your goal then is to complete the outline by filling in the missing details. **Figure 10.8** shows an example of an instructor's outline presented before the lecture begins.

Partial outlines are valuable learning tools for several reasons. First, the outline organizes the different levels of information for you. Second, more than not, the instructor's lecture will follow the outline without sidetracking to other topics. Third, knowing that you need to listen carefully for the appropriate details to complete the outline increases concentration and active listening skills.

Listening and taking lecture notes are two complex processes that require a repertoire of strategies for understanding, interpreting, organizing, and recording important information. What strategies do you use in lecture classes to capture important information for your notes?

©Digital Vision/Jupiter Images

FIGURE 10.7 Ways to Take Notes on Sidetracking

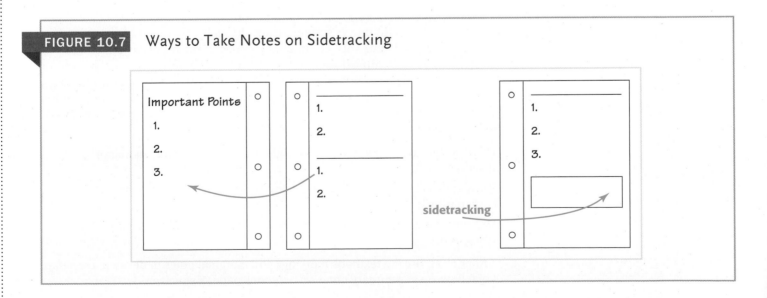

FIGURE 10.8   Example of an Instructor's Lecture Outline

Outline for Feb. 5 Lecture

Practice Effective Listening

I. Direct and Indirect Listening
    A. Direct Listening Cultures
        1. Def-
        2. Countries
            a.
            b.
            c.
    B. Indirect Listening Cultures
        1. Def-
        2. Countries
            a.
            b.
    C. Culturally Sensitive Words
        1.
        2.
        3.
    D. Gender-Sensitive Words
        1.
        2.

The Book Notes System

> The Book Notes System is a form of notetaking that involves marking your textbook as the lecturer moves systematically through a chapter.

The Book Notes System is a form of notetaking that involves marking your textbook as your instructor moves systematically through a chapter. Lecturing straight from the textbook is not very common, but does occur on occasion, such as in technical, reading, composition, and some math courses. When an instructor moves systematically through the textbook chapter, discussing various headings, emphasizing certain details, demonstrating how to solve problems, or working textbook exercises with you in class, you can take notes directly in your textbook. Use the following strategies to take book notes:

- Use a specific colored marker to highlight the information the instructor discusses.
- Write notes in the margins to reflect any additional information or explanations.
- Use symbols, such as arrows or stars, to draw your attention to sections discussed.

After class, use the textbook markings and marginal notes to develop a separate set of follow-up or summary notes on notebook paper if you wish.

CONCEPT CHECK 10.10

What is the Book Notes System and when can you use it effectively?

CHECK POINT 10.2

Answers Appear in BXX

True or False?

_____ 1. Effective notetakers use Cornell notes for lectures, outline notes for math courses, and two- or three-column notes only for discussions.

_____ 2. The content of the lecture and the instructor's lecture style often determine which notetaking system would be the most effective to use.

_____ 3. Every student should master one specific notetaking system so he or she can use that system consistently for taking notes in every class that term.

_____ 4. The Book Notes System is designed to be used when you read a textbook before the instructor discusses the information in class.

 Access Chapter 10 Practice Quiz 2: Notetaking Options under "Interactive Quizzes" in your College Success CourseMate, accessed through *CengageBrain.com*.

GROUP PROCESSING

A COLLABORATIVE LEARNING ACTIVITY

Form groups of three or four students. Then complete the following directions.

1. On a large chart, make two columns. In the left column, brainstorm problems that students encounter when they take lecture notes. List as many problems as you can think of within a ten-minute period.

2. In the right column, brainstorm possible solutions for each of the problems. Include solutions you know from personal experience and solutions that appear in this chapter.

Effective Notetaking Strategies

 Discuss effective strategies for taking and working with lecture notes, including Power Point notes and math lectures notes, and strategies to solve common notetaking problems.

The major difference between taking textbook notes and taking lecture notes is the rapidity with which you need to respond to stimuli, understand words and ideas, organize information in meaningful ways, and transfer it into notes—while at the same time taking in new information presented by the speaker. When taking lecture notes, keeping up with the speaker replaces the comfortable pace you use when taking textbook notes. Taking lecture notes definitely challenges your working memory.

CONCEPT CHECK 10.11

What is the average rate of speaking, rate of thinking, and rate of writing? How do these rates affect taking lecture notes?

Speaking, Thinking, and Writing Rates

The *rate of speaking* (or rate of speech) indicates an average number of words a speaker says per minute. In personal conversations, for example when you want to discuss serious issues or want to be sure the listener understands your points, you may speak slower than 100 words per minute. Other times in casual conversations, for example when you have exciting news to share, you may speak much faster than the normal rate of 125–150 words per minute for conversations. The average rate of speech during a lecture is 100–125 words per minute—a rate that provides a little more time to create basic understanding and to take notes.

Taking lecture notes requires you to adjust to your instructor's *rate of speech*. You will likely encounter three general speaking rates instructors use during lectures: too slow, comfortable, or too fast. When the speaking rate is fast, you will have to increase your level of concentration and increase your rate of writing. When an instructor speaks too slowly, you may have difficulty staying focused, so you will need to make a concerted effort to increase concentration and avoid distractions.

The *rate of thinking* indicates an average number of words or small units of information a person thinks per minute. The average is 400 words per minute. When an instructor speaks slowly, your *rate of thinking* far outpaces the instructor's rate of speech, so your mind tends to wander off the subject.

The *rate of writing* indicates the average number of words a person writes per minute. An average rate of writing is thirty words per minute. When an instructor speaks too fast, your *rate of writing* is too slow to capture the instructor's ideas on paper. When an instructor speaks at a comfortable pace, taking notes will still be demanding, but the discrepancies among speaking, writing, and thinking rates will not create as many notetaking difficulties. **Figure 10.9** summarizes average speaking, writing, and thinking rates.

Rate Discrepancies

Dealing with the discrepancies among the rate of speech in lectures, rate of writing, and rate of thinking requires flexibility and familiarity on your part with a variety of strategies you can use to adjust to specific lecture situations. **Figure 10.10** shows nine Essential Strategies for Dealing with Rate Discrepancies.

Maintain Undivided Attention

When your mind wanders, you start daydreaming, or you start doodling or tending to other tasks because of the large discrepancy between the speaker's slow rate of speech and your much faster rate of thinking, you may miss important information and find switching back into the listening mode more difficult to do. Your listening goal is to use strategies to keep your mind focused on the speaker and to maintain undivided attention, even though the presentation of information is not demanding. Use the

> The rate of speaking (or rate of speech) indicates an average number of words a speaker says per minute. (100–125 words per minute)

> The rate of thinking indicates an average number of words or small units of information a person thinks per minute. (400 words per minute)
> The rate of writing indicates the average number of words a person writes per minute (30 wpm).

FIGURE 10.9 Speaking, Writing, and Thinking Rates

Average Rates	Words per Minute (wpm)
Average Rate of Speaking During Lectures	100–125 wpm
Average Rate of Writing	30 wpm
Average Rate of Thinking	400 wpm

following three strategies to deal with the discrepancy between a slow rate of speech and a fast rate of thinking:

- **Strategy 1: Keep Writing.** Even if the details do not seem vital to your notes, write them down anyway. You can always cross out or eliminate them later. By continuing to write, you keep your working memory active and focused on the content of the lecture.

- **Strategy 2: Mentally Summarize.** In your mind, run through the main ideas and the supporting details that have been discussed. Try to mentally summarize and list the details while you wait for new information to be introduced. You can also ask yourself basic questions, such as *Do I agree with this information? Is this the way it was presented in the textbook?*

- **Strategy 3: Predict the Next Point or an Answer to a Question.** With active listening, you can often "mentally tune in" to the speaker's outline or organizational plan for the lecture. Predict the next point that would naturally follow the sequential development of information, or mentally ask yourself a question that you think the next section of information will answer. Then listen carefully to determine if your prediction was correct or if your question was answered.

Increase Your Writing Rate

More often than not, notetaking problems occur because the rate of speech during a lecture is faster than your rate of writing. Your notetaking goal is *not* to write fast enough to write word for word; that is not feasible, practical, nor useful as notes should be *condensed* versions of information. Your goal is to develop a writing fluency or speed that is fast enough to write important information in your notes. Writing fluency is an essential notetaking skill; in fact, research studies show that writing fluency has the greatest impact on the quality of your notes. The following three time-saving strategies can improve your writing rate and fluency:

- **Strategy 4: Paraphrase the Speaker.** *Paraphrasing* is the process of using your own words to rephrase or shorten a speaker's verbal information. Paraphrasing begins as a mental process that must be done quickly. As soon as you capture the speaker's words, interpret the information quickly, condense it using your own words, and write the shortened form in your notes. Your "sentences" do not need to be grammatically correct. You may omit words such as *the, an, and, there,* and *here* and other words that do not add to the overall meaning. Paraphrasing is perhaps one of the most difficult parts of notetaking, but with practice and familiarity with different instructors' lecture styles, your skills at paraphrasing will improve, and so will your writing fluency.

- **Strategy 5: Use Abbreviations and Symbols.** Using abbreviations and symbols increases your writing speed. When you find content-related words that you use frequently, create your own abbreviations for the terms or use common abbreviations, such as the following:

BC. For *because*	**PRES.** For *president*
EX. For *example*	**SOC.** For *social or sociology*
IMP. For *important*	**SOL.** For *solutions*
POL. For *politics*	**W/Out** for *without*

FIGURE 10.10 Essential Strategies for Dealing with Rate Discrepancies

- Keep writing.
- Mentally summarize.
- Predict the next point or an answer to a question.
- Paraphrase the speaker.
- Use abbreviations and symbols.
- Use modified printing.
- Leave a gap and start writing again.
- Shift to paragraph form.
- Tape the lecture.

CONCEPT CHECK 10.12

What strategies can you use to minimize problems created by discrepancies between speaking and writing rates? Speaking and thinking rates?

Access Chapter 10 Practice Quiz 3: Keeping Up with the Speaker under "Interactive Quizzes" in your College Success CourseMate, accessed through *CengageBrain.com.*

Paraphrasing is the process of using your own words to rephrase or shorten a speaker's verbal information.

CONCEPT CHECK 10.13

What is writing fluency? How can you increase your writing fluency when taking lecture notes?

Symbols are another form of abbreviations to use to increase your writing speed. Symbols frequently appear in math notes, but you can use symbols for other words as well. Following are common symbols you can use in your notes:

&	And	→	Leads to; causes
@	At	<	Less than
↓	Decreases	>	More than; greater than
≠	Doesn't equal	#	Number
=	Equals	+/−	Positive/negative
↑	Increases	∴	Therefore
+	Add; also	−	Subtract
×	Times	/	Divide; per
( )	Quantity	$p \wedge q$	Conjunction *and*
~p	Negation (not p)	$p \vee q$	Disjunction *or*

- **Strategy 6: Use Modified Printing.** Modified printing is a style of handwriting that is functional and increases writing speed by using a mixture of cursive writing and printing. While taking notes, you can relax your handwriting standards and experiment with switching back and forth from printing and cursive writing to see if this increases your writing speed.

Do Not Stop When You Fall Behind

Most students at one time or another experience frustration when they are not able to keep up with the speaker—even when using strategies to increase their writing speed. A normal tendency is to simply give up—stop taking notes and just listen. Sometimes that may not be a bad option, but later you may regret not having a written record of the information. Try using the following three strategies when you fall behind.

- **Strategy 7: Leave a Gap and Start Writing Again.** Instead of giving up, leave a gap in your notes and start taking notes again for as long as you can keep up with the instructor. After class, ask another student or the instructor to help fill in the gaps.

- **Strategy 8: Shift to Paragraph Form.** Sometimes becoming overly concerned with the notetaking format slows you down. If you find yourself spending too much time trying to decide how to number, label, or indent a detail, stop using your notetaking format and shift instead to writing paragraphs. Continue to paraphrase and use abbreviations or symbols in your paragraphs when possible. Later, when you have more time, you can reread the paragraph and organize it in a more meaningful way, such as making the recall column in Cornell notes or highlighting headings and numbering main ideas.

CONCEPT CHECK 10.14

How do you react to a note taking situation in which you can no longer keep up with the instructor? What other ways can you deal with the situation?

- **Strategy 9: Tape the Lecture.** If you consistently have difficulties keeping up with one instructor's style and rate of speech in lectures, ask your instructor for permission to tape the lectures. If permission is granted, sit near the front of the room. Start your tape recorder, and then begin taking notes on paper. If your tape recorder has a counter on it, when you run into notetaking problems or fall behind in your notes, jot down the counter number as it appears right then on your recorder. After class, return to specific sections of the tape so you can listen to the information one more time and add missing details in your notes. Your tape recorder should supplement, *not* replace, notetaking during the lecture.

 Access Chapter 10 Practice Quiz 4: Organizing Notes under "Interactive Quizzes" in your College Success CourseMate, accessed through *CengageBrain .com*.

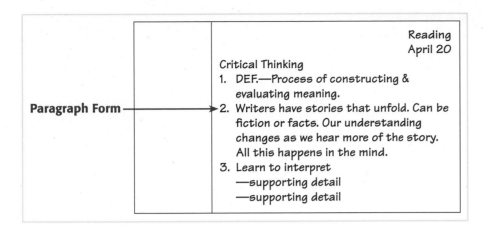

Paragraph Form →

Reading
April 20

Critical Thinking
1. DEF.—Process of constructing &
   evaluating meaning.
2. Writers have stories that unfold. Can be
   fiction or facts. Our understanding
   changes as we hear more of the story.
   All this happens in the mind.
3. Learn to interpret
   —supporting detail
   —supporting detail

EXERCISE 10.3

Matching Problems to Solutions

DIRECTIONS: Go to Exercise 10.3 in Appendix C. In this matching exercise, you will see textbook reading and lecture notetaking problems that students frequently encounter in their classes. In the right column, you will find solutions for each of the problems. Match the solutions to the problems.

Instructor Clues

As you become accustomed to your different instructors and their lecture styles, you will be able to use their verbal, visual, and nonverbal clues to help identify important information to place in your notes. At the beginning of the chapter, you learned about listening for instructor verbal clues to help you identify important information for your notes. These verbal clues include key words, direct statements, and other speaking patterns such as intonation, volume, and rate of speech. In additional to verbal clues, instructors also provide you with visual clues and nonverbal clues that can help you identify the information to include in your lecture notes.

CONCEPT CHECK 10.15

What kinds of clues do instructors often provide for you during a lecture to help you identify important information to record in your notes?

Watch for Visual Clues

Information that instructors write on the chalkboard or visual graphics that instructors display on a screen are visual clues that information is important. Include visual information as much as possible in your notes. If you recall seeing the same chart or visual information in your textbook, jot down a quick reminder to yourself to refer to the textbook chapter. If the visual information does not appear in your textbook, sketch the visual graphic and jot down as many details as possible about the visual graphic as the instructor presents it. Asking questions about the visual materials provides you with the opportunity to get more information from the instructor as to what information from the visual graphic is important to place in your notes.

Watch for Nonverbal Clues

Watch your instructor's *nonverbal clues* or patterns as well. Body stance, hand gestures, and facial expressions (forehead wrinkles, eyebrows rise) are nonverbal clues that communicate to observant listeners. If the instructor pauses to look at his or her notes or simply pauses to allow you time to write, the pauses are nonverbal clues. These nonverbal clues may signal that the instructor is shifting to another heading or main idea, or that he or she wants to verify that all the important details have been mentioned. Writing information on the board, pointing to parts of it over and over, and circling words on the board are also nonverbal clues indicating that information is important.

EXERCISE 10.4

DIRECTIONS

1. Read each case study carefully. Respond to the question at the end of each case study by using *specific* strategies discussed in this chapter. Answer in complete sentences.

2. Write your responses on paper or online at the CourseMate student Web site, Textbook Case Studies. You will be able to print your online response or e-mail it to your instructor.

CASE STUDY 1: Kimberly is very uncomfortable sitting in a classroom. She often feels like other students are watching her, so she sits in the back corner. She has a lot of problems taking notes. Her notes are too brief and ineffective for studying. She does not include information written on the board because she cannot see it clearly. At other times, she simply loses her concentration. When she does try taking notes, she cannot write fast enough to get all of the instructor's words on her paper. What would you recommend Kimberly do to improve her notetaking skills?

CASE STUDY 2: Alex prefers to listen to a lecture on a topic before reading his textbook. He believes the lecture will highlight for him the important points he should learn when he reads the chapter. During a lecture, he frequently annoys his classmates and instructors by interrupting the instructor to ask irrelevant questions or to ask the instructor to repeat information or to slow down. He always seems confused. Consequently, he spends more time talking than listening and taking notes. What techniques does Alex need to learn in order to be a more effective listener and leave lectures with more effective lecture notes?

 Access Chapter 10 Textbook Case Studies and Web-Only Case Studies in your College Success CourseMate, accessed through *CengageBrain.com*.

CONCEPT CHECK 10.16

Why is it necessary to take notes on Power Point slides? What are different ways to take notes on Power Point slide presentations?

Power Point Notes

Power Point slides are a form of visual graphics that has become popular and widely used for classroom lectures and presentations. A special projector hooked to a computer projects individual slides created by using the Power Point program. Instructors click through a series of slides. As a slide with words, pictures, and possibly other special effects appears on the wall or screen, the instructor refers to the slide in his or her lecture. Sometimes the instructor reads what is on the slide and then clarifies or expands with details; other times the instructor discusses the slide but does not read word-for-word what appears on the slide.

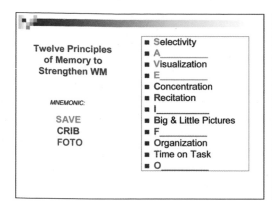 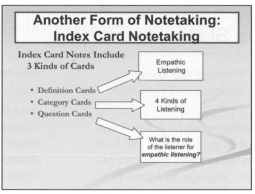

Instructors use Power Point slides in a variety of ways, which means you will need to be familiar with a variety of methods for taking notes on Power Point slides. Even though you may have access to the entire Power Point presentation, your instructor will provide additional details or explanations about the content in the slides. Do not sit back and rely solely on the slides; take notes to capture additional key points.

Multiple Slides on a Page

When your instructor provides you with a printed copy of multiple Power Point slides on a page, usually 4–6 slides per page, listen carefully for explanations or details not included on the slides. Use lines to branch off each slide; place key words at the end of each line or branch. If sufficient space is not available to connect key ideas to each slide, write the slide number on notebook paper. Write details about each slide under the slide number on your paper. The two-column notetaking systems works effectively for Power Point notes.

Power Point Slides with a Notes Column

Your instructor may provide you with a printed copy of the Power Point slides, usually two or three slides per page, with a "notes" column on the right. In the notes column, take notes on explanations and details that are not included in the original slide.

Partial Power Point Slides

When your instructor provides you with a printed copy of partially completed Power Point slides, listen carefully for and watch for the missing details. Write the details on the lines provided on the partial Power Point slides. This strategy is similar to completing a partial outline of a lecture. Add additional details to the pictures of the slides.

Power Point Outline

Some instructors may provide you with a printed outline of the Power Point slides, but not the slides themselves. As with lecture outline notes, add details to the end of the lines of the outline. If there is sufficient space and if you have sufficient time, sketch the Power Point slide to show any additional details that do not appear in the outline.

Power Point Slides to Download

If your instructor announces that the Power Point Slides used in class will be available to download online after class, select a notetaking system to take notes on each Power Point slide. Again, the two-column notetaking system is efficient to use for taking notes on Power Point presentations. After class, when you download the slides, attach your notes to the printed slides or attach details to the pictures of each slide.

CONCEPT CHECK 10.18

Why is it important to work with your notes soon after a lecture? What activities should you do when you work with your lecture notes?

Working with Your Notes

Taking lecture notes helps you stay focused on the lecture and keeps your mind from wandering. The most significant purpose of taking notes, however, is to create study tools to use *after* the class has ended. As you learned in Chapter 4, scheduling a study block as soon after a lecture as possible gives you the opportunity to work with your notes while the information is still fresh in your mind. Use the following five strategies as soon after class as possible.

- **Complete Your Notes.** Add missing details, fill in gaps, and correct any misspelled key terms that appear in your notes. Confer with other students or your instructor, or refer to your textbook for missing information or correct spellings. If you chose to use the Cornell Notetaking System, complete the reduce step by creating the recall column.

- **Add More Structure to Your Notes.** If your notes lack a clear structure or appear disorganized, insert headings or number the individual details. Highlight specific concepts or key words or use a colored pen to circle terminology to create more structure for your notes.

- **Supplement Your Notes.** As you work with your notes, you may want to make lists of information, brief outlines of main ideas, or clarifying questions that you would like to ask in class. Each type of notetaking system recommends that you write only on the front side of your notebook paper. Use the back sides for adding supplementary notes or questions.

- **Rewrite Your Notes When Justified.** Do not spend valuable time rewriting lecture (or textbook) notes simply for the sake of producing a neater set of notes. However, students who are kinesthetic or highly visual learners may find value in rewriting or typing their notes on a computer. The physical process of rewriting boosts memory and encodes information in a form that is easier to recall. In such cases, rewriting notes, which may include reorganizing information, is a meaningful and effective use of time.

- **Recite, Reflect, and Review Your Notes***:* The true value of your notes involves using them *after* the lecture. Spend time digesting the information, reciting the information, reworking problems, rehearsing, and reflecting. At the beginning of your next study block for the class, you can use your notes as a *warm-up activity*. Schedule time each week to use your notes for *ongoing review*.

New Lecture Notes

EXERCISE 10.7

DIRECTIONS

1. For this assignment, your instructor will provide you with a new lecture situation. This may involve taking notes for a lecture presented by a guest speaker, taking notes on a specific video, taking notes from one of your lecture classes, or taking notes on a lecture your instructor presents on a new topic.

2. Select the most appropriate notetaking system to use to take a complete set of notes.

3. Go to **Appendix C** for the **Lecture Notetaking Checklist.** This is the same checklist that you may have used in Exercise 10.6. Complete the checklist and refer to the "Scoring Your Responses" to evaluate the effectiveness of your notes. This notetaking checklist is also available on the student CourseMate Web site.

4. If your new notetaking situation involves taking notes from one of your lecture classes, you may be asked to also complete the Exercise 10.6 Instructor Questionnaire.

CHECK POINT 10.3

Answers appear on page B4

True or False?

_____ 1. The most common cause of notetaking problems is the discrepancy between thinking and writing rates.

_____ 2. If you think at 400 wpm and your instructor speaks at 80 wpm you may need to use strategies, such as mentally summarizing, to stay attentive to the lecture.

_____ 3. Paraphrasing, using abbreviations, and modified printing are strategies to help you increase your writing fluency.

_____ 4. Following a lecture, it is important to take time to complete and refine your notes and then rewrite each set of notes to use for further review.

 Access Chapter 10 Practice Quiz 5: Lecture Notes under "Interactive Quizzes" in your College Success CourseMate, accessed through *CengageBrain.com*.

CHAPTER 10 REFLECTIVE WRITING 2

 On separate paper, in a journal, or online at this textbook's CourseMate Web site, respond to the following questions.

1. Which strategies in this chapter were the most beneficial for helping you become a more effective listener? Be specific.

2. Which strategies in this chapter were the most beneficial for helping you take more effective lecture notes? Be specific.

 Access Chapter 10 Reflective Writing 2 in your College Success CourseMate, accessed through *CengageBrain.com*.

ACTIVITY

Chapter 10 Critical Thinking

BACKGROUND: Critical reading, critical listening, and critical thinking all involve working with information on deeper levels, analyzing the development of information for logic, consistency, accuracy, and sufficient details to support an argument or develop an idea.

DIRECTIONS

1. Review "Evaluating Internet Information" and Figure 8.2 in Chapter 8. Read Excerpt 9: How to Listen Critically and Guidelines for Critical Listening in Appendix D.

2. What do critical reading of online materials and critical listening have in common? Create a list of key words or key actions that are common to critical readers as they evaluate Internet information and critical listeners as they apply critical listening skills to a speech.

Terms to Know

By yourself or with a partner, practice reciting or writing definitions for the following terms. You may also practice defining these terms by using the online flashcard programs or comparing your answers to the online glossary.

listening p. 288

active listening p. 294

critical listening p. 294

empathic listening p. 294

appreciative listening p. 295

the Book Notes System p. 302

rate of speaking (rate of speech) p. 304

rate of thinking p. 304

rate of writing p. 304

paraphrasing p. 305

 Access Chapter 10 Flashcard Drills and Online Glossary in your College Success CourseMate, accessed through *CengageBrain.com*.

Learning Objectives Review

1 *Discuss factors that influence the quality of listening, the four kinds of listening, and essential listening strategies for lectures.*

- Listening skills are often the weakest of the four verbal communication skills.
- Listening is more than hearing; listening involves attaching meaning to a speaker's words.
- Lack of training or instruction as well as functions of our memory system are two reasons listening is a difficult process. In addition, both listener interferences and speaker interferences affect one's ability to listen effectively.
- Each of the following four kinds of listening involves different listening goals: active listening, critical listening, empathic listening, and appreciative listening.
- Learning to use a variety of essential listening strategies for lectures can strengthen your listening skills and improve the quality of your lecture notes.

2 *Explain how to use Cornell, Two-Column, Three-Column, and Outline Notes for taking lecture notes; explain how to use the Book Notes System.*

- The subject matter, the instructor's lecture style, and your personal preference will help determine the most appropriate notetaking system to use in a lecture.
- Notetaking options for lectures include Cornell Notes, Two-Column Notes, Three-Column Notes, Outline Notes, and the Book Notes System.

3 *Discuss effective strategies for taking and working with lecture notes, including Power Point notes and math lectures notes, and strategies to solve common notetaking problems.*

- Some listening and notetaking difficulties occur due to discrepancies among rate of speaking (100–125 wpm for average lectures), rate of thinking (400 wpm average), and rate of writing (30 wpm average).

- Nine strategies help students deal with rate discrepancies and deal with common notetaking problems for lectures.

- Using instructor verbal, visual, and nonverbal clues helps students identify important information to include in your lecture notes.

- Several forms of notetaking work effectively to take notes for lectures based on Power Point slides.

- Math lectures often involve both declarative and procedural knowledge. Taking notes on steps to solve problems requires accuracy and attention to details, patterns, and explanations.

- For notes to be effective, students need to work with their notes shortly after a lecture and spend time reciting, reflecting, and reviewing their notes.

Chapter 10 Review Questions

Answers appear on page BX

Multiple Choice

_____ 1. Which of the following is the most frequently used form of communication?

    a. writing

    b. listening

    c. reading

    d. speaking

_____ 2. Your listening efficiency or ability may be influenced by

    a. your attitude toward the subject and familiarity with the subject.

    b. listener interferences.

    c. the speaker's style of delivery, tone of voice, and rate of speech.

    d. all of the above.

_____ 3. Which of the following is *not* true about writing fluency?

    a. Your writing fluency has minimal effect on the quality of your notes.

    b. Writing fluency refers to a person's rate of writing.

    c. A person with high writing fluency most likely knows how to paraphrase.

    d. A person with low writing fluency may fall behind taking notes during a lecture.

_____ 4. Listening goals

    a. vary for each of the four kinds of listening.

    b. involve understanding different kinds of information for different purposes.

    c. for critical listening involve higher-level thinking skills such as analysis.

    d. involve all of the above.

_____ 5. Which of the following is *not* true?

    a. Linear listeners prefer a broad, open-ended discussion of a topic.

    b. Empathic listeners focus on a person's feelings without giving too much input.

    c. Global listeners prefer to get an overview followed by examples and discussion.

    d. Familiarizing yourself with the topic before class promotes active listening.

_____ 6. When taking lecture notes, strive to

    a. capture main ideas and important details.

    b. increase writing speed by using abbreviations and modified printing.

    c. listen for word clues that help you organize levels of information.

    d. do all of the above.

_____ 7. The best notetaking system to use in lecture classes is

    a. always the Cornell system.

    b. a notetaking system that works well with the lecturer's style and content.

    c. two-column notes with the topic or question on the right.

    d. a formal outline that shows specific levels of information.

_____ 8. Paraphrasing

    a. involves rephrasing and shortening a speaker's words.

    b. is an effective strategy to use to keep up with the speaker during notetaking.

    c. can be used to pose questions to the speaker.

    d. involves all of the above.

Short-Answer Questions

Write your answers on separate paper.

1. What strategies can you use to combat the effects of a discrepancy between the rate of speech and the rate of writing?

2. Explain the different notetaking systems that you would select to take lecture notes for a sociology class, lecture notes for a math class, and lecture notes for a Power Point presentation.

 Access Chapter 10 Chapter Quizzes 1-4 and Enhanced Quiz under "Interactive Quizzes" in your College Success CourseMate, accessed through *CengageBrain* .com.

Access all Chapter 10 Online Materials in your College Success CourseMate, accessed through *CengageBrain.com*.

Chapter Notes

11 Creating and Using Visual Notes and Study Tools

©Stockbyte/Getty Images

Tailoring your approach to learning involves becoming familiar with an array of strategies, learning to use the strategies, and then selecting those strategies that work most effectively for you and the content or course you are studying. Visual notetaking provides you with an avenue to use your visual skills and creativity to capture important information in the form of visual mappings, hierarchies, comparison charts, and index card notes. By learning to use all of these notetaking options, you will be better equipped to individualize the process of learning to achieve greater success.

LEARNING OBJECTIVES

1. *Describe strategies you use to tailor your approach to learning.*

2. *Explain and demonstrate how to create and use visual mappings.*

3. *Explain and demonstrate how to create and use hierarchies.*

4. *Explain and demonstrate how to create and use comparison charts.*

5. *Explain and demonstrate how to create and use index card notes.*

Access Chapter 11 Expanded Chapter Outline and Objectives in your College Success CourseMate, accessed through *CengageBrain.com.*

YOUR CHAPTER MAPPING

After reading information under each heading, return to the chapter visual mapping below. Add key words to show subheadings and important details related to each heading.

 Access Chapter 11 Visual Mapping in your College Success CourseMate, accessed through *CengageBrain.com.*

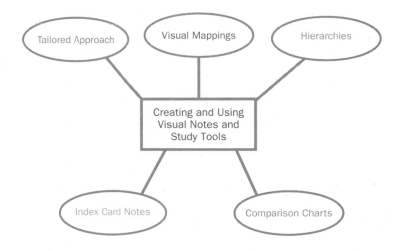

Creating Visual Notes and Study Tools

ANSWER, SCORE, and **RECORD** your profile before you read this chapter. If you need to review the process, refer to the complete directions given in the profile for Chapter 1 on page 4.

ONLINE: You can complete the profile and get your score online at this textbook's CourseMate Web site.

Access Chapter 11 Profile in your College Success CourseMate, accessed through CengageBrain.com.

	YES	NO
1. I use one specific notetaking system in all notetaking situations.	_____	_____
2. I tailor my approach to learning by selecting different learning strategies and study tools to match the learning situation and materials.	_____	_____
3. I draw various kinds of pictures to help me remember what I have read.	_____	_____
4. I close my eyes or look up into the air to visualize or picture information.	_____	_____
5. I recite information in diagrams and get immediate feedback on the accuracy and completeness of the information I recited.	_____	_____
6. I try to visually memorize all the information in charts or diagrams.	_____	_____
7. I know how to organize my notes into charts designed to compare and contrast information for different topics.	_____	_____
8. I avoid making flashcards because they are too cumbersome to manage.	_____	_____
9. I create index card notes that include definition cards, study question cards, and category cards with lists of information to memorize.	_____	_____
10. I am confident in my ability to convert printed information into meaningful visual notes to study and learn new information.	_____	_____

QUESTIONS LINKED TO THE CHAPTER LEARNING OBJECTIVES:

Questions 1, 2: objective 1   Question 7: objective 4

Questions 3, 4: objective 2   Questions 8, 9: objective 5

Questions 5, 6: objective 3   Question 10: all objectives

Tailored Approach

❶ *Describe strategies you use to tailor your approach to learning.*

> Metacognition is the process of understanding *how* you learn, *what* you need to learn, and *which* strategies or techniques would be the most effective or the best matched to the learning task and your learning process.

Metacognition is the process of understanding *how* you learn, *what* you need to learn, and finally, *which* strategies or techniques would be the most effective or the best matched to the learning task and your learning process. In Chapter 1, you learned a variety of strategies for visual, auditory, and kinesthetic learners; in Chapters 2 and 3, you learned how your memory works and Memory Principles to use to enhance your memory systems; in Chapter 6, you were introduced to a variety of study tools for summary notes; in Chapter 7, you learned to create definition cards and vocabulary sheets; in Chapter 8, you learned strategies for learning from your textbooks, and in Chapters 9 and 10, you learned to use annotation, Cornell notes, two- and three-column notes, outline notes, and book notes for taking textbook or lecture notes.

Needless to say, using *all* of these study strategies for one chapter is not feasible. Instead, after experimenting with the various strategies, you should become increasingly more comfortable about *tailoring* or *personalizing* your approach to learning by selecting the combinations that work best for you in particular learning situations. After using a specific strategy to begin the learning process with new materials, you may at times choose to create additional notes or study tools to encode the information in new ways, elaborate or rehearse in greater depth to "cement" the information in memory, or to add more interest and creativity to the learning process. The following are possible combinations you may at times choose to use:

- Create Cornell notes, then create a form of visual notes.
- Highlight and annotate, then create Cornell notes or outline notes.
- Create two-column notes, then create a set of index card notes.
- Create Power Point notes, then create a visual mapping or a hierarchy.

The various combinations of notetaking systems and study tools are extensive; however, the choices are yours to make based on your preferences and effectiveness of various formats for specific information you are studying. In this chapter, you will learn additional strategies to add to your repertoire of strategy resources: visual mappings, hierarchies, comparison charts, and index card notes.

Creating Visual Notes

Visual notes are a form of notetaking that organizes information into diagrams that use colors, pictures, and shapes to help imprint information into visual memory. Visual notes, also called *graphic organizers*, include visual mappings, hierarchies, comparison charts, and index card notes. Many students prefer using visual notetaking systems to create reflect activities or study tools to review specific sections of information; however, some students become so proficient with visual notetaking that they can use it to take textbook and lecture notes. Visual notes are powerful and effective because they:

Visual notes are a form of notetaking that organizes information into diagrams that use colors, pictures, and shapes to help imprint information into visual memory.

- Incorporate Memory Principles that boost your ability to learn new information
- Utilize colors, pictures, symbols, and graphic formats that provide you with visual images and associations that work as memory retrieval cues
- Provide structures to organize and rearrange information logically, show relationships, and clarify different levels of information (topics, main ideas, supporting details)
- Utilize right-brain or global approaches to learning, with emphasis on creativity and visual memory skills
- Provide a way to personalize information in original, creative ways
- Promote effective recitation, lead to elaborative rehearsal, and increase concentration
- Involve multisensory approaches to learning
- Provide you with effective study tools to use for ongoing review

Level-one information reflects the subject or the topic for the information you are studying.

- A topic or a subject presented in several chapters and lectures
- Lecture information
- Test review information in the form of summary notes
- Ideas brainstormed for a paper or a speech

Level-One Information: The Topic

Level-one information reflects the subject or the topic for the information you are studying. The topic may be the title of a chapter, the name of a lecture, or a specific subject. The first step for creating a visual mapping is to identify the topic or the subject for your visual mapping and then place it inside a geometric shape (circle, oval, triangle, or rectangle) or inside a picture shape in the center of the page. For example, if you are creating a visual mapping on the Brain Dominance Theory, you may want to use the picture in **Figure 11.2** as the center of your visual mapping.

Level-Two Information: Main Ideas or Headings

Level-two information reflects the main ideas associated with a specific topic. If you are creating a visual mapping for a textbook chapter, use the headings in the chapter for level-two information. Use the following guidelines for writing level-two information on your visual mapping:

- **Create your own headings.** In addition to the headings indicated in the printed materials, you can add headings, such as "Introduction" or "Summary." You can create a special heading to show a specific chart or diagram if it does not fit elsewhere on your visual mapping.

Level-two information reflects the main ideas associated with a specific topic.

FIGURE 11.2   The Topic for Brain Dominance Theory Visual Mapping

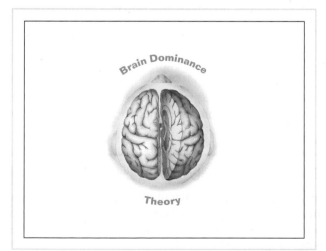

Source: Bernstein/Nash, *Essentials of Psychology.* Houghton Mifflin Company, © 2008, page 59. Reprinted with permission.

- **Use effective spacing.** Visually appealing and uncluttered mappings are easier to visualize or memorize. Before you begin adding the level-two information, count the number of main ideas to decide how to space them evenly around the page. Place them relatively close to the topic so you will have room to add details later.

- **Use clockwise organization.** The most common organization for level-two information is clockwise, beginning at the eleven o'clock position. If there is a definite sequence to the information, such as steps that you must learn in order, you may add numbers to the lines that extend from the topic or add numbers inside the borders of level-two information.

- **Use connectors.** Draw a line from the topic in the center to each main idea to connect the level-two subtopics to the main topic.

- **Add borders, shapes, or pictures.** To make the main ideas or categories stand out, you can place a border or shape around each item on level two. You may use a different shape or a picture for each main idea if you wish.

- **Use colors.** Colors strengthen visual memory and create a stronger visual impression. Experiment with the use of colors: shade in the main ideas, use different colors for different levels of information, or add colors to pictures used as retrieval cues.

Keep in mind that visual mappings involve creativity, so a visual mapping that you create will be unique. Other students' visual mappings of the same topic will include similar information, but the visual presentations will vary because of different kinds of drawings or pictures, shapes, and use of color. For example, compare this visual mapping in **Figure 11.3** to the SQ4R visual mapping in Exercise 8.3, Chapter 8 (page 231).

Access Chapter 11 Topics In-Depth: Expanded SQ4R Visual Mapping in your College Success CourseMate, accessed through *CengageBrain.com.*

CONCEPT CHECK 11.6

What guidelines can you use so the details you add to a visual mapping are organized, easy to read, and stand out?

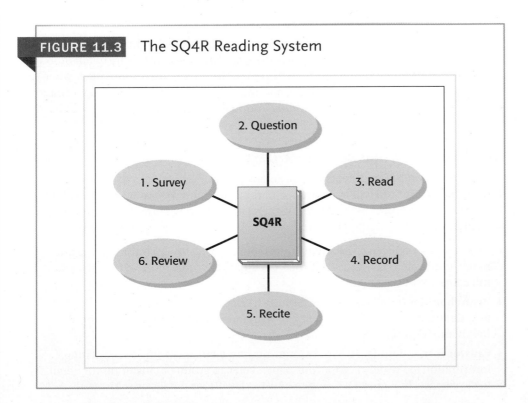

FIGURE 11.3   The SQ4R Reading System

Level-Three Information: Supporting Details

> Level-three information reflects the major supporting details that explain, support, or prove the main idea.

Level-three information reflects the major supporting details that explain, support, or prove the main idea. Major supporting details are key words that work as retrieval cues to trigger recall of information. Later when you study your visual mapping and recite, you will convert these key words into full sentences to explain the information in greater detail. Use the following guidelines for adding level-three information to your visual mapping:

- **Add key words.** Use only key words on level three. Avoid using long phrases or full sentences as they will clutter your visual mapping.

- **Decide how to organize details.** You can arrange the details in any order; they do not need to be organized in a clockwise direction.

- **Space details evenly.** Space details somewhat evenly around the main idea so each detail is clear and easy to read. Cluttered or crowded level-three details become distractions and are difficult to use to check your accuracy after reciting.

- **Select details carefully.** Be selective. Include only as many major details as you need to help you remember key information about each main idea.

- **Write on a horizontal plane.** To make your mapping easy to read, keep all your writing horizontal. Avoid writing at a slant or sideways or turning the paper as you write, resulting in words written upside down. Our visual memories are trained to recall writing that appears on horizontal lines.

- **Add optional borders.** You do not need to add borders around level-three information if the details stand out clearly; however, including borders is an option.

- **Personalize with pictures.** Pictures help imprint information in your visual memory and are often easier to recall than words, so include pictures when appropriate.

In Chapter 5, you learned about four coping strategies to manage stress. **Figure 11.4** shows a visual mapping of textbook information with more details about each of the four coping strategies. Notice how much you can learn about the textbook information simply by studying the visual mapping. If you wish, you may expand the Figure 11.4 visual mapping by adding additional details you learned about each coping strategy in Chapter 5, pages 138–139.

Level-Four Information: Minor Details

> Level-four information reflects minor details that directly explain or support level-three information.

Level-Four Information reflects minor details that directly explain or support level-three information. You will encounter situations in which you want to include level-four information on your visual mapping. Use the following guidelines for level-four information:

- **Be extremely selective.** Too many minor details will clutter your mapping and make it difficult to use as a study tool. Use only key words or short phrases, not full sentences.

- **Branch minor details off major details.** In Figure 11.4, notice the level-four details that extend down from "time management" in the section about Behavioral Coping Strategies.

- **Cluster minor details.** To avoid cluttering your visual mapping or branching information too widely across your paper, you can group or cluster minor details to save space. In Figure 11.4, notice how the level-four details are clustered

CONCEPT CHECK 11.7

What is "level-four" information and how can you include it in a visual mapping without cluttering up your visual notes?

FIGURE 11.4 Visual Mapping for Coping Strategies

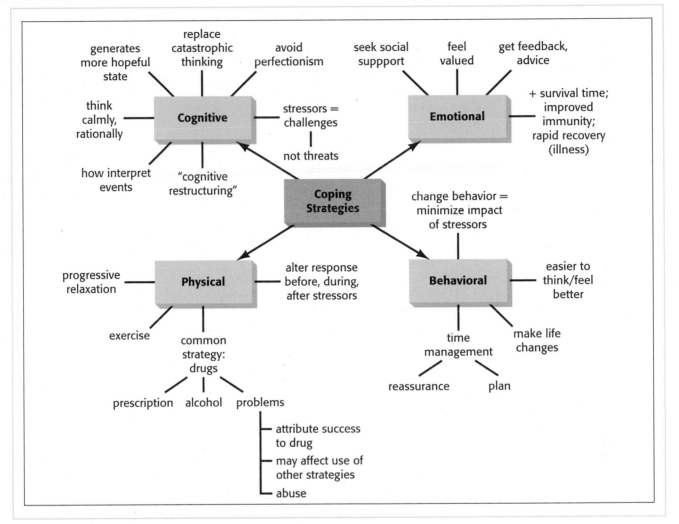

Source for information used in the visual mapping: Bernstein/Nash, *Essentials of Psychology* 2ED. Houghton Mifflin Company, © 2002, pp. 370–371. Reprinted with permission.

together as they branch down from "problems" in the section about Physical Coping Strategies.

- **Use larger paper.** When you plan to create more extensive visual mappings, work on unlined legal paper, drawing paper, or poster-sized paper. Crowded, cluttered visual mappings lose their purpose and their power if they are difficult to visualize.

- **Create separate visual mappings.** When you create a visual mapping for a chapter, you may find that you frequently need four or more levels of information to capture the important points. When this is the case, consider reorganizing the information into several different visual mappings; narrow the scope of each mapping by chunking the information into more meaningful units.

Creating a Visual Mapping

DIRECTIONS

1. Follow your instructor's directions to do one of the following:
   a. Expand the Visual Mapping for SQ4R shown in Figure 11.3.
   b. Expand a specific chapter mapping for any one chapter in this textbook.

2. In your visual mapping, include at least three levels of information.

3. Visualize the skeleton of your visual mapping. Then practice reciting and explaining details for each main heading. Glance back to your visual mapping to check your accuracy of the details.

CONCEPT CHECK 11.8

How does the process of creating a visual mapping improve memory? What strategies can you use to increase memory even more by studying the visual mapping?

Studying from Visual Mappings

Studying from visual mappings strengthens your visual memory skills and provides you with visual images you can use to retrieve important information from memory. Even though you will learn details about a topic during the process of creating the visual mapping, you will gain the most benefit by using the Essential Strategies for Studying Visual Notes in Figure 11.1 on page 322. For example, to study the visual mapping you created in Exercise 11.1, do the following:

1. Create a mental image of the skeleton of your mapping. Visually memorize the skeleton with only the topic and the main headings.

2. Without looking at the visual mapping, visualize the skeleton. Recite the topic and then each of the main headings.

3. Then begin reciting or explaining what you remember about each of the main headings. Glance down at the details in the mapping to check your accuracy.

4. Use a reflect activity for elaborative rehearsal. For example, recreate the visual mapping from memory. Draw it on paper. Check your accuracy.

5. Use ongoing review to mentally rehearse and recite the visual mapping.

Understanding Levels of Information

DIRECTIONS

1. Work with a partner. Examine and discuss the visual mapping shown on the next page. This information comes from Excerpt 6: Other Solar System Objects in Appendix D.

2. Answer the following questions about the "Other Solar System Objects."

   a. What are the level-two headings for this visual mapping?

   b. Which parts of the mapping would you visually memorize as the skeleton?

   c. What details are provided for the heading "Background"?

   d. What level-three details are provided for asteroids?

   e. Where in the mapping do pictures help clarify information?

   f. Where are level-four details in this visual mapping?

   g. Which parts of the visual mapping should you not visually memorize, but you should refer to after you recite so you can check your accuracy?

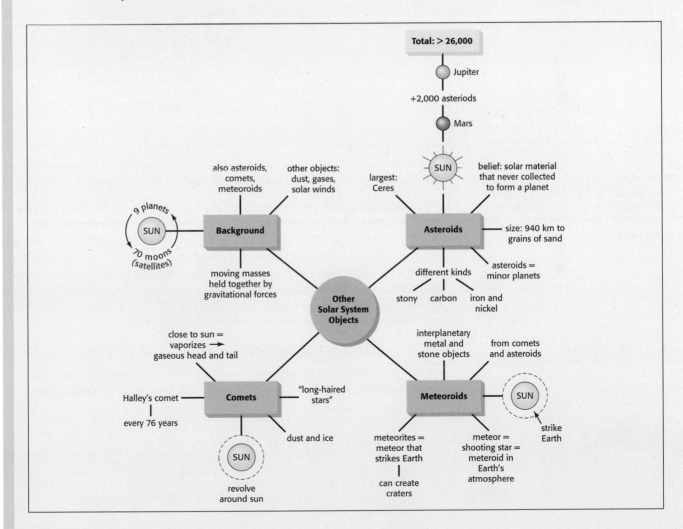

CHECK POINT 11.2

Answers appear on page B4

Multiple Choice

_____ 1. Which statement is *not* true about visual mappings?

  a. To avoid clutter, visual mappings should include only two levels of information.

  b. In a well-developed mapping, different levels of information are easy to identify.

  c. For consistency in "reading" a visual mapping, a standard format for ordering level-two information is recommended.

  d. Pictures, shapes, and colors strengthen visual memory and recall of information.

_____ 2. In visual mappings, level-one and level-two information

  a. should be visually memorized as the skeleton of the visual mapping.

  b. show the topic and its main headings.

  c. are the only levels of information that you should visually memorize.

  d. should do all of the above.

 Access Chapter 11 Practice Quiz 2: Visual Mappings under "Interactive Quizzes" in your College Success CourseMate, accessed through *CengageBrain.com*.

Hierarchies

Hierarchies are diagrams that place the topic on the top line of a diagram with main ideas branching down from the topic followed by details branching down from the main ideas.

 Explain and demonstrate how to create and use hierarchies.

Hierarchies are diagrams that place the topic on the top line of a diagram with main ideas branching down from the topic followed by details branching down from the main ideas. Hierarchies arrange information in levels of size and importance from the top down. If visualizing mappings with lines extending in all directions is difficult for you, you may prefer the more organized structure of hierarchies. **Figure 11.5** shows two different ways to organize level-one and level-two information. SQ4R is the topic, so it appears on the top line. The six steps of SQ4R are the main ideas or headings, so they appear on the second level.

Level-One and Level-Two Information: The Hierarchy Skeleton

You can use hierarchies to show the same kinds of information that you can show in visual mappings. The skeleton of a hierarchy, the parts of the hierarchy that you will

FIGURE 11.5   Organizing Level-One and Level-Two Information

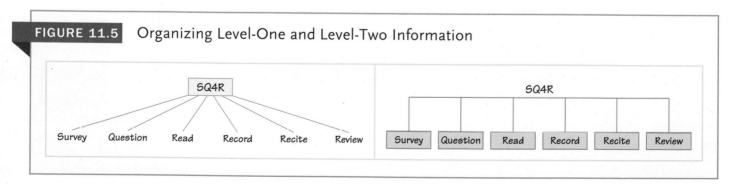

visually memorize, are the topic and the level-two headings or main ideas. Begin by placing the topic or the subject on the top line. Then determine the number of main ideas to be placed under the topic. Branch *downward* to level two to write the main ideas. Use the following guidelines for writing level-two information on your hierarchy.

CONCEPT CHECK 11.9

Which levels of information in a hierarchy form the skeleton? How is this skeleton similar to and different from the skeleton in a visual mapping?

- **Use legal-size paper.** To have adequate room for the level-two and later the level-three information, consider using 8 1/2 " × 14" or legal size paper.

- **Space the main ideas evenly.** Spacing level-two information evenly helps avoid a cluttered or crowded look.

- **Use connectors.** Clearly connect levels of information by using lines.

- **Always write horizontally.** Your visual memory is not set up to visualize slanted writing, so imagine horizontal lines on your paper so you print on a horizontal plane.

- **Add colors, shapes, or pictures.** These visual features strengthen the visual image.

- **Add other level-two headings if necessary.** You can add headings, such as "Intro." or introductory information, or you may want a heading to show a specific graph or chart. If the printed material has a summary, you may want to add a final heading, "Summary."

Level-Three and Level-Four Information: Supporting Details

Be very selective. Use only key words or short phrases for level-three and level-four details. Because the lower levels on your hierarchy tend to have numerous supporting details, consider different ways to place the details on the paper. To avoid a cluttered or crowded look, you can stagger or arrange the details in a variety of layouts, as shown in **Figure 11.6**. As with visual mappings, do not attempt

---

FIGURE 11.6   Arranging Details in Hierarchies

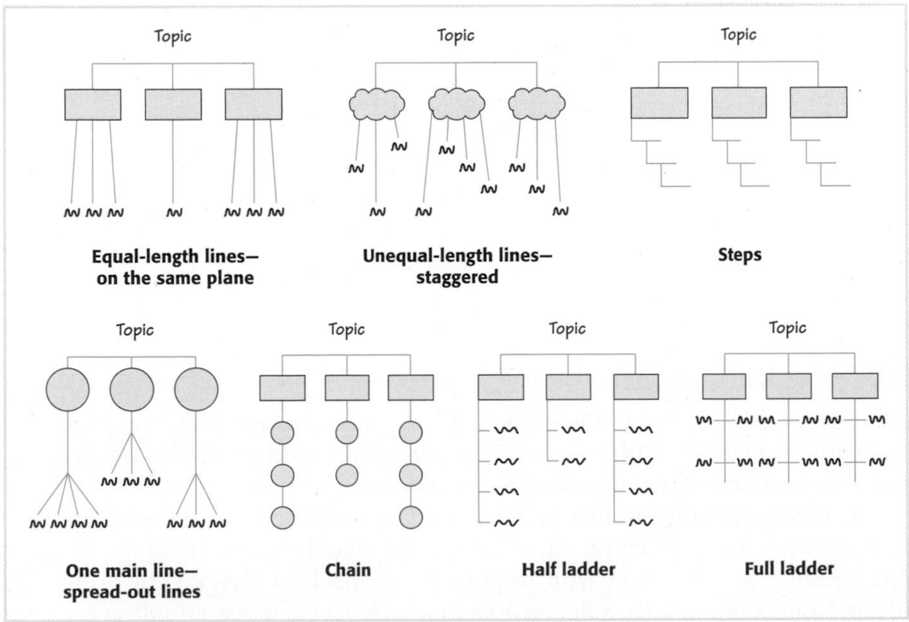

Equal-length lines— on the same plane   Unequal-length lines— staggered   Steps

One main line— spread-out lines   Chain   Half ladder   Full ladder

to visually memorize the supporting details. When you study your hierarchy, you will only glance down at the supporting details for feedback after you recite the information.

Converting a Visual Mapping to a Hierarchy

PURPOSE: Hierarchies are a "top down" visual representation of information. Hierarchies contain the same information that you would find in visual mappings.

DIRECTIONS:

1. The following visual mapping reflects a student's lecture notes about vocabulary skills. The student showed two kinds of vocabulary: expressive and receptive. The student then showed six strategies for finding definitions for new vocabulary words.

2. On your own paper or on a large chart if you are working in a group, convert the visual mapping into a hierarchy. Show the three levels of information.

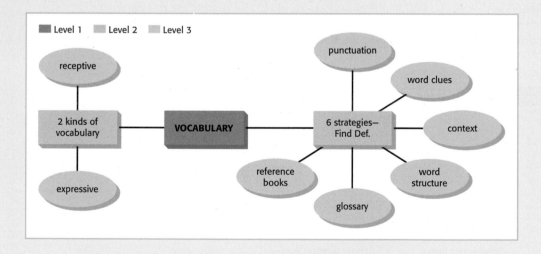

Studying from Hierarchies

Use the Essential Strategies for Studying Visual Notes in Figure 11.1 on page 322 to study your hierarchy. With frequent practice, you should be able to recall quickly and accurately the skeleton with the first two levels of information in your hierarchy. By reciting as you practice, you activate your auditory channel and strengthen your auditory memory and ability to recall the details. Glancing at the hierarchy after reciting provides you with important feedback to check your accuracy of information about details. Select a meaningful reflect activity, and then use ongoing review.

Access Chapter 11
Chapter Exercises:
Exercise 11.4 in your
College Success
CourseMate,
accessed through
CengageBrain.com.

EXERCISE 11.4

Transfer These Skills

DIRECTIONS

1. Follow your instructor's directions to do one of the following:

a. Select a topic from a section of one of your textbooks or select a set of lecture notes for any one of your classes this term.

b. Read and use Excerpt 4: Procrastination and Its Causes in Appendix D.

c. Read and use Excerpt 7: Theories of Forgetting in Appendix D.

2. Create either a visual mapping or a hierarchy for the topic, its headings, and its supporting details. Include at least three levels of information.

3. Visually memorize and practice reciting the skeleton from memory. You may be asked to recite your skeleton in class.

4. Evaluate your visual notes by using the Visual Notes Checklist online on the CourseMate Web site, Exercise 11.4 or go to Appendix C and photocopy the same Visual Notes Checklist that appears in Part II of Exercise 11.7.

CHECK POINT 11.3

Answers appear on page B4

True or False?

_____ 1. On hierarchies, larger concepts appear on the top levels and details appear on lower levels.

_____ 2. When you study hierarchies, you begin by visually memorizing the skeleton and then using the memorized skeleton to guide the reciting of details.

_____ 3. Unlike visual mappings, hierarchies usually do not include pictures or color.

_____ 4. Hierarchies tend to be more linear-learner oriented than visual mappings.

Access Chapter 11 Practice Quiz 3: Hierarchies under "Interactive Quizzes" in your College Success CourseMate, accessed through *CengageBrain.com*.

EXERCISE 11.5

Textbook Case Studies

DIRECTIONS

1. Read each case study carefully. Respond to the questions at the end of each case study by using *specific* strategies discussed in this chapter. Answer in complete sentences.

2. Write your responses on paper or online at the CourseMate student Web site, Textbook Case Studies. You will be able to print your online response or e-mail it to your instructor.

Exercise 11.5 (cont.)

CASE STUDY 1: Monica, a graphic arts student, feels that visual notetaking suits her learning style. The diagram below is her first attempt at creating a visual mapping for a section in her textbook about *Chronemics.* Monica was disappointed with the results. She found that her mapping was difficult to study from because it seemed "too busy" and "too disorganized." What techniques could Monica try that might result in a visual mapping that would be easier to use and study?

CASE STUDY 2: Mickey creates many visual mappings and hierarchies as a second form of notetaking after she has taken Cornell notes for a textbook or a lecture. She finds that the process of reorganizing and writing information in her own handwriting makes studying more interesting. However, she then sets them aside because she is not sure how to study from them. What strategies can Mickey use to study effectively from her visual notes?

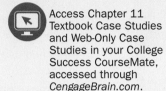 Access Chapter 11 Textbook Case Studies and Web-Only Case Studies in your College Success CourseMate, accessed through *CengageBrain.com.*

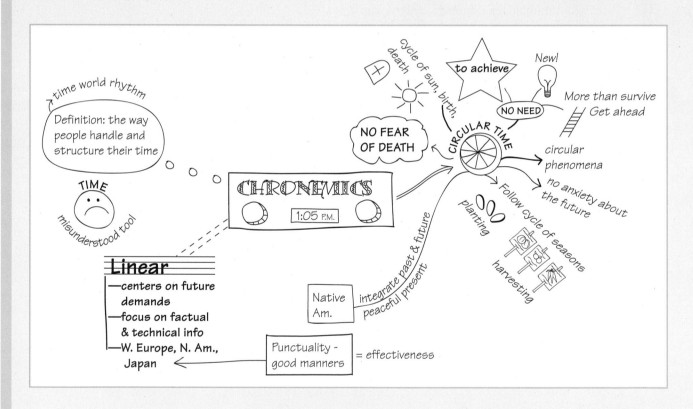

Comparison Charts

④ *Explain and demonstrate how to create and use comparison charts.*

Comparison charts are diagrams that organize information for two or more subjects into a chart or a grid with columns and rows.

Comparison charts are diagrams that organize information for two or more subjects into a chart or a grid with columns and rows. Comparison charts, also known as matrixes, grids, or tables, organize a large amount of information into a format that clearly compares and contrasts information for two or more subjects. You can easily create comparison charts on a computer by using the *tables* feature.

Labeling a Comparison Chart

The title of the comparison chart appears above the chart. **Figure 11.7** shows the categories or the characteristics that are being compared or contrasted placed at the top of each column. The subjects that are being compared or contrasted are placed at the beginning of each row.

In a comparison chart, *columns* run up and down, and *rows* run across the page. Important information about each subject is written inside boxes called *cells*. The number of columns and rows is determined by the information being covered.

Identify the Subjects

Begin by identifying the number of subjects discussed in the printed text information. Write the names of the subjects on the rows. If you have two subjects, your chart will have only two rows. The following are important points about identifying the subjects:

- You may use comparison charts for information within a paragraph or group of paragraphs. Look carefully to identify the individual subjects.

- You may also use comparison charts to capture related information from several chapters, or in comparative reading, to show information from several sources.

- Some tables or informational charts in textbooks place the subjects at the top of the columns instead of at the beginning of the rows, and they label the rows with the characteristics. You can also use this alternative format if it seems more effective for specific kinds of information.

Identify Categories

Identifying categories requires you to think carefully about and analyze the information you have read. What categories of information were discussed for all or most of the subjects? You can use the general category "Characteristics," but more specific categories are more useful. The number of categories you select determines the number of columns in your comparison chart. Once you have identified the categories, label the top of each column.

Sometimes finding appropriate labels for the columns is difficult. Use the following process to help organize information and identify column headings:

- List each of the subjects across the top of a piece of paper.
- Under each subject, list important details associated with that subject.
- Look at your list of details. Can you group the details into larger categories?
- If you see a logical category of information under one subject, is that same kind of information also given for other subjects? If so, you have discovered an appropriate title for a category.

©Steve Cole/Photodisc/Jupiter Images

Graphic programs on computers often facilitate the process of converting printed materials into visual graphics or visual notes. In what ways do you use a computer to create study tools?

FIGURE 11.7   The Structure of a Comparison Chart

categories→ subjects ↓	column 1 Characteristics	column 2 Uses	column 3 Advantages:
Subject 1			
Subject 2			
Subject 3			

CONCEPT CHECK 11.11

What strategies can you use to identify meaningful categories to label the columns in a comparison chart? Why will labels you use vary from one chart to another?

Figure 11.8 shows general categories that often appear in specific subject disciplines. You can use several of these categories if you are not able to identify more specific categories for your comparison chart.

Completing a Comparison Chart

Once you have created the structure or the skeleton of the comparison chart, complete the chart by writing key details in the cells (the boxes). To avoid confusion, frustration, or errors with details, approach this task in an organized, systematic manner.

One approach: Focus on one subject at a time. Reread the textbook or source of your information on that one subject. Identify and then write key words or short phrases to fill in the cells for each category or column listed across the top of your chart. After you finish the cells for the first subject, move to the second subject and continue the process until you have filled as many of the cells on the chart as possible.

Another approach: Focus on one *column* of information. For example, if the first column is labeled "time period," then fill in the time period for each subject. Then identify the details to complete the cells in the second column. Continue until you have added information in the cells under each category.

Remember that your goal is to work in an organized, systematic manner to complete the cells in the comparison chart. Use the following guidelines for completing your comparison chart:

- **Be selective.** Include only significant words or phrases. Avoid using full sentences.
- **Use dashes or bullets.** When you have two or more significant details in one cell, use dashes or bullets to separate the individual details.

FIGURE 11.8   Common Categories for Subject Disciplines

Literature	author	tone	theme	setting	main plot	characters/traits	actions
Sociology and Anthropology	culture family	location economy	government transportation	religion foods	beliefs tools	education imports/exports	tribe
History	events	time period	location	leaders/rulers	wars/conflicts	influences	
Psychology	kinds/types	traits	problems	frequency	duration		
Science	terminology equations	kinds/types theorems	causes problems	effects solution	relationships applications		

- **Leave cells blank if necessary.** On occasion, some cells will remain empty due to lack of details for individual categories of information. However, if information is not available for numerous cells under one category, the category is ineffective and needs to be renamed or eliminated.

Attaching Other Forms of Notes

On occasion, a printed section of material will contain important information that does not fit within the categories of your chart. When you encounter the following kinds of information, you may write a paragraph, create a list of the important points, or redraw the diagram outside of your comparison chart:

- An introductory paragraph that "sets the scene" for the information
- Definitions for terminology
- Diagrams or charts with valuable information
- A summary paragraph or conclusion

   You can place these additional notes before or after the comparison chart, or if they are brief, between the title and the comparison chart. Remember, these are *your notes,* so you can modify or attach information in any way that is meaningful to you.

CONCEPT CHECK 11.12

How can you add important information to comparison charts when the information does not fit or belong in your rows, columns, or cells?

GROUP PROCESSING

A COLLABORATIVE LEARNING ACTIVITY

Form groups with three or four students. Then complete the following directions. Write your work on chart paper.

DIRECTIONS

1. For Exercise 11.2, you examined a visual mapping based on information from Excerpt 6: Other Solar System Objects in Appendix D. Go to Appendix D and read Excerpt 6. Use the information for this group processing activity.

2. Creating a comparison chart often involves critical thinking skills in order to identify labels for the col-

umns. In the following chart, notice the categories of information that were selected to represent the kinds of details in Excerpt 6.

3. On chart paper, copy the skeleton for the comparison chart that appears below. Leave ample space in the cells to add information.

4. As a group, discuss key words or phrases to place in each cell of the comparison chart. Complete the chart. Remember, you may need to leave some cells empty if some subjects do not give details for the category of information.

5. You may be asked to present your chart to the class.

Other Solar System Objects

Objects	Location	Size	Origin	Kinds	Also Called	Other Characteristics
Asteroids						
Meteroroids						
Comets						

CONCEPT CHECK 11.13

How are the strategies for studying from comparison charts similar to and different than studying graphic materials and tables as discussed in Chapter 8? (Review Figure 8.7 and Figure 8.12.)

Studying from Comparison Charts

Use the *Essential Strategies for Studying Visual Notes* in Figure 11.1 on page 313. The skeleton that you need to imprint in your visual memory and visualize consists of the labels used for the columns and the rows. Do not focus your attention on visually memorizing the details within the cells.

Reciting from Comparison Charts

Reciting from comparison charts is more demanding than for other types of visual notes. To facilitate the process, recite in a systematic way by using one of these approaches:

One Approach: Begin with the first subject in row 1. Recite what you remember about each category of information for that subject. Check your accuracy by looking at your chart. Continue in this manner for each of the subjects. For example, in the "Other Solar System Objects" Group Processing chart, you would begin by reciting information about *asteroids:* the location, size, origin, kinds, also called, and other characteristics.

Another Approach: Begin with the first category of information in column 1. Recite the information you remember about the category for each of the subjects in your chart. Check your accuracy by looking at your chart. Continue in this manner for each of the columns. For example, in the "Other Solar System Objects" Group Processing chart, you would begin by reciting information about *location* for *asteroids, meteoroids,* and *comets.* Continue then to recite about the *size* of each subject.

EXERCISE 11.6

Diabetes Comparison Chart

DIRECTIONS: Read and highlight the following excerpt. Then convert the information into a comparison chart. You will need to identify categories to label the columns.

Type I And Type II Diabetes

Though both Type I diabetes and Type II diabetes are metabolic disorders that affect the way the body uses food, they are more dissimilar than similar. Type I diabetes, the insulin-dependent diabetes, affects 5% to 10% of the 16 million Americans who have diabetes. Type I diabetes surfaces during childhood or young adulthood; for that reason it is called *juvenile onset diabetes.* With Type I diabetes, the immune system attacks the pancreas and destroys its ability to make insulin. As a result, diabetics need to track the food they eat, their activity levels, and their blood sugar levels several times during the day. They must inject themselves with insulin to keep the body's sugar levels in balance.

Type II diabetes has different characteristics. Type II diabetes, the non-insulin-dependent diabetes, affects 90% to 95% of Americans who are diagnosed with diabetes. Type II diabetes usually surfaces after the age of forty. It is called *adult onset diabetes.* With this form of diabetes, the pancreas produces insulin, but the body and its tissues, especially its muscles, do not use the insulin effectively. Type II diabetes is linked to inactivity, weight gain, and obesity. Eighty percent of the people with Type II diabetes are overweight. Type II diabetics can reduce or eliminate the health threats related to diabetes by lifestyle changes, more exercise, better nutritional habits, and possibly medication.

Even though Type I and Type II diabetes differ considerably in their time of onset, effects on the body, and forms of treatment, both are autoimmune disorders that must be diagnosed and treated in order to avoid serious, life-threatening health problems.

Source: Modified from Wong, *Paragraph Essentials,* Houghton Mifflin (2002), p. 259.

Thinking Critically about the Information

Comparison charts provide an opportunity to think critically about the information compiled in the chart. To understand relationships among subjects and details in your comparison chart, take time to compare and contrast information in the cells of the chart. Ask yourself questions, such as the following:

How is the first subject similar to the second subject? How is it different?
How is the first category of information different for each subject?
Which subjects have characteristics in common?

Then go a step further to look for cause-effect relationships. For example, ask yourself questions, such as the following:

Why does this occur for the first subject but not for the second subject?
Why does this subject not have information in a specific cell of the chart?
Did something in a cell for one subject cause something to occur that is listed in the cell of a different subject?

Using these kinds of critical thinking questions will increase your understanding of the subjects and their relationships to each other. Such information forms stronger impressions of the information in your memory.

CHECK POINT 11.4

Answers Appear on Page B4

True or False?

_____ 1. A standard format for comparison charts is to label the rows with the subjects, the columns with the topics or characteristics, and the cells with key words for details.

_____ 2. Comparison charts are limited to comparing or contrasting characteristics for one, two, or three subjects.

_____ 3. A completed comparison chart always has information in each cell of the chart.

_____ 4. A main difference between comparison charts and hierarchies or visual mappings is that likenesses and differences are more pronounced in comparison charts.

_____ 5. Study strategies for all forms of visual notes involve visually memorizing skeletons, reciting supporting details, and using feedback to check your learning accuracy.

 Access Chapter 11 Practice Quiz 4: Comparison Charts under "Interactive Quizzes" in your College Success CourseMate, accessed through *CengageBrain.com*.

EXERCISE 11.7

Creating Visual Study Tools

DIRECTIONS

1. Go to Part 1 in Exercise 11.7 in Appendix C, page C28, to read, highlight, and create visual notes for "Industries That Attract Small Businesses."

2. Select one of the following kinds of visual notes to create: visual mapping, hierarchy, or comparison chart. Then, if you chose to create a visual mapping or a hierarchy, complete the Visual Notes Checklist in Part 2 of Exercise 11.7.

3. You may be asked to share your visual notes in class and compare the results of each type of visual notes created by members of your class.

Index Card Notes

⑤ *Explain and demonstrate how to create and use index card notes.*

Index card notes involve creating three types of flashcards to use as study tools: definition cards, category cards, and question cards. Index card notes are effective study tools for learning definitions for terminology, lists of items under a specific category, steps in a process, or answers to questions you predict will appear in one form or another on an upcoming test. Index card notes work effectively to study both *declarative knowledge* (facts, dates, formulas, rules) and *procedural knowledge* (doing or applying steps to perform a process).

A Comprehensive Set of Index Card Notes

In Chapter 7, page 208, you learned that one way to study terminology is to create definition cards. Effective definition cards include three parts or kinds of information: the category, the formal definition, and then one more detail. In addition to definition cards, a comprehensive set of index card notes also includes *question cards* and *category cards*.

- **Question cards:** Pose study questions for information that you are expected to learn. To prepare for a test, predict and write test questions on your index cards with the answers on the back. Question cards become excellent summary notes for test preparation.

- **Category cards:** Write a category or topic on the front. On the back, list the items that belong to the category. To work effectively, do not clutter the back of the card with any additional details; you want to be able to visually memorize the list of items. **Figure 11.9** shows four examples of question, definition, and category index card notes.

To create stronger visual impressions of information on your index cards, use colors to write different kinds of information, and add pictures that you can use as retrieval cues. With practice, you can look up and to the left to picture the information on your cards.

> Index card notes involve creating three types of flashcards to use as study tools: definition cards, category cards, and question cards.

CONCEPT CHECK 11.14

What are the three kinds of cards used in a comprehensive set of index card notes? What are the benefits of having all three kinds of notes?

FIGURE 11.9   Kinds of Index Card Notes

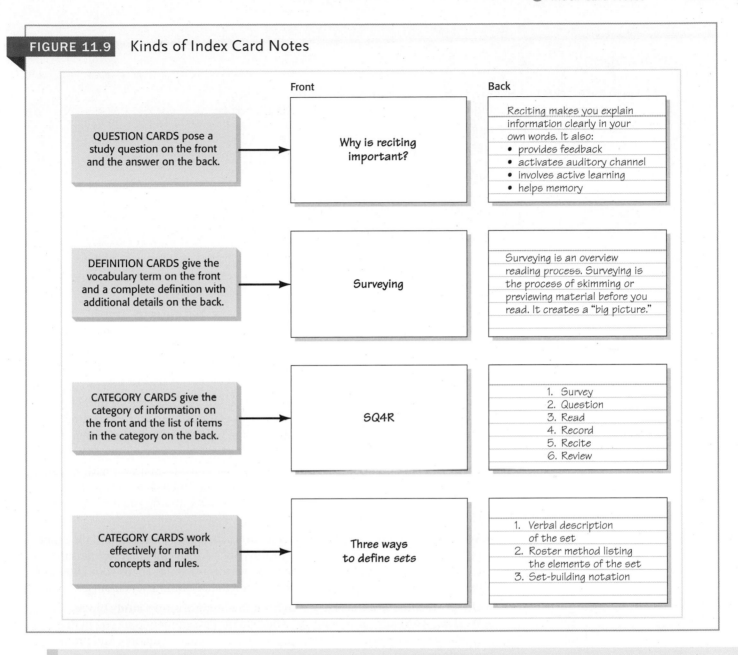

Front   Back

QUESTION CARDS pose a study question on the front and the answer on the back.

Front: Why is reciting important?

Back: Reciting makes you explain information clearly in your own words. It also:
- provides feedback
- activates auditory channel
- involves active learning
- helps memory

DEFINITION CARDS give the vocabulary term on the front and a complete definition with additional details on the back.

Front: Surveying

Back: Surveying is an overview reading process. Surveying is the process of skimming or previewing material before you read. It creates a "big picture."

CATEGORY CARDS give the category of information on the front and the list of items in the category on the back.

Front: SQ4R

Back:
1. Survey
2. Question
3. Read
4. Record
5. Recite
6. Review

CATEGORY CARDS work effectively for math concepts and rules.

Front: Three ways to define sets

Back:
1. Verbal description of the set
2. Roster method listing the elements of the set
3. Set-building notation

Creating Index Card Notes

PURPOSE: Index card notes, which include definition, question, and category cards, provide you with effective study tools to use to review important information.

EXERCISE 11.8

Exercise 11.8 (cont.)

DIRECTIONS

1. Go to the excepts in Appendix D. Follow your instructor's directions to create a *comprehensive* set of index card notes for one of the following excerpts:
    - Excerpt 5: Muscular System
    - Excerpt 7: Theories of Forgetting
    - Excerpt 8: Maslow's Hierarchy of Needs
    - Excerpt 10: Kinds of Managers
2. Include *at least one question card, two category cards,* and as many *definition cards* as you think are important.

Studying from Index Card Notes

Index card notes are portable and convenient to use. You can carry them in small plastic bags or hold them together with a rubber band and place them in the front of your binder. If you wish, you can also punch a hole in the top of the cards and attach them to a large metal ring. Use the following suggestions to study your index card notes:

- **Use the cards for self-quizzing.** Look at one side of the card and recite the information on the reverse side. Check the reverse sides of the cards for immediate feedback on the accuracy and completeness of the information you recited. Use your cards to self-quiz between classes, while waiting for transportation or for other events to occur, or any time when you have a few spare minutes.

- **Ask others to quiz you.** You can practice explaining information clearly by asking study partners, friends, or family members to use your cards to quiz you. Because all the information appears on the card, the person quizzing you does not necessarily need to know the information.

- **Sort the cards into two piles.** One pile shows the cards you know and the other pile shows cards you need to study further. Set aside the pile that contains the cards that you can explain accurately and with confidence. Focus your attention on the pile of cards that you need to study further. Continue rehearsing.

- **Use your cards as a warm-up activity at the beginning of a study block.** Working with your cards before you begin a new assignment puts you in the mindset for the subject, activates previously learned information, and promotes ongoing review.

- **Create reflect activities with your note cards.** You can use your cards in creative ways for elaborative rehearsal:

    1. Shuffle all your cards together. Begin sorting them by meaningful *categories* of information. Sorting into categories provides practice grouping or reorganizing related items. **Figure 11.10** shows possible categories for note cards created for this course.

    2. Then, select one category of cards and spread those cards out on a table. Make a verbal or written summary that includes information from all of the cards. Stringing the ideas together logically and coherently provides you with practice associating related information.

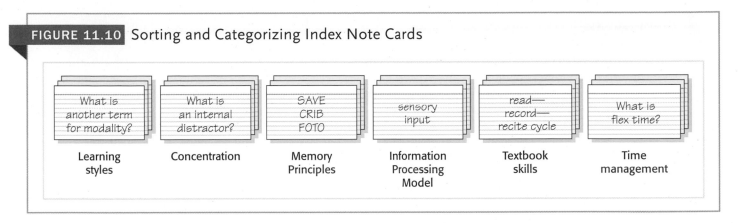

FIGURE 11.10 Sorting and Categorizing Index Note Cards

| Learning styles | Concentration | Memory Principles | Information Processing Model | Textbook skills | Time management |

Cards: "What is another term for modality?" / "What is an internal distractor?" / "SAVE CRIB FOTO" / "sensory input" / "read— record— recite cycle" / "What is flex time?"

CHECK POINT 11.5

Answers appear on page B4

True or False?

_____ 1. You can use index card notes for elaborative rehearsal of definitions, lists, and study questions.

_____ 2. Index card notes are basically flashcards that include more than definitions for terminology.

_____ 3. When creating category cards, you should include brief details or definitions for each item that appears in the list of items.

_____ 4. Studying from index card notes involves recitation, feedback, and ongoing review.

Access Chapter 11 Practice Quiz 5: Index Card under "Interactive Quizzes" Notes in your College Success CourseMate, accessed through *CengageBrain.com*.

Chapter 11 Critical Thinking

In Chapter 12, you will learn more about critical thinking skills and Bloom's Taxonomy, which is a classification system for types of questions and levels of processing information. Bloom's Taxonomy consists of the following six levels of questions. Work with a partner or in a small group to answer the questions that follow.

1. **Knowledge:** How do visual notes help you memorize and learn basic information (declarative and procedural knowledge) for materials you are studying?

2. **Comprehension:** Why is reciting an effective strategy to use to check how well you understand information in your visual notes?

3. **Application:** For each of the types of visual notes you have learned in this chapter, can you demonstrate how to apply the steps to create your own visual notes?

4. **Analysis:** To analyze something, you need to be able to break it into its smaller parts and levels of information. Why is analysis an essential process for creating visual notes?

5. **Synthesis:** To synthesize, you need to connect related information, see relationships, and compile related information in meaningful ways. How do you use synthesis when you study from comparison charts?

ACTIVITY

Chapter 11 critical thinking (cont.)

6. **Evaluation:** Evaluation involves judging information, assessing processes or progress, and selecting the appropriateness of information, processes, or actions. What is the relationship between metacognition and the process of evaluation?

CHAPTER 11
REFLECTIVE WRITING 2

On separate paper, in a journal, or online at this textbook's CourseMate Web site, respond to the following questions:

1. Which visual notetaking systems in this chapter appeal to you the most? Why?

2. How does creating visual notes and study tools affect your level of motivation and confidence for learning subject matter? Be specific.

Access Chapter 11 Reflective Writing 2 in your College Success CourseMate, accessed through *CengageBrain.com.*

Terms to Know

By yourself or with a partner, practice reciting or writing definitions for the following terms. You may also practice defining these terms by using the online flashcard programs or comparing your answers to the online glossary.

metacognition p. 320

visual notes p. 321

visual mappings p. 323

level-one information p. 324

level-two information p. 324

level-three information p. 326

level-four information p. 326

hierarchies p. 330

comparison charts p. 334

index card notes p. 340

Access Chapter 11 Flashcard Drills and Online Glossary in your College Success CourseMate, accessed through *CengageBrain.com.*

Learning Objectives Review

1 *Describe strategies you use to tailor your approach to learning.*

- You are using metacognition when you personalize or tailor your approach to learning by using a variety of learning strategies. Visual notes, which include visual mappings, hierarchies, comparison charts, and index card notes, expand your repertoire of strategy resources for tailoring your approach to learning.
- To create effective visual notes, you need to understand and be able to identify different levels of information: topics, main ideas, and supporting details.
- Five essential strategies work effectively to study all forms of visual notes. Strategies involve imprinting skeletons, visualizing, reciting, reflecting, and using ongoing review.

2 *Explain and demonstrate how to create and use visual mappings.*

- Visual mappings show levels of information: level one shows the topic; level two shows the headings; and levels three and four show supporting details.
- Using borders, shapes, pictures, and colors in visual mappings creates a stronger visual image to memorize.
- Studying from visual mappings involves using the five essential strategies used for all visual notes.

3 *Explain and demonstrate how to create and use hierarchies.*

- Hierarchies arrange levels of information from the top down. They also use borders, shapes, pictures, and colors to create strong visual images.
- You can use a variety of strategies to organize lower-level details to avoid cluttering the hierarchy and to facilitate the process of getting feedback after reciting.
- Studying from hierarchies involves using the five essential strategies used for all visual notes.

4 *Explain and demonstrate how to create and use comparison charts.*

- Comparison charts compare and contrast characteristics for two or more subjects. These charts consist of rows, columns, and cells.
- Creating comparison charts involves understanding printed information, analyzing it, and then identifying subjects and categories of information to compare or contrast.
- You can attach additional notes to your charts if important information does not fit within the categories you are using.
- Studying from comparison charts involves using a systematic approach to recite and think critically about the information that appears within the cells.

5 *Explain and demonstrate how to create and use index card notes.*

- A comprehensive set of index card notes includes flashcards for definitions, categories, and study questions. The key term, category, or question appears on the front; information or answers appear on the back.
- Index card notes are effective study tools to use for self-quizzing, elaborative rehearsal, warm-up activities, reflection activities, and ongoing review.

Chapter 11 Review Questions

Answers appear on page B4

Multiple Choice

_____ 1. You can use visual mappings, hierarchies, and comparison charts to
   a. take lecture or textbook notes.
   b. create summary notes before a test.
   c. create study tools for elaborative rehearsal.
   d. do all of the above.

_____ 2. Visual notes involve which of the following Principles of Memory?
   a. Selectivity, Association, Visualization, Elaboration
   b. Concentration, Recitation, Intention, Big and Little Pictures
   c. Feedback, Organization, Time on Task, Ongoing Review
   d. All Twelve Principles of Memory

_____ 3. When you visualize your notes, you should
   a. first create a visual image of the skeleton.
   b. be creative and make changes each time you visualize.
   c. stare at the paper for at least fifteen minutes.
   d. keep your eyes focused on the notes when you recite.

_____ 4. Feedback
   a. is nonessential when you work with visual notes.
   b. lets you know how well you are learning.
   c. comes only in auditory form.
   d. requires that you work with a partner.

12 Carrying Your Skills Forward

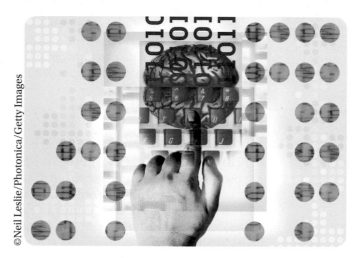

©Neil Leslie/Photonica/Getty Images

You have already learned an extensive set of study skills and strategies from Chapters 1–11. This chapter provides you with new strategies for carrying those skills forward into the next term. Reading in content areas, understanding Bloom's Taxonomy, and familiarizing yourself with critical thinking skills will benefit you as you progress through your course requirements and enroll in higher level required courses. This chapter ends with culminating activities to prepare you for your final exam in this course and the upcoming term.

LEARNING OBJECTIVES

1. *Discuss strategies to use when reading college textbooks for different disciplines and content areas.*

2. *Explain the six levels of cognitive processing in the original and the revised Bloom's Taxonomy.*

3. *Define the term "critical thinking" and discuss characteristics of critical thinkers and the steps in the Scientific Method of Inquiry.*

4. *Complete the Culminating Activities for Essential Study Skills.*

Access Chapter 12 Expanded Chapter Outline and Objectives in your College Success CourseMate, accessed through *CengageBrain.com*.

YOUR CHAPTER MAPPING

After reading information under each heading, return to the chapter visual mapping below. Add key words to show subheadings and important details related to each heading.

 Access Chapter 12 Visual Mapping in your College Success CourseMate, accessed through *CengageBrain. com*.

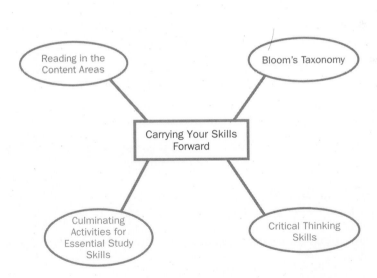

Carrying Your Skills Forward

ANSWER, SCORE, and **RECORD** your profile before you read this chapter. If you need to review the process, refer to the complete directions given in the profile for Chapter 1 on page 4.

ONLINE: You can complete the profile and get your score online at this textbook's CourseMate Web site.

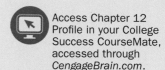

Access Chapter 12 Profile in your College Success CourseMate, accessed through *CengageBrain.com*.

	YES	NO
1. I am familiar with basic differences among composition, literature, social science, science, and math textbooks.	_____	_____
2. I use the 2:1 ratio for reading and studying for all of my courses.	_____	_____
3. I use the same study strategies for factual and process knowledge in my courses.	_____	_____
4. I understand different levels of thinking that are involved in course materials and test questions.	_____	_____
5. I use my study time to focus only on learning information that I need to remember and understand.	_____	_____
6. I take time when I study to break information into smaller parts (analyze) and also put details together to form a "big picture" (synthesize).	_____	_____
7. I accept textbook information as it is presented without questioning or evaluating its accuracy or usefulness.	_____	_____
8. I am open-minded and willing to adjust my opinions or decisions after evaluating data or relevant information.	_____	_____
9. I select appropriate strategies to review course material for this textbook and prepare for the final exam.	_____	_____
10. I am confident in my abilities to transfer skills and strategies I learned this term to new courses next term.	_____	_____

QUESTIONS LINKED TO THE CHAPTER LEARNING OBJECTIVES:

Questions 1–3: objective 1   Question 9: objective 4

Questions 4–6: objective 2   Question 10: all objectives

Questions 7, 8: objective 3

Reading in the Content Areas

 Discuss strategies to use when reading college textbooks for different disciplines and content areas.

Understanding the differences among textbooks from various content areas can help you select the most appropriate reading and study skills strategies to use for each textbook. Increasing your awareness of characteristics of different kinds of textbooks

and the kinds of reading skills required for different content areas increases your understanding of the options you have for selecting appropriate strategies to use. **Figure 12.1** summarizes common reading skills and strategies for different content areas and kinds of textbooks.

Notice in Figure 12.1 that each of the content areas and subject matters involve working with declarative (factual) knowledge and procedural knowledge, two kinds of knowledge you first learned about in Chapter 3. The following are reminders about working with *declarative knowledge* and *procedural knowledge:*

- *Declarative knowledge* is factual information. It involves learning definitions, names, dates, significant events, facts, symbols, formulas, rules, patterns, and specific kinds of organizational structures. It also involves learning ways to analyze or interpret materials and memorizing prototypes (models) that you can use to compare against other paragraphs or math problems.

- **Use elaborative rehearsal study strategies for declarative information.** Elaborative rehearsal strategies involve working with information in new and creative ways. These strategies may involve creating associations, mnemonics, visual mappings, and notes, as well as using processes that involve reciting and other Look-Away Techniques for feedback.

- *Procedural knowledge* is process information. It involves learning to apply steps or processes to achieve an outcome. In composition classes, you use procedural knowledge each time you generate ideas, gather and organize information, write drafts, edit, proofread, revise, analyze styles of writing, and critique work. In science and math classes, you use procedural knowledge each time you apply a series of steps to solve an equation or a problem.

- **Use repetition for procedural information.** Strategies to learn procedural knowledge involve reworking and solving problems *multiple times*. Repetition increases your problem-solving speed and accuracy; it helps you internalize the process so you can perform it automatically. Repetition also helps you develop the ability to generalize the steps so you can apply them to new problems. Working problems multiple times also provides you with feedback and the opportunity to correct any calculation or application errors.

> **CONCEPT CHECK 12.1**
>
> *How do the strategies to study factual knowledge differ from strategies to study procedural knowledge?*
>
> Declarative knowledge is factual information.
>
> Procedural knowledge is process information.

FIGURE 12.1   Common Reading Skills in Content Areas

Subjects	Declarative Knowledge	Procedural Knowledge	Organizational Patterns	Graphic Materials	Survey Chapter	Optional Overview Reading	SQ4R	Triple Q	Customized
Composition	X	X	X		X	X			X
Literature	X	X	X		X	X		X	X
Social Sciences	X	X	X	X	X	X	X	X	
Science	X	X	X	X	X	X	X	X	X
Mathematics	X	X	X	X	X	X			X

- **Learning procedural knowledge requires time.** Trying to learn procedural knowledge quickly without using practice and repetition often leads to partial and inaccurate learning, "skill gaps" that cause problems later when you try to work with higher level skills, rote memory without understanding the how and why a process works, and a sense of confusion and frustration.

CHAPTER 12
REFLECTIVE WRITING 1

On separate paper, in a journal, or online at this textbook's CourseMate Web site, respond to the following questions.

is difficult and strategies you have already used to learn from these textbooks.

1. What are the major differences you have noticed about the different textbooks you are using this term for different courses? Be specific and provide details.

2. Which of your textbooks have the most difficult content for you to master? Explain why the content

Access Chapter 12 Reflective Writing 1 in your College Success CourseMate, accessed through *CengageBrain* .com.

CONCEPT CHECK 12.2

What are examples of factual information and process information that you will need to learn in a composition class?

Composition Textbooks

Composition courses encompass a wide range of writing skills—from grammar and sentence structure skills, to paragraph level skills, to essay skills involving writing for specific audiences, specific purposes, and within specific contexts. Becoming an accomplished writer involves acquiring:

- The foundation skills of grammar, punctuation, usage, and sentence structures
- A well-developed expressive vocabulary
- Broad background knowledge of many subjects
- Skills in organizing information and ideas effectively
- Analytical reading and critical thinking skills
- Effective research skills

Notice in Figure 12.1 that a *customized reading system* is effective for composition textbooks. Your instructors and authors of composition textbooks are aware of the difficulties and challenges many students experience with written expression. To address students' needs, composition textbooks include a variety of student-friendly features that you can use to work your way through a chapter: step-by-step explanations, clear examples, and ample exercises to practice skills.

Literature Textbooks

Most colleges offer a variety of literature courses with different purposes, content, and *genre* (categories of literature, such as poetry, drama/plays, and types of fiction). *Survey courses* involve the study of major writers and literary works from a specific period of time, nationality, or culture. Other literature courses may focus on specific genres, such as short stories, poetry, mythology, essays, or novels. For many courses, *Cliff Notes,* a special series of handbooks to help you interpret pieces of literature, are available study tools that you can use.

Literature textbooks use imagery and figurative language—such as symbolism, multiple meanings, and figures of speech—to convey images, evoke emotions, develop themes and characters, and engage readers in the action of the plots. Following are common figures of speech and terminology you will encounter and need to learn to interpret in literature textbooks:

- *Metaphors* compare one object to another *without* using the words *like* or *as.*
- *Similes* compare one object to another by *using* words such as *like* or *as.*
- *Personification* gives human qualities or capabilities to objects, ideas, or animals.
- *Alliteration* is the repetitive use of one letter sound at the beginning of a series of words.
- *Hyperbole* is the use of exaggeration to create a specific effect.

Read Two or More Times

For the full emotional impact of the writing, read the selection at least two times. For the *first reading,* read through the complete selection, uninterrupted, to get an overview; do not stop to analyze or take notes. Let yourself get immersed in the content and the flow of the action. For novels, your overview reading may involve reading one chapter at a time. For the *second,* and possibly the *third reading,* read with the goal to use thorough reading strategies to analyze and interpret the key literary elements. Write comments next to important passages, take notes on paper, or create visual mappings or charts to show important details. With each reading, you comprehend on a deeper level and create a stronger impression of the information.

Create Schemas

Studying literature involves creating schemas for different literary forms. These schemas identify specific sets of conventions or standards, characteristics, and literary terminology used to think about and analyze the structure, content, and purpose of different kinds of literature. As you study different literary forms, you can create visual mappings to show schemas with key elements to use in analyzing or discussing each of the various literary forms. To construct schemas, pay close attention to the standard features, frameworks, patterns, and aspects of literature emphasized by your instructor. **Figure 12.2** shows a visual mapping (schema) you could use to read and analyze short stories. After reading a story once to get an overview and an emotional response from the story, read to identify important details and attach those details to the visual mapping.

Look for Organizational Patterns

The information you learned in Chapter 8 about organizational patterns directly applies to reading literature textbooks. In literature textbooks, you may encounter the term *rhetorical mode,* which means styles of writing based on specific purposes.

CONCEPT CHECK 12.3

What is the relationship between composition courses and literature courses? What do they have in common? How do they differ?

FIGURE 12.2   Key Elements in a Short Story

Theme: The main point, the subject, the meaning, or the purpose

Setting: The location and the time of the story

Characters: The main character and the minor characters

 ▌ **Physical characteristics:** age, gender, body type, facial features, race or ethnic group

 ▌ **Social characteristics:** family, occupation, economic status, religion, political point of view, cultural background

 ▌ **Psychological characteristics:** beliefs, motives, attitudes, personality, likes/dislikes, mental state of mind

 ▌ **Moral characteristics:** values, conflicts, beliefs, ethics

Plot: Sequence of events from beginning to a turning point, and finally to a climax or conclusion

Point of View: Who tells the story, first, second, or third person

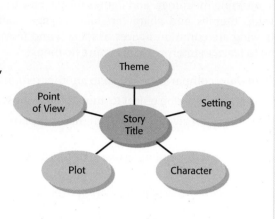

Notice that many of the following rhetorical modes are the same or similar to the organizational patterns discussed in Chapter 8:

- Description
- Narration
- Definition
- Illustration and Example
- Division and Classification
- Comparison and Contrast
- Cause and Effect
- Analysis
- Argumentation

Social Science Textbooks

The term *social science* refers to a large category of academic disciplines that study societies and humanity from different perspectives. Many social science textbooks include topics that will be somewhat familiar to you because of your personal experiences. However, reading and studying social science textbooks involve moving beyond personal experiences and into an academic look at aspects of human relationships in and to society. Social scientists pose theories, create models, and examine trends based on research, scientific methods, and observational studies. Following are common fields of social science.

Common Fields of Social Science		
Anthropology	Finance	Marketing
Archaeology	Foreign Policy	Philosophy
Business	Geography	Political Science
Counseling	History	Psychology
Criminal Justice	Information Science	Public Administration
Economics	International Relations	Sociology
Education	Law	Women's Studies
Ethnic Studies	Linguistics	

Use the Textbook Features

Each social science textbook has its own "style or personality." After working through one or two chapters in a specific social science textbook, you will become familiar with the format and standard features characteristic of your textbook. You will notice quickly that social science textbooks are rich with graphic materials designed to create interest and curiosity, explain concepts and theories, and condense statistics and data into visual forms that are easy to read and understand. As you work with social science textbooks, spend ample time reading and studying the graphic materials and relating them to the paragraphs that contain the more extensive details and explanations.

Create Time Lines for History Textbooks

History textbooks portray an event or series of events that occurred in the past. Unlike other social science textbooks, history textbooks use a narrative, storytelling approach to explain the unfolding of events influenced by specific individuals, groups, governments, and cultural factors, such as economics, religion, art, and social structures. **Figure 12.3** shows the basic structure of a time line and the steps to use to create a time line that can increase your understanding of historical events and relationships.

FIGURE 12.3   Creating a Time Line

Steps for Creating and Using Time Lines:

1. In equal intervals of time, label the horizontal line.
2. Above the horizontal line and the corresponding year, write the historical events, such as a war, treaty, economic shift, or political leadership that occurred in that time period.
3. Continue to add events to your time line as you work through the chapters.
4. Look for patterns, trends, and cause-and-effect relationships among the political, social, and cultural events.

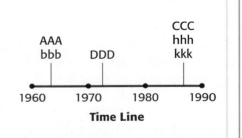

Science Textbooks

The "hard sciences" or natural sciences include biology, chemistry, computer science, engineering, environmental science, geology, and physics. Science textbooks are densely written and filled with declarative knowledge and procedural knowledge. The study of the sciences also includes:

- Inductive arguments: observable experiments, evidence, or proof to arrive at a conclusion.
- Hands-on, personal laboratory demonstrations, experiments, or observations.
- Emphasis on understanding how parts relate to whole concepts or frameworks.
- Conceptual understanding: understanding scientific concepts in order to solve problems in the appropriate context.
- Problem-solving skills and analysis: knowing how to approach a problem, steps to solve a problem, and problem-analysis to explain the thinking processes used to reach a solution.
- Applications: using concepts and problem-solving skills in everyday applications.
- The scientific method: experimentation, hypotheses, collect and analyze data, and draw conclusions. See *The Scientific Method of Inquiry*, page 357

Acquire Background Knowledge

When topics or concepts are new to you, you may lack background knowledge or experiences with the subject matter. Learning basic information about a subject creates a schema in memory upon which you can attach more in-depth or complex concepts and details. To lay a foundation for the new material, use the following suggestions:

- *Videos:* Check your science lab and library for available videos to view.
- *Internet:* Conduct Internet searches to locate and read articles about the subject.
- *Magazines:* Locate magazine articles related to the topic.
- *Surveying the chapter:* Survey the chapter before thorough reading and *before* the lecture on the topic.
- *Overview reading:* Conduct an uninterrupted overview reading of a chapter or a section of a chapter before thorough reading and *before* the lecture on the topic if possible.

Read Slowly and Thoroughly

Science textbooks are dense with complex scientific processes and reasoning, theories, predictions, explanations, evidence, patterns, numbers, symbols, formulas, graphic materials, and definitions. Because of the complexity of information in science textbooks and the critical thinking skills associated with the study of science, your reading goal for science textbooks is to read slowly, sometimes sentence by sentence, to comprehend, process, and integrate information. Another goal is to use your repertoire of reading and study strategies so you can adjust to the content and the textbook level of difficulty.

CONCEPT CHECK 12.5

Define the term 3:1 ratio. Why is the 3:1 ratio often essential to use for science courses? Be specific.

Use a 3:1 Study Ratio for Some Science Classes

After surveying and possibly conducting an overview reading of a chapter, begin the process of thorough reading. For reading and studying science textbooks, you may need to use a 3:1 ratio in order to have ample time to read slowly and carefully, comprehend and integrate information, create notes or study tools, complete lab assignments, and finish textbook assignments.

Mathematics Textbooks

Studying mathematics is similar to studying a foreign language: it involves learning a language of symbols and formulas. Studying mathematics is also similar to studying fields of science: it involves learning and using formulas, equations, proofs, and problem-solving steps to reach solutions. The following points about studying math and using your math textbooks are important to remember:

- Studying mathematics involves learning a progression of concepts and skills, each building on previously learned information and setting a foundation for higher level skills. The process is ongoing, for there is always another higher level of mathematics to master.

- In learning math concepts, you often need to direct your mind to switch back and forth between new information and information stored in long-term memory. The process is complex and involves many cognitive processes, so strive to maintain undivided attention as you work with your math textbooks and notes.

- Utilize all available resources: math lab videos, tutors, tutorials, or other supplemental materials.

- Using a Customized Reading System is often the most effective system to use for math textbooks. Use the three steps on page 234 to devise a step-by-step system to read and work with your math textbooks. See Figure 8.6, page 234 for an example of a Customized Reading System for a math textbook.

Use Effective Time Management Strategies

Working memory requires time to understand new abstract concepts, connect chunks of information, create associations, retrieve learned information, and perform a variety of functions to complete steps of a process. Use the following time-management strategies to create ample time to process math skills and work with procedural knowledge.

- Study math every day of the week. Working with math problem sets and reviewing key terms, formulas, and steps enhance the learning process.

- Use a 3:1 study ratio to provide ample time to practice problem-solving steps, recall prototypes, rework previous problems, increase problem-solving speed, and increase accuracy.

- Provide time in your study blocks to survey chapters or topics before lectures so you are familiar with key terms and familiar with the examples and prototypes that appear in the textbook.

- Schedule a study block shortly after class to begin working problem sets.

- Schedule time to work with a study partner, with a tutor, or in a study group.

Study Examples and Memorize Prototypes

A *prototype* is a model of a specific type of math problem. By memorizing and understanding a prototype, you can then use it as a reminder of the steps to use to solve that problem type. Prototypes often appear when the textbook introduces you to a new type of math problem or equation. Explanations and examples accompany the prototype. Study each example carefully, step by step, until you can follow the steps and understand the logic behind the process. Practice verbally explaining each step of the process to solve that type of problem; then express the same information using mathematical symbols and equations. Read the equation out loud. **Figure 12.4** shows a prototype for dividing fractions.

A *prototype* is a model of a specific type of math problem.

Cognitive Levels in Bloom's Taxonomy

DIRECTIONS

1. Writing practice test questions is one effective strategy to prepare for tests and review course materials. Work with a partner or by yourself to create practice test questions for an end-of-the-term review.

2. On separate paper, list all six levels of Bloom's Taxonomy.

3. Refer back to the information for each level in the model: Knowledge, Comprehension, Application, Analysis, Synthesis, and Evaluation. Review the key words frequently associated with each level.

4. Write *two* review questions that use key words from the Knowledge Level. Then continue by writing *two* review questions for each of the remaining five cognitive levels.

5. You may be asked to use your questions in class to help other students review information for the final exam in this course.

The Revised Bloom's Taxonomy

Educators on all levels of our education system use Bloom's Taxonomy as a tool to define educational objectives and create curriculum. In the mid-1990's, a group of educators, which included Dr. Lorin Anderson, a former student of Benjamin Bloom, and Dr. David Krathwohl, who co-authored with Bloom, revised Bloom's Taxonomy so it reflects the current emphasis on using the cognitive levels to write educational objectives. **Figure 12.6** shows the revised model for Bloom's Taxonomy. Note the following changes:

- The names of the levels were changed from nouns to verbs to represent a more active form of thinking.
- "Knowledge" now appears as "Remembering."
- "Comprehension" now appears as "Understanding."
- The top two levels have been rearranged, so "Evaluating" is now the fifth, not the sixth level of thinking.
- "Synthesis" has been renamed to "Creating," which appears as the highest order of thinking skills.

In *Theory of Practice, Autumn 2002*, Dr. David R. Krathwohl, one of the co-authors of the revised Bloom's Taxonomy, provides additional information about the significant changes that now appear in the revised Bloom's Taxonomy:

- Knowledge, now referred to as Remembering, has several subdivisions:
  - ***Factual Knowledge:*** The basic elements that students must know to be acquainted with a discipline or solve problems. This includes, for example, knowledge of terminology and knowledge of specific details.
  - ***Conceptual Knowledge:*** The interrelationships among the basic elements within a larger structure that enable them to function together. This includes,

CONCEPT CHECK 12.8

In terms of wording and position of specific levels, what changes were made in the revised version of Bloom's Taxonomy?

FIGURE 12.6   The Revised Bloom's Taxonomy

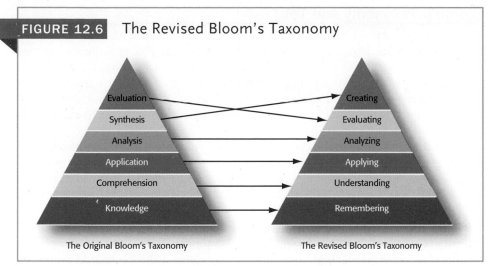

Anderson & Krathwohl, *A Taxonomy for Learning, Teaching, and Assessing,* © 2001 by Addison Wesley Longman, Inc. Reproduced by permission of Pearson Education, Inc.

for example, knowledge of classifications, categories, principles, generalizations, theories, models, and structures.

- *Procedural Knowledge:* How to do something; methods of inquiry, and criteria for using skills, algorithms, techniques, and methods. This includes, for example, knowledge of subject-specific skills, algorithms, techniques, methods, and criteria for determining when to use appropriate procedures.

- *Metacognitive Knowledge:* Knowledge of cognition in general as well as awareness and knowledge of one's own cognition. This includes, for example, knowing how to use strategies, understanding cognitive tasks, and self-knowledge.

- The Creating Level involves putting elements together to form a novel, coherent whole or make an original product. It includes generating, planning, and producing.

Modified from Source: "*A Revision of Bloom's Taxonomy: an Overview—Benjamin S. Bloom,*" Theory into Practice, Autumn, 2002. ©2002 The Ohio State University, College of Education ©2003 Gale Group (Cengage Learning)

GROUP PROCESSING

A COLLABORATIVE ACTIVITY

Form groups of three or four students. Complete the following directions.

1. On a large paper, create the following chart.

2. Under each of the levels of the revised Bloom's Taxonomy, brainstorm to list as many processes, activities, and strategies that you recall learning and using in this course that worked on the levels shown on the chart. Ask yourselves questions, such as *What did we do that required us to remember information? What strategies focus on remembering different kinds of information?*

3. Each group may be asked to share its chart with the class.

Remembering	Understanding	Applying	Analyzing	Evaluating	Creating

Bloom's Taxonomy and You

Essential Study Skills is based on a metacognitive approach to learning. The focus began by learning about cognitive processes and how you specifically process information most effectively. This provided you with the skills to *apply* your understanding to new situations and new materials and to *analyze* information in order to work with it as you read textbooks, created notes, and developed study tools. Many of the study tools you developed involved *creating* new forms to express the information.

Even though this textbook did not specifically identify the levels of thinking in Bloom's Taxonomy, you have learned to use the levels of Bloom's Taxonomy in a multitude of ways. Each chapter contains terminology and strategies that you needed to *remember*.

You learned strategies for *understanding* what you read and *applying* what you learned to this textbook and to textbooks from other courses. You learned to break information into smaller units, identify organizational patterns, and interpret visual graphics; in other words, you have already experienced the process of *analyzing* information. Each time you created study tools, such as comparison charts with multiple subjects, or flashcards for multiple chapters, you *created* (or synthesized) information. Even though this textbook did not include extensive reading skills for *evaluating* information, in Chapter 8, you learned about evaluating Internet information in terms of reliability, quality and usefulness.

Being aware of the levels of thinking in Bloom's Taxonomy will benefit you by helping you to:

- Understand textbook and test questions and understand the lower-order or higher-order information expected of you when you answer the questions

- Create effective questions on multiple levels when you predict and practice writing your own test questions to review course information and prepare for tests

- Realize that every course has basic learning and more complex learning, all of which require you to push yourself to learn more thoroughly and think more deeply

Transfer These Skills

EXERCISE 12.3

DIRECTIONS

1. Look at chapter questions in three or more of your textbooks.

2. Create a list of at least 10 questions from those textbooks. Strive to locate questions that demonstrate use of different levels of questioning.

3. Identify the level of questioning you believe is used in each question. Write the level next to each question.

4. Bring your list of questions to class. You may be asked to turn them in to your instructor, or you may be asked to share them in a small group or with the class.

CHECK POINT 12.2

Short-Answer Questions

On separate paper, answer each of the following questions.

1. Compare the original Bloom's Taxonomy to the revised Bloom's Taxonomy. Summarize the changes that appear in the revised levels of cognition.

2. Why do you think the authors of the revised Bloom's Taxonomy believe the new levels of cognition are more effective and better suited for contemporary use?

3. How can you use Bloom's Taxonomy to improve your academic performance?

 Access Chapter 12 Practice Quiz 2: Bloom's Taxonomy under "Interactive Quizzes" in your College Success CourseMate, accessed through *CengageBrain.com*.

Critical Thinking Skills

> ③ *Define the term "critical thinking" and discuss characteristics of critical thinkers and steps in the Scientific Method of Inquiry.*

In an age of information overload, we often feel the need to remember and understand a vast amount of information, yet research continually changes previously learned information and provides us with new information that was unknown or undiscovered in the past decade. As we earnestly strive to remember and understand new information, to be an effective thinker requires that we learn the lower-order cognitive skills of Bloom's Taxonomy but then push ourselves to think more deeply, more seriously, and more critically about the information we encounter. With access to the Internet and endless databases, we easily can locate information, but to understand, use, and evaluate the information effectively requires us to know how to think critically.

Critical thinking is higher-order, purposeful, skillful thinking that focuses on gathering, understanding, and utilizing relevant information to reach logical, trustworthy conclusions about what to believe, what to do, or what decisions to make in everyday life.

Critical Thinkers

Critical thinking involves a wide range of cognitive and behavioral skills. Following are goals for you to use to become a more powerful critical thinker:

- Be inquisitive and ask questions before evaluating information as trustworthy, accurate, or useful.
- Use reflective judgment about what is observed or what appears in writing.
- Engage in processes that evaluate the quality of thinking, decision-making criteria, and personal decision-making skills.
- Use self-assessment and self-regulatory skills to adjust thinking, modify problem-solving strategies, and make decisions about what to think or what to do.
- Distinguish between facts or valid arguments and opinion and biased information.
- Use a clearly defined set of criteria to analyze and evaluate information or decision-making processes.
- Examine information and situations in order to find new solutions.

CONCEPT CHECK 12.9

What is the relationship between Bloom's Taxonomy and critical thinking skills?

Critical thinking is higher-order, purposeful, skillful thinking that focuses on gathering, understanding, and utilizing relevant information to reach logical, trustworthy conclusions about what to believe, what to do, or what decisions to make in everyday life.

- Use metacognitive strategies, which includes thinking about one's own thinking.
- Show open-mindedness and willingness to explore and evaluate your own thinking.
- Engage intellectually in discussions and debates by using logical arguments and trustworthy information.
- Recognize problems and examine and evaluate possible solutions or conclusions.
- Use Bloom's higher-order cognitive processes, which include the following kinds of thinking activities:

analyze	*convince*	*explain*	*outline*
apply	*create*	*formulate*	*persuade*
appraise	*critique*	*generalize*	*plan*
argue	*debate*	*grade*	*prepare*
arrange	*decide*	*hypothesize*	*propose*
assess	*defend*	*illustrate*	*rank/rate*
categorize	*design*	*infer*	*rearrange*
classify	*determine*	*integrate*	*recommend*
collaborate	*develop*	*interpret*	*revise*
combine	*devise*	*invent*	*select*
compare	*diagram*	*investigate*	*summarize*
compile	*differentiate*	*judge*	*support*
compose	*discriminate*	*justify*	*synthesize*
conclude	*evaluate*	*measure*	*test*
construct	*examine*	*modify*	*validate*

The Scientific Method of Inquiry

Critical thinking skills are essential cognitive skills to use in all of your courses as well as in your personal life as you strive to understand, evaluate, and make choices or decisions. In the fields of science and mathematics, critical thinking skills are essential and emphasized each time you use the Scientific Method of Inquiry. Curriculum in these fields of study center around understanding and applying the Scientific Method.

The *Scientific Method of Inquiry* is a process based on observation, experimentation, and the development of theories or natural laws. Following is an explanation of the Scientific Method of Inquiry from *An Introduction to Physical Science:*

> The Scientific Method of Inquiry is a process based on observation, experimentation, and the development of theories or natural laws.

> The process of investigating nature is known as the **scientific method**, which holds that no concept or model of nature is valid unless the predictions are in agreement with experimental results. That is, all hypotheses—tentative answers—should be based on as much relevant data as possible and then should be tested and verified. If a hypothesis does not withstand rigorous testing, it must be modified and retested, or rejected and replaced by a new hypothesis. An attitude of curiosity, objectivity, rationality, and willingness to go where the evidence leads is associated with use of the scientific method. Note carefully that the scientific method not only is used in scientific work but also is applicable in many areas of our daily lives.

> Source: Shipman et al. *An Introduction to Physical Science*, 10ED. Houghton Mifflin Company, © 2003, p. 3. Reprinted with permission.

The following points in the explanation of the Scientific Method are essential critical thinking skills that you can apply to academic as well as to personal life situations:

- No concept or model is valid unless based on experimental results.

- All tentative answers, conclusions, or solutions should be based on as much relevant data as possible.

- You should test and verify the data.

- If the answers, conclusions, or solutions do not withstand testing and verification, they must be modified, retested, rejected, or replaced by another model.

- An attitude of curiosity, objectivity, rationality, and willingness to go where the evidence leads is an essential part of the Scientific Method.

Figure 12.7 shows the steps used in the Scientific Method. To increase you understanding of this essential process, read the explanation that appears next to the figure.

CONCEPT CHECK 12.10

Explain how you can use the principles and steps in the Scientific Method to make decisions in your personal life. Be specific.

FIGURE 12.7 | The Scientific Method is a formal procedure that scientists use to answer questions

The scientific method

The **scientific method** of inquiry is based on three main concepts: observation, experimentation, and the development of theories or natural laws. The first step in the scientific method is the actual observation and recording of facts. Much of the work of a scientist involves **observation** and the collection of data. This helps scientists to gain as much information as they can about the natural phenomena they are studying and then record that information in an organized way. Observation also involves conducting experiments. **Experiments** are controlled observations that help to answer questions about what scientists are trying to discover. The next step in the scientific method is the formulation of a **theory** that might explain how or why the natural phenomenon that is being studied is occurring. This is also called a **hypothesis**, which is an explanation that is supported by a set of facts. The final step in the scientific process is the formulation of a natural law that explains the phenomenon that is being studied. The formulation of a natural or a physical law helps to explain how certain aspects of the natural world operate and, more importantly, how they can be used to make predictions. Scientists often use observations they have made in the past to make inferences about what might occur in the future. An **inference** is a prediction or conclusion that is made about a future event based on previous scientific observations. The scientific method is a formal and organized procedure that scientists around the world use to make accurate investigations of the natural world.

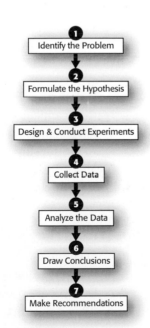

1. Identify the Problem
2. Formulate the Hypothesis
3. Design & Conduct Experiments
4. Collect Data
5. Analyze the Data
6. Draw Conclusions
7. Make Recommendations

Source: Copyright © 2000 Howard Gardner. Reprinted by permission of Basic Books, a member of the Perseus Books Group.

CHECK POINT 12.3

Answers appear on page B4

True-False

_____ 1. Critical thinking is the process of criticizing other people's ideas.

_____ 2. Critical thinkers contemplate, evaluate, and judge information instead of focusing on memorizing or remembering information.

_____ 3. Critical thinking skills occur frequently in science and math courses but seldom are required in literature or social science courses.

_____ 4. Critical thinkers use a variety of skills and strategies to develop their points of view and opinions about a specific topic.

_____ 5. Critical thinking also involves metacognitive strategies.

 Access Chapter 12 Practice Quiz 3: Critical Thinking under "Interactive Quizzes" in your College Success CourseMate, accessed through *CengageBrain* *.com*.

ACTIVITY

Chapter 12 Critical Thinking

DIRECTIONS

1. Read the Excerpt 11: The Species Called Homo-Simpsons in Appendix D. After expressing some interesting points about people's dislike of critical thinking skills, author Randy Alcorn carries his thesis into the political arena.

2. After you have read Excerpt 11, read the following questions that appeared with the excerpt in the textbook *Viewpoints*. (Only seven of the sixteen questions used in the textbook appear below.)

- Can you identify which level of Bloom's Taxonomy is used in each question?
- Do the questions give you a better understanding of what is meant by "critical thinking" skills?

3. Your instructor may ask you to answer the following questions that appeared with the excerpt or to discuss answers in class.

QUESTIONS FROM THE TEXTBOOK:

a. According to Alcorn, what is the homo-simpson's thought process?

b. What is the thesis of this selection? Rewrite it in your own words.

c. Does Alcorn provide enough evidence to support his thesis?

d. What is the organizational pattern used in paragraphs 4 and 5?

e. What is the author's attitude towards his subject? How can you tell?

f. Do you agree or disagree with the author that "too many people seem to find rational, analytical thought unpleasant, difficult and too-time consuming?" Why?

g. What can you infer about Alcorn's opinion of George W. Bush as president?

(Source of questions: From Adams. *Viewpoints*, 7E. © 2010 Heinle/Arts & Sciences, a part of Cengage Learning, Inc. Reproduced by permission. www.cengage.com/permissions.

©Barry Austin Photography/Riser/Getty Images

Throughout this term you have learned an array of study skills strategies to improve your academic performance. The true value of these skills will be apparent next term when you apply these skills to new courses and new learning situations. What essential skills will you use consistently next term to continue increasing your academic performance and success?

Culminating Activities for Essential Study Skills

4 *Complete the Culminating Activities for Essential Study Skills.*

You have worked hard this term to acquire new study skills strategies and new ways of learning, processing, remembering, and applying these strategies to course-work materials. The overall process required you to examine your habits, behaviors, attitudes, and strategies and then be willing to try new ways of processing information and performing in the classroom. Throughout this term, you also have increased your understanding of "what it takes" to succeed in the world of academics. However, the true value of this course will be known only in the following terms when you make a conscious decision to continue using what you have learned this term. Carrying these skills forward will contribute to your continued successes in your life as a student.

Planning to Carry Skills Forward

As soon as the next term begins, you will be swept into the process of becoming familiar with new textbooks, new instructors, and new course content. Before you begin the process of a new term, plan to carry skills forward that you learned this term. You can begin by doing the following:

- Preview your new textbooks. Become familiar with the front matter and the back matter of each textbook.

- Begin to organize your monthly and your weekly time-management schedules for the new term.

- Create an Essential Study Skills Resource Notebook. Exercise 12.4 provides you with directions for compiling essential strategies, charts, and information that you know will be valuable to have at your fingertips next term.

Exercise 12.6 (cont.)

DIRECTIONS

1. If you have not already done so, use one color of pen to connect the responses that show your original profile scores. Your Master Profile chart will then appear as a line graph that connects the twelve points on the chart.

2. Complete the directions for the "End-of-the-Term Profile" located in Appendix B.

3. Compare your pre- and your post-profile scores.

CHAPTER 12
REFLECTIVE WRITING 2

On separate paper, in a journal, or online at this textbook's CourseMate Web site, respond to the following questions.

1. Examine your pre- and post- profile scores on your Master Profile Chart in Appendix B. In which areas did you show the most progress or gain? What strategies did you learn to use to produce the change? Be specific.

2. Which areas on your Master Profile Chart show the least gains? Why do you think this is so? What strategies do you still need to use more effectively for those categories?

 Access Chapter 12 Reflective Writing 2 in your College Success CourseMate, accessed through *CengageBrain.com*.

Terms to Know

By yourself or with a partner, practice reciting or writing definitions for the following terms. You may also practice defining these terms by using the online flashcard programs or comparing your answers to the online glossary.

declarative knowledge p. 351

procedural knowledge p. 351

prototype p. 357

Knowledge (Remembering) Level p. 359

Comprehension (Understanding) Level p. 360

Learning Objectives Review

1 *Discuss strategies to use when reading college textbooks for different disciplines and content areas.*

- Composition, literature, social science, science, and math textbooks each have unique characteristics. You can select the most appropriate reading systems and strategies for textbooks when you understand the characteristics and skills commonly associated with specific fields of study.

- A Reading in the Content Areas Inventory helps you identify effective reading strategies that you are using and strategies that you can begin using to increase your reading performance.

2 *Explain the six levels of cognitive processing in the original and the revised Bloom's Taxonomy.*

- Bloom's Taxonomy is a classification system for levels of cognitive processes or thinking. Knowledge, Comprehension, Application, Analysis, Synthesis, and Evaluation are the six levels in the original Bloom's Taxonomy.

- The first three levels involve lower-order thinking skills; the final three levels involve higher-order, critical thinking skills.

- The revised Bloom's Taxonomy renamed some of the levels and converted the titles of levels from nouns to verbs. Remembering, Understanding, Applying, Analyzing, Evaluating, and Creating are the six levels of the revised version.

- Understanding the levels of thinking and knowing key words frequently used in questions on each level help you better understand textbook and test questions and realize the importance of engaging in both basic and complex forms of thinking.

3 *Define the term "critical thinking" and discuss characteristics of critical thinkers and the steps in the Scientific Method of Inquiry.*

- Critical thinking is higher-order, skillful, and more complex form of thinking that involves the higher level thinking skills in Bloom's Taxonomy.

- Critical thinking, which involves gathering and understanding information and then evaluating the information, results in drawing reasonable, logical conclusions about what to believe, what to do, or what decisions to make in every day life.

- The Scientific Method of Inquiry is a process based on observation, experimentation, and the development of theories or natural laws. The steps in the Scientific Method involve critical thinking skills that you can use in the academic world and in your personal life.

4 *Complete the Culminating Activities for Essential Study Skills.*

- The effectiveness of this course will be determined next term and future terms as you carry forth the skills you have learned. You can plan now to continue using essential strategies next term in your new courses.

- Culminating activities include creating a resource notebook, preparing for your final exam, reviewing terminology, and completing your Master Profile chart.

Terms to Know

Application (Applying) Level p. 360
Analysis (Analyzing) Level p. 360
Synthesis (Creating) Level p. 361
Evaluation (Evaluating) Level p. 361
critical thinking p. 365
Scientific Method of Inquiry p. 366

Chapter 12 Review Questions

Answers appear on page B4

Multiple-Choice

_____ 1. Which of the following is not true about elaborative rehearsal? Elaborative rehearsal works effectively to:

    a. study special terminology in literature courses.

    b. interpret passages and identify organizational patterns.

    c. learn factual information in science and social science textbooks.

    d. reorganize and practice information in new ways.

_____ 2. Understanding ways to learn procedural knowledge will help you with coursework in

  a. math classes.

  b. science classes.

  c. composition classes.

  d. all classes that include steps and processes to learn.

_____ 3. Which of the following statements is not true about Bloom's Taxonomy?

  a. In order to think on the higher-order levels, you must have the skills from the Remembering and Understanding levels.

  b. The Evaluation Level is the highest level of thinking in both the original and the revised model.

  c. In the revised version of Bloom's Taxonomy, factual, conceptual, procedural, and metacognitive knowledge are subdivisions of the Remembering Level.

  d. The Synthesis Level in the original model was changed to the Creating Level in the revised model; the Knowledge Level was changed in the revised version to the Remembering Level.

_____ 4. Critical thinking

  a. involves gathering, understanding, and using relevant information to draw conclusions or make decisions.

  b. includes the use of the Scientific Method of Inquiry.

  c. involves being inquisitive, questioning what you hear or read, and using clear criteria to analyze and evaluate information.

  d. involves all of the above.

_____ 5. Which of the following key words are least likely to be used for questions that require you to analyze, evaluate, or create?

  a. assess, classify, and convince

  b. define, match, and label

  c. hypothesize, interpret, and defend

  d. design, recommend, and validate

Short-Answer

1. Draw and label the revised model of Bloom's Taxonomy. Next to each level, write three key words that show the types of questions or activities associated with that level.

2. Create your own definition for the term *critical thinking*. Because critical thinking involves an array of skills, many answers are possible.

 Access Chapter 12 Chapter Quizzes 1-4 and Enhanced Quiz under "Interactive Quizzes" in your College Success CourseMate, accessed through *CengageBrain.com*.

Access all Chapter 12 Online Material in your College Success CourseMate, accessed through *CengageBrain.com*.

Appendixes

Essential Test-Taking Skills Pull-Out Section

Learning to use Essential Study Skills involves an array of skills designed to increase your academic performance. Test-taking skills are essential as you will encounter tests throughout your college years. Chapter 6 focuses your attention on the following essential test-preparation and test-taking skills to prepare you for upcoming tests:

- Identify and explain effective strategies for preparing for tests.
- Identify and explain effective strategies for performing well on tests.
- Identify and explain effective strategies for managing test anxiety.
- Identify and explain ways to use mnemonics to prepare for tests.

Exercise 6.4 in Appendix C provides you with course-specific questions to evaluate your understanding and recall of course concepts, terminology, and strategies. At the end of term, include Exercise 6.4 as a review tool to prepare for your final exam.

The Essential Test-Taking Skills Pull-Out Guide

Are you confused by true-false, multiple-choice, matching, short-answer, or essay questions? Do you sometimes feel the need to find ways to understand what the questions are really asking, how to interpret them, or how to respond effectively? The *Essential Test-Taking Skills Guide* provides you with essential skills to understand and apply to objective, recall, math, and essay questions that may appear on tests in all of your courses. At an appropriate time during this term, your instructor will assign this *Essential Test-Taking Skills Guide* for you to study and discuss. However, you may choose an independent study approach any time during the term to learn important test-taking skills to prepare you for an upcoming test in any of your other courses. At the end of the term, remove this guide and place it in your notebook to use in future terms.

CourseMate - Essential Test-Taking Skills

Go to this textbook's CourseMate Web site. On the Web site menu, click on Appendix A **"Essential Test-Taking Skills."** Select **Interactive Quizzes** for supplementary practice quizzes and chapter quizzes to strengthen your test-taking skills:

- 12 Practice Quizzes
- 8 Chapter Quizzes

Yes, You Can!

Test-taking is an "art" that consists of sets of valuable skills that can make your life as a student less frustrating and more rewarding. By practicing the strategies recommended in Chapter 6 and in the Essential Test-Taking Skills Guide, you can join the ranks of students who "know how to take tests" and who see themselves as "good test-takers."

Becoming an effective test-taker increases confidence, reduces test anxiety, and rewards you with test results that better reflect your understanding and your hard work to master course content.

ESSENTIAL TEST-TAKING SKILLS

Young man doing homework on rug/© Frank & Helena/ Cultura/ Getty Images RF; Girl with study group/© Masterfile RF; Students at desk/© Image Source/ Image Source/ Getty Images RF

LINDA WONG

Appendix A

Table of Contents for Essential Test-Taking Skills

Introduction

Throughout your college years, you will encounter many different kinds of tests and a variety of test-taking situations. This guide, *Essential Test-Taking Skills*, will help you recognize and understand different types of test questions and key elements in different test-question formats. Understanding how to read and respond to a variety of test questions will increase your test-taking performance and your grades. Remove this handy test-taking guide and place it in your notebook. In addition, review these essential test-taking skills throughout the term—before you enter test-taking situations—and in future terms throughout your college career.

Essential Test-Taking Skills provides you with **sixty-five** specific, easy-to-use strategies for understanding, interpreting, and answering the following kinds of test questions:

- **Objective test questions**, which include true-false, multiple-choice, and matching questions

- **Recall test questions**, which include fill-in-the-blanks, listing, definition, and short-answer questions

- **Math test questions**, which involve solving problems, applying equations, and answering word or story problem questions

- **Essay questions**, which involve using a series of paragraphs to develop a thesis statement for an answer

Twelve Essential Test-Taking Skills

To strengthen your ability to perform well on tests, and as a first step, carefully read and consider the following twelve Essential Test-Taking Skills. The first four skills are important to use to prepare for upcoming tests. The final eight test-taking skills help you focus, organize your time, and set the stage to perform well on a variety of tests.

Twelve Essential Test-Taking Skills

1. **Identify specific topics and chapters.** Find out exactly what topics and chapters will be covered on an upcoming test. Organize your textbook and lecture notes, homework and lab assignments, and study tools with all relevant materials.

2. **Schedule study blocks throughout the week.** Identify specific times you will set aside to study the materials you gathered to prepare for an upcoming test. To avoid one major cause of test anxiety—under-preparedness—plan sufficient time to review thoroughly.

3. **Use self-quizzing strategies when you review.** Include Look-Away Techniques: look away from the printed materials, recite and visualize the information, then look back at the printed materials to check your accuracy and completeness of information.

4. **Create meaningful study tools.** For major tests, prepare a separate set of flashcards or summary notes that focus on information you need to review further right before the test.

5. **Jot down items on your test.** As soon as you receive the test, on the back of the test or in the margins, jot down important information, such as formulas, lists, or specific facts that you predict you will need to use and that you want to have available at your fingertips.

6. **Survey the test.** Glance through the test to become familiar with the types of questions on the test, the different point values for each section of the test, and the overall length of the test.

7. **Budget your time.** Quickly estimate the amount of time to spend on each section of the test. This is especially important if the test includes essay questions that require more time to answer.

8. **Decide on a starting point.** You do *not* need to begin on the first page and work through the test in the presented order. You can begin with the part of the test that feels the most comfortable, has the highest point value, or with which you feel most confident.

9. **Read all the directions and questions carefully.** The number one cause of students' unnecessary errors on tests has to do with hastily reading directions and questions. Read slowly and carefully. Circling any key words in test directions and specific questions helps you maintain your focus on the essential elements.

10. **Use your test time wisely.** If you finish the test early, use the remaining time to check your answers. Do *not* change answers if you are panicking or feeling time is running out. *Do* change answers if you can justify the change; perhaps other questions on the test gave you clues or helped you recall information that affects your original answer.

11. **Do not leave answer spaces blank.** If you start to run out of time, pick up your pace, read faster, and spend less time pondering answers. When pinched for time, you can make quicker choices or use the educated selection options discussed in the following section. For essay questions, if you do not have time to write a complete answer, provide an outline or list of points you would have included in a complete answer.

12. **Use the four levels of response for answering test questions.** Systematically use *immediate, delayed, assisted,* and *educated selection* responses as you work your way through to the completion of a test. These levels of response are explained in the following section.

Objective Test Questions

Objective test questions, also called recognition questions, require that you recognize whether or not information is correct, and then apply skills to identify the correct answer. The following easy-to-use strategies discuss each type of objective test question: true-false, multiple choice, and matching. Applying these strategies will build your confidence for taking objective tests and improve your test performance.

Four Levels of Response to Answer Test Questions

Do you move through tests by reading questions, answering them with certainty or hesitancy, and then moving on to the next question? Many students use this approach of plowing through tests—question after question—feeling confident about some answers and doubtful about others. Using the following four levels of response to answer test questions provides you with a structured, step-by-step process that leads to more correct answers and more self-confidence in your ability to perform well on tests.

- **Immediate response:** Read the question carefully. If you immediately know the answer, write the answer with confidence and move to the next question.

- **Delayed response:** If you do not immediately know the answer, reread the question carefully, and then conduct a memory search. Recall what you do know about the topic; strive to trigger an association that will link you to the answer. If you cannot answer with certainty, *leave the answer space empty.* Place a check mark next to the question and return to it after you have answered as many questions as possible on the remainder of the test.

- **Assisted response:** Return to the unanswered questions, the ones with the check mark reminder next to them. Identify one or two key words in the question. Scan through the other parts of the test for these key words and for other clues or associations that may help trigger recall of information to help you select an answer.

- **Educated selection:** Use an educated-selection strategy (educated guessing) to select an objective test-question answer if all else fails. In the following sections, Essential Test-Taking Skills provides you with educated selection strategies to use with true-false, multiple choice, and matching questions.

Familiarize Yourself with Terminology for Objective Tests

To lay a foundation of understanding for objective test questions, read through the following glossary of terms. These terms are used throughout the sections for true-false, multiple-choice, and matching questions.

- **Modifiers:** Modifiers are words that tell to what degree or frequency something occurs. Absolute (100 percent) and in-between modifiers appear in objective test questions.

- **Definition Clues:** Definition clues are words that signal that the question is testing your understanding of the meaning or the definition of terminology.

- **Relationship Clues:** Relationship clues are words that signal the question is testing your understanding of the relationship between two subjects.

- **Negatives:** Negatives are words or prefixes in words that carry the meaning of "no" or "not."

- **Stems:** Stems are the beginning part of a multiple-choice question that appear before the options for answers.

- **Options:** Options are the choices of answers to use to complete a multiple-choice question.

- **Distractors:** Distractors in multiple-choice questions are the incorrect answers or incorrect options.

True-False Questions

True-false questions are the most basic kind of objective test question. Because they are usually one-sentence questions, students tend to read and respond too quickly without paying sufficient attention to the following key elements in true-false questions:

- items in a series

- the smaller words called modifiers

- definition and relationship clues

- negative words that affect overall meaning

FIGURE 2:   Learn to Recognize These Definition Clues

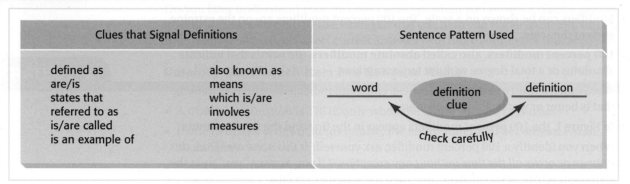

Clues that Signal Definitions		Sentence Pattern Used
defined as	also known as	
are/is	means	
states that	which is/are	
referred to as	involves	
is/are called	measures	
is an example of		

- Word phrases such as *defined as, states that,* or *also known as* may be working as clues for definitions.
- **Figure 2** shows common definition clues and the sentence pattern often used in statements that test your understanding of definitions.
- Circle definition clues when you see them in true-false statements.
- Then, underline the terminology word and ask yourself: *What is the definition I learned for this word?*
- Compare your definition to the definition that appears in the statement. If your definition matches the test question definition, answer TRUE.
- If there is a discrepancy, analyze the test question definition carefully because it may be saying the same thing but simply using different words. If the definitions are not the same, answer FALSE.
- In the following sample test questions, the definition clue appears in boldface print. Notice that the definition clue appears between the terminology word and the definition.

  __T__ 1. Annotating **is** the active learning process of marking textbooks to show main ideas and supporting details.

  __F__ 2. Marathon studying **is also known as** distributed practice.

  __T__ 3. A traditional IQ test **measures** intellectual abilities in the areas of verbal, visual-spatial, and logical mathematics.

STRATEGY 6   Look for Relationship Clues

- **Relationship clues** are words that signal the question is testing your understanding of the relationship between two subjects.
- Relationships often show cause/ effect—one item causes another item to occur.
- Relationships may also show other organizational patterns: chronological, process, comparison/contrast, and whole/parts.

FIGURE 3:   Learn to Recognize These Relationship Clues

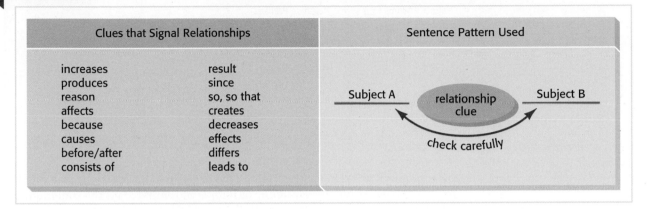

- **Figure 3** shows common relationship clue words and a sentence pattern often used in statements that show relationships.
- Circle relationship clues when you see them in true-false statements.
- Then, underline the key words for the two subjects involved in the relationship.
- Ask yourself: *What do I know about how these two subjects are related to each other?*
- Compare your relationship idea with the relationship presented in the question.
- If the relationship in the statement is logical, answer TRUE.
- If the relationship statement varies considerably from your thoughts about the relationship, analyze the accuracy and logic of the statement more carefully. If the statement shows a faulty relationship, answer FALSE.
- In the following examples, the relationship clue appears in boldface print. Notice that the relationship clue appears between the two subjects in all but the last example, which shows a second sentence pattern that places the relationship clue in the front of the sentence.

  __T__ 1. Linking a picture to a word **creates** an association that you can use as a retrieval cue.

  __F__ 2. Rote memory is effective for learning textbook information **because** it promotes comprehension and memorization of important facts.

  __F__ 3. **Because** rote memory promotes comprehension and memorization of important facts, it is effective for learning textbook information.

Identify the Impact of Negatives   **STRATEGY 7**

- **Negatives** are words or prefixes in words that carry the meaning of "no" or "not."
- Negatives affect the meaning of the sentence; if you ignore or miss them, the meaning of the sentence is the opposite of the correct meaning.

FIGURE 4:   Learn to Recognize These Common Negatives

Negative Words	Negative Prefixes
no	dis (disorganized)
not	im (imbalanced)
but	non (nonproductive)
except	il (illogical)
	in (incomplete)
	ir (irresponsible)
	un (unimportant)

- For example, if you skip over and ignore the negative in the following statement, *The ABC Method is **not** a goal-setting technique* your mind reads the statement as *The ABC Method is a goal-setting technique.*

- **Figure 4** shows words and common prefixes often used as negatives in true-false statements.

- Negatives can cause some confusion in understanding or interpreting a statement accurately.

- If a question with a negative word or prefix confuses you, use the *Negative Cover-Up Technique: cover up the negative* and reread the statement without the negative. If the sentence has two negatives, cover up *only one* negative.

- When you use the Negative Cover-Up Technique, if the statement without the negative makes a *true* statement, the answer to the original question will be the opposite: *false.*

- When you use the Negative Cover-Up Technique, if the statement with the negative removed is a false statement, the answer to the original question will be the opposite: *true.*

- In the following examples, the negatives appear in boldface print. You may notice that sometimes questions with one or more negatives can be confusing and can leave you wondering what the question really means. In such cases, use the *Negative Cover-Up Technique* to better understand the question.

___F___ 1. A **dis**organized desk is **not** an external distractor.

___F___ 2. The Principle of Selectivity is **not** used during the fourth step of SQ4R.

___T___ 3. Using chained associations is **not im**practical during a test when you need to conduct a memory search to find an answer to a question.

STRATEGY 8   Use Essential Test-Taking Strategies for True-False Questions

- **Read each statement carefully.** Pay attention to every word in the statement. If you tend to misread questions, point to each word as you read and circle the key words.

- **Be sure you completely understand the statement.** Read it a second time if necessary. For clarity, translate difficult words into more informal words. Create a visual picture of the information.

- **Pay close attention to key elements: items in a series, modifiers, definition clues, relationship clues, and negatives.** One single word can affect the meaning and the accuracy of a statement.

- **Be objective when you answer.** Do not personalize the question by interpreting it according to what you do or how you feel. Instead, answer according to the information presented by the textbook author or your instructor in class.

- **Mark a statement as TRUE only when the statement is completely true.** If any part of a statement is inaccurate or false, you must mark the entire statement as FALSE.

- **Do not add your reasoning or argument to the side of a question.** Frequently, the only information that the instructor will look at is the T or the F answer, so other notes, comments, or clarifications will be ignored during grading.

- **Make a strong distinction between the way you write a T and an F.** Trying to camouflage your answer so it can be interpreted as a T or an F will backfire. Unclear letters usually are marked as incorrect.

- **Use the Four Levels of Response.** Avoid feeling the need to provide an immediate answer if you do not understand the question or do not know an immediate answer. Use the four levels of response.

Use Educated Selection as a Last Resort

STRATEGY 9

- Educated selection, sometimes referred to as *educated guessing*, is the fourth level of response for answering objective test questions.

- Educated selection is more than random guessing because it often involves using common sense, basic logic, critical thinking skills, and specific test-taking strategies to improve your odds for supplying the correct answers for objective test questions.

- Even though educated-selection strategies may help you gain a few additional points on a test, the strategies do not always result in correct answers so do not become overly confident about taking tests simply because you know how to use educated-selection strategies.

- **Figure 5** summarizes five educated-selection strategies that apply to true-false questions.

FIGURE 5   Educated-Selection Strategies for True-False Questions

1. Select *true* if there is an in-between modifier.
2. Select *true*, the "wild-shot guess," if there are no other clues in the true-false statement.
3. Select *false* if there is a 100 percent modifier.
4. Select *false* if there is a relationship clue.
5. Select *false* if the statement is obviously incorrect, silly, or ridiculous.

STRATEGY 10

Select True: In-Between Modifiers

- The *in-between modifiers* allow for exceptions or for the statement to sometimes apply and sometimes not apply.
- If you are using educated selection, and you see an in-between modifier in a true-false question, or in an option in a multiple-choice question, select *true*.
- Notice how the in-between modifiers work in the following true-false questions. Also notice how you use a variety of thinking skills other than random guessing to select answers.

T	1. Reviewing notes from a previous paragraph can **sometimes** be used to help understand a difficult paragraph.
T	2. People **often** use empathic listening to try to understand another person's feelings.

STRATEGY 11

Select True: The "Wild-Shot Guess"

- For true-false questions, if there are no modifiers to use, and there is no relationship shown, you may need to use *true*, the "wild-shot guess."
- If you run out of time on a test and simply must guess, select true. There is a logical reason for this. When instructors write tests, they often prefer to leave the correct, accurate information in your mind. Therefore, they tend to write more true statements than false statements.

STRATEGY 12

Select False: 100 Percent Modifiers

- The *100 percent modifiers* are the *absolutes,* meaning that they are the extremes; no exceptions are allowed.
- Few things happen or exist without exceptions, so the odds are in your favor that true-false questions, or options in multiple-choice questions with 100 percent modifiers, will be false. Select *false*.
- Notice how the 100 percent modifiers work in the following true-false questions.

F	1. Classroom attendance in college is required for **every** class.
F	2. **Always** begin by studying your favorite subject first.

STRATEGY 13

Select False: Relationship Clues

- If you cannot determine the correct answer for a cause-effect or relationship question, select *false*. Why? Relationship questions often involve higher-level thinking skills, and test writers can easily write questions that show false relationships.
- Notice how the following true-false questions do not show a true or accurate relationship.

___F___ 1. Lack of motivation is the **reason** unsuccessful students avoid using time management.

___F___ 2. Cramming is ineffective **because** it uses only ten of the Twelve Principles of Memory.

Select False: Obviously Incorrect Answers

- If you read statements that are ridiculous, foolish, or insulting, mark them *false* in true-false statements or in options for multiple-choice questions.
- If you read statements that have unfamiliar terms, mark them *false*. If you have attended class regularly and have done all the reading assignments, odds are in your favor that statements with unfamiliar terms are false.
- Notice how this works in the following examples.

___F___ 1. Howard Gardner's Multiple Intelligences Theory applies only to people with IQs over 175. *(ridiculous)*

___F___ 2. Howard Gardner added an eighth intelligence called psychic/intuitive to his Multiple Intelligence Theory. *(unfamiliar terms)*

Multiple-Choice Questions

Multiple-choice questions begin with a **stem** followed by **options** to use to complete the statements correctly. Usually there are four options, but multiple-choice questions may have only three options or more than four options. Unless the directions say otherwise, there will be only one correct answer. The **distractors** are the options that are *not* the correct answer.

Eleven Easy-to-Use Strategies for Multiple-Choice Questions

Do you sometimes answer multiple-choice questions incorrectly because you select the first possible answer without reading the other options? Do you have difficulty selecting the best answer from the list of options? The following eleven easy-to-use strategies provide you with step-by-step processes to use to analyze multiple-choice questions and select the best option to answer the questions.

Use the Three-Step Approach for Answering Multiple-Choice Questions

Step One: Finish the Stem in Your Mind

- Read the stem carefully and, without looking at the options, quickly finish the stem in your mind. This step puts you in retrieval mode and into a long-term memory schema related to the statement.
- Then glance down to see if any of the options are similar to what you had in mind.
- For practice, how would you complete each of the following stems in your mind?

1. A mnemonic is _____
2. When you trade time on your weekly schedule, you _____
3. Howard Gardner's eighth intelligence is _____

Step Two: Create True-False Statements

- Create a true-false statement by reading the stem of a multiple-choice question with the "a" option in the list of options.

- Continue by creating true-false statements by reading the stem with each of the remaining options. If you have four options, you will have four true-false questions to examine.

- Following is an example of creating three true-false statements for a question with three options:

  _____ 1. Schemas in long-term memory are
  - a. small details attached to larger impressions.
  - b. clusters of related information or concepts.
  - c. visually encoded impulses.

By combining the stem and the options, you create three true-false statements:

1. Schemas in long-term memory are small details attached to larger impressions.
2. Schemas in long-term memory are clusters of related information or concepts.
3. Schemas in long-term memory are visually encoded impulses.

Step Three: Identify the Distractors and Select the Answers

- Examine each of the true-false statements you create by combining the stem with each option. Use the true-false test-taking strategies you have learned.

- Cross off the **distractors**, the options that you know are false.

- Examine the remaining statements and select the *best* answer from those options.

- The following example shows how to use *step three* of this process.

  ~~1.~~ Schemas in long-term memory are small details attached to larger impressions.   *This is false, so cross off this option.*
  2. Schemas in long-term memory are clusters of related information or concepts.   *This forms a true statement.*
  ~~3.~~ Schemas in long-term memory are visually encoded impulses.   *This is false, so cross off this option.*

STRATEGY 16　　**Choose the Most Inclusive or Comprehensive *TRUE* Statement**

- When you combine a stem with the options, the result may be some *true* and some *false* statements.

- In such situations, you must then carefully examine the *true statements* to decide which statement is the most inclusive, most comprehensive, or most accurate and thus, is the correct answer.

- The following example shows how two of the true-false statements created by adding the options to the stem form true statements (*b* and *d*), and two form false statements (*a* and *c*). However, *b* is the *best* option as it is more comprehensive and includes the information stated in option d.

<u> b </u> 1. The Incentive Theory of Motivation suggests that

       a. a person must receive monetary rewards in order to be motivated. *(F)*

       b. both positive rewards and negative consequences may activate specific behaviors and increase motivation. *(T)*

       c. unobtainable rewards are the greatest motivators to push for higher goals. *(F)*

       d. positive rewards active specific behaviors and kinds of motivation. *(T)*

Carefully Examine "Not" Questions

STRATEGY 17

- One type of multiple-choice question you may encounter is a *"not"* question.
- A "not" question asks you which of the options is *not true* or does *not belong* in the same category as the other options.
- To answer this type of multiple-choice question, convert each option into a true-false statement.
- Then carefully examine the statement or statements marked *false* as these statements will reflect what is *not true* or what *does not belong* in a given category.
- Notice how the *false* statement is the correct answer:

<u> c </u> 1. Which of the following statements is ***not*** true about systematic desensitization?

       a. It is a strategy to use to decrease test anxiety. *(T)*

       b. It replaces negative emotional responses with positive ones. *(T)*

       c. It involves a four-step process to use during a test to reduce procrastination. *(F)*

       d. It may involve visualizing a different response to words that trigger anxiety. *(T)*

Use Essential Test-Taking Strategies for Multiple-Choice Questions

STRATEGY 18

- **Read the directions carefully.** Unless indicated otherwise, select only one answer. Realize, however, that some directions may state that you should mark all the correct answers.
- **Use the three-step approach** for answering multiple-choice questions. Identify which options form true statements when used with the stem and which options form false statements when used with the stem.
- **Read all of the options** before you select your answer. Do not stop reading and analyzing as soon as you find an acceptable answer. A later option may be more comprehensive or a better answer.
- **Pay attention to modifiers, definition clues, relationship clues, and negatives**. After you combine the stem with each option to create true-false statements, use the same strategies you use for answering true-false questions.
- **Choose the *best* answer**. One or more of the answers may be correct, but only the most inclusive (with the broadest information), most accurate, or most complete is the best answer.

- **In a "not" question the option that forms the false statement is the correct answer**. The *false* statement shows inaccurate information or information that does not belong in a given category.

- **Select "All of the Above"** only when every option is correct. Only choose the option that says "All of the above" when every option is accurate and forms a true statement when combined with the stem. If any one option forms a false statement, you cannot select "All of the above" as your answer.

- **Avoid careless mistakes.** To avoid writing the wrong letter on the line, circle the letter of the best answer and then write the letter on the line. You may not need to use this strategy all the time, but it is effective when you get nervous, tend to respond too quickly, or your eyes skip around during a bout with test anxiety.

- **Use the Four Levels of Response**. If you do not immediately know the answer, conduct a memory search. Cross off options you know are distractors. If you cannot confidently select an answer, use assisted response to later look through the test for assistance. As a last resort, use educated selection to write an answer to a multiple-choice question.

STRATEGY 19   Use the True-False Educated-Selection Strategies

- The educated-selection strategies you use for true-false questions (Figure 5) also work for multiple-choice questions when you combine the stem with the options to form your own true-false statements.

- Select TRUE for options with in-between modifiers and FALSE for statements that have 100 percent modifiers, relationship clues, or options that obviously are incorrect answers.

- Remember to cross off and then ignore all the distractors.

- In the first example that follows, both *b* and *c* have in-between modifiers. However, before randomly guessing between these two options, think carefully. Option *c* does not show accurate information; option *b* makes sense and is the correct answer.

- In the second and third examples, notice the key words that you can use to analyze the question and select the best answer.

  _b_ 1. Intrapersonal intelligence is an intelligence that
   a. **always** shows leadership and group charisma.   *(F)*
   b. **often** involves a special interest in personal growth and insights.   *(T?)*
   c. **seldom** is combined with linguistic or interpersonal intelligence.   *(T?)*
   d. is **never** taught in schools.   *(F)*

  _d_ 2. Systematic desensitization
   a. **causes** a person to react more mildly to criticism.   *(F)*
   b. works **because** the immune system is strengthened.   *(F)*
   c. should **never** be used to avoid undesirable situations.   *(F)*
   d. **helps** a person change his or her negative reaction to specific events.   *(T)*

  _a_ 3. Interpersonal intelligence is
   a. **often** seen in people with social and leadership skills.   *(T)*
   b. **associated** with immaturity. *(ridiculous)*   *(F)*

c. **not** a useful quality in school beyond the first grade. *(silly)*　(F)

d. a form of **type B behavior**. *(unfamiliar term)*　(F)

Use Five Educated-Selection Strategies for Multiple-Choice Questions

STRATEGY 20

In addition to the educated-selection strategies in Figure 5 that also apply to multiple-choice questions, **Figure 6** shows five additional educated-selection strategies for multiple-choice questions. Even though these strategies help you analyze questions more carefully and guide you to selecting an answer, do not feel overly confident or rely on these strategies except as a last resort as they will not always produce a correct answer.

FIGURE 6　Educated-Selection Strategies for Multiple-Choice Questions

1. Select one of the **middle numbers** when numbers are the options.
2. Select one of the "**look-alikes**" when two options are almost identical.
3. Select the **longest** or the **most inclusive** option.
4. Select c, the "wild-shot guess" if there are no other clues.
5. Select "**All of the above**" in specific situations.

Select a Middle Number

STRATEGY 21

- When the options in a multiple-choice question are numbers, chances are better that the correct answer is one of the numbers in the middle range.
- Therefore, treat the highest and the lowest numbers as distractors; eliminate them.
- That leaves you with two options. Try to reason through to make the better choice from the remaining two options.
- If any one of the other educated-selection strategies applies (such as choose *c*), consider that strategy as well to choose your answer.

__c__　1. An average rate of thinking speed is

a. 800 words per minute. (Eliminate the highest.)

b. 600 words per minute. ⎰Choose between

c. 400 words per minute. ⎱these two options.

d. 200 words per minute. (Eliminate the lowest.)

Select One of the "Look-Alikes"

STRATEGY 22

- Some questions have two options that look almost identical except for one or two words. Chances are good that the correct answer is one of these two options.
- Eliminate the other options and focus on these two "look-alikes."
- Carefully think through and associate the information with what you have learned. If you can't decide, choose either one.

- In the following example, focus on *c* and *d* because they are "look-alikes." Now try to reason your way through this. You have already eliminated *a*, which deals with language. Because *c* also relates to language, it, too, must be incorrect. This leaves you with *d* as the correct answer, which it is. (Notice in this case how the guessing strategy to use *c* does not work—there are no guarantees!)

  d 1. Compared to the left hemisphere of the brain, the right hemisphere of the brain
      a. understands spoken language better.
      b. has better logical abilities.
      c. perceives words better.
      d. perceives emotions better.

STRATEGY 23   Select the Longest or Most Inclusive Option

- Look at the *length* of the options. If one option is much longer than the others, choose it. Sometimes more words are needed to give complete information, so selecting the longest option may result in a correct answer.
- Also look at the *content* of the options. An option that covers a wider range of possibilities is more likely to be correct.
- Sometimes two or three options may be correct to some degree, but one option contains more information or is a broader idea. This answer is the most inclusive, so choose it.
- Notice in the following example how all of the options are correct to some degree. However, *d* is the longest and includes a wider range of information. The answers *a, b,* and *c* fit under the information given in *d*. Therefore, *d* is the best option.

  d 1. You can reduce test anxiety by focusing on:
      a. the test and not other students. *(T)*
      b. conducting careful memory searches. *(T)*
      c. positive statements and affirmations. *(T)*
      d. effective test-taking skills related to both your actions and your thoughts. *(T)*

STRATEGY 24   Select C: The "Wild-Shot Guess"

- For multiple-choice questions, many instructors favor the *c* answer for the correct answer. If you try writing some of your own multiple-choice questions, you may find that you, too, tend to put more correct answers in the *c* position than in any other position.
- The position of *c* seems to hide the answer best and force the reader to read through more of the options.

STRATEGY 25   Select "All of the Above" in Specific Situations

- If you know for certain that two options are correct, but you are not sure about the third option, and the fourth option is "All of the above," choose "All of the above."

- If you do not know for certain that two are correct, and you have found no other clues to help you, you can choose "All of the above." However, be aware that this strategy is not very reliable, especially if the option "All of the above" is used throughout the test.

Matching Questions

Matching questions consist of two columns of information. The left column often consists of key words or terminology. The right column contains definitions, descriptions, events, examples, or other factual information that matches with the items in the left column. Matching questions are created through the use of *paired associations.* The following are examples of paired associations you may encounter on matching tests:

- Words and their definitions

- Dates and events

- Problems and their solutions

- People and what they did

- Terms and their function or purpose

- Causes and effects

Five Easy-to-Use Strategies for Matching Questions

Do you tend to get confused and frustrated with the process of matching items from two columns? Do you sometimes use answers more than once or almost finish the matching tests only to find that the remaining items do not belong together or match? If so, the following five strategies will provide you with a systematic method to use to avoid confusion, frustration, and incorrect matches.

Examine the Matching Format Carefully   **STRATEGY 26**

- Read the directions carefully. Usually you can use each item on the right only once. If you can use an item on the right more than once, the directions usually indicate this.

- Count the number of items in each column. If both columns show an equal number of items, each item will be used once. If the right column contains *more* items than the column on the left, some items on the right will be extra and will not be used.

Work Systematically   **STRATEGY 27**

- Use a systematic approach for matching items on the two lists. If you *incorrectly* match an item on the right with an item on the left, the result will be two or more incorrect answers rather than one.

- Read through the list with the shortest entries to familiarize yourself with the topics and get a glimpse of the kinds of paired associations in the matching test. If the items in each column are about equal length, read the left column.

- Start with "a," the first item at the top of the right column. Scan the items in the left column to find a match.

- Once you see a definite match, write the letter on the line and *cross off the letter you used so you do not reuse it.* Crossing off used letters also helps avoid confusion.
- Do *not* make a match unless you are confident that the item on the right matches the item on the left. When in doubt, leave the item unmatched and move to the next letter in the column to look for its match.
- After you have matched as many items as possible by using immediate and delayed response, return to the unmatched items. Use assisted response by looking through other parts of the test for related information that may help you match up the remaining items.
- **Figure 7** shows the systematic approach to matching items on a matching test.

FIGURE 7   Steps for Answering Matching Questions

Matching

① Directions say to use each answer once.

Match the items on the left to the items on the right. Write the letter of each answer on the line. Each item on the right may be used only one time.

② Two answers are extra and won't be used.

③ Read the shorter list. ↘   ④ Start with "a." Do only the ones you know.

⑤ Use delayed response. Use helper words to try to connect the items that you do not know well.

⑥ Use assisted response. Use the rest of the test for assistance in finding more answers.

⑦ Use educated guessing. Fill in any remaining blanks with letters you did not already use.

	Left	Right
_h_	1. working memory	a. permanent storage center
___	2. motivation	b. associating items together
_a_	3. long-term memory	c. short-term memory and feedback loop
_j_	4. affirmations	d. feeling, emotion, or desire that elicits an action
_f_	5. chunking	e. feedback
___	6. sensory stimuli	f. group into bigger units or break into smaller units
_b_	7. linking	g. procedural memory
_i_	8. central executive	h. conscious mind
___	9. self-efficacy	i. manager/organizer of WM
___	10. result of self-quizzing	j. positive statements written in present tense
		k. belief in one's own abilities
		l. words, sounds, pictures

Look for Word Clues and Grammar Clues   STRATEGY 28

- Word clues (helper words) can help you find correct matches. For example, if you see a word such as *system, technique, process,* or *rule* in the right column, narrow your focus by searching for choices in the left column that deal specifically with a system, technique, process, or rule.

- Grammar clues can help you find correct matches. If an item in the right column is a *plural,* the match in the left column will also refer to a plural. Similarly, singular items in the right column are matched with singular items in the left column.

- In the following example, notice how the word clues *technique* and *response* and the grammar clues *style, two kinds* and *subintelligences* in the right column help you find the matches in the left column.

__c__ 1. core abilities		a. **two kinds** of locus of control
__e__ 2. assisted response		b. a cognitive learning **style**
__d__ 3. relaxation technique		c. **subintelligences**
__a__ 4. internal and external		d. soothing mask **technique**
__b__ 5. visual learnere		e. third level of **response** for test questions

Connect Items in Each Column By Making Logical Sentences   STRATEGY 29

- As you look at an item in the right column, ask yourself questions to find logical matches. For example, in Figure 7, item *k,* ask yourself, "What item on the left has something to do with belief in one's abilities?"

- When you think you have found a match, connect the two items by forming a sentence. For example, for *k* in Figure 7, you could say, "Self-efficacy is the belief in one's own abilities."

- If you cannot form a logical sentence by connecting an item on the right with an item on the left, chances are that the two items are not a match.

Write an Answer in Every Space   STRATEGY 30

If you have not been able to match all the items after using the above strategies, fill in the missing blanks with the remaining letters. Refrain from the urge to start changing answers that you previously marked with certainty. An empty answer line obviously will be wrong, so filling in the remaining answers with "left-over" letters may result in one or more correct answers, but this strategy is risky and should only be used as a last resort.

Recall Test Questions

Recall questions are questions that require you to retrieve (recall) information from your memory in order to respond with an answer. The recall tasks required often involve conducting memory searches to locate and retrieve information from your long-term memory.

- Unlike objective test questions, recall questions do not provide you with direct clues or answers to recognize as accurate or not.

- Recall questions require higher levels of thinking and processing information.

Kinds of Recall Questions

Following are the kinds of questions that will require you to recall or retrieve answers from your long-term memory. By using effective study strategies that include creating associations that link two or more items in memory, you will be able to recall correct answers for the following kinds of questions:

Fill-in-the-blanks to complete sentences

List items or steps in a process

Define specific terminology

Write a short paragraph or short answer

Solve a word problem or an equation (See math tests)

Familiarize Yourself with Terminology for Recall Tests

In strategies for recall questions, you will encounter terms that are specific to recall questions. Read through the following glossary of terms before proceeding to the strategies for recall tests.

- **Closed questions:** Closed questions are questions that require specific answers. Sometimes the answers must appear in a specific order, such as giving the steps of a process. Other times the answers are limited to course-specific concepts, topics, or details that may appear in any order.

- **Open-ended questions:** Open-ended questions are questions that have many possible answers. A variety of answers may be correct if they reflect course content, show logical connections to course material, or reflect understanding of concepts, topics, or details.

- **Direction words:** Direction words are words in test questions that signal a specific kind of answer that is required. *List, define, discuss, tell, describe, explain why,* and *when* are a few examples of direction words.

Fill-in-the-Blanks Questions

Fill-in-the-blanks questions are recall questions in the form of sentences that have one or more missing words. The words used to "fill in the blanks," or to complete the statement usually are key terms that appear in your textbook, course materials, or lectures.

- In most cases, fill-in-the-blanks questions are *closed questions*, which means you must use specific words rather than a variety of possible words for a correct answer.

- Spelling is important. Usually your instructors require you to spell words correctly to receive full points.

- When you read the completed sentence with the filled in words, the sentence must make sense and be grammatically correct.

Three Easy-to-Use Strategies for Fill-in-the-Blanks Questions

Do you sometimes go blank and have difficulty thinking of the exact word needed to complete fill-in-the blanks questions? When you receive your graded test and see the correct answer, do you recognize the word? Using the following three strategies will help you recall the words needed to complete this type of question.

Study Course Terminology

STRATEGY 31

- Many key words used to fill-in-the-blanks will be course vocabulary.
- Use flashcards to study. Read the definition side of your flashcards. *Recite* the key term and *spell* it. Turn the card over to check your answer and the spelling of the key word.
- If your textbook provides a list of terms, use the terms to write your own fill-in-the-blanks test questions. Practice completing your own questions. Check your spelling.
- Use any textbook or online exercises that include practice filling in missing words and spelling key terms correctly.

Determine the Number of Words Required in the Sentence

STRATEGY 32

- You can write only one word on each blank line. If there is only one blank line, you will write only one word. Trying to write a two-word response on a single line will result in an incorrect answer.
- In the following examples, only one word completes each statement. Remember, you must spell answers correctly.

  1. A _____ learner is a "right-brain dominant person" who tends to be intuitive, creative, and visual. (Answer: global)
  2. _____ motivation is the driving force to take action that comes from within you. (Answer: Intrinsic)

- When you see two or more blank lines, a comma between each blank line signals that your response will require a series of separate items.
- If no commas separate the blank lines, your response is a two- or a three-word answer.
- The following examples show both types of statements that require more than one-word answers:

  1. _____ _____ is also known as your conscious mind. (Two-word answer: Working memory)
  2. You can use the Increase-Decrease Method to adjust the time you plan to spend in the three main areas of your Pie of Life: _____, _____, and _____. (Answers in any order: school, work, leisure in any order)
  3. _____, _____, _____ on _____, and Ongoing _____ are the last four Principles of Memory represented by the mnemonic "FOTO." (Answers: Feedback, Organization, Time (on) Task, (ongoing) Review)

Use Essential Test-Taking Strategies to Fill in the Blanks

STRATEGY 33

- **Identify the kind of word needed for the answer.** Based on the position of the word in the sentence, you often can recognize that the missing word is a noun (naming an object, concept, step, process, or person) or a verb stating some type of action.

- **Conduct memory searches for answers.** Use key words in the statement to trigger associations. Ask yourself the following kinds of questions: *What do we call.... Who...Where did I learn this? What is this related to?* This type of memory search and questioning works well during the delayed response to answering a question.
- **If you cannot answer after delayed response, leave the question unanswered.** Place a check mark next to the question. Return to it later.
- **Use assisted response to fill in blanks.** If you cannot recall the necessary word, identify other key words in the statement, skim through the rest of the test to look for those key words. Try inserting a possible word into the statement, then read the statement, remembering that the completed sentence must be grammatically correct, make sense, and be logical.
- **Write a substitute word, a synonym, or even a phrase to complete the sentence.** A **synonym** is a word with a similar meaning. Even though a substitute word, a synonym, or a short phrase is not the exact answer for the fill-in-the-blanks statement, you may receive partial points for your effort.

Listing Questions

Listing questions are recall questions that ask for a specific list of ideas, items, or steps that belong together in a specific category. Unless the directions say otherwise, answers on listing questions are words or phrases, not complete sentences.

Three Easy-to-Use Strategies for Listing Questions

Do you have problems providing the number of items required to complete a listing question? Do you tend to include items in your list that do not answer the question? The following three easy-to-use strategies will help you complete listing questions with appropriate answers.

STRATEGY 34   Predict Listing Questions When You Study

- As you read and take notes, watch for items that appear in lists or steps in a process.
- Create study tools, such as flashcards, for these lists. Practice reciting these lists from memory.
- Predict listing questions when you prepare for an upcoming test. Write your own test questions that require you to list specific items or steps in a process.
- Use chapter objectives and chapter summaries as additional sources for lists of information to learn.

STRATEGY 35   Identify Questions as Closed or Open-Ended Questions

- Listing questions use two kinds of questions: closed questions and open-ended questions.
- **Closed questions** are questions that require specific answers. Some closed questions, such as questions about the steps used in a specific process, require that you list the items in their original order.
- The following are examples of *closed* listing questions:

  1. What are the Four Levels of Response to use for answering objective questions? (*Specific order required: Immediate, Delayed, Assisted, Educated Selection*)

2. List the four most common ways to encode information to process into memory. (*Nonspecific order:* linguistic, visual, motor, semantic)

- **Open-ended questions** are questions that have a variety of possible answers.

- To answer open-ended questions, you can list a variety of answers as long as the items in your answers relate to or belong in the category of the question. Items in your list may come from different chapters and different parts of the course.

- Often answers to open-ended questions were not studied as a specific list of information. Instead, you must pull together information that relates to the question. For this reason, students who rely on rote memory often find open-ended questions challenging.

- The following are examples of open-ended questions that have a variety of possible correct answers:

1. List four subintelligences of Gardner's musical intelligence.
2. List five *reflect activities* a student could use during the fourth step of the Cornell notetaking system.
3. List three statements a student with an external locus of control might make after performing poorly on a test.

Use Essential Test-Taking Strategies for Listing Questions

STRATEGY 36

- **Underline the key words in the question.** This helps you focus on what kind of information you need to include in your answer.

- **Identify the question as a closed or an open-ended question.**

- **Conduct memory searches for answers.** Use the key words you underlined in the question to trigger associations and answers. Ask yourself questions: *What else belongs here? What other things are related to the answers I already listed?*

- **Place a check mark next to the list if you were not able to complete it.** After you have answered the questions on the remainder of the test, use assisted response by using other parts of the test to locate items to complete your list.

- **Write a substitute word, synonym, or phrase to complete the list.** An empty space brings only one result: no points for your answer—so attempt to complete the list. Avoid restating an item already listed as duplicate answers will not receive points.

Definition Questions

Definition questions are recall questions that ask you to define and expand upon a word or terminology. For definition questions, a one-sentence answer that simply provides a formal definition of a term often is insufficient and does not earn you the maximum points for the question.

Four Easy-to-Use Strategies for Definition Questions

Do you tend to have problems recalling definitions for course-specific terminology? Do you tend to receive only partial points for short answers to definition questions? The following four easy-to-use strategies provide you with a step-by-step process to write strong answers that define terminology.

STRATEGY 37	**Predict and Study for Definition Questions**

- Use key words in boldface print or lists of important terms in each chapter to predict definition questions.
- Spend ample time reciting definitions and explaining what terms mean and how they are used. With a strong understanding of course-specific terminology, you will have a solid foundation for other concepts and skills in the course.
- Create flashcards or vocabulary study sheets for vocabulary terms you need to know. Use your textbook and glossary to clarify definitions.
- Work with a partner or in a study group to practice reciting and explaining terminology out loud.
- Use self-quizzing and practice writing definitions as you prepare for tests. Use feedback throughout the process to evaluate your understanding.

STRATEGY 38	**Practice Writing Definitions with Three Levels of Information**

1. **Name the category associated with the term.** To identify the category, ask yourself: In what group or category of information does this belong? *In what chapter (topic) did this appear? What is the "big picture" word or schema for this word*?

2. **Give the formal definition.** Give the course-specific definition you learned from your textbook or from class lectures.

3. **Expand the definition with one more detail. Figure 8** shows seven methods and examples for expanding an answer for a definition question.

FIGURE 8	Methods to Expand a Definition Answer

Method	Example
Add one more fact.	Distributed practice often occurs when the 2:1 ratio is used.
Give a synonym.	Distributed practice is the same as spaced practice.
Give an antonym, a contrast, or a negation.	Distributed practice is the opposite of marathon studying or massed practice.
Give a comparison or an analogy.	Distributed practice is like working on a goal a little every day instead of trying to complete all the steps in one block of time.
Define the structure of the word.	The root of neuron is neuro, which means nervous system.
Give the etymology.	The term locus comes from the Latin loci, which means place, so locus of control refers to a place where there is the control.
Give an application.	Surveying can be used to become familiar with a new textbook, chapter, article, or test.

STRATEGY 39	**Study Examples of Weak and Strong Answers**

Any opportunity you get, examine other students' responses to definition questions. Notice how they develop their definitions and the kinds of information they include. Notice in the following example the difference between a weak answer and a strong answer for a definition question.

Question:	**Define the term *distributed practice.***
Weak Answer:	It means you practice at different times.
Strong Answer:	Distributed practice is a time-management strategy that is also related to the Memory Principle of Time on Task. (Category) It means that study blocks are spread or distributed through the week. (Formal definition) Distributed practice, also known as spaced practice, is the opposite of marathon studying. (Expanded definition)

Use Essential Test-Taking Strategies for Definition Questions

STRATEGY 40

- **Read the question carefully; underline the word you need to define.**
- **Use paired associations.** When you studied the term, you paired it with the definition. Say the word to yourself; conduct a memory search for the definition. Try to recall hearing yourself reciting or reading the definition on your flashcard or vocabulary sheet. Try to visualize the information in your notes.
- **Include three or more sentences in your answer.** Use the category-definition-one additional detail format for your definition answer.
- **Use assisted response.** If you are not able to define the word after conducting a memory search, place a check mark next to the question, and move to another question. Later, use other parts of the test for clues you can use to complete your answer.

Short-Answer Questions

Short-answer questions are recall questions that require a short paragraph for an answer. Five to seven sentences usually suffice; writing information in lists instead of full sentences usually does not suffice.

- Answers to short-answer questions are often graded on not only the content, but also on your writing skills.
- Answer in complete sentences. Use correct grammar, punctuation, and spelling.
- Write legibly.

Six Easy-to-Use Strategies for Short-Answer Questions

Do you tend to have difficulty expressing your ideas in a clear, well-organized way? Do you sometimes write answers that do not directly answer the short-answer question? The following six strategies show how to organize and develop answers for short-answer questions.

Pay Attention to and Circle Direction Words

STRATEGY 41

- **Direction words** are words in test questions that signal a specific kind of answer is required.
- To get full points for your answer, your response must reflect the expectation associated with the question word.
- As soon as you identify a direction word in a question, *circle it.* Review in your mind what is required by this direction word.
- **Figure 9** shows common direction words used for short-answer questions.

FIGURE 9	Direction Words for Short-Answer Questions
Direction Word	**What Is Required**
Discuss/Tell	Tell about a particular topic.
Identify/What are?	Identify specific points. (This is similar to a listing except that you are required to answer in full sentences.)
Describe	Give more specific details or descriptions than are required by "discuss."
Explain/Why?	Give reasons. Answer the question "Why?"
Explain how/How?	Describe a process or a set of steps. Give the steps in chronological (time sequence) order.
When?	Describe a time or a specific condition needed for something to happen, occur, or be used.

- Notice in the following examples how each of the test questions has the same subject: *visual mappings*. However, think how answers will vary slightly because of the different direction words used.

> Why is recitation important to use while studying a visual mapping?
>
> Explain how to create a visual mapping.
>
> How should you study from a visual mapping?
>
> When should you use visual mappings?

STRATEGY 42   Pay Attention to and Underline Key Words

- Read each question carefully. Identify key words in the question that indicate the subject or topics that must appear in your answer.
- Underline key words in the question. Underlining helps you maintain a focus on what is important to include in your answer and helps you avoid wandering off course with nonessential information.
- Plan to include these key words in your response.

STRATEGY 43   Make a Mental Plan or a Short List of Key Ideas

- Determine if the question is a *closed question* with specific answers or an *open-ended question* with a variety of possible answers.
- Conduct a *memory search* for appropriate details related to the key words and the direction word in the question.
- Make a quick mental plan or jot down a short list of points to develop into sentences. Plan to develop these ideas into sentences and then into a paragraph.

Write a Strong, Focused Opening Sentence

STRATEGY 44

- Begin your answer with a sentence that is direct and to the point. Do not beat around the bush or save your best information for last.
- The first sentence, when well written, lets your instructor know right away that you are familiar with the subject and your answer is "on target."
- The first sentence of your answer should clearly state the main idea of your answer and include the key words from the question.
- The first sentence should also show that you are responding appropriately to the direction word and providing the required kind of information.
- Your opening sentence may indicate the number of items that you will discuss or even possibly list the series of items you will explain further.
- **Figure 10** shows differences in quality in three opening sentences. The first one does not get to the point. The second and third examples are direct, focused, and show confidence.

FIGURE 10   Examples of Opening Sentences

Question:	(Why) is <u>recitation</u> important in the <u>learning process</u>?
Weak:	Recitation is important because it helps a person learn better.
Strong:	Recitation, one of the Twelve Principles of Memory, is important in the learning process for three reasons.
Strong:	Recitation is important in the learning process because it involves the auditory channel, feedback, and practice expressing ideas.

Expand Your Answer with Details

STRATEGY 45

- Support your opening sentence by expanding into a paragraph with details.
- For a strong answer, use course-related terminology and/or examples used in class or in your textbook.
- Stick to the point. Do not pad the answer with unrelated information or attempt to write too much or to write an essay.
- **Figure 11** shows a weak answer and a strong answer to the question, *"Why is recitation important in the learning process?"*

| FIGURE 11 | Weak and Strong Answers |

Weak: Recitation is important because it helps a person learn. Everyone wants to do the very best possible, and recitation helps make that happen. When you recite, you talk out loud. You practice information out loud before a test.

Strong: Recitation is important in the learning process because it involves the auditory channel, gives feedback, and provides practice expressing ideas. When a person states information out loud and in complete sentences, he/she encodes information linguistically and keeps information active in working memory. Reciting also gives feedback so that a person knows immediately whether or not the information is understood accurately and on the level that can be explained to someone else. Taking time to recite also provides the opportunity to practice organizing and expressing ideas clearly.

| STRATEGY 46 | **Use Essential Test-Taking Strategies for Short-Answer Questions** |

- **Determine if the question is closed or open-ended.** For a closed question, conduct a memory search to locate specific information in long-term memory. For open-ended questions, conduct a memory search for a variety of possible details to include in your answer.
- **Use your mental plan or a short list of ideas as an easy-to-use guide to write your answer.** This helps you keep your answer focused and avoid wandering off the topic. If for some reason you run out of time to write a paragraph answer, turn in your list of ideas for possibly partial points for your answer.
- **Use a short-answer format for your answer.** Start with a strong, focused opening sentence. Expand your answer by adding sentences that support the opening sentence, provide additional details, use course terminology, and reflect the expectations of the direction word.
- **Use assisted response if necessary.** Scan through other parts of the test to identify additional details to include in your answer.
- **Proofread and correct any spelling or grammatical errors.**

Math Test Questions

Performing well on math tests requires an alert mind ready to manage a variety of thinking processes and tasks that result in an exact correct answer. Studying mathematics involves learning a progression of concepts and skills, each building on previously learned information that sets the foundation for higher level skills. Questions on math tests:

- Emphasize using problem-solving skills that you acquired through practice and repetition, skills that you cannot memorize or master the night before a test.

- Involve applying *prototypes* you have learned to new problems of the same type but problems that you have not previously seen or solved.

- Involve understanding and defining mathematical terms and understanding how to express information in mathematical terms, formulas, or algebraic equations.

- Math test questions appear in more than tests for math courses. You will find math questions on tests for science courses, health occupation courses, as well as social science courses, or any other courses that involve the use of formulas to solve problems.

Understand Procedural Knowledge

Unlike tests for many other subjects that assess your understanding and ability to recall specific *declarative knowledge,* math tests assess your ability to apply *procedural knowledge* you have learned to *new* problems. **Procedural knowledge** is information that involves steps or processes to use to solve problems or create specific products with accuracy and speed. Unlike factual knowledge that you can memorize and work with in a variety of ways, procedural knowledge involves using strategies that emphasize repetition, repetition, and more repetition.

- Learning procedural knowledge requires time. Trying to learn it quickly without practice and repetition often leads to partial and inaccurate learning---"skill gaps" that cause problems later when you try to work with higher level skills.

- Effective studying of procedural knowledge requires repeating the original process multiple times over a period of days, weeks, and sometimes several months until the process of applying specific steps becomes automatic.

- When you rework familiar math problems multiple times, the steps and processes become more internalized, more solidified in memory, and a more familiar routine to apply to new problem sets.

- As you rework problems multiple times, you increase your problem-solving speed and accuracy.

- To avoid rote memory, explain each step to yourself or to others to demonstrate that you understand the process and are not simply memorizing without attaching meaning to the steps.

Familiarize Yourself with Terminology for Math Tests

Your math textbooks include a wide range of special terminology required to understand, explain, and use mathematical operations and formulas. For example, you may be required to understand terms such as associative property, adjacent angles, area, axis, circumference, common denominators, commutative property, denominator, distributive property, or division of integers. Due to the vast range of mathematical skills, subjects, and terminology, you will need to use your specific textbooks to identify important terminology to learn. For now, read through the following glossary of terms before proceeding to the strategies for questions on math tests.

Algebraic symbols: Algebraic symbols are marks or signs used in mathematical expressions and equations to represent specific processes or functions. For example, the symbol / may mean: divide, quotient, or per.

Algebraic expressions: Algebraic expressions are statements that show values by using letters, symbols, and numerals. Examples include: x – 5 (means a number decreased by 5) and x + 8 (means eight more than x).

Equations: Equations are linear arrangements of mathematical symbols used to show equalities on each side of an equal sign.

Prototypes: Prototypes are original formulas or examples of problems that serve as models to use to solve new problems with similar characteristics.

RSTUV Problem-Solving Method: RSTUV is a five-step approach to use to solve math word problems: read, select, think, use, and verify.

Word Problems or Story Problems: In sentence format, the test question presents you with a variety of facts that you need to use to solve a problem.

Nine Easy-to-Use Strategies for Math Tests

When you review graded math tests, do you see a pattern of errors? For example, did you forget to show all your work, did you omit mathematical signs, or did you use incorrect steps to problem solve? The following nine strategies will help you increase your performance on math tests.

STRATEGY 47 · Memorize Prototypes When You Study

- A prototype is a model of a specific type of math problem. By memorizing and understanding a prototype, you can use this model to apply the necessary steps to solve a new problem that is of the same problem type.

- Prototypes often appear in textbooks when you are introduced to a new type of math problem or equation. Explanations and examples accompany the prototype.

- Study prototypes carefully. Memorize them. Practice explaining them. Your goal is to be able to recognize when to use the prototype and to be familiar enough with its steps that you can apply them without hesitation to new problems.

- To prepare for upcoming math tests, without looking at the correct answers, rework textbook examples multiple times. Check your accuracy.

- **Figure 12** shows examples of prototypes. In each textbook, example problems followed the prototype.

STRATEGY 48 · Learn the Terminology

Every math course has specific terminology that you must understand in order to communicate and explain steps or processes. Terms that you need to know often are indicated by bold or colored print in the textbook.

- Create flashcards to study and explain terminology. On the front sides of the cards, write the terms. On the back sides of the cards, write the definition. Include an example.

- Use self-quizzing. Look at the front and recite the back. Check your accuracy.

FIGURE 12:   Examples of Prototypes

EXAMPLE 1: TEMPERATURE SCALE CONVERSION

Table 5-14   Temperature Scale Conversion Formulas

Convert From	Fraction Formula	Decimal Formula
Centigrade to Fahrenheit	$(°C \times 9/5) + 32 = °F$ Example: 37°C $(37 \times 9/5) + 32 = °F$ $333/5 + 32 = 98.6°F$	$(°C \times 1.8) + 32 = °F$ Example: 37°C $(37 \times 1.8) + 32 = °F$ $66.6 + 32 = 98.6°F$

EXAMPLE 2: DOSAGE FORMULA

The first method is to use the *dosage formula*, which is

$$\frac{\text{desired dose}}{\text{on-hand dose}} \times \text{Vehicle} = \text{amount to give.}$$

In short-hand notation, this formula is expressed as

$$\frac{D}{H} \times V = A.$$

EXAMPLE 5-10: A physician orders: *Keflex 750 mg p.o. stat.* However, the label on the medicine bottle states the dosage strength is 250 mg (per tablet). What is the correct amount to give the patient?

1) *Applying the dosage formula:* The desired dose is 750 mg. The amount on hand is 250 mg. The vehicle is one tablet. Substitute this information into the dosage formula.

$$\frac{D}{H} \times V = \frac{750 \text{ mg}}{250 \text{ mg}} \times 1 \text{ tablet} = 3 \times 1 \text{ tablet} = 3 \text{ tablets}$$

EXAMPLE 3: VOLTAGE CHANGE

The voltage change for a transformer is given by

$$V_2 = \left(\frac{N_2}{N_1}\right) V_1 \qquad 8.10$$

transformer voltage change

Where $V2$ = secondary voltage
        $V1$ = primary voltage
        $N1$ = number of turns in primary coil
        $N2$ = number of turns in secondary coil.

Finding Voltage Output for a Transformer

A transformer has 500 windings in its primary coil and 25 in its secondary coil. If the primary voltage is 4400 V, find the secondary voltage.

SOLUTION

Using Eq. 8.10 with $N_1 = 500$, $N_2 = 25$, and $V_1 = 4400$ V, we have

$$V_2 = \left(\frac{N_2}{N_1}\right) V_1 = \left(\frac{25}{500}\right) (4400 \text{ V}) = 220 \text{ V}$$

Sources: Example 1: From Mitchell/Haroun. *Introduction to Health Care*, 2E. © 2007 Delmar Cengage Learning, a part of Cengage Learning, Inc. Reproduced by permision. www.cengage.com/permissions. 2. From Helms, *Mathematics for the Health Sciences*, 1E. © 2010 Delmar Learning, a part of Cengage Learning, Inc. Reproduced by permission. www.cengage.com/permissions. 3. Shipman et al. *An introduction to Physical Science*, 10ED. Houghton Miffin Company, © 2003, p. 103. Reprinted with permission.

- In addition to regular terminology, you will need to know how to read and translate into words the symbols used in formulas or equations. On the fronts of cards, write symbols. On the backs, translate the symbols into words. Use self-quizzing to practice naming symbols and reading formulas.

STRATEGY 49   Identify and Think about the Pattern of the Problem

- Read the problem carefully. Ask yourself: *What do I already know about this kind of problem? What problems did I study that are similar? What steps did I use to solve similar problems? What prototypes did I memorize that I can use to solve this problem?*
- Conduct a memory search or use associations to recall the prototype (model) problem you memorized for this pattern and the steps or formula you used to solve that problem.
- Focus your attention on the specific steps used in the prototype and then apply those steps to the new math test problem.

STRATEGY 50   Devise a Strategy to Solve Word Problems

- Carefully examine all the details in word problems. Underline key words.
- Identify what information is needed, what information is missing, and what information is irrelevant to solving the problem.
- List or underline the known relevant facts that you will need to solve the equation or problem. Ignore the nonessential details.
- Draw a simple picture of the problem to get a clearer understanding of the information.
- Identify the algebraic formula you can use to solve the problem.
- Mentally talk or explain to yourself the steps you will use to solve the problem.
- Apply the steps. Show your work for each problem-solving step.

STRATEGY 51   Use RSTUV to Read and Solve Problems

The **RSTUV Problem-Solving Method** is a five-step approach to solve math word problems. Each letter of RSTUV represents one step of this problem-solving approach.

- **R = READ** the problem, not once or twice, but until you understand it. Pay attention to key words or instructions such as *compute, draw, write, construct, make, show, identify, state, simplify, solve,* and *graph.*
- **S = SELECT** the unknown; that is, find out what the problem asks for. One good way to look for the unknown is to look for the question mark (?) and carefully read the material preceding it. Try to determine what information is given and what is missing.
- **T = THINK** of a plan to solve the problem. Problem solving requires many skills and strategies. Some of them are *look for a pattern; examine a related problem; make tables, pictures, and diagrams; write an equation; work backward;* and *make a guess.*

- **U = USE** the techniques you are studying to carry out the plan. Look for procedures that can be used to solve specific problems. Then carry out the plan. Check each step.
- **V = VERIFY** the answer. Look back and check the results of the original problem. *Is the answer reasonable? Can you find it some other way?*

  From Bello and Britton, *Topics in Contemporary Mathematics, 6th ed.,* pp. 5-6. Copyright © 1997. Reprinted by permission of Houghton Mifflin, Inc

Mentally Visualize or Reconstruct Information

STRATEGY 52

- If you are working on an application problem or a word/story problem, picture the known information and the information you need to find to solve the problem.
- As you read the following example, try visualizing the story. Then use your skills to answer the questions.

  Question: After playing tennis for 2 hr, Ruben ate a banana split containing 650 calories and a fudge brownie containing 250 calories. Playing tennis uses 720 calories per hour. (Visualize this story scene.)

  a. Without doing the calculations, did the banana split and the fudge brownie contain more or fewer calories than Ruben burned off playing tennis?

  b. Find the number of calories Ruben gained or lost from these two activities.

Avoid Getting Stuck on One Problem

STRATEGY 53

- When you feel stuck and not sure how to solve a problem, shake your head a few times, look away from the problem, take a few deep breaths, and ask yourself a few questions to help change your thought processes. *Why does this problem look familiar? What prototype do I know that looked similar? What processes are we studying that apply here?*
- To solve math problems often requires your mind to shift back and forth rapidly and multiple times between the problem and the information in your long-term memory. Reread the problem, shift your eyes away a few seconds, do a memory search to scan memory for possible ways to solve a specific problem, and then look back at the problem.
- If you have tried a variety of strategies without success, or if you have spent too much time on one individual problem, place a check mark next to the question and move on.
- After completing as many questions on the test as possible, return to the questions with the check marks. You may be able to see the problem differently and recall a strategy to use to complete the problem-solving steps.

Use Essential Test-Taking Strategies for Math Tests

STRATEGY 54

- **Survey the test and create a plan for budgeting your test time.** Skim through the test to familiarize yourself with the types of questions, test question point values, and the length of the test. Create a quick plan for budgeting your time for each section.

- **Begin with familiar problems.** You do *not* need to work problems in the order that they appear in the test. By starting with familiar problems, you create a mind-set for the material, and you build self-confidence.
- **Circle direction words and underline key words.** These two actions help you maintain a focus on what is required and what is essential for a complete answer.
- **Check your work one final time.** If time permits, checking your work and answers helps you eliminate common errors: omitting labels on story problem answers, using incorrect mathematical signs of operation, or making careless calculation errors.

STRATEGY 55   Avoid the Ten Common Test-Taking Errors

- When you receive your graded tests, do an error analysis on the test. Look at the kinds of errors you made on the test.
- Correct the errors so you replace the incorrect thinking about the problem or the process with the correct information.
- The following are ten common test-taking errors students discover during error analyses.

1. *Missing more questions in the first third or the last third of a test:* Errors in the first third of a test (the easiest problems) can be due to carelessness. Errors in the last part of the test can be due to the fact that the last problems are more difficult or due to increasing your test speed to finish the test.

2. *Not completing a problem to its last step:* Take time to review the last step to be sure you show all your work right up to the end of the problem.

3. *Changing test answers from correct to incorrect:* Changing answers without a logical reason for doing so is a sign of panic or test anxiety. Keep your original answer unless you locate an error in your work when you review your work a final time.

4. *Getting stuck on one problem and spending too much time on it:* Set a time limit for each problem. Working too long on a problem without success will increase your test anxiety and waste valuable time that could be better used solving other problems or reviewing your test.

5. *Rushing through the easiest part of the test and making careless errors:* Work more slowly and carefully. Review the easiest problems first if you have time to go back over your work during the allotted test time.

6. *Miscopying an answer from your scratch work to the test:* Systematically compare your last problem step on scratch paper with the answer written on the test. Always hand in your scratch work with your test.

7. *Leaving answers blank:* If you cannot figure out how to solve a problem, rewrite the problem and try to do at least the first step.

8. *Solving only the first step of a two-step problem:* Write *two* in the margin of the test when you first read the problem. This reminds you that you need to show two steps or two answers to the problem.

9. *Not understanding all the functions of your calculator:* To avoid major testing problems, take time to learn all the functions of your calculator *before* the test.

10. *Leaving the test early without checking your answers:* Use the entire allotted test time. Remain in the room and use the time to check each problem.

Adapted from Paul Nolting, *Math Study Skills Workbook,* pp. 92–95. Copyright © 2000. Reprinted with permission of Houghton Mifflin, Inc.

Essay Test Questions

Essay questions require an organized composition that develops several main ideas that are related to one thesis sentence. The thesis sentence directly states the main point of the entire essay. Following are additional points about essay test questions.

- Answering essay questions is demanding as it requires you know information thoroughly, be able to pull the information from your memory, and know how to integrate facts to show relationships.

- The way you express the information and the relationships you show need to follow a logical line of thinking and include sufficient details to develop an effective essay answer.

- Essays also require a sound grasp of writing skills (grammar, syntax, and spelling) and a well-developed, expressive vocabulary.

Familiarize Yourself with Terminology for Essay Test Questions

The structure of essays involves key concepts that you will also encounter in composition classes. Carefully read through the following terms before focusing your attention on the specific strategies.

- **Thesis statement:** A thesis statement is a strong, focused sentence that states the main point of an entire essay. The thesis statement often appears as the first sentence of the essay but may appear other places in the introductory paragraph.

- **Direction words:** Direction words are words in test questions that signal a specific kind of answer that is required. *List, define, discuss, tell, describe, explain why,* and *when* are a few examples of direction words.

- **Organizational plan:** An organizational plan is an outline, a hierarchy, a visual mapping, or a list of main ideas the writer intends to use in an essay to develop the thesis of the essay.

- **Five-paragraph format:** The five-paragraph essay format consists of an introductory paragraph, three paragraphs in the body of the essay to develop three separate main ideas, and a concluding paragraph.

- **Main idea:** A main idea is the most important point in a paragraph that the writer wishes to make about a topic. Each paragraph has only one main idea. The main idea supports or helps develop the thesis statement.

- **Supporting details:** Supporting details are facts, examples, or definitions that are related to the subject of a paragraph. A paragraph has adequate development when sufficient details appear in the paragraph to support the main idea.

Familiarize Yourself with Different Kinds of Essay Test Formats

Instructors may use a variety of formats for essay tests, some of which provide you with greater opportunities to prepare your essay answer in advance. Following are essay formats and situations you may encounter in your courses.

- **Topics are announced in advance.** If you know the topics that will be used for essay questions, generate detailed notes on the topics. Gather pertinent information; use the index of your textbook to locate information on the topic; and prepare a set of summary notes. Predict possible questions, organize your information, and practice writing answers to the questions you predicted.

- **Questions are announced in advance.** When the questions are announced in advance, use the index in your textbook to locate and organize pertinent information. Create and memorize an outline or organizational plan for your answers. Practice writing essay answers for each question.

- **Books may be used for the essay test.** Open-book essay tests require less retrieval of information from memory and more organizational skills to locate information in the textbook. Become familiar with the index of your book so you can look up topics quickly. Use a special highlighter to mark important facts (dates, names, events, statistics, and terminology) and quotations you may wish to use in your answer. Use tabs to mark significant pages such as those with important summary charts, tables, lists, steps, or visual materials.

- **Essay test is done at home.** Take-home essay tests provide you with more time to organize and develop your essay answer. Create a plan of action that provides you with sufficient time to develop a polished essay answer. Set your completed essay aside for a day; then, reread it; proofread for spelling, grammar, and mechanics; revise if you see ways to strengthen it; and type the final version.

Ten Easy-to-Use Strategies for Essay Test Questions

Do your essay answers tend to lack sufficient supporting details or wander off course by including information that does not answer the question? Do you have difficulty clearly organizing your answers and expressing your ideas? The following ten easy-to-use strategies will guide you through the process of developing strong answers for essay test questions.

STRATEGY 56   **Prepare for In-Class Essay Tests**

When you do not receive information about the topics or the essay questions that will appear on a test, your challenge will be to retrieve and organize information from memory. Sometimes you will be required to answer one or more essay questions; other times you may be instructed to select one or more essay questions from a list of questions. The following tips can help you prepare for this type of essay test.

- **Predict test questions.** Use your course syllabus to identify concepts, trends, themes, or categories of information that you are expected to learn. Write practice test questions based on these materials.

- **Create summary notes.** Essay questions often require you to compare, contrast, summarize, explain, discuss, or apply information about major topics, themes, theories, or models. Create summary notes with important supporting details for topics that you predict may be on essay test questions.

- **Practice writing essay answers.** Work with a partner or in a study group to create practice essay questions and answers. When you practice organizing information and presenting your ideas *before* an actual essay test, you become more comfortable with the essay-writing process.

Understand the Question and the Direction Words   STRATEGY 57

- Read the question carefully and identify the question as a closed or an open-ended question.
- Underline key words in the question as a reminder to include these key words in your introductory paragraph and to emphasize these words throughout your essay.
- Be sure you understand the direction word as it signals the type of response required. Circle the direction word to maintain a focus on the direction of your answer.
- **Figure 13** shows direction words frequently used for essay questions.

Carefully Select Which Questions to Answer When You Have a Choice   STRATEGY 58

- Examine the questions carefully. Do not automatically choose the questions that look the shortest or the easiest. They are usually more general and more difficult to answer than longer questions that tend to be more specific.
- Select the questions that contain the topics that you are most familiar with and topics for which you can recall specific and sufficient supporting details.
- After you select the questions to answer, begin with the question that is the most familiar as this tends to boost your confidence level and puts you in the "essay writing mode."

Write a Strong, Focused Thesis Sentence   STRATEGY 59

A **thesis sentence** is a strong, focused sentence that states the main point of an entire essay. The thesis sentence for an essay test answer usually appears as the first sentence on your paper. The following points about your thesis statement are important to remember:

- Clearly state the topic of the essay. Include key words that are a part of the question. If you wish, you may indicate the number of points you plan to develop.
- Show that you understand the direction word and plan to focus your answer in the direction indicated by the direction word.
- Your thesis statement serves as a guide for developing the rest of your essay. It suggests the basic outline of main ideas to develop with important supporting details.
- Your thesis statement serves as an immediate indicator for your instructor that you understand the question and know the answer.

FIGURE 13   Direction Words for Essay Questions

Direction Word	What Is Required
Compare	Show the similarities and differences between two or more items.
Contrast	Present only the differences between two or more items.
Define	Give the definition and expand it with more examples and greater details.
Trace/Outline	Discuss the sequence of events in chronological order.
Summarize	Identify and discuss the main points or the highlights of a subject. Omit in-depth details.
Evaluate/Critique	Offer your opinion or judgment and then back it up with specific facts, details, or reasons.
Analyze	Identify the different parts of something. Discuss each part individually.
Describe	Give a detailed description of different aspects, qualities, characteristics, parts, or points of view.
Discuss/Tell	Tell about the parts or the main points. Expand with specific details.
Explain/Explain why	Give reasons. Tell why. Show logical relationships or cause/effect.
Explain how	Give the process, steps, stages, or procedures involved. Explain each.
Illustrate	Give examples. Explain each example with details.
Identify/What are	Identify specific points. Discuss each point individually. Include sufficient details.
When	Describe a time or a specific condition needed for something to happen, occur, or be used. Provide details and any relevant background information.

- Because of the significance of the thesis statement, take time to create a strong, direct, confident opening sentence.
- **Figure 14** shows examples of two essay test questions, the meaning of the directions words, and examples of strong thesis statements.

STRATEGY 60   Develop An Organizational Plan

- After you have developed a strong thesis statement, take the time to develop an organizational plan.
- Your organizational plan provides an overview of the main ideas you plan to include in your essay. Once you conceptualize and develop your plan, you will be able to write your response faster and avoid wandering off course or becoming confused about the next point to write in your answer.

FIGURE 14   Thesis Sentences

Question	Direction	Possible Thesis Statement
(Discuss) the characteristics of each of Howard Gardner's multiple intelligences.	Discuss = tell about What are the eight intelligences?	Each of Howard Gardner's eight intelligences has clearly recognizable characteristics.
(Explain why) elaborative rehearsal is more effective for college learning than rote memory strategies.	Explain why = give reasons What are the reasons? How many reasons?	Elaborative rehearsal is more effective than rote memory because more Memory Principles are used and information in memory is in a more usable form.

- Your organizational plan becomes your step-by-step outline that guides the writing process.
- Your plan may be an outline, a visual mapping, a hierarchy, or a basic list of main ideas. **Figure 15** shows the four basic kinds of organizational plans to use.

FIGURE 15   Organizational Plans for Essay Questions

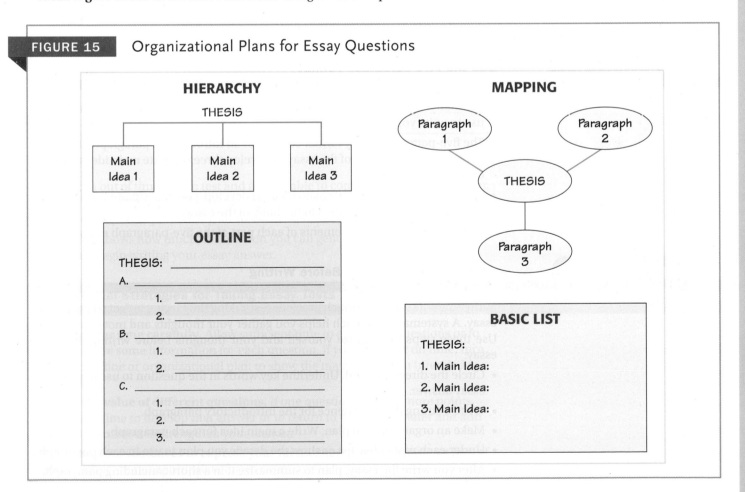

- **Include supporting details so your essay will not be underdeveloped.** Include facts such as names, dates, events, and statistics; include definitions, examples, or appropriate applications of the information you are presenting. Do not make the mistake of assuming that information is obvious or that your instructor knows what you are thinking or clearly sees the connection.

- **Include quotations for details.** For some courses, you may want to memorize important quotations that appear in your textbook and you predict you may be able to use to develop an essay test answer. Remember to place quotation marks around the quoted material and cite the source.

- **Use key words in the question and course-specific terminology in your answers as much as possible.**

- **Strive to write as neatly as possible.** Illegible handwriting will hurt your grade. If you need to delete some of the information, delete it by crossing it out with one neat line or by using correction fluid.

STRATEGY 64   Strengthen Your Essay and Revise if You Have Time

As you recall, writing effective essays involves understanding and using effective vocabulary, writing, and spelling skills. Following are revisions you can make in your essays if you have time available during the testing period. If you do not have time to revise, familiarize yourself with the following writing tips so you can strive to implement them the next time you face an essay test.

- Replace slang or informal language with formal language or course terminology.
- Reword to avoid using the word *you.* Replace the word *you* with the word it represents, the specific noun, such as *students.*
- Replace vague pronouns such as *it* with the name of the specific item.
- Reword sentences to avoid weak "sentence starters" such as *There is... There are... Here is...* or *Here are.*
- Use sentence variety in your essay: simple, compound, complex, and compound-complex sentences. Knowing how to use sentence combining is also an economical way to combine and develop ideas. Using effective sentence variety results in an essay that is interesting to read and understand.

STRATEGY 65   Learn from Your Tests

- Writing strong essay answers becomes easier with practice.
- When you get your essay tests back, read the comments and suggestions.
- Analyze your essays and ask yourself questions: *Did I predict this question? Did I answer questions directly and in an organized way? Did I include sufficient details? How could I have strengthened my answer?*
- Adjust your studying and test-taking skills as needed to improve your performance on the next essay test.

Conclusion

This Essential Test-Taking Skills Guide is designed to equip you with essential skills and strategies to improve your test-taking skills and performance. Using the sixty-five specific test-taking strategies will strengthen your ability to read, understand, interpret, and respond appropriately to a variety of test questions and test-taking situations. Becoming an effective test-taker requires practice and attention to details. Each time you receive a graded test, take time to examine your answers and learn from your tests. Return to this guide to prepare for upcoming tests as well as refresh and refine your skills so your tests more truly reflect how well you have mastered the content of your courses.

Use the following self-assessment inventory to evaluate your general test-taking skills and identify areas you can strengthen. Strive to achieve the perfect score of 60.

Test-Taking Skills Inventory

Read each statement about test-taking skills. Circle the degree to which you use these test-taking skills. 1 = seldom or never   2 = sometimes   3 = always or almost always

1. I complete all of my assignments and reading prior to a test.   1 2 3
2. I set ample time aside to study specifically for a test.   1 2 3
3. I use self-quizzing and feedback methods when I study.   1 2 3
4. I know definitions for all course-specific terminology.   1 2 3
5. I feel confident that I studied sufficiently to do well on a test.   1 2 3
6. I use the four levels of response for answering test questions.   1 2 3
7. I rehearse factual information using a variety of strategies, and I rehearse procedural information by using ample repetition.   1 2 3
8. I read directions carefully and understand direction words.   1 2 3
9. I read carefully and pay attention to modifiers, clue words, negatives, and other details in test questions.   1 2 3
10. I use the essential strategies for answering objective questions: true-false, multiple-choice, and matching test questions.   1 2 3
11. I use educated selection (guessing) only as a last resort.   1 2 3
12. I use the essential strategies for answering recall questions: fill-in-the-blanks, definition, and listing questions.   1 2 3
13. I include sufficient details to answer short-answer questions.   1 2 3
14. I respond with the correct kind of information for closed questions and open-ended questions.   1 2 3
15. I memorize prototypes for different kinds of math problems.   1 2 3
16. I create an organizational plan for essay test answers.   1 2 3
17. I develop a strong thesis statement for essay test answers.   1 2 3
18. I include ample details in essays to support the thesis.   1 2 3
19. I use available test-taking time to check my answers and work.   1 2 3
20. I analyze error patterns and learn from my tests.   1 2 3

Your Total Score: _____

Appendix B

Answer Keys

Master Profile Chart

Beginning-of-the-Term Profiles

1. As you begin a new chapter, complete the chapter profile chart in your textbook or online at the CourseMate Web site.

2. Score your profile. (See Chapter 1, page 4.) Find the chapter number above. Circle your score to show the number of correct responses.

3. Connect the circles with lines to create a graph (your Master Profile Chart).

	Learning Styles	Processing Memory	Twelve Memory Principles	Time Manager; Goal Setter	Self-Management	Upcoming Tests	Reading Skills	College Textbooks	Notetaking Skills	Listening; Lecture Notes	Visual Notes	Carrying Forward
Chapter:	1	2	3	4	5	6	7	8	9	10	11	12
100%	10	10	10	10	10	10	10	10	10	10	10	10
90%	9	9	9	9	9	9	9	9	9	9	9	9
80%	8	8	8	8	8	8	8	8	8	8	8	8
70%	7	7	7	7	7	7	7	7	7	7	7	7
60%	6	6	6	6	6	6	6	6	6	6	6	6
50%	5	5	5	5	5	5	5	5	5	5	5	5
40%	4	4	4	4	4	4	4	4	4	4	4	4
30%	3	3	3	3	3	3	3	3	3	3	3	3
20%	2	2	2	2	2	2	2	2	2	2	2	2
10%	1	1	1	1	1	1	1	1	1	1	1	1
0%	0	0	0	0	0	0	0	0	0	0	0	0

Profile Answer Keys

CHAPTER 1: Learning Styles

1. Y	2. Y	3. Y	4. N	5. Y
6. Y	7. N	8. Y	9. Y	10. Y

CHAPTER 2: Processing Memory

1. Y	2. Y	3. N	4. Y	5. Y
6. Y	7. Y	8. N	9. Y	10. Y

CHAPTER 3: Twelve Memory Principles

1. Y	2. N	3. Y	4. N	5. Y
6. Y	7. Y	8. Y	9. N	10. Y

CHAPTER 4: Time Manager; Goal Setter

1. Y	2. Y	3. N	4. N	5. Y
6. Y	7. N	8. Y	9. Y	10. Y

CHAPTER 5: Self-Management

1. N	2. N	3. Y	4. Y	5. Y
6. Y	7. N	8. Y	9. N	10. Y

CHAPTER 6: Upcoming Tests

1. Y	2. Y	3. Y	4. N	5. N
6. Y	7. N	8. N	9. Y	10. Y

CHAPTER 7: Reading Skills

1. Y	2. N	3. N	4. Y	5. Y
6. Y	7. N	8. Y	9. Y	10. Y

CHAPTER 8: College Textbooks

1. N	2. Y	3. Y	4. N	5. Y
6. Y	7. N	8. Y	9. Y	10. Y

CHAPTER 9: Notetaking Skills

1. Y	2. N	3. Y	4. Y	5. N
6. Y	7. N	8. Y	9. N	10. Y

CHAPTER 10: Listening; Lecture Notes

1. Y	2. N	3. Y	4. Y	5. N
6. N	7. Y	8. N	9. Y	10. Y

CHAPTER 11: Visual Notes

1. N	2. Y	3. Y	4. Y	5. Y
6. N	7. Y	8. N	9. Y	10. Y

CHAPTER 12: Carrying Forward

1. Y	2. N	3. N	4. Y	5. N
6. Y	7. N	8. Y	9. Y	10. Y

End-of-the-Term Profiles

1. Redo all the profile questions so you can see the changes that you have made this term. Cut a two-inch-wide strip of paper to cover up the original answers on the profile questions at the beginning of each chapter. Write Y or N *next to the number of each profile question.* If you prefer, you may complete the profile questions on the CourseMate Web site for this textbook.

2. Score your profile answers using the answer key listed at the beginning of this appendix.

3. Chart your scores on the Master Profile Chart. Use a different color ink so that you can compare these scores with your original scores.

Chapter Answer Keys

CHAPTER 1: Learning Styles

CHECK POINT 1.1
1. F   2. F   3. T   4. F   5. T

CHECK POINT 1.2
1. F   2. T   3. T   4. F   5. F

CHECK POINT 1.3
1. T   2. F   3. F   4. T   5. T

CHAPTER 1 REVIEW QUESTIONS
True or False?
1. F   2. T   3. T   4. T   5. T

Multiple Choice
1. c   2. d   3. b   4. d

Definitions
Answers will vary.*

Short-Answer Question
Answers will vary.*

CHAPTER 2: Processing Memory

CHECK POINT 2.1
1. F   2. F   3. F   4. T   5. F

CHECK POINT 2.2
1. d   2. a   3. d   4. b

CHECK POINT 2.3
1. T   2. F   3. T   4. F   5. F

CHAPTER 2 REVIEW QUESTIONS
Matching
1. g   2. h   3. f   4. i   5. a
6. b   7. d   8. c   9. j   10. e

True or False?
1. F   2. T   3. T   4. T   5. T
6. F   7. T   8. T   9. T   10. T

Recall Question
Compare to Figure 2.1.

CHAPTER 3: Twelve Memory Principles

CHECK POINT 3.1
1. T   2. T   3. F

CHECK POINT 3.2
1. F   2. T   3. T   4. T   5. T

CHECK POINT 3.3
1. d   2. d   3. b

CHECK POINT 3.4
1. Feedback
2. Organization
3. Time Task
4. Review

CHAPTER 3 REVIEW QUESTIONS
Matching
1. g   2. h   3. b   4. a   5. e
6. j   7. c   8. f   9. d   10. i

True or False?
1. F   2. F   3. T   4. T   5. F

Short-Answer Question
Answers will vary.*

CHAPTER 4: Time Manager; Goal Setter

CHECK POINT 4.1
1. T   2. F   3. F   4. F   5. T

CHECK POINT 4.2
1. g   2. i   3. d   4. b   5. j
6. a   7. h   8. c   9. e   10. f

CHECK POINT 4.3
1. T   2. F   3. T   4. F   5. F

CHECK POINT 4.4
1. F   2. F   3. T   4. T   5. T

CHAPTER 4 REVIEW QUESTIONS
True or False?
1. T   2. T   3. T   4. T

Multiple Choice
1. b   2. b   3. b   4. b
5. a   6. d   7. d   8. b

Short-Answer Questions
Answers will vary.*

CHAPTER 5: Self-Management

CHECK POINT 5.1
1. T   2. T   3. F   4. F

CHECK POINT 5.2
1. F   2. F   3. T   4. T   5. T

CHECK POINT 5.3
1. b   2. d   3. a

CHECK POINT 5.4
1. T   2. T   3. T   4. F   5. F

CHAPTER 5 REVIEW QUESTIONS
Fill-in-the-Blanks
1. External
2. Stressors
3. Incentive
4. Intrinsic
5. efficacy
6. coping
7. exercise
8. Procrastination

Multiple Choice
1. d   2. d   3. d   4. a   5. c
6. d

Short-Answer Questions
Answers will vary*

CHAPTER 6: Upcoming Tests

CHECK POINT 6.1
1. T   2. F   3. F   4. T

CHECK POINT 6.2
1. T   2. F   3. T   4. F   5. T

CHECK POINT 6.3
1. F   2. T   3. F   4. T   5. T

CHECK POINT 6.4
1. F   2. F   3. T   4. T

CHAPTER 6 REVIEW QUESTIONS
True-False?
1. F   2. T   3. F   4. F   5. F

Multiple Choice
1. d   2. d   3. b   4. a   5. d

Definitions
Answers will vary.*

Short-Answer Questions
Answers will vary.*

*Answers will vary. Check your answer with another student or with your instructor.

CHAPTER 7: Reading Skills

CHECK POINT 7.1
1. d   2. d

CHECK POINT 7.2
1. T   2. F   3. T   4. F

CHECK POINT 7.3
1. T   2. F   3. F   4. T

CHECK POINT 7.4
1. T   2. T   3. T   4. F

CHAPTER 7 REVIEW QUESTIONS
True or False?

1. T   2. T   3. T   4. F
5. F   6. F   7. T   8. F

Locating Definitions
Discuss your answers with other students or your instructor.

Short-Answer Questions
Answers will vary.*

Chapter 8: College Textbooks

CHECK POINT 8.1
1. T   2. F   3. T   4. F   5. F

CHECK POINT 8.2
1. T   2. F   3. T   4. T

CHECK POINT 8.3
1. F   2. T   3. F

CHECK POINT 8.4
1. T   2. T   3. F   4. T

CHAPTER 8 REVIEW QUESTIONS
True or False?
1. T   2. F   3. T   4. F
5. T   6. T   7. F   8. T

Multiple Choice
1. b   2. d   3. a   4. d

Short-Answer Questions
Answers will vary.*

Chapter 9: Notetaking Skills

CHECK POINT 9.1
1. F   2. T   3. T   4. T

CHECK POINT 9.2
1. a   2. d

CHECK POINT 9.3
1. F   2. T   3. T   4. T

CHECK POINT 9.4
1. F   2. T   3. T   4. F

CHECK POINT 9.5
1. T   2. F   3. T   4. F

CHAPTER 9 REVIEW QUESTIONS
True or False?
1. F   2. T   3. F   4. F
5. T   6. T   7. T   8. T

Application
Answers will vary.*

Chapter 10: Listening; Lecture Notes

CHECK POINT 10.1
1. F   2. T   3. T   4. T   5. F

CHECK POINT 10.2
1. F   2. T   3. F   4. F

CHECK POINT 10.3
1. F   2. T   3. T   4. F

CHAPTER 10 REVIEW QUESTIONS
Multiple Choice
1. b   2. d   3. a   4. d
5. a   6. d   7. b   8. d

Short-Answer Questions
Answers will vary.*

Chapter 11: Visual Notes

CHECK POINT 11.1
1. F   2. T   3. T   4. F

CHECK POINT 11.2
1. a   2. d

CHECK POINT 11.3
1. T   2. T   3. F   4. T

CHECK POINT 11.4
1. T   2. F   3. F   4. T   5. T

CHECK POINT 11.5
1. T   2. T   3. F   4. T

CHAPTER 11 REVIEW QUESTIONS
Multiple Choice
1. d   2. d   3. a   4. b   5. c

Application
Answers will vary.*

Chapter 12: Carrying Forward

CHECK POINT 12.1
1. T   2. T   3. F   4. T

CHECK POINT 12.2
Answers will vary.*

CHECK POINT 12.3
1. F   2. T   3. F   4. T   5. T

CHAPTER 12 REVIEW QUESTIONS
Multiple Choice
1. b   2. d   3. b   4. d   5. b

Short Answer
1. Check your work by using the textbook.
2. Answers will vary.*

*Answers will vary. Check your answer with another student or with your instructor.

Appendix C

Exercises, Inventories, and Checklists

EXERCISE 2.5

Working Memory Inventory

Think back to the last time you sat down to study. Answer the following questions.

Circle **1** if you did not use the working memory strategy during the study block.

Circle **2** if you used the working memory strategy occasionally during the study block.

Circle **3** if you used the working memory strategy consistently during the study block.

1.	I was aware of the kinds of sensory stimuli from the physical world that I was receiving.	1	2	3
2.	I used selective attention to focus on important stimuli and ignored the unimportant stimuli and distractions.	1	2	3
3.	As I studied, I was aware of different ways I encoded the information.	1	2	3
4.	I studied without the interference of visual or auditory stimuli from a television or background music.	1	2	3
5.	To avoid information dropping out of my short-term memory, I started thinking about or working with information as soon as I read it.	1	2	3
6.	I limited the number of items I studied at one time by working with no more than five chunks of information at one time.	1	2	3
7.	I rehearsed or repeated the information in some form at least one time.	1	2	3
8.	I worked slowly to give my working memory time to work effectively.	1	2	3
9.	I broke large chunks of information in my notes or in the textbook into smaller units to study.	1	2	3
10.	I freed up some working memory by removing intrusive thoughts.	1	2	3
11.	I paid attention to categories of information or schemas connected to the new information I was studying.	1	2	3
12.	I maintained a positive attitude toward studying and toward the subject matter and materials.	1	2	3
13.	I was aware of using retrieval cues and conducting memory searches to locate information in my long-term memory.	1	2	3
14.	I intentionally created new retrieval cues so I could recall the information more quickly at later times.	1	2	3
15.	I spent extra time rehearsing the items in the middle of a list of items because I know the first items and the last items are often easier to recall.	1	2	3
16.	I used some form of self-quizzing and "chatted my way" to answers.	1	2	3
17.	I took time to connect different pieces of information to each other.	1	2	3
18.	I either felt a natural interest or created an interest in studying.	1	2	3
19.	I set a learning goal when I studied so I knew what I wanted to accomplish.	1	2	3
20.	I used multisensory strategies to work with the information.	1	2	3

TOTAL SCORE: _____

YOUR SCORE

20–35   You can make better use of your working memory. Look at all the items that received a "1."
Strive to include these strategies when you study.

36–50   You are making average use of your working memory, but there is room to improve. Strive to
include the strategies marked with a "1" or a "2" on a more consistent basis when you study.

51–60   You are using your working memory effectively. Continue to use all of the strategies
consistently when you study.

Memory Principles Inventory

DIRECTIONS: Complete the following inventory by answering YES or NO to each question. Be honest with your answers so they reflect your *current* use of the principles.

SELECTIVITY   YES   NO

1. Do you spend a lot of time studying but seem to study the "wrong information" for tests?   _____   _____

2. Do you get frustrated when you read because everything seems important?   _____   _____

3. Do you tend to highlight too much when you read textbooks?   _____   _____

4. Do your notes seem excessively long and overly detailed?   _____   _____

5. Do you avoid making study tools such as flashcards because you are not sure what
    information to put on the study tools?   _____   _____

ASSOCIATION   YES   NO

1. Do you tend to memorize facts or ideas in isolation?   _____   _____

2. When you try to recall information you have studied, do you sometimes feel "lost"
    because there is no direct way to access the information in your memory?   _____   _____

3. Do you feel that you are memorizing numerous lists of information but not really
    understanding what they mean or how they are connected?   _____   _____

4. Do you "go blank" on tests when a question asks for information in a form or context
    different from the way you studied it?   _____   _____

5. Do you lack sufficient time to link difficult information to familiar words or pictures?   _____   _____

VISUALIZATION   YES   NO

1. When you finish reading, do you have difficulty remembering what paragraphs were even about?   _____   _____

2. Do you have difficulty remembering information that appeared in a chart your
    instructor presented on the chalkboard or on a screen?   _____   _____

3. Do you find it difficult to recall a visual image of printed information?   _____   _____

4. When you try to recall information, do you rely mainly on words rather than pictures?   _____   _____

5. When your instructor explains a new concept by giving a detailed example or anecdote
    (story), do you have difficulty recalling the example or anecdote after you leave class?   _____   _____

ELABORATION   YES   NO

1. Do you learn individual facts or details without thinking about the schema in which they belong?   _____   _____

2. Do you frequently attempt to use rote memory to memorize facts, definitions, or rules?   _____   _____

3. Do you complete a math problem and immediately move on to the next problem?   _____   _____

4. Do you study information in the same order and in the same form in which it was presented?   _____   _____

5. Do you avoid creating new study tools that involve reorganizing information?   _____   _____

CONCENTRATION

		YES	NO

1. Do you often experience divided attention because too many unrelated thoughts disrupt your thinking?

2. Do you have so many interruptions when you study that you are not quite sure what you have accomplished at the end of a study block?

3. Do you miss important information during a lecture because your mind tends to wander or daydream?

4. When you are reading, do you find it difficult to keep your mind focused on the information in the textbook?

5. Do you study with the television, radio, or stereo turned on?

RECITATION

		YES	NO

1. When you review for a test, do you do all or most of your review work silently?

2. Do you have difficulty defining new terminology out loud?

3. Do you have difficulty clearly explaining textbook information to another person?

4. When you rehearse information out loud, do you often feel that your explanations are "fuzzy," unclear, or incomplete?

5. Do you feel awkward or uncomfortable talking out loud to yourself?

INTENTION

		YES	NO

1. When you sit down to study, do you set a goal to complete the assignment as quickly as possible?

2. Do you always have the same purpose in mind when you sit down to study?

3. Do you lack curiosity, interest, or enthusiasm in the course content for one or more of your classes?

4. When you begin learning new information, do you find setting a specific learning goal difficult to do?

5. Do you study facts, details, or concepts in the same way that you study steps or processes for a procedure?

BIG AND LITTLE PICTURES

		YES	NO

1. Do you have problems distinguishing between main ideas and individual details in textbook passages?

2. Do you understand general concepts but oftentimes have difficulty giving details that relate to the concept?

3. Do you grasp specific details but oftentimes have difficulty connecting them together to form a larger picture or a concept?

4. Do your lecture notes capture main ideas but lack details?

5. Do your notes include running lists of details without a clear method of showing main ideas?

FEEDBACK

		YES	NO

1. Do you use tests as your main means of getting feedback about what you have learned?

2. Do you keep taking in new information without stopping to see whether or not you are trying to learn too much too fast?

3. When you are rehearsing, do you "keep on going" even if you sense that you have not clearly understood something?

C6   APPENDIX C Exercises, Inventories, and Checklists

Exercise 4.1 (cont.)

DAY 3				
Time	Activity		Time	Activity
midnight			noon	
12:30 A.M.			12:30 P.M.	
1:00 A.M.			1:00 P.M.	
1:30 A.M.			1:30 P.M.	
2:00 A.M.			2:00 P.M.	
2:30 A.M.			2:30 P.M.	
3:00 A.M.			3:00 P.M.	
3:30 A.M.			3:30 P.M.	
4:00 A.M.			4:00 P.M.	
4:30 A.M.			4:30 P.M.	
5:00 A.M.			5:00 P.M.	
5:30 A.M.			5:30 P.M.	
6:00 A.M.			6:00 P.M.	
6:30 A.M.			6:30 P.M.	
7:00 A.M.			7:00 P.M.	
7:30 A.M.			7:30 P.M.	
8:00 A.M.			8:00 P.M.	
8:30 A.M.			8:30 P.M.	
9:00 A.M.			9:00 P.M.	
9:30 A.M.			9:30 P.M.	
10:00 A.M.			10:00 P.M.	
10:30 A.M.			10:30 P.M.	
11:00 A.M.			11:00 P.M.	
11:30 A.M.			11:30 P.M.	

THREE-DAY TIME LOG			
Activity	Day 1	Day 2	Day 3
School: Classes, labs, studying, test preparation			
School: Meetings, practices			
Work: Job			
Work: Parenting, chores, other work			
Leisure: Family			
Leisure: Friends			
Leisure: Personal time; recreation			
Naps, Sleep			
Snacks, Meals			
Other/Unaccounted for Hours			
	TOTAL HOURS	**TOTAL HOURS:**	**TOTAL HOURS**

Part I: Weekly Time-Management Schedule

EXERCISE 4.4

FOR THE WEEK OF			NAME				
TIME	MONDAY	TUESDAY	WEDNESDAY	THURSDAY	FRIDAY	SATURDAY	SUNDAY
12–6 A.M.							
6–7:00							
7–8:00							
8–9:00							
9–10:00							
10–11:00							
11–12 NOON							
12–1:00 P.M.							
1–2:00							
2–3:00							
3–4:00							
4–5:00							
5–6:00							
6–7:00							
7–8:00							
8–9:00							
9–10:00							
10–11:00							
11–12 A.M.							

Exercise 4.4 (cont.)

Part II: Time-Management Self-Assessment Checklist

Name _____   Date _____

Check only the statements that are true for your weekly time-management schedule.

STUDY BLOCKS

My schedule shows:

_____ Sufficient study blocks set aside for *each* class using the 2:1 ratio.

_____ Each study block labeled with the subject to be studied at that time.

_____ Study blocks spread throughout the week (spaced practice).

_____ Two or more study blocks scheduled on the weekend.

_____ No marathon studying (no more than 3 study hours in a row).

_____ The majority of study hours are during the day or early evening hours.

_____ Two or more FLEX blocks scheduled throughout the week.

_____ Study times for most difficult classes scheduled earlier in the day.

_____ Study blocks for lecture and math classes scheduled shortly after class.

FIXED ACTIVITIES

My schedule shows:

_____ Sufficient hours of sleep each night.

_____ A fairly regular sleep schedule throughout the week.

_____ Time set aside for three meals a day.

_____ My work schedule.

_____ Specific meetings or appointments that occur on a weekly basis.

BALANCING YOUR LIFE

My schedule shows:

_____ Time set aside to spend with family and friends.

_____ Time set aside for exercise, hobbies, or recreation.

_____ Time set aside for necessary errands, chores, or personal responsibilities.

_____ Time set aside to work on specific goals.

GENERAL GUIDELINES

Check only the statements that apply to you or your schedule.

_____ I walked through each day in my mind and believe it is realistic.

_____ As much as is possible, I used my peak energy times during the day to study.

_____ I color-coded my schedule so different activities are easier to identify.

_____ Using a schedule will help me have a more organized week.

_____ Using a schedule will help me achieve more tasks during the week.

_____ I will strive to follow this schedule to my greatest abilities this week.

_____ I will note problem areas on the schedule and use this information to adjust next week's schedule.

_____ I will use a "star system" to track the blocks of time I follow successfully.

QUESTIONS/COMMENTS/EXPLANATIONS

Stress Test

EXERCISE 5.2

PURPOSE: Good and bad events in one's life can increase stress levels. Knowing how to manage stress reduces the chances that stress will take a negative toll on your health and emotional well-being. In 1967, Dr. Thomas H. Holmes and Dr. Richard H. Rahe developed the following "stress test" to help individuals identify their stress levels. By knowing stress levels, people can make an even greater asserted effort to use strategies to manage stress effectively.

DIRECTIONS

1. In the following list of events, circle every experience that you have had in the *last twelve months*.

2. Total the point values next to each of the experiences you circled. Use that total to find your stress level in the scoring section that follows.

Event	Point Value
Death of a Spouse	100
Divorce	73
Marital Separation	65
Jail Term	63
Death of a Close Family Member	63
Personal Injury or Illness	53
Marriage	50
Fired at Work	47
Marital Reconciliation	45
Retirement	45
Change in Health of a Family Member	44
Pregnancy	40
Sex Difficulties	39
Gain of a New Family Member	39
Business Readjustments	39
Change in Financial State	38
Death of a Close Friend	37
Change to a Different Line of Work	36
Change in Number of Arguments with Spouse	35
Mortgage over $50,000	31
Foreclosure of Mortgage	30

Event	Point Value
Change in Responsibilities at Work	29
Son or Daughter Leaving Home	29
Trouble with In-Laws	29
Outstanding Personal Achievements	28
Partner Begins/Stops Work	28
Begin or End School	26
Change in Living Conditions	25
Revision of Personal Habits	24
Trouble with Boss	23
Change in Work Hours or Conditions	20
Change in Residence	20
Change in School	20
Change in Recreation	19
Change in Religious Activities	19
Change in Social Activities	18
Loan Less than $50,000	17
Change in Sleeping Habits	16
Change in Number of Family Gatherings	15
Change in Eating Habits	15
Vacation	13
Holidays	12
Minor Violation of Laws	11

TOTAL SCORE

SCORING

Low Stress Level <149

Mild Stress Level 150–200

Moderate Stress Level 200–299

Major Stress Level >300

Source: Reprinted from *Journal of Psychosomatic Research, 11* (2), Holmes, T. H. & Rahe, R. H., "The social readjustment rating scale," pp. 213–218. © 1967 with permission from Elsevier.

EXERCISE 6.1

Assessing Your Strategies Inventory

DIRECTIONS: To assess how you are preparing for any test, check the Memory Principles that you are currently using.

_____ 1. **Selectivity:** I carefully select the main ideas and the important details to learn.

_____ 2. **Association:** I link new information to previously learned information, and I create and practice paired associations and chained associations.

_____ 3. **Visualization:** I create and picture images and movies in my mind of information from my textbook and my notes.

_____ 4. **Elaboration:** I encode information in new ways and use elaboration by asking and answering _Why_ and _How_ questions.

_____ 5. **Concentration:** I use strategies to keep my mind focused on studying.

_____ 6. **Recitation:** I recite information without looking at printed materials.

_____ 7. **Intention:** I create learning goals and plans of action each time I study.

_____ 8. **Big and Little Pictures:** I create study tools that show the relationship between big pictures (concepts) and little pictures (details).

_____ 9. **Feedback:** I use self-quizzing strategies and respond to the positive and the negative feedback that I receive.

_____ 10. **Organization:** I personalize the learning process by rearranging or reorganizing the information into meaningful groups or clusters of related information.

_____ 11. **Time on Task:** I schedule ample time to study, rehearse, and review; I spread studying over different periods of time.

_____ 12. **Ongoing Review:** I practice retrieving and reviewing information on an ongoing basis.

EXERCISE 6.3

Academic Preparation Inventory

DIRECTIONS: After identifying a specific class and the most recent test grade you received in that class, think back to the days prior to that test. Check **YES** or **NO** for each statement.

What is the specific class you are using for this inventory? _____

What was the last test grade you received in this class? _____

	YES	NO
1. I had all the reading assignments and homework assignments done on time.	_____	_____
2. I attended class regularly and was prepared for each class.	_____	_____
3. I reviewed comments and my responses on my homework assignments when they were returned.	_____	_____
4. I asked questions about information I did not understand.	_____	_____
5. I worked with a tutor, with a study partner, or in a review group to prepare for the test.	_____	_____
6. I participated in class discussions, asked questions, and responded to questions during class.	_____	_____
7. I followed my time-management schedule and used the 2:1 ratio.	_____	_____
8. I was an active learner and created a variety of study tools to rehearse and review information.	_____	_____
9. I spent time each week reviewing information that I had previously studied.	_____	_____
10. I knew the definitions for all the textbook terminology.	_____	_____
11. I used study techniques that gave me feedback; I used both positive and negative feedback constructively.	_____	_____
12. I read my textbook carefully and took notes on important textbook information.	_____	_____
13. I was able to stay fairly motivated about the class and the work.	_____	_____
14. I was organized, understood assignments, and had the materials necessary to study and review.	_____	_____
15. I created a specific plan of action to prepare for the test.	_____	_____
16. I avoided cramming the night before the test.	_____	_____
17. I felt confident that I was prepared for the test.	_____	_____
18. I can honestly say that I gave it my best.	_____	_____

All the **YES** responses for the above strategies indicate you are using those strategies effectively.

All the **NO** responses indicate strategies that you could use more effectively to achieve better test results.

EXERCISE 6.4

Practice Test-Taking Skills

After reading the **Essential Test-Taking Skills** guide in **Appendix A,** work by yourself, with a partner, or in a small group to practice your test-taking skills. Read the directions for each set of questions.

Part A: True-False Questions

DIRECTIONS: Write *T* for true statements and *F* for false statements. Carefully check each statement for the accuracy of each item in a series, relationship clues, and use of modifiers.

_____ 1. You can create associations by using visualizations, acronyms, acrostics, and the Loci Method.

_____ 2. Students with strong study skills always use the 2:1 ratio for studying.

_____ 3. Declarative knowledge involves working with factual details while procedural knowledge works with applying steps, procedures, and formulas.

_____ 4. Some form of assessment is used in all college-level, graded courses.

_____ 5. Students with a high self-efficacy are often self-motivated and goal-oriented.

_____ 6. Students who procrastinate and who experience test anxiety never perform well on tests.

_____ 7. Intrusive thoughts, stress, and use of selective attention cause working memory to overload and work less efficiently.

_____ 8. The central executive is the part of working memory that holds stimuli for less than two seconds.

_____ 9. The Principle of Elaboration involves working with information in new ways.

_____ 10. Performing well on tests is often the result of creating strong retrieval cues, using ongoing review, and using effective test-taking strategies.

_____ 11. When you create a goal organizer, you identify benefits you will gain, obstacles you may encounter, and resources you could use to complete a goal.

_____ 12. Concentration is defined as the ability to focus on two or more things at one time without being distracted.

_____ 13. Reciting is important because it utilizes the auditory channel and creates associations.

_____ 14. You should always begin by studying your favorite subject first so that you can get motivated.

_____ 15. The central executive in the Information Processing Model is not a part of long-term memory.

_____ 16. The right hemisphere of the brain coordinates movement on the right side of the body and processes mental activities that involve creativity and generalized thinking.

_____ 17. In true-false questions, it is important to read every word because a single word can change the meaning of the statement.

_____ 18. Some true-false statements may have more than one answer depending on your personal experiences.

_____ 19. *Always, best, larger, never,* and *none* are 100 percent or absolute modifiers.

_____ 20. One effective strategy for true-false questions involves circling clue words for definitions, relationships, and false statements.

Part B: Multiple-Choice Questions

DIRECTIONS: Use the three-step approach for answering multiple-choice questions: Read the stem and finish it in your mind; create true-false statements; and identify distractors and select the answer. Write the letter for the *best* answer on the line.

_____ **1.** Options in a multiple-choice question may

    a. contain definition or relationship clues.

    b. form true statements.

    c. include items in a series separated by commas.

    d. involve all of the above.

_____ **2.** Which of the following is *not* a recommended strategy for multiple-choice tests?

    a. Circle correct answers instead of writing them on the line.

    b. Turn each option into a true-false statement.

    c. Finish the stem in your mind before looking at the options.

    d. Cross off and eliminate distractors and then focus on the remaining options.

_____ **3.** Objective test questions

    a. require students to pay careful attention to all the words in the question.

    b. involve recognition level tasks.

    c. often are answered best after comparing the information in the question to information in one's memory.

    d. involve all of the above.

_____ **4.** Which of the following parts of a multiple-choice question should you use with each option to form a true-false statement?

    a. distractors

    b. directions

    c. stem

    d. modifiers

_____ **5.** Educated selection (educated guessing) should be used after

    a. the recall step of response.

    b. the immediate response step.

    c. all other options have been tried.

    d. the delayed response step.

_____ **6.** When you first read the stem of a multiple-choice question, you should

    a. decide you really do not like the question.

    b. turn it into one or two true-false questions.

    c. finish the stem with your own words and then see whether an option matches your words.

    d. identify the distractors immediately by using educated-selection strategies.

_____ **7.** Which of the following is *not* true about modifiers?

    a. 100 percent modifiers are also called absolute modifiers.

    b. The words *always, everyone, never,* and *every* are not absolute modifiers.

    c. The words *maybe, sometimes, most,* and *seldom* are not absolute modifiers.

    d. Modifiers indicate the degree or the frequency that something occurs.

Exercise 6.4 (cont.)

_____ **8.** The central executive in your memory system

    a. coordinates most brain activities and cognitive functions.

    b. manages the flow of information into and out of long-term memory.

    c. initiates goal-directed behavior.

    d. integrates sensory information.

_____ **9.** Which of the following statements is *not* true about visualization?

    a. You can use it to visualize the skeleton of a visual mapping or hierarchy.

    b. It never involves staring at an object as a way to make a visual impression.

    c. You can use visualization as a Look-Away Technique, to increase comprehension when you read, or to reduce stress.

    d. It involves picturing information in your mind without looking at the physical form.

_____ **10.** Look-Away Techniques

    a. always involve reciting.

    b. are used mainly when you read.

    c. help you ignore unimportant information.

    d. provide feedback.

_____ **11.** The five steps in the Feedback Model are

    a. action, goal, feedback, comparison, yes.

    b. goal, action, feedback, comparison, results.

    c. feedback, action, comparison, yes, no.

    d. goal, feedback, comparison, action, results.

_____ **12.** The principle of Big and Little Pictures

    a. encourages you to identify individual facts and details.

    b. is based completely on rote memory.

    c. recommends that you process information only in clusters.

    d. recommends that you try to "see the trees" *and* "see the forest" when you study.

Part C Matching Questions

DIRECTIONS: Match the items on the left to the items on the right, writing the letter answer on the line. You may use each answer only once.

_____ **1.** Paired associations

_____ **2.** 100 percent modifiers

_____ **3.** In-between modifiers

_____ **4.** Relationship clues

_____ **5.** Prefixes with negative meanings

_____ **6.** Recognition questions

_____ **7.** Delayed response

_____ **8.** Assisted response

_____ **9.** Stem

_____ **10.** Distractors

  a. words such as *sometimes, often, some, perhaps*

  b. units of meaning at the beginning of words that mean "no" or "not"

  c. guessing *true* or the letter *c*

  d. the linking of two ideas together

  e. the beginning part of a multiple-choice question

  f. answers that you immediately know

  g. options that are incorrect answers

  h. involves rereading, looking for clues, and doing memory searches

  i. words that are absolutes

  j. objective questions

  k. a response you give after you skim the test for clues

  l. words that often show cause/effect

Part D: Fill-in-the-Blanks Questions

DIRECTIONS: Complete each statement by writing one word on each blank line.

1. The _____ _____ technique is a concentration technique for letting other people know that you do not want to be disturbed.

2. The beginning part of a multiple-choice question is called the _____ _____.

3. _____ _____ time consists of a few hours each week added to your time-management schedule to allow for any extra study time beyond your regular study blocks.

4. The _____ _____ Method helps you prioritize goals according to their degree of importance.

5. The _____ _____ effect states that you will recall more easily information that you most recently studied or reviewed.

6. Each time you link together two items in memory, you create an _____ _____ that then works as a retrieval cue to retrieve information at a later time.

7. An _____ _____ is a "memory trick" or a memory tool that you can create by taking the first letter of each of the key words in a list to create a mnemonic sentence.

8. _____ _____ are situations or actions that cause stress.

9. The Memory Principle of _____ _____ involves setting goals and creating action plans.

10. The _____ _____ Theory of Motivation states motivation is linked to a person's intensity or desire to achieve a goal and belief in the likelihood of achieving the goal.

Part E: Listing Questions

DIRECTIONS: On separate paper, list answers for each question without referring to other pages in your textbook or your notes.

1. What are the steps, in order, for the Feedback Model?

2. List five strategies to reduce or eliminate procrastination.

3. List five traits or characteristics of linear learners.

4. What are the eight intelligences in Howard Gardner's Theory of Multiple Intelligences?

Part F: Definition Questions

DIRECTIONS: On your own paper, define each of the following terms. Use the three-part format for your answers: category, definition, and expansion with one more detail.

1. Define the term *reciting*.

2. You have learned many study strategies in this course. Many of these strategies have one common characteristic: they all emphasize elaborative rehearsal. Define *elaborative rehearsal*.

3. Learning involves intellectual and emotional growth. Positive self-talk has the power to enhance the learning process, but negative self-talk can hinder the learning process. In this course, the focus has been on the power of positive self-talk. Define *positive self-talk*.

Part G: Short-Answer Questions

DIRECTIONS: Answer any *two* of the following questions. On separate paper, write your answers in paragraph form.

1. Explain why *rote memory* is not a reliable method for studying most college materials.

2. Discuss important functions of the central executive in working memory.

3. Describe situations when marathon studying can be effective.

4. Discuss types of time-management schedules students can create to organize their time more effectively.

5. Identify any three sets of self-management skills and explain how each provides students with the opportunity to enhance their academic performance.

Test Anxiety Inventory

DIRECTIONS: Check the responses that seem to best describe you this term.

	NEVER	SOMETIMES	ALWAYS
1. I have trouble sleeping the night before a test.	_____	_____	_____
2. I can feel a lot of tension in my shoulders, arms, or face on the day of a test.	_____	_____	_____
3. My heart beats fast during a test, and I feel hot, clammy, or downright sick during a test.	_____	_____	_____
4. I am irritable, snappy, impatient, and sometimes even rude right before a test.	_____	_____	_____
5. I try to find excuses not to go to school on the day of a test.	_____	_____	_____
6. I prepare for tests by cramming the day or the night before the test.	_____	_____	_____
7. I read my textbook, but when I start to review for tests, I get worried about how much I do not remember.	_____	_____	_____
8. I procrastinate so much about studying that I am always behind in my assignments.	_____	_____	_____
9. I find myself blaming the teacher, my family, or my friends for the fact that I am not prepared for tests.	_____	_____	_____
10. I run short on time to study and do not make summary notes or review effectively.	_____	_____	_____
11. My negative voice is quick to remind me that I never do well on tests.	_____	_____	_____
12. I cannot seem to forget how disappointed I was with my last grade on a test; I really blew it.	_____	_____	_____
13. It is difficult for me to get motivated to study for tests because the results are always discouraging.	_____	_____	_____
14. I fear the consequences of failing a test because so much is riding on getting good grades.	_____	_____	_____
15. I get so nervous about tests because anything less than my personal standards deflates my self-esteem.	_____	_____	_____
16. I get stuck on one question and do not want to move on until I remember the answer.	_____	_____	_____
17. I get distracted and annoyed by the littlest things others do in class during a test.	_____	_____	_____
18. I am so anxious to get out of the classroom, that I seldom check my answers or proofread.	_____	_____	_____
19. I turn in tests that are incomplete even when I have more time.	_____	_____	_____
20. Without knowing why, I panic and start changing answers right before I turn the test in.	_____	_____	_____
21. I make careless mistakes on tests. Sometimes I can't believe the answers that I marked.	_____	_____	_____
22. My mind goes blank, but as soon as I leave the classroom after taking a test, I remember the answers.	_____	_____	_____

Answers in the **NEVER** column	=	Not major indicators of test anxiety.
Answers in the **SOMETIMES** column	=	Possible indicators; seek ways to alter your approach.
Answers in the **ALWAYS** column	=	Strong indicators of test anxiety; use strategies to reduce test anxiety.

EXERCISE 7.3

Identifying Topic Sentences and Supporting Details

Directions: Highlight the topic sentence and important supporting details in each paragraph. Remember, only highlight one complete sentence (the topic sentence) in each paragraph.

1. In a family with two adults and children, for example, one of the adults may already have a job and the other may be choosing between working at home or working outside the home. This decision may be very sensitive to the wage and perhaps the cost of child care or consuming more prepared meals. In fact, the increased number of women working outside the home may be due to the increased opportunities and wages for women. The increase in the wage induces workers to work more in the labor market. Economists have observed a fairly strong wage effect on the amount women work.

From Taylor, *Economics*, Houghton Mifflin Company, © 2004, p. 327, 329. Reprinted with permission.

2. The human brain in late adulthood, however, is smaller and slower in its functioning than the brain in early adulthood. This reduction is thought to be caused by the death of neurons, which do not regenerate. Neurons die at an increasing rate after age 60. The proportion of neurons that die varies across different parts of the brain. In the visual area, the death rate is about 50 percent. In the motor areas, the death rate varies from 20 to 50 percent. In the memory and reasoning areas, the death rate is less than 20 percent. The production of certain neurotransmitters also declines with age.

From Payne/Wenger. *Cognitive Psychology,* Houghton Mifflin Company, © 2004, p. 359. Reprinted with permission.

3. A solid has a definite shape and volume. In a *crystalline* solid, the molecules are arranged in a particular repeating pattern. This orderly arrangement of molecules is called a *lattice*. The molecules are bound to each other by electrical forces. Upon heating, the molecules gain kinetic energy and vibrate about their positions in the lattice. The more heat that is added, the stronger the vibrations become. When the melting point is reached, additional energy breaks apart the bonds that hold the molecules in place. As bonds break, holes are produced in the lattice, and nearby molecules can move toward the holes. As more and more holes are produced, the lattice becomes significantly distorted.

From Shipman et al., *An Introduction to Physical Science, 10th ed.,* p. 103. Copyright © 2003. Reprinted by permission of Houghton Mifflin Co.

EXERCISE 8.1

Textbook Reading Inventory

Textbook Reading Inventory

Think about the way you read your college textbooks. Answer the following questions.

Circle **1** if you do not use this strategy when you read your textbooks.

Circle **2** if you use this strategy occasionally when you read your textbooks.

Circle **3** if you use this strategy consistently when you read your textbooks.

1.	I create a plan of action before I begin reading a new textbook chapter.	1	2	3
2.	I identify main ideas and the important supporting details in each paragraph that I read.	1	2	3
3.	I use word, punctuation, definition, word structure, and context clues to identify definitions of terminology and unfamiliar words.	1	2	3
4.	I interact with printed materials by taking notes, making diagrams, writing questions, and creating study tools.	1	2	3
5.	I read out loud or verbalize as I read.	1	2	3
6.	I visualize information as I read.	1	2	3
7.	I identify the organizational patterns to understand how the author organized the details in paragraphs.	1	2	3
8.	I identify levels of information by differentiating between topics, headings, main ideas, and details.	1	2	3
9.	I ask questions throughout the reading process.	1	2	3
10.	I carefully examine graphic materials, such as charts, tables, illustrations, and graphs.	1	2	3
11.	I use available resources and online materials that are available for the textbook.	1	2	3
12.	I stay with a paragraph until I understand its meaning or content.	1	2	3
13.	I look for relationships within paragraphs as well as relationships among previously discussed topics.	1	2	3
14.	I adjust my reading rate to a rate that is comfortable for making associations and understanding content.	1	2	3
15.	I "chunk up," or look to see how a paragraph fits into the larger picture or relates to previous paragraphs.	1	2	3
16.	I "chunk down" or break difficult sections of information into smaller units until I understand the material.	1	2	3
17.	I convert information into pictures to understand the content more clearly.	1	2	3
18.	I am an active reader, not a passive reader.	1	2	3
19.	I avoid reading in an "automatic pilot" mode, which involves reading but not processing or remembering information.	1	2	3
20.	I use a metacognitive approach to reading textbooks: I adjust my strategies as needed to understand the textbook information.	1	2	3

SCORE: [ ][ ][ ]

YOUR SCORE   TOTAL SCORE: _____

20–35   You need to apply effort to using active reading strategies to understand your college textbook material more thoroughly. Look at all the items that received a "1." Strive to increase comprehension by adding these strategies to your textbook reading strategies.

36–50   You are using many active reading strategies effectively, but there is room to improve. Strive to include the strategies marked with a "1" or a "2" on a more consistent basis when you read your textbooks.

51–60   You are using active reading strategies effectively. Continue to use all of the strategies consistently when you study.

Triple Q and Organizational Patterns

DIRECTIONS: Read one paragraph at a time. Complete the two directions below. Continue the same process for paragraphs 2 and 3.

1. In the Triple Q Reading System, Q_2 involves writing one or more test questions in the margins next to the paragraph and then highlighting key words that answer the question. Use this process for each paragraph.

2. Identify the primary organizational pattern used in the paragraph. Write it on the line below the paragraph.

Paragraph 1: The earth system contains a number of interconnected subsystems, often described as "environmental spheres." The four major subsystems are the *atmosphere*, or the ocean of air that overlies the entire earth's surface; the *hydrosphere*, or the water of the surface and near-surface regions of the earth; the *lithosphere*, or the massive accumulation of rock and metal that form the solid body of the planet itself; and the *biosphere*, or the layer of living organisms of which we are a part. All four respond in various ways to the flow of energy and materials through the earth system.

Source: Holt Atkinson, *Reading Enhancement and Development,* 5th ed., Houghton Mifflin Company, © 1995, p. 218–219. Reprinted with permission.

Organizational Pattern: _____

Paragraph 2: The Celsius scale is the temperature scale for general use in much of the world and for scientific use worldwide. On this scale, the freezing point of water is 0°C, and the boiling point of water at normal barometric pressure is 100°C. On the Fahrenheit scale, *the scale in common usage in the United States,* the freezing point of water is 32°F, and the boiling point of water at normal barometric pressure is 212°F. Negative temperatures are possible with both of these scales. For example, liquid nitrogen boils at –321°F and –196°C.

Source: From Darryll D. Ebbing and Rupert Wentworth, *Introductory Chemistry*, 2nd ed., pp. 33–34. Copyright © 1998 Houghton Mifflin Company. Used with permission.

Organizational Pattern: _____

Paragraph 3: Visual discomfort is commonly reported as a result of computer work. Eyestrain and headaches are the most common problems. The eyes tire more quickly when looking at a computer screen than when reading printed materials. This is because of the different characteristics of the type. Printed material has dark, dense, consistent lines that are easy to focus on. Computer screens display images with a less consistent density, and this results in the eyes having to work much harder to focus. This extra effort can result in eyestrain.

From Mitchell, Haroun, *Introduction to Health Care, 2e,* © 2007 Delmar Learning, a part of Cengage Learning, Inc. Reproduced by permission. www.cengage.com/permissions.

Organizational Pattern: _____

EXERCISE 9.1

Annotation Checklist

DIRECTIONS: After annotating a passage, use the following checklist to assess your work.

	NO	SOMEWHAT	YES
1. I completely highlighted only one sentence, the topic sentence, in every paragraph.	___	___	___
2. I selectively highlighted key words or phrases to show details that support the topic sentence.	___	___	___
3. I circled all terminology.	___	___	___
4. I highlighted key words or phrases that define terminology.	___	___	___
5. I numbered details in the paragraphs that appear with ordinals.	___	___	___
6. The notes I wrote in the margins are brief.	___	___	___
7. I used abbreviations for some of the information that I wrote in the margins.	___	___	___
8. To avoid highlighting too much, I used brackets to remind me about larger blocks of important text.	___	___	___
9. For important graphic materials, I marked them and their captions in some meaningful way.	___	___	___
10. At a glance, I can quickly pick out the important points when I review each paragraph.	___	___	___
11. I used colors effectively.	___	___	___
12. I was selective and did not over-mark the paragraphs.	___	___	___

EXERCISE 9.2

Part I: Cornell Notetaking Self-Assessment Checklist

Name _____   Date _____

Topic of Notes _____   Assignment _____

RECORD STEP	YES	NO
1. Did you clearly show headings in your notes so you can see the main topics?	_____	_____
2. Did you underline the headings and avoid putting numbers or letters in front of the headings?	_____	_____
3. Did you leave a space between headings or larger groups of information so that your notes are not cluttered or crowded?	_____	_____
4. Did you include sufficient details so that you do not need to return to the textbook to study this information?	_____	_____
5. Did you use numbering for the different details under the headings?	_____	_____
6. Did you indent and use dashes or other symbols to show minor supporting details?	_____	_____
7. Did you use meaningful phrases or shortened sentences that will be clear at a later time?	_____	_____
8. Did you paraphrase or shorten the information so that your notes are not too lengthy?	_____	_____
9. Did your notes refer to important charts, diagrams, or visual materials in the chapter, or did you make reference to the textbook pages in your notes?	_____	_____
10. Did you write on only one side of the paper, leaving the back side blank?	_____	_____
11. Did you label the first page of your notes (course, chapter number, and date) and use page numbers on the other pages?	_____	_____
12. Did you write your notes so that they are neat and easy to read?	_____	_____

RECALL COLUMN (REDUCE STEP)	YES	NO
1. Did you move each heading into the recall column and underline it?	_____	_____
2. Did you use a two-and-one-half-inch margin on the left for the recall column?	_____	_____
3. Did you include study questions in the recall column for the key points in your notes?	_____	_____
4. Did you include enough information in the recall column to guide you when you recite your notes?	_____	_____
5. Did you include in the recall column some key words that you need to define or explain?	_____	_____
6. Did you write the questions and the key words directly across from the corresponding information in your notes column?	_____	_____
7. Did you avoid writing too much information or giving yourself all of the information in the recall column, thus leaving you with little to recite from memory?	_____	_____
8. Did you try using the recall column?	_____	_____
9. Did you add or delete information in the recall column after you tried using that column for reciting?	_____	_____

Exercise 9.2 (cont.)

Part II: Cornell Notetaking Instructor Assessment Form

Name _____   Date _____

Notes for _____

Check the statements that apply to a specific set of Cornell notes.

YOUR NOTES COLUMN

_____ You clearly showed and underlined the headings.

_____ Your notes will be easier to study because you left a space between new headings or sections of information.

_____ Your notes show accurate and sufficient details.

_____ You used meaningful phrases or shortened sentences effectively so that the information is clear and understandable.

_____ You shortened information effectively and captured the important ideas.

_____ Your notes are well organized. You effectively used numbering and indentations for supporting details.

_____ You included important visual graphics from the textbook.

_____ Your notes are neat and easy to read.

_____ You used notetaking standards effectively: you wrote on one side of the paper, you included a heading on the top of the page, and you numbered pages.

YOUR RECALL COLUMN

_____ You used a $2\frac{1}{2}$-inch column.

_____ You placed your headings, questions, and key words directly across from the information in your notes.

_____ Your questions and key words are effective.

_____ Use the recall column to check its effectiveness. Add more self-quizzing questions, visual cues, or hints to guide reciting if necessary.

_____ Use a $2\frac{1}{2}$-inch column on the left.

_____ Place the headings, questions, and key words directly across from the information in your notes.

_____ You need more meaningful questions and key words in the recall column.

_____ You are giving yourself too much information in the recall column; use questions without answers so that you will have more to recite.

AREAS FOR IMPROVEMENT IN YOUR NOTES

_____ Strive to identify and underline headings.

_____ Leave a space before you begin a new heading or section of information so your notes will be less crowded or cluttered.

_____ Include more information in your notes. Your notes lack some important details.

_____ Short phrases or isolated words lose meaning over time. Use more sentences or more detailed phrases to capture important ideas.

_____ Use shortened sentences to capture the important ideas. Your notes are unnecessarily lengthy.

_____ Strive for clearer organization. Number and indent supporting details.

_____ Include graphic information in your notes.

_____ Strive for neater penmanship and readability.

_____ Write on one side of the paper. Include a heading on the first page. Number all the pages of your notes.

OTHER COMMENTS

Photocopy this form before you use it.

Classroom Listening Factors Inventory

EXERCISE 10.1

DIRECTIONS: Read each set of statements carefully. Check the statement that most reflects your behavior or attitude in a typical lecture class in which you are enrolled.

1. **Interest Level**
   _____ A. I am not interested in the topic; in fact, it bores me.
   _____ B. I do not have a genuine interest in the topic, but I know it is important to learn.
   _____ C. I find ways to expand my interest in the topic, such as discussing it with others.

2. **Seating Location**
   _____ A. I sit in the back of the classroom so I can see everything that goes on.
   _____ B. I sit in the middle of the classroom so I can see the screen or chalkboard clearly.
   _____ C. I sit in the front of the classroom so I have fewer distractions and a clearer view of visual materials.

3. **Materials and Preparedness**
   _____ A. I often arrive to the classroom just as the lecture begins; I am seldom tardy.
   _____ B. I arrive with sufficient time to select a good seat and "settle in."
   _____ C. I arrive a few minutes early and prepared with sufficient paper, pens, my textbook, and class work.

4. **Familiarity with the Topic**
   _____ A. I am curious at the beginning of each class about the topic for that day's lecture.
   _____ B. I use the course syllabus to identify the topic for the day's lecture; then I survey the corresponding pages in the textbook.
   _____ C. I read the textbook section or chapter for the lecture before class so I am familiar with the topic, definitions, and the kind of information I can find in the textbook.

5. **Focused Attention**
   _____ A. I tend to "tune out" when the information is too technical or difficult to follow.
   _____ B. I am aware that my concentration fades in and fades out multiple times during the lecture; I refocus as quickly as possible.
   _____ C. I block out distractors so my concerted effort can be directed toward following the instructor's thinking and explanations.

6. **Emotional Responses**
   _____ A. I immediately let an instructor know if I disagree with or dislike something he or she says during a lecture.
   _____ B. I am aware during a lecture of the times when I do not agree with the instructor's information or point of view.
   _____ C. I put my personal opinions aside so I can listen carefully to the information presented by an instructor before questioning or disagreeing with the information.

Exercise 10.1 (cont.)

7. Asking Questions

_____ A. I like to challenge the instructor by asking any questions as they pop into my mind.

_____ B. I jot down questions during a lecture and then ask them at an appropriate time.

_____ C. I ask open-ended clarifying questions to learn more about the topic; for example, I might ask: *What are some ways this could be used? or Why is it important to…?*

8. Checking Understanding

_____ A. I wait until after class to look at my notes to see what I understand.

_____ B. I ask questions or show my confusion at the point during a lecture when I do not understand what the instructor is presenting.

_____ C. At an appropriate time, I rephrase or paraphrase information that I do not understand clearly; for example, I might ask: *Do you mean that…? Is it correct then to say that…?*

9. Levels of Information

_____ A. I know that everything the instructor presents is important to remember.

_____ B. I use verbal and nonverbal clues to identify the main points of a lecture.

_____ C. I use verbal, nonverbal, and visual clues, such as information the instructor writes on an overhead or presents on a slide, to identify important information.

SCORING YOUR INVENTORY

How many responses did you have in each category? Write the number of responses:

A _____   B _____   C _____

RESPONSES FOR A represent ineffective listening behaviors and attitudes.

RESPONSES FOR B represent adequate listening behaviors and attitudes that you can further strengthen.

RESPONSES FOR C indicate effective active learning behaviors and attitudes to use during lectures.

EXERCISE 10.3

Matching Problems to Solutions

DIRECTIONS: Read each problem on the left. Then find the solution on the right. Write the letter of the solution on the line. You may use each answer only once.

____ 1. I highlight too much.

____ 2. I don't know how to study from underlining.

____ 3. I fall behind during a lecture because I spend too much time trying to figure out how to organize the minor details in my formal outline notes.

____ 4. I have trouble finding the topic sentence in paragraphs.

____ 5. I have problems finding definitions for key words in the book.

____ 6. I don't feel like I really understand how to use the text-book features very well.

____ 7. I need a fast way to look up page numbers to find information in my book.

____ 8. The instructor said to check our work with the answer keys in the book, but I can't find any answer keys in my chapters.

____ 9. I get frustrated taking lecture notes because I don't understand the topics or the terminology used in the lecture.

____ 10. I go into automatic pilot every time I try to read pages in my textbook.

____ 11. I can't write fast enough to write down every thing the instructor says in a lecture.

____ 12. When the instructor talks too slowly, my mind wanders to other things.

____ 13. My notes are a jumbled mess. The information all runs together.

____ 14. When the instructor "walks through the chapter" section by section in her lecture, there is too much information to write in my Cornell notes.

a. Switch to another form of notetaking that is less confusing.

b. Survey the book at the beginning of the term.

c. Use punctuation clues, word clues, word structure clues, and context clues.

d. Try to organize with headings and numbered details. Leave spaces between headings.

e. Only mark the main idea and the key words for details.

f. Read one paragraph at a time. Stop. Take time to comprehend what you read.

g. Use your own words to string together the ideas you marked.

h. Use the index.

i. Survey the chapter before the lecture, or if there is time, read the chapter to acquire basic understanding of new topics or concepts.

j. Paraphrase with shortened sentences. Abbreviate. Use symbols.

k. Instead of taking lecture notes on separate paper, take notes directly in the textbook.

l. Keep writing, anticipate new points, question ideas, or mentally summarize.

m. Check the appendix of the book.

n. Check the first and the last sentences to see if one has the main idea that controls the paragraph.

EXERCISE 10.6

Part I: Lecture Notetaking Checklist

DIRECTIONS: Select any set of lecture notes you have for any one of your courses. Rank the quality of each of the following items in your notes, with **3** representing the highest quality.

1. The notetaking system I used was effective for the lecture.   1   2   3
2. The headings or main ideas are clear in my notes.   1   2   3
3. I paraphrased the instructor's words.   1   2   3
4. I used shortened sentences but did not lose the meaning.   1   2   3
5. I used abbreviations and/or symbols in my notes.   1   2   3
6. I used a combination of printing and cursive writing.   1   2   3
7. I left a gap or shifted to paragraph form when I started falling behind taking notes.   1   2   3
8. My notes include definitions for important terminology.   1   2   3
9. My notes include supporting details: dates, names, facts, or statistics.   1   2   3
10. My notes summarize examples without including every detail.   1   2   3
11. I numbered individual details so they are easy to identify.   1   2   3
12. I used the instructor's verbal, visual, and nonverbal clues to help identify important
    information for my notes.   1   2   3
13. My notes include explanations for details or for steps in a process.   1   2   3
14. My notes either include visual materials or references to textbook pages that
    have those visual materials.   1   2   3
15. My notes are well-organized and have sufficient details so I will be able to use
    them for studying and review.   1   2   3

TOTAL SCORE: _____

SCORING YOUR RESPONSES: Total all the circled numbers for your final score.

15–20   Strive to use more effective strategies; your notes may lack sufficient
            information to be effective as a study tool to review lecture content.

21–40   Continue developing your notetaking skills for the areas ranked 1 and 2;
            your notes include adequate information for studying, but they could be
            stronger.

41–45   Continue using your notetaking skills; you have quality notes that you can
            use to study and review.

Part II: Instructor Questionnaire

DIRECTIONS TO THE INSTRUCTOR

In the _____ course, students are developing their lecture notetaking skills. One of your students, _____, chose to use your lecture class to practice notetaking skills. Your feedback on the student's notes would be greatly appreciated. Please take a few minutes to review the student's notes and answer the following questions. Students are asked to turn in this questionnaire with their practice notes.

Instructor's Name _____

Class _____

1. Do the notes appear to include the important information presented in the lecture?

    ____ Yes   ____ No   ____ Somewhat

    Comments:

2. Do the notes also show information that was presented on the overhead projector, blackboard, Power Point slides, or other form of visual presentation?

    ____ Yes   ____ No   ____ Somewhat

    Comments:

3. In what way could this student improve his or her notes for your lecture?

Exercise 12.1 (cont.)

_____ **5.** I create associations by linking pictures, familiar situations, visual images, or mnemonics to important concepts or charts. I practice the associations so they become retrieval cues for memory.

_____ **6.** I create visual materials to show schemas. I draw visual mappings, diagrams, or charts to show relationship among key concepts. I rehearse, recite, and review my drawings.

_____ **7.** I think out loud. I verbally explain information, processes, or scientific reasoning to myself, my lab partner, or my study partner. I check my accuracy and use feedback.

_____ **8.** I visualize. I create strong visual impressions of processes, charts, or diagrams. I practice looking away from the material and recalling the images from memory.

_____ **9.** I use elaborative rehearsal strategies for factual information. I use repetition for procedural knowledge.

_____ **10.** I realize that understanding processes occurs in stages and that each time I rework problem sets, lab procedures, or steps to solve a problem, my comprehension deepens. Each time I rework problems, I compare the steps I use and my solution to the original problem and answer.

MATH TEXTBOOKS

_____ **1.** I recognize which information is factual and which is procedural. I use appropriate strategies to read and study the two different kinds of knowledge.

_____ **2.** I carefully read examples and create prototypes (models) that I memorize and use to recall characteristics of a specific type of problem as well as the steps to use to solve that type of problem.

_____ **3.** I translate verbal information into visual forms. As I read word or story problems, I create pictures or charts to show the known information and information I need to find.

_____ **4.** I translate visual information into verbal forms. I explain to myself what charts or diagrams represent and how they can be used.

_____ **5.** I use math symbols and equations to form sentences. I practice converting numbers and symbols into verbal sentences.

_____ **6.** I create strong visual images of equations, formulas, and charts that I can use as retrieval cues.

_____ **7.** I practice visualizing and reconstructing images of problem prototypes, patterns, formulas, steps, illustrations, or diagrams.

_____ **8.** I rework textbook examples, lecture problems, and homework problem sets and then compare my work to the original problems.

_____ **9.** I use repetition, repetition, and repetition to increase my speed and accuracy and understand processes sufficiently that I am able to form generalizations and apply the skills to new problems.

_____ **10.** I recognize information may appear in different forms: verbal explanations, symbols and formulas, tables and graphs, or real world story problems.

Appendix D

Excerpts

Excerpt 1:   Models of Memory

Models of Memory

We remember some information far better than other information. Suppose your friends throw a surprise party for you. When you enter the room, you might barely notice the flash of a camera. Later, you cannot recall it at all. And you might forget in a few seconds the name of a person you met at the party. But if you live to be a hundred, you will never forget where the party took place or how surprised and pleased you were. Why do some things stay in memory forever, whereas others barely make am impression? Each of four ways of thinking about memory, called *models* of memory, provides a somewhat different explanation. Let's see what the levels-of-processing, transfer-appropriate processing, parallel distributed processing, and information-processing models have to say about memory.

Levels of Processing   The **levels-of-processing model** suggests that memory depends on the extent to which you encode and process information when you first encounter it. Consider, for example, the task of remembering a phone number you just heard on the radio. If you were unable to write it down, you would probably repeat the number over and over to yourself until you could get to a phone. This repetition process is called **maintenance rehearsal.** It can be an effective method for encoding information temporarily, but what if you need to remember something for hours, months, or years? In that case, you would be better off using **elaborative rehearsal**, a process in which you relate new material to information you already have stored in memory. For example, instead of trying to remember a new person's name by simply repeating it to yourself, you could try thinking about how the name is related to something you know well. So if you introduced to a man named Jim Crews, you might think, "He is as tall as my Uncle Jim, who always wears a crew cut."

Study after study has shown that memory is improved when people use elaborative rehearsal rather than maintenance rehearsal (Jahnke & Nowaczyk, 1998). According to the levels-of-processing model, the reason is that material is processed more "deeply" when elaborative rehearsal is used (Lockhart & Craik, 1990; Roediger & Gallo, 2001). The more you think about new information, organize it, and relate it to something you already known, the "deeper" the processing, and the better your memory of the information becomes. Teachers use this idea when they ask students not only to define a new word but also to use it in a sentence. Figuring out how to use the new word takes deeper processing than does merely defining it. (The next time you come across an unfamiliar word in this book, don't just read its definition. Try to use the word in a sentence by coming up with an example of the concept that is related to your knowledge and experience.)

Transfer-Appropriate Processing   Level of processing is not the only factor that affects memory. Another critical factor, suggested by the **transfer-appropriate processing model** of memory, is how the encoding process matches up with what is later retrieved. In one study, for example, half the students in a class were told that their next exam would contain multiple-choice questions. The rest of the students were told to expect essay questions. Only half the students actually got the type of exam they expected, however. These students did much better on the exam than those who took an unexpected type of exam. Apparently, in studying for the exam, the two groups used encoding strategies that were most appropriate to the type of exam they expected. Those who tried to retrieve the information in a way that did not match their encoding method had a harder time (d'ydewalle & Rosselle, 1978). Results such as these indicate that how well the encoding method transfers to the retrieval task is just is important as the depth of processing.

Parallel Distributed Processing   A third way of thinking about memory is based on **parallel distributed processing (PDP) models** (Rumelhart & McClelland, 1986). These models of memory suggest that new experiences do more than provide specific facts that are stored and later retrieved one at a time. Those facts are also combined with what you already know, so that each new experience changes your overall understanding of the world and how it operates. For example, when you first arrived at college, you learned lots of specific facts,

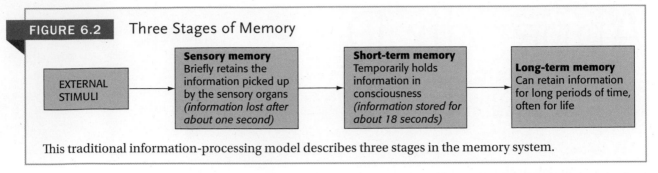

FIGURE 6.2   Three Stages of Memory

EXTERNAL STIMULI → **Sensory memory** Briefly retains the information picked up by the sensory organs *(information lost after about one second)* → **Short-term memory** Temporarily holds information in consciousness *(information stored for about 18 seconds)* → **Long-term memory** Can retain information for long periods of time, often for life

This traditional information-processing model describes three stages in the memory system.

such as where classes are held. what time the library closes, and where to get the best pizza. Over time, these and many other facts about college life form a network of information that creates a more general understanding of how the whole college system works. The development of this network makes experienced students not only more knowledgeable than new students, but also more sophisticated. It allows them to, say, allocate their study time in order do well in their most important courses and to plan a schedule that doesn't conflict with work commitments and maybe even avoids morning class—and certain professors.

Using this network concept, PDP models of memory see each unit of knowledge as connected with every other unit. The connections between units become stronger as they are experienced together more frequently. In other words, your knowledge about the world is distributed across a network of associations that all operate at the same time, in parallel. This network allows you to quickly and efficiently draw inferences and generalizations about the world. For example, because of your network of associations, just seeing the word *chair* allows you to know immediately what a chair looks like, what it is used for, where it tends to be located, who might buy one, and the like. PDP models of memory explain this process very effectively.

Information Processing   The **information-processing model** is probably the most influential and comprehensive model of memory. It suggests that for information to be firmly implanted in memory, it must pass through three stages of mental processing: sensory memory, short-term memory, and long-term memory.

In *sensory memory*, information from the senses—sights or sounds, for example—is held very briefly before being lost. But if information in sensory memory is attended to, analyzed, and encoded as a meaningful pattern, we say that it has been *perceived* (see the chapter on sensation and perception). Information in sensory memory that has been perceived can now enter *short-term memory*. If nothing further is done with it, that information will disappear in less than twenty seconds. However, if the information in short-term memory is further processed, it may be encoded into *long-term memory*, where it may remain indefinitely.

The act of reading illustrates all three stages of memory processing. As you read any sentence in this book, light energy reflected from the page reaches your eyes, where it is converted to neural activity and registered in your sensory memory. If you pay attention to these visual stimuli, your perception of the patterns of light can be held in short-term memory. This stage of memory holds the early parts of the sentence so that they can be integrated and understood as you read the rest of the sentence. As you read, you are constantly recognizing words by matching your perceptions of them with the patterns and meanings you have stored in long-term memory. In other words, all three stages of memory are necessary for you to understand a sentence.

"In Review: Models of Memory" summarizes the four memory models we have discussed. Each of these models provides an explanation of why we remember some things.

in review

MODELS OF MEMORY

Model	Assumptions
Levels of processing	The more deeply material is processed, the better our memory of it.
Transfer-appropriate processing	Retrieval is improved when we try to recall material in a way that matches how the material was encoded.
Parallel distributed processing (PDP)	New experiences add to and alter our overall knowledge base; they are not separate, unconnected facts. Networks of associations allow us to draw inferences and make generalizations about the world.
Information-processing	Information is processed in three stages: sensory memory, short-term memory, and long-term memory.

Excerpt 2:   Practice Visualization

Practice Visualization

Sometimes, when we imagine giving a speech, we see the worst-case scenario. We see ourselves trembling, forgetting what we planned to say, dropping our notes, tripping on the way to the podium, and so on. Although a speech rarely goes this badly, these negative images stay in our minds. They increase our anxiety and often set up what is called a self-fulfilling prophecy: If you see yourself doing poorly in your mind before your speech, you set yourself up to do so in the speech. There are two solutions to this negative dynamic: visualization and affirmations.

Visualization. Visualization is a process in which you construct a mental image of yourself giving a successful speech. Research on the benefits of visualization before giving a speech suggests that one session of visualization (about fifteen minutes) has a significant positive effect on communication apprehension. The techniques of visualization are used by a wide range of people—athletes, performers, executives—and can range from elaborate to quite simple processes. For public speakers, the most effective process works as follows:

Find a quiet, comfortable place where you can sit in a relaxed position for approximately fifteen minutes. Close your eyes and breathe slowly and deeply through your nose, feeling relaxation flow through your body. In great detail, visualize the morning of the day you are to give your speech.

You get up filled with confidence and energy, and you choose the perfect clothing for your speech. You drive, walk, or ride to campus filled with this same positive, confident energy. As you enter the classroom, you see yourself relaxed, interacting with your classmates, full of confidence because you have thoroughly prepared for your speech. Your classmates are friendly and cordial in their greetings and conversations with you. You are *absolutely* sure of your material and your ability to present that material in the way you would like.

Next, visualize yourself beginning your speech. You see yourself approaching the place in your classroom from which you will speak. You are sure of yourself, eager to begin, and positive in your abilities as a speaker. You know you are organized and ready to use all your visual aids with ease. Now you see yourself presenting your speech. Your introduction is wonderful. Your transitions are smooth and interesting. Your main points are articulated brilliantly. Your evidence is presented elegantly. Your organization is perfect. Take as much time as you can in visualizing this part of your process. Be as specific and positive as you can.

Visualize the end of the speech: It could not have gone better. You are relaxed and confident, the audience is eager to ask questions, and you respond with the same talent as you gave your speech. As you return to your seat, you are filled with energy and appreciation for the job well done. You are ready for the next events of your day, and you accomplish them with success and confidence.

Now take a deep breath and return to the present. Breathe in, hold it, and release it. Do this several times as you return to the present. Take as much time as you need to make this transition.

Research on visualization for public speakers suggests that the more detail we are able to give to our visualizations (what shoes we wear, exactly how we feel as we see ourselves, imagining the specifics of our speech), the more effective the technique is in reducing apprehension. Visualization has a significant effect on reducing the nervousness we feel because it systematically replaces negative images with positive ones.

Griffin. *Invitation to Public Speaking*, 3e. © 2009 Wadsworth, a part of Cengage Learning, Inc. Reproduced by permission. www.cengage.com/permissions.

Excerpt 3   Maintaining a Normal Weight

Maintaining a Normal Weight

Good nutrition and a healthy weight have been repeatedly proven to contribute to wellness and the prevention of disease. However, it is estimated that at least 64% of adults in the United States are overweight or obese and 30% of adults age 20 and above are obese (National Center for Health Statistics). This number may actually be higher because official statistical reports lag by several years and the trend is toward growing numbers of overweight individuals. Of particular concern is the increasing number of children and adolescents who are overweight or obese. Young people who are overweight tend to have weight problems as adults. Researchers believe that poor diet and physical inactivity are now among the leading causes of preventable deaths in the United States, possibly contributing to as many as 365,000 deaths in 2000.

Height—weight charts were used for many years to determine if a person was overweight, but the body mass index (BMI) is being increasingly used. BMI measures the relationship of weight to height using the following mathematical formula:

1. Multiply weight in pounds by 703.
2. Divide the result by height in inches.
3. Divide the result from step 2 by height in inches.

A BMI of 25.0 to 29.9 is defined as overweight. A BMI of 30.0 is considered obese.

Excess body weight contributes to a number of uncomfortable conditions and serious diseases:

- High blood pressure
- Elevated levels of fats in the blood, including **cholesterol** (fatty substance that can clog the arteries)
- Type 2 diabetes
- Heart disease
- Stroke
- Gallbladder disease
- Osteoarthritis
- Sleep apnea (condition in which a person stops breathing while sleeping)
- Respiratory problems
- Cancers: endometrial, breast, prostate, and colon

Researchers are investigating why the percentage of overweight and obese Americans continues to grow even as we learn more about the health benefits of maintaining a healthy weight. It is believed there are a number of reasons why Americans continue to gain weight:

- Increase in the total amount of food consumed
- Increased consumption of high-calorie and high-fat foods
- Heavy use of the automobile as a means of transportation
- Increased number of hours watching television, using the computer, and playing video games
- Lack of active recreational exercise
- Increases in technology and decreases in tasks that require manual labor

Calories are the energy content of foods. When more calories are taken in than are needed by the body to function, the unused energy is stored as fat. Thus an increase in calories with a corresponding decrease in physical activity almost certainly results in weight gain.

Another contributing factor to weight gain is that decreased activity results in a loss of muscle mass, which in turn leads to a decreased number of calories needed to maintain the body's weight. This is because muscle tissue uses more energy to support itself than does fat tissue. Lack of exercise then contributes to increased weight both by lowering the number of calories burned throughout the day *and* by reducing the body's caloric requirements.

Dozens of diets and methods have been proposed for losing weight. Many of the most popular diets contradict each other, and it can be difficult to sort fact from fiction. Most nutrition experts believe that excess calories cause excess body weight. Any diet that provides fewer calories than are burned is likely to result in weight loss.

Calories, however, are not the only consideration in healthy eating. It is important that the foods eaten provide all the necessary **nutrients**, substances the body uses to grow and function properly. There are six classes of nutrients:

1. **Proteins:** food substances containing amino acids, which are necessary to both building and maintaining the structural components of the body. Common sources are meat, fish, and eggs.

2. **Carbohydrates:** food substances composed of units of sugars that provide the body with immediate energy. Common sources are fruits, breads, cereals, and pasta.

3. **Fats:** consist of fatty acids, which provide the most concentrated forms of energy for the body. In addition to oils and butter, fats are found in meats, fish, nuts, eggs, and certain plants such as olives and avocados.

4. **Vitamins:** organic (related to or derived from living organisms) substances found in foods that are essential (in very small quantities) for growth, health, and life.

5. **Minerals:** inorganic (not derived from living matter) substances that must be supplied to the body in the diet.

6. Water

Weight-loss diets that emphasize one type of food over another or eliminate a whole category of foods can result in a shortage of one or more essential nutrients. Therefore a balanced diet that includes a variety of foods is generally recommended. The U.S. Department of Agriculture has developed an eating plan, which is updated every few years, to help Americans eat for wellness. The plan, known as the **food guide pyramid**, divides foods into six major groups and gives recommended daily servings from each group. Following are the six groups:

1. Grains
2. Vegetables
3. Fruits
4. Oils
5. Milk products
6. Meat, fish, beans, and nuts

Improving eating habits sometimes requires individuals to make significant adjustments, because the typical American diet contains many processed foods that are high in calories and low in nutritive value and **fiber** (food contents that cannot be fully digested). To add to the problem, many people eat on the run and depend on fast-food suppliers–or worse, vending machines–for at least one of their daily meals.

From Mitchell/Haroun, *Introduction to Health Care*, 2E. © 2007 Delmar Learning, a part of Cengage Learning, Inc. Reproduced by permission. www.cengage.com/permissions.

Excerpt 4:   Procrastination and Its Causes

Procrastination and Its Causes

Author Maia Szalavitz in the following article, "Stand & Deliver" (*Psychology Today,* August 2003, pp. 50–54), provides information about procrastination and its causes.

Procrastination is not just an issue of time management or laziness. It's about feeling paralyzed and guilty as you channel surf, knowing you should be cracking the books or reconfiguring your investment strategy. Why the gap between incentive and action? Psychologists now believe it is a combination of anxiety and false beliefs about productivity.

Tim Pychyl, PhD, associate professor of psychology at Carleton University in Ottawa, Canada, tracked students with procrastination problems in the final week before a project was due. Students first reported anxiety and guilt because they had not started their projects. "They were telling themselves[,] 'I work better under pressure' or 'this isn't important,'" says Pychyl. But once they began to work, they reported more positive emotions; they no longer lamented wasted time, nor claimed that pressure helped . . . Psychologists have focused on procrastination among students because the problem is rampant in academic settings; some 70 percent of college students report problems with overdue papers and delayed studying, according to Joseph Ferrari, associate professor of psychology at Chicago's DePaul University.

Pychyl also found that procrastination is detrimental to physical health. College students who procrastinate have higher levels of drinking, smoking, insomnia, stomach problems, colds, and flu. So why can't people just buckle down and get the job done?

False Beliefs: Many procrastinators are convinced that they work better under pressure, or they'll feel better about tackling the work later. But, tomorrow never comes and last-minute work is often low quality. In spite of what they believe, "Procrastinators generally don't do well under pressure," says Ferrari. The idea that time pressure improves performance is perhaps the most common myth among procrastinators.

Fear of Failure: "The main reason people procrastinate is fear," says Neil Fiore, PhD, author of *The Now Habit.* Procrastinators fear they'll fall short because they don't have the requisite talent or skills. "They get overwhelmed and they're afraid they'll look stupid." According to Ferrari, "Procrastinators would rather be seen as lacking in effort than lacking in ability." If you flunk a calculus exam, better to loudly blame it on the half-hour study blitz than admit to yourself that you could have used a tutor the entire semester.

Perfectionism: Procrastinators tend to be perfectionists—and they're in overdrive because they're insecure. People who do their best because they want to win don't procrastinate; but those who feel they must be perfect to please others often put things off. These people fret that "No one will love me if everything I do isn't utter genius." Such perfectionism is at the heart of many an unfinished novel.

Self-Control: Impulsivity may seem diametrically opposed to procrastination, but both can be part of a larger problem: self-control. People who are impulsive may not be able to prioritize intentions, says Pychyl. So, while writing a term paper[,] you break for a snack and see a spill in the refrigerator, which leads to cleaning the entire kitchen.

Thrill-Seeking: Some procrastinators enjoy the adrenaline "rush." These people find perverse satisfaction when they finish their taxes minutes before midnight on April 15 and dash to the post office just before it closes.

Task-Related Anxieties: Procrastination can be associated with specific situations. "Humans avoid the difficult and boring," says Fiore. Even the least procrastination-prone individuals put off taxes and visits to the dentist.

Unclear Expectations: Ambiguous directions and vague priorities increase procrastination. The boss who asserts that everything is high priority and due yesterday is more likely to be kept waiting.

Depression: The blues can lead to or exacerbate procrastination—and vice versa. Several symptoms of depression feed procrastination. Because depressed people can't feel much pleasure, all options seem equally bleak, which makes getting started difficult and pointless.

Excerpt 5:   The Muscular System

MUSCULAR SYSTEM

More than 600 muscles make up the system known as the **muscular system.** Muscles are bundles of muscle fibers held together by connective tissue. All muscles have certain properties or characteristics:

- **Excitability:** irritability, the ability to respond to a stimulus such as a nerve impulse

- **Contractibility:** muscle fibers that are stimulated by nerves **contract,** or become short and thick, which causes movement

- **Extensibility:** the ability to be stretched

- **Elasticity:** allows the muscle to return to its original shape after it has contracted or stretched

There are three main kinds of muscle: cardiac, visceral, and skeletal. **Cardiac muscle** forms the walls of the heart and contracts to circulate blood. **Visceral**, or **smooth**, **muscle** is found in the internal organs of the body, such as those of the digestive and respiratory systems, and the blood vessels and eyes. Visceral muscle contracts to cause movement in these organs. Cardiac muscle and visceral muscle are **involuntary**, meaning they function without conscious thought or control **Skeletal muscle** is attached to bones and causes body movement. Skeletal muscle is **voluntary** because a person has control over its action. Because cardiac muscle and visceral muscle are discussed in sections on other systems, the following concentrates on skeletal muscle.

Skeletal muscle perform four important functions:

- Attach to bones to provide voluntary movement

- Produce heat and energy for the body

- Help maintain posture by holding the body erect

- Protect internal organs

Skeletal muscles attach to bones in different ways. Some attach by **tendons**, which are the strong, tough, fibrous connective-tissue cords. An example is the gastrocnemius muscle on the calf of the leg which attaches to the heelbone by the Achilles tendon. Other muscles attach by **fascia**, a tough, sheet-like membrane that covers and protects the tissue. Examples include the deep muscles of the trunk and back, which are surrounded by the lumbodorsal fascia, When a muscle attaches to a bone, the end that does not move is called the **origin**. The end that moves when the muscle contracts is called the **insertion**. For example, the origin of the shoulder muscle, called the *deltoid*, is by the clavicle and scapula. Its insertion is on the humerus. When the deltoid contracts, the area by the scapula remains stationary, but the area by the humerus moves and abducts the arm away from the body.

A variety of different actions or movements performed by muscles are described as follows:

- **Adduction:** moving a body part toward the midline

- **Abduction:** moving a body part away from the midline

- **Flexion:** decreasing the angle between two bones, or bending a body part

- **Extension:** increasing the angle between two bones, or straightening a body part

- **Rotation:** turning a body part around its own axis; for example, turning the head from side to side

- **Circumduction:** moving in a circle at a joint, or moving one end of a body part in a circle while the other end remains stationary, such as swinging an arm in a circle

Muscles are partially contracted at all times, even when not in use. This state of partial contraction is called **muscle tone** and is sometimes described as a state of readiness to act. Loss of muscle tone can occur in severe illness such as paralysis. When muscles are not used for a long period, they can *atrophy* (shrink in size and lose strength). Lack of use can also result in a **contracture**, a severe tightening of a flexor muscle resulting in bending of a joint. Foot drop is a common contracture, but the fingers, wrists, knees, and other joints can also be affected.

From Simmers et al., *Introduction to Health Science Technology*, 2E. © Delmar Learning, a part of Cengage Learning, Inc. Reproduced by permission. www.cengage.com/permissions.

Excerpt 6:   Other Solar System Objects

Background

The *solar system* is a complex system of moving masses held together by gravitational forces. At the center of this system is a star called the Sun. Revolving around the Sun are nine rotating planets and over 70 satellites (moons). In addition to the planets and the satellites, the solar system consists of thousands of asteroids, vast numbers of comets, meteoroids, and other solar objects such as interplanetary dust particles, gases, and a solar wind.

Asteroids

Ceres, the first of many planetary bodies between the orbits of Mars and Jupiter, was discovered by an Italian astronomer in 1801. Ceres is the largest of more than 2000 solar objects named and numbered that orbit the Sun between Mars and Jupiter. These objects are called **asteroids**, or *minor planets*.

The diameters of the known asteroids range from that of Ceres (940 kilometers) down to only a few kilometers, but most asteroids are probably less than a few kilometers in diameter. There are perhaps thousands the size of boulders, marbles, and grains of sand.

Asteroids are believed to be early solar-system material that never collected into a single planet. One piece of evidence supporting this view is that there seem to be several different kinds of asteroids. Those at the inner edge of the belt appear to be stony, whereas those farther out are darker, indicating more carbon content. A third group may be composed mostly of iron and nickel.

Like the planets, asteroids revolve counterclockwise around the Sun. More than 26,000 have been cataloged. Although most asteroids move in an orbit between Mars and Jupiter, some have orbits that range beyond Saturn or inside the orbit of Mercury.

Meteoroids

Meteoroids are interplanetary metallic and stony objects that range in size from a fraction of a millimeter to a few hundred meters. They are probably the remains of comets and fragments of shattered asteroids. They circle the Sun in elliptical orbits and strike the Earth from all directions at very high speeds.

A meteoroid is called a **meteor**, or "shooting star," when it enters the Earth's atmosphere and becomes luminous because of the tremendous heat generated by friction with the air. Most meteoroids are vaporized in the atmosphere, but some larger ones survive the flight through the atmosphere and strike the Earth's surface, in which case they become known as **meteorites**. When a large meteorite strikes the Earth's surface, a large crater is formed.

Comets

Comets are named from the Latin words *aster kometes,* which mean "long-haired stars." They are the solar system members that periodically appear in our sky [for] a few weeks or months and then disappear. A **comet** is a reasonably small object composed of dust and ice and revolves about the Sun in a highly elliptical orbit. As it comes near the Sun, some of the surface vaporizes to form a gaseous head and a long tail.

Halley's comet, named after the British astronomer Edmond Halley (1656–1742), is one of the brightest and best-known comets. Halley was the first to suggest and predict the periodic appearance of the same comet (he did not discover it). Halley observed the comet that bears his name in 1682, and correctly predicted its return in 76 years. Halley's comet has appeared every 76 years, including 1910 and 1986.

Adapted from Shipman, Wilson, and Todd, *An Introduction to Physical Science,* 10th ed. (Boston: Houghton Miffin Company, 2003), p. 381, pp. 404–408. Copyright © 2003. Reprinted by permission of Houghton Miffin Co.

Excerpt 7   Theories of Forgetting

Five theories of forgetting offered by psychologists explain some of the reasons information may be forgotten or inaccessible in memory. These theories describe forgetting that occurs at various stages in the learning process.

The *Decay Theory* suggests that stimuli received by short-term memory (a part of working memory) may be too weak or unattended to, resulting in the stimuli simply decaying or fading away. Unattended or ignored stimuli decay from short-term memory within eighteen seconds, and thus are never processed or truly learned.

A second theory, the *Displacement Theory,* suggests another type of forgetting that also occurs in short-term memory. If too much information comes into short-term memory too rapidly, the short-term memory system in working memory becomes overloaded. Some of the stimuli already in short-term memory are shoved aside or displaced to make room for new stimuli. Displacement occurs because of short-term memory's limited capacity to hold, on the average, no more than seven chunks of information at one time. Once displaced, the stimuli drop out of the memory and processing centers.

The *Interference Theory* suggests two forms of forgetting that occur with learned information in long-term memory: retroactive and proactive interference. Interference can occur between items studied in the same session or between items studied many years apart. Both forms of forgetting are caused by interferences between old and new information during the imprinting or retrieval stages of learning. Forgetting due to interference often occurs when old and new information are similar in nature and characteristics of each are not highly differentiated.

Retroactive interference occurs when new information in working memory interferes with the retrieval process of old, previously learned information. The new information is fresher in working memory and overrides the ability to recall old information. For example, new information you are learning in a history class this term may hinder your ability to recall information you learned the previous term in a different history class.

Proactive interference occurs when old, previously learned information in long-term memory interferes with the ability to recall newly learned information, especially when the new information contradicts or does not integrate logically with previously learned information. For example, if you have spent several terms studying Spanish, this knowledge may make it difficult for you to switch to different language patterns to learn a language such as Japanese.

The *Incomplete Encoding Theory* suggests forgetting occurs due to incomplete encoding during the rehearsal process in working memory. If learning information is interrupted, information is only partially learned or understood. Strong enough impressions, retrieval cues, or associations are not created to recall information accurately. If some form of self-quizzing is not used, the learner may not be aware that information is not encoded clearly. When the stimuli are not imprinted clearly in long-term memory, recall produces partial or unusable information.

The *Retrieval Failure Theory* refers to the inability to conduct successful memory searches to locate information stored in long-term memory. Failure to retrieve information may be attributed to a weak organizational system for storing or filing the information, a lack of retrieval cues or associations, or it may be due to lack of use or practice pulling information back into working memory. Information that is not rehearsed or practiced still exists in memory, but it is not accessible. Anxiety, excessive stress, or emotionally disruptive thoughts may also hinder a person's ability to recall learned information.

Fortunately, a variety of study strategies that support the functions of working memory can be used to combat each of the five types of forgetting.

Excerpt 8   Maslow's Hierarchy of Needs

MASLOW'S HIERARCHY OF NEEDS

Surviving is about meeting needs, and learning to thrive is about learning how to meet more and more complicated needs well. This is far too complex to do all at once, so the brain moves through stages of development, each in turn devoted to interacting with the environment and learning behaviors to meet ever more complex needs. An American psychologist, Abraham Maslow, described these needs as a hierarchy, meaning that we move through them one step at a time from the least to the most complex (Maslow, 1970). The lowest need that is chronically unmet will grow larger and more insistent until it dominates the person's feelings, thoughts, emotions, and actions. Stop breathing for three minutes and see how concerned you are about anything other than getting another breath of air. This hierarchy can be illustrated in a stair-step arrangement (Figure 2.2).

Needs

Physical needs are the basic needs and they are easy to identify; if they aren't met well enough, you die. They include air, food, water, warmth, and pressure. If these needs are not met they quickly grow to dominate behavior, centering the person around the effort to meet the need and relieve the distress. Safety and security is more complicated. If you are unsafe you may not die, but you are in danger of harm or death. Security is the feeling of being able to stay safe, and it depends on learning to understand your environment and developing the ability to negotiate it well enough to believe yourself capable of avoiding harm. Love is acceptance, appreciation, and affection from one or a few important individuals in your life. Belonging is acceptance and inclusion; it begins in the family and then extends out of the family into a group. Esteem in recognition and respect first from others in the group, and then from your self. Self-actualization is motivation and direction from within, being guided by your own principles and your own conscience.

Moral Levels

Maslow's hierarchy establishes multiple levels of needs that must be met in order. Over time the lowest-level need that is consistently unmet grows ever more powerful until it motivates thoughts, emotions, and actions at that level. This motivation is the key to what Lawrence Kohlberg (1984) termed moral levels. **Moral Levels** are defined not by what we do, but by why we do it. As the lowest order need that is chronically unmet grows powerful it motivates behavior that can most often be defined and predicted by the morals at that level. Moral levels can be correlated with the unmet need that motivates behavior at that level (Figure 2.3).

The domination of physical needs drives behavior at the power moral level. At this level "might makes right"; we do something because we want to, we can, and no one can stop us. Our actions are controlled only by someone with greater physical or material power who can provide punishments and rewards. The domination of safety and security needs drives behavior at the deals moral level. At this level we still take what we want if we can, but with those who have more power we make self-serving bargains and compromises in order to get what we want or avoid what we don't want. The domination of the need for love drives behavior at the good boy/good girl moral level. At this level we do what someone

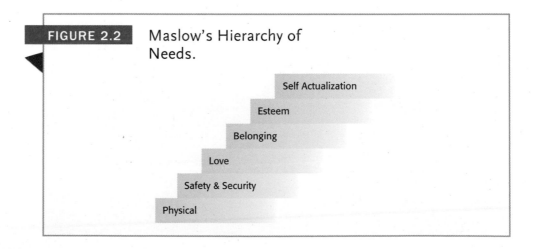

FIGURE 2.2   Maslow's Hierarchy of Needs.

Self Actualization

Esteem

Belonging

Love

Safety & Security

Physical

else wants in order to be a "good boy" or a "good girl" and win their acceptance, approval, and love. The domination of belonging needs drives behavior at the rules or authority moral level. At this level we follow the rules of the group so that its members will accept and approve of us and we will belong. Identity is solidified in conjunction with the group and the rules become such an integral part of who we are that they guide long after we have moved away from the particular group. The domination of esteem needs drives behavior at the social contracts moral level. At this level we work for the general welfare, for the most good for the most people, not for personal interest. This is the level of the U.S. Constitution. The domination of self-actualization needs drives behavior at the individual conscience moral level. At this level we are guided and motivated by the worth of each individual and by principles of life such as dignity, justice, responsibility, freedom, and equality.

From Wilbanks, APPLIED PSYCHOLOGY IN HEALTH CARE, 1E. © 2009 Delmar Learning, a part of Cengage Learning, Inc. Reproduced by permission. www.cengage.com/permissions.

FIGURE 2.3   Maslow's Hierarchy of Needs Correlated with Kohlberg's Moral Levels.

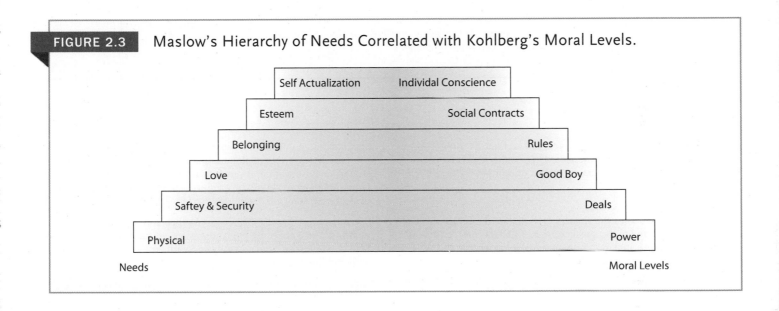

Excerpt 9:   How to Listen Critically

HOW TO LISTEN CRITICALLY

When you listen to a speech critically, you mentally check it for accuracy, comparing what the speaker says with what you personally know and what your own research tells you. You also listen to assess the strengths and weaknesses of the reasoning and supporting materials presented in a speech. Note that listening critically is different from listening to judge or find fault with a message. Rather, **critical listeners** listen for the accuracy of a speech's content and the implications of a **speaker's message**. Critical listeners benefit by remaining open to new ideas, but they also listen carefully to how speakers develop those ideas into arguments. Additionally, they consider the impact of a speaker's ideas and how they may affect immediate audiences as well as larger communities.

To help you listen to speeches critically, ask yourself the questions in Table 3.1 and then follow the suggested guidelines. Asking these questions will help you assess a speaker's claims and arguments before you make decisions about their value or strength.

When we listen critically, we allow for dialogue because we avoid making quick decisions about good and bad, right and wrong. Listening critically encourages us to ask questions about ideas so we are better able to respond to claims and explore issues with others.

Table 3.1   Guidelines for Critical Listening

QUESTION	GUIDELINE
• How fully has the speaker developed an idea? Is something left out, exaggerated, or understated? Does the speaker use sound reasoning? Are claims based on fact or opinion?	• Speakers must develop all major arguments fully rather than present them without explanation and development. Speakers should not exaggerate arguments or understate their importance. Major ideas should be supported by evidence in the form of examples, statistics, testimony, and the like.
• What sources does the speaker rely on? Are they credible? How are they related to the speaker's topic? Will the sources benefit if facts are presented in a certain way? For example, is the tobacco industry arguing that smoking isn't harmful?	• Speakers must use credible sources that are as unbiased as possible. Speakers must cite sources for all new information. Sources should be cited carefully and with enough detail so the audience knows why the source is acceptable.
• Are the claims the speaker makes realistic? What are the implications of those claims? Who is affected by them? In what way? Has the speaker acknowledged these effects, or are they left unstated? Are there other aspects of the issue the speaker should address?	• Speakers must make realistic and logical claims and acknowledge different perspectives. They must also acknowledge those affected by their arguments and acknowledge the effects of their proposed solutions. When speakers take a position, they must not present their position as absolute or the only one possible.
• How does this speech fit with what I know to be true? What is new to me? Can I accept this new information? Why or why not?	• When speakers make claims that go against your personal experience, see if you can discover why. Sometimes, the answer lies in cultural differences or in a speaker's research. Try to be open to different views of the world while at the same time assessing the speaker's evidence and reasoning objectively. Before you reject a speaker's claims, engage the speaker in a civil discussion to find out why your perspective differs.
• What is at stake for the speaker? How invested is the speaker in the topic and the arguments being made? How will the speaker be affected if the audience disagrees?	• All speakers are invested in some way in their topics and arguments. However, some arguments benefit a speaker more than anyone else. Identify the speaker's motives so you can better understand why she or he is making particular claims.

Excerpt 10: Kinds of Managers

KINDS OF MANAGERS

Managers can be classified two ways: according to their level within the organization and according to their area of management. In this section we use both perspectives to explore the various types of managers.

Levels of Management

For the moment, think of an organization as a three-story structure. Each story corresponds to one of the three general levels of management: top managers, middle managers, and first-line managers.

Top Managers A **top manager** is an upper-level executive who guides and controls the overall fortunes of the organization. Top managers constitute a small group. In terms of planning, they are generally responsible for developing the organization's mission. They also determine the firm's strategy. It takes years of hard work, long hours, and perseverance, as well as talent and no small share of good luck, to reach the ranks of top management in large companies. Common job titles associated with top managers are president, vice president, chief executive officer (CEO), and chief operating officer (COO).

Middle Managers Middle management probably comprises the largest group of managers in most organizations. A **middle manager** is a manager who implements the strategy developed by top managers. Middle managers develop tactical plans and operational plans, and they coordinate and supervise the activities of first-line managers. Titles at the middle-management level include division manager, department head, plant manager, and operations manager.

First-Line Managers A **first-line manager** is a manager who coordinates and supervises the activities of operating employees. First-line managers spend most of their time working with and motivating their employees, answering questions, and solving day-to-day problems. Most first-line managers are former operating employees who, owing to their hard work and potential, were promoted into management. Many of today's middle and top managers began their careers on this first management level. Common titles for first-line managers include office manager, supervisor, and foreman.

Areas of Management

Organizational structure can also be divided into areas of management specialization. The most common areas are finance, operations, marketing, human resources, and administration. Depending on its mission, goals, and objectives, an organization may include other areas as well—research and development, for example.

Financial Managers A **financial manager** is primarily responsible for the organization's financial resources. Accounting and investment are specialized areas within financial management. Because financing affects the operation of the entire firm, many of the CEOs and presidents of this country's largest companies are people who got their "basic training" as financial managers.

Operations Managers An **operations manager** manages the systems that convert resources into goods and services. Traditionally, operations management has been equated with manufacturing—the production of goods. However, in recent years many of the techniques and procedures of operations management have been applied to the production of services and to a variety of nonbusiness activities. Like financial management, operations management has produced a large percentage of today's company CEOs and presidents.

Marketing Managers A **marketing manager** is responsible for facilitating the exchange of products between the organization and its customers or clients. Specific areas within marketing are marketing research, advertising, promotion, sales, and distribution. A sizable number of today's company presidents have risen from the ranks of marketing management.

Human Resources Managers A **human resources manager** is charged with managing the organization's human resources programs. He or she engages in human resources planning; designs systems for hiring, training, and evaluating the performance of employees; and ensures that the organization follows government regulations concerning employment practices. Because human resources management is a relatively new area of specialization in many organizations, few top managers have this kind of background. However, this situation should change with the passage of time.

Administrative Managers An **administrative manager** (also called a *general manager*) is not associated with any specific functional area but provides overall administrative guidance and leadership. A hospital administrator is a good example of an administrative manager. He or she does not specialize in operations, finance, marketing, or human resources management but instead coordinates the activities of specialized managers in all these areas. In many respects, most top managers are really administrative managers.

Whatever their level in the organization and whatever area they specialize in, successful managers generally exhibit certain key skills and are able to play certain managerial roles. But, as we shall see, some skills are likely to be more critical at one level of management than at another.

Pride/Hughes/Kapoor: *Business,* 5E. Houghton Mifflin Company, © 1996, p. 180–182. Reprinted with permission.

Excerpt 11   The Species Called Homo-Simpsons

The Species Called Homo-Simpsons

RANDY ALCORN

As a freelance journalist, Randy Alcorn has spent 23 years writing weekly columns for the Santa Barbara News Press. *This article appeared in* Noozhawk.com.

1   One of nature's curious ironies is how the defining gift that she bestowed on the human species is so sparingly used by so many of its members. The "sapiens" in homo-sapiens is Latin for "wise," but judging by the brainless behavior that humans increasingly exhibit, the biological classification for human beings might more aptly be homo-simpsons.

2   Too many people seem to find rational, analytical thought unpleasant, difficult and too time-consuming. Logic requires a mental discipline that applies a process of inference, inquiry and examination—a process that lazy or easily distracted minds quickly abandon.

3   Homo-simpsons want quick, short, simple answers to life's imposing questions. Therefore, they prefer to substitute critical thinking with standard philosophies to which they can adhere without the discomfort of doubt. They are contented with the conventional wisdom. As Oscar Wilde once noted, such people are not really individuals, "their thoughts are someone else's opinions, their lives a mimicry, their passions a quotation."

4   There are few instances where the lack of intellectual diligence and the unquestioning acceptance of conventional wisdom are more apparent than in American political behavior. It certainly explains how George W. Bush could be elected president not just once, but twice. It explains how a nation could be led into a misbegotten and unnecessary war in Iraq, and, most disturbingly, how a nation could so easily be persuaded to surrender its founding principles of civil rights and individual liberty.

5   Boneheaded public polices and corrupt, incompetent politicians continue to be inflicted upon this nation in great part because so many people have succumbed to the delusion that they are thinking correctly if they accept commonly accepted reasoning and beliefs, especially those endorsed by celebrities and by political and religious leaders.

6   A recent study conducted by Germany's Max Planck Institute revealed that people will continue to believe gossip and rumors—especially if those are malicious—even when they are presented with clear evidence refuting the gossip and rumors. The German researchers speculated that people may be genetically programmed to base decisions on hearsay rather than on a rational evaluation of the evidence.

7   The disastrously lethal and costly war in Iraq may corroborate the German study. Ignoring all the evidence to the contrary, millions of Americans abandoned common sense, did not question authority, and accepted the politically motivated malicious gossip that Iraq was directly involved in the 9/11 terrorist attacks. Additionally, ordinary citizens, much of the mainstream media and most of Congress succumbed to groupthink and accepted the Bush administration's fallacious assertions that Iraq had weapons of mass destruction that would be made available to al-Qaeda terrorists.

8   Eventually, the rationale offered for continuing the Iraq debacle was the removal of a murderous tyrant and the establishment of democracy in Iraq. If that were the justification for war, Cuba would have been a more convenient place to start spreading democracy. But then, we don't need Cuba's sugar, we need oil.

9   Islamic terrorism against the United States was incited in great measure by the U.S. military presence in the Middle East—there to protect the oil supplies. Ironically, the money that is being spent on the war in Iraq and on the U.S. military presence in the Middle East could be better spent on weaning America from its dependence on foreign oil and on oil in general. For the cost of this war, nearly $500 billion already, how many homes in America could be made energy-independent with solar electric technology? How much research and development of alternate energy could be funded?

10   American politics and, therefore, its government are dominated by ideologues whose capability for rational thought and analysis is crippled by adherence to dichotomous doctrine—left or right, Democrat or Republican. It is no mystery why nothing that makes much sense gets done in Washington, D.C.—there is little clear, impartial thinking that happens there, We have ciphers in Congress and incompetents in the White House (doh!), but no real leaders, no cynosures guiding the nation to real solutions to its real problems. Just partisan bickering, ideological platitudes, and reckless, salivating, venality.

11   There are certainly more rational approaches to the issues this nation confronts, but finding them would require many more citizens to have vigorous, independent minds engaged in logical thinking.

More people would have to question conventional thinking, especially when it derives from authority figures and calcified ideologies.

12   When surveying the political landscape our vision has been conditioned to see only left or right, liberal or conservative. What we should be looking for is rational or irrational, intelligence or stupidity. Today, rational discretion is seldom found in the same old place—left or right, Democrat or Republican. We need to look with clear vision in new places. We must stop behaving like homo-simpsons and start living up to our namesake, home-sapiens.

Reprinted with permission from Randy Alcorn.

Index

Abbreviations, 261, 306
ABC method, 111, 112f, 114
Absolute modifiers. *See* 100 percent modifiers
Abstract coding. *See* Semantic encoding
Academic preparation inventory, C11, 164
Achievement motivation, development, 233f
Acoustical coding. *See* Linguistic coding
Acquired background knowledge, 356
Acronyms, 179
  creating, 180
Acrostics, 179
  creating, 180
Active learner, 124
Active learning, 70, 124, 194f
Active listening, 294, 294f
Active reading, 220
  strategies, 221, 223f
Affirmations, 132
Alliteration, 353
All of the above, guessing, A18
Analogies, 212f
Analysis, 360
  of errors, A38
  of information, 221
Analysis Level, 360
Anderson, Lorin, 362
Annotation, 259, 266, 321
  checklist, C20
  strategies, 259f, 261, 261f
Answers. *See also* Short-answer questions
  expansion of, A31
  memory search, A7
  miscopying, A38
  weak/strong, A32f
Antonyms, 212f
Anxiety, 134
  task-related, D6
  test, 172–174, 173f, C16
Appendix, 196
Application, of information, 158
Application Level, 360
Appreciative listening, 294f, 295
Assisted response, 168, A7
Association, 65–66, 82
  chained, A12
  of chunks, 221
  creation of, 52
  of information, 65
  memory principles, 65–66
  paired, 65, 206
  picture, 181, 181f
  practice, 163
  strategies, 66f
  vividness/detail, 66f
  word, 180–181

Attention
  control of, 222
  to details, 158
  rehearsal, 55–56, 55f
  selective, 42, 44, 57
Attitude, positive/negative, 55, 292f
Auditory learners, 5
  characteristics of, 11–12
  strategies, 11–12
Auditory learning style, 5, 11–12
Authoritative information, 225
Automatic pilot, 70, 192

Background knowledge, acquired, 356
Bar graphs, 242, 246
  double bar, 246
  horizontal, 247
Beliefs, false, D6
Big and little pictures, 17–18, 40, 266
  memory principles, 74
  schema, 74
  strategies, 74f
Bloom's Taxonomy, 363–364
  Analysis Level, 360
  Application Level, 360
  Comprehension Level, 360
  Evaluation Level, 361
  Knowledge Level, 359
  revised, 362, 363f
  Synthesis Level, 361
Bodily-kinesthetic intelligence, 26
Book Notes System, 302, 310
Brackets, 261
Brain
  division, 49
  left, 2, 15–18, 18f, 49
  right, 2, 15–16, 18, 19f, 49
Brain Dominance Theory, 16, 19
  involvement of hemispheres, 16f
  visual mapping, 324f
Brainstorming, 91
Breathing by threes technique, 140

Captions, 242
Categories
  cards, 340
  of cards, 343f
  identification of, 335
  of words, 209
Cause/effect (causal) pattern, 239–240
Central executive, 41–42
  functions of, 43
  scan, 46
Chained association, A12
Change

  adjustment to, 100
  willingness, 122
Chapter
  outlines, 160f
  surveying of, 197–198, 229
Check mark technique, 126
Chronological patterns, demonstration of, 236–237
Chunking, 124
  of information, 63–65, 68f, 79, 83, 192
  up/down, 223
Chunks, 63–65, 79, 83
  association of, 221
  similarities/differences, 68f
Closed test questions, 156, A24, A26
Clues
  context, 212–213, 213f
  definition, A7, A9, A10f
  grammar, A23
  instructor, 307–308
  punctuation, 207–208
  relationship, A7, A10, A11f, A14
  verbal, 298–299
  visual, 307
  word, 206–208, 206f, 280, A23
  word structure, 210–211, 211f
Clue words, 206–208, 206f, 280, A23
Codes, kinds of, 39f
Coding. *See also* Encoding
  linguistic, 39f
  motor, 39f
  semantic, 39f
  visual, 39f
Cognitive coping strategies, 138
Cognitive learning styles, 5
Cognitive modalities, 14
Communication activities, time used, 289f
Comparative reading, 273
Comparison charts, 321, 334. *See also* Tables
  completing, 336
  labeling, 335
  structure of, 336f
  studying, 160f, 338
Comparison/contrast pattern, 237
  demonstration of, 238
Comparisons, 212f
Composition textbooks, 352
Comprehension Level, 360
Comprehension skills, 218
Computerized tests
  advantages/disadvantages, 169
  rules, 169
  strategies, 169f, 170
Concentration, 82, 118, 120–121, 177
  distraction, 125
  increase of, 70